Marriage Notices from Steuben County New York Newspapers 1797-1884

Mary S. Jackson
and
Edward F. Jackson

HERITAGE BOOKS
2007

HERITAGE BOOKS

AN IMPRINT OF HERITAGE BOOKS, INC.

Books, CDs, and more—Worldwide

For our listing of thousands of titles see our website
at
www.HeritageBooks.com

Published 2007 by
HERITAGE BOOKS, INC.
Publishing Division
65 East Main Street
Westminster, Maryland 21157-5026

International Standard Book Number: 978-0-7884-0995-0

List of Newspapers

Addison Advertiser	1858 - 1884
Voice of the Nation (Addison, NY)	1855
Bath Gazette and Genessee Advertiser	1797 - 1798
Steuben American (Bath, NY)	1856 - 1857
Steuben Democrat (Bath, NY)	1843 - 1849
The Constitutionalist (Bath, NY)	1837 - 1842
Steuben Courier (Bath, NY)	1843 - 1884
Steuben Farmers Advocate (Bath, NY)	1831 - 1866
Canisteo Times	1880 - 1884
Corning and Blossburg Advocate	1840 - 1843
Corning Journal	1847 - 1872
Hammondsport Herald	1874 - 1884
Hornellsville Daily Times	1879 - 1881
Steuben Signal (Hornellsville, NY)	1883 - 1884
Painted Post Times	1870 - 1871
Prattsburgh News	1872 - 1884

Introduction

Newspapers are probably one of the most valuable and interesting sources for genealogy and are too often overlooked by researchers. Not only for the marriage and death notices that are published but many other articles are a valuable source of information. Some newspapers carry family histories of many of the local people. They also print sale of properties, notices of probate, advertising, personal items such as who is ill this week or who visited who, reunions, etc. They can be very entertaining as well as informative.

This volume contains nearly 8,000 marriage notices from Steuben County New York newspapers from 1797 to 1884 abstracted from microfilm copies available at the New York State Library. Other copies may be available elsewhere. Although these newspapers were published in Steuben County, they include notices for the surrounding counties and Pennsylvania. They also include many notices for those people who moved to other towns in New York or to other states.

Vital records were being recorded by the Town Clerks in New York State beginning in the 1880's. However, recording was not mandatory until 1906. Before 1880 one of the best sources for these vital records are local newspapers for that time period. Verification of the information contained in these newspapers should be made by using a primary source whenever possible. Sometimes mistakes were made in printing and these newspapers are very old and sometimes very difficult to read. It is still one of the best sources available.

Marriages from Steuben County, NY Newspapers

1797 - 1884

Addison Advertiser

March 10, 1858 - December 25, 1884

HOUGHENTOUGLEN Theoerastus (Newspaper date) March 10, 1858
VAN OZZLEDOZZLE Adriana Augustina Elmira, NY

CHRISTJOHN Stephen March 12, 1858
BARNES Susan Addison, NY

FEITH Nicolas of Corning, NY March 30, 1858
KRUMBOLE Monica of Corning, NY Addison, NY

HIGGINS Henry of Flint, Mi. April 15, 1858
TAYLOR Augusta F. of Geneva, NY Geneva, NY

BISHOP Nathan of Warren Co., NY April 23, 1858
COLBURN Johanna of Addison, NY Addison, NY

SPRING George of Elkland, Pa. April 3, 1858
MAY Martha of Knoxville, Pa. Knoxville, Pa.

JONES Henry S. of Addison, NY June 7, 1858
ATHERTON Maria of Elkland, Pa. Elkland, Pa.

PECK John of Addison, NY June 23, 1858
OSMUN Esther of Addison, NY Addison, NY

CORSE Luther S. of Osceola, Pa. July 3, 1858
MARVIN Martha of Osceola, Pa. Addison, NY

SEAMAN J. M. July 1, 1858
EATON Charlotte Towanda, Pa.

SHORT Robert of Addison, NY September 26, 1858
KING Nancy of Addison, NY

MOSE William of Addison, NY September 30, 1858
RIAL Rachael E. of Addison, NY at res. of Simon S. Rial

ELWOOD Lyman of Addison, NY October 7, 1858
BLANCHARD Maria N. of Addison, NY at res. of James Blanchard

PARSONS James A. of Corning, NY   October 13, 1858
LAND Mary E. of Corning, NY   Corning, NY

REYNOLDS Edwin M. of Addison, NY   November 19, 1858
SMITH Freelove of Addison, NY

YOUNG Charles C. of Addison, NY   November 22, 1858
HORN Almira dau of E. J. Horn of Addison, NY Addison, NY

CRANE Francis L. of Addison, NY   October 24, 1858
MC HENRY Mary A. of Covington, Pa.

EVANS George A. of Rathbone, NY   November 19, 1858
WILLSON Sarah C. of Addison, NY

GRAVES Charles O. of Waverly, NY   November 23, 1858
SEAMAN Phebe A. of Addison, NY

WEAVER Daniel of Erwin, NY   December 29, 1858
MC BEATH Emma of Erwin, NY   Addison, NY

SANFORD Alvin O. of Corning, NY   December 28, 1858
WILKES Mary Ann of Corning, NY

WINTON David B. of Chicago, Ill.   January 12, 1859
GILLETT Frances J. dau of J. D. of Addison, NY Addison, NY

MANLEY N. V.   January 23, 1859
CLINTON E. C.

missing issues

GRAHAM Richard of Ramseys, NJ   March 14, 1861
THORPE Julia of Ellenville, NY   Ramseys, NJ

MORSE Cyrus B. of Addison, NY   April 5, 1861
BARR Ada E. of Addison, NY   Addison, NY

NETTLETON Charles   June 2, 1861
GIBSON Maria   Addison, NY

MILLER Samuel of Addison, NY   June 9, 1861
CRANE Clarissa E. of Addison, NY   Addison, NY

TALIES John M. of Tuscarora, NY   May 25, 1861
LACKEY Mrs. Susan of Tuscarora, NY   Tuscarora, NY

COOK Fayette F. of Addison, NY   June 13, 1861
WOOLEVER Mary of Addison, NY   Addison, NY

VAN HOUSEN Edward of Pulteney, NY   May 27, 1861
WILLIAMS Amanda of Pulteney, NY

ALLES Elijah   June 4, 1861
HAYES Emily O.   Pulteney, NY

ORDWAY James M. of Adrian, NY   June 6, 1861
BAILEY Elzina of Urbana, NY   Urbana, NY

BULLOCK John of Tuscarora, NY   August 22, 1861
FROMAN Julia of Jasper, NY   Tuscarora, NY

STONE Joel of Troupsburg, NY   August 24, 1861
BROTZMAN Martha Ann of Troupsburg, NY   Addison, NY

MONTGOMERY Charles E.   October 17, 1861
KELLOGG Emma E.   Addison, NY

FLUENT Teneyck of Rathbone, NY   November 18, 1861
ROSENCRANCE Amanda of Brookfield, Pa.   Addison, NY

SHERER Rev. Francis of Fremont, NY   December 10, 1861
HILL Helen A. of Addison, NY   Addison, NY

WARRINER W. A. of Addison, NY   December 22, 1861
THOMPSON Bertha J. of Knoxville, NY   Addison, NY

SLADE Judson D. of Rathbone, NY   January 4, 1862
WILSON Mary E. of Woodhull, NY   Addison, NY

HURDICK Franklin L. of Addison, NY   December 26, 1861
KINGKADE Mira E. of Virgil, NY   Virgil, NY

LEWIS C. E.   January 10, 1862
THURBER Jane O. of Caton, NY   Caton, NY

VEAZIE Jason R. of Caton, NY   January 10, 1862
BABCOCK Phoebe A. of Caton, NY   Caton, NY

VAN ORSDALE James C. of Addison, NY   January 1, 1862
DUNN Emma A. of Addison, NY   Osceola, Pa.

SANDERS George J. of W. Addison, NY   February 23, 1862
SCUTT Anna of W. Cameron, NY

LUDINGTON William S. of Addison, NY   July 14, 1862
JONES Laura A. of Addison, NY   Addison, NY

SEARS Gilbert T. of Freemansburg, NY   July 13, 1862
WILBUR Alice N. dau of Martin of Addison, NY   Addison, NY

CHAPMAN Henry of Otisville, NY   August 20, 1862
OTIS Frances C. of Otisville, NY   Addison, NY

FAIRBANKS Russell L. of Addison, NY   August 3, 1862
EYGEBROAT Elizabeth of Addison, NY   Addison, NY

BROWN Frank B. of Corning, NY   September 9, 1862
DE VOE Nellie M. of Owasco, NY   Buffalo, NY

PAYNE Levi V. of Woodhull, NY   November 2, 1862
BOLYEN Elizabeth A. of Rathbone, NY   Addison, NY

TEFT C. B.   October 29, 1862
HILL H. C. dau of Rev. H. F. Hill   Corning, NY

AMEY Frederick of Corning, NY   (Newspaper date) November 19, 1862
YALE Catherine of Knoxville, NY   Knoxville, NY

TOWNSEND George A. of Hornellsville, NY   November 1, 1862
BRIMMER Louisa V. of Hornellsville, NY   Hornellsville, NY

WARREN Robert Harper of Owego, NY   November 9, 1862
VAN CAMPEN Eliza Ann of Hornellsville, NY   Hornellsville, NY

VAN CAMPEN Hamilton of Hornellsville, NY   November 9, 1862
EDWARDS Maryette of Hornellsville, NY   Hornellsville, NY

CARPENTER Charles V. of Dundee, Ill.   October 15, 1862
SHERMAN Hulda of Urbana, NY   Bath, NY

PIERCE Stephen A. of New York City   November 20, 1862
KING Mrs. Sarah E. of Addison, NY   Addison, NY

GRANT Leroy of Corning, NY   November 9, 1862
WOODWARD Helen of Corning, NY   Corning, NY

SMITH James P. of Caton, NY   November 13, 1862
CROSS Sarah J. of Caton, NY   Corning, NY

BROWN Byron C. of Tuscarora, NY   November 15, 1862
HIGGINS Hulda A. of Tuscarora, NY   Tuscarora, NY

HURLBURT Daniel L. of Addison, NY   November 27, 1862
MOORE Adelaide D. of Tuscarora, NY   Tuscarora, NY

TUBBS Hugh of Woodhull, NY   November 16, 1862
BULLEN Jane of Woodhull, NY   Woodhull, NY

CARPENTER Uriah A. of Cameron, NY   November 23, 1862
MERCHANT Frances A. of Merchantville, NY   Merchantville, NY

EASTERBROOK Andrew J. of Hornby, NY	November 25, 1862
NEWMAN Minerva R. of Tuscarora, NY	Tuscarora, NY
CROCKER Edmond of Addison, NY	December 24, 1862
MARLATT Sarah V. of Woodhull, NY	Addison, NY
PARKER A. J. of Dryden, NY	March 15, 1863
WILCOX M. C. of Addison, NY	Addison, NY
CARR Alvin D. of Tuscarora, NY	March 12, 1863
SPICER Harriet of Tuscarora, NY	Tuscarora, NY
JONES Aruna of Rathbone, NY (Newspaper date)	March 25, 1863
CRANE Mrs. Sarah of Addison, NY	Rathbone, NY
BATES Rufus of Ithaca, NY	April 2, 1863
DOOLITTLE Flora Melissa dau of Anson of Addison, NY	Addison, NY
BOOTH S. A. J. of Addison, NY	April 11, 1863
SMITH Angie of Addison, NY	Addison, NY
SEAMAN Horace of Addison, NY	May 16, 1863
FOX Mercena M. of Addison, NY	Lawrenceville, Pa.
BALL Charles of Lawrenceville, Pa.	May 13, 1863
STODDARD Harriet of Lawrenceville, Pa.	Tuscarora, NY
JONES James E. of Addison, NY	June 9, 1863
BROWN Betsey B. of Addison, NY	Addison, NY
JACKSON John T. of Addison, NY	September 8, 1863
HOLMES Rachel of Addison, NY	Addison, NY
FOX John of Addison, NY	September 27, 1863
HUTCHINS Ermina of Addison, NY	Addison, NY
FERROW George of Alexandria, Va.	September 25, 1863
STEPHENS Annie G. dau of Jacob of Addison, NY	Addison, NY
LYON Augustus W. of Addison, NY	October 22, 1863
BERRY Gertrude of Addison, NY	Addison, NY
AMES Howard 2nd of Addison, NY	October 28, 1863
JONES Ruth E. of Addison, NY	Addison, NY
ALLEN Fernando of Rathbone, NY	November 2, 1863
CHURCH Helen of Rathbone, NY	Cameron, NY
STONE Samuel F. of the 86th NY Vol.	January 13, 1864
SEARLES Anna M.	Addison, NY

HAMMOND John W. of Tuscarora, NY — March 10, 1864 — Woodhull, NY
DELAMATER Adelaide M. of Woodhull, NY

JONES Llewellyn M. of Addison, NY — May 5, 1864 — Erwin, NY
ERWIN Mary E. dau of Arthur of Erwin, NY

GILLETT Charles W. of Addison, NY — September 1, 1864 — Laurens, NY
COMSTOCK Augusta R. of Laurens, NY

PECK Charles of Elmira, NY — October 19, 1864 — Addison, NY
BONHAM Josepha B. of Addison, NY

missing issues

ANSON Junior W. of Addison, NY — February 27, 1866 — Addison, NY
CURRAN Emily of Addison, NY

DAVIS Thomas C. of Brookfield, Pa. — March 10, 1866 — Addison, NY
WILBUR Mary F. of Addison, NY

WARD Thomas of Rathbone, NY — March 22, 1866 — Addison, NY
STROUD Mary of Woodhull, NY

MINARD John H. of Troupsburgh, NY — March 22, 1866 — Addison, NY
OLMSEY Cornelia P. of Troupsburgh, NY

SMITH William B. of Knoxville, Pa. — March 25, 1866 — Knoxville, Pa.
SHOVE Sarah H. of Farmington, Pa.

BREWSTER Orvil of Addison, NY — April 6, 1866 — Addison, NY
EASTWOOD Helen of Addison, NY

RICHARDSON William W. of Beecher's Corners, Pa. — April 12, 1866 — Addison, NY
SMITH Emma of Beecher's Corners, Pa.

ATHERTON Thomas R. of Osceola, Pa. — April 17, 1866 — Addison, NY
GORDON Margaret K. of Tuscarora, NY

AUSTIN Charles — May 26, 1866 — Hornellsville, NY
BOVIER Hannah of Canisteo, NY

CRANDALL Walter of Addison, NY — July 3, 1866
CRANE Mary of Addison, NY

CRANE George of Addison, NY — July 3, 1866
ORR Mary of Addison, NY

WALTY William of Lindley, NY — July 4, 1866
WARD Rachel of Erwin, NY

BUDD John S. of Addison, NY

AMES Sarah of Rochester, NY

July 12, 1866

Rochester, NY

CROWL George W. of Tuscarora, NY

ALBEE Catherine M. dau of Stephen T. of Tuscarora, NY

July 4, 1866

Tuscarora, NY

CLARK Isaac P. of Corning, NY

CASE Sarah A. of Corning at Father's

July 11, 1866

Knoxville, NY

GIBBS Albert V. of Addison, NY

GIBSON Lavina of Gibson, NY

July 4, 1866

Painted Post, NY

HARDIE T. E. of Syracuse, NY

BENNETT M. of Corning, NY

August 5, 1866

Corning, NY

COOK M. P.

CODDINGTON Jennie of Elmira, NY

July 30, 1866

Corning, NY

PETERS H. H.

CODDINGTON E. A. of Elmira, NY

July 30, 1866

Corning, NY

DAVIS H. H.

CASTOR Louisa J. dau of William

July 1, 1866

Caton, NY

KOON Jacob

MOORE Alma L. of Lawrenceville, Pa.

July 4, 1866

Corning, NY

BOATWRIGHT James H. of Rathbone, NY

CLEMENTS Catherine A. of Rathbone, NY

August 5, 1866

Thurston, NY

JONES Ross S.

MULLEN Alice E. dau of Seth of Addison, NY

August 20, 1866

Addison, NY

JAYNES Eugene of Corning, NY

BROWN Julia F. of Corning, NY

August 26, 1866

ELDER Henry J. of Fulton, NY

RICE Martha L. of Gibson, NY

August 13, 1866

Gibson, NY

EDWARDS William H. of Addison, NY

SHEPHERD Helen E. of Addison, NY

August 30, 1866

Addison, NY

VAN ORSDALE Charles A.

COUNTRYMAN Helen C. dau of Solomon of Jasper, NY

October 5, 1866

Jasper, NY

PARK Rufus

COUNTRYMAN Catherine C. dau of Solomon of Jasper, NY

October 3, 1866

Jasper, NY

MAGEE Hugh J. of Lawrenceville, Pa.

ELDRICH Mary of Lawrenceville, Pa.

September 30, 1866

Lawrenceville, Pa.

NYE Obed of W. Union, NY   October 17, 1866
BOARDMAN Eliza Ann of Clymer, Pa.   Addison, NY

O'CONNELL William B. of Dunkirk, NY   October 31, 1866
DE PUY Mary S. dau of Mrs. C. COWLEY of Addison, NY Lawrenceville, Pa.

WALDO William A. of Prattsburgh, NY   December 19, 1866
WAKEMAN Gertrude dau of Rev. Joel Wakeman of Addison Addison, NY

HOWARD Harlow J. of Woodhull, NY   December 2, 1866
CLARK Nettie of Woodhull, NY

NEWTON Willett C. of Woodhull, NY   December 6, 1866
FULLER Juliett of Woodhull, NY

JOHNSON Hon. Thomas A. of Corning, NY   December 18, 1866
PARKER Mrs. Sarah W. dau of Henry WELLS of Penn Yan Penn Yan, NY

HILTON Sylvester B. of Hornby, NY   December 19, 1866
DICKINSON Louisa of Hornby, NY   Hornby, NY

WILSON John of Jackson, Pa.   December 10, 1866
BUCANON Mrs. Emma E. of Corning, NY   Corning, NY

ROGERS Richard H. of Hornby, NY   December 2, 1866
BACKER Delephine of Dix, NY   Hornby, NY

PERRY Albert J. of Galesburg, Ill.   December 9, 1866
HUGHES Albina S. of Savona, NY   Savona, NY

HARLOW James S. Md. of Bath, NY   December 12, 1866
DUDLEY Sarah of Bath, NY

TOWNSEND Josiah of Urbana, NY   December 2, 1866
ANGEL Diantha of Urbana, NY

SPAULDING H. G. of Corning, NY   January 2, 1867
BROWN Jennie F. dau of John N. Brown of Addison, NY Addison, NY

FINCH John of Woodhull, NY   January 19, 1867
MEAD Mrs. Rebecca M. of Woodhhull, NY at res. of Moses FINCH

MORRIS Jacob of Williamsport, Pa.   February 9, 1867
HOLMES Harriet A. of Addison, NY

TEMPLAR William H. of Schenectady, NY   March 21, 1867
STEWART Elizabeth of Addison, NY

WRIGHT James   April 4, 1867
DEMAND Mary of Addison, NY

SWARTWOOD Llewelyn of Cameron, NY
LANPHEAR Harriet of Addison, NY

April 10, 1867

PARK James H. of Addison, NY
REYNOLDS E. A. of Addison, NY

April 23, 1867

FALKNER William A. of Knoxville, Pa.
FRASER Julia of Knoxville, Pa.

April 30, 1867
Addison, NY

REYNOLDS Cyrus J. of Addison, NY
GRAY Jennie of Greene, NY

April 23, 1867
Greene, NY

DICKINSON Francis A. of Thurston, NY
JACK Minerva of Risingille, NY

May 16, 1867
Bath, NY

BEECHER John D. of Avoca, NY
CASE Ellen of Kanona, NY

May 1, 1867
Kanona, NY

TRACY John of Addison, NY
YOUNG Lucilla of Addison, NY

June 16, 1867
Addison, NY

DUDLEY James T. of Elmira, NY
BRONSON Ida dau of A. H. of Painted Post, NY

June 18, 1867
Painted Post, NY

HYDE William F. of Hornellsville, NY
ANDERSON Helen M. of Hornellsville, NY

June 18, 1867
Hornellsville, NY

JUDSON A. H. Esq. of Fredonia, NY
FAIRMAN Sarah A. dau of S. B. of Elmira, NY

June 12, 1867
Fredonia, NY

SAYLES Albert R.
MC MULLEN Fanny dau of James of Corning, NY

June 13, 1867
Painted Post, NY

HOOKER Augustus S. of Troy, Pa.
DONAHE Anna adopt. dau of P. S. of Bath, NY

July 8, 1867
Bath, NY

ROBINSON Oliver S. of Corning, NY
BLISS Katie M. of Addison, NY

July 18, 1867
Addison, NY

SOLES Stephen H. of Bath, NY
WRIGHT Eliza Ann of Thurston, NY

July 4, 1867
Addison, NY

HENDRICK Orva of Hornby, NY
CLARK Bella of Hornby, NY

July 13, 1867

CRAM Henry D. of Meadville, Pa. late of Caton, NY
VEAZIE Eva A. dau of Stephen Veazie

June 30, 1867
Caton, NY

HARRIS George W. of Southport, NY
WIDGER Samantha of Caton, NY

July 31, 1867
Caton, NY

COLEGROVE Albert
LEACH Clara dau of I. C.

September 7, 1867
Woodhull, NY

NICHOLSON William W. of Bath, NY
PRATT Cora of Bath, NY

September 7, 1867
Corning, NY

FORD John K. of Campbell, NY
WHITENACK Marilla A. of Centreville, NY

September 9, 1867
Centreville, NY

ELDRICH Amos of Italy, NY
JORNEON Huldah

August 25, 1867
Prattsburg, NY

RICHARDS Robert of Caton, NY
HOWE Helen of Beecher's Island, Pa.

September 19, 1867
Addison, NY

MC CAIG John E. of Penn Yan, NY
WARD Sarah Jane of Rathbone, NY

October 29, 1867
Rathbone, NY

WHEELER Edward Ransom
MURRAY Mary Isabelle of Beloit, Wis.

November 13, 1867
Addison, NY

BRAUGHT Henry of Bath, NY
HOTCHKISS Sarah A. of Bath, NY

October 30, 1867

DAWSON Robert B. of Hornellsville, NY
AMIDON Sarah of Hornellsville, NY

October 16, 1867
Hornellsville, NY

BAKER W. H. of Corning, NY
VAN ZINE Jennie of St. Louis, Mo.

November 13, 1867
Bath, NY

FERENBAUGH S. H.
PATCHIN Tina E. dau of Dr. L. W. of Carbondale, Pa.

November 12, 1867
Carbondale, Pa.

REYNOLDS J. S. of De Kalb, Ill.
JONES J. Matilda of Addison, NY

December 14, 1867
Addison, NY

BENEDICT William A. of Addison, NY
CRANE Matilda A. of Addison, NY

November 24, 1867
Cooper's Plains, NY

HAYES Byron of Prattsburgh, NY
KENNEDY Margaret of Italy, NY

December 5, 1867
Italy, NY

MC GOWAN Albert S. of Hornellsville, NY
STAINER Adelaide E. of Hornellsville, NY

November 28, 1867
Hornellsville, NY

JONES Charles H. of Addison, NY   (Newspaper date) March 4, 1868
MILES Helen L. of Covington, Pa.   Covington, Pa.

WELTON James P. of Cameron, NY
SMITH Amanda of Cameron, NY

February 24, 1868
Bath, NY

GRIFFIN Thomas of Rathbone, NY   February 28, 1868
JONES Ann E. of Rathbone, NY

GIBSON Mason J. of Addison, NY   March 9, 1868
TINGLEY Mariah E. of Liberty, Va.   Selma, Ala.

BRIMMER John A. of Elkland, Pa.   March 31, 1868
BEAGLE Alice of Elkland, Pa.   Addison, NY

RUSSELL Charles of Ft. Edward, NY   (Newspaper date) May 13, 1868
GUINNIP Mary of Rochester, NY at sis. Mrs. Henry **LAMBERTONS**

MAYHU John of Jasper, NY   May 17, 1868
STILES Lodosky of Troupsburgh, NY   Troupsburgh, NY

VAN DINE Vanrensalaer of Troupsburgh, NY   May 17, 1868
STILES Loretta of Troupsburgh, NY   Troupsburgh, NY

MINARD Isaac of Troupsburg, NY   May 17, 1868
STILES Losiea of Troupsburgh, NY   Troupsburgh, NY

STILES Albert of Troupsburgh, NY   May 17, 1868
GURNSEY Amelia of Troupsburgh, NY   Troupsburgh, NY

BAILEY George of Urbana, NY   August 27, 1868
VAN GELDER Sarah of Prattsburgh, NY   Prattsburgh, NY

OATLEY Ward of S. Dansville, NY   August 13, 1868
BROWN Anna of Burns, NY   Canasaraga, NY

WILSON Milton J. of Cohocton, NY   August 20, 1868
HALL Mary E. of Cohocton, NY   Liberty, NY

CLARK Heman of Rathbone, NY   September 10, 1868
YOUNGS Florence of Rathbone, NY   Rathbone, NY

REYNOLDS Dwight N. of Addison, NY   October 13, 1868
PRICE Mary E. of Addison, NY   Addison, NY

EWING Alexander L. of Corning, NY   October 15, 1868
LANNING Almira H. dau of J. H. of Corning, NY   Corning, NY

PATTISON Charles L. of Fall Brook, Pa.   October 21, 1868
PARKHURST Anna S. dau of Joel of Elkland, Pa.   Elkland, Pa.

WAGNER Lewis C. of Wheeler, NY   November 14, 1868
SHULTS Eliza M. of Prattsburgh, NY   Prattsburgh, NY

O'DELL Theodore of Urbana, NY   November 2, 1868
BARRETT Louisa of Urbana, NY   Bath, NY

GOFF Lucien   November 5, 1868
COASTON Irena of Greenwood, NY   Greenwood, NY

COASTON Casper M. of Canisteo, NY   November 5, 1868
GRACE Sarah A. of Canisteo, NY   Greenwood, NY

SPENCER Alonzo of Nelson, Pa.   November 29, 1868
ORSER Matilda of Addison, NY   Nelson, Pa.

MANLY H. M. of Albert Lee, Mn.   (Newspaper date) December 16, 1868
HALL Electa of Monroe, Wis. at Father's Leonard **JACOBS**   Jasper, NY

ANGEL Byron P. of Exeter, NY   December 17, 1868
BONHAM Gertrude E. of Addison, NY   Addison, NY

WALLACE William of Blossburg, Pa.   December 26, 1868
MUMFORD Deborah widow of Dr. Mumford of Corning   Corning, NY

BATCHELDER John R. of Corning, NY   December 31, 1868
REED Frances R. of Corning, NY   Corning, NY

SMITH Benjamin of Corning, NY   January 5, 1869
WHEAT Minnie A. of Corning, NY   Corning, NY

GOLDEN Francis W. of Painted Post, NY   January 6, 1869
DICKENS Sarah of Painted Post, NY   Painted Post, NY

VEAZIE Arthur of Caton, NY   December 23, 1868
HOYER Mrs. Marion of Caton, NY   Caton, NY

FORCE Edward H. of Caton, NY   December 24, 1868
CONKLIN Julia of Big Flats, NY

DE WATER Yokk H. of Southport, NY   December 24, 1868
CLEVELAND Stella of Caton, NY

WILLIAMS Levi of Corning, NY   December 23, 1868
KNISELEY Catherine A. dau of John C. of Corning, NY

HALEY Solomon of Corning, NY   December 23, 1868
WILLIAMS Henrietta dau of George of Corning, NY

BABCOCK Julian of Caton, NY   December 19, 1868
ENNIST Rebecca of Shokan, NY   Shokan, NY

MORLY G. W. of Mansfield, Pa.   December 24, 1868
JEROLD S. A. of Mansfield, Pa.   Corning, NY

CARRIER George of Elmira, NY   January 19, 1869
TALBOT Mirivia J. of Jasper, NY   Jasper, NY

VEDDER Hiram of Norway, NY
YOUNGS Electa of Rathbone, NY

January 14, 1869
Rathbone, NY

SMITH Alfred C. of Corning, NY
WOOLSEY Izora J. of Addison, NY

December 5, 1868
Hornellsville, NY

DENNIS Peter of Jasper, NY
GOSPER Hannah of Jasper, NY

February 5, 1869
Jasper, NY

SWART Charles of Addison, NY
CONGDON Sarah of Addison, NY

February 20, 1869
Corning, NY

TROOP Eugene of Erwin, NY
BURLINGAME Orinda of Erwin, NY

February 11, 1869
Corning, NY

O'BRIAN Robert of Howard, NY
COOPER Sarah Jane of Bath, NY

January 25, 1869
Howard, NY

SCOTT Samuel W. of Green Bay, Wis.
MALETTE Hattie A. of Avoca, NY

March 17, 1869
Avoca, NY

BRAND J. C. of Thurston, NY
SANDFORD Elizabeth dau of Daniel of Urbana, NY

March 17, 1869
Urbana, NY

JOHNSTON Charles of Caton, NY
WININS Lovicea of Caton, NY

April 18, 1869
Caton, NY

BROWN Edwin of Caton, NY
DONNELL Nellie M. of Elmira, NY

March 30, 1869
Elmira, NY

HOWARD Daniel of Southport, NY
CROSS Libbie of Caton, NY

April 4, 1869
Caton, NY

SANDS Erastus of Hornby, NY
WILDER Hattie E. of Painted Post, NY

April 1, 1869
Painted Post, NY

SHANE Leonard
BARENTHALER Lucy

April 6, 1869
Corning, NY

VANCE James
VERMILYEA S. M.

May 4, 1869
Addison, NY

COLE A. G. of Rathbone, NY
BROMLEY Mira A. of Rathbone, NY

May 20, 1869

BROWN Rush P. son of Dr. R. P. of Addison, NY
COWLEY Georgie of Addison, NY

June 2, 1869
Addison, NY

CRANDALL George of Addison, NY
KENNEDY Anna of Addison, NY

May 27, 1869
Addison, NY

WADSWORTH A. J. of Rochester, NY	June 9, 1869
PERRY Katie dau of Henry C. of Corning, NY	Bath, NY
ARNOLD Henry A. of Ithaca, NY	June 3, 1869
WILKIES Elizabeth of Corning, NY	Corning, NY
HUNT William of Corning, NY	June 6, 1869
HEED Carrie of Caton, NY	Caton, NY
PLACE A. C.	June 8, 1869
SAVORY Miss Frank of Corning, NY	Corning, NY
HAVENS William P. of Corning, NY	June 7, 1869
ROBINSON Susan M. of Corning, NY	Corning, NY
LEARNED William C. of Painted Post, NY	June 8, 1869
SETCHELL Adda of Cuba, NY	Cuba, NY
CORNWELL George E. of Bath, NY	June 6, 1869
SCHENCK S. Jeannette of Bath, NY	Bath, NY
PRESLER William of Riker Hollow, NY	June 6, 1869
DRAKE Lydia of Riker Hollow, NY	Riker Hollow, NY
CROSS Curtis D.	June 1, 1869
CARTER Libbie A. of Canisteo, NY	
BUCK James of Addison, NY	August 8, 1869
YOUNG Mary of Rathbone, NY	Great Bend, Pa.
WALKER Henry of Lindley, NY	July 4, 1869
MATHEWS Matilda L. of Lindley, NY	Addison, NY
EDDY Jerry F. of Campbell, NY	July 3, 1869
CONGDON Emma of Addison, NY	Corning, NY
NOLEN John W. of Binghamton, NY	July 5, 1869
SCOTT Margaret of Corning, NY	Corning, NY
FENTON Morris of Cameron, NY	June 30, 1869
STOCUM Mary of Cameron, NY	Cameron, NY
BAILEY T. S. of Iowa City, Iowa	July 8, 1869
GEE Nellie M. of Council Bluff, Iowa	Council Bluff, Iowa
PARK T. R. of Canisteo, NY	July 20, 1869
BROWN Mary Annie of Canisteo, NY	Niagara Falls, NY
SLINGLAND Orlon of Almond, NY	June 21, 1869
CORNISH Antoinette of Troupsburgh, NY	Troupsburgh, NY

STRAIGHT Dennis of Woodhull, NY	July 11, 1869
GARDINER Martha of Woodhull, NY	Troupsburgh, NY
HARPENDING A. A. of Dundee, NY	July 11, 1869
GRISWOLD Tavie of Addison, NY	Wayne, NY
LEE Lemuel F. of Corning, NY	July 19, 1869
PETERSON Sabina of Corning, NY	Corning, NY
HALBERT Eli of Almond, NY	August 1, 1869
COWAN Elizabeth of Almond, NY	Almond, NY
WILLIAMS James A. of Sheridan, NY	July 31, 1869
WALLACE H. Libbie of Hornellsville, NY	
EDWARDS Milo N. of Hartsville, NY	July 31, 1869
VAN BUSKIRK Eliza J. of Hartsville, NY	
MORROW Robert D. of Thurston, NY	July 24, 1869
STOCKING Amelia of Thurston, NY	
CLARK Eli S. of Altay, NY	July 29, 1869
DRAKE Mattie E. of Watkins, NY	Lake Keuka, NY
BOSTWICK Marshall of Lawrenceville, Pa.	August 4, 1869
ELLISON Emma of Lawrenceville, Pa.	Corning, NY
GODDEN Samuel of Rathbone, NY	August 7, 1869
LANNING Minerva of Rathbone, NY	Addison, NY
FENTON Ezra D. of Tuscarora, NY	August 22, 1869
ALDRICH Marietta of Tuscarora, NY	Tuscarora, NY
BALLARD Alvah of Hammondsport, NY	August 10, 1869
LARROWE Levina E. of Pulteney, NY	Pulteney, NY
SMITH Richard of Woodhull, NY	August 1, 1869
JEFFREY Charlotte of Woodhull, NY	Osceola, Pa.
VAN PELT William of Caton, NY	August 7, 1869
BUTLER Olive of Addison, NY	
SANFORD Daniel T. of Cameron, NY	September 13, 1869
SELLECK Emma J. of Cameron, NY	Addison, NY
MILLER Isaac of Addison, NY	September 15, 1869
ROOT Ida of Addison, NY	Addison, NY
CHAMBERLAIN Benjamin of E. Randolph, NY	October 5, 1869
MILES Margaret of Rathbone, NY	Rathbone, NY

BOWYER John of Rathbone, NY   November 3, 1869
MATHER Emily of Rathbone, NY   Rathbone, NY

FAULKNER Henry of Hammondsport, NY   November 3, 1869
MATHER Eliza of Rathbone, NY   Rathbone, NY

DWIGHT Sylvester of Addison, NY   October 20, 1869
BAKER Mrs. Seraphina dau of Elias H. **SMITH** Corning, NY

SCUDDER Frank T.   November 3, 1869
BRAY Gustie N. dau of James B.   Waverly, NY

CRAME C. C. of Addison, NY   November 9, 1869
BLADES Mrs. Helen A. of Penn Yan, NY   Syracuse, NY

WELLINGTON Samuel B. of Corning, NY   November 17, 1869
HALL Emma F. dau of Isaac of Owego, NY   Owego, NY

SANDERSON W. N. of Painted Post, NY   November 10, 1869
WESSELS Mary of Painted Post, NY   Painted Post, NY

HUGHSON Simeon A. of Big Flats, NY   November 10, 1869
VAN ORDER Emily A. of Big Flats, NY   Oramel, NY

BROWN William M. son of Rev. William B. of Newark, NJ   November 16, 1869
BAXTER Nellie M. of Corning, NY   Corning, NY

LOWELL O. B.   November 16, 1869
ETZ Mrs.Sarah M. dau of Mrs. A. **WELLINGTON** Tioga, Pa.

CROWL Alvin of Addison, NY   December 12, 1869
MOURHESS Cynthia of Addison, NY

HATHAWAY Edgar M.   December 1, 1869
TUBBS Julia D.   Woodhull, NY

WELTA Jacob   December 17, 1869
BAXTER Susan O.   Woodhull, NY

GOULD William H.   December 1, 1869
BRIGGS Elsie J. of Woodhull, NY   Woodhull, NY

STURDEVANT Thomas of Knoxville, Pa.   December 15, 1869
DELANY Elizabeth of Knoxville, Pa.   Knoxville, Pa.

WARD Ashbel A. of N. Almond, NY   December 21, 1869
DUNNING Jennie of N. Almond, NY

CLEAVELAND Bradford   December 20, 1869
KAPLE Hattie of Hornellsville, NY

CHASE Chandler W. of Cameron, NY
SABIN Clara A. of Cameron, NY
January 1, 1870
Addison, NY

LEE James E. of Binghamton, NY
GRISWOLD Mattie of Addison, NY
December 28, 1869
Elmira, NY

SEELEY Dr. A. H. of Woodhull, NY
SULLIVAN Maggie of Woodhull, NY
January 9, 1870
Addison, NY

SMITH Lewis of Burdette, NY
CARMAN Phoebe of Mechlinburgh, NY
December 30, 1869
Mechlinburgh, NY

THURBER Joseph of Caton, NY
FORCE Alice of Caton, NY
January 1, 1870
Mechlinburgh, NY

ROSS Thomas of Cooper's Plains, NY
SHULTZ Alvira of Cooper's Plains, NY
December 28, 1869
Painted Post, NY

LITTLE Thomas H. of Torrey, NY
COVERT Hannah M. of Painted Post, NY
December 30, 1869
Painted Post, NY

CORNISH William of Van Etten, NY
PAUL Laura of Erwin, NY
December 31, 1869
Erwin, NY

JACOBS Lemuel K. of Corning, NY
JONES Ida dau of I. P. of Corning, NY
December 30, 1869
Corning, NY

HODSON William J. of Waverly, NY
JOHNSON Emma of Wellsboro, Pa.
January 3, 1870
Corning, NY

BURKE Thomas W. of Tioga, Pa.
BUCK Hettie M. of Addison, NY
December 13, 1869
Addison, NY

LANE John C. of Big Rapids, Mi.
NORTHRUP Arminda of Rathbone, NY
February 16, 1870
Rathbone, NY

BRUNDAGE James W. of Urbana, NY
BRONSON Sarah of Urbana, NY
February 10, 1870
Urbana, NY

MEADE Benjamin F. of Corning, NY
SAVORY Adda of Corning, NY
February 20, 1870
Corning, NY

LOVELL George L.
DOANE Isabella F. of Erwin, NY
March 2, 1870
Erwin, NY

GIFFORD James R. of Hornby, NY
COYE Alice D. of Hornby, NY
February 23, 1870
Corning, NY

DENTON James H. of Painted Post, NY
GRANT Mary of Painted Post, NY
February 28, 1870
Corning, NY

SHOEMAKER Samuel O. of Corning, NY
HOWARD Mary E. of Big Flats, NY
March 2, 1870
Big Flats, NY

SAVORY James W. of Painted Post, NY
WOOD Edith A. of Painted Post, NY
February 16, 1870
Painted Post, NY

LANGDON Smith H. of Canisteo, NY
WARNER Eliza L. of Canisteo, NY
February 22, 1870
Hornellsville, NY

CRANE Cyrus of Addison, NY
SAXTON Ella of Addison, NY
March 18, 1870
Addison, NY

BROUGHM John H. of Horseheads, NY
HAMILTON Frank of Horseheads, NY
March 3, 1870

GRINNELL Ira N. of Lindley, NY
BENJAMIN Ann E. of Tuscarora, NY
March 30, 1870
Addison, NY

BAKER Myron L. of Torrey, NY
NORMAN Eliza Ann of W. Dryden, NY
March 26, 1870
Addison, NY

EVANS Clark of Corning, NY
JAMES Alice S. of Corning, NY
April 27, 1870
Corning, NY

EASTERBROOK George H. of Painted Post, NY
THROOP Dora of Painted Post, NY
April 20, 1870
Painted Post, NY

GEE James of Nelson, Pa.
WARNER Julia A. of Corning, NY
April 14, 1870
Corning, NY

GUNSOLOS Tunis
COLLIER Martha H. of Avoca, NY
(Newspaper date) May 11, 1870
Avoca, NY

HORTON Ira of Pulteney, NY
THOMPSON Mrs. Cynthia of Prattsburgh, NY
(Newspaper date) May 11, 1870
Prattsburgh, NY

GREGG Joshua C. of Hornellsville, NY
WOMBOUGH Olive A. of Addison, NY
May 18, 1870
Addison, NY

WITTER D. P. formerly of Addison, NY
LA GRANGE Ella M. of Harrisville, Mi.
April 29, 1870
Harrisville, Mi.

RANDALL John S. of Cohocton, NY
CADY Helen M. of Avoca, NY
April 25, 1870
Avoca, NY

HALL Stephen of Corning, NY
BARBER Anna of Corning, NY
May 14, 1870
Corning, NY

DE WOLF Peter J. of Little Flats, NY
CLARK Carrie E. of Little Flats, NY
May 12, 1870
Corning, NY

HUGGINS John of Lindley, NY   May 12, 1870
WATSON Winnie of Lindley, NY   Corning, NY

LATHROP William of Corning, NY   May 24, 1870
BISSELL Arvesta of Corning, NY   Corning, NY

COBB F. H. of Dunkirk, NY   May 18, 1870
ANDERSON Etta of Hornellsville, NY

SOULE Thomas of Caton, NY   May 21, 1870
MURCY Jane of Caton, NY   Caton, NY

BEATON George S.   May 11, 1870
ALLERTON Emma of Thurston, NY   Thurston, NY

WHITTEMORE Moses Faller of Jasper, NY   May 18, 1870
HATCH Sarah Abigail of Jasper, NY   Jasper, NY

CASE Eugene B. of Lawrenceville, Pa.   February 1, 1870
NEWTON Eunice of Addison, NY   Addison, NY

ORR Robert B. of Tuscarora, NY   June 22, 1870
PATRICK Mary A. of Lindley, NY   Addison, NY

NEWTON George of Addison, NY   July 4, 1870
POTTER Mary of Addison, NY   Addison, NY

BROWN George of Corning, NY   July 5, 1870
CLARK Arlena of Corning, NY   Corning, NY

POLMATEER Harrison H. of Prattsburgh, NY   July 4, 1870
HENDRICK Agnes C. of Hornby, NY   Corning, NY

HOOD Orrin D. of Savona, NY   July 3, 1870
GARRISON Frances A. of Wheeler, NY   Bath, NY

BAIN Alphus D. of Wheeler, NY   June 22, 1870
HOFFMAN Parmelia of Bath, NY   Bath, NY

DANIELS Norman of Bath, NY   (Newspaper date) July 13, 1870
GILLETT Frances M. of Bath, NY

SMITH John L. of Kanona, NY   June 29, 1870
BARTLETT Sarah of Horseheads, NY   Bath, NY

PUFFER S. M. of Canisteo, NY   July 2, 1870
THOMPSON Susannah of Howard, NY   Hornellsville, NY

STEVENS Lee of Hartsville, NY   July 3, 1870
WILLIAMS Theresa of Hartsville, NY   Hornellsville, NY

BATES Joseph M. of Hornellsville, NY   July 2, 1870
WENBEN Josephine of Hornellsville, NY   Hornellsville, NY

LYON Walker S. of Catherine, NY   August 11, 1870
BLISS Mary of Addison, NY   Addison, NY

GOODBY J. H. of Addison, NY   July 31, 1870
TAFT Lydia of Addison, NY   Portage, NY

WHITTENHALL Charles Theodore of Seneca, Ks.   September 13, 1870
STEVENS Frank L. of Hornellsville, NY   Hornellsville, NY

CLARK Lyman D. of Hornellsville, NY   September 8, 1870
WHEELER Mary I. of Hornellsville, NY   Hornellsville, NY

RUMSEY Peter of Thurston, NY   September 21, 1870
NORTHRUP Alice J. of Thurston, NY   Thurston, NY

SMITH Oliver of Hammondsport, NY   September 25, 1870
STRAIT Anna of Hammondsport, NY at res. of Ira Smith   Bath, NY

HOUSE Jacob of Bath, NY   September 22, 1870
REYNOLDS Mrs. ____ of Bath, NY   Bath, NY

HOAG D. S. of Chicago, Ill.   October 6, 1870
COOK Aggie dau of F. F. Cook of Addison, NY   Addison, NY

VAUGHN Harvey I. of Cameron, NY   October 2, 1870
MANLY Almira of Painted Post, NY   Corning, NY

KETCHUM W. of Towlesville, NY   Newspaper date) October 12, 1870
GAY Sarah J. of Towlesville, NY   Towlesville, NY

PATTERSON John G. of Bath, NY   September 27, 1870
DOBBIN Mary Jane of Bath, NY

SPAFFORD S. A. of Canisteo, NY   October 13, 1870
KIMBERLIN Mary A. of Dryden, NY   Addison, NY

CRAWFORD William of Rathbone, NY   October 5, 1870
NORTHRUP Delia of Rathbone, NY   Cameron Mills, NY

SMYTH George M. of Corning, NY   September 29, 1870
WELLS Isabella S. of Corning, NY   Corning, NY

DANIELS Joseph W. of Bath, NY   September 28, 1870
FIELDS Sarah E. of Chemung, NY   Chemung, NY

ERWIN Arthur H. of Painted Post, NY   October 19, 1870
BROWN Gertie M. dau of Reuben P. of Addison, NY   Addison, NY

BROOKS Clark of Addison, NY   October 20, 1870
WILBER Emma Adell of Addison, NY   Addison, NY

HARRINGTON Eugene N. of Rathbone, NY   October 20, 1870
BURLINGAME Seraphine of Rathbone, NY   Addison, NY

GRAY F. E. of Addison, NY   October 26, 1870
CARTER Ritie L. of Greene, NY   Greene, NY

BROWN Myron A. of Corning, NY   (Newspaper date) November 9, 1870
WHEELER Mary A. of Candor, NY   Candor, NY

GILBERT James A.   October 23, 1870
HILL Julia E. dau of Ephraim of Caton, NY   Caton, NY

DAVIS Edwin F. of Corning, NY   October 26, 1870
DOW Jennie M. of Corning, NY

BONHAM Myron L. of Deerfield, Pa.   November 2, 1870
BOSARD Susie A. of Osceola, Pa.   Osceola, Pa.

HARDENBURG Chester M. of Corning, NY   October 29, 1870
RUTHERFORD Nellie M. of Corning, NY

WARNER Mathew of Lindley, NY   November 14, 1870
BARRON Elizabeth of Tuscarora, NY   Corning, NY

THORNE Charles E. of Horseheads, NY   November 9, 1870
BAKER Minnie (Amanda) of Corning, NY   Corning, NY

KENT John of Big Flats, NY   November 16, 1870
GRAVES Ellen of Elkland, Pa.   Addison, NY

CONGDON George W. of Addison, NY   December 3, 1870
WEBSTER Rosa of Addison, NY   Addison, NY

RANDALL George W. of Benton, NY   November 29, 1870
MERRIFIELD Florence A. of Benton, NY   Addison, NY

BARRETT Frank A. of Maine   November 17, 1870
HINDS Ella F. formerly of Corning, NY   Washington DC

FENDERSON Frank A. of Corning, NY   November 23, 1870
PATCHIN Mary H. of Painted Post, NY   Painted Post, NY
    (sister of Mrs. S. H. **FERENBAUGH**)

HORTON John C.   November 16, 1870
SEYMOUR Effie M.   Tioga, Pa.

PADDOCK Phillip of Jerusalem, NY   December 8, 1870

COGSWELL Caroline E. of Jerusalem, NY   Jerusalem, NY

WALLACE Joseph H. of Hornellsville, NY   November 30, 1870
HAMMOND Nancy of Belmont, NY   Hornellsville, NY

PARSELLS Charles E. of Addison, NY   January 3, 1871
HARDEE Hannah M. of Rathbone, NY   Rathbone, NY

MC FALL Henry of Bath, NY   January 18, 1871
LINDSEY Lizzie of Bath, NY

BRUNDAGE Lewis of Thurston, NY   January 19, 1871
ADAMS Lizzie of Bath, NY

BAILEY Joseph of N. Cameron, NY   January 18, 1871
LE SURE Mrs. Malinda of N. Cameron, NY   N. Cameron, NY

BEAM Isaac of Mitchellville, NY   January 23, 1871
HIGGINS Mrs. Hannah of Cameron, NY   Cosse's Corners, NY

COOK Jacob of Thurston, NY   April 2, 1871
ROZELL Libbie of Caton, NY   Caton, NY

CLARK John W. of Addison, NY   April 6, 1871
DODGE Mary L. of Addison, NY   Addison, NY

PERKINS Wallace of Tuscarora, NY   March 26, 1871
ALDRICH Alice L. of S. Addison, NY   Addison, NY

CRAWFORD Lewis D. of Rathbone, NY   April 2, 1871
KELLY Sarah M. of Rathbone, NY   Addison, NY

MOREHESS James of Tuscarora, NY   April 21, 1871
THOMAS Cornelia of Tuscarora, NY   Addison, NY

COLE George F. of Woodhull, NY   April 23, 1871
BRION Clara M. of Woodhull, NY   Addison, NY

DENNING Dyer W. of Corning, NY   April 30, 1871
JOHNSON Catherine Amelia of Olean, NY   Addison, NY

ROBERTSON Almon of Corning, NY   April 26, 1871
SHEPHERD Lovinia of Corning, NY   Corning, NY

JENNINGS William B. of Addison, NY   April 25, 1871
BAKER Mary A. of Painted Post at Mrs. Elizabeth **VOAK** Painted Post, NY

SHAW John of Campbell, NY   April 29, 1871
SMITH Mamie of Campbell, NY   Painted Post, NY

COVELL Edward S. of Elmira, NY April 27, 1871
RATHBONE Mary B. dau of Henry

BRONSON Isaac H. of Urbana, NY May 3, 1871
MC FIE Elizabeth M. of Urbana, NY Bath, NY

COOPER Charles J. of Hornellsville, NY May 2, 1871
FITZGIBBONS Mary E. of Hornellsville, NY

HOLT George C. April 26, 1871
WHITTENHALL Mary E. dau of Capt. D. S. Rulo, Neb.

TOWSLEY Charles A. of Jasper, NY July 4, 1871
TOWSLEY Elsie of Jasper, NY

BAUTER John M. of Wheeler, NY June 6, 1871
SHULTS Minerva C. of Wheeler, NY Wheeler, NY

BROWNELL T. K. of Waterville, NY June 14, 1871
UPSON Phebe A. of Canisteo, NY Canisteo, NY

MILLER William of Howard, NY June 18, 1871
SWARTWOOD Angeline of Howard, NY Hornellsville, NY

BLANK John Jr. of Dansville, NY June 24, 1871
PETERS Mary Jane of Hornellsville, NY Hornellsville, NY

HEPWORTH George E. of Addison, NY July 4, 1871
MITCHELL Sarah of Addison, NY Addison, NY

HARRISON John D. of Canisteo, NY July 7, 1871
HARRINGTON Lavina of Addison, NY

ECKER John of Wellsville, NY July 29, 1871
REMLEY Margaret of Wellsville, NY Addison, NY

COLEGROVE William H. of Arkport, NY August 2, 1871
SPAULDING Mary J. of Chatham, Pa. Hornellsville, NY

GRANT James O. of Addison, NY August 19, 1871
MILLS Elizabeth of Cameron, NY Addison, NY

NICHOLS William M. of Bath, NY September 7, 1871
MORROW Caroline B. of Tyrone, NY Tyrone, NY

SMEAD Benjamin formerly of Bath, NY August 31, 1871
DODGE Annie of Albany, NY Albany, NY

KILBURN I. G. August 30, 1871
WAKELEY Libbie of Brookfield, Pa. Corning, NY

PATCHALL John G. of St. Louis, Mo.
SAXTON Mary of Addison, NY
September 27, 1871
Addison, NY

DUNN Frank Albert of Goodland, Ind.
GROY Frank
September 21, 1871
Bath, NY

BENNETT James E. of Bath, NY
RUTHERFORD Rose A. of Bath, NY
September 21, 1871
Bath, NY

FINCH Isaac of Tuscarora, NY
KNAPP Mrs. E. of Addison, NY at res of S. Knapp
September 3, 1871
Cameron, NY

MC MULLEN or (**MC COLLUM**) Jacob of Caton, NY
COLE Hannah of Caton, NY
October 7, 1871
Addison, NY

CHASE Roswell of Cameron, NY
RUFF Helen of Cameron, NY
October 2, 1871
Bath, NY

HALLOCK Jesse of Campbell, NY
SNYDER Ella of Bath, NY
October 3, 1871
Bath, NY

THOMAS A. L. of Addison, NY
HARRINGTON Mrs. E. of Addison, NY
October 15, 1871
Addison, NY

BASLEY James H.
CROSS Mrs. Henrietta of Tioga, Pa.
October 6, 1871
Gibson, NY

KELTS Delos
MIDDAW Harriet of Lawrenceville, Pa.
October 4, 1871

CAPLE Charles H. of Alfred, NY
PERKINS Mary E. of Andover, NY
October 5, 1871
Hornellsville, NY

RIDDELL Joseph of Canisteo, NY
LAUDER Aggie of Hornellsville, NY
October 5, 1871
Canisteo, NY

THOMAS Lemuel of Bath, NY
WILSON Georgiana of Bath, NY
October 11, 1871

LATTIMER Ferris W. of Addison, NY
CONDERMAN Emma S. of Hornellsville, NY
October 17, 1871
Hornellsville, NY

MC GRAW Alonzo S. of Hartsville, NY
WHITFORD Olive of Hornellsville, NY
October 15, 1871
Hartsville, NY

TERBELL W. D. Md. of Corning, NY
WEST Mary C. of Corning, NY
October 16, 1871
Elmira, NY

ROWLEY Elijah of Titusville, Pa.
THOMPSON Kate of Corning, NY
October 11, 1871
Corning, NY

JOHNSON Ithuel M. of Corning, NY   October 11, 1871
MORGAN Louisa A. of Corning, NY   Corning, NY

STANTON L. J. of Hornby, NY   October 12, 1871
VAN HOESON Melissa of Hornby, NY   Hornby, NY

HILL George B. of Corning, NY   October 18, 1871
CARR Mary G. of Corning, NY   Corning, NY

STODDARD Dr. Charles of Wis.   October 10, 1871
MYRTLE Belle   Hammondsport, NY

MC INTOSH Hiram of Almond, NY   October 11, 1871
O'CONNOR Mrs. L. W. of Almond, NY   Almond, NY

PECK William M. of Fabins, NY   October 25, 1871
ELDRICH Ellen D. of Groton, NY formerly of Addison   Groton, NY

RHODES B. Franklin of Elmira, NY   December 31, 1871
BREES Nettie of Caton, NY   Corning, NY

STRATTON George W. of Lindley, NY   November 22, 1871
THURBER Julia A. of Lindley, NY   Lindley, NY

FORCE Oscar of Caton, NY   December 5, 1871
WOLCOTT Frances J. of Caton, NY   Caton, NY

NELLIS George W. of Cambletown, NY   November 11, 1871
VELIE Martha J. of Cambletown, NY

TORRENCE Marcus L. of Thurston, NY   December 4, 1871
JACKSON Mrs. C. J. of Bath, NY

ROWLEY Frank L.   December 12, 1871
GREGORY Jane I. of Caton, NY   Caton, NY

MC LEOD D. of Hornellsville, NY   December 2, 1871
BROWN Eliza of Hornellsville, NY   Hornellsville, NY

OWEN A. J. of Corning, NY   December 6, 1871
WENTZ Mrs. Louise M. of Corning, NY

SCHOONOVER Mansel of Clymer, Pa.   January 1, 1872
SMITH Mary J. of Tuscarora, NY   Addison, NY

CONNOR Theodore W. of Painted Post, NY   (News. date)   January 3, 1872
CLEMONS Frances A. of Painted Post, NY   Addison, NY

FLINT James M. of Dansville, NY   December 17, 1871
DAVIS Emma at res. of William B. **STEVENS**   Steven's Mills, NY

MAJOR John J. of Hornellsville, NY
BEACH Sarah of Dansville, NY
December 19, 1871
Dansville, NY

DENNIS Sidney H. of Jasper, NY
MC NEIL Kate F. of Oxford, NY
December 4, 1871
Jasper, NY

MERRIHEW Delvin A. of Plattsburg, NY
PARSONS Gertrude A. of Hartsville, NY
December 21, 1871

HELM Willis of Elmira, NY
ROWLEY Cecelia of Addison, NY
January 27, 1872
Addison, NY

FARNHAM George of Addison, NY
REYNOLDS Mary dau of late Nathan of Elmira, NY
January 17, 1872
Elmira, NY

SMITH S. T. of Emporium, Pa.
MC NEIL Mary E. dau of Willis
January 11, 1872
Campbell, NY

SCHOONOVER R. P. of S. Troupsburgh, NY
LEROY Eliza of S. Troupsburgh, NY
February 26, 1872
S. Troupsburgh, NY

PRICE L. S. of Addison, NY
WHEELER Lois E. of Cameron, NY
March 31, 1872

DOBBIN Samuel R. of Bath, NY
WILSON Martha Jane of Howard, NY
April 3, 1872
Howard, NY

RANDALL Franklin E. of Painted Post, NY
BENN Adelia of Painted Post, NY
March 31, 1872
Erwin, NY

WAGNER Hiram R. of Hornellsville, NY
SNELL Celestia of Avoca, NY
April 10, 1872
Avoca, NY

MC CLAY Joseph of Maquoketa, Iowa
BARTON Catherine L. of Addison, NY
May 7, 1872
Monticello, Iowa

EASTERBROOK E. Josiah of Hornby, NY
DICKINSON Delinda E. of Hornby, NY
May 1, 1872
Corning, NY

PENCE Jacob S. of Lock Haven, Pa.
BUCK Kate J. of Addison, NY
June 18, 1872
Addison, NY

TRUE George of Addison, NY
TURNER Louisa of Addison, NY
June 19, 1872
Addison, NY

VAN GORDON Cornelius of Addison, NY
DE PUY Mrs. Zada E. of Addison, NY
June 22, 1872
Addison, NY

COLE Alpheus B.
DOLTEN Mary A. of Tuscarora, NY
July 1, 1872
Corning, NY

RICE Asahel E. of Farmington, Pa.　　July 22, 1872
TEACHMAN Jennie of Farmington, Pa.　　Addison, NY

SCHINDER Andrew of Michawaka, Ind.　　August 21, 1872
COLVIN Kate of Hornellsville, NY　　Hornellsville, NY

ANDREWS Charles of Avoca, NY　　August 25, 1872
STINSON Mary E. of Bath, NY　　Kanona, NY

STARKS J. C.　　August 29, 1872
WRIGHT Ella C. of Campbell, NY

PERKINS John G. of Tuscarora, NY　　September 26, 1872
ORVIS Fronie of Tuscarora, NY　　Tuscarora, NY

TANNER John of Troupsburgh, NY　　September 29, 1872
BENTON Mary E. of Troupsburgh, NY　　Troupsburgh, NY

NICHOLSON Henry J. of Rathbone, NY　　August 15, 1872
WOOD Elizabeth　　Addison, NY

WILSON James E. of Addison, NY　　October 2, 1872
WOMBOUGH Elizabeth of Tuscarora, NY　　Tuscarora, NY

BANNIFIELD Capt. S. A.　　June 13 1872
CLINTON Frances L. formerly of Addison, NY　　Eureka, Cal.

FARNHAM George W. of Addison, NY　　October 30, 1872
NYE Minnie of Addison, NY　　Addison, NY

GREEN Frank of Addison, NY　　November 3, 1872
PHOENIX Esther of Rathbone, NY　　Rathbone, NY

BORDEN S. B. of Addison, NY　　December 8, 1872
HARRISON Lizzie of Addison, NY　　Addison, NY

WOOD John T. formerly of Montgomery, NY　　December 8, 1872
ADAMS May of Hornellsville, NY　　Addison, NY

ORR B. F. of Addison, NY　　December 3, 1872
MORSE Alice M. of Randolph, Ohio　　Randolph, Ohio

LOVELESS Charles W.　　November 30, 1872
DAVIS Sarah E. of Corning, NY　　Corning, NY

CHAPMAN Frank of Corning, NY　　December 24, 1872
TAYLORSON Christine of Painted Post, NY　　Painted Post, NY

BEARDSLEY Albert J. of Addison, NY　　December 22, 1872
WOODCOCK Jennie of Addison, NY　　Woodhull, NY

BRENNEN James of Lindley, NY
MONKS Mary Ann of Lindley, NY

January 1, 1873
Addison, NY

ROOT Henry E. of Addison, NY
BEARDSLEY Ruth A. of Addison, NY

January 1, 1873
Addison, NY

BENSON Herman A. of Addison, NY
JOHNSON Carrie of Addison, NY

January 8, 1873
Addison, NY

HUNTER Charles of Addison, NY
HULSIZER Mara of Addison, NY

January 25, 1873
Addison, NY

DAVISON George L. of Caton, NY
BENSON Emma E. of E. Groveland, NY

January 22, 1873
Addison, NY

GARRABRANT William E. of Baldwin, NY
BROWN Libbie E. of Woodhull, NY

January 15, 1873
Woodhull, NY

CASSIDY Thomas of Elmira, NY
FITZPATRICK Katie of Elmira, NY

February 25, 1873
Bath, NY

SEELEY Judd
REDFIELD Mrs. Mary of Farmington, Pa.

February 26, 1873
Osceola, Pa.

FORD Adelbert of Troupsburg, NY
DAWLEY Hannah of Woodhull, NY

February 24, 1873
Westfield, Pa.

BROWN Dr. Franklin of Binghamton, NY
LAWTON Aggie of Rochester, NY

March 1, 1873
Elmira, NY

MORSE Lee
LASHURE Kate of Lindley, NY

March 4, 1873
Corning, NY

ALDRICH Thomas S. of Rathbone, NY
PARKER Mary A. of Rathbone, NY

March 18, 1873
Addison, NY

VAUGHN H. of Cameron, NY
BROWNELL Lucinda of Cameron, NY

March 17, 1873
Cameron, NY

STRAIT Luke of Tuscarora, NY
CORNWELL Alice A. of Tuscarora, NY

February 29, 1873
Tuscarora, NY

SWAN Lyman A.
WELLS Martha M.

April 3, 1873
Tuscarora, NY

BEARDSLEY Sylvester W. of Orleans Co. NY
WRIGHT Azuba A. of Tuscarora, NY

April 5, 1873
Tuscarora, NY

METCALF Christopher of Huron, NY
PERKINS Mary A. dau of P. W. of Tuscarora, NY

March 27, 1873
Tuscarora, NY

WEEKS William H. of Tuscarora, NY   March 27, 1873
PERKINS Jennie of Tuscarora, NY   Tuscarora, NY

WHITE Charles F. Editor of Allegany Democrat   April 3, 1873
MILLEN Jennie E. dau of H. W.   Wellsville, NY

NADO Eli of Addison, NY   April 5, 1873
CONGDON Eve of Addison, NY   Addison, NY

MONKS Richard of New York City   April 9, 1873
TENBROECK Clara of Big Flats, NY   Addison, NY

RICKY John of Addison, NY   April 9, 1873
CHRISTIAN Frankie of Addison, NY   Addison, NY

SHEPARD Frank of Chicago, Ill.   May 6, 1873
KATHAN Agnes of Oxford, NY formerly of Addison, NY   Oxford, NY

VAN GORDON Dewitt   May 25, 1873
DAY Lizzie E. of Dansville, NY   Addison, NY

HOFFMAN Norman D. of Addison, NY   May 13, 1873
RUSSELL Ellen L. dau of late Joseph of Warrensburg, NY   Chestertown, NY

HUNT E. J. of Woodhull, NY   May 5, 1873
COOK Nancy I. of Woodhull, NY   Woodhull, NY

PEYNE Mathias S. of Jackson Co. Ind.   (Newspaper date) July 23, 1873
DAVID Ann of Addison, NY

LEWIS Hiram D. of Belmont, NY   (Newspaper date) July 30, 1873
TALBOT Delephine of Jasper, NY

REDWOOD Hamilton L. of Corning, NY   August 23, 1873
THOMAS Betsey L. of Troupsburgh, NY

WORMLEY Frank of Addison, NY   August 27, 1873
LAWTON Addie of Addison, NY   Addison, NY

HUBBARD T. S. of Fredonia, NY   July 29, 1873
GILBERT Carrie M. of Fredonia, NY   Fredonia, NY

HUBBARD Rev. A. W. of Cameron, NY   August 25, 1873
SPENCER Emma R. of Corning, NY   Corning, NY

FULKERSON John of Addison, NY   September 1, 1873
HATHAWAY Julia of Addison, NY

AMES Francis R.   September 3, 1873
COOLEY D. Denton of Eldred, Neb. dau of Charles   Addison, NY

ORMSBY Wilmot M. of Troupsburgh, NY   September 28, 1873
VOSE Julia A. of Addison, NY   Coopers Plains, NY

BENSON William W. of Woodhull, NY   September 13, 1873
MC DOWELL Laura C. of Addison Hill, NY   Osceola, Pa.

TUBBS John of Osceola, Pa.   September 24, 1873
PHELPS Mrs. D. C. of Osceola, Pa.   Osceola, Pa.

CLARK Joel of Canisteo, NY   September 10, 1873
HALLETT Addie of Cameron, NY   Cameron, NY

JOHNSON Alza H. of Jasper, NY   September 17, 1873
TAYLOR Ella C. of Jasper, NY   Cameron, NY

PURDY Frank Md. of Corning, NY   October 9, 1873
O'DELL Julia E. of Addison, NY   Cameron, NY

STUART Norman of Addison, NY   October 14, 1873
SPENCER Jane of Rathbone, NY   Rathbone, NY

CURTIS James Z. of Thurston, NY   October 15, 1873
BUCK Loretta Ann of Thurston, NY   Addison, NY

MC INTOSH John W. of S. Addison, NY   October 20, 1873
CARR Nellie E. of S. Addison, NY   S. Addison, NY

WYGANT J. L. of Cameron Mills, NY   October 26, 1873
TUBBS Susan P. of Cameron Mills, NY   Cameron Mills, NY

DICKEY Charles B. of Cameron, NY   October 30, 1873
JOHNSTON Melissa of Cameron, NY   Cameron, NY

WESTCOTT J. E. of Addison, NY   November 9, 1873
JONES Emma of Osceola, Pa.

DININNEY H. J. of Danbury, Conn.   November 19, 1873
AMBLER Sarah O. of Danbury, Conn.

COLEGROVE Charles A. of Hornellsville, NY   November 25, 1873
DAVISON Louie E. of Bath, NY   Bath, NY

LEWIS James S. of Mansfield, Pa.   December 7, 1873
RUSHMORE May of Mansfield, Pa.   Mansfield, Pa.

SMITH Albert D. of Woodhull, NY   December 4, 1873
SIMONS Emma of Addison, NY   Addison, NY

FOX Alanson J. of Painted Post, NY   December 10, 1873
STEBBINS Cornelia of Plainfield, NJ   Plainfield, NJ

WOODMANSE Melvin of Canisteo, NY   December 18, 1873
BUNN Emma Estella of Canisteo, NY   Canisteo, NY

SEARS Uriah P. of Thurston, NY   December 24, 1873
ORR Edna L. of Monestique, Mi.   Monestique, Mi.

MYERS Christian of Townline, NY   January 22, 1874
SHAVER Rosetta of Rathbone, NY   Addison, NY

GREEN Samuel of Addison, NY   January 29, 1874
DIKE Mary J. of Elmira, NY   Addison, NY

TAFT Theodore R. of Tuscarora, NY   February 8, 1874
MOOR Emerjene of Pa.

STICKLES John W. of Jasper, NY   February 19, 1874
FORT Phoebe J. of Thurston, NY   Hedgesville, NY

SIMPSON James F. of Tuscarora, NY   December 30, 1873
ALDRICH Eva M. of Tuscarora, NY   Tuscarora, NY

SMITH Oscar A.   February 19, 1874
KITTLE Frances I.   Tuscarora, NY

SMITH Joseph H. of Sidney Plains, NY   February 17, 1874
SOUTHWORTH Agnes A. of Aetna, NY   Addison, NY

BALCOM I. Goodrich   March 3, 1874
WOOSTER Jane E. of Olympia, Washinton Terr.   Addison, NY

STEPHENS Robert of Tuscarora, NY   March 1, 1874
JORDAN Mary E. of Addison, NY   Addison, NY

COOK Varnum of Lindley, NY   March 5, 1874
MULFORD Licetta of Lindley, NY   Addison, NY

HARDER H. D. of Woodhull, NY   February 27, 1874
MERING Priscilla of Rathbone, NY

HIBBARD William of Addison, NY   March 7, 1874
MILLER Ida of Addison, NY   Addison, NY

KIMBALL Madison C. of Osceola, Pa.   March 8, 1874
ALBEE Arvilla A. of Addison, NY   Addison, NY

BILLS William H. of Lindley, NY   March 1, 1874
BAKER Hannah C. of Lindley, NY at Mrs. Hannah Bills   Tuscarora, NY

HARRISON Charles M. of Lindley, NY   March 4, 1874
MANLEY Leona N. of Tuscarora, NY   Tuscarora, NY

BILLS Zacra of Erwin, NY
BRIGGS Harriet E. of Bridgemanville, NY

April 1, 1874
Bridgemanville, NY

REYNOLDS Nathaniel of Troupsburgh, NY
HORTON Mrs. May of Troy, Pa.

March 31, 1874
Troy, Pa.

HARRISON John H. of Lindley, NY
MANLEY Elnora P. of Tuscarora, NY

April 19, 1874
Tuscarora, NY

DATES William of Rathbone, NY
WOOD Mrs. Elizabeth L. of Rathbone, NY

April 27, 1874
Addison, NY

CRANE Richard K. of Elmira, NY
LEWIS Eleanah of Addison, NY

May 20, 1874
Addison, NY

SPAULDING William L. of Rockingham Co. NC
LAURDER Jennie formerly of Hornellsville, NY

May 3, 1874
Rockingham Co. NC

LANE George of Addison, NY   (Newspaper date) June 18, 1874
DRAKE Clara of State Line, Pa.

State Line, Pa.

DE GROAT Charles of Lindley, NY
MANDEVILLE Helena A. of Tuscarora, NY

July 6, 1874
Tuscarora, NY

DODGE Harvey A.
CHAPMAN Leafy

June 27, 1874
Woodhull, NY

SULLIVAN Charles of Addison, NY
JEFFRIES Lucy Ann of Woodhull, NY

July 8, 1874
Woodhull, NY

VAN HORN B. C. of Wellsboro, Pa.
MORGAN Addie of Columbia, Pa.

July 1, 1874
Wellsboro, Pa.

HALLINAN Thomas of Tuscarora, NY
SMITH Jennie of Charleston, Pa.

July 6, 1874
Charleston, Pa.

KINNER Albert
NOTTINGHAM Sarah M.

July 22, 1874
Hedgesville, NY

MOSIER Joseph of Lindley, NY
APGAR Emma of Tuscarora, NY

July 28, 1874
Tuscarora, NY

MILLIGAN Marcus of Jasper, NY
SMITH F. E. of Cameron, NY

July 5, 1874
Cameron, NY

MOSCO Elihu of Tuscarora, NY
POTTER Jennie of Woodhull, NY

August 8, 1874
Cameron, NY

SMITH William A. of Addison, NY
CROSBY Mrs. Almira

August 11, 1874
Otisville, NY

FENTON L. W. of Elkland, Pa. August 12, 1874
BRIGGS Clara L. of Middlebury, Pa. Wellsboro, Pa.

LOSIER Frank of Cameron Mills, NY (Newspaper date) August 27, 1874
PROTZMAN Henrietta of Jasper, NY

GODDARD Samuel of Rathbone, NY August 22, 1874
HOUGHTALING Esther of Hornellsville, NY Addison, NY

HARRISON Gilbert L. of Hornellsville, NY August 25, 1874
ROOT Theresa O. of Addison, NY Addison, NY

RINDGE Edwin C. of Cortland, NY September 1, 1874
BENEDICT Mattie of Addison, NY Addison, NY

EYGEBROAT John of Addison, NY September 4, 1874
PARSONS Mary C. of Addison, NY Addison, NY

HILL Harlan H. of Nunda Station, NY September 16, 1874
NICHOLS Rebecca of Whitney's Crossing, NY Birdsall, NY

MC CHESNEY W. H. of Rathbone, NY September 16, 1874
LOPER Mary S. of Rathbone, NY Rathbone, NY

WHEELER Marcus of Cameron, NY September 17, 1874
SMITH Louisa M. of Cameron, NY Cameron, NY

BIERLY W. L. of Williamsport, Pa. September 24, 1874
BOSARD Sarah Louisa of Wellsboro, Pa. Wellsboro, Pa.

BROOKMAN W. Albert of Elmira, NY September 20, 1874
SHAW Lucy of Elkland, Pa. Knoxville, Pa.

NOLAN James of Rathbone, NY September 20, 1874
YALE Frankie J. of Clymer, Pa. Clymer, Pa.

SHUFELT Stephen of Troupsburgh, NY September 27, 1874
FENTON Ada of Troupsburgh, NY Troupsburgh, NY

ARNOLD F. September 29, 1874
ORR Minnie dau of James Wabashaw, Mn.

POTTER Wesley of Troupsburgh, NY October 18, 1874
MASCHO Jane of Brookfield, Pa.

ROBERTS Amos of Glen's Falls, NY October 22, 1874
WHITMORE Gertie C. of Rathbone, NY Rathbone, NY

CROWL Frank R. of Tuscarora, NY November 6, 1874
ALBEE Rhoda V. of Tuscarora, NY

PIERCE George W. of Trumansburg, NY   November 3, 1874
GAY Elnora A. of Canisteo, NY   Addison, NY

GAGE Charles W. of Addison, NY   November 19, 1874
CRANS Adell of Addison, NY   Addison, NY

MILES Levi of Rathbone, NY   November 26, 1874
WILHELM Helen L. of Rathbone, NY

HILL Oscar J. of Addison, NY   December 23, 1874
SHOCKEY Bella E. of Addison, NY   Addison, NY

SPENCER Gilbert of Addison, NY   December 23, 1874
SHOCKEY Mary of Addison, NY   Addison, NY

BROOKS Charles   December 18, 1874
HOLT Mary of Troupsburgh, NY   Troupsburgh, NY

SHORT Marcus of Troupsburgh, NY   November 23, 1874
EYMER A. M. of Troupsburgh, NY   Brookfield, Pa.

SMITH Elbert of Addison, NY   December 29, 1874
WEBB Clara M. of Tuscarora, NY   Tuscarora, NY

JACK William O. of Thurston, NY   January 18, 1875
TORRENCE Jozuna I. of Thurston, NY   Addison, NY

PARSELLS Parlee of Thurston, NY   December 31, 1874
HUGG Mary of Thurston, NY   Addison, NY

PEASE Walter L. of Deerfield, Pa.   January 21, 1875
SMITH Frank of Nelson, Pa.   Addison, NY

EDMINSTER Dallas of Erwin, NY   February 10, 1875
WORMLEY Helen M. of Addison, NY   Addison, NY

MC CONNELL H. S. of Horseheads, NY   February 24, 1875
DARRIN Sarah of Corning, NY   Addison, NY

BORT William W. of Onieda Valley, NY   March 7, 1875
KITTLE Nellie of Tuscarora, NY   Addison, NY

RESUE Nelson of Addison, NY   March 8, 1875
ANDRUS Helen of Addison, NY   Addison, NY

STUART John E. of Cameron, NY   (Newspaper date) March 25, 1875
WALRATH Martha of Cameron, NY   Hedgesville, NY

SWAN Alanson of Tuscarora, NY   March 11, 1875
SNAY Mrs. Harriet of Addison, NY   Tuscarora, NY

COBURN E. H. of Addison, NY	March 24, 1875
NEWMAN Nellie E. of Toledo, Ohio	Toledo, Ohio
PRENTICE Charles of Butternuts, NY	March 2, 1875
HOLLIS Lizzie of Butternuts, NY	Gilbertsville, NY
DEXTER W. J. of Hornellsville, NY	April 5, 1875
ANDERSON Frank of Hornellsville, NY	Hornellsville, NY
PRICE William of Addison, NY	April 11, 1875
BUNDY Nellie of Andover, NY	Andover, NY
ROBINSON Mr. ____ of Thurston, NY	April 13, 1875
YOST Melinda of Thurston, NY	Rathbone, NY
ALLEN William Delos of Cameron, NY	May 16, 1875
REYNOLDS Minnie E. of Cameron, NY	Hedgesville, NY
RICE Rev. Francis F. of Addison, NY	May 27, 1875
CAMERON Lucy of Addison, NY	Binghamton, NY
HATHAWAY Amos M. of Tuscarora, NY	June 3, 1875
MANDEVILLE Anna A. of Tuscarora, NY	Tuscarora, NY
RODBERNSON Henry of Hornellsville, NY	June 26, 1875
BAKER Clara J. of Hornellsville, NY	Cameron, NY
STID Calvin of Tuscarora, NY	June 27, 1875
NEWMAN Mrs. Elizabeth of Tuscarora, NY	Corning, NY
LINES Charles J. of Woodhull, NY	June 13, 1875
RICE Mrs. Lucy P. of Troupsburgh, NY	Woodhull, NY
MACK D. V. of Elkland, Pa.	July 18, 1875
VAN ZILE E. M. of Elkland, Pa.	Addison, NY
BRUNSON Philo of Woodhull, NY	August 7, 1875
MILES Louise M. of Rathbone, NY	Cameron, NY
SIMONS J. of Woodhull, NY	July 25, 1875
TOWNER Martha A. of Cohocton, NY	Liberty, NY
WESTCOTT James H. Md. of Norwich, NY	August 2, 1875
ARNOLD Gertrude S. of Lindley, NY	Norwich, NY
PERRY Edwin of Addison, NY	September 8, 1875
ARLINGTON Delephine of Addison, NY	Addison, NY
WALKER L. C. of Addison, NY	August 25, 1875
HAWLEY Elizabeth of Chatham, Pa.	Wellsboro, Pa.

BROWN Frank S. of Addison, NY
KINYON Anna A. of Athens, Pa.

October 13, 1875
Athens, Pa.

NORWOOD Herbert E.
COSS ____ (illegible)

October 26, 1875
Hedgesville, NY

PURCELL Michael H. formerly of Addison, NY
DICKSON Mary Agnes

October 7, 1875
Buffalo, NY

MOORE Joseph H. of Cameron, NY
WHEATON May A. of Cameron, NY

November 21, 1875
Hedgesville, NY

WAGNER Edward of Albany, NY
TRACY Keziah of Knoxville, NY

November 25, 1875
Addison, NY

DICKINSON Samuel of Addison, NY
GRIFFIN Ann E. of Addison, NY

December 4, 1875
Addison, NY

COOK Dallas D. of Clarendon, NY
MULLIKIN Mary J. of Clarendon, NY

December 30, 1875
Clarendon, NY

HAMMOND M. F. of Osceola, Pa.
OWEN M. E. of Blossburg, Pa.

December 21, 1875
Blossburg, Pa.

CRANS Romain B. of Rathbone, NY
BRINK Sarah A. of Rathbone, NY

February 5, 1876
Westfield, Pa.

GRAHAM Miles G. Editor of Hornellsville Herald
RUTHERFORD Mary A. of Hornellsville, NY

February 2, 1876
Hornellsville, NY

HAND Perry of Tuscarora, NY
MANTLE Mary of Rathbone, NY

February 20, 1876
Addison, NY

HOWARD Lester of Erwin, NY
DOANE Sarah of Erwin, NY

February 9, 1876

HOWLAND William of Cameron, NY   (Newspaper date) February 24, 1876
DRAKE Olive of Canisteo, NY

MC KAY James of Grand Rapids, Mi.
CAMERON Jennie L. of Osceola, Pa.

February 23, 1876
Osceola, Pa.

PERRY William of Troupsburgh, NY
DAVIS Laura L. of Troupsburgh, NY

February 6, 1876

TEW George J. of Troupsburgh, NY
MOROY Susan E. of Troupsburgh, NY

February 29, 1876
Troupsburgh, NY

BOALDMAN G. F. of Woodhull, NY
HEPWORTH Martha of Addison, NY

March 12, 1876
Woodhull, NY

COLE Oscar J. son of Jacob of Rathbone, NY | March 15, 1876
KENT Emma F. only child of R. T. of Jasper, NY | Jasper, NY

WAFLER William of W. Almond, NY | March 26, 1876
LYON Barbara L. of Woodhull, NY | Woodhull, NY

HANNAH Charles of Rathbone, NY | March 30, 1876
WHEELER Addie of Rathbone, NY | Woodhull, NY

MILLER William B. of Jasper, NY | April 7, 1876
TIMMERMAN Martha A. of Jasper, NY | Woodhull, NY

FULKINSON William M. of Woodhull, NY | April 9, 1876
HOPPER Sarah E. (or Anvernett) of Woodhull, NY | Woodhull, NY

STUART Edward F. of Cameron, NY | April 9, 1876
HOPPER Sarah E. of Woodhull, NY | Woodhull, NY

MARLATT Gaylord C. of Woodhull, NY | April 9, 1876
BLANE Emma J. of Woodhull, NY | Woodhull, NY

FLEMING William C. of Addison, NY | April 16, 1876
SCOFIELD Emma M. of Addison, NY | Addison, NY

LUCKEY George W. of Philadelphia, Pa. | April 11, 1876
ANDERSON Etta C. dau of Horatio G. K. of Patterson, NJ | Patterson, NJ

MITCHELL Dr. John D. of Hornellsville, NY | April 18, 1876
MORRIS Artilissa of Hornellsville, NY | Hornellsville, NY

RUMSEY Adson J. of Rathbone, NY | April 26, 1876
HASELTINE Henrietta L. of Cameron, NY | Addison, NY

NORTHRUP C. D. of Troupsburgh, NY   (Newspaper date) May 4, 1876
WEEKS E. Naoma of Orange, NY | Orange, NY

THOMPSON Daniel A. of Addison, NY | May 7, 1876
NEWCOMB Frances H. of Addison, NY | Addison, NY

DARRIN Delmar M. of Addison, NY | June 22, 1876
HILL Mary dau of Charles C. **DAWSON** | Plainfield, NJ

BEERS R. O. of Addison, NY | July 3, 1876
DELAMATER Helen E. of Addison, NY | Addison, NY

WRIGHT Henry N. of Tuscarora, NY | July 5, 1876
HARRISON Sarah E. of Lindley, NY | Addison, NY

STEVENS Percy C. of Addison, NY | July 11, 1876
TAFT Lena E. of Addison, NY | Addison, NY

ADAMS S. B. of Woodhull, NY　　　　　　　July 3, 1876
SPOOR Isabell of Woodhull, NY　　　　　　　Woodhull, NY

WILCOX Delano of Mc Donough, NY　　　　July 3, 1876
BARTLE Emma of Troupsburgh, NY　　　　　Woodhull, NY

BARTLE William R. of Troupsburgh, NY　　　July 3, 1876
RICE Emily J. of Troupsburgh, NY　　　　　　Woodhull, NY

ORDWAY Clarence E. of Covington, Pa.　　　July 3, 1876
VAN DUYN Eva of Troupsburgh, NY　　　　　Woodhull, NY

HOLMES John Burt　　　　　　　　　　　July 12, 1876
DOWNS Kate H. formerly of Addison, NY　　　Philadelphia, Pa.

CURRIER John　　　　　　　　　　　　　August 2, 1876
HORN Dora of Addison, NY　　　　　　　　Addison, NY

JOHNSON Frank of Coopers Plains, NY　　　July 15, 1876
DECKER Sarah of S. Addison, NY　　　　　　Corning, NY

BROWN William H. of Woodhull, NY　　　　August 16, 1876
CARPENTER Flora E. of Woodhull, NY　　　　Woodhull, NY

VAN ORSDALE Lieut. J. T. of the 7th Inf.　　July 30, 1876
LOGAN Emily dau of Capt. William Logan of US Army　　Fort Shaw, M. T.

MERMOUD Francis of New York City　　　　August 20, 1876
SANDERS Ellen F. dau of Rev. WIlliam of Tuscarora　　Tuscarora, NY

BURDICK Clarence L.　　　　　　　　　　August 27, 1876
BOST Augusta　　　　　　　　　　　　　Woodhull, NY

WILBER Rev. W. C. of Angelica, NY　　　(Newspaper date) September 14, 1876
MITCHELL Mary V. dau of Dr. John of Addison, NY　　Addison, NY

MURRAY Henry A. of Addison, NY　　　　　September 20, 1876
BENEDICT Emma L. of Addison, NY　　　　　Addison, NY

REBOUT William of Corning, NY　　　　　　October 4, 1876
DODGE Charlotte R. of Addison, NY　　　　　Addison, NY

GOODRICH Charles F. of Elmira, NY　　　　October 11, 1876
KINNEY Ermina M. of Addison, NY　　　　　Addison, NY

MITCHELL John H. of Addison, NY　　　　　October 9, 1876
DODGE Flora E. of Rochester, NY　　　　　　Rochester, NY

STEVENS Alonzo C. of Havana, NY　　　　　October 24, 1876
SMITH Mary A. of Cameron, Mills, NY　　　　Cameron Mills, NY

HARDER Robert Jr. of Woodhull, NY   November 29, 1876
JONES Lena of Woodhull, NY

COOK Samuel H. of Van Metter, Iowa   December 19, 1876
HATHAWAY Lois Adelaide of Addison, NY   Chicago, Ill.

RIGBY J. W. of Troupsburgh, NY   December 20, 1876
BARTLE Sarah U. of Troupsburgh, NY   Rathbone, NY

BAXTER Clark of Troupsburgh, NY   January 21, 1877
SCHOONOVER Martha P. of Troupsburgh, NY   Troupsburgh, NY

HOLMES Charles A. of Tuscarora, NY   January 21, 1877
SCHOONOVER Ella L. of Troupsburgh, NY   Troupsburgh, NY

MOSELY S. of Wilmington, Del.   January 25, 1877
HINCHMAN Mrs. E. of Oswego, Ill.   Addison, NY

HORNSBY George B. of Whitesville, NY   February 4, 1877
BURNSIDE Emma of Troupsburgh, NY   Troupsburgh, NY

STEWART John K. of Woodhull, NY   January 31, 1877
GOODWIN Emma S. of Woodhull, NY   Canisteo, NY

HARGROVE Thomas J. of Cameron, NY   February 8, 1877
JACKSON Serena L. of Cameron, NY   Addison, NY

ROWEN Hamilton J.   March 1, 1877
ALLEN Nancy M. dau of George of Cameron, NY   Cameron, NY

GLEASON Ezra of Osceola, Pa.   March 22, 1877
PERKINS Sarah S. dau of Samuel of Addison, Hill, NY   Addison Hill, NY

HILL Byron T.   March 28, 1877
PRICE Mary T. at brother's William Price

BURT Samuel J. of Tuscarora, NY   March 29, 1877
MILLER Lottie A. of Addison, NY   Addison, NY

GLENDENNING Thomas R. of Fayette, NY   March 21, 1877
GRINNELL Sarah L. of Monistique, Mi. formerly of Addison, NY

ERWIN James of Bradford, Pa.   April 10, 1877
KNAPP Densa A. of Cameron, NY   Cameron, NY

HOWARD Hiram J. of Dayton, NY   April 11, 1877
COLVIN Julia of Dayton, NY   Addison, NY

SHEAN Patrick of W. Union, NY   April 17, 1877
O'MARA Mary E. of Troupsburgh, NY   Rexville, NY

TOWSLEY Adelbert of Jasper, NY   May 5, 1877
CLEMMONS Mary of Painted Post, NY   Painted Post, NY

FOSTER Albert B. of Woodhull, NY   May 27, 1877
ALDRICH Adelia of Woodhull, NY   Addison, NY

MANLEY Lucius N. of Long Island City, NY   May 29, 1877
WEATHERBY Olive P. of Addison, NY   Addison, NY

PARKS Hollis of Alpena, Mi.   May 10, 1877
HOUSE Bertha E. of Jasper, NY   Jasper, NY

HENDERSON Arthur M. of Woodhull, NY   June 17, 1877
WELCH Nancy of Woodhull, NY   Woodhull, NY

PARSON Frank G. of Rochester, NY   June 28, 1877
GRAHAM Clara Adeline dau of J. V. of Addison, NY   Addison, NY

KENT Emery L. of Addison, NY   June 15, 1877
DANIELS Alice J. of Campbell, NY

WARDEN W. H. of Veteran, NY   July 4, 1877
FREELAND Maria of Woodhull, NY   Addison, NY

HILTON W. M. Md. of Van Etten, NY   August 15, 1877
ATWOOD Mary A. dau of Rev. William of Big Flats, NY Big Flats, NY

BALCOM Fred L. of Addison, NY   July 30, 1877
VROOMAN Ida F. of Dunkirk, NY   Dunkirk, NY

DUNHAM Albert C. of Sequiot, NY   September 4, 1877
COLE Jennie of Woodhull, NY   Woodhull, NY

DININNY Owen R. of Tuscarora, NY   September 25, 1877
BEERS Betsey U. of Tuscarora, NY   Addison, NY

COWLEY Millard C. of Addison, NY   October 30, 1877
MULLEN Nellie M. of Addison, NY   Addison, NY

ANDREWS William of Elmira, NY   November 16, 1877
SPAULDING Ella of Elmira, NY   Addison, NY

HARDER Uri S. of Woodhull, NY   October 10, 1877
COLE Sarah A. of Rathbone, NY   Rathbone, NY

LLOYD George M. of Rathbone, NY   November 27, 1877
MILES Lucinda of Rathbone, NY   Rathbone, NY

WELLES Edward M. of Addison, NY   November 29, 1877
SMITH Mattie of Addison, NY   Addison, NY

WEBB Wallace of Nelson, Pa.
TRIM Cora of Elkland, Pa.

November 29, 1877
Tuscarora, NY

CRANCE Leroy of Cowanesque Valley, Pa.
FRINKNER Florence of Cowanesque Valley, Pa.

December 31, 1877
Addison, NY

DOWNES Eli of Canisteo, NY
FAILING Ella of W. Union, NY

December 26, 1877
W. Union, NY

HARRISON Theodore of Lindley, NY   (Newspaper date) January 3, 1878
PRITCHARD Sarah of Lawrenceville, Pa.

Lawrenceville, Pa.

MC PHERSON W. J. of Rathbone, NY
SWARTS Addie C. of Woodhull, NY

December 26, 1877

WARNER Samuel of Lindley, NY
BENJAMIN Dell H. of Tuscarora, NY

December 31, 1877
Addison, NY

FURMAN Dallas of Potter Brook, Pa.
WILLIAMSON Ada of Cameron, NY

January 1, 1878
Cameron, NY

ROBINSON William A. of Addison, NY
MONROE Libbie L. of Hornellsville, NY

January 2, 1878
Hornellsville, NY

SWAN Ephraim of Lindley, NY
MANLEY Annie of Tuscarora, NY

December 23, 1877
Lindley, NY

MARR A. K. of Milton, Pa.
SCOFIELD Ella of Addison, NY

January 16, 1878
Addison, NY

CURTIS Monroe of Addison, NY
CUMMINGS Celia A. of Milford, NY

January 22, 1878
Milford, NY

HARRIS George L. of Woodhull, NY
CISCO Mary E. of Elkland, Pa.

January 27, 1878
Osceola, Pa.

MITCHELL Frank D. formerly of Addison, NY
BROWN Belle of Haywood, Cal.

January 30, 1878
Haywood, Cal.

HOLLENBECK Dr. George G. of Corning, NY
SLEEPER Jennie dau of Hiram of Big Flats, NY

February 14, 1878

BOYD D. W. of Woodhull, NY
WELTY Mary of Troupsburgh, NY

March 6, 1878
Canisteo, NY

THOMAS Edgar of Addison, NY
CONEY Mary A. of Addison, NY

February 26, 1878
Addison, NY

DEMING Lucien of Jackson, Pa.
MONTGOMERY Ursala of Tuscarora, NY

March 14, 1878
Tuscarora, NY

RITCHIE Daniel of W. Union, NY   March 17, 1878
COLEGROVE Mrs. Jane of Troupsburgh, NY   Addison, NY

PHOENIX Samuel of Rathbone, NY   March 9, 1878
ROSENCRANCE Mrs. Anna of Rathbone, NY   Rathbone, NY

REYNOLDS Charles W. of Rathbone, NY   February 28, 1878
LEWIS Martha of Rathbone, NY   Rathbone, NY

ELLISON George of Hornby, NY   April 14, 1878
BURNSIDE Charity of Addison, NY   Addison, NY

HALL James C. of Addison, NY   April 21, 1878
HARRISON Irena N. of Addison, NY   Addison, NY

PARSONS Henry C. of Corning, NY   April 25, 1878
BENJAMIN Maria H. of Corning, NY   Addison, NY

SARGENT Sumner of Jasper, NY   May 7, 1878
SMITH Frances of W. Union, NY   W. Union, NY

WILLIAMSON Alvah H. of Cameron, NY   April 28, 1878
BRADY Ann dau of Robert of Cameron, NY   Cameron, NY

BURLINGAME Edgar of Rathbone, NY   June 1, 1878
YOST Villie of Rathbone, NY

MILES Samuel of Rathbone, NY   June 6, 1878
LLOYD Maggie M. of Rathbone, NY

WILHELM John of Addison, NY   June 21, 1878
KNAPP Mrs. Jane of Addison, NY   Addison, NY

WHITE John C. of Knoxville, Pa.   June 23, 1878
KNOX Laura M. of Deerfield, Pa.   Deerfield, Pa.

NEWMAN Charles of Tuscarora, NY   July 19, 1878
STARNER Phebe of Tuscarora, NY   Tuscarora, NY

BARKER Charles H. of Thurston, NY   August 3, 1878
SMITH Percilla Emeline of Thurston, NY   Thurston, NY

ALBEE Stephen E. of Tuscarora, NY   August 18, 1878
ALDRICH Frances V. of Tuscarora, NY   S. Addison, NY

MC MURDY William J. of Stamford, NY   September 4, 1878
JONES Adelaide V. dau of Ettsel of Addison, NY   Addison, NY

WEEKS Atwood of Tuscarora, NY   September 10, 1878
BEERS Frone Z. of Tuscarora, NY   Addison, NY

GRIGGS John of Troupsburgh, NY
POTTER Libbie of Troupsburgh, NY

September 12, 1878
Austinville, Pa.

JUNE Charles E. of Addison, NY
CADY Georgia of Tioga, Pa.

(Newspaper date) October 3, 1878
Tioga, Pa.

BALDWIN Henry D. of Addison, NY
KLINE Eva L. of Woodhull, NY

November 3, 1878
Addison, NY

ERWIN Samuel of Corning, NY
TUPPER Emma A. of Corning, NY

October 15, 1878
Elmira, NY

ERWIN Francis A. of Corning, NY
CLUTE Hattie D. dau of I. M. of Corning, NY

October 10, 1878
Corning, NY

HAMMOND James M. of Westfield, Pa.
FARNHAM May of Westfield, Pa.

October 31, 1878
Knoxville, Pa.

NORTHRUP Dewitt of Rathbone, NY
CRAWFORD Mattie of Cameron Mills, NY

October 23, 1878
Cameron, NY

TIMMERMAN Levi D. of Jasper, NY
DENNIS Mary E. of Jasper, NY

October 16, 1878
Jasper, NY

CARR Charles H. of Jerusalem, NY
ROBINSON Olive S. of Jasper, NY

October 24, 1878
Rathbone, NY

CLOSE Newberry of Addison, NY
PAYNE Mrs. Lodema C. of Addison, NY

October 9, 1878
Rathbone, NY

CRANE Ferrel J. of Addison, NY
BRIGGS Amy E. of Addison, NY

November 10, 1878
Addison, NY

NEWMAN Frank of Tuscarora, NY
TINEY Nellie J. of Addison, NY

October 20, 1878
Rathbone, NY

THOMPSON Joseph A. of Addison, NY
MEAD Sarah A. of Addison, NY

November 10, 1878
Addison, NY

BROWNELL Charles T. of Troupsburgh, NY
ROUSE Helen M. of Addison, NY

November 14, 1878
Addison, NY

KINNE Erwin of Addison, NY
OLIN Jennie M. of Woodhull, NY

November 20, 1878
Woodhull, NY

BURRELL Sylvester of Tuscarora, NY
PRENTISS Ida of Tuscarora, NY

November 14, 1878
Tuscarora, NY

LANNING Millard A.
DODGE Adelle of Addison, NY

December 24, 1878
Addison, NY

DAVIDSON W. D. formerly of Addison, NY   December 24, 1878
VAN AUKEN Sara   Voorheesville, NY

ADAMS David L. of Woodhull, NY   January 1, 1879
JONES Cordelia of Woodhull, NY   Addison, NY

DEATS Theodora of Lawrenceville, Pa.   January 1, 1879
CROFFORD Lizzie of Lawrenceville, Pa.   S. Addison, NY

STEPHENS Charles A. of Addison, NY   January 15, 1879
ALLYN Edith L. of Addison, NY   Addison, NY

ORR Ellsworth W. of Addison, NY   February 12, 1879
CORNELISON Clara of Addison, NY   Addison, NY

WHEATMORE Loren of Tioga Co. Pa.   (Newspaper date) February 13, 1879
BLEND Clarissa of Woodhull, NY   Woodhull, NY

BARROWS J. M. of Cameron, NY   January 29, 1879
COATES Lillie V. of Cameron, NY   Cameron, NY

ALLEN Moses N. of Rathbone, NY   February 12, 1879
SELLECK Sylvia I. of Rathbone, NY   Rathbone, NY

BRUNSON John of Brookfield, Pa.   February 24, 1879
MARKHAM Imogene L. of Brookfield, Pa.   Knoxville, Pa.

JONES Robert of Addison, NY   February 26, 1879
TAYLOR Maggie of Park Station, NY   Park Station, NY

PIERCE Francis M. of Painted Post, NY   March 11, 1879
ALBEE Eva M. of Addison, NY   Addison, NY

COLE Daniel A. of Cameron, NY   March 23, 1879
PENNEY Tinnie E. of Wellsville, NY   Addison, NY

HOBER Darius W. of Troupsburgh, NY   March 19, 1879
HOLT Martha A. of Troupsburgh, NY   Knoxville, Pa.

SMITH William A. formerly of Greene, NY (Newspaper date) March 27, 1879
SMITH Mrs. Clara of Tuscarora, NY   S. Addison, NY

RATHBUN George E. of Williamsport, Pa.   April 9, 1879
RICH Rhoda M. of Knoxville, Pa.   Knoxville, Pa.

GIBSON Joseph A. of Addison, NY   April 19, 1879
CURTIS Cora B. of Addison, NY   Addison, NY

WOMBOUGH Charles H. of Addison, NY   April 24, 1879
GREENHOW Maggie dau of J. of Hornellsville, NY   Hornellsville, NY

BALDWIN Rufus C. of Addison, NY   June 18, 1879
SMITH Lettie M. at uncle's C. W. **NOBLE**   Addison, NY

CROSBY John W. of Canisteo, NY   June 11, 1879
BAKER Chloe W. of Canisteo, NY   Canisteo, NY

RICE William E. of Troupsburgh, NY   June 29, 1879
TUBBS Sarah V. of Westfield, Pa.   Troupsburgh, NY

ALBEE Alpheus C. of Addison, NY   July 3, 1879
COON M. E. of Addison, NY   Addison, NY

JANES George H. of Addison, NY   May 19, 1879
MILLER Emma A. of Addison, NY   Rathbone, NY

SMITH William A. of Addison, NY   June 15, 1879
RICHARDS Ella of Addison, NY   Rathbone, NY

WORKS Charles of Troupsburgh, NY   July 2, 1879
BOWEN Eva L. of Knoxville, Pa.   Knoxville, Pa.

WHITE James B. of Knoxville, Pa.   August 3, 1879
WILLHELM Emma E. of Knoxville, Pa.   Knoxville, Pa.

SWAN Alvin J. of Tuscarora, NY   August 18, 1879
O'BRYAN Ellen A. of Tuscarora, NY   Tuscarora, NY

GREER William H. of Rathbone, NY   August 14, 1879
DUEL Rosalina E. of Rathbone, NY

STRAIGHT Joseph H. of Almond, NY   August 31, 1879
MERRING Amanda of Rathbone, NY   Rathbone, NY

CARPENTER Hanry A. of Tuscarora, NY   August 31, 1879
CHAMPLAIN C. of Woodhull, NY   Knoxville, Pa.

CHURCH John M. of Addison, NY   September 10, 1879
DICKINSON Emma L. dau of A. B. C. of Addison, NY   Addison, NY

MIX Brennett J. of Hamilton, NY   September 14, 1879
WILBUR Hulda dau of D. C. of Woodhull, NY   Woodhull, NY

ALDRICH Henry S. of Osceola, Pa.   September 23, 1879
SMITH Lillie V. dau of James E. of Tuscarora, NY   Tuscarora, NY

ALLEN Joseph of Cameron, NY   September 17, 1879
SANFORD Mary Ann of Cameron, NY   Cameron, NY

COOK Ezekiel of Rathbone, NY   September 28, 1879
BATES Amarette of Rathbone, NY   Addison, NY

STUART Zeri D. of Cameron, NY
WHITE Mary W. of Cameron, NY

October 5, 1879
Cameron, NY

SMITH Rulif J. of Tuscarora, NY
ROWLEY Delila of Tuscarora, NY

October 21, 1879
S. Addison, NY

ALDRICH Almond O. of Midland Mi.
SIMONS Nettie J. of Woodhull, NY

October 26, 1879
Tuscarora, NY

DININNY John E. of Tuscarora, NY
SMITH Adelia N. of Tuscarora, NY

October 23, 1879
Addison, NY

WHITMORE Clarence S.
CRAWFORD Belle F.

October 23, 1879
Rathbone, NY

MALLORY Eugene E. of Addison, NY
BROWN F. May of Hammondsport, NY

October 22, 1879
Hammondsport, NY

MILLS Rev. W. T. of Knoxville, NY/Pa.
WOOSTER Mary E. of Addison, NY

October 20, 1879
Knoxville, NY/Pa.

TUBBS Charles of Osceola, Pa.
BACON Sylvania of Osceola, Pa.

October 22, 1879
Osceola, Pa.

HARRIS Oscar F. of Tyrone, NY
SIMMONS Eliza of Tyrone, NY

November 8, 1879
Addison, NY

WHITING Leslie B. of Jasper, NY
ORDWAY Brunett of Cameron, NY

October 31, 1879
Cameron, NY

WILLARD H. Burr of Campbell, NY
NORTHRUP Amelia dau of Norman of Rathbone, NY

October 30, 1879
Rathbone, NY

KINNEY Barney of Woodhull, NY
KINNEY Mrs. Sally of Annin Creek, Pa.

November 13, 1879
Woodhull, NY

DATES W. W. of Pa.
MORRISON Nancy E. of Tuscarora, NY

November 23, 1879
Tuscarora, NY

JACKSON John H. of Cameron, NY
BROWN Sarah M. of Cameron, NY

November 6, 1879
Tuscarora, NY

YAGER Willard E.
JOHNSON Jane Whittingham dau of Edward M. & Fannie A.

November 19, 1879
Oneonta, NY

DUDLEY O. A. of Tuscarora, NY
DAGGETT Florine of Tioga, Pa.

November 26, 1879
Tioga, Pa.

BERRY Abner of Lindley, NY
LOVELL Hattie E. of Lindley, NY

December 7, 1879
Lindley, NY

KING Aaron P. of Westfield, Pa.   December 7, 1879
STEPHENSON Nellie of Westfield, Pa. Knoxville, Pa.

SHORT Darius S. of Deerfield, Pa.   December 7, 1879
KING Electa L. of Westfield, Pa.   Knoxville, Pa.

CLARK H. H. of Owego, NY   December 27, 1879
BURNSIDE Mrs. Louisa of Addison, NY Addison, NY

HURD Norman of Woodhull, NY   December 24, 1879
KNAPP Jennie E. of Tuscarora, NY Tuscarora, NY

RULOFSON Isaac of New Britain, Ct. December 24, 1879
PRICE Mrs. Lois E. dau of James B. **WHEELER** Cameron, NY

SWAN Lanson of Addison, NY   December 17, 1879
JONES Mary J. of Addison, NY   Tuscarora, NY

ALDRICH Clifton J. of Tuscarora, NY January 1, 1880
WILLIAMS Lillie L. of Tuscarora, NY Tuscarora, NY

SCHERMERHORN James T. of Addison, NY January 10, 1880
PIERCE Hattie M. of Addison, NY

ANGLE Stephen L. of Addison, NY January 21, 1880
SWAYZE Alice D. of Hope, NJ   Hope, NJ

HAVEN George W. of Woodhull, NY February 8, 1880
FLANDERS Luna Z. of Woodhull, NY Addison, NY

COOPER A. R. of Addison, NY   January 27, 1880
BEEBE Emma F. of Addison, NY   Addison, NY

HILL Arthur P. of Addison, NY   February 17, 1880
PECK Anna of Addison, NY   Addison, NY

SPRAGUE Alton J. of Eldred, Pa.   February 14, 1880
SIMONS Hattie T. of Woodhull, NY Addison, NY

TUBBS Henry of Osceola, Pa.   January 28, 1880
BULKLEY Mirce of Osceola, Pa.   Osceola, Pa.

RARRICK Anthony H. of Alpine, NY February 23, 1880
RARRICK Mrs. Catherine of Addison, NY

LYON A. W. of Addison, NY   February 5, 1880
LANDIS Sarah E. of Erwin Center, NY Erwin Center, NY

TRANSO William A. of Big Flats, NY February 18, 1880
CARPENTER Grace L. of Erwin Center, NY Erwin Center, NY

STACY William of Addison, NY   April 19, 1880
BARRON Ida dau of W. P. of Addison, NY   Addison, NY

BLADES John W. of Addison, NY   April 14, 1880
MERRITT Emma M. of Lindley, NY   Lindley, NY

YONG Claude H. of Big Flats, NY   May 5, 1880
SHELBY Celissa M. of Big Flats, NY   Addison, NY

THOMPSON Leonard of Clymer, Pa.   May 2, 1880
SUTTON Jennie of Deerfield, Pa.   Knoxville, Pa.

TEMPLAR George K. of Schenectady Co. NY   June 15, 1880
STEWART Mary E. of Addison, NY

CORWIN Henry A. of Farmington, Pa.   July 3, 1880
DREW Linnie of Farmington, Pa.   Knoxville, Pa.

MAGOON Isaac of Hedgesville, NY   June 30, 1880
CLINTON Clara M. of Addison, NY   Addison, NY

LANDERS J. J. of Erwin Center, NY   July 14, 1880
CAREY Belle of Lindley, NY   Lindley, NY

CLARK Virgil of Deerfield, Pa.   July 28, 1880
SMITH Mary T. of Chatham, Pa.   Chatham, Pa.

STEWART George of Rathbone, NY   (Newspaper date) August 12, 1880
WOODCOCK Fannie of Tuscarora, NY   Tuscarora, NY

SMITH Edwin J. of Woodhull, NY   August 22, 1880
GUILES Sarah J. of Woodhull, NY   Woodhull, NY

BRAVO Ira of Erwin Center, NY   September 4, 1880
GARDNER Eliza of Erwin Center, NY   Woodhull, NY

JUNE Frank of Jasper, NY   September 1, 1880
GARDNER Sarah of Woodhull, NY   Hedgesville, NY

STEPHENS Frank N. of Addison, NY   September 15, 1880
ALLYN Ella M. of Addison, NY   Addison, NY

JACKSON John T. of Addison, NY   July 30, 1880
HANSCOM Jennie T. of Lock Haven, Pa.   Corning, NY

SHEEHAN James of Addison, NY   September 19, 1880
MC TAMNY Maggie A. of Addison, NY   Addison, NY

HILL Stephen L. of Lindley, NY   September 22, 1880
BAXTER Lucy A. of Tuscarora, NY   Tuscarora, NY

MAYO T. A. of Lindley, NY
JORDAN Theresa of Tuscarora, NY

September 22, 1880
Tuscarora, NY

HILL Orrin F. of Lindley, NY
BAXTER Rebecca M. of Tuscarora, NY

October 1, 1880
Lindley, NY

CHURCH Leon A. of Deerfield, Pa.
CORWIN Eleanor C. of Deerfield, Pa.

September 28, 1880
Deerfield, Pa.

BULLOCK William W. of Osceola, Pa.
VAN ZILE Hannah of Osceola, Pa.

September 25, 1880
Knoxville, Pa.

JONES Henry S. of Addison, NY
JONES Sarah Elizabeth of Addison, NY

October 13, 1880
Addison, NY

RUMSEY Isaac of Campbell, NY
PARCELL Anna E. of Addison, NY

September 26, 1880
Addison, NY

WILEY Lyman of Emporium, Pa.
ROWLEY Villa L. of S. Addison, NY

November 9, 1880
S. Addison, NY

FINCH Joseph of Tuscarora, NY
DININNY Mary of Tuscarora, NY

September 25, 1880
S. Addison, NY

ORR Augustus L. of Tuscarora, NY
LACKSY Emma S. of Tuscarora, NY

November 17, 1880
Tuscarora, NY

GARDNER Willard W. of Tuscarora, NY
ORR Alice L. of Tuscarora, NY

November 17, 1880
Tuscarora, NY

BARRY James L. of Grand Rapids, Mi.
FREEMAN Estella A. of Tuscarora, NY

November 22, 1880
Tuscarora, NY

BEEK John of Jackson, Pa.
WYGANT Martha A. of Liberty, Pa.

November 23, 1880

CAMPBELL Joseph B. of Lindley, NY
TAFT Amelia E. of Addison, NY

November 8, 1880
Addison, NY

CASTLE Erwin of Rathbone, NY
BEST Lizzie of Colesville, NY

November 15, 1880

WARNER Austin E. of Addison, NY
EVERTS Christina of S. Addison, NY

December 27, 1880
Addison, NY

VAN DUSEN Charles W. of Farmington, Pa.
SEELEY Alice B. of Osceola, Pa.

December 23, 1880
Knoxville, Pa.

VAN DUSEN Walter of Farmington, Pa.
VAN DUSEN Jennie of Farmington, Pa.

December 23, 1880
Knoxville, Pa.

MC BURNEY John B. of Corning, NY
BRYAN Rose B. of Canandaigua, NY

August 4, 1880
Painted Post, NY

ORR Fred of Erwin Center, NY
ROSENCRANS Effie of Erwin Center, NY

January 25, 1881
Addison, NY

ORR Phillip W. of Addison, NY
SHIPMAN Louisa M. of Addison, NY

March 1, 1881
Addison, NY

WADE Franklin D.
ROBINSON Ada M. dau of Charles

May 16, 1881
Rathbone, NY

SEVERANCE Luther Jr. of Thurston, NY
MARTYN Ida G. of Thurston, NY

July 18, 1881
Thurston, NY

HUBBELL S. B. Jr.
BEARDSLEY C. Louisa of Elmira, NY

August 5, 1881
Elmira, NY

CONOVER F. B. of Hornellsville, NY
SHAW Ella of Alfred, NY

August 6, 1881
Arkport, NY

HUNTER Nathaniel Perry of Jasper, NY
HALLETT Vinnie of Jasper, NY

July 30, 1881
Jasper, NY

BEECHER Fary B. of Fremont, NY
JOHNSON Emma A. of N. Cohocton, NY

July 27, 1881
Wayland, NY

FENTON Sylvester of Bath, NY
YOUNG Emma J. of Tuscarora, NY

August 14, 1881
Tuscarora, NY

PARSELLS George W. of Tuscarora, NY
RICHARDS Jerusha A. of Addison, NY

July 31, 1881
Addison, NY

ROBINSON Charles W. of Addison, NY
PRUTZMAN Flora E. of Tioga, Pa.

October 3, 1881
Tioga, Pa.

PALMER Charles W. of Elmira, NY
MANNING Anna of Campbell, NY

September 13, 1881
Painted Post, NY

VAN WIE Airy of Bloods, NY
BURGESS Ann Eliza of Geneva, NY

September 17, 1881
Geneva, NY

COLLINS Clayton W. of Hornellsville, NY
BRIGGS Minnie S. of Fremont, NY

September 13, 1881
Fremont, NY

MALLORY Dennis of Franklin, Pa. formerly of Savona, NY
DUNN Matie L. of Meadville, Pa.

September 15. 1881
Meadville, NY

WILLIAMS Allen E.
STANTON Emma B.

September 14, 1881
Hornby, NY

CHEESBROUGH Charles of Addison, NY	October 6, 1881
NOBLE Mollie of Addison, NY	Nelson, Pa.
BOWERS William E. of Campbell, NY	September 29, 1881
GREEK Minnie D. of Savona, NY	Savona, NY
ALLEN Charles B. of S. Addison, NY	September 27, 1881
STONEMETTS Mattie A. of Big Flats, NY	Big Flats, NY
BURRELL William of Farmington, Pa.	September 12, 1881
HOYT Ida of Farmington, Pa.	Addison, NY
EDWARDS Charles A. of Lindley, NY	September 29, 1881
RANDALL Shay of Lindley, NY	Addison, NY
WHIPPLE George F. of Carlton, NY	October 23, 1881
FORD Alice A. of Carlton, NY	E. Carlton, NY
SHERWOOD Wesley of Cameron, NY	October 19, 1881
HARGRAVE Hattie of Cameron, NY	Cameron, NY
POST James D. of Oswasso, Mi.	October 26, 1881
SUTTON Mattie E. of Cameron, NY	Cameron, NY
TURNER Robert E. of Waverly, NY	October 30, 1881
ROE Lizzie of Canisteo, NY	Canisteo, NY
HAND E. Turner of Addison, NY	November 2, 1881
HARRISON Dell of Woodhull, NY	Borden, NY
JONES Emerson J. of Thurston, NY	November 2, 1881
YOST Millie J. of Thurston, NY	Thurston, NY
FAILING Frank of W. Union, NY	November 19, 1881
MARLATT Della of Troupsburgh, NY	Troupsburgh, NY
ALDRICH Frank of Addison, NY	December 5, 1881
NEWCOMB Ettie of Addison, NY	Addison, NY
BABCOCK S. C. of Fremont, NY	November 24, 1881
ACOMB Mary A. of Dansville, NY	Canisteo, NY
CHASE Solomon of Addison, NY	November 22, 1881
HUMISTON Mrs. Margaret dau of David **LONGWELL**	Bath, NY
TUBBS James of Osceola, Pa.	December 15, 1881
WIGGINS Mrs. Laura of Chicago, Ill.	Chicago, Ill.
SANDFORD Robert M. of Thurston, NY	November 28, 1881
FOLLANSBEE Jennie M. of Cohocton, NY	Bath, NY

HUBBARD Winfield S. of Troupsburgh, NY — August 28, 1881 — Brookfield, Pa.
NOBLES Emma P. of Brookfield, Pa.

HOUCK Dr. J. C. of Addison, NY — December 21, 1881 — Elkland, Pa.
BEAGLE Jennie of Elkland, Pa.

VAN GELDER Charles F. of Tuscarora, NY — December 4, 1881 — Tuscarora, NY
CARLTON Jennie E. of Elmira, NY

STODDARD Wallace of Elkland, Pa. — December 22, 1881 — Elkland, Pa.
RICE Jennie of Elkland, Pa.

BURDICK Uriah T. of Osceola, Pa. — December 27, 1881 — Osceola, Pa.
WEBSTER Celinda B. of Addison, NY

COOK William of Addison, NY — December 27, 1881 — Dunkirk, NY
PROUTY Jennie M. of Dunkirk, NY

CAMPBELL James of Savona, NY — December 25, 1881 — Cameron, NY
BABCOCK Laura of Cameron, NY

STONE H. J. of Garfield, Ks. — December 25, 1881 — Woodhull, NY
HUDSON Mrs. Julia of Woodhull, NY

PARSELLS J. B. of Addison, NY — December 25, 1881 — Woodhull, NY
CHAPMAN M. L. of Woodhull, NY

HALLOCK Albert A. of Troupsburgh, NY — January 1, 1882 — Troupsburgh, NY
SCHOONOVER Emma of Troupsburgh, NY

BEEM C. S. of Dundee, NY — December 31, 1881 — Painted Post, NY
INGERSOLL Minnie of Addison, NY

WATKINS Herbert N. of Deerfield, Pa. — January 16, 1882 — Woodhull, NY
CHILSON Allie V. of Jasper, NY

ROWLEY Richard H. of Troupsburgh, NY — January 1, 1882 — Troupsburgh, NY
COOK Emma of Troupsburgh, NY

SCHOONOVER Irwin of Troupsburgh, NY — January 7, 1882
GARDNER Mary Ettie of Troupsburgh, NY

RICE Charles C. of Troupsburgh, NY — January 9, 1882 — Westfield, Pa.
LA BAR Agnes of Westfield, Pa.

DAVIS Marion C. of Painted Post, NY — December 25, 1881 — Osceola, Pa.
VAN ORSDALE Amadelia of Woodhull, NY

CONVERSE Caleb of the Swale, NY — January 13, 1882 — Troupsburgh, NY
COLEMAN Dora of the Swale, NY

VAN GELDER Frank M. of Bath, NY	January 25, 1882
EARLY Ruvy J. of Prattsburgh, NY	Prattsburgh, NY
BENAWAY Melvin F. of Jasper, NY	January 22, 1882
DECK Laura A. J. of Jasper, NY	Greenwood, NY
BIXBY Rufus W. of S. Addison, NY	February 25, 1882
COATS Charity of Bath, NY	Savona, NY
STILES John	February 18, 1882
LA BAR Amanda	Troupsburgh, NY
CAMPBELL William	February 25, 1882
NUDD Nora L.	Troupsburgh, NY
FARNHAM Lee of Canisteo, NY	February 22, 1882
HILL Mary E. of Canisteo, NY	Hornellsville, NY
EVERITT Good of Troups Corners, Pa.	February 23, 1882
JORDAN Sylvia M. of Woodhull, NY	Woodhull, NY
JACKSON William F. of Cameron, NY	February 28, 1882
WOOD Ermine E. of Bradford, NY	Cameron, NY
HARWOOD F. S. of Hedgesville, NY	March 22, 1882
WILEY Martha S. of Woodhull, NY	Woodhull, NY
LINDSAY Robert T. of Bath, NY (Newspaper date)	April 6, 1882
JACKSON Mrs. E. A. of Bath, NY	
BAKER A. M. of Hornby, NY (Newspaper date)	April 6, 1882
FISHER Laura of Caton, NY	
TOBIAS Frank B. of Thurston, NY	March 22, 1882
HAGGERTY Frances A. of Thurston, NY	Thurston, NY
SNELL Horace of Towlesville, NY	March 23, 1882
HECOX Ida of Avoca, NY	Avoca, NY
TENSLER Edward of Campbell, NY	March 23, 1882
HUBBARD Emma of Campbell, NY	Savona, NY
DILDINE V. S. of Almond, NY	March 26, 1882
BARRETT Carrie of Thurston, NY	Thurston, NY
HOFFMAN O. E. of Hornellsville, NY	March 22, 1882
ELLISON Ella dau of Frank of Cameron, NY	Cameron, NY
SCHANCK Jonathan E. of Jasper, NY	April 8, 1882
DENNIS Olive of Jasper, NY	Greenwood, NY

MOORE Morris
PUTNAM Audie

April 3, 1882
Troupsburgh, NY

BALDWIN Horace D. of Addison, NY
BIRDSALL Adelaide F. dau of H. H. of Addison, NY

April 18, 1882
Afton, NY

PIPER Anson of Townsend, NY
DUDLEY Emma E. of Tuscarora, NY

April 16, 1882
Tuscarora, NY

GARDNER G. A. of Tuscarora, NY
DICKINSON Julia of Tuscarora, NY

April 9, 1882
Tuscarora, NY

CLARK George W. of Addison, NY
CHASE Kittie L. of Cameron, NY

April 12, 1882
Addison, NY

SIMONS Philo od Tuscarora, NY
RUNYAN Addie of Tuscarora, NY

April 16, 1882
Tuscarora, NY

HURD Truman of Woodhull, NY
KNAPP Ida A. of Corning, NY

May 21, 1882
Tuscarora, NY

CROSBY Lorenzo of Jasper, NY
UPTON Mrs. Fannie of Canisteo, NY

May 3, 1882
Canisteo, NY

CALKINS Anthony B. of Addison, NY
BRIDGEMAN Emma F. of Addison, NY

May 24, 1882
Painted Post, NY

ALBEE Franklin G. of Tuscarora, NY
ALDRICH Lizzie of Tuscarora, NY

July 4, 1882
Hammondsport, NY

WEAVER John of Nelson, Pa.   (Newspaper date) August 31, 1882
MERRICK Minnie of Gaines, Pa.

Lindley, NY

POTTER Archibald of Troupsburgh, NY
CADY Mrs. Charlotte of Troupsburgh, NY

August 13, 1882
Knoxville, Pa.

DENNIS Samuel F. of Jasper, NY
BOWEN Mrs. Mary A. of Addison, NY

September 12, 1882
Addison, NY

BUNDY Fred W. of Andover, NY
HEZELINE Flora E. of W. Union, NY

September 9, 1882
W. Union, NY

SWARTHOUT A. H. of Owego, NY
TOWNLEY Grace dau of C. C. of Mansfield, Oh.

September 25, 1882
Mansfield, Oh.

SMITH George W. of Buffalo, NY
SMITH Addie

September 27, 1882
Addison, NY

HUGGINS James T. of Lindley, NY
WATSON Nellie B. of Lindley, NY

October 4, 1882
Addison, NY

HILDRETH O. A. of Addison, NY	September 28, 1882
BROWN Flora of Addison, NY	Addison, NY
MARTIN Mr. ____ of Canisteo, NY	October 1, 1882
WHITMORE Emma V. of Addison, NY	Addison, NY
BURNSIDE R. F. of Jasper, NY	October 15, 1882
HADLEY Arania of Jasper, NY	Jasper, NY
VAN DYKE Daniel W. of Nelson, Pa.	October 11, 1882
HEYSHAM Mary of Nelson, Pa.	Nelson, Pa.
FENTON Heman J. of Woodhull, NY	October 30, 1882
SIMONS Anna E. of Woodhull, NY	Corning, NY
PARSON Charles W. of Rochester, NY	November 5, 1882
YOUNG Hattie M. of S. Addison, NY	S. Addison, NY
ROCHE W. of Renova, Pa.	November 30, 1882
DURKIN Mary A. of Addison, NY	Addison, NY
SACKRIDER Daniel A. of Randolph, NY	November 28, 1882
BEECHER Lucia E. of Addison, NY	Addison, NY
HURD Ellis S. of Woodhull, NY	November 29, 1882
ALDRICH Nettie J. of Woodhull, NY	
BACHELDER Martin of Jasper, NY	November 29, 1882
DOTY Theresa of Jasper, NY	Cameron Mills, NY
FULTS Henry M. of Rathbone, NY	December 13, 1882
DORTHY Bertha Anna of Wayne, NY	Addison, NY
PLAISTED Charles F. of W. Union, NY	November 22, 1882
WILCOX Lizzie of Troupsburgh, NY	Troupsburgh, NY
HALLEY H. R. of Bath, NY	December 15, 1882
BACHELLOR Hattie M. of Merchantville, NY	Merchantville, NY
SAXTON William D. of Addison, NY	December 22, 1882
BECKWITH Edith A. of Addison, NY	
WOODCOCK John of Elkland, Pa.	December 30, 1882
BLISS Louisa of Elkland, Pa.	Osceola, Pa.
SALISBURY George of Woodhull, NY	December 24, 1882
BROWN Sarah M. dau of S. G. of Woodhull, NY	Woodhull, NY
QUAKENBUSH Emanulet of Woodhull, NY	December 24, 1882
MC CASLIN Emma of Woodhull, NY	Lindley, NY

NORTON Charles H. of Hartsville, NY   December 2, 1882
FOSTER Martha A. of Hartsville, NY   Greenwood, NY

ZIMMERMAN J. F. of Elk, Pa.   January 14, 1883
ANDERSON Mrs. Susanna of Elk, Pa.   Elk, Pa.

SYMONDS G. H. of S. Oxford, NY   January 10, 1883
OLMSTEAD Nettie of Troupsburgh, NY   Troupsburgh, NY

PRICE Alonzo R. of Harrisburg, Pa.   January 22, 1883
JOHNSON Danna of Addison, NY   Addison, NY

HIBBARD Cherick of New Albany, Pa.   January 10, 1883
FERGUSON Mary M. formerly of Cameron, NY   New Albany, Pa.

PARSHALL J. W. of Waverly, NY   January 21, 1883
WILLIAMS Emma of Waverly, NY   Knoxville, Pa.

SMITH Albert M. of Tuscarora, NY   January 28, 1883
LEAVY Libbie M. of Tuscarora, NY   Tuscarora, NY

BRIDGEMAN Judson of Addison, NY   (Newspaper date) March 15, 1883
WHITE Libbie of Addison, NY   Addison, NY

JOHNSON Frank of Woodhull, NY   March 14, 1883
NORTHRUP Ella of Rathbone, NY   Rathbone, NY

FENTON Albert of Tuscarora, NY   March 11, 1883
CORNELL Ida L. of Woodhull, NY   Elk Creek, NY

REYNOLDS Eugene W. of Troupsburgh, NY   March 17, 1883
HOBER Myra B. of Troupsburgh, NY   Troupsburgh, NY

BURNSIDE Sammy Jr.   March 27,1883
SHELLY Mrs. Jennie

CORNELL Willard B. of Woodhull, NY   March 31, 1883
NEWMAN Ruth of Tuscarora, NY

JUNE Isaac of Addison, NY   June 6, 1883
HOLLIS Mrs. Lucretia W. of Grand Rapids, Mi.   Grand Rapids, Mi.

HARRISON James L. of Addison, NY   June 6, 1883
GRISWOLD Carrie of Addison, NY   Addison, NY

HOUGHTALING Adelbert L. of Addison, NY   June 6, 1883
BESSE Alice F. of Addison, NY

BAKER A. B. of Knoxville, Pa.   June 6, 1883
MOTT Estella A. of Knoxville, Pa.   Knoxville, Pa.

GEE Clark of Keeneyville, Pa. **DAILEY** Emma of Westfield, Pa.	June 10, 1883 Gaines, Pa.
MOERDYKE Peter of Grand Rapids, Mi. **PERRY** Marie of Troupsburgh, NY	June 4, 1883 Troupsburgh, NY
WHITE E. B. of Troupsburgh, NY **HALL** Sarah of Troupsburgh, NY	June 3, 1883 Troupsburgh, NY
HALL A. C. of Troupsburgh, NY **HERRINGTON** Mary of Troupsburgh, NY	June 3, 1883 Troupsburgh, NY
WHITEHEAD Delos E. of Addison, NY **WOOLEVER** Fanny E. of Addison, NY	June 13, 1883 Addison, NY
ROSS Charles A. of Bath, NY **SMITH** Lillie of Cameron, NY	June 17, 1883 Canisteo, NY
KANE T. W. of Omaha, Neb. **ELTON** Annie B. of Chicago, Ill.	June 7, 1883 Council Bluffs, Io.
HOLLANDS William Jr. **CADY** Eliza dau of E. Cady of Elkland, Pa.	June 21, 1883 Elkland, Pa.
ALBEE Leonard of S. Addison, NY **COOK** Sabrina of Rathbone, NY	June 7, 1883 Rathbone, NY
EDWARDS James of Addison, NY **MC TAMNEY** Rebecca of Tuscarora, NY	July 30, 1883 Addison, NY
BEARD James of Bath, NY **GOFORTH** Mary Jane of Addison, NY	August 1, 1883
DE LEURY William of Addison, NY **DE GROFF** Ella of Addison, NY	August 1, 1883 Addison, NY
STICKLES J. V. of Addison, NY **PHELPS** Mrs. Mary Louisa of Addison, NY	September 5, 1883 Addison, NY
YOUNG Frank D. of Addison, NY **CHAMBER** Lizzie of New Haven, Ct	October 3, 1883 New Haven, Ct.
VANDERWARKER George of Addison, NY **WEBSTER** Lillie of Addison, NY	September 30, 1883 Addison, NY
NICKET John Jr. of Syracuse, NY **BURRELL** Nellie of Knoxville, NY/Pa.	October 17, 1883
BUSH George of Addison, NY **SOLES** Annie Jeanett of Campbell, NY	October 13, 1883

SMITH W. N. of Coopers Plains, NY   (Newspaper date) October 18, 1883
NEWMAN Mrs. E. J. of Addison, NY

BROWN Chauncey P. of Cameron, NY   October 24, 1883
JUNE Ida M. of Jasper, NY   Jasper, NY

MALLORY N. E. of Addison, NY   October 18, 1883
ELDRICH Cornie of New York City   New York City

SIMMONS Lew H. of Olean, NY   October 24, 1883
MERCEREAU E. Belle of Addison, NY   Addison, NY

STERNER Edward of Lindley, NY   (Newspaper date) November 15, 1883
RODGERS Carrie dau of Capt. J. A. of Lindley, NY

SHOEMAKER Frederick H. of Lawrenceville, Pa.   November 3, 1883
WELDEN Bessie of Lindley, NY   Elmira, NY

NORTHRUP Eugene of Woodhull, NY   November 15, 1883
PERKINS Nellie of Tuscarora, NY   Tuscarora, NY

RICHARDSON Cassius M. of Nelson, Pa.   November 15, 1883
BONHAM Carrie of Osceola, Pa.   Osceola, Pa.

GROVER W. J. of Ulysses, Pa.   November 15, 1883
KNAPP Nellie M. of Westfield, Pa.   Westfield, Pa.

KETCHUM Charles of Jasper, NY   November 15, 1883
BULLOCK Sada of Harrison Valley, Pa.   Harrison Valley, Pa.

KIRTLAND Charles C. of Knoxville, Pa.   December 1, 1883
DOANE Arvilla S. of Knoxville, Pa.   Knoxville, Pa.

WRIGHT John M. of Erwin Center, NY   December 17, 1883
VAN GORDEN Mary S. of Addison, NY   Addison, NY

WHITLEY Delos   December 7, 1883
WHITE Mrs. Almira   Cameron, NY

CLARKSON John H. of Brookfield, Pa.   December 23, 1883
DOANE Alice P. of Brookfield, Pa.   Troupsburgh, NY

WAFLER John of Angelica, NY   January 1, 1884
LYON C. of Woodhull, NY   Woodhull, NY

WELTY Jacob of Troupsburgh, NY   December 9, 1883
MILLER Zelda of Troupsburgh, NY   Woodhull, NY

BRAZEE Barnham of Campbell, NY   January 9, 1884
HOWLAND Estella A. of Rathbone, NY   Rathbone, NY

HUNT Lincoln E. of Troupsburgh, NY   January 30, 1884
WHEATON Minnie M. of Troupsburgh, NY   Jasper, NY

PALMER W. H. of Toronto, Canada   January 16, 1884
SMITH Ella M. of Addison, NY

CALINAN John of Corning, NY   February 7, 1884
QUINN Katie of Corning, NY   Addison, NY

ESTEE Prof. D. M. of Canisteo, NY   March 20, 1884
PIERPONT Nettie W. of Allen's Hill, NY

SCOTT Peter of Addison, NY   April 20, 1884
KNAPP Hattie   Addison, NY

DODGE Frank of Addison, NY   April 17, 1884
BEADLE Jennie of Elkland, Pa.   Addison, NY

STOCUM Charles of N. Hector, NY   May 14, 1884
TITUS Louise E. of Erwin Center, NY   Addison, NY

SNELL Herman W. of Addison, NY   June 13, 1884
HUNT Estella H. of Addison, NY   Addison, NY

NELSON Charles H. of Coudersport, Pa.   June 12, 1884
EVANS Mary of Addison, NY   Addison, NY

BROWN Ernest W. of Friendship, NY   June 18, 1884
PARKHURST Lena A. of Friendship, NY   Friendship, NY

BECKWITH Chester J. of Addison, NY   July 26, 1884
TOTTEN Jennie of Woodhull, NY   Addison, NY

HUBBARD Nathaniel of Troupsburgh, NY   August 17, 1884
MATTESON Minnie of Troupsburgh, NY   Brookfield, Pa.

WRIGHT James of Lindley, NY   August 22, 1884
VAN GORDON Orpha of Addison, NY   Addison, NY

STICKLER Oscar of Knoxville, NY/Pa,   August 3, 1884
BRIGGS Ella of Knoxville, NY/Pa.   Addison, NY

GROSS Gustave of W. Branch, Pa.   September 25, 1884
SCHAAR Emma of W. Branch, Pa.   Gaines, Pa.

BANKS Samuel of Jasper, NY   September 7, 1884
BUTLER Annetta of Jasper, NY   Jasper, NY

BALOU Daniel of Clymer, Pa.   September 21, 1884
COON Jennie of Troupsburgh, NY   Troupsburgh, NY

LATTIMER James L. of Chatham, Pa.   September 26, 1884
GLOVER Carrie of Troupsburgh, NY   Troupsburgh, NY

CHAPMAN Edward W. of Woodhull, NY   (Newspaper date) October 9, 1884
WOOD Ida E. of Lawrenceville, Pa.

SLITER Joseph D. of Lindley, NY   September 24, 1884
TUCKER Hattie of Troupsburgh, NY   Woodhull, NY

BURDICK U. T. of Osceola, Pa.   November 15, 1884
STEVENS Flora V. of Nelson, Pa.

CROFT Wayne M. of Keeneyville, Pa.   November 15, 1884
POTTER Louisa M. of Troupsburgh, NY   Woodhull, NY

HARE William H. of Painted Post, NY   November 13, 1884
REYNOLDS Alice R. of Cameron, NY   Jasper, NY

SPRAGUE Lewis of Westfield, Pa.   November 27, 1884
COOPER Elvis of Westfield, Pa.

HALLINAN James of Tuscarora, NY   December 1, 1884
FRAWLEY Mary of Thurston, NY   Addison, NY

PARK Henry of Rathbone, NY   December 4, 1884
YOUNG Mary B. of Rathbone, NY   Rathbone, NY

Voice of the Nation (Addison, NY)

January 10, 1855 - December 19, 1855

GRINNELL Zelotus of Addison, NY   January 3, 1855
COLWELL Caroline of Addison, NY   Addison, NY

BRIDGEMAN Otis of Addison, NY   December 30, 1854
WRIGHT Ann E. of Addison, NY   Addison, NY

BLISS Charles of Corning, NY   December 31, 1854
MILLIGAN Ann of Corning, NY   Corning, NY

WOLCOTT Charles 3rd of Corning, NY   January 1, 1855
GILLETT Huldah Jane of Corning, NY   Corning, NY

CHAPMAN Silas of Addison, NY   January 10, 1855
HIGGINS Abigail of Addison, NY   Addison, NY

CHASE Edward C. of Wayne, NY   January 18, 1855
CHASE Mrs. Hannah M. of Wis.   Prattsburgh, NY

MINER Harrison C. of Wayland, NY	January 16, 1855
HAMLIN Ellen M. of Wayland, NY	Wayland, NY
NORRIS S. R. of Kanona, NY	January 26, 1855
SMITH H. Mariah of Urbana, NY	Urbana, NY
BENTON G. R. of Pulteney, NY	January 24, 1855
ARMSTRONG Lydia A. dau of Andrew of Pulteney, NY	Pulteney, NY
ABER Henry G. of Bath, NY	January 28, 1855
PANGBURN Nancy L. of Bath, NY	Bath, NY
LOVELESS Andrew of Bath, NY	January 30, 1855
GUSTIN Lucy of Bath, NY	Bath, NY
COWELL Henry of Monterey, NY	January 18, 1855
DAWSON Mary M. of Monterey, NY	Monterey, NY
WAGONER Inglehart of Wheeler, NY	February 12, 1855
SHAY Mary E. of Italy, NY	Liberty Corners, NY
WAUGH William of Orange, NY	February 11, 1855
HUGHEY Margaret dau of Joseph of Orange, NY	Orange, NY
BRUNDAGE Andrew J. Atty.	February 20, 1855
KELLOGG Frances A. dau of Russell Kellogg	Kanona, NY
FAUCETT Robert of Livingston Co. Mi.	February 20, 1855
FAUCETT Mary of Bath, NY	Bath, NY
WOODWARD F. W. of Bath, NY	February 19, 1855
KELLEY Elizabeth of Elmira, NY	Elmira, NY
LOUCKS Richard of Avoca, NY	February 22, 1855
MORSE Elizabeth of Avoca, NY	Avoca, NY
VAN DEMARK Joseph H. of Junius, NY	March 5, 1855
HUNT Jane A. of Prattsburgh, NY	Prattsburgh, NY
PRATT Nelson of Tioga, Pa.	March 1, 1855
ABBOTT Ann of Tioga, Pa.	Corning, NY
TOWNER Oliver R. of Avoca, NY	February 25, 1855
SQUIRE Sarah J. of Avoca, NY	Avoca, NY
SHERWOOD Henry of Addison, NY	March 14, 1855
ROBINSON Eleanora of Ithaca, NY	Ithaca, NY
MYERS James D. of Waverly, NY	March 14, 1855
KRESS Elizabeth A. of Corning, NY	Corning, NY

WALKER John of Howard, NY
MARSH Elizabeth L. of Bath, NY

March 7, 1855
Bath, NY

SAWTELL Henry P. of Canisteo, NY
TOTTEN Caroline of Canisteo, NY

March 16, 1855
Canisteo, NY

MONROE John of Woodhull, NY
STEPHENS Margaret of Addison, NY

March 20, 1855
Addison, NY

ALBEE Eleazor of Addison, NY
BROOKS Eunice of Addison, NY

March 25, 1855
S. Addison, NY

DICEY Elmer C. of Grand Haven, Mi.
LEWIS Emeline of Bath, NY

March 18, 1855
Bath, NY

GAYLORD Leroy of Savona, NY
MC ELWEE N. Caroline of Savona, NY

February 28, 1855
Savona, NY

GOODSELL John of Thurston, NY
CORBETT Elizabeth S. of Thurston, NY

March 18, 1855
Thurston, NY

BECKWITH Griffin of Tioga, Pa.
CUSHION Margaret E. of Schuyler Co. NY

March 28, 1855
Corning, NY

DILLENBACK Jacob of Wheeler, NY
UPTHEGROVE Mrs. Adeline of Prattsburgh, NY

April 5, 1855
Prattsburgh, NY

ANDRUS Ambrose F. of Addison, NY
FLYNN Permelia of Bath, NY

April 10, 1855
Bath, NY

PHIPPS William R. of Jasper, NY
POMERLY Julia A. of Woodhull, NY

April 8, 1855
Savona, NY

THOMPSON Giles B. of Worcester, Mass. (newspaper date) May 2, 1855
CHASE Catherine of Elkland, Pa.

Addison, NY

WHITTENHALL Thomas A. of Addison, NY
SHOEMAKER Sarah of Bath, NY

May 11, 1855
Bath, NY

WOMBOUGH George W. of Addison, NY
CLARK Caroline E. of Addison, NY

May 3, 1855
Addison, NY

HATCH Austin S. of Addison, NY
FAIRBANKS Juliett of Addison, NY

May 12, 1855
S. Addison, NY

STEWART Anthony (Newspaper date) May 16, 1855
SHERWOOD Ann H.

Corning, NY

STRONG James of Addison, NY
SHEARER Silly of Addison, NY

May 21, 1855
Addison, NY

BRAMBLE George S.	May 15, 1855
ROBBINS Mary	Prattsburgh, NY
HILL Harvey	May 16, 1855
WILSON Susan Jane	Prattsburgh, NY
OTTARSON Thomas J. of Thurston, NY	May 19, 1855
MARTIN Harriet Eliza of Thurston, NY	Thurston, NY
CALL Levi N. of Hartsville, NY	May 26, 1855
GUYON Mary of Hartsville, NY	Addison, NY
STEPHENS Albert S. of Hartsville, NY	May 27, 1855
HOAG Sarah E. of Hartsville, NY	
BURDICK Mr. ____ of Bainbridge	July 4, 1855
MC PHERSON L. of Jasper, NY	Addison, NY
HOWELL James Faulkner	July 10, 1855
SHEPHERD Lydia	Bath, NY
REES Martin A.	July 4, 1855
EDSON Ruby J.	Prattsburgh, NY
GORDON Whitman of S. Addison, NY	July 22, 1855
MC MINDS Sarah of S. Addison, NY	S. Addison, NY
GILLAN William W. of Addison, NY	August 17, 1855
O'NEIL Harriet of Addison, NY	Addison, NY
FORTNER William of Addison, NY	September 29, 1855
GEE Martha of Addison, NY	Addison, NY
DAWSON R. B. of Addison, NY	September 19, 1855
JOHNSON Miss ____ of Bath, NY	Bath, NY
BALDWIN James of Addison, NY	October 10, 1855
COWLEY Emma L. dau of C. Cowley of Addison, NY	Addison, NY
ROLESON Alfred of Hornby, NY	September 20, 1855
KNOWLTON Mary of Hornby, NY	Hornby, NY
WHITAKER James L. of Troupsburgh, NY	September 27, 1855
MALLORY Nancy M. of Troupsburgh, NY	Prattsburgh, NY
STEWART Charles D. of Tecumseh, Mi.	September 27, 1855
READ Roella of Urbana, NY	Urbana, NY
BAILY George S. of Urbana, NY	September 22, 1855
WIXOM Sarah Jane of Urbana, NY	Urbana, NY

MC COLLUM William H. of Farmington, Pa.   November 25, 1855
GEE Rachel G. of Middleburg, Pa.   S. Addison, NY

BAILEY Sylvester S. of Woodhull, NY   December 7, 1855
DALLEY Sally Elizabeth of Woodhull, NY   Addison, NY

Bath Gazette and Genessee Advertiser

June 1, 1797 - April 12, 1798

WOODRUFF James of Bath, NY   (Newspaper date) October 12, 1797
HUFF Hannah of Bath, NY   (Thursday last)

AULLS Ephraim of Steuben Co. NY   January 25, 1798
SANFORD Ann of Steuben Co. NY

WILSON John   February 22, 1798
DUNN Betsey dau of Robert of Yorktown, Pa.

Steuben American (Bath, NY)

January 2, 1856 - May 6, 1857

HIBBARD John of Woodhull, NY   January 1, 1856
WORDEN Ellen of Woodhull, NY   Woodhull, NY

ANDERSON Horatio G. K. of Addison, NY   January 19, 1856
CRANS Juliet of Woodhull, NY   Woodhull, NY

BOYD John of Pulteney, NY   February 5, 1856
HOTCHKIN Eunice   Bath, NY

FLETCHER Myron H. of Bath, NY   February 14, 1856
HAVEN Hannah of Bath, NY   Bath, NY

STRATTON Charles of Hammondsport, NY   February 19, 1856
LYON Sophia of Bath, NY

SAMMONS I. D. of Painted Post, NY   February 28, 1856
WHITTENHALL Adelaide of Addison, NY   Addison, NY

BAXTER Peter of Addison, NY   April 8, 1856
WELCH Louisa of Addison, NY   Addison, NY

CURTIS Josiah of Addison, NY   (Newspaper date) April 16, 1856
SMITH Caroline of Addison, NY

RHODA Peter of Hornby, NY   April 2, 1856

CHAPIN Adeline of Campbell, NY — Corning, NY

STETSON Reuben of Corning, NY — April 10, 1856
GIFFORD Elsie of Corning, NY — Corning, NY

LAMAN John J. of Toledo, Ohio — April 9, 1856
RUMSEY Carolyn of Kanona, NY — Kanona, NY

OVERHISER Abram of Wheeler, NY — May 1, 1856
WRAIGHT Alice of Wheeler, NY — Kanona, NY

BRUNDAGE James L. — July 3, 1856
BRUNDAGE Caroline — Bath, NY

CHASE Rev. L. D. — August 28, 1856
LARROWE E. dau of Judge Larrowe of Hammondsport, NY — Urbana, NY

MANCHESTER H. D. of Bath, NY — August 31, 1856
DANIELS Elizabeth of Bath, NY — Bath, NY

HALL Rev. Uria S. — August 13, 1856
PARKHILL Elizabeth of Avoca, NY — Avoca, NY

POWERS William D. Md. of Hammondsport, NY — October 2, 1856
BARRETT Lovisa M. dau of Seth W. of Hammondsport, NY — Hammondsport, NY

HALL Philander J. of Addison, NY — September 21, 1856
CHASE Melissa R. of Rathbone, NY — Thurston, NY

FOOTE Franklin C. of E. Pembroke, NY — October 22, 1856
NORTON Frances L. of E. Pembroke, NY — Kanona, NY

BURNHAM Joseph L. of Buena Vista, NY — October 20, 1856
CAPLE Sarah Jane of Prattsburgh, NY — Prattsburgh, NY

HARDENBROOK Frank of Bath, NY — September 30, 1856
MC ELWEE M. J. of Bath, NY — Bath, NY

DONAHE Menzer D. of Avoca, NY — November 5, 1856
SMITH Margaret J. dau of John J. of Bath, NY — Bath, NY

EDWARDS C. H. of Brown, Pa. — November 11, 1856
JONES A. A. of Addison, NY — Addison, NY

BALDWIN Henry of Addison, NY — November 5, 1856
BLISS Bella of Hornellsville, NY — Hornellsville, NY

ARNOLD Edwin P. of Lisle, NY — November 18, 1856
KINNEY Melissa of Painted Post, NY — Painted Post, NY

MURRAY James H. of Hornby, NY   February 15, 1857
THOMAS Alvira of Addison, NY   Addison, NY

CHASE Isaac N. of Elkland, Pa.   February 15, 1857
BENNETT Helen of Elkland, Pa.   Addison, NY

JOHNSON E. M. of Addison, NY   March 10, 1857
WHITTENHALL Frances M. of Addison, NY   Addison, NY

HOTCHKIN James H.   March 5, 1857
LEWIS Mrs. Clarissa Jane   Prattsburgh, NY

GLEASON Ezra formerly of Luzerne, NY   March 1, 1857
CLARK Sarah F. dau of H. R. of Thurston, NY   Merchantville, NY

FAY Lewis D. Sheriff of Bath, NY   March 30, 1857
ZIELLY Nancy of Bath, NY   Bath, NY

Steuben Democrat

November 15, 1843 - May 22, 1849

MATHEWSON John M. of Benton, NY   November 18, 1843
NASH Jane E. of Bath, NY   Bath, NY

NORTHROP Eli of Tyrone, NY   November 29, 1843
CRAFT Rachel of Tyrone, NY   W. Tyrone, NY

SARGEANT William   December 4/5, 1843
DILLISTON Laura   E. Tyrone, NY

EARLY Jackson of Prattsburgh, NY   January 3, 1844
TRENCHARD Patience of Wheeler, NY   Wheeler, NY

MITCHELL Walter   (Newspaper date) January 17, 1844
ZIMMERMAN Catherine dau of John   Bradford, NY

LEGRO Samuel   January 24, 1844
TIFFANY Elmira   Bath, NY

DISBROW Caleb R. of Bath, NY   February 19, 1844
GRISWOLD Electa of S. Dansville, NY   S. Dansville, NY

RARRICK Anthony H. of Tyrone, NY   February 29, 1844
CAMPBELL Sarah of Bath, NY   Bath, NY

HOTCHKIN Joseph T. of Prattsburgh, NY   April 3, 1844
DUNNING Desiah of S. Pulteney, NY   S. Pulteney, NY

BRAMBLE Ezra C. of Prattsburgh, NY   April 11, 1844
LINDSLEY Lydia G. of Prattsburgh, NY   Prattsburgh, NY

VAN HOUTEN James of Bath, NY   April 17, 1844
JOHNSON Nancy K. of Bath, NY   Bath, NY

DUDLEY James R. of Bath, NY   April 22, 1844
EDWARDS Clarissa R. of Bath, NY   Bath, NY

PALMER Milo of Bath, NY   May 15, 1844
MORE Azilla of Bath, NY

ROWLAND Norman of Avoca, NY   April 20, 1844
TOWNER Hannah of Avoca, NY

LEE Leicester of Bath, NY   May 15, 1844
BRUNDAGE Salina of Pulteney, NY   Pulteney, NY

missing issues

OLMSTEAD Jeremiah of Avoca, NY   June 29, 1848
DYGERT Charlotte of Wheeler, NY   Wheeler, NY

SMITH Rufus of Bath, NY   July 5, 1848
CHASE Polly of Bath, NY   Bath, NY

KELLY John of Bath, NY   July 10, 1848
COLLINS Margaret of Bath, NY   Bath, NY

JENKS Watermore of Bath, NY   August 3, 1848
RICHARDSON Eliza Ann of Bath, NY   Bath, NY

RIPLEY Francis of Milwaukee, Wis.   August 9, 1848
FOWLER Christina G. dau of John W. of Bath, NY   Bath, NY

LOOK J. B. formerly of Bath, NY   August 31, 1848
FAY Sarah M. dau of A. Fay of Havana, NY   Havana, NY

SEYMOUR Mr. ____ of Mass.   September 12, 1848
BINGHAM Miss Eugene   Bath, NY

FRENCH Jefferson of Bath, NY   September 14, 1848
WARREN Mary dau of Col. Phineas Warren of Bath, NY   Bath, NY

FORDYCE Seymour of Scipio, NY   September 12, 1848
ALEXANDER Susan M. of Howard, NY   Howard, NY

HOUSE P. R. of Bath, NY   September 19, 1848
GUIWITS Mary of Wheeler, NY   Wheeler, NY

COOK Henry H. of Bath, NY
MC CAY Mary
September 27, 1848
Bath, NY

HOWELL N. H. Jr. of Canandaigua, NY
MC CAY Frances dau of W. W. of Bath, NY
September 27, 1848
Bath, NY

WHITE P.
CLISDELL Eliza
August 8, 1848
Bath, NY

GAMBLE Col. William of Bath, NY
SOUTHERLAND Mrs. Amelia of Bath, NY
October 17, 1848
Bath, NY

LOSIER John P.
GOULD Louisa H. of Bath, NY
October 11, 1848
Bath, NY

CALIENS Philander
COLCORD Emily
November 15, 1848
Thurston, NY

WHEELER Mr. ____ of Bath, NY
HALLIDAY Emma of Thurston, NY
November 16, 1848
Thurston, NY

BEEMER Thomas F. of Cohocton, NY
WILLIAMS Maria E. of Ithaca, NY
November 20, 1848
Cohocton, NY

ALLEN Samuel T. D. of Cohocton, NY
SKUTT Catherine E. of Naples, NY
November 21, 1848
Geneva, NY

HEAD James
BENNETT Ann
October 26, 1848
Howard, NY

TOLLIVER D. T. of Bath, NY
NICHOLS Elizabeth of Bath, NY
November 29, 1848
Kennedyville, NY

DININNY Feril C. of Addison, NY
HARFORD Adia of New York City
December 12, 1848
Bedford, NY

MC CRAW Daniel of Greenwood, NY
BRUNDAGE Caroline E. of Greenwood, NY
December 30, 1848
Greenwood, NY

CALKINS John C. of Avoca, NY
MACK Abigail of Bath, NY
January 30, 1849
Bath, NY

STEWART Andrew of Howard, NY
BRACKER Susan of Bath, NY
January 30, 1849
Bath, NY

FLEMING Dr. J. B. of Bath, NY
BROWN Hannah C. of Bath, NY
March 7, 1849
Bath, NY

SWEET Edward A. of Urbana, NY
GREGORY Meribah of Urbana, NY
March 3, 1849
Avoca, NY

VANDERWARKIN Jacob of Wheeler, NY   March 3, 1849
ELLIOTT Mrs. Temma of Wheeler, NY   Wheeler, NY

LONGWELL James of Urbana, NY   March 15, 1849
LONGWELL Mrs. Elizabeth of Urbana, NY

HARRIS Hiram of Bath, NY   March 15, 1849
INGERSOLL Sally Ann of Bath, NY   Bath, NY

NICHOLSON Ambrose of Howard, NY   March 27, 1849
ELLIS Sophia of Lodi, NY   Lodi, NY

WILLOUR Alonzo   April 4, 1849
NICHOLDS Adeline of Bath, NY

STINSON George of Mud Creek, NY   (Newspaper date) April 18, 1849
JOHNSON Catherine of Dansville, NY (Wednesday last) Bath, NY

LONG William of Great Britain   March 15, 1849
WALLACE Nancy of Prattsburgh, NY   Prattsburgh, NY

BURD George   April 21, 1849
DYGERT Nancy   Cameron, NY

PETERS Charles   May 3, 1849
CROSBY Lucinda   Bath, NY

HELMER Andrew of Addison, NY   May 26, 1849
SMITH Mrs. Thankful of Thurston, NY   Thurston, NY

PATTERSON Robert   May 29, 1849
ANTHONY Miss ____   Addison, NY

MC CALL Dr. ____ of Rushford, NY   May 29, 1849
SMITH Miss ____ dau of Ancel of Erwin, NY Erwin, NY

ROWE Anson of Bath, NY   June 4, 1849
SMITH Lucy Jane of Bath, NY   Prattsburgh, NY

MORGAN William of Bath, NY   May 26, 1849
SMITH Cordelia M. of Bath, NY   Wayne, NY

The Constitutionist (Bath, NY)
Wednesday
August 23, 1837 - February 16, 1842

FAULKNER John of Urbana, NY   August 29, 1837
MYRTLE Angeline of Wheeler, NY   Hammondsport, NY

STEWART James A. of Howard, NY   September 22, 1837
STEWART Margaret dau of Henry of Bath, NY   Bath, NY

MORTON Eben L. of Cameron, NY   (Newspaper date) October 11, 1837
GUSTIN Lucy dau of Gardner of Cameron, NY (Sunday last) Cameron, NY

JAMISON Louis T. of the US Army   November 16, 1837
MC CLURE Mary E. dau of Gen. George Mc Clure   Grove, Ill.

HASTINGS Lemuel of Hammondsport, NY   December 13, 1837
BARNARD Mary of Geneva, NY   Geneva, NY

MORSE Phillip of Bath, NY   December 24, 1837
GRAMES Jane of Bath, NY   Painted Post, NY

KETCHUM William R. of Bath, NY   January 17, 1838
GIFFORD Ruth E. of Bath, NY   Bath, NY

SATTLE William formerly of Chenango Co. NY   January 28, 1838
WELLS Laura   Addison, NY

WATKINS Joseph   January 14, 1838
BAILEY Eliza   Bath, NY

CHAMBERLAIN Henry W. of Bath, NY   February 14, 1838
BACON Angeline dau of Col. Simeon Bacon   Howard, NY

SHIPMAN Dr. Daniel M. of Bath, NY   February 20, 1838
TOWNSEND Sarah C. of Bath, NY   Bath, NY

STEWART Richard B.   February 21, 1838
METCALFE Charlotte dau of Thomas   Bath, NY

RIDER Samuel   (Newspaper date) February 28, 1838
CONNOR Elizabeth   Howard, NY

ROSE Sherman   March 23, 1838
STRYKER Mahala G.   Wheeler, NY

WHITNEY Abraham Jr.   February 15, 1838
WARNER Mercy dau of Alpheus   Hornby, NY

DENNIS Franklin   March 20, 1838
LAMSON Martha E.   Jasper, NY

READ Lazurus Hammond of Hammondsport, NY   April 3, 1838
WOODS Elizabeth L. dau of late William   Bath, NY

PAYNE Arnold of Cameron, NY	April 12, 1838
ARNOLD Phebe C. of Cameron, NY	Bath, NY
GOODSELL George	April 19, 1838
FULSOM Sally Ann	Bath, NY
BROWN Lucien M. of Dansville, NY	May 9, 1838
BESLEY Susan T. dau of Samuel of Campbell, NY	Campbell, NY
ELLIS George Washington of Tyrone, NY	May 8, 1838
POTTS Amelia Alexandrina of Seneca Falls, NY	Seneca Falls, NY
WILLIAMS Nathaniel P.	May 16, 1838
QUICK Elizabeth	Hammondsport, NY
ELLAS Francis S. of Onieda Co. NY	May 9, 1838
HOYT Sarah E. formerly of Buffalo, NY	Stamford, Conn.
MASTEN Joseph G. of Buffalo, NY	June 12, 1838
CAMERON Christina of Greene, NY	Greene, NY
WOLVERTON William of Bradford, NY (Newspaper date)	July 4, 1838
HAUSE Betsey of Tyrone, NY	Tyrone, NY
POWERS Cyrus of Urbana, NY	July 4, 1838
RICHMOND Nancy of Wayne, NY	Wayne, NY
ALLEN Samuel of Howard, NY	July 1, 1838
STEVENS Ann of Howard, NY	Howard, NY
NIPHER Michael of Howard, NY	July 1, 1838
PERSONS Hannah of Howard, NY	Howard, NY
ALLEN Hubbart of Howard, NY	July 1, 1838
BALDWIN Lydia of Howard, NY	Howard, NY
BENNETT Jeremiah of Howard, NY	July 1, 1838
WINNE Anne of Howard, NY	Howard, NY
STRONG Stephen Judge of Tioga, Co. NY	July 10, 1838
CAMP Mrs. Abigail of Owego, NY	Owego, NY
COSS Minor of Bath, NY	July 30, 1838
DE WITT Harriet of Bath, NY	Bath, NY
SHUMWAY Charles N. of Addison, NY	July 16, 1838
GILE Margaret A. dau of William of Oxford, NY	Oxford, NY
BRIGGS William of Bath, NY	August 20, 1838
TOWLE Cecelia B. of Holley, NY	Holley, NY

OTIS Ralph of Almond, NY   August 25, 1838
SMITH Mary   Hornellsville, NY

LINDSLEY Edward   September 13, 1838
JOHNSON Mary B.   Bath, NY

BONHAM Charles   September 18, 1838
GOODWIN Mary B.   Campbell, NY

EASLING Dayton of Hornby, NY   September 27, 1838
MASTERS Emeline dau of Nehemiah of Hornby, NY   Hornby, NY

DENNIS Samuel F.   September 27, 1838
WOODWARD Sarah S.   Jasper, NY

KNOX John of Painted Post, NY   (Newspaper date) October 10, 1838
GUSTIN Mrs. Fanny widow of Maj. Gustin of NH   Pulteney, NY

MILLARD Josiah   September 19, 1838
CORNELL Elizabeth   Canisteo, NY

WALRATH Abraham I.   October 9, 1838
HOUSE Sarah Rodela dau of George I.   Cameron, NY

COYE Levi   October 11, 1838
GOODSELL Hannah A.   Hornby, NY

RANDALL Alford of Orange, NY   October 18, 1838
SAYER Sally Ann of Hornby, NY   Hornby, NY

CLASON Henry P.   (Newspaper date) October 24, 1838
LILLY Harriet   Hornellsville, NY

HASTINGS George H. of Bath, NY   October 8, 1838
BARTLETT Sarah E. dau of Montgomery of Utica, NY Chilicothe, Ohio

TALBOT Jarvis   November 1, 1838
DENNIS Fidelia Jane   Jasper, NY

ROSE Martin H. of Hammondsport, NY   November 22, 1838
MARSHALL Eliza Ann dau of Gen. Otto F. Marshall   Wheeler, NY

BIXBY Alanson   November 17, 1838
ROWE Cornelia   Hornby, NY

BECKWITH Joseph of Hornby, NY   November 28, 1838
GORTON Hannah of Painted Post, NY

STRATTON David   November 1, 1838
HAWKENBURY Eliza

TUTTLE William H.
BROOKS Mary J.
December 27, 1838
Bath, NY

LOUCKS Adam of Avoca, NY
COLLIER Jane M. of Avoca, NY
December 25, 1838
Avoca, NY

DECK Daniel I.
MERRIAM Eliza
January 1, 1839
Jasper, NY

MAY Dr. Joseph Adams form. of Bath, NY (Newspaper date) January 23, 1839
STUART Mary
Baton Rouge, La.

CLASON G. W. of Hornellsville, NY (Newspaper date) January 30, 1839
SEWARD N. of Almond, NY
Hornellsville, NY

ANDRUS W. (Newspaper date) January 30, 1839
RUSSELL P.
Hornellsville, NY

FERRIS George of Tyrone, NY
HUDINOT Ann of Tyrone, NY
January 28, 1839
Wayne, NY

JOHNSON John of Guilford, NY
January 29, 1839
BUCKINGHAM Harriet of Medina, NY formerly of Bath, NY

SITAMEN John of Wheeler, NY
HARRIS Maria of Wheeler, NY
January 30, 1839
Wheeler, NY

BISHOP Charles of Troupsburgh, NY (Newspaper date) February 13, 1839
BROTZMAN Charity
Jasper, NY

WISS David (Newspaper date) February 13, 1839
HECKMAN Elizabeth
Jasper, NY

HECKMAN Robert H. (Newspaper date) February 13, 1839
DECK Betsey
Jasper, NY

STONE Amos of Urbana, NY
MILLS Jane of Bath, NY
February 20, 1839
Bath, NY

BULL Harvey
TOWLE Lucinda
March 6, 1839
Bath, NY

WIXSON James M.
STOUT Margaret W.
February 27, 1839
Urbana, NY

WOODWARD David Francis of Jasper, NY
WEBSTER Phebe of Bath, NY
March 27, 1839
Bath, NY

CHASE Solomon of Bath, NY
HUDSON Tripheny of Bath, NY
March 28, 1839
Bath, NY

SHANNON Mathew of Bath, NY   March 26, 1839
FOSSETT Martha of Bath, NY   Bath, NY

COSTEN Frederick of Bath, NY   March 31, 1839
LATTA Nancy of Bath, NY

HAIGHT Samuel S. of Angelica, NY   April 7, 1839
CHEESEMAN Maria of Allegany Co. NY   Allegany Co. NY

ROSE John of Bath, NY   April 25, 1839
MASON Eliza H. of Bath, NY   Almond, NY

FLUENT Rufus   May 21, 1839
ROSS Mary Jane   Howard, NY

ROSS James   May 22, 1839
FLUENT Mehitabel   Canisteo, NY

HINCKLEY John of Naples, NY   May 12, 1839
STEWART Sophia   Prattsburgh, NY

HOPKINS Erastus of White Lake, Mi.   May 21, 1839
CLARK Climena   Prattsburgh, NY

EDDY John S. of Campbell, NY   May 30, 1839
ALDRICH Jude of Cameron, NY   Bath, NY

TALBOT Warren   June 9, 1839
TRAVACE Esther Ann   Jasper, NY

PATCHIN E. W. Md. of Sparta, NY   (Newspaper date) July 17, 1839
EWERTS Mary of Geneseo, NY   Geneseo, NY

GOODRICH James of Columbia, Pa.   July 24, 1839
BELL Polly of Bath, NY   Bath, NY

WARREN George formerly of Bath, NY   July 27, 1839
ROBERTS Rachel of Geneseo, NY   Dansville, NY

GILLETT Samuel   August 18, 1839
HELMER Anna   Bath, NY

KEELER Joseph   August 14, 1839
BLOOD Lucita   Bath, NY

COBB Zenos   August 20, 1839
BAKER Julia dau of Samuel   Urbana, NY

SMITH A. L. Jr. of Hornellsville, NY   August 31, 1839
YOUNG Sarah of Painted Post, NY   Painted Post, NY

BURTON William
HELIKER Mary

August 12, 1839
Jasper, NY

POMEROY Nelson
HUTCHINSON Jemima

August 12, 1839
Woodhull, NY

BACKMAN Edmond of Pulteney, NY
VORHEES Mary of W. Fayette, NY

September 10, 1839
W. Fayette, NY

VORHEES Sebring of Van Burke, Mi.
BACKMAN Sarah of Pulteney, NY

September 11, 1839
Pulteney, NY

MOORE Francis Jr. Mayor of Houston, Tx. (Newspaper date) October 2, 1839
WOOD Elizabeth dau of Benjamin

Bath, NY

GRISWOLD C. M.
MOSIER Sophronia

September 1, 1839
Addison, NY

BUCK E. A.
JONES Catherine A.

September 5, 1839
Addison, NY

BROWN Elnathan G.
KANE Betsey

September 8, 1839
Addison, NY

SPAULDING Erastus of Howard, NY
WALKER Eliza of Howard, NY

September 4, 1839
Howard, NY

ALLEN Stephen of Howard, NY
MEEKS Caroline of Howard, NY

September 10, 1839
Howard, NY

RANDLE Alford of Orange, NY
SAYER Sally Ann of Hornby, NY

October 18, 1839
Hornby, NY

CLASON Henry P.   (Newspaper date) October 24, 1839
LILLY Harriet

Hornellsville, NY

BROWNELL John
TRENCHER Sally Ann

October 19, 1839
Wheeler, NY

GILBERT William J. of Painted Post, NY
ERWIN Rachel A. dau of late Capt. Samuel Erwin

October 30, 1839

RATHBUN Chauncey
MC NAUGHTON Jane

December 4, 1839
Howard, NY

TOWLE John D. of Howard, NY
ASER Elizabeth of Howard, NY

December 15, 1839

SILLICK Samuel D. of Cameron, NY
LLOYD Julia Ann of Cameron, NY

December 15, 1839

SWARTHOUT James of Leicester, NY
December 29, 1839
WELLS Julia of Leicester, NY
Addison, NY

MILLER Henry of Mt. Morris, NY
December 19, 1839
TOWNSEND Sarah of Urbana, NY
Urbana, NY

SMALL Hiram
January 1, 1840
EMERSON Clarissa
Bath, NY

FERRIS Lewis G. Md. of Mt. Morris, NY
January 2, 1840
HOLMES Sophronia dau of Simeon of Cohocton, NY
Cohocton, NY

HALLETT Dilsevan of Canisteo, NY
January 8, 1840
SWIFT Harriet of Cameron, NY
Cameron, NY

RUTHERFORD Andrew
January 9, 1840
EMERSON Roxana
Bath, NY

VANESS Ira of Hammondsport, NY
January 12, 1840
ROBINSON Angeline of Bath, NY
Bath, NY

CROSS Capt. Asa of Bath, NY
January 28, 1840
BOWLSBY Catherine of Bath, NY
Bath, NY

MC CAY James Stuart late of Mosside, Co. Antrim, Ire.
March 12, 1840
HAMLIN Hester
Bath, NY

THOMPSON William
March 26, 1840
STRYKER Hester Ann
Wheeler, NY

THOMPSON Dr. John W. formerly of Bath, NY
April 8, 1840
JACKSON Cordelia dau of Gen. D. of Burdett, NY
Burdett, NY

PARKER Ansel of Bath, NY
April 29, 1840
NILES Elizabeth G. of Bath, NY
Kennedyville, NY

HAMILTON Daniel
May 6, 1840
BENNETT Marilla dau of Gen. D. Bennett
Howard, NY

SNIDER Daniel
June 7, 1840
SOUTHARD Betsey Ann
Howard, NY

MINGAS Henry of Wayne, NY
June 7, 1840
CRISTLER Maria of Tyrone, NY
Tyrone, NY

FREEMAN Lewis of Bath, NY
August 22, 1840
HICKS Jane of Bath, NY

BABCOCK Dr. Brayton of Scottsville Cortland Co. NY
September 2, 1840
SMITH Eunice of Avoca, NY
Avoca, NY

DE LONG Harry of Wayne, NY
TOLBERT Mary Ann of Wayne, NY

September 23, 1840

BECKWITH A. B. of Bath, NY
THOMPSON Martha C. of Painted Post, NY

September 29, 1840
Painted Post, NY

LOZIER Abram
CONEHITE (?) Mary (illegible)

November 10, 1840
Wayne, NY

CHASE Peter
MC COLLUM Sarah

November 26, 1840
Cameron, NY

DEWEY L. H. of Sackett's Harbor, NY
MERRIAM Harriet Y. of Auburn, NY

December 29, 1840
Auburn, NY

SWARTHOUT William D.
NORTHRUP Amanda

December 30, 1840
Cameron, NY

RUMSEY David Jr. of Bath, NY
BROWN Jane E. dau of A. C. of Ogdensburg, NY

January 19, 1841
Ogdensburg, NY

STOCKBRIDGE Levi of N. Hadley, Mass.
LAWTON Syrena of Jasper, NY

January 20, 1841
Jasper, NY

HESS Alexander
SEELY Martha T. dau of late Samuel S.

January 10, 1841
Elmira, NY

LONGWELL Lewis of Urbana, NY
RATTAN Rachael of Pulteney, NY

January 28, 1841
Pulteney, NY

MARKHAM Charles
RIDER Olive of Howard, NY

February 16, 1841
Dansville, NY

BEBEE Daniel D.
HOBART Almira M.

March 24, 1841
E. Bloomfield, NY

DORSEY Dennis of Elmira, NY
HIGGINS Cecelia M. of Bath, NY

March 30, 1841
Bath, NY

TAPPING Winfield Scott
TICKNER Mary

March 27, 1841
Prattsburgh, NY

WHITTEMORE Moses F.
WEBSTER Sarah

April 8, 1841
Bath, NY

JENKS Waterman
EGGLESTON Keziah

April 11, 1841
Cohocton, NY

BARBER Melancton
RATHBUN Lucinda

May 2, 1841
Howard, NY

BATCHELDER Elwin J.   May 19, 1841
SHARP Sally   Jasper, NY

SIMMONS Orson of Fredonia, NY   June 9, 1841
GOULD Maria E. of Prattsburgh, NY   Prattsburgh, NY

ELLAS George S. of Bath, NY   June 16, 1841
LOOMIS Amanda D. dau of Chester of Rushville, NY   Rushville, NY

WHEELER William of Wheeler, NY   June 17, 1841
JOHNSON Henrietta dau of S. A. of Prattsburgh, NY   Prattsburgh, NY

LAMSON Charles E. formerly of Jasper, NY   May 26, 1841
COOK Elizabeth of Hadley, Mass.   Hadley, Mass.

GREENFIELD Jerome of Bath, NY   June 27, 1841
GIFFORD Mary of Bath, NY   Bath, NY

RICE Orrin of Bath, NY   June 27, 1841
MORSE Sarah of Bath, NY   Bath, NY

COVELL Jacob   July 11, 1841
EMERSON Mary Ann   Bath, NY

SHADDUCK Daniel H.   July 11, 1841
EMERSON Harriet   Bath, NY

PIKE John   August 29, 1841
LAKE Helen   Bath, NY

COOK George of Campbell, NY   September 1, 1841
BONHAM Sarah of Campbell, NY   Campbell, NY

JOHNSON William H. of Trenton, NY   September 6, 1841
WILLIAMS Jane of Pulteney, NY   Pulteney, NY

BOGARDUS Richard of Geneva, NY   September 1, 1841
LYON Mary Jane of Bath, NY   Bath, NY

FRASER James of York, NY   September 9, 1841
MC PHERSON Agnes Jane of Bath, NY   Bath, NY

WHITE George of Albany, NY   September 9, 1841
TAYLOR Helen A. of Bath, NY   Bath, NY

PELLET N. Editor of Chenango Telegraph   (Newspaper date)September 15, 1841
BOWEN Malvina dau of Ira of Homer, NY   Homer, NY

ADSIT Martin of Hornellsville, NY   September 8, 1841
CHARLES Esther Jane of Angelica, NY   Angelica, NY

MOORE William	September 12, 1841
FISHER Elizabeth of Prattsburgh, NY	Prattsburgh, NY
NILES Simeon P. of Prattsburgh, NY	August 16, 1841
SMITH Hannah of Bath, NY	Bath, NY
HAUSE Alvin C. of Tyrone, NY	October 28, 1841
NOBLE Fidelia of Wayne, NY	Wayne, NY
PECK Lucius	October 28, 1841
DAY Mary	Howard, NY
HOBART Albert M. of Prattsburgh, NY	November 17, 1841
BLODGETT Mary of Rushville, NY	Rushville, NY
ARMSTRONG Ackerson of Pulteney, NY	November 18, 1841
WHEELER Eliza dau of G. W. of Wheeler, NY	Wheeler, NY
WHEELER Capt. Silas of Wheeler, NY	November 28, 1841
FRISBEE Phidelia of Wheeler, NY	Wheeler, NY
MILLER William H. of Cameron, NY	December 8, 1841
GREGORY Eleanor of Cameron, NY	Kennedyville, NY
WHIPPLE J. Eustace of Lansingburgh, NY	December 2, 1841
VELIE Maria E. E. of Albany, NY	W. Troy, NY
CHENEY Dr. Walter S. of Prattsburgh, NY	December 23, 1841
AINSWORTH Sarah L. of Prattsburgh, NY	Prattsburgh, NY
COOK Capt. William A. of Bath, NY	December 28, 1841
COOK Ellen C. of Pike, NY	Pike, NY
KIP Dyer S. of Pulteney, NY	January 9, 1842
PARKER Jane A. of Pulteney, NY	Pulteney, NY
BAXTER Caleb	February 13, 1842
MANN Sophia	Prattsburgh, NY
HOFFMAN John S.	February 3, 1842
LOGAN Lydia formerly of Bath, NY	Elmira, NY

Steuben Courier (Bath, NY)

September 20, 1843 - December 26, 1884

BATCHELDER Joseph	September 5, 1843
BALCH Hannah	Jasper, NY

KENNEDY Edward of Burns, NY   (Newspaper date) October 4, 1843
KENNEDY Adeline dau of L. P. of Burns, NY   Burns, NY

SABINS Bennett   September 23, 1843
CRANDALL Jenet   Howard, NY

HIGGINS Loren   September 24, 1843
JONES Polly   Howard, NY

DORSEY Samuel of Otsego Co. NY   September 27, 1843
HIGGINS Amanda of Howard, NY   Howard, NY

CAMPBELL Robert J. Atty. of Bath, NY   October 10, 1843
FOWLER Frances C. dau of Jno. W. Fowler of Bath, NY   Bath, NY

BIRDSALL Henry of Urbana, NY   October 1, 1843
CRAWFORD Amanda of Urbana, NY   Urbana, NY

WILKINS Isaac   October 15, 1843
BRUNER Rebecca Elizabeth of Starkey, NY   Bath, NY

HENDERSON Barnet B. formerly of Washington Co. NY   October 9, 1843
COLLIER Eliza Ann of Avoca, NY   Avoca, NY

GRISWOLD Ira   October 11, 1843
WISE Anna   Bath, NY

MC CASLIN Henry   October 11, 1843
ROBINSON Lucinda   Avoca, NY

ROBINSON Henry   October 11, 1843
MC CASLIN Nancy   Avoca, NY

HOTCHKIN John D. of Prattsburgh, NY   October 19, 1843
SHERWOOD Eveline of Woodhull, NY   Prattsburgh, NY

MUNFORT David of Rush, NY   October 19, 1843
HENDRYX Elizabeth D. of Cohocton, NY   Cohocton, NY

CLARK Robert   October 29, 1843
RHODES Caroline   Corning, NY

SMITH Thomas of S. Corning, NY   November 30, 1843
BARNARD Mary of S. Corning, NY   S. Corning, NY

CARR Francis B. of Addison, NY   December 25, 1843
SHARP Lycena of Jasper, NY   Jasper, NY

SHELDON Philo B. of Huron, NY   December 28, 1843
WALDO Mary B. dau of Aaron Waldo of Pulteney, NY   Pulteney, NY

BRUNDAGE Capt. Abraham	January 1, 1844
WILLIAMS Sally	Urbana, NY
WHITING Lieut. Henry of US Army	November 29, 1843
RICE Pamelia dau of Dr. J. Rice of Mackinac, Mi.	Mackinac, Mi.
BROWN Ira of Dundee, NY	January 8, 1844
GLASS Mrs. Cornelia of Bath, NY	Bath, NY
FENTON Dr. E. of Prattsburgh, NY	January 18, 1844
GUSTIN E. J. dau of A. W. Gustin of Cohocton, NY	Cohocton, NY
RICHARDSON Thomas	January 18, 1844
WILLIAMSON Amanda	Bath, NY
AECKER James C. of Palatine, NY	February 1, 1844
SHAVER Catherine of Avoca, NY	Avoca, NY
CROCKER Dr. W. R.	February 5, 1844
DOWNS Jane R.	S. Cameron, NY
SMITH James S. of Ulysses, NY	February 8, 1844
DUDLEY Sally Ann of Bath, NY	Bath, NY
HALLIDAY William H.	February 8, 1844
CHASE Hannah M.	Cameron, NY
WEBSTER James	January 17, 1844
BECKWITH Caroline	Bath, NY
ADAMS John	February 14, 1844
EMERSON Melissa	Bath, NY
POST Curtis M	January 31, 1844
NICHOLS Mary B.	Georgia, Vt.
DELAMATER Isaac C. of Corning, NY	April 2, 1844
WATKINS Harriet F. dau of T. W. Watkins of Corning, NY	Corning, NY
JACKSON S. A. of Prattsburgh, NY	April 20, 1844
ROACE Charlotte of Prattsburgh, NY	Prattsburgh, NY
GILLETT William of Caton, NY	May 9, 1844
ANDREWS Frances E. of Mud Creek, NY	Mud Creek, NY
SCOTT Uriah of Tompkins Co. NY	May 19, 1844
TYLER Sally of Bath, NY	Bath, NY
BABCOCK Naboth C.	June 8, 1844
REEVES Mary Ann	Caton, NY

WEBSTER Lonson formerly of Bath, NY   May 15, 1844
MERROW Maria C.   Richfield, Mi.

HAYT James A. of Corning, NY   July 1, 1844
HURD Flora A. of Marshall, Mi.   Marshall, Mi.

HOLLIS Harvey of Avoca, NY   June 23, 1844
HOSMER Fannie of Kennedyville, NY   Kennedyville, NY

MORRISON William   July 3, 1844
SIMONS Selina   Avoca, NY

HARNEY Henry   July 4, 1844
PEAK Mrs. Christina

MC BURNEY John of Painted Post, NY   July 1, 1844
EDWARDS Mrs. Julia Ann dau of Cornelius **YOUNGLOVE** Urbana, NY

COLCORD David D. of Thurston, NY   July 4, 1844
PEET Sarah of Coudersport, Pa.   Coudersport, Pa.

SMITH Andy L. of Hornellsville, NY   August 6, 1844
MC HENRY Sarah of Almond, NY

YOUNG Martin of Prattsburgh, NY   August 17, 1844
BURLEW Mary of Prattsburgh, NY   Bath, NY

ROWE Rev. A. of Michigan   August 12, 1844
VAN NESS Mary F.   Urbana, NY

BARKER Ezra of Italy, NY   August 20, 1844
MAGEE Emily of Wheeler, NY   Wheeler, NY

THOMAS John   September 1, 1844
UNDERHILL Augusta   Castleton, NY

GRANDIN Rev. J. L. S. of Genessee Conference   September 21, 1844
KNAPP Elizabeth of Elkland, Pa.   Elkland, Pa.

PETERSON Jerome of Fairport, NY   October 2, 1844
HORTON Maria F. dau of Daniel Horton of Campbell, NY   Urbana, NY

MC CULLOR Alfred   October 1, 1844
BURST Delane   Painted Post, NY

TOWNSEND Belden   September 7, 1844
STRATTON Laura   Kennedyville, NY

WATERBURY William of Italy, NY   October 9, 1844
HAIGHT Almira of Cohocton, NY   Hornellsville, NY

BAKER H. T. of Warren, Pa.   October 9, 1844
HUNTER Mary A. of Bath, NY   Bath, NY

GREGG Robert   October 9, 1844
HOPPER Sally   Orange, NY

SHEFFIELD William H. of Cattaraugus Co., NY   October 3, 1844
STEWART Helen A. of Bath, NY   Bath, NY

SMITH P. P. of Wheeler, NY   October 15, 1844
DONAHE Alice dau of John Donahe   Avoca, NY

SISSON William of Yates Co. NY   October 30, 1844
GENNING Melissa of Yates Co. NY   Italy, NY

CHAMBERLAIN James of Talmadge, Ohio   October 24, 1844
HEATH Harriet of Geneseo, NY   Geneseo, NY

JEFFREY Edwin A. of Corning, NY   October 5, 1844
LEE Mary F. of Corning, NY   Corning, NY

LONGWELL George of Urbana, NY   October 31, 1844
BENJAMIN Adeliza of Bath, NY   Bath, NY

WINNE Benjamin L. of Boston, Mass.   October 17, 1844
DENNIS Nancy of Hancock, NH

BAKER T. J. of Urbana, NY   October 10, 1844
TUNNICLIFF Louisa of Warren, NY   Warren, NY

LONGWELL Capt. J. C. of Urbana, NY   November 13, 1844
HENDERSON Rachel A. of Milo, NY   Milo, NY

VAN HEUSEN A. H. of Howard, NY   December 11, 1844
JONES Mary Ann of Howard, NY   Howard, NY

JOHNSON Schuyler D.   December 11, 1844
CALKINS Mrs. Nancy   Corning, NY

KNICKERBOCKER Gen. N. V. of Bath, NY December 19, 1844
MC KISSON Catherine of Bath, NY   Urbana, NY

DISBROW Ira   December 26, 1844
HAUSE Mary Jane of Tyrone, NY   Tyrone, NY

DICKINSON Amos B. C.   December 1, 1844
JONES Ann   Bath, NY

OWENS Jesse T. of Hector, NY   December 25, 1844
ELLIS Almira of Bath, NY   Bath, NY

HILL Ephraim of Caton, NY   December 31, 1844
REED Mary M. of Caton, NY   Corning, NY

HALL Austin of Bath, NY   January 16, 1845
CALKINS Rachael of Cohocton, NY   Cohocton, NY

PRATT William C. of Campbell, NY   January 16, 1845
MATTESON Tarrissa M. of Campbell, NY   Campbell, NY

ROBERTS Henry of Reading, NY   January 1, 1845
HURD Eliza O. of Reading, NY   Reading, NY

MC PHERSON John of Bath, NY   January 16, 1845
FOSSERT Mary Anne of Bath, NY

VAN GELDER Benjamin   January 15, 1845
LOOK Lucy E.   Bath, NY

LAKE G. W.   January 1, 1845
PARKHILL Eliza Ann   Avoca, NY

SQUIRE Seth W.   January 23, 1845
ALLEN Catherine

SQUIRE Philo   January 23, 1845
DAVIS Harriet

PETERS Charles   January 26, 1845
SANFORD Elizabeth   Bath, NY

COTTON Edward   January 9, 1845
EGGLESTON Phebe Ann   Bath, NY

FERENBAUGH John of Painted Post, NY   January 29, 1845
ADAMS Phebe of Painted Post, NY   Painted Post, NY

TOPPING Perry of Bath, NY   February 23, 1845
BUNDY Elizabeth dau of Nathaniel Bundy of Cameron, NY   Cameron, NY

HADDEN Gilbert of Urbana, NY   February 22, 1845
BROWN Hester of Wheeler, NY   Wheeler, NY

WEAVER Lewis of Catlin, NY   February 13, 1845
KIMBALL Sally Ann of Catlin, NY   Corning, NY

BARNES John of Corning, NY   February 23, 1845
TUTTLE Susan of Corning, NY   Corning, NY

TALLMADGE Ira S. of Corning, NY   February 23, 1845
MURPHY Sarah of Corning, NY   Corning, NY

HARTSHORN Charles of Hornellsville, NY   March 2, 1845
HART Cordelia dau of Charles N. Hart of Hartsville, NY   Hartsville, NY

UNDERHILL Henry of Bath, NY   March 4, 1845
SCOTT Henrietta S. of Vienna, NY   Vienna, NY

SMITH Thomas of S. Corning, NY   February 26, 1845
WILCOX Ann of Corning, NY   Corning, NY

HAUSE (or **HAWES**) Lewis K. of Tyrone, NY   March 25, 1845
STEWART Fanny of Bath, NY   Bath, NY

WHITE Dr. Joseph of Canajoharie, NY   March 20, 1845
ROSEBOOM Marietta dau of Abraham of Cherry Valley, NY   Cherry Valley, NY

CUTHELL James of New York City   May 28, 1845
GANTZ Mary of New York City   New York City

JENKINS W.   March 27, 1845
MATTESON Lydia   Campbell, NY

HART Dr. Henry of Avoca, NY   May 1, 1845
WAY Sarah Helen of S. Dansville, NY   S. Dansville, NY

CHITTENDEN Rev. W. E. of Bellville, Ill.   April 24, 1845
SMITH A. E. of Prattsburgh, NY   Prattsburgh, NY

BADGER Henry E. of Corning, NY   May 7, 1845
CLARK Catherine of Corning, NY   Geneva, NY

FANTON Melwin of Weston, Ct.   May 13, 1845
BONHAM Mary O. of Campbell, NY   Campbell, NY

COMSTOCK H. S. Atty. of Hammondsport, NY   May 8, 1845
IVES Jane O. of Guilford, NY   Guilford, NY

CUMPSTON D. B.   May 28, 1845
FRASIER Ann   Corning, NY

BORST Ira   May 28, 1845
COATS Laura of Elmira, NY   Painted Post, NY

TENSLER Thomas   May 28, 1845
BORST Jane of Painted Post, NY   Painted Post, NY

BELKNAP Jonathan S. of Corning, NY   May 25, 1845
CREAMER Lucinda M. of Corning, NY   Corning, NY

GOFF Dr. Potter G. H. of Mc Henry Co. Ill.   June 23, 1845
HALSEY Lavantia of Avoca, NY   Bath, NY

ZIELLY Henry E. of Bath, NY
OLMSTEAD Laura E. of Howard, NY
June 22, 1845
Howard, NY

ERWIN Samuel of Painted Post, NY
KERN Mary of Painted Post, NY
June 11, 1845
Painted Post, NY

CROW William of Bath, NY
ANGEL Emily S. of Cameron, NY
June 11, 1845
Cameron, NY

WATERS Gilbert E. of Prattsburgh, NY
VORHEES Hannah E. of Pontiac, Mi.
June 19, 1845
Prattsburgh, NY

WILLOUR James of Bath, NY
PALMER Lydia of Bath, NY
July 20, 1845
Bath, NY

HODGEMAN Lansing D. of Stillwater, NY
COOK Abby C. dau of Constant Cook of Bath, NY
August 5, 1845
Bath, NY

RUSSELL John A. of Jersey, NY
MC DONALD Margaret of Weemsburgh, NY
August 28, 1845
Troy, NY

JONES George of Prattsburgh, NY
UMSTED Jane of Wheeler, NY
September 17, 1845
Avoca, NY

KING George Henry
TOBIAS Amelia Ann
September 1, 1845
Bradford, NY

CLARK Jonathan
MILLS Mary Ann
September 7, 1845
Bath, NY

ERWAY Ezra of Burdett, NY
GARDINER Charlotte E. of Corning, NY
September 21, 1845
Bath, NY

MASON Enoch L. of Cameron, NY
RICHMOND Mary A. of Independence, NY
October 1, 1845
Independence, NY

HAIGHT George W. of Cohocton, NY
STETSON Mary A.
September 23, 1845
Campbell, NY

STEVENS Elias
BEEBE Mrs. Elizabeth
September 25, 1845
Corning, NY

KENT Vine of Big Flats, NY
SCOFIELD Amira of Big Flats, NY
October 2, 1845

SMITH Jerard of Pa.
HOOD Phebe Ann of Wheeler, NY
October 7, 1845
Wheeler, NY

PECK Ripley of Avoca, NY
DAVIS Eliza dau of Daniel H. Davis of Cohocton, NY
October 12, 1845
Cohocton, NY

HICKS Benjamin F. of N. Bristol, NY
VANCE Margaret of Urbana, NY

October 22, 1845
Urbana, NY

GOFF Steven of Big Flats, NY
SCOFIELD Hila Ann of Big Flats, NY

October 10, 1845
Painted Post, NY

BAUTER A. of Avoca, NY
BENNETT Annis of Hornellsville, NY

October 19, 1845
Hornellsville, NY

LOW Thomas S. of Patterson, NJ
DECKER Susan Ann of Bath, NY

November 6, 1845
Bath, NY

PALMER Rufus W. of Lindley, NY
THURBER Sophia dau of Abner Thurber of Lindley, NY

November 3, 1845
Lindley, NY

HOPKINS Franklin P. of Vermontville, Mi.
BRIDGES Jane of Prattsburgh, NY

November 6, 1845
Prattsburgh, NY

GILLETT William B. of Bath, NY
FOX Catherine of Bath, NY

November 12, 1845
Bath, NY

BENNETT Henry T. of Portage, NY
WOOD Eliza Jane of Portage, NY

November 13, 1845
Bath, NY

SHEEHAN John of Bath, NY
MC CANN Betsey Ann of Howard, NY

November 9, 1845
Bath, NY

CONDERMAN John D. of Howard, NY
SPAULDING Aseneth of Howard, NY

November 16, 1845
Howard, NY

RYNO D. S.
LEFFERTS Abigail S.

November 18, 1845
Hornellsville, NY

BARBER Jonathan of Cameron, NY
BURNS Adaline of Cameron, NY

November 16, 1845
Cameron, NY

CASTER William of Painted Post, NY
PIERCE Mary of Painted Post, NY

November 16, 1845
Painted Post, NY

TUELL S. R. of Bath, NY
POTTER Sarah of Bath, NY

December 23, 1845
Bath, NY

WILLHELM Joseph
CAMPBELL Sarah

December 22, 1845
Bath, NY

CARR John of Bulley Hill, NY
SMITH Sarah late of Rochester, NY

December 25, 1845
Bath, NY

MOORE James
GOODSELL Jane

December 25, 1845
Bath, NY

HOLMES Caleb   December 26, 1845
STEPHENS Angeline M.   Avoca, NY

BAILEY George S. of Urbana, NY   December 31, 1845
HILL Susan of Pulteney, NY   Pulteney, NY

DYER George W. of Corning, NY   January 1, 1846
MC KINNEY Olive S. dau of John of Great Bend, Pa.   Great Bend, Pa.

MILLER Franklin K. of Bath, NY   January 19, 1846
TERRELL Clarinda M. of Bath, NY   Bath, NY

MORRIS M. of Penn Yan, NY   January 14, 1846
SPENCER Laura of Penn Yan, NY   Bath, NY

COTTON Silas of S. Dansville, NY   December 31, 1845
MACK Sarah A. of S. Dansville, NY   S. Dansville, NY

BAILEY John   January 10, 1846
NIXON Hannah of Starkey, NY   Bath, NY

JACKSON John   January 10, 1846
KNAPP Mary H. of Elkland, Pa.   Painted Post, NY

WHITNEY Nelson of Painted Post, NY   (Newspaper date) January 21, 1846
PARCELL Susan C. of Painted Post, NY   Painted Post, NY

STEPHENS Joseph H. of Cameron, NY   January 18, 1846
VANDERWARKER Charlotte of Campbell, NY   Cameron, NY

ROSE Rev. L. of Howard, NY   January 17, 1846
BENNETT Rachel of Hornellsville, NY   Hornellsville, NY

BAKER Marvin of Bath, NY   January 22, 1846
DOWD Lucinda of Bath, NY

KENDALL John R. of Havana, NY   January 20, 1846
BISHOP Amy of Havana, NY   Knoxville, NY

JACKSON Edward of Tyrone, NY   January 10, 1846
CLARK Amanda of Tyrone, NY

SMITH Daniel of Tyrone, NY   January 7, 1846
PERRY Elizabeth of Tyrone, NY

GABRIEL John P. of Starkey, NY   January 1, 1846
CLEVELAND Elizabeth of Reading, NY

DORSEY Edwin of Bath, NY   February 1, 1846
MILLS Phebe Ann of Bath, NY

FISK F. A. of Bath, NY   January 27, 1846
MC HENRY Mary of Big Flats, NY   Big Flats, NY

WALKER Hiram P. of Bath, NY   January 27, 1846
SHEFFIELD Sarah Ann of Jasper, NY   Bath, NY

WILLSON Thomas of Broome Co. NY   January 14, 1846
HORTON Henrietta A. of Campbell, NY

WILLIAMSON John D. of Bath, NY   February 7, 1846
SMITH Betsey M. dau of Rev. David Smith of Bath, NY   Bath, NY

DE GROAT J. D. of Corning, NY   February 8, 1846
TUTTLE Hannah of Corning, NY   Corning, NY

COLE John of St. Joseph Co. Mi. formerly Steuben Co.   January 5, 1846
COLMS Lydia M. formerly of Steuben Co.   Warsaw, Ind.

MC CLURE V. C. Md. of Bath, NY   March 4, 1846
GRAVES Caroline S. dau of late Randall Graves of Howard Howard, NY

BURLEY William of Bath, NY   March 8, 1846
MERRILL Mrs. Anna of Bath, NY   Thurston, NY

SHAFER Edward of Avoca, NY   March 4, 1846
CONNOR Mary of Avoca, NY   Avoca, NY

THOMPSON Isaac   April 2, 1846
SCANLAN Elizabeth of Gloucestershire, England   Caton, NY

KINGMAN Nelson of Corning, NY   April 22, 1846
WRIGHT S. D. of Addison, NY   Addison, NY

FISHER Asa   April 21, 1846
DENNIS Mrs. Elizabeth   Jasper, NY

LOCKWOOD John   March 4, 1846
GLENN Nancy   Urbana, NY

DOUGLAS Albert   (Newspaper date) April 29, 1846
TAYLOR Jane E.   Urbana, NY

CANFIELD Ebenezer   (Newspaper date) April 29, 1846
MILLS Mary Ann (or Miriam)   Urbana, NY

STRATTON David of Bath, NY   April 29, 1846
EMERSON Esther Ann of Bath, NY   Bath, NY

LYON James of Bath, NY   May 12, 1846
ROBIE Harriet A. of Bath, NY   Bath, NY

WILLIAMS Charles D. Md. of Cleveland, Oh.　　　May 6, 1846
COWLES Cornelia of Corning, NY　　　Corning, NY

ROISE Charles of Big Flats, NY　　　May 3, 1846
HARRISON Charlotte of Corning, NY　　　Corning, NY

BIDWELL George H. Editor of Dansville Republican　　　May 3, 1846
MOSES Mary E. of Hartford, Ct.　　　Hartford, Ct.

SKINNER Sidney M of Prattsburgh, NY　　　May 14, 1846
RUMSEY Lydia Jane of Dansville, NY　　　Dansville, NY

BRUNDAGE Robert L. Atty of Hornellsville, NY　　　May 26, 1846
VAN SICKLE Hannah A. of Greenwood, NY　　　Greenwood, NY

TOMPKINS Charles S. of Dundee, NY　　　June 7, 1846
ROUSE Susan of Barrington, NY　　　Bath, NY

FOX David D. of Avoca, NY　　　May 28, 1846
DIXON Harriet of Cohocton, NY　　　Cohocton, NY

FISH David of Cohocton, NY　　　May 29, 1846
SMITH Sally L. of Cohocton, NY　　　Cohocton, NY

RIDER Ira S. of Warren, Pa.　　　June 15, 1846
BEVERLY Mary Ann of Howard, NY　　　Howard, NY

LONGCORE James of Barrington, NY　　　July 4, 1846
MORSE Mrs. E. J. of Bath, NY　　　Bath, NY

ENOS Levi of Painted Post, NY　　　June 24, 1846
HILL Catherine of Painted Post, NY　　　Painted Post, NY

MC ELWEE John　　　June 25, 1846
RUTHERFORD Mrs. Jane　　　Mud Creek, NY

HUNT Dr. Lewis　　　June 16, 1846
FULKINSON Eliza

SHELTON Thomas F. of Bath, NY　　　July 5, 1846
PLACE Eliza of Bath, NY

FREY Elisha　　　June 15, 1846
GLENN Rhoda of Urbana, NY　　　Urbana, NY

LOVELAND J. P. of Addison, NY　　　July 16, 1846
DEAN Jane of Corning, NY　　　Corning, NY

JANSEN De Witt of Catlin, NY　　　July 4, 1846
ROGERS Almira of Catlin, NY　　　Corning, NY

FOSTER Dugald C. of Cohocton, NY
BLINN Laura E. of Howard, NY

July 19, 1846
Howard, NY

COON William
EARL Annah of Danby, NY

July 20, 1846
Corning, NY

BASHFORD John Jr. of Cohocton, NY
DOUSET Mary of Bath, NY

August 13, 1846
Bath, NY

HAWLEY Henry of Wayne, NY
LESTER Mariah of Urbana, NY

August 13, 1846
Urbana, NY

WHITE Henry of Corning, NY
BRAZEE Phebe of Corning, NY

August 20, 1846
Corning, NY

VAN KEUREN Dr. Eser of Urbana, NY
BAKER Sarah H. of Urbana, NY

August 20, 1846
Urbana, NY

COOPER C. J. of Cooper's Plains, NY
PIERCE Martha A. of Campbell, NY

September 15, 1846

STACK A. E. of Cohocton, NY
TERRY Elizabeth of Cohocton, NY

September 8, 1846
Cohocton, NY

BUGBE James R. of Boston, Mass.
ROBINSON Amanda P. of Corning, NY

October 6, 1846
Corning, NY

LYON David W. of Bath, NY
FAY Hopia of Uniontown, Pa.

September 22, 1846
Uniontown, Pa.

MC CAY William B. of Bath, NY
ELLSWORTH Sabra of Penn Yan, NY

September 29, 1846
Penn Yan, NY

HUNTER Samuel D.
WHIPPLE Augusta A. dau of late Rev. P. L. Whipple

October 1, 1846
Bath, NY

HOYT William C. of Coventry, NY
GILMORE Emeline S. of Bath, NY

October 1, 1846
Bath, NY

YOST Nicholas
CARPENTER Mary Ann

September 29, 1846
Cameron, NY

PRATT Dr. George W. of Corning, NY
HAYT Helen M. dau of Harry Hayt of Patterson, NY

September 19, 1846
Patterson, NY

VAN ORDER Nathaniel of Catlin, NY
DRAKE Mary Ann of Hornby, NY

September 30, 1846
Hornby, NY

SEELEY Reuben L. of Prattsburgh, NY
WHEATON Susan of Prattsburgh, NY

September 20, 1846
Prattsburgh, NY

MILLER Rev. L. Merrill of Bath, NY   October 13, 1846
RUMSEY Lydia of Bath, NY   Bath, NY

BOYD Alexander   October 4, 1846
QUANT Catherine   Bath, NY

PRATT Claudius P. of Marshall, Mi.   October 12, 1846
PHELPS Mary E. dau of H. G. Phelps of Corning, NY   Corning, NY

STEELE Edward A. of Romney, Va.   October 14, 1846
HARROWER Martha dau of Benjamin of Lindley, NY   Lindley, NY

COOLEY Calvin W. of Dansville, NY   October 15, 1846
DAVIS Celinda of Avoca, NY   Avoca, NY

ROSE Levi of Chemung, NY   October 29, 1846
GREEN Jerusha of Fairport, Chemung Co. NY   Fairport, NY

LARUE George of Cohocton, NY   October 8, 1846
WILLIAMSON Gitty Ann of Avoca, NY   Avoca, NY

WILLIAMSON John J. of Avoca, NY   October 24, 1846
LARUE Sarah Jane of Cohocton, NY   Avoca, NY

DRAPER Solomon of Cohocton, NY   October 29, 1846
WOOD Loritia of Cohocton, NY   Dansville, NY

MILLIGAN Col. Robert J. of Steuben Co. NY   November 24, 1846
FLETCHER Hannah S. of Saratoga Springs, NY   Saratoga Springs, NY

FORD George W. of New York City   December 9, 1846
VAN DUSEN Ann dau of William Van Dusen of Veteran, NY Veteran, NY

LEWIS John V. of Prattsburgh, NY   December 17, 1846
LYON Helen Ann dau of Abner Lyon of Prattsburgh, NY   Prattsburgh, NY

PATCHIN Myron of Cohocton, NY   December 23, 1846
PARMATER Rozilla of Cohocton, NY   Cohocton, NY

DANIELS Asa B. of Bath, NY   December 31, 1846
WALKER Gratia Ann of Bath, NY   Bath, NY

FOX Miller of Towanda, Pa.   January 6, 1847
EVANS Margaret C. of Cooper's Plains, NY   Cooper's Plains, NY

WHEELER N. Sanger of Bath, NY   January 7, 1847
LEWIS Barbara of Bath, NY   Bath, NY

LEWIS Daniel D. of Wheeler, NY   November 26, 1846
WHEELER Jane Frances of Wheeler, NY   Wheeler, NY

STEPHENS Nathan of Thurston, NY
SCHENCK Ellen of Bath, NY
January 6, 1847
Bath, NY

DE WITT David of Bath, NY
STEVENS Eliza of Chenango Co. NY
January 13, 1847
Bath, NY

SHAW Col D. J. Jr. of Elkland, Pa.
DAVENPORT Harriet A. dau of Lemuel of Elkland, Pa.
December 30, 1846

BENNETT Daniel of Howard, NY
ROSE Maria of Burton, Oh.
January 20, 1847
Howard, NY

SIMPSON A. B. of Jasper, NY
FISHER Antoinette of Jasper, NY
January 17, 1847
Jasper, NY

VAN CAMPEN William R. of Almond, NY
HOWARD Harriet A. of Howard, NY
January 31, 1847
Howard, NY

CHUBBOCK John of Lockport, NY
RATHBUN Frances B. of Howard, NY
February 7, 1847
Howard, NY

PUNCHES George W. of Cameron, NY
DENNIS Martha of Jasper, NY
February 18, 1847
Jasper, NY

GRIFFITH John Jr. of Bath, NY
PIKE Almira of Bath, NY
February 23, 1847
Bath, NY

BILES Hezekiah S. of Bath, NY
GRISWOLD Olive S. of Penn Yan, NY
February 27, 1847

MATHEWSON Joseph H.
HOLMES Polly dau of S. Holmes
February 21, 1847
Avoca, NY

CLARK John of Dix, NY
PATCHIN Laura J. of Greenwood, NY
February 27, 1847
Greenwood, NY

MACK Elisha of S. Dansville, NY
NILES Mrs. Hannah of Bath, NY
March 2, 1847

BIDWELL Eli Jr. of Bath, NY
DUDLEY Louisa dau of Benjamin P. Dudley of Bath, NY
March 4, 1847
Bath, NY

HEDGES Isaac
VOSBURGH Mary
March 6, 1847
Cameron, NY

CHAPMAN Andrew F. of Benton, NY
HICKS Mary E. of Benton, NY
March 4, 1847
Benton, NY

TURNER Simeon C. of Canisteo, NY
FAIRBANKS Sarah E. of Canisteo, NY
March 6, 1847
Canisteo, NY

LYON Abner P. of Prattsburgh, NY
SHELDON Sarah (or Laura) of Huron, NY

March 4, 1847
Huron, NY

EMERSON Joseph of Bath, NY
JAQUA Harriet late of Hamilton, NY

March 14, 1847
Thurston, NY

WHITE William of Bath, NY
HILTON Angeline of Oakland Co. Mi.

February 13, 1847
Oakland Co. Mi.

GORTON James H. of Howard, NY
SMITH Laura M. of Howard, NY

March 16, 1847
Howard, NY

TAYLOR Isaac of Thurston, NY
BRIGGS Mrs. ____ of Thurston, NY

February 24, 1847
Thurston, NY

WARNER Hiram of Wheeler, NY
OSTERHOUT Susan of Urbana, NY

March 28, 1847
Bath, NY

CROSS John
BOZZARD Fanny of Dix, NY

March 24, 1847

LONGWELL David
CAMPBELL Laura

March 25, 1847
Bath, NY

CAMPBELL Jesse of Thurston, NY
QUANT Sarah M. of Bath, NY

(Newspaper date) April 14, 1847
Thurston, NY

SARGENT James R.
WHITTEMORE Parmelia

April 20, 1847
Jasper, NY

NICHOLAS Harvey of Orange, NY
DURLAND Hannah J. of Bradford, NY

April 21, 1847
Bradford, NY

COLBURN Schuyler of Addison, NY
SEARS Anna Mariah of Cameron, NY

April 29, 1847
Cameron, NY

WHEAT Charles B. of Hornby, NY
WELLS Polly J. of Jackson, Pa.

(Newspaper date) May 5, 1847
Jackson, Pa.

BELLOWS George C. of Bath, NY
ABER Jane of Bath, NY

May 10, 1847
Bath, NY

HAMLIN Edward of Naples, NY
BABCOCK Maria of Prattsburgh, NY

May 4, 1847
Prattsburgh, NY

SEARS James of Cameron, NY
HATHAWAY Elizabeth of Campbell, NY

May 27, 1847

HOPKINS Henry of Bath, NY
STOCKING Henrietta of Bath, NY

June 19, 1847
Avoca, NY

WILCOX Joseph of Troupsburgh, NY   July 4, 1847
WEBSTER Jane of Jasper, NY   Jasper, NY

MONELL Oliver of Bath, NY   July 20, 1847
SKINNER Ann of Bath, NY

PERINE Henry W. of Bath, NY   August 18, 1847
READ Elizabeth S. dau of Capt. James Read of Urbana, NY   Urbana, NY

VAN NESS William   August 22, 1847
DE WITT Sarah   Bath, NY

BAKER Franklin of Republic, Oh.   October 12, 1847
BRUNDAGE Mary dau of William Brundage of Urbana, NY   Urbana, NY

EMMONS Carlos of Springville, NY   October 21, 1847
POWERS Mrs. Caroline widow of Rev. Philander Powers   Bath, NY

BABCOCK James of Bath, NY   October 23, 1847
VAN GELDER Catherine of Bath, NY

FERRIS Albert P. Atty. of Bath, NY   October 20, 1847
READ Catherine dau of Capt. Read of Bath, NY   Bath, NY

DICKINSON R. E. of Pleasant Valley, NY   October 24, 1847
NOBLE Lucy V. of Pleasant Valley, NY   Bath, NY

THARP Joseph of Bath, NY   October 31, 1847
TOWRE Mary of Bath, NY   Bath, NY

JEFFREY D. A. of Ransomville, NY   November 10, 1847
MESSEREAU Dinah A. of Erwin Center, NY   Erwin Center, NY

ROW D. F. of Urbana, NY   December 12, 1847
SHAW Sarah A. of Ithaca, NY   Bath, NY

PRATT W. B. of Prattsburgh, NY   December 10, 1847
MC NAIR Martha J. of W. Sparta, NY   W. Sparta, NY

BABBITT William S. Md.   December 15, 1847
CARY Caroline dau of Johnson Cary of Arkport, NY   Arkport, NY

VAN NESS Peter of Bath, NY   January 2, 1848
HART Lucy of Cohocton, NY   Avoca, NY

LUMBARD Avro C. formerly of Bath, NY   January 1, 1848
LEWIS L. Maria of Southport, NY   Southport, NY

SPENCER William of Rochester, NY   December 26, 1847
WALDRON Mary of Cohocton, NY   Liberty, NY

HINMAN J. M. of Monroton, Pa.   January 19, 1848
DUDLEY Frances M. of Painted Post, NY   Painted Post, NY

GUSTIN Reuben of Cohocton, NY   January 26, 1848
TERRY Abigail Jane of Cohocton, NY   N. Cohocton, NY

FERRIS Delanson of Bath, NY   February 23, 1848
NICKSON Eliza of Elmira, NY   Bath, NY

NICHOLSON John of N. Cohocton, NY   February 16, 1848
ANDREWS Clarissa of N. Cohocton, NY   N. Cohocton, NY

RICKEY Alpheus of Greenwood, NY   March 1, 1848
STARR Phebe of Greenwood, NY   Greenwood, NY

CRANE Charles of Cameron, NY   March 26, 1848
BRUNDY Harriet O. of Cameron, NY   Bath, NY

PHELPS William J. of Bath, NY   May 10. 1849
MILLER Elizabeth of Bath, NY   Bath, NY

O'BRIAN George of Howard, NY   May 17, 1849
WOOD Maria of Bath, NY   Bath, NY

SHARP Mason W. of Campbell, NY   May 23, 1849
MEAD Louisa C. formerly of Big Flats, NY

SAILOR Rev. John of Elkland, Pa.   May 30, 1849
BALCOM Margaret dau of Lyman Balcom of Campbell, NY   Campbell, NY

STRAWN H. T. of Ogden, NY   June 6, 1849
PHILLIPS Amanda E. dau of Samuel Phillips of Tyrone, NY   Tyrone, NY

GOSS Daniel of Lynden, NY   June 9, 1849
NICHOLDS Savana of Bath, NY   Bath, NY

FRENCH John of Cameron, NY   June 5, 1849
OVERHISER Mary of Big Flats, NY   Big Flats, NY

CRANDALL P. M. of Canandaigua, NY   June 6, 1849
CLARK Charlotte Maria dau of late Ira C. Clark   Prattsburgh, NY

BRACE William B. of Ottawa, Ill   June 19, 1849
STRAIT Alvira of Bath, NY   Bath, NY

WATTERMAN Joshua W. Atty. of Detroit, Mi.   July 4, 1849
DAVENPORT Eliza C. dau of Ira Davenport of Bath, NY   Bath, NY

LOZIER William T. of Tyrone, NY   June 28, 1849
CARPENTER Mary Ann dau of Benjamin of Tyrone, NY   Tyrone, NY

ASHBINWALL Levi of Cohocton, NY | July 4, 1849
SIMONS Dolly Jane of Cohocton, NY | Avoca, NY

ROGERS John L. of Penn Yan, NY | July 6, 1849
EVANS Catherine of Hammondsport, NY | Avoca, NY

YOUNG Stephen of Bath, NY | July 4, 1849
GOULD Ellen dau of A. R. Gould of Bath, NY | Bath, NY

RICHARDSON E. G. of Dansville, NY | July 22, 1849
STRIKER Mary Ann of Dansville, NY | Oak Hill, NY

GLANN Drew of Urbana, NY | August 5, 1849
ATWELL Mary L. of Urbana, NY | Wayne, NY

BECKMAN John of Wayne, NY | August 5, 1849
GREEK Aseneth of Bath, NY | Wayne, NY

STARR Dr. D. of Wisconsin | August 15, 1849
ABBOTT D. Ann of Michigan | Howard, NY

SMITH William Md. of Oswego, Ill. | September 9, 1849
BLOOD Rebecca P. dau of Capt. Blood of Bath, NY | Bath, NY

LOOMIS Henry | September 18, 1849
SWART Ann Eliza dau of Peter Swart of Bath, NY | Bath, NY

BEGOLE Devan | September 11, 1849
WALLACE Margaret C. dau of James of Cohocton, NY | Cohocton, NY

FIELD Darius | September 12, 1849
KNICKERBOCKER Maria

BALLARD Thomas E. of Attica, NY | September 12, 1849
FRENCH Susan E. R. of Bath, NY | Bath, NY

POWELL Stephen B of Livonia, NY | September 13, 1849
POWELL Lodassa E. of Livonia, NY

SHAVER John F. of Howard, NY | September 12, 1849
LOUCKS Amanda of Avoca, NY | Avoca, NY

HULBERT Silas of Cohocton, NY | September 16, 1849
WATKINS Sophia of Cohocton, NY | Cohocton, NY

HUDSON C. W. of Bath, NY | September 13, 1849
ELLAS Julia Ann of Bath, NY | Bath, NY

ELLIOTT Benjamin of Bath, NY | September 19, 1849
SMALLEY Sarah of Bath, NY | Bath, NY

WILBUR Thomas of Friendship, NY   September 10, 1849
BELDEN Ann of Hornellsville, NY   Hornellsville, NY

GREGORY Christopher of Hornellsville, NY   September 11, 1849
REDFIELD Betsey Jane of Hornellsville, NY   Hornellsville, NY

WILSON Stephen L. of Hornellsville, NY   September 27, 1849
SMITH Harriet of Hornellsville, NY   Hornellsville, NY

AYRES Stewart of Arkport, NY   September 27, 1849
ALLEN Martha of Hornellsville, NY

DECKER Hezekiah of Bath, NY   September 26, 1849
SMITH Jane dau of Charles Smith of Bath, NY   Bath, NY

HURLBURT William S. of Arkport, NY   October 3, 1849
CARTER (?) Susan dau of Johnson of Arkport, NY   Arkport, NY

ROSE William L. of Ithaca, NY   October 3, 1849
HELME D. R. of Ithaca, NY   Ithaca, NY

EDWARDS Alexander formerly of Bath, NY   October 2, 1849
MC CURDY Elizabeth of Dansville, NY   Dansville, NY

DRAKE Joseph H. of Wheeler, NY   October 7, 1849
CASTER Catherine of Prattsburgh, NY   Prattsburgh, NY

EGGLESTON John of Bath, NY   October 18, 1849
EMERSON Mrs. Harriet of Bath, NY

SELDEN J. F. of Stockbridge, Mi.   August 4, 1849
DAVISON Eliza of Henrietta, Jackson Co. Mi.

CRANE Joseph N. of Wayne, NY   October 16, 1849
MITCHELL Helena Ann dau of John B. of Wayne, NY   Wayne, NY

WHITING Thomas Jefferson   October 11, 1849
GAY Nancy Ann   Bath, NY

SQUIRE Jason of Italy Hill, NY   October 20, 1849
RANDALL Emeline of Jerusalem, NY   Hammondsport, NY

DIVEN Truman of Bath, NY   November 15, 1849
HOVEY Julia Ann of Bath, NY   Bath, NY

MORSE F. Md. of Barrington, NY   December 30, 1849
PIERCE Mary A. dau of A. Pierce of Cooper's Plains, NY Cooper's Plains, NY

SWICK Constant of Bath, NY   January 1, 1850
PLAISTED Harriet of Thurston, NY   Bath, NY

BENNETT George of Bath, NY	December 31, 1849
WARREN Phebe Ann of Bath, NY	Bath, NY
ALDERMAN Sylvester of Tyrone, NY	January 8, 1850
HOTCHKIN S. of Rochester, NY	
ARNOLD Lyman of Avoca, NY	January 8, 1850
MC NEIL Mary Jane of Wheeler, NY	Wheeler, NY
PINNEO Rev. James R.	February 21, 1850
LINSLEY Mrs. Melissa	Prattsburgh, NY
STODDARD Peter of Wheeler, NY	February 10, 1850
WELCH Thankful of Wheeler, NY	Wheeler, NY
CHEENEY W. S. of Prattsburgh, NY	March 12, 1850
FALLS Louise of Prattsburgh, NY	
MARSH Davis	December 9, 1849
POWELL Harriet	Bath, NY
CHASE Solomon	December 30, 1849
EMERSON Annis	Bath, NY
EMERSON Perry	March 3, 1850
CHASE Harriet Ann	Bath, NY
GURNSEY Joel	March 13, 1850
BISHOP Martha H.	Bath, NY
WALKER John	March 14, 1850
BISHOP Mary	Bath, NY
FERRIS Lemuel H. of Bath, NY	March 23, 1850
MC DOWELL Eliza Ann of Howard, NY	Bath, NY
GRAVES Horace of Howard, NY	March 29, 1850
WILLIS Dorcas M. dau of Orrin Willis of Bath, NY	Bath, NY
CLIZBE Joseph of Avoca, NY	March 26, 1850
CHAPIN Rachel B. dau of Judge E. Chapin of Prattsburgh	Prattsburgh, NY
PAGE James of Cohocton, NY	April 2, 1850
LOOMIS Lucinda A. of Cohocton, NY	Cohocton, NY
FOSTER William S.	April 2, 1850
FAY Helen W.	Prattsburgh, NY
NICHOLS George W. of Hammondsport, NY	April 10, 1850
HASTINGS Clarissa A. of Hammondsport, NY	Hammondsport, NY

SHERWOOD John H. of Hammondsport, NY — April 6, 1850
TAYLOR Mrs. Betsey of Hammondsport, NY — Hammondsport, NY

FORD Henry — April 16, 1850
WILSON Mrs. Electa — Prattsburgh, NY

BAIN Nathan — October 13, 1849
MILLARD Nancy E. of Bath, NY — St. Charles, Ill.

COTTON Samuel S. of Howard, NY — April 17, 1850
CARRINGTON Sarah of S. Dansville, NY — S. Dansville, NY

BRIGGS Alanson E. — April 24, 1850
HILTON Betsey E. — Prattsburgh, NY

WALDO Otis H. of Milwaukee, Wis. — April 20, 1850
VAN VALKENBURGH Gertrude C. dau of J. of Oakley, Mi. — Oakley, Mi.

ABER T. J. of Bath, NY — May 1, 1850
BRAMBLE Samantha B. of Bath, NY — Bath, NY

TOULS Daniel H. of Bath, NY — May 8, 1850
VELEY Sally of Bath, NY — Bath, NY

ROSS William of Reading, NY — May 16, 1850
REED Sarah E. of Hornellsville, NY — Hornellsville, NY

RAWSON Isaac of Almond, NY — May 16, 1850
RICHARDSON Sarah E. of Almond, NY — Almond, NY

WHITING T. W. of Bath, NY — May 21, 1850
LAMBERT M. J. of Bath, NY — Bath, NY

STARR Salmon S. of Campbell, NY — June 6, 1850
JUMP Caroline of Campbell, NY — Campbell, NY

STARKS Henry L. of Bath, NY — June 30, 1850
STARKS Almira of Bath, NY — Bath, NY

LODER Job of Bath, NY — June 19, 1850
MAXWELL Jane of Bath, NY — Bath, NY

HOAGLAND Jacob — July 2, 1850
PARSONS Mrs. Harriet C. — Prattsburgh, NY

STODDARD Philo K. Md. — July 4, 1850
LEWIS Sarah Jane — Prattsburgh, NY

PANGBURN Edward S. — July 4, 1850
SMALL Catherine — Wheeler, NY

DAVIS Samuel D. of Hammondsport, NY July 4, 1850
POWERS Eliza B. dau of John Powers of Hammondsport, NY Hammondsport, NY

LADO William of Hornby, NY (Newspaper date) July 10, 1850
MANWARING Phebe of Hornby, NY Hornby, NY

CHAPIN Joseph of Campbell, NY June 26, 1850
PLATT Elizabeth of Campbell, NY Campbell, NY

BENNETT Trumbull L. Md. of Lima, NY July 17, 1850
PAINE Elizabeth S. dau of Maj. E. L. Paine of Canisteo, NY

BIRD Samuel O. of Canisteo, NY July 27, 1850
DYGERT Mary Ann of Cameron, NY Cameron, NY

WATSON Seneca of Bath, NY August 12, 1850
MILLS Lydia of Bath, NY Bath, NY

HULL Henry H. Editor of Steuben Courier August 15, 1850
WILLISTON Clara dau of Horace Williston of Athens, Pa. Athens, Pa.

GUIWITS William H. of Wheeler, NY August 8, 1850
KELLY Mary J. of S. Dansville, NY S. Dansville, NY

CHAPMAN George H. of N. Urbana, NY September 10, 1850
WALLING Amanda M. of Liberty, NY Liberty, NY

HIGGINS Charles of Howard, NY September 11, 1850
RICE Lorena dau of Seth Rice of Howard, NY Howard, NY

CONKLIN Ambrose of Addison, NY September 14, 1850
FLUENT Lucy E. of Addison, NY Bath, NY

CHASE Rev. A. B. of Cameron, NY September 17, 1850
TOWLE Elizabeth B. of Howard, NY Bath, NY

HOWELL Edward Jr. of Bath, NY September 18, 1850
GANSEVOORT Mary L. dau of Capt. John R. of Bath, NY Bath, NY

TUCKER Daniel of Mud Creek, NY September 29, 1850
BRINK Susanna C. of Mud Creek, NY Mud Creek, NY

BIDWELL William E. of Bath, NY September 29, 1850
BROWN Sarah M. of Cleveland, Oh. Mud Creek, NY

RYNDERS Abel L. of Cohocton, NY September 29, 1850
VANDERWARKER Nancy of Prattsburgh, NY N. Cohocton, NY

BROWN Alva Ellis of Bath, NY October 9, 1850
HAMILTON Sarah Halsey dau of William of Bath, NY Bath, NY

SMITH Harmon of Bath, NY
COMINGS Elizabeth of Bath, NY

October 13, 1850
Hammondsport, NY

THOMPSON Robert
SWARTHOUT Juliette

October 14, 1850
Addison, NY

COOK James N. of Hornellsville, NY
SQUIRE Susan of Cooperstown, NY

October 14, 1850
Addison, NY

GLOYD S. V. R.
SMITH Louisa

October 17, 1850
Newville, NY

BAXTER Henry B. of Italy, NY
SMITH Hannah of Woodhull, NY

October 17, 1850

EVERITT Isaac of Troupsburgh, NY
WILSON Jane A. of Troupsburgh, NY

October 19, 1850
Troupsburgh, NY

VAN HOUSEN Joseph H. of Prattsburgh, NY
VAN WIE Catherine of Howard, NY

October 16, 1850
Howard, NY

CROSBY Maj. T. S. of Cohocton, NY
WOOD Abby S. of Norwich, NY

September 15, 1850
Norwich, NY

SHERMAN Isaac A. of Middletown, NJ
SHERMAN Comelia J. of Urbana, NY

November 7, 1850
Urbana, NY

HART Reuben of Hornellsville, NY,   (Newspaper date) November 27, 1850
CHARLES Margaret of Hornellsville, NY

Hornellsville, NY

GOODRICH A. M. of Albany, NY
REED Omanda C. of Bath, NY

November 24, 1850
Bath, NY

HAZARD John
EDSALL Elvina F.

December 1, 1850
Thurston, NY

HOLTON Elisha of Bath, NY
WRIGHT Mary A. of Grafton, Vt.

November 30, 1850
Geneva, NY

DYGERT John of Avoca, NY
TERRIL Arista of Howard, NY

December 8, 1850
Bath, NY

GOULD John W. of Bath, NY
MORGAN Jane A. of Bath, NY

December 14, 1850
Bath, NY

STEWART Myron W. of Thurston, NY
STEWART Calcina E. of Campbell, NY

December 11, 1850
Campbell, NY

ABEL William H. of Savona, NY
VAN AMBURG Sarah F. of Savona, NY

December 14, 1850
Savona, NY

HAMILTON Harmon M. teacher at Haverling in Bath, NY	December 23, 1850	
SMITH Annis S. dau of Orrin Smith of Bath, NY	Bath, NY	
ELLISON George F. of Corning, NY	December 25, 1850	
SANDERSON Mary E. of Corning, NY	Savona, NY	
HERRINGTON Alonzo of Corning, NY	December 25, 1850	
PIERCE Ellen H. of Corning, NY	Savona, NY	
MILLER Andrew of Savona, NY	December 29, 1850	
BARTHOLOMEW Nancy E. of Savona, NY	Savona, NY	
CURTIS Alvin	December 25, 1850	
JACOBUS Sophronia of Wayne, NY	Wayne, NY	
THOMAS John C. of Bath, NY	January 8, 1851	
WILHELM Margaret of Bath, NY	Bath, NY	
ALLEN Asaph of New Hudson, NY	January 13, 1851	
PERINE Mrs. Marietta of S. Dansville, NY	Bath, NY	
PERRY Glbert N. of Canadice, NY	January 27, 1851	
ELLIS Martha of Bath, NY	Bath, NY	
AINSWORTH George R. R. of Prattsburgh, NY	January 23, 1851	
SMITH Mary E. adopted dau of L. D. **HASTINGS**	Hammondsport, NY	
CLISDELL William of Bath, NY	February 26, 1851	
MC CHESNEY Hannah of Howard, NY	Bath, NY	
CRAWFORD Nathaniel of Wayne, NY	March 5, 1851	
BRUNDAGE Emily of Urbana, NY	Urbana, NY	
KINNEY Theodore B. of Wheeler, NY	March 5, 1851	
VAN NESS Elizabeth of Urbana, NY	Wayne, NY	
EACKER John G. of Palatine, NY	March 27, 1851	
SHAVER Elizabeth dau of Henry Shaver	Avoca, NY	
INGALLS Newcomb of S. Dansville, NY	March 27, 1851	
PRESTON Elizabeth of S. Dansville, NY	Almond, NY	
JENKS Oliver	April 6, 1851	
PARKER Rebecca Ann	Cohocton, NY	
YOUNG Sebastian of Memphis, Mi.	April 21, 1851	
ROYCE Maria of Starkey, NY	Cameron, NY	
UNDERHILL Anthony L. of Dansville, NY	May 2, 1851	
MC BEATH Charlotte L. of Bath, NY	Bath, NY	

LYON Robert M. of Bath, NY　　　　　　May 20, 1851
BROTHER Rebecca P. of Bath, NY　　　　Bath, NY

HORTON William Jr. of Pulteney, NY　　May 15, 1851
BEDELL Hannah of Pulteney, NY　　　　Savona, NY

VAN NESS Peter of Savona, NY　　　　　May 15, 1851
WHITTAKER Susan of Campbell, NY　　　Campbell, NY

GLOVER Alexander of Howard, NY　　　　May 20, 1851
STEWART Julia Adelaide of Howard, NY　Howard, NY

CROOKS Samuel J. Atty. of Hornellsville, NY　May 29, 1851
MEDBURY Adelaide C. dau of Charles Medbury　New Berlin, NY

BLOOMINGDALE William H. of Albany, NY　　June 18, 1851
HART Phebe Ann dau of Charles Hart of Hornellsville, NY　Hornellsville, NY

QUICK J. of Canisteo, NY　　　　　　　June 19, 1851
RIDDLE Mary of Canisteo, NY　　　　　Canisteo, NY

FRENCH Charles late of California　　　July 6, 1851
READ Mary of Campbell, NY　　　　　　Savona, NY

HUNT Warren of Bath, NY　　　　　　　July 6, 1851
BROWN Elizabeth of Bath, NY　　　　　Avoca, NY

CARPENTER James of Troupsburgh, NY　July 13, 1851
SIMMONS Elizabeth of Oxford, NY　　　Troupsburgh, NY

BRAYTON Henry　　　　　　　　　　　July 17, 1851
LOUCKS Hannah C. of Dansville, NY　　Howard, NY

ABEL David O. of Savona, NY　　　　　July 23, 1851
STILES Rhoda of Bradford, NY　　　　　Bradford, NY

BRONSON George A. of Beaver Dams, NY　September 11, 1851
BENEDICT Margaret of Campbell, NY　　Campbell, NY

GUINNIPS Francis H. of Wheeler, NY　　August 19, 1851
CLAWSON Sarah J. of Avoca, NY　　　　Avoca, NY

WOODS David　　　　　　　　　　　　September 10, 1851
ROBIE Olive dau of Reuben Robie　　　Bath, NY

ADAMS A. Atty. of Cohocton, NY　　　　September 19, 1851
RAYMOND Mary of Cohocton, NY　　　　Cohocton, NY

VAN TUYL John of Cameron, NY　　　　September 15, 1851
LAWRENCE Nancy Jane of Cameron, NY

WILLIS H. of Bath, NY September 25, 1851
WHITING Nancy of Howard, NY Howard, NY

HADLEY John A. of Avoca, NY October 2, 1851
FIFE Electa J. of Bath, NY Bath, NY

SHOEMAKER Phillip K. of Bath, NY October 4, 1851
GIBBS Mary of Bath, NY Bath, NY

DECKER J. Rensselaer of Bath, NY September 25, 1851
BULLARD Hannah Ann dau of Joel Bullard of Howard, NY Howard, NY

KINMORE Charles of Andover, NY September 28, 1851
COMFORT Sarah Elizabeth adopted dau of Eli Comfort Howard, NY

HASKINS Isaac J. of Dansville, NY October 1, 1851
BENNETT Amanda of Howard, NY Howard, NY

LAWRENCE Alphonso H. of Bath, NY August 6, 1851
VOSBURGH Caroline of Bath, NY Bath, NY

SANDERS George W. of Bath, NY September 20, 1851
SINCLAIR Mary Ann of Bath, NY Bath, NY

KINNER William T. October 2, 1851
CHAPMAN Clarissa A.

EGGLESTON Ira H. of Urbana, NY (Newspaper date) October 29, 1851
COVELL Delilah of Urbana, NY Bath, NY

DONAHE Horace G. of Bath, NY October 29, 1851
HAMILTON Mary Helen of Bath, NY Bath, NY

SNOOK Tunis November 9, 1851
GAWENS Cynthia Thurston, NY

STILTS Jacob H. November 5, 1851
BAKER Sarah Ann of Bradford, NY Bradford, NY

MILLS Daniel A. of Bath, NY November 15, 1851
EGGLESTON Esther Eliza of Bath, NY

BLAKESLEY George of Bath, NY November 22, 1851
DYKINS Charlotte of Bath, NY

MITCHELL Dr. J. of Lisle, NY November 20, 1851
HUBBARD Alma B. of Cameron, NY Cameron, NY

GOFF F. of Howard, NY November 20, 1851
MITCHELL Nancy A. of Lisle, NY Cameron, NY

FREEMAN John W. of Bath, NY   November 26, 1851
COVELL Cynthia A. of Bath, NY

TAYLOR Daniel L. of Savona, NY   November 30, 1851
HARVEY Esther of Savona, NY   Savona, NY

MAY Henry R. of Bath, NY   December 3, 1851
CLAYSON Adeline of Cohocton, NY   Cohocton, NY

CLEMENT Henry N.   December 5, 1851
COATS Ursala A. of Bradford, NY   Weston, NY

MILLER Sylvester S. of Bath, NY   December 9, 1851
HOOD Caroline C. of Bath, NY   Bath, NY

HARRIS James P. of Bath, NY   December 11, 1851
BUTLER Prudence R. of Prattsburgh, NY   Bath, NY

DUDLEY John Q. of Buffalo, NY   December 10, 1851
WALKER Helen M. of Buffalo, NY   Buffalo, NY

RAPLEE Daniel of Starkey, NY   December 29, 1851
BEARD Catherine of Bath, NY   Savona, NY

BRONSON Charles S. of Beaver Dams, NY   January 1, 1852
BENEDICT C. Elizabeth of Campbell, NY   Campbell, NY

TREMAIN Theodore of Lawrence, Pa.   December 31, 1851
SPRAGUE Josephine of Westfield, Pa.   Lindley, NY

WETMORE Elijah of E. Springwater, NY   January 22, 1852
ROTH Louisa of Bath, NY   Bath, NY

SNYDER Henry M. of Barrington, NY   January 26, 1852
BARTON Fannie M. of Bath, NY

SEBRING Nelson of Tyrone, NY   January 8, 1852
YOUNG Mary of Tyrone, NY   Weston, NY

TENANT Horace of Jefferson, NY   January 18, 1852
FENNO C. E. of Tyrone, NY   Weston, NY

BARNEY Nelson of Bath, NY   February 15, 1852
VAN DUSEN Polly Ann of Bath, NY   Bath, NY

ERLS James of Avoca, NY   February 25, 1852
DAVIS Ortha A. of Avoca, NY   Avoca, NY

NEALLY James   March 14, 1852
GRAY Eunice dau of L. Gray of Wheeler, NY

GOODSELL Daniel of Bath, NY
HEWLETT Susan of Bath, NY

February 18, 1852
Bath, NY

GREEN John F. of Penn Yan, NY
KING Cynthia dau of George B. King of Bath, NY

March 16, 1852
Bath, NY

FAIRFIELD John of Urbana, NY
MC CARNY Elizabeth of Bath, NY

January 10, 1852
Savona, NY

WIXON Alfred of Wayne, NY
BENNETT Thankful of Bradford, NY

January 27, 1852
Savona, NY

HEWLITT Emory T. of Savona, NY
MOORE Caroline of Savona, NY

March 18, 1852
Savona, NY

MOORE Jefferson of Savona, NY
WING Julia T. of Savona, NY

March 31, 1852
Savona, NY

HITCHCOCK Norman of York, NY
RYAN Mary Ann of York, NY

March 11, 1852
York, NY

CASEY William E. G. of York, NY
BIDWELL Eveline E. of York, NY

March 29, 1852
York, NY

DREW James S. of Urbana, NY
CLARK Mary of Urbana, NY

May 13, 1852
Hammondsport, NY

BEAGLE Stephen S. of Hammondsport, NY
LOGHRY Sarah Ann of Bath, NY

April 17, 1852
Bath, NY

EMERSON John of New York City
LOGHRY Ruhamah of Bath, NY

May 16, 1852
Bath, NY

THOMAS Charles D. of Bath, NY
SOUTHARD Emeline of Bath, NY

May 25, 1852

SNOW David of Wheeler, NY
SHULTS Margarey of Wheeler, NY

May 29, 1852

MAGEE Thomas Jefferson of Hornellsville, NY
WHIPPLE Ellen P. L. dau of late Rev. Phineas Whipple

June 1, 1852
Bath, NY

PLATT C. F. Atty. of Painted Post, NY
ERWIN Mary E. dau of Gen. F. E. Erwin of Painted Post

May 26, 1852
Painted Post, NY

RANGER Jason of Howard, NY
HICKOX Mrs. Janette of Thurston, NY

June 8, 1852
Thurston, NY

CHAPIN Addison of Prattsburgh, NY
STEWART Rachel at res. of Capt. William H. Stewart

June 26, 1852
Penn Yan, NY

BURLEY O. F. of Cameron, NY   June 27, 1852
HALL Jane of Thurston, NY   Thurston, NY

LEWIS B. Vrooman of Prattsburgh, NY   July 1, 1852
STODDARD Esther J. of Jerusalem, NY   Jerusalem, NY

SWARTHOUT Minor of Wayne, NY   July 4, 1852
HORTON Ann Eliza of Cameron, NY   Cameron, NY

HURLBURT Smith of Oramel, NY   May 26, 1852
LOVELL Almira of Nunda, NY   Bath, NY

MINIER Goerge of Thurston, NY   June 9, 1852
SMITH Elvira dau of H. Smith

PATTERSON George of Florida, NY   June 14, 1852
MAXWELL Susan of Riga, NY   Avoca, NY

KNOWLES Jeremiah S. of Upper Gilmantown, NH   July 4, 1852
NASH Sarah Jane dau of L. Nash of Bath, NY   Bath, NY

PARKER Ransom G. of Avoca, NY   July 4, 1852
HOLLIS Susan D. of Avoca, NY   Avoca, NY

KEYSER Levi of Avoca, NY   July 5, 1852
COOK Margaret of Avoca, NY   Avoca, NY

CORNUE John of Avoca, NY   (Newspaper date) July 14, 1852
COOPER Mirandy of Avoca, NY   Avoca, NY

TILTON David of Avoca, NY   July 13, 1852
MOORE Jane of Avoca, NY   Avoca, NY

MACKIE Robert of Avoca, NY   July 8, 1852
HOWARD Jane V. of Howard, NY   Howard, NY

CRAMMER Peter of Cohocton, NY   July 11, 1852
WOODARD Jane of Cohocton, NY   Cohocton, NY

HOLZMAIER Sebastian   August 4, 1852
FUNK Dorothea   Bath, NY

EDDY Horatio P. of Prattsburgh, NY   August 12, 1852
BELLOWS Mary Jane dau of Dr. M. B. Bellows   Seneca Falls, NY

OLNEY Parmenas F. Md. of Prattsburgh, NY   August 12, 1852
BELLOWS Helen Mar dau of Dr. M. B. of Seneca Falls, NY   Seneca Falls, NY

PURINGTON William F. Pastor Baptist Ch. Prattsburgh, NY   August 9, 1852
SMITH Rhoda Jane of Prattsburgh, NY   Prattsburgh, NY

PARSONS J. F. of Whitney's Point, NY — August 12, 1852
HUBBARD Nettie of Cameron Mills, NY — Cameron Mills, NY

GARNET John of Michigan — September 18, 1852
CORYELL Sarah of Pulteney, NY — Hammondsport, NY

PRATT William Beach of Prattsburgh, NY — September 16, 1852
PRATT Cornelia dau of Henry BROTHER of Bath, NY — Bath, NY

BENEDICT David E. of Campbell, NY — August 22, 1852
LOVE Harriet of Thurston, NY — Thurston, NY

BILLINGHURST Lucien of Corning, NY — September 26, 1852
PALMER Mary Jane of Corning, NY — Savona, NY

CHASE A. B. of Townsend, NY — October 11, 1852
HORTON M. Cordelia of Cameron, NY — Cameron, NY

SHEPARD Otis Atty. of Prattsburgh, NY — October 28, 1852
AULLS Lydia Ann dau of Ephraim Aulls of Wheeler, NY — Wheeler, NY

EARLY Thomas of Prattsburgh, NY — October 29, 1852
HORR Betsey Jane of Prattsburgh, NY — Prattsburgh, NY

FISHER George F. of Wellsville, NY — November 9, 1852
DAVIS Mary of Greenwood, NY — Hornellsville, NY

KINNE George P. of Addison, NY — November 11, 1852
JONES Catherine of Rathbone, NY — Hornellsville, NY

WILBUR Gilbert L. of Addison, NY — November 11, 1852
PHOENIX Parmelia of Addison, NY — Hornellsville, NY

BRECK George W. of Bath, NY — November 10, 1852
RUTHERFORD Mrs. R. E. of Bath, NY — Bath, NY

LITTLE Charles G. — November 10, 1852
DUDLEY Susan — Bath, NY

ELLIS Chester — November 10, 1852
SMITH Elizbeth at res. of John J. Smith — Bath, NY

ERWIN Edward E. — November 22, 1852
GAMBLE Susan J. — Bath, NY

WARREN Dwight of Bath, NY — November 18, 1852
GRANT Angeline of Bath, NY — Bath, NY

STEBBINS Joseph of Pulteney, NY — November 30, 1852
CLARY Almira B. of Prattsburgh, NY — Prattsburgh, NY

DAVIDSON Thomas
LINDSAY Elizabeth

December 23, 1852
Bath, NY

CLISDELL George
CLISDELL Maria

December 23, 1852
Bath, NY

DONAHE P. S.
MC BEATH Mary Elizabeth

December 22, 1852
Bath, NY

NILES Austin of Prattsburgh, NY
STEVENS Laura A. dau of Asa Stevens of Birdsall, NY

December 16, 1852
Birdsall, NY

PALMER James E. of Savona, NY
MILLER Melinda of Monterey, NY

January 6, 1853
Savona, NY

SEAMANS Devolrou of Savona, NY
STEWART Amelia of Campbell, NY

January 6, 1853
Savona, NY

READ Stephen S. of Bath, NY
MONELL Elizabeth at res. of Peter Monell of Bath, NY

December 30, 1852
Bath, NY

RICHARDSON Roswell of Bath, NY
WILLOUR Mary E. of Bath, NY

January 10, 1853
Bath, NY

SIMONS Halsey of Bradford, NY
ELMENDORPH Elizabeth of Olive, NY

December 9, 1852
Savona, NY

COVELL Amasa of Bath, NY
BIRKETT Jane of Bath, NY

January 19, 1853
Eagle Valley, NY

ARNOLD Lyman
SHULTS Magdalene

February 10, 1853
Avoca, NY

WHEELER Addison
SHEPARD Olive

February 24, 1853
Wheeler, NY

STEVENS George of Campbell, NY
SOUTHWICK Olive of Owego, NY

February 23, 1853
Centreville, NY

STEVENS Harmon of Campbell, NY
JILLETT Martha J. of Corning, NY

February 23, 1853
Corning, NY

LANE Samuel of Bath, NY
SIMONS Louisa of Bath, NY

March 10, 1853
Bath, NY

BALDWIN Abraham of Howard, NY
FORRESTER Elizabeth of Howard, NY

March 16, 1853
Howard, NY

BALDWIN Henry of Howard, NY
PARKHILL Rachael A. of Howard, NY

March 17, 1853
Howard, NY

MORROW Robert of Bath, NY
LEIGHTON Elizabeth dau of John Leighton of Bath, NY
March 22, 1853
Bath, NY

TOPPING Perry of Bath, NY
LARROWE Mary Jane of Wheeler, NY
March 30, 1853
Wheeler, NY

BRUNDAGE Edward of Urbana, NY   (Newspaper date)
ROBINSON Mary Ann of Hammondsport, NY
April 13, 1853
Hammondsport, NY

MORSE Willard C. of Painted Post, NY
COOPER Mary E. dau of John of Coopers Plains, NY
April 6, 1853
Coopers Plains, NY

GRAHAM John L. of Bath, NY
SLOSSON Mary Jane of Maine, NY
April 7, 1853
Maine, NY

BOYD John A. of Woodhull, NY
BAILY Fanny of Prattsburgh, NY
April 16, 1853
Bath, NY

MASON Charles Wesley of Cameron, NY
HICOK Eleanor of Bath, NY
April 17, 1853
Bath, NY

BROOKS William of Bath, NY
NASH Mary E. of Bath, NY
April 17, 1853
Avoca, NY

CUMPSTON Peter of Tyrone, NY
ARMSTRONG Mary A. of Bath, NY
April 17, 1853
Savona, NY

BURLINGHAM Roswell R. of Liberty, NY
FULLER Alletha Ann of Thurston, NY
March 31, 1853
Thurston, NY

MAGEE Duncan S. of Bath, NY
GANSEVOORT Catherine E. dau of late Ten Eyck
May 3, 1853
Bath, NY

JENKINS Edward S. of Elmira, NY
PARKER Mary E. of Pulteney, NY
May 15, 1853
Pulteney, NY

CHANEY Allen of Ogdensburg, NY
RUMSEY Candace C. dau of late David Rumsey of Bath, NY
May 17, 1853
Ogdensburg, NY

SANFORD John of Thurston, NY
COLLIER Sophia R. of Bath, NY
March 29, 1853
Savona, NY

DIMMICK Edmond of Campbell, NY
THOMPSON Jane of Bath, NY
May 18, 1853
Eagle Valley, NY

ALLEN John Jr. of Avoca, NY
STEVENSON Helen E. of Avoca, NY
May 26, 1853
Avoca, NY

VAN HOUSEN Charles R.
LEWIS Mary E.
May 26, 1853
Prattsburgh, NY

WYGANT Hiram
FAY Samantha A.
June 7, 1853

RICE Burrage of Bath, NY
SMITH Mary F. dau of Orren Smith of Bath, NY
June 8, 1853

STEWART Washington (or Wellington) of Corning, NY
DAVIS Elizabeth of Corning, NY
June 7, 1853
Corning, NY

TERWILLIGER Job of Elmira, NY
CARY Eliza of Elmira, NY
June 6, 1853

PHELPS John C. of Corning, NY
STEVENS Sarah C. of Little York, NY
June 6, 1853
Little York, NY

PEASE Edwin of Gibson, NY
ROUSE Sophia E. of Gibson, NY
June 5, 1853
Gibson, NY

WILLIAMS Edward of New York City
HARROWER Susan dau of B. Harrower of Lindley, Pa.
June 7, 1853
Lindley, Pa.

WHEELER James P. of Bath, NY
PIER Elizabeth B. of Bath, NY
June 22, 1853

VAN HOUSEN Samuel of Avoca, NY
HERRINGTON Olive of Avoca, NY
July 4, 1853
Avoca, NY

COOK Charles of Alfred, NY
BRADLEY Harriet of Cohocton, NY
July 4, 1853

CROOKSTON Charles of Wayne, NY
HARRISON Henrietta of Wayne, NY
July 3, 1853
Wayne, NY

LEMM Henry Lafayette of Bath, NY
WILBUR Sarah Jane of Thurston, NY
July 3, 1853
Thurston, NY

MATTICE George B. of Prattsburgh, NY
CORMELL Sarah of Wheeler, NY
July 9, 1853
Wheeler, NY

GILES Levi
SPRAUL Letitia
July 13, 1853
Orange, NY

PERRY James of Tyrone, NY
POWELL Mary of Tyrone, NY
May 29, 1853
Pine Grove, NY

WALLEN Anthony of Tyrone, NY
BUMP Rachael of Tyrone, NY
July 17, 1853

STELLER Henry of Rochester, NY
VAN PELT Mary F. of Bath, NY
August 2, 1853

RODGERS Wisner of Thurston, NY	May 2, 1853
LEWIS Elizabeth of Thurston, NY	Thurston, NY
WOODS Freeman Whipple of Buffalo, NY	August 10, 1853
BRIGHAM Caroline Whitney of Liberty, NY	Bath, NY
GATES Edwin of Candor, NY	August 25, 1853
PERT Mary of Candor, NY	Ithaca, NY
CLARK Daniel R. of Howard, NY	September 4, 1853
SMITH Brulah of Bath, NY	Bath, NY
CHAPMAN Berkley of Tyrone, NY	September 14, 1853
FREEMAN Cornelia of Bath, NY	
CAMPBELL C. W. of Bath, NY	September 20, 1853
DEUSENBERRY A. L. of Cohocton, NY	Cohocton, NY
MC MASTER Guy H. of Bath, NY	October 18, 1853
CHURCH Amanda dau of R. W. Church of Bath, NY	Bath, NY
KEYSER Henry	September 11, 1853
VROOMAN Mary A.	Avoca, NY
VUNCK Alonzo	October 2, 1853
DOUD Ruth E.	Avoca, NY
BLAKESLEY Abram of Wheeler, NY	October 13, 1853
ANGELL Catherine E.	Avoca, NY
BRAMBLE Sylvester E.	October 11, 1853
CLIZBE Mary M.	Prattsburgh, NY
ACKERSON Charles of Wheeler, NY	October 16, 1853
ROSE Ruth Ann dau of S. H. Rose of Howard, NY	Howard, NY
DORR J. D. Md.	November 1, 1853
KELLOGG Jane E. dau of Russell Kellogg	Kanona, NY
PECK John A. of Avoca, NY	November 21, 1853
ALLEN Sarah A. of Avoca, NY	Avoca, NY
KENDALL A. S. of Jasper, NY	November 21, 1853
LATTIMER Carrie of Groveland, NY	Groveland, NY
MC CLARY Daniel of Avoca, NY	November 27, 1853
OXX Hannah C. of Avoca, NY	Avoca, NY
HUBBARD William of Campbell, NY	November 30, 1853
WILLIAMS Sarah Ann of Bath, NY	Thurston, NY

LIPE Ambrose of Bath, NY
WAGONER Nancy M. of Avoca, NY

November 24, 1853
Avoca, NY

EMERSON Alpheus of Bath, NY
SHEARER Fanny of Bath, NY

November 16, 1853
Thurston, NY

HARROWER H. G. of Tioga, Pa.
DONLEY Lizzie of Starkey, NY

December 21, 1853
Starkey, NY

CONNOR Leonard D. of Cohocton, NY
KENDALL Mrs. Lucy of Brooks Grove, NY

December 26, 1853
Brooks Grove, NY

VAN HOUSEN John H. of Bath, NY
TORREY Charlotte A. dau of P. B. Torrey of Naples, NY

January 12, 1854
Naples, NY

ALBRO William Henry of Buffalo, NY
GREGORY Sarah Hammond dau of James of Urbana, NY

January 16, 1854
Urbana, NY

MASON Nathan E. of Kane Co. Ill.
HITT Esther L. of Savona, NY

January 16, 1854
Savona, NY

EVERETT Levi of Wheeler, NY
SAMSON Mrs. Caroline of Wheeler, NY

January 29, 1854
Wheeler, NY

MC PHERSON William H. of Cameron, NY
KNAPP Eveline of Cameron, NY

February 12, 1854
Cameron, NY

SCOTT Calvin of Bradford, NY
CHASE Sarah L. of Wayne, NY

February 7, 1854
Wayne, NY

WOMBOUGH Addison of Addison, NY
CHASE Velnette of Wayne, NY

February 14, 1854
Wayne, NY

HUGHES George of Buffalo, NY
WEEKS Mary R. of Prattsburgh, NY

February 20, 1854
Prattsburgh, NY

TANNER Joseph H. of Branchport, NY
TUBBS Esther of Branchport, NY

February 25, 1854
Bath, NY

NOBLE William of Bath, NY
HUNTER Lucinda Jane at res. of Peter Hunter

March 9, 1854
Bath, NY

KELSEY William F. of Bath, NY
EELLS Eunice E. of Wheeler, NY

March 13, 1854
Avoca, NY

ALLEN James H. Md. of Gorham, NY
STEVENSON Phebe E. of Avoca, NY

March 16, 1854
Avoca, NY

BROWN Abraham of Seneca Co. Ohio
GRAY Lucretia dau of L. Gray of Wheeler, NY

March 8, 1854
Wheeler, NY

WHEELER Heiro of Cameron, NY   March 21, 1854
DRAKE Mary Emily dau of Allen Drake of Jasper, NY   Jasper, NY

LEWIS Daniel D. of Wheeler, NY   March 22, 1854
WEBB Deborah H. of Wheeler, NY   Wheeler, NY

HOPKINS Joseph M. of Prattsburgh, NY   March 30, 1854
LINSLEY Laura A. of Republic, Ohio   Republic, Oh.

STEWART Thomas of Howard, NY   April 18, 1854
HOWEY Mary of Howard, NY   Bath, NY

CALKINS Calvin G. of Avoca, NY   April 19, 1854
HASKINS Mary A. of Howard, NY   Howard, NY

SEABRING Daniel of Tyrone, NY   April 25, 1854
SMITH Seany of Tyrone, NY   Weston, NY

WILLIS Philander G. of Bath, NY   April 4, 1854
HOAGLAND Ellen of Howard, NY   Howard, NY

MILLER Charles of Bath, NY   July 4, 1854
WOODARD Elizabeth of Bath, NY   Avoca, NY

ROBARDS John of Avoca, NY   July 6, 1854
EDWARDS Clarissa of Avoca, NY   Haskinsville, NY

MIX (or **MEEKS**) Christopher of Howard, NY   July 13, 1854
HEAD Melissa of Howard, NY   Avoca, NY

WAGNER Charles   July 23, 1854
NEWKIRK Mary Catherine   Avoca, NY

JOHNSON Richard M. of Wheeler, NY   July 30, 1854
SNOW Louisa of Wheeler, NY   Avoca, NY

HAGADORN Jacob of Bath, NY   June 19, 1854
PECK Helen M. of Bath, NY   Coopers Plains, NY

PINDER Lawrence W. of Lima, NY late of New Orleans   August 10, 1854
BARNHOUSE Susan of Lima, NY   Avoca, NY

SOULE James K. Md. of Hammondsport, NY   August 28, 1854
BARKER Nancy J. of Prattsburgh, NY   Prattsburgh, NY

MORRIS Oscar F. of Howard, NY   August 26, 1854
MC GONEGAL Jane A. dau of Orren of Avoca, NY   Avoca, NY

STOUT Alvin of Avoca, NY   September 6, 1854
GONSOLUS Susan E. of Avoca, NY   Avoca, NY

BLACK James W. Md. of Almond, NY   September 6, 1854
WARDEN E. C. dau of Dr. James Warden of Orange, NY   Orange, NY

LUKE William R. of Bath, NY   September 10, 1854
HAVENS Elizabeth of Bath, NY   Corning, NY

WALES Francis F.   September 12, 1854
ALDERMAN Chloe E.   Prattsburgh, NY

COLE Franklin   September 20, 1854
FOSTER Mary Ann dau of Capt. W. W. Foster   Prattsburgh, NY

WALDO John D. of Prattsburgh, NY   September 21, 1854
STEWART Charlotte dau of late Capt. Stewart   Jerusalem, NY

PATRIDGE Leander of Jamestown, Ind.   October 3, 1854
MINER Mary A. of Prattsburgh, NY   Prattsburgh, NY

CAUTE Sanford of S. Dansville, NY   October 11, 1854
TIMMERMAN Charlotte of Howard, NY   S. Dansville, NY

WILLIAMS John of Weston, NY   October 9, 1854
JONES Eunice of Weston, NY   Weston, NY

WHITING Otis Jr. of Watkins, NY   October 4, 1854
BARNES Harriet N. dau of Dr. Enos Barnes of Philadelphia   Monterey, NY

HENDRICK Orva of Hornby, NY   October 12, 1854
GAYLORD Sophia L. dau of Willis Gaylord of Hornby, NY   Hornby, NY

ALLIS John P.   October 17, 1854
DEMING Mary J.   Prattsburgh, NY

WARREN Chancey of Bath, NY   October 26, 1854
BENNETT Polly S. of Bath, NY   Bath, NY

SMITH Reuben C. of Williamsport, Pa.   November 1, 1854
BALCOM Sue F. dau of Judge Balcom of Painted Post, NY   Painted Post, NY

WOLF Carl of Bruchsal Grand Duchy of Baden, Germany   November 27, 1854
CLEMENT Anna dau of late Schuyler **STRONG**   Bath, NY

INGALSBE Royal of Hartford, NY   November 30, 1854
WATERBURY Jane M. of Avoca, NY   Avoca, NY

FAY Franklin   December 13, 1854
VAN HOUSEN Lydia Jane   Prattsburgh, NY

DURHAM Charles of Branchport, NY   December 18, 1854
CAMERON Helen of Prattsburgh, NY   Prattsburgh, NY

TYLER John G. of Pulteney, NY	December 15, 1854
SULLIVAN Catherine M. of Pulteney, NY	Pulteney, NY
GILBERT William of Urbana, NY	January 1, 1855
HICKS Catherine of Wayne, NY	
ADAMS Douglas of Tyrone, NY	January 11, 1855
EATON Selinda dau of Julius Eaton of Tyrone, NY	
MERRITT Gilbert of Wheeler, NY	January 11, 1855
ACKERSON Mary Elizabeth of Prattsburgh, NY	Prattsburgh, NY
WALDO James Augustine of Manitowoc, Wis.	February 14, 1855
WHEATON M. Amelia dau of John M. of Prattsburgh, NY	Bath, NY
WEEKS Caradon O. of Wheeler, NY	February 14, 1855
DILLENBACK Catherine of Wheeler, NY	Avoca, NY
MAXFIELD Andrew J. of Wheeler, NY	February 22, 1855
DILLENBACK Lany A. of Wheeler, NY	Wheeler, NY
MC LEAN George of Pulteney, NY	March 13, 1855
WYGANT Mrs. Ann Maria of Prattsburgh, NY	Prattsburgh, NY
VAN AUKEN J. B. of Hammondsport, NY	March 12, 1855
WISE Mary A. of Hammondsport, NY	
HAYS Clark of Saltille	March 7, 1855
THOMPSON Sally M. of Saltille	Orange, NY
BEALS J. Sylvester of Wheeler, NY	March 15, 1855
JONES Sophia of Prattsburgh, NY	Avoca, NY
KEYES Thomas K. of Corning, NY	April 11, 1855
UPDIKE Sarah C. of Corning, NY	Big Flats, NY
PUTNAM Joel of Avoca, NY	April 18, 1855
STEVENS Eliza M. of Thurston, NY	Bath, NY
BENNETT Daniel M.	April 11, 1855
CLARK Susan dau of M. Clark	Urbana, NY
RICE Horace A. of Avoca, NY	May 31, 1855
SHULTS Sarah M. of Avoca, NY	Avoca, NY
HAZEN Alexander T. of Cameron, NY	May 14, 1855
WHITE Melissa of Canisteo, NY	Canisteo, NY
QUICK Hiram of Campbell, NY	May 26, 1855
BUDGET Lydia of Campbell, NY	Cameron, NY

TERRY Zenas Jackson
HOPKINS Flaville S.

May 31, 1855
Prattsburgh, NY

MC WHORTER James of Avoca, NY
BULLARD Arthusa of Howard, NY

June 14, 1855
Howard, NY

SHULTS Lyman of Avoca, NY
LYKE Emeline of Kanona, NY

June 14, 1855
Kanona, NY

ACKERSON Henry of Wheeler, NY
HOTCHKISS Mrs. Mary of Prattsburgh, NY

June 21, 1855
Prattsburgh, NY

BRIGGS Sidney of Campbell, NY
CONVERSE Harriet of Campbell, NY

June 13, 1855
Campbell, NY

NORRIS Samuel H. of Pulteney, NY
HALLIDAY Clarinda L. of Thurston, NY

June 28, 1855
Bath, NY

HOWELL James Faulkner
SHEPHERD Lydia dau of late Schuyler **STRONG**

July 10, 1855
Bath, NY

HEES Martin A.
EDSON Ruby J.

July 4, 1855
Prattsburgh, NY

MONELL Chauncey L. of Bath, NY
HALL Philinda of Bath, NY

July 4, 1855
Bath, NY

MC PHERSON George W. L. of Cameron, NY
POWERS Ester Ann of Addison, NY

July 4, 1855
Addison, NY

GARLINGHOUSE Daniel of Urbana, NY
MARGESON Sarah of Urbana, NY

July 22, 1855
Savona, NY

ROBIE Levi of San Francisco formerly of Bath, NY
PERKINS Annie dau of late Asa Perkins of Dover, NH

June 30, 1855
San Francisco, Ca.

WALKER Newton of Woodhull, NY
VOSE Amanda of Thurston, NY

August 5, 1855
Bath, NY

GRAVES Jerome of Albion, Mi.
AINSWORTH Adelaide of Bath, NY

August 20, 1855
Bath, NY

SHULTS Charles of Avoca, NY
ECKER Mrs. Catherine of Avoca, NY

August 30, 1855
Avoca, NY

YOUNG Jacob of Avoca, NY
SIMONS Amelia A. of Howard, NY

September 2, 1855
Howard, NY

BARBER Henry of Monterey, NY
FULKERSON Mary Augusta of Monterey, NY

September 26, 1855
Monterey, NY

WHEATON Samuel W. of Bingham, Pa.   September 27, 1855
MALLORY Betsey Ann of Troupsburgh, NY   Troupsburgh, NY

HOLLENBECK B. P. of Corning, NY   September 24, 1855
DYER Nancy S. of Cameron, NY   Cameron, NY

MANCHESTER J. N. of Wayne Co. Pa.   October 1, 1855
ALLISON Mary A. of Bath, NY   Bath, NY

STODDARD Philo K. Md. of Prattsburgh, NY   September 29, 1855
COWING Sarah Ida of Jerusalem, NY   Jerusalem, NY

ALDEN De Witt C. of Bath, NY   October 9, 1855
CHURCH Mary Josephine dau of L. V. Church of Bath, NY

WOODHOUSE Leonard of Thurston, NY   October 7, 1855
BANCROFT Mary Jane dau of B. B. of Thurston, NY   Risingville, NY

MULLIGAN Eugene of New York City   October 17, 1855
MC CAY Sophie dau of late W. W. Mc Cay of Bath, NY   Bath, NY

LINDSAY William   October 11, 1855
FAUCETT Mary Elizabeth at res. of Robert Fausett   Bath, NY

FRIEDMAN Frank of Bath, NY   October 23, 1855
WIEDEMER Katherine of Bath, NY   Bath, NY

STEPHENS John G. of Prattsburgh, NY   October 24, 1855
CRAFT Climena of Urbana, NY   Bath, NY

EDWARDS John of Avoca, NY   November 13, 1855
OLMSTEAD Hannah Magdalen of Wheeler, NY   Wheeler, NY

COOK Henry of Prattsburgh, NY   November 13, 1855
VORHEES Elizabeth of Wheeler, NY   Wheeler, NY

WEBSTER Newell P. of Delmar, Pa.   November 5, 1855
WALLEN Chloe Ann of Savona, NY   Savona, NY

WING Luther A. of Campbell, NY   November 14, 1855
BENEDICT Eunice A. of Campbell, NY   Campbell, NY

WAGNER Manley T. of Wheeler, NY   November 14, 1855
GOODSELL Elizabeth Jane of Bath, NY   Bath, NY

SMITH Otis B. of Pulteney, NY   November 19, 1855
BANCROFT Ruth of Thurston, NY   Thurston, NY

RAY John W. of Avon Springs, NY   November 28, 1855
EENSTERMOCKER Jennie dau of Isaac of Dansville, NY   Dansville, NY

BARNES W. W.   November 29, 1855
TERRY Happy De Ette dau of Dr. M. Terry   Savona, NY

SMITH Bishop   December 5, 1855
LEWIS Fanny M.   Prattsburgh, NY

MOORE James N. of Avoca, NY   November 29, 1855
DAWSON Rachel of Kanona, NY   Kanona, NY

DEPEW James of Milo, NY   November 14, 1855
HUTCHES Mary of Urbana, NY   Urbana, NY

HUNTER George   December 12, 1855
LITTLE Catherine Ann

METCALF Benjamin F. of New York City   December 26, 1855
SEELEY Zerviah R. of Bath, NY   Bath, NY

RICE William A. of Albany, NY   December 26, 1855
SEELEY Hannah of Bath, NY   Bath, NY

HESS Solomon Francis of Wayland, NY   December 27, 1855
CHICHESTER Helen Mar dau of H. Chichester   Wheeler, NY

BECKWITH Collins   December 27, 1855
CHICHESTER Charity Eliza dau of H. Chichester   Wheeler, NY

STRANG A. T. of Woodhull, NY   December 31, 1855
MARRING Huldah of Thurston, NY   Thurston, NY

CAMPBELL Charles E. of Campbell, NY   January 1, 1856
BENEDICT Celestia M. of Addison, NY   Thurston, NY

WARNER Horatio H. of Hornellsville, NY   December 31, 1855
NORTHRUP Jane of Hornellsville, NY   Savona, NY

LEE Alfred of Jeffersonville, Ind.   January 10, 1856
WATROUS Sarah A. of Cameron, NY   Cameron, NY

ROBINSON Homer G. of Rochester, NY   January 10, 1856
WOODWARD Helen Sophia of Bath, NY   Bath, NY

SPRAKER Henry   January 15, 1856
JOHNSON Elizabeth at res. of Chester Johnson   Bath, NY

HOWARD William of Bath, NY   February 6, 1856
GEORGE Elizabeth M. of Corning, NY   Coopers Plains, NY

BROWN John of Corning, NY   February 24, 1856
BARBER Lucy Jane of Corning, NY   Corning, NY

FITTS John of Rochester, NY	February 10, 1856
STEVENS Mrs. Mary Ann of Painted Post, NY	Painted Post, NY
COON Harrison	February 21, 1856
PRINDLE Mary Jane	Wayne, NY
WHITNEY Benjamin F. of Burns, NY	March 16, 1856
KUDER Mary Ellen of Burns, NY	Hornellsville, NY
WILBER Harry of Dansville, NY	March 18, 1856
BLANK Angelina A. of Burns, NY	Hornellsville, NY
SEGAR George W. of California (Newspaper date)	March 26, 1856
SHERWIN Sarah M of Wayne, NY	Wayne, NY
FULLER George B. of Prattsburgh, NY	March 20, 1856
CAWARD Mary E. dau of George Caward	Pulteney, NY
MANN William H. of Petersham, Mass.	March 6, 1856
BANCROFT Susan dau of B. B. Bancroft of Thurston, NY	Thurston, NY
HALL James H. of Thurston, NY	March 23, 1856
KNICKERBOCKER Mary Ann of Lawrenceville, NY	Lawrenceville, Pa.
DOWNS George W.	March 26, 1856
CLEMENS Ruth A.	Prattsburgh, NY
KROSINSKEY Augustus of Corning, NY	March 24, 1856
SAMSEL Catherine of Corning, NY	
ALBERTS Walter of Corning, NY	March 24, 1856
KROSINSKEY Joanna of Corning, NY	
VERMILYEA E. G. of Caton, NY	March 13, 1856
HARMON Elizabeth C. of Campbell, NY	Campbell, NY
LAWREY W. C. of Caton, NY	March 26, 1856
RIDER Sarah Ann of Corning, NY	Corning, NY
LUCA John W. (Newspaper date)	April 2, 1856
GREEN Sarah L. (member of Luca Family singers)	Ellicotville, NY
SCOFIELD Lewis K. of Elgin, Ill.	March 26, 1856
ALVORD Ellen M. of Freeport, Ill. formerly of Bath, NY	Freeport, Ill.
HOTCHKIN James J.	April 23, 1856
LEWIS Hannah M.	Prattsburgh, NY
CALKINS Abner C. of Bath, NY	June 25, 1856
JUMP Annis of Savona, NY	Corning, NY

WALKER William
BILLINGTON C. A.

June 25, 1856
Howard, NY

CHAPMAN Amos
VOAS Emeline

June 29, 1856
Thurston, NY

COOK Adam P. of Prattsburgh, NY
EDWARDS Eleanor of Avoca, NY

June 26, 1856
Avoca, NY

CHAPELL N. A.
FOSTER Sarah J. formerly of Prattsburgh, NY

July 10, 1856
Bradford, Iowa

MC CALL Anson J. Atty. of Bath, NY
ELLAS Mary A. dau of Dr. S. Ellas of Bath, NY

August 21, 1856
Bath, NY

MONELL Gilbert W. of Bath, NY
CAREY Kate of Bath, NY

September 29, 1856

HEWITT Alonzo S. of Bath, NY
BILLINGTON Sarah J. of Bath, NY

October 2, 1856
Bath, NY

HARRISON William K. of Wayne, NY
SANFORD Ann of Bath, NY

November 3, 1856
Bath, NY

HALLETT Charles L. of Canisteo, NY
SUTTON Louise of Cameron, NY

November 2, 1856
Cameron, NY

ROSE Hubert D. of Hammondsport, NY
HAMMOND Mary of Hammondsport, NY

November 19, 1856
Hammondsport, NY

CHAMPOLAN Addison of Hammondsport, NY
ROSENCRANCE Ann E. of Hammondsport, NY

November 17, 1856
Hammondsport, NY

BALDWIN Lathrop Jr. Editor Elmira Republican
TILLOTSON Helen dau of D. L. Tillotson of Elmira NY

November 17, 1856
Elmira, NY

SMITH Augustus T.
EVERETT Sarah Jane

November 21, 1856
Prattsburgh, NY

CRONK George
WALRATH Mary J.

December 9, 1856
Prattsburgh, NY

ROWLEY Edward   (Newspaper date)
BARR Eliza S.

December 17, 1856
Addison, NY

QUICK P.
WILEY C. E.

December 21, 1856
Addison, NY

ERWIN Samuel C.
THOMPSON Elizabeth

December 24, 1856
Erwin, NY

HALL James S. formerly of Howard, NY — January 1, 1857
WHITE Elizabeth of Cameron, NY — Bath, NY

KINNEY Christopher — December 30, 1856
FOOTE Elizabeth — Addison, NY

CARR Alexander — January 1, 1857
VAN GORDER Mary — Addison, NY

FISHER William C. of Rushville, NY — December 28, 1856
CLARK Anna dau of John Jr. of Prattsburgh, NY — Geneva, NY

WATERBURY A. M. — January 15, 1857
HUBBLE Frances S. dau of William S. Hubble — Bath, NY

MAY Charles A. of Clinton, Wis. — January 27, 1857
DANN Ann Louise of Avon, NY — Avon, NY

MILLER Henry R. of Mt. Morris, NY — February 4, 1857
STRONG Eliza C. dau of late Schuyler Strong of Bath, NY — Bath, NY

BLAKESLEE George of Bath, NY — March 25, 1857
LA FORGE Mrs. Susan M. of Bath, NY — Bath, NY

BLAKESLEE Chauncey of Hammondsport, NY — March 25, 1857
BAIN Mary E. of Bath, NY — Bath, NY

NOLEN Lemuel of Painted Post, NY — April 14, 1857
GILL Hannah of Painted Post, NY — Addison, NY

PLAISTED E. H. of Bath, NY — May 11, 1857
ABER Rachel of Bath, NY — Bath, NY

STICKNEY J. of Wheeler, NY — May 10, 1857
ALLS Eliza of Wheeler, NY — Wheeler, NY

ORR Levi — May 28, 1857
ALDRICH Ann — Addison, NY

ALLEN Perlee — May 28, 1857
ORR Ann Eliza — Addison, NY

WILCOX James of Bath, NY — May 27, 1857
SPRAKER Jane of Bath, NY

HEALY Joshua Jr. of S. Dansville, NY — June 25, 1857
CHICHESTER Julia A. of Wheeler, NY — Wheeler, NY

CRANDALL Simeon of Baraloo, Wis. — June 15, 1857
BRIDGES Mary B. — Prattsburgh, NY

WILLIAMSON George P.
PRATT Amansa S. dau of Joel F. Pratt of Bath, NY

July 2, 1857
Cameron, NY

BELL Clark of Hammondsport, NY
TAYLOR Helene S. of Wheeler, NY

September 8, 1857
Hammondsport, NY

GUTHRIE Edwin of Humphrey, NY
MACK Mary S. of Bath, NY

October 12, 1857

MILLS Charles of Hume, NY
POWERS Julia dau of John Powers of Avoca, NY

October 7, 1857
Avoca, NY

DORSEY Henry of Bath, NY
PUTNAM Jennie M. dau of George Putnam of Salem, Mass.

October 7, 1857
Bath, NY

RETAN Barrett L. of Mt. Washington, NY
BRUNDAGE Catherine H. of Pleasant Valley, NY

June 17, 1857
Pleasant Valley, NY

LONGWELL David of Mt. Washington, NY
BRUNDAGE Mary E. of Pleasant Valley, NY

October 20, 1857
Pleasant Valley, NY

EDWARDS George of Bath, NY
SHERWOOD Sarah H. of Woodhull, NY

October 29, 1857
Addison, NY

HAMMEL Jacob of Bath, NY
HAMMEL Julia of Bath, NY

October 26, 1857

POOLE James of Bath, NY
SCOTT Jenette of Bath, NY

October 21, 1857
Bath, NY

HOLLEY James of Bradford, NY
PARKER Mary M. of Bradford, NY

November 15, 1857
Savona, NY

PETERS Elezer C.
LENHART Sarah Matilda

November 4, 1857
Bath, NY

ACKERMAN James P. of Bath, NY
DECKER Amelia M. of Bath, NY

November 14, 1857
Bath, NY

COON A. L. of Pulteney, NY
DANIELS Mary L. of Bath, NY

November 25, 1857
Bath, NY

ARNOLD Asa of Woodhull, NY
COOK Margaret M. of Spencer, NY

November 24, 1857
Spencer, NY

HUTCHES David of Urbana, NY
DIKES Malvina A. of Urbana, NY

December 1, 1857
Urbana, NY

BARTHOLOMEW David L. of Bradford, NY
SANFORD Nancy of Bath, NY

December 2, 1857

REYNOLDS P. B. of Prophetstown, Ill.　　　　November 26, 1857
MAY Lizzie G. dau of Gen. S. S. May of Bath, NY　　Davenport, Iowa

STURDEVANT Edward M.　　　　　　　　　December 8, 1857
ARDELL Sarah Ann　　　　　　　　　　　Prattsburgh, NY

WOOLVERTON Theodore M. of Bath, NY　　　October 17, 1857
TULLY Ama Catherine of Bath, NY　　　　　Bath, NY

FREEMAN Baskin of Bath, NY　　　　　　　December 10, 1857
ELLISON Phebe Ann of Urbana, NY

MC HENRY James of Erwin, NY　　　　　　December 23, 1857
CUTLER Susan M. dau of Dr. J. and Mary Cutler　Corning, NY

MILLER Elisha　　　　　　　　　　　　　November 23, 1857
WOODS Harriet　　　　　　　　　　　　Bath, NY

SHEARER Daniel of Howard, NY　　　　　　December 16, 1857
WARREN Mary Ann of Bath, NY　　　　　　Bath, NY

SMALLIDGE Jerome of Bath, NY　　　　　　January 12, 1858
CALKINS Mary J. of Bath, NY　　　　　　　Bath, NY

LOUCKS George of Bath, NY　　　　　　　January 28, 1858
BRUNDAGE Henrietta dau of Charles Brundage of Thurston, NY

EGGLESTON Harrison of Bath, NY　　　　　February 3, 1858
BARRETT Emma T. dau of Seth Barrett of Hammondsport　Hammondsport, NY

CASE Dr. George F. of Howard, NY　　　　　January 27, 1858
OSBORN Mary L. of Pulteney, NY　　　　　Pulteney, NY

TIFFANY Ezra of Kanona, NY　　　　　　　February 18, 1858
BROWN Lucy Ann dau of Russell Brown　　　Belfast Mills, NY

CHAPMAN Levi of Urbana, NY　　　　　　March 13, 1858
EDSON Antoinette of Prattsburgh, NY　　　　Prattsburgh, NY

SCARVELL Thomas of Bath, NY　　　　　　March 14, 1858
NASH Harriet of Bath, NY　　　　　　　　Bath, NY

DUDLEY Charles of Bath, NY　　　　　　　May 12, 1858
CROSS Mary C. of Bath, NY　　　　　　　Bath, NY

WHEELER C. J. of Bath, NY　　　　　　　June 9, 1858
BUSHNELL Susan S. of Bath, NY　　　　　Bath, NY

PARSONS Charles W.　　　　　　　　　　June 10, 1858
OVERHISER Ruth Adeline　　　　　　　　Prattsburgh, NY

ROBIE Jonathan
CHURCH M. Amelia at res. of L. V. Church

June 9, 1858
Bath, NY

ALLEN John B.
BRAMBLE Julia Amira

June 15, 1858
Prattsburgh, NY

SCOTT James P.
PLATT Jane Irving

August 1, 1858
Prattsburgh, NY

ELWARD John H.
CLARKSON Ann Jane of Bath, NY

July 3, 1858
Wheeler, NY

WILCOX Adam A.
CLARKSON Mary of Bath, NY

July 3, 1858
Bath, NY

PATTERSON Henry P. of Bath, NY
RAPPALYEA Catherine B. of Bath, NY

July 3, 1858
Bath, NY

DICKINSON Charles J. of Bath, NY
HOLDEN Elizabeth of Bath, NY

July 10, 1858
Bath, NY

FLYNN Martin A. of Bath, NY
ANDREWS S. A. of Addison, NY

July 3, 1858
Coopers Plains, NY

BUSHNELL Watts
WHEELER Harriet

July 22, 1858
Bath, NY

DUDLEY Prof. George E. of Mi. State Normal School
BEAUMONT Mary H. of Jonesville, Mi,

July 15, 1858
Jonesville, Mi.

CARPENTER Alva of Thurston, NY
SHARP Mary R. of Thurston, NY

August 4, 1858
Thurston, NY

SPRAGUE Samuel of Hammondsport, NY
MILLS Sally Ann

August 1, 1858
Bath, NY

HODGE Jacob N. of Canisteo, NY
CHISSOM Almira R. of Canisteo, NY

September 9, 1858

LAWRENCE Andrew J. of Canisteo, NY
CHISSOM Alma of Canisteo, NY

September 9, 1858

INGERSOLL Samuel of Wheeler, NY
SPRAGUE Hulda J. of Urbana, NY

September 18, 1858
Urbana, NY

BAKER George P. of Corning, NY
SMITH Seraphina dau of Elias H. Smith of Corning, NY

September 8, 1858
Savona, NY

HARADON Isaac C. of Corning, NY
DICKINSON Mary A. at res. of A. B. Dickinson

September 15, 1858
Hornby, NY

SAYLES Martin V. of Corning, NY
PRITCHARD Mary M. dau of H. Pritchard of Corning, NY

September 9, 1858
Corning, NY

MILLER Andrew J. of Corning, NY
COLE Almira of Corning, NY

September 9, 1858
Corning, NY

BROWN William Henry of Corning, NY
PATTENGILL Lettie Theresa dau of Rev. H. Pattengill

September 7, 1858
Hornellsville, NY

PERHAM Leander of Dansville, NY
MOREY Mary of Dansville, NY

September 25, 1858
Bath, NY

TOWNSEND Elijah of Urbana, NY
BUCHER Mary of Bath, NY

October 10, 1858
Bath, NY

WALKER A. of Thurston, NY
MC DOWELL Harriet of Westfield, Pa.

October 18, 1858
Westfield, Pa.

AINSWORTH A. C. of Madison, Wis.
READ Phebe M. of Pleasant Valley, NY

October 17, 1858
Hammondsport, NY

WHEELER James of Wheeler, NY
HOPKINS Speedy of Avoca, NY

October 11, 1858
Bath, NY

NELLIS A. J. of Bath, NY
BRUNDAGE Eliza M. dau of late Jesse of Bath, NY

October 20, 1858
Bath, NY

CLARK Barnet R. of Pulteney, NY
BEDELL Lydia of Pulteney, NY

October 21, 1858
Bath, NY

WIXOM Bradford of Prattsburgh, NY
GRAHAM Helen E. of Italy, NY

October 21, 1858
Italy, NY

PRATT Jared of Campbell, NY
BROOKS Amy A. of Bath, NY

October 20, 1858
Bath, NY

MC CONNELL Eli of Penn Yan, NY
RANDALL Mary F. of Hammondsport, NY

October 21, 1858
Hammondsport, NY

HILL Cyrus C. of Pulteney, NY
HULTZ Mary E. of Pulteney, NY

October 16, 1858
Bath, NY

MONELL George W. of Bath, NY
ALGAR Celina of Bath, NY

October 18, 1858
Bath, NY

HOAGLAND Charles of Urbana, NY
FREEMAN Eliza of Bath, NY

October 27, 1858
Bath, NY

ALDRIDGE Rev. S. H. of E. Genessee Conference
PIERCE Harriet A. of Westfield, Pa.

October 22, 1858
Harrison, Pa.

GILLETT Martin H. Md. of Springville, NY
LEWIS Elizabeth F. of Prattsburgh, NY

November 2, 1858
Prattsburgh, NY

HEIST George
WEBBER Elizabeth

October 13, 1858
Monterey, NY

ERWIN Francis son of Gen. F. E. Erwin
CAMPBELL Helen M. dau of Bradford Campbell of Mi.

October 27, 1858
Painted Post, NY

PARKER Edwin Van Dore
AUSTIN Charlotte Jane

November 20, 1858
Pulteney, NY

LITTLE James of Bath, NY
LONGWELL Sarah of Bath, NY

November 17, 1858
Bath, NY

ROSENCRANTS Garrett of Pulteney, NY
GILBERT Harriet E. of Urbana, NY

October 28, 1858
Urbana, NY

BENNETT ___ F. (illegible)
TOWNSEND Frank of Bath, NY

September 26, 1858
Savona, NY

VANDERWARKER Washington of Cameron, NY
LEECH Hannah L. of Cameron, NY

December 29, 1858
Bath, NY

BEAM John of Urbana, NY
CHILSON Ann of Wheeler, NY

November 30, 1858
Prattsburgh, NY

FOSTER Isaac
CURTIS Sarah Jane of Wheeler, NY

December 30, 1858
Prattsburgh, NY

ROGERS Samuel of Reed's Corners, NY
PIERCE Elizabeth of Pulteney, NY

January 1, 1859
Prattsburgh, NY

BROWN Asa O. of Painted Post, NY
VROOMAN Gertrude V. of Prattsburgh, NY

January 4, 1859
Prattsburgh, NY

BAXTER Orren B. of Woodhull, NY
HERRICK Maria A. of Woodhull, NY

January 6, 1859
Woodhull, NY

WHITFORD Robert of Charleston, Mi.
LOCKWOOD Ruth R. of Wheeler, NY

December 25, 1858
Richland, Mi.

OTIS J. Tilton of Kanona, NY
BARNES Rebecca W. of Bath, NY

January 23, 1859

SNELL Levi of Bath, NY
BILLINGTON Lucinda S. of Bath, NY

January 27, 1858

HALL Ornan of Hammondsport, NY
YOST Eliza of Thurston, NY

January 30, 1859
Thurston, NY

EMERSON J. Calvin — January 30, 1859
SMEAD Mary — Bath, NY

LANE James of Phelps, NY — February 14, 1859
IRWIN Sarah L. of Chicago, Ill. — Chicago, Ill.

MAXFIELD Levi of Wheeler, NY — February 24, 1859
SHAUT Sarah J. of Wheeler, NY — Bath, NY

CREVELING Samuel R. of Thurston, NY — February 23, 1859
CONKLIN Kate of Reading, NY — Reading, NY

THOMPSON John of Wheeler, NY — January 20, 1859
STRYKER Irena of Wheeler, NY — Wheeler, NY

FREEMAN William of Bath, NY — March 10, 1859
HUNT Joanna of Bath, NY — Bath, NY

VUNCK Alonzo of Avoca, NY — March 16, 1859
RUTHERFORD Jane A. of Bath, NY — Bath, NY

STEPHENS Francis H. of Bath, NY — March 26, 1859
LINDSAY Emeline of Bath, NY

RILEY Truman of Caton, NY — April 2, 1859
ROGERS Sarah of Bath, NY — Bath, NY

PRESHO John of Bath, NY — April 13, 1859
SUTHERLAND Agnes of Bath, NY — Bath, NY

CLARKE Charles Cameron of New York City — May 9, 1859
MC CUTCHIN Sarah R. at res of Col. Davenport — Bath, NY

EDDY E. Chapin — May 15, 1859
HOLTON Mrs. Lemira dau of Israel SKINNER — Prattsburgh, NY

CARSON James of Springwater, NY — May 15, 1859
ROBERTS Lucretia of Liberty, NY

SMITH Orrin — May 16, 1859
FITCH Mrs. Elizabeth — Bath, NY

MANCHESTER John N. of Lisbon, Iowa — May 17, 1859
RICE Mary M. at res. of James M. EDWARDS — Bath, NY

MC CAY T. M. of Bath, NY — June 2, 1859
DUNN Fanny S. of Brooklyn, NY — New York City

NORRIS Levi of Pulteney, NY — June 22, 1859
CLARK Phebe of Pulteney, NY — Bath, NY

DOUBLEDAY Elisha of Yates Co. NY   July 9, 1859
WILLIAMS Mrs. Caroline of Chemung Co. NY   Prattsburgh, NY

EDGETT Andrew J. of Howard, NY   (Newspaper date) July 13, 1859
SHEARER Betsey J. of Howard, NY   Howard, NY

BOWER Justus of Campbell, NY   July 4, 1859
COOK Avis of Campbell, NY   Corning, NY

TERBELL James G. of Campbell, NY   June 19, 1859
KNOX Frances F. dau of John P. Knox of Campbell, NY Campbell, NY

CLARK E. L. of Owego, NY   July 21, 1859
SPRINGER Hannah E. of Owego, NY

GREENLEAF J. B. of Cleveland, Ohio   July 30, 1859
OLMSTEAD Sarah of Bath, NY   Bath, NY

MAY Dr. Henry C. of Corning, NY   September 14, 1859
AGGETT Phebe M. dau of James Aggett of Lyons, NY   Lyons, NY

WOODRUFF Wilson   September 25, 1859
YOUMANS Lucinda   Bath, NY

DEAN Darius of Pulteney, NY   September 11, 1859
STEWART Mary E. of Medina, NY   Bath, NY

BEERS George A. of Bath, NY   October 15, 1859
BREWSTER Anna of Bath, NY   Bath, NY

ROBIE Charles H. of Bath, NY   October 11, 1859
MC ELWEE Lizzie dau of Henry Mc Elwee of Bath, NY

SCOTT John V. R.   October 5, 1859
BANTA Helen D.   Wheeler, NY

PURDY John H. of Des Moines, Io. formerly Bath, NY September 28, 1859
GREGG Mary E. of Bath, NY   Mt. Pleasant, Io.

POWERS Ambrose S.   October 27, 1859
WATERBURY Caroline L.   Avoca, NY

GIBSON Ira of Pulteney, NY   November 1, 1859
BEADON Caroline of Pulteney, NY   Pulteney, NY

STURDEVANT Daniel Butler   November 2, 1859
PARKER Mary Ann   Prattsburgh, NY

SUTHERLAND James of Bath, NY   November 9, 1859
LINDSEY Fanny of Bath, NY

MALTBY Charles R. of Orange, NY   November 9, 1859
STONE Eliza A. dau of Jason Stone of Bath, NY

BISHOP George W. of Thurston, NY   November 6, 1859
PHILLIPS Harriet M. of Thurston, NY

THOMPSON Calvin L. of Wheeler, NY   December 15, 1859
WILCOX Mrs. Catherine   Prattsburgh, NY

THOMAS Stephen of Prattsburgh, NY   December 29, 1859
TOWNSEND Martha M. of Prattsburgh, NY   Prattsburgh, NY

NEVINS Arthur of Bradford, NY   January 9, 1860
WELLS Harriet of Bradford, NY   Bradford, NY

STRAIT Cornelius of Beaver Dams, NY   (Newspaper date) January 18, 1860
COMPTON Catherine of Bradford, NY

HIGGINS A. R. of Howard, NY   January 17, 1860
BALDWIN Julia E. of Pulteney, NY   Pulteney, NY

RICHTMYER William of Thurston, NY   January 7, 1860
SPENCER Mary J. of Thurston, NY   Thurston, NY

VANDERHOVEN F. De C. of Bath, NY   January 25, 1860
HAZLETT Jennie I. of New York City   Keyport, NY

MERRITT William S. of Wheeler, NY   January 24, 1860
BIRDSEYE Phebe R. of Prattsburgh, NY   Prattsburgh, NY

ALLEN Henry E. of Prattsburgh, NY   January 26, 1860
HOLCOMB Charlotte J. of Seneca, NY   nr Geneva, NY

HODGEMAN W. S. of Painted Post, NY   February 1, 1860
BALCOM Jennie dau of Lyman Balcom of Painted Post, NY   Painted Post, NY

EDWARDS C. Y. of Mc Henry Co. Ill.   February 8, 1860
SEELEY Antoinette S. dau of Col. H. H. Seeley   Erwin, NY

FORD Wallace D. of Hornellsville, NY   February 14, 1860
GARRISON Sarah Jane of Prattsburgh, NY   Prattsburgh, NY

FOWLER John W.   February 15, 1860
NEFF Margaret S.   Prattsburgh, NY

BOUTON Eli F.   March 8, 1860
WALDO Fannie dau of H. H. Waldo   Prattsburgh, NY

MOORE John D. of Savona, NY   March 12, 1860
TOWNER Dorcas of Wheeler, NY   Wheeler, NY

FAY Franklin of Prattsburgh, NY
HUTCHISON Clara of Prattsburgh, NY

February 20, 1860
Prattsburgh, NY

FINCH Hiram R. of Columbus, Ga.
DAWSON Eliza

March 14, 1860
Bath, NY

RICHARDSON William of Ingersoll, Canada W.
GAMBLE Louisa dau of William Gamble of Bath, NY

March 28, 1860
Painted Post, NY

WILKES Robert of Bath, NY
ERWIN Harriet M. dau of Gen. F. E. Erwin of Erwin, NY

March 27, 1860
Erwin, NY

DE PEW Abram of Urbana, NY
LAYTON Sarah of Urbana, NY

March 3, 1860
Urbana, NY

HICKS Lewis of Urbana, NY
LAYTON Margaret of Urbana, NY

March 3, 1860
Urbana, NY

SWARTHOUT Anthony of Milo, NY
VAN NESS Ellen of Urbana, NY

March 25, 1860
Urbana, NY

LONGWELL Randall of Urbana, NY
BRUNDAGE Eliza of Urbana, NY

March 27, 1860
Urbana, NY

THOMAS George of Bath, NY
BUTLER Mary of Bath, NY

February 12, 1860
Bath, NY

BRUNDAGE William of Urbana, NY
DE WITT P. E. of Bath, NY

March 21, 1860
Bath, NY

WALKER John of Bath, NY
CROSIER Caroline of Howard, NY

March 29, 1860
Howard, NY

EARNEST Wallace H. of Wayne, NY
CLARKE Phebe A. of Barrington, NY

March 29, 1860

BRIGLIN W. W. Harrison
SHAUT Estelle S.

March 24, 1860
Prattsburgh, NY

DREW J. Milton of Urbana, NY
GRAHAM Hannah G. of Prattsburgh, NY

April 12, 1860
Prattsburgh, NY

HARRIS Samuel T.
SAGAR Martha J.

February 26, 1860
Prattsburgh, NY

BROWN Robert D.
LAING Elizabeth

April 13, 1860
Prattsburgh, NY

VAN GORDER Allen of Canisteo, NY
HEADLEY Betsey of Canisteo, NY

February 26, 1860
Canisteo, NY

ROGERS William of Wheeler, NY	March 31, 1860
ABER Ruth Ann of Wheeler, NY	Howard, NY
HAIRE Ezra of Branchport, NY	April 22, 1860
GARDNER Sarah of Wheeler, NY	Wheeler, NY
GOODRICH Timothy B. of Stiles, Wis.	May 9, 1860
MAGEE Mary of Bath, NY	Bath, NY
FRENCH James R. of Bath, NY	May 17, 1860
BREWSTER Othelia of Bath, NY	Bath, NY
STOKES Thomas of Watkins, NY	June 13, 1860
WELLS Miranda of Bradford, NY	Bradford, NY
PRENTISS Luther W. of Pulteney, NY	June 24, 1860
VAN SYCKLE Ella A. of Pulteney, NY	Harmonyville, NY
STRONG David of Prattsburgh, NY	June 24, 1860
CLELAND L. Jennie of Cohocton, NY	Avoca, NY
PETTIBONE W. H. of Attica, NY	June 28, 1860
WARREN Etta of Attica, NY	Attica, NY
DE PUY John S. of Thurston, NY	July 12, 1860
BOSFORD Kate M. of Thurston, NY	Thurston, NY
BARBER T. W. of St. Paul, Mn.	July 24, 1860
CROSS F. A. of Cameron, NY	Thurston, NY
MC CASKEY John P. of Lancaster, Pa.	August 8, 1860
CHASE Ellen M. of Bath, NY	Bath, NY
WETMORE Justus F. of Hornellsville, NY	August 13, 1860
BROWNELL Cornelia dau of Martin Brownell of Bath, NY	Bath, NY
MILLER E. L.	September 2, 1860
ROWE Caroline	Bath, NY
WILCOX George	September 15, 1860
CROSS Mrs. Elizabeth	Bath, NY
VELEY Peter	September 18, 1860
TICHENOR Mary	Bath, NY
MILES Darwin	September 26, 1860
QUAKENBUSH Mary	Bath, NY
RUGER Moses A. of Greenwood, NY	September 23, 1860
COLBATH Mary L. of Bath, NY	Bath, NY

CLASON Luther of Cohocton, NY September 26, 1860
WHEELER Helen dau of Luther Wheeler Prattsburgh, NY

UNDERHILL Charles A. of Bath, NY October 17, 1860
PARKS Adda H. of Kanona, NY Kanona, NY

JIMERSON Thomas of Bradford, NY October 17, 1860
CLARK Mrs. Amanda Prattsburgh, NY

VAN VALKENBURGH Frank V. of Milwaukee, Wis. October 8, 1860
PRATT Emeline W. at Mother's Bloomfield, Mn.

METCALF Clarence H. October 6, 1860
DICKEY Louise Buffalo, NY

WILLIAMS William J. of Bath, NY October 24, 1860
FRINK Susan R. dau of Elain Frink of Bath, NY Bath, NY

SNYDER Isam of S. Jackson, Mi. October 22, 1860
WAITE Sarah of Cohocton, NY Cohocton, NY

YOUNG James of Chicago, Ill. November 1, 1860
BROTHER Ellen M. dau of Henry Brother of Bath, NY Bath, NY

MC ELWAIN William of Bath, NY November 2, 1860
WEDGE Lucinda of Bath, NY Bath, NY

BILES Ten Eyck of Bath, NY November 8, 1860
VODGES Kate R. of Pittsburg, Pa. Pittsburg, Pa.

MERRITT Wesley S. of Parma, NY November 8, 1860
BROWN Lydia Jane of Pulteney, NY Pulteney, NY

HALL Granville of Elmira, NY (Newspaper date) November 14, 1860
MACK Eliza

MILLS George of Urbana, NY November 19, 1860
RICHARDSON Nancy of Bath, NY

LEWIS Harrison W. of Savona, NY December 8, 1860
SMITH Jenette of Savona, NY

DURNIAN Richard of Bath, NY December 5, 1860
STEWART Elizabeth L. of Bath, NY

THOMAS James M. of Bath, NY December 5, 1860
WILLIAMS Ellen H. of Bath, NY

RETAN Nelson of Pulteney, NY December 15, 1860
BALL Esther S. of Pulteney, NY

DRAKE Alex   December 12, 1860
CORNISH Louisa E.   Prattsburgh, NY

COLCORD Albert of Thurston, NY   December 23, 1860
SHEARER Elizabeth of Bath, NY   Bath, NY

JACOBUS James D. of N. Urbana, NY   December 24, 1860
DAVIS Mary A. of Sonora, NY   Sonora, NY

DUNKLEE Eli F. of Coopers Plains, NY   December 31, 1860
LEWIS Jane J. of Bath, NY formerly of Brooklyn, NY Kanona, NY

ST JOHN William H. of Pulteney, NY   December 26, 1860
FRAZER Fannie of Hammondsport, NY   Hammondsport, NY

ROSE Isaac of Corning, NY   January 1, 1861
ARWAY Rhoda A. of Bath, NY at res of Peter **MONELL**   Bath, NY

EDGER Jacob of Corning, NY   January 1, 1861
ARWAY Sarah A. of Corning, NY   Bath, NY

SMITH Lemual H. of Bath, NY   January 20, 1861
HADLEY Mary C. of Bath, NY   Bath, NY

CHISSOM Robert of Cameron, NY   January 24, 1861
WILLIAMSON Julia Ann of Cameron, NY

ORR Peter A. of Jerusalem, NY   January 24, 1861
STURDEVANT Lucy P. of Prattsburgh, NY   Prattsburgh, NY

HOPT Ramor   December 1, 1860
HUBER Louisa   Bath, NY

SMITH Ira L. of Deerfield, Pa.   February 3, 1861
SMITH Phylinda

WALES Francis   January 31, 1861
TERRY Jane Eliza   Prattsburgh, NY

TAYLOR N. C. of Canisteo, NY   February 11, 1861
BARTLETT Lura A.   Prattsburgh, NY

WAGONER Peter of Wheeler, NY   February 23, 1861
FREEMAN Mary of Bath, NY

FOSTER Henry D. of Cohocton, NY   January 26, 1861
WINDNAGLE Martha A. of Cohocton, NY   Kanona, NY

ADAMS John D. of Bath, NY   March 12, 1861
NILES Viorna E. of Bath, NY   Bath, NY

CRAWFORD Edwin of Savona, NY
CRAWFORD Mary of Savona, NY

March 12, 1861
Bath, NY

DEAN John of Pulteney, NY
BOSS Sarah of Pulteney, NY

March 24, 1861
Pulteney, NY

KING William of Hammondsport, NY
SAYRES Sarah of Hammondsport, NY

February 26, 1861

WILBER S. K. of Thurston, NY
MINIER Alvira of Bath, NY at res of Harlow SMITH

March 21, 1861
Bath, NY

WALDO Edward F.
CAWARD Hattie A.

April 3, 1861
Prattsburgh, NY

DUDLEY Albert D. of Bath, NY
SEDGEWICK May Jane of Bath, NY

May 22, 1861
Bath, NY

GREEN D. H. of Pulteney, NY
DRUM Frances of Pulteney, NY

May 16, 1861
Prattsburgh, NY

ROWE James M. of Bath, NY
ACLABOYER Mary of Dansville, NY

June 1, 1861

SMITH George W. of Bath, NY
TUTTLE Elizabeth of Bath, NY

April 24, 1861
Bath, NY

MOREY Robert C. of Woodhull, NY
BAKER Elizabeth A. of Woodhull, NY

May 27, 1861

CAMPBELL Thomas of Cameron, NY
CLYDE Mrs. Mary of Cameron, NY

June 5, 1861
Bath, NY

YOUNG Charles H.
KELLOGG Marion dau of Robert Kellogg

June 5, 1861
Kanona, NY

MILLS Harmon of Savona, NY
CHAMPLAIN Sarah of Savona, NY

June 9, 1861
Bath, NY

WARD Benjamin of Stark, NY (Herkimer Co.)
MOUNT Rose Ellen of Kanona, NY at Father's

June 24, 1861
Howard, NY

HARRIS William of Bath, NY
ROBINSON Celestia V. of Hornellsville, NY

June 23, 1861
Hornellsville, NY

DILDINE Zechariah of Hornellsville, NY
ROBINSON Ann of Avoca, NY

June 23, 1861
Hornellsville, NY

CLARK John M. of Pulteney, NY
WILSON Mrs. Catherine of Hammondsport, NY

August 1, 1861
Kanona, NY

WALDO D. P. September 5, 1861
HOTCHKIN Hannah Marie Prattsburgh, NY

BULL George Robie September 4, 1861
WAGONER Louisa Ann dau of Charles Wagoner of Bath, NY Bath, NY

SMITH Andrew K. September 2, 1861
PHILLIPS H. Marilla dau of Chauncey Phillips Prattsburgh, NY

SHAW Charles B. of Penn Yan, NY September 9, 1861
REED Ellen J. of Hammondsport, NY

ROSE George W. of Bath, NY September 12, 1861
ADAMS Matilda of Bath, NY

HIGGINS Orson of Bath, NY October 9, 1861
BENTON Mary Jane of Bath, NY Bath, NY

KNIGHT Chester of Bath, NY October 24, 1861
GILMORE Harriet R. dau of Perez Gilmore of Bath, NY Bath, NY

BEEKMAN Abram of Bath, NY October 31, 1861
MC CAY Sarah dau of John W. **FOWLER** of Bath, NY Bath, NY

ALLEN William W. October 30, 1861
GANSEVOORT Helen M. dau of late John R. Gansevoort

BARTLETT Norman of Viennna, Mi. October 28, 1861
FOX Mary Jane of Wheeler, NY Wheeler, NY

CHASE Thomas C. of Avoca, NY November 21, 1861
HEES Mary of Avoca, NY Avova, NY

WOODARD David of Bath, NY November 18, 1861
CUMMINGS Mrs. Nancy of Bath, NY Hammondsport, NY

PECK M. A. of Avoca, NY November 26, 1861
JANES M. L. of Avoca, NY Avoca, NY

HUNTER Samuel D. of Bath, NY November 21, 1861
FERRIS Caroline of Bath, NY Bath, NY

CAWARD N. Haynes December 5, 1861
WALDO Harriet N. dau of Henry H. Waldo Prattsburgh, NY

GREGG Frederick of Thurston, NY December 1, 1861
FLUENT Lucinda of Thurston, NY Coe's Corners, NY

BAILEY James N. of Urbana, NY December 22, 1861
COOLEY Mary H. of Wayne, NY Bath, NY

MURPHY Elias of Pulteney, NY　　　　　　　　　November 10, 1861
SIMPSON Sarah of Pulteney, NY

BELLOWS Edward of Prattsburgh, NY　　(Newspaper date) December 25, 1861
MURPHY Catherine of Pulteney, NY　　　　　　　　Pulteney, NY

FAULKNER Frazier of Urbana, NY　　　　　　　　December 21, 1861
BRUNDAGE Cornelia A. dau of Charles Brundage of Thurston, NY

GREEK Barrett S. of Savona, NY　　　　　　　　December 24, 1861
TROVENGER Susan C. 3rd dau of John Trovenger of Sonora, NY

HOPKINS Charles E. of Bath, NY　　　　　　　　December 28, 1861
BRYANT Catherine of Bath, NY

BARTHLOMEW Joshua F. of Bradford, NY　　　　December 23, 1861
SCOTT Mary A. dau of Thomas Scott of Bradford, NY

ROWLES Eli of Bradford, NY　　　　　　　　　　January 1, 1862
TOBIAS Rachel dau of Amos Tobias of Bradford, NY　Bradford, NY

PERRY Frank Lindley of Bridgeport, Ct.　　　　　January 1, 1862
CHIDSEY Rebecca J. dau of Capt. Chidsey of Pulteney, NY　Branchport, NY

HESS Jeremiah J. of Pulteney, NY　　　　　　　　January 7, 1862
PRENTISS Florence A. of Pulteney, NY　　　　　　Pulteney, NY

BROWN H. Clay formerly of Bath, NY　　　　　　December 26, 1861
BLACK Minerva of Canton, Ill.　　　　　　　　　Canton, Ill.

WEARE John of Cedar Rapids, Io.　　　　　　　December 26, 1861
ROGERS Martha Campbell dau of Dr. G. A. Rogers　Clinton City, Io.

EDDY R. W. of Towanda, Pa.　　　　　　　　　January 8, 1862
BILES Fannie N. 2nd dau of Lewis Biles of Bath, NY　Bath, NY

YOST A. C. of Bath, NY　　　　　　　　　　　January 14, 1862
O'HARE Mary of Bath, NY　　　　　　　　　　Bath, NY

HALL Mathew R. of Pulteney, NY　　　　　　　January 8, 1862
CORYELL Sarah of Pulteney, NY　　　　　　　　Pulteney, NY

HESS Hiram R. of Bath, NY　　　　　　　　　　January 15, 1862
HOWELL Mrs. Mary G. of Bath, NY　　　　　　Bath, NY

MATHER Charles S. of Bath, NY　　　　　　　　January 28, 1862
TOWLE Sarah Maria dau of Jonathan of Bath, NY

SMITH Pitt M. of Thurston, NY　　　　　　　　January 1, 1862
PURDY Harriet of Bath, NY

HARTMAN Charles of W. Sparta, NY	January 29, 1862
SMITH Mary E. of Bath, NY	Bath, NY
WATTS Joseph of Hammondsport, NY	February 1, 1862
LAYTON Martha of Hammondsport, NY	
KELLY Amos J. of Thurston, NY	December 22, 1861
ROYCE Jane M. of Thurston, NY	Savona, NY
COLE Theron of Carmel, NY	January 30, 1862
HOUCK Mrs. Amanda of Urbana, NY	Savona, NY
YOUNG Elphonso of Thurston, NY	February 16, 1862
SAYER Kate S. of Thurston, NY	Thurston, NY
GRAY Richard of Wheeler, NY	February 13, 1862
BARNEY Candace J. of Wheeler, NY	Wheeler, NY
SULLIVAN John Jr. of Pulteney, NY	January 26, 1862
CLARK Loley of Pulteney, NY	Pulteney, NY
SPENCER N. R. of Penn Yan, NY	February 6, 1862
LYON Maggie of Penn Yan, NY	Penn Yan, NY
MORTON James M. of Bath, NY	February 26, 1862
WHEELER Sarah A. of Cameron, NY	Cameron, NY
FARR Erastus B.	February 26, 1862
BROWNELL Ellen dau of Martin Brownell	Bath, NY
SILSBEE T. A. of Bath, NY	February 13, 1862
CHARLESWORTH Elvira C. of Avoca, NY	Avoca, NY
SICKLES Anson of Milo, NY	February 26, 1862
HATHAWAY Mary Elizabeth of Prattsburgh, NY	
ABEL John of Bath, NY	March 26, 1862
WISEWELL Mrs. Arabella of Hornellsville, NY	Corning, NY
HOVEY William H.	March 16, 1862
WILLOUR Martha A.	Grand Rapids, Mi.
OSBORN John D. of Merchantville, NY	April 7, 1862
HUNT Mary A. of Bath, NY	Bath, NY
SHATTUCK Harvey S. of N. Cohocton, NY	April 10, 1862
BAILEY Belinda dau of Mrs. Elizabeth A. Bailey	Urbana, NY
SHAUT Alvah of Wheeler, NY	February 6, 1862
FOX Lucretia of Avoca, NY	Avoca, NY

WORTSER John of Prattsburgh, NY
OVERHISER Marilla of Wheeler, NY

April 27, 1862
Wheeler, NY

GARDNER H. R. of Wilmington, Ill.
WHEELER Eliza J. of Hammondsport, NY

June 4, 1862
Hammondsport, NY

VAN WIE Alonzo of Howard, NY
WYGANT Sarah

May 29, 1862
Prattsburgh, NY

BEND Otis of Urbana, NY
SPRAGUE Sarah Ann of Urbana, NY

June 13, 1862
Bath, NY

BEULPIN Charles of Branchport, NY
DUNNING June

July 14, 1862
Prattsburgh, NY

WILSON Lieut. B. C. of Corning, NY
BILES Mattie D. dau of Lewis Biles of Bath, NY

August 10, 1862

WILLIAMS Frank of Prattsburgh, NY
CLARK Jennie of Urbana, NY

August 9, 1862

LOVELL James W. of Thurston, NY
ABER Lizzie of Bath, NY

August 10, 1862
Bath, NY

STRATTON John E. of Bath, NY
WARREN Laura Ann of Bath, NY

August 7, 1862
Bath, NY

HERRINGTON James H. of Avoca, NY
ARMSTRONG Alma C. of Bath, NY

August 10, 1862
Bath, NY

BARBER Lloyd of Rochester, Mn.
DE BOW Mary Jane of Almond, NY

August 20, 1862
Hammondsport, NY

WHEELER Jacob W. of Urbana, NY
BROWN Edify C. of Bradford, NY

August 20, 1862

PERKINS Edward of Thurston, NY
BEATON Rosa of Thurston, NY

August 20, 1862

HARRINGTON Isaac of Rathbone, NY
BARAER Emily of Cameron, NY

August 25, 1862

SPRAGUE Tobias of Urbana, NY
CASS Margaret of Southport, NY

(Newspaper date) September 10, 1862
Bath, NY

SWITZER A. J. of Hammondsport, NY
HASTINGS Fidelia of Hammondsport, NY

September 2, 1862

VROOM George
HUTCHES Mrs. Almira

September 7, 1862
Hammondsport, NY

SMITH Charles of Bath, NY   September 13, 1862
SHULTS Euphrasia C. of Canisteo, NY

STEVER Frank of Prattsburgh, NY   (Newspaper date) September 24, 1862
TODD Lydia L. of Branchport, NY

SCOTT J. F. of Philadelphia, Pa.   September 11, 1862
MAXWELL Jennie E. of Bath, NY

SMITH Austin B. of Cameron Mills, NY   September 20, 1862
CLYDE Almira of Cameron, NY

BELDEN Capt. G. H. of San Francisco, Cal.   September 20, 1862
CARPENTER Anna M. of Port Dover, Canada W.   Elmira, NY

PEACOCK James of New York City   September 20, 1862
LOGHRY Fanny A. of Bath, NY   Bath, NY

BEERS Uri of Canisteo, NY   September 24, 1862
WARREN Louisa of Bath, NY

KNIFFEN John of Bath, NY   September 24, 1862
SMITH Julia E. of Bath, NY   Bath, NY

HOAGLAND Martin of Urbana, NY   September 25, 1862
FAUCETT Mary of Bath, NY   Bath, NY

ALICE John of Chicago, Ill.   October 7, 1862
ROSENCRANCE Eliza Ann of Hammondsport, NY

JOHNSON Henry A.   October 22, 1862
LEWIS Alida dau of John Lewis of Prattsburgh, NY

DAVIS Porter J. of Little Falls, NY   October 22, 1862
GOODSELL Julia A. of Thurston, NY   Thurston, NY

MILLER John of Howard, NY   October 15, 1862
WILLIAMS Elizabeth of Bath, NY

WETMORE Bela of Springwater, NY   September 13, 1862
LENHART Elizabeth H. of Bath, NY   Bath, NY

FRY Charles of Urbana, NY   October 21, 1862
SECKEE Susana

HAYNES David of S. Dansville, NY   October 23, 1862
DEMERY Sarah of Fremont, NY

STUART Alexander of Bath, NY   October 8, 1862
OXX Sarah Dorathy of Howard, NY   Bath, NY

HOUEY Alexander of Bath, NY   October 8, 1862
STUART Sarah of Bath, NY   Bath, NY

HEERMANS George of Bath, NY   October 22, 1862
SEDGEWICK Hattie C. dau of William Sedgewick of Bath, NYBath, NY

JOHNSTON John M. of Bath, NY   October 21, 1862
MC CANN Lizzie D. of Bath, NY

GANSEVOORT James   November 10, 1862
OGDEN Eliza E. dau of Col. G. **LOOMIS** of US Army   Gobernors Is., NY

RARRICK Abel of Pulteney, NY   November 5, 1862
LAKBOTH Emily of Pulteney, NY   Bath, NY

FISK James E. of Hammondsport, NY   November 7, 1862
CARR Henrietta of Hammondsport, NY   Hammondsport, NY

AVERELL Oscar J. of Bath, NY   November 19, 1862
THOMPSON Helen C. dau of Jared H. of Bath, NY   Bath, NY

CARPENTER Uriah A. of Cameron, NY   November 23, 1862
MERCHANT Frances E. dau of H. Merchant   Merchantville, NY

SEDGEWICK William P. of Bath, NY   December 3, 1862
SHULTS Fannie E. dau of Conrad Shults of Bath, NY   Bath, NY

SMITH Prof. F. E. of Prattsburgh, NY   December 3, 1862
NEWMAN Emmie dau of late Edwin of Unadilla, NY   Unadilla, NY

LEARY Edward of New York City   December 2, 1862
CROSIER Sarah Elizabeth dau of William of Howard, NY   Bath, NY

SMITH Joseph L. of Urbana, NY   December 3, 1862
SCOFIELD Rhoda of Urbana, NY   Urbana, NY

GRAVES C. C. of Howard, NY   December 3, 1862
WILLIAMS Jane J. of Howard, NY   Howard, NY

ALDERMAN Flavel B.   December 31, 1862
WHITEHEAD Miami   Bath, NY

WILBER John M. of Bath, NY   November 29, 1862
GRANT Lucinda of Bath, NY   Bath, NY

MORGAN William D. of Bath, NY   December 22, 1862
ALGER Mary of Bath, NY   Bath, NY

SLAGHT Jeremiah of Hector, NY   December 31, 1862
VAN GELDER Almada of Bath, NY   Bath, NY

KETCHUM Levi of Barrington, NY	January 1, 1863
SMITH Angeline of Pulteney, NY	Bath, NY
BRUNDAGE Lewis of Urbana, NY	January 1, 1863
COVERT Sarah of Urbana, NY	Bath, NY
SMALLY Zachariah of Urban, NY	January 3, 1863
STEWART Mrs. Julia of Thurston, NY	Bath, NY
ALLEN John J. of Corning, NY	December 31, 1862
MERRILL Sarah Jane of Cameron, NY	
HUNT Henry A. of Bath, NY	January 10, 1863
HARRIS Hattie E. of Scio, NY	Bath, NY
BARTON Edwin C. of Buffalo, NY	January 21, 1863
TURNER Sarah D.	Prattsburgh, NY
SWART Ten Eyck G. of Bath, NY	February 1, 1863
ABEL Ellen T. of Bath, NY	Bath, NY
HUNT Norman of Jerusalem, NY	January 28, 1863
PRENTISS Lilly G. dau of William Prentiss of Pulteney	Pulteney, NY
WELSH James of Wheeler, NY	January 10, 1863
EVERETT Sarah M. of Wheeler, NY	Avoca, NY
TAYLOR L. W. of Towanda, Pa.	January 28, 1863
HESS Ann S. at res of James Hess	Avoca, NY
BRIGGS C. V. of Springwater, NY	December 22, 1862
LAMONT Maryette of Springwater, NY	Avoca, NY
GOFF William S. of Howard, NY	February 1, 1863
VAN WIE Nancy of Howard, NY	
CONNOR Harvey of Avoca, NY	February 12, 1863
SHULTS Maggie of Avoca, NY	
TALBOT J. Montgomery of Rochester, Mn.	February 11, 1863
ERWIN Nancy	
LINDSAY John W. of Bath, NY	March 4, 1863
FAUCETT Matilda Ann dau of Robert Faucett of Bath, NY	
LEE Cyrus Jr. of Cohocton, NY	December 24, 1862
POLMATEER Elizabeth A. of Cohocton, NY	
SMITH Henry of Naples, NY	December 25, 1862
STANTON Susan P. of Cohocton, NY	

YOKUM Swan of Cohocton, NY
VAN KLECK Jane of Cohocton, NY

January 4, 1863

LARROWE Alburtus of Liberty, NY
DRAPER Julia A. of Liberty, NY

February 25, 1863

SMITH Zalmon W. of Addison, NY
YOUNG Adelaide A. of Addison, NY

February 21, 1863

HERRON James of Bath, NY
RUTHERFORD Mary Jane of Bath, NY

March 16, 1863

HARRIS Marcus S. of Bath, NY
GREGG Maggie E. of Bath, NY

March 31, 1863

EDWARDS A. C. of Bradford, NY
NEAR Flora A. of Savona, NY

February 18, 1863
Savona, NY

MORSE William H. of Campbell, NY
HUBBARD Sarah Eveline of Campbell, NY

March 14, 1863
Campbell, NY

SHARP William Pastor Baptist Church Bennettsburg, NY
PATCHIN Rosaltha of Dix, NY

March 4, 1863
Dix, NY

DAVIS Theodore T. of Chicago, Ill.
GUINNIP Sarah C. of Savona, NY

March 27, 1863
Savona, NY

LACOST Charles of Savona, NY
SMITH Mary Frances of Tyrone, NY

March 27, 1863
Savona, NY

BARNES Rev. J. D. of Bath, NY
CORBETT Mary R. of Binghamton, NY

April 2, 1863
nr Binghamton, NY

COVAL Jackson of Bath, NY
ROSS Phebe Ann of Canisteo, NY

April 5, 1863

BECKWITH John of Bath, NY
SCOTT Jane of Bath, NY

April 7, 1863
Bath, NY

MOORE John W. of Milo, NY
COSS Eliza A. of Bath, NY

April 9, 1863
Bath, NY

CURTIS Daniel of Campbell, NY
BROWN Mary A.

May 6, 1863
Bath, NY

HAW Henry of Cohocton, NY
DUNN Sarah M. of Cohocton, NY

May 19, 1863
Bath, NY

HOFFMAN Jacob C. of the 174th Reg. NY Vol.
MEYER Catherine of Baton Rouge, La.

April 28, 1863
Baton Rouge, La.

DUVALL Abram of Hornby, NY   May 29, 1863
YOUMANS Eunice S. of Savona, NY   Bath, NY

PIERCE Sylvester of Urbana, NY   (Newspaper date) June 3, 1863
WHITCOMB Mary E. of Bath, NY   Bath, NY

HAGADORN Stephen H. of Bath, NY   June 2, 1863
WILLIAMS Hulda H. of Naples, NY   Naples, NY

RICE Alfred of Pulteney, NY   June 7, 1863
RILEY Maria B. of Pulteney, NY   Pulteney, NY

ST JOHN Frederick   June 16, 1863
CHAMPLAIN Jennie of Hammondsport, NY

TOMPKINS S. G. Jr. of Gorham, NY   June 14, 1863
TOWNER Vinnie A. of Prattsburgh, NY   Wheeler, NY

HEES Henry of Avoca, NY   June 24, 1863
DWELLE Maggie of Rushville, NY   Rushville, NY

GELDER James U. D. of Canisteo, NY   May 19, 1863
COVELL Mary Ann of Bath, NY   Bath, NY

WILLSON James A. of Wayland, NY   July 13, 1863
WISE Nancy A. of Cameron, NY   Cameron, NY

GLEASON David of Thurston, NY   July 3, 1863
FULLER Susan J. of Thurston, NY   Bath, NY

TOWNSEND Henry L. of Bath, NY   August 13, 1863
FERRIS Allace M. of Bath, NY   Bath, NY

WOOD Pierson E. of Auburn, NY   August 25, 1863
FRENCH Clarissa E. of Bath, NY

COBURN L. James   August 26, 1863
PUTNAM Helen N.   Prattsburgh, NY

GANSEVOORT Conrad of Bath, NY   September 6, 1863
FINN Nellie M. of Mentor, Ohio   Mentor, Oh.

CAMPBELL Charles of Bath, NY   September 17, 1863
WAGNER Samantha of Bath, NY   Bath, NY

STEWART Warren of Campbell, NY   September 15, 1863
VAN HOUSEN Catherine   Prattsburgh, NY

MOREY Henry   September 6, 1863
LENHART Mary   Bath, NY

BALMORE Thomas   September 26, 1863
O'DAY Mary

BOTTRIEL John W. of Bath, NY   September 29, 1863
ABER Susan M. of Bath, NY   Bath, NY

HALL Franklin of Savona, NY   September 25, 1863
MC GLOTHEN Ruby A. of Bath, NY   Bath, NY

WOODRUFF William of Savona, NY   October 3, 1863
BREWSTER Caroline of Savona, NY

SEARS Ezra S. of Oramel, NY   October 4, 1863
STOCKING Debbie A. of Cameron, NY

KNAPP Frank of Dansville, NY   September 6, 1863
TOWNSEND Martha of Urbana, NY   Urbana, NY

SPRAGUE Alanson W. of Bath, NY   September 23, 1863
CHAPIN Lucy E. of Bath, NY

BRUNDAGE Morris of Urbana, NY   October 14, 1863
WYGANT Maria F. of Urbana, NY   Urbana, NY

BEEBE George W. of Dansville, NY   October 21, 1863
MC CAY Jennie youngest dau of Mrs. W. W. Mc Cay   Bath, NY

COLLINS William W. of Denver City   October 22, 1863
ALDRICH Lucinda L.   Dansville, NY

SMEAD James B. of Bath, NY   October 10, 1863
AYLER Anna E. of Baltimore, Md.

WHITEHEAD Hudson J. of Bath, NY   October 17, 1863
ALLISON Caroline of Bath, NY   Bath, NY

HARRIS William H. of Wheeler, NY   October 25, 1863
BAKER Eliza A. of Wheeler, NY   Bath, NY

BOGARDUS Henry E. of Tuscarora, NY   September 27, 1863
CARR Mary E. of Tuscarora, NY   Knoxville, NY

GRIM George W. of Tuscarora, NY   November 3, 1863
KITTLE Jane H. of Tuscarora, NY   Knoxville, Pa.

WYCKOFF R. S. of Jasper, NY   November 12, 1863
KNIFFEN Clara L. of Bath, NY   Bath, NY

STANTON Alpha S. of Avoca, NY   November 14, 1863
MONROE Harriet L. of Avoca, NY   Bath, NY

CADMUS Lieut. J. M. of 161st Reg. of Bath, NY   October 21, 1863
TOMPKINS Hannah A. of Bath, NY

HESS George P. formerly of Bath, NY   November 12, 1863
MURRY Ella L. of Iowa City, Io.   Iowa City, Io.

LEWIS William of Painted Post, NY   November 22, 1863
PAINE Sarah J. of Bath, NY

DAMOTH Addison G. of Bradford, NY   November 19, 1863
JEWELL Sarah A. of Wayne, NY

FREEMAN Baskin of Bath, NY   November 25, 1863
WYCKOFF Elizabeth S. of Bath, NY

PECK Joel S. of Tyrone, NY   November 19, 1863
CULVER Lola of Tyrone, NY   Altay, NY

BENHAM Martin of Reading, NY   November 22, 1863
KRESS Elizabeth C. of Reading, NY

MC NAMARA James of Hammondsport, NY   November 24, 1863
HOUGHTALING Mrs. B. of Tyrone, NY

WARREN Frank of Bath, NY   November 26, 1863
WILLIS Sophia of Towlesville, NY   Towlesville, NY

HURLBURT H. F. of Hammondsport, NY   December 17, 1863
BENHAM Helen A. of Hammondsport, NY

CRAWFORD Nelson of Reading, NY   December 8, 1863
CULVER Hattie of Reading, NY

ARNOLD A. J. of Wheeler, NY   November 26, 1863
ARNOLD Esther D. of Wheeler, NY

CUMMINGS Martin M. of Bath, NY   December 24, 1863
MORTON Rosina of Bath, NY   Bath, NY

LEE Cyrus of Cohocton, NY   December 26, 1863
HALL Catherine of Cohocton, NY   N. Cohocton, NY

CRANS Jackson   December 23, 1863
INGERSOLL Jennie   Bath, NY

BLACKMAN Frederick   December 25, 1863
PROUTY Harriet   Bath, NY

STANTON Beverly M. of Avoca, NY   January 1, 1864
MONROE Diana A. of Rathbone, NY   Bath, NY

HOPKINS Lewis R.   December 29, 1863
VAN VALKENBURGH Catherine   Prattsburgh, NY

CLARK Eugene K. of Bath, NY   (Newspaper date) January 6, 1864
GRAVES Frances Adelia of Prattsburgh, NY   Prattsburgh, NY

BARNES Enos W. of Bath, NY   January 12, 1864
HURD Sarah A. of Bath, NY   Bath, NY

GRISWOLD John of Tyrone, NY   January 21, 1864
WASHBURN Augusta of Wayne, NY   Hammondsport, NY

DRUM Amos B. of Kanona, NY   January 1, 1864
STRAIT Minerva of Beaver Dams, NY   Bradford, NY

MOSHER George D. of Millport, NY   January 3, 1864
SCOTT Charlotte A. of Bradford, NY   Bradford, NY

BATES Henry   January 18, 1864
HOGARTY Mary   Bath, NY

WILBER James   February 3, 1864
WATROUS Marietta D.

BAIRD Rev. J. R. of the Jasper Circuit   January 29, 1864
SCUTT Eunice of Cameron, NY   W. Cameron, NY

WHITE William A. of Howard, NY   February 3, 1864
GOLIVER Mary A. of Bath, NY   Bath, NY

PRATT William M.   February 11, 1864
WHITE Esther J.   Bath, NY

JENNINGS L. A. of Addison, NY   February 10, 1864
MATHER Mary of Rathbone, NY   Rathbone, NY

ROBINSON Silas of Urbana, NY   February 17, 1864
DYKES Catherine E. of Urbana, NY   Urbana, NY

KNAPP James B. of Canisteo, NY   January 18, 1864
CRONKRITE Nancie J. of Tyrone, NY   Tyrone, NY

CHEESEMAN Charles L. of Jasper, NY   January 18, 1864
KNAPP Hattie S. of Cameron, NY   Tyrone, NY

GRAVES Asher   February 23, 1864
LEWIS Christina   Prattsburgh, NY

BARTO William S. of Caton, NY   March 1, 1864
WARNER Mary E. of Bath, NY   Bath, NY

TORRENCE W. B. of Cameron, NY	March 5, 1864
SEARS Martha D. of Cameron, NY	Thurston, NY
BAILEY Daniel E. of Rathbone, NY	March 17, 1864
KNAPP Catherine of Cameron, NY	Cameron, NY
WILBER George of Bath, NY	March 9, 1864
TOWNSEND Mary J. of Bath, NY	Bath, NY
MC CAIG Richard of Rathbone, NY	March 22, 1864
LAING Grace of Penn Yan, NY	Bath, NY
BURTON G. E. of Corning, NY	March 27, 1864
SMITH Mrs. Althea of Otisco, NY	Prattsburgh, NY
ORR Samuel of Orange, NY	March 21, 1864
ROLSTON Ruth of Howard, NY	Howard, NY
GOULD Garret C. of Bath, NY	April 10, 1864
MILLER Sarah E. of Bath, NY	Savona, NY
VAN LOON Jeremiah C. of Bath, NY (Newspaper date)	April 20, 1864
WARREN Ellen M. of Bath, NY	
RITCHMYER John H. of Thurston, NY	April 13, 1864
NILES Azalia S. of Bath, NY	Bath, NY
MATHEWS Manly T. of Watkins, NY	April 21, 1864
OSTRANDER Sarah of Kanona, NY	Kanona, NY
BRECK George W.	May 19, 1864
RANDALL Angie dau of Jacob Randall of Harlem, NY	Bath, NY
BENNETT Wallis of Howard, NY	June 9, 1864
EMSLEY F. Eloise of Greenwood, NY	Greenwood, NY
SEXTON Mike of Bath, NY	June 2, 1864
MC CONE Ophelia Elmore of Vincennes, Ind.	St. Louis, Mo.
EDGETT Andrew I. of Howard, NY	June 16, 1864
STRATTON Laura A. of Bath, NY	Prattsburgh, NY
WILCOX Thomas F. of Bath, NY	July 4, 1864
FAY Flora A. of Bath, NY	Bath, NY
HENDERSON James M. of Buffalo, NY	June 20, 1864
GILLETT Mrs. Frances Elizabeth dau of John **LEWIS**	Prattsburgh, NY
CROSSMAN George of Pulteney, NY	July 4, 1864
CLARK Mary of Pulteney, NY	Pulteney, NY

BARBER Cpl. John W. Co. K. 86th Reg. of Rathbone, NY   May 29, 1864
BAILEY Mrs. Sally E. of Rathbone, NY   Rathbone, NY

TOMPKINS A. J. of Sonora, NY   July 17, 1864
TEEPLE Emma M. of Sonora, NY   Sonora, NY

ALLEN William of Bath, NY   July 22, 1864
CRARY Ellen of Bath, NY   Bath, NY

PUGSLEY William H. of Thurston, NY   August 17, 1864
MINIER Almira J. of Thurston, NY   Thurston, NY

ROGERS Delvan of Bath, NY   August 22, 1864
STRATTON Maggie of Urbana, NY   Bath, NY

MATHER Cornelius B. formerly of Bath, NY   August 10, 1864
RADEKER Mary M. of Lawrenceville, Pa.   Lawrenceville, Pa.

WIXOM Alonzo J. of Wayne, NY   August 15, 1864
WELLES Maggie of Wayne, NY   Wayne, NY

GARRISON John T. of Urbana, NY   September 7, 1864
SPRAGUE Harriet of Urbana, NY   Bath, NY

FISK Phineas of Campbell, NY   September 14, 1864
SWEEZEY Fanny of Hammondsport, NY   Kanona, NY

SMITH Edward M. of Bath, NY   September 14, 1864
EVANS Idella of Hammondsport, NY   Kanona, NY

WHEELER William H. of Wheeler, NY   September 15, 1864
MC NULTY Maggie of Bath, NY   Bath, NY

BARKER James M. of Pittsfield, Ma.   September 21, 1864
WHITING Helena of Bath, NY   Bath, NY

DUNTON Julius C. of Bath, NY   September 11, 1864
WOODWARD Philenda A. of Bath, NY   Savona, NY

ROYER William H.   October 21, 1864
WILCOX Phonetta   Bath, NY

RUTHERFORD Daniel of Bath, NY   October 19, 1864
BECKWITH Martha C. of Bath, NY   Bath, NY

HITCHCOCK Charles A. of Auburn, NY   October 19, 1864
GREEN Celestia A. adopted dau of D. H. **BURROUGHS**   Bath, NY

OLIVER F. X. of Lawrence, Ks.   October 25, 1864
MARCY Anna M. of Avoca, NY   Avoca, NY

STRONG Seth   November 15, 1864
COOK Kate R. of Prattsburgh, NY   Prattsburgh, NY

OLMSTEAD John of Avoca, NY   November 26, 1864
VAN WIE Lucinda of Howard, NY   Howard, NY

HUDSON Richard V. of Auburn, NY   December 1, 1864
CHEENEY Louisia dau of Dr. Walter S. Cheeney   Prattsburgh, NY

WILBUR A. D. of Auburn, NY formerly of Bath, NY   December 8, 1864
KERR Kittie of Seneca Falls, NY   Seneca Falls, NY

GARRISON Emanuel of Hamilton, Oh.   December 6, 1864
OTIS E. Sophia of Avoca, NY   Avoca, NY

GREGG THomas W. of Thurston, NY   December 14, 1864
WILBUR Lucinda A. dau of Samuel Wilbur of Thurston, NY Thurston, NY

JOHNSON Sylvester E. W. of Avon, NY   December 21, 1864
ELLAS Minerva H. of Bath, NY   Bath, NY

BEARD Aaron of Bath, NY   November 8, 1864
HONEY Mrs. Arminda of Dundee, NY   Savona, NY

STEVENS Benjamin of Blairstown, NJ   December 4, 1864
THOMPSON Kate M. of Bath, NY   Savona, NY

RAYMOND Simon S. of Italy Hill, NY   December 5, 1864
GREGORY Sarah E. of Campbell, NY   Campbell, NY

LARROWE Stewart of Wheeler, NY   January 1, 1865
CLARK Libbie of Wheeler, NY   Mitchellville, NY

FAIRCHILD Edward   December 26, 1864
VORHIS Carrie   Hammondsport, NY

HOPKINS E. H. of Prattsburgh, NY   (Newspaper date) January 11, 1865
MC KAY Jennie H. of Naples, NY   Norwich, Ct.

GILLSON Frank E. of Hornellsville, NY   January 4, 1865
ADAMS Mary Jane of Bath, NY   Bath, NY

BALDWIN D. W.   December 24, 1864
LEWIS Anna Y. dau of Sebastian Lewis   Prattsburgh, NY

HOWELL Ambrose Spencer of Bath, NY   January 26, 1865
DUTCHER Mary Woods of Bath, NY   Bath, NY

PADDOCK Thomas S. of Cleveland, Oh.   January 1, 1865
DE WOLFE Jennie E. of Bath, NY   Bath, NY

WOHLGEMUTH Rev. William E. of E. Genesee Conf.   February 9, 1865
WILLIS Sarah of Rochester, NY   Rochester, NY

BENNETT Peter of Urbana, NY   February 19, 1865
HORTON Ann E. of Pulteney, NY   Pulteney, NY

COWLES Francis N. of Wellsville, NY   March 5, 1865
SMALLIDGE Saloma A. of Bath, NY   Bath, NY

PARKER George W. of Sonora, NY   March 5, 1865
MILLS Sarah E. of Campbell, NY   Bath, NY

CALDWELL R. of Brooklyn, NY   February 20, 1965
BELL Ollie of Harford, NY   Harford, NY

EDSON Benjamin S.   March 2, 1865
CARSON Mary Jane   Prattsburgh, NY

HAND William G. of Bath, NY   March 16, 1865
SPENCER Harriet A. of Vestal, NY

DAMOTH George of Bradford, NY   March 28, 1865
DILDINE Eliza of Hammondsport, NY   Bath, NY

LEONARD Solymon M. of Troy, Pa.   April 13, 1865
HASTINGS Libbie M. of Hammondsport, NY

COOK Warner of Avoca, NY   March 30, 1865
LAFLIN Nellie of Bath, NY

BRINK William H. of Savona, NY   April 30, 1865
SHANNON Helen dau of Dr. Thomas Shannon of Savona, NY Savona, NY

STORY John of Bath, NY   April 20, 1865
LUCAS Emeline D. of Bath, NY   Bath, NY

BROWN Valentine of Galen, NY   May 8, 1865
CLOSS Eliza Ann of Galen, NY   Bath, NY

PIERCE George of Bath, NY   May 17, 1865
WOODRUFF Mary J. of Bath, NY   Bath, NY

WHITWOOD Deo of Canisteo, NY   June 1, 1864
POTTER Amelia F. of Addison, NY   Bath, NY

STROWBRIDGE Lyman M. of Potter, NY   June 7, 1865
BAKER Emma S. of Prattsburgh, NY   Pulteney, NY

FAULKNER Dorr of Dansville, NY   May 22, 1865
GROVER Letetia A. of Hornellsville, NY   Hornellsville, NY

SNELL Andrew P. of Bath, NY	June 22, 1865
KINKADE Susan E. of Avoca, NY	Avoca, NY
NUTT Edwin H. of Dresden, NY	June 21, 1865
CHEENEY Abby	Prattsburgh, NY
BIRD David F. of Urbana, NY	July 11, 1865
TRAVIS Eleanor A. of Howard, NY	Bath, NY
ROBINSON James of Hudson, NJ	July 23, 1865
JUDD Emily of Cameron, NY	Painted Post, NY
MILLER G. A. of Corning, NY	July 24, 1865
DE GROAT Alice of Erwin, NY	Painted Post, NY
BULLOCK George W. of Addison, NY	July 25, 1865
DEVOE Amelia C. of New York City	Painted Post, NY
SAMPSON Samuel of Eagle Harbor, NY	August 19, 1865
THOMAS Georgianna of Bath, NY	Bath, NY
FLYNN Lester of Bath, NY	August 20, 1865
LYMAN Mary L. of Bath, NY	Bath, NY
DUNTON Stephen B. of Lyons, NY	August 24, 1865
BLYNN Eliza M. of Bath, NY	Bath, NY
THOMPSON William H. of Howard, NY	August 29, 1865
VANDERLINDER Sarah J. of Howard, NY	Bath, NY
FAUCETT Samuel of Bath, NY	August 20, 1865
WOOLAND Jane of Bath, NY	Bath, NY
JEFFREY Nathan C. of Avoca, NY	September 4, 1865
PARKHILL Alberta of Avoca, NY	Avoca, NY
GOULD Abram S. of Bath, NY	September 8, 1865
PLAISTED Lizzie A. of W. Union, NY	W. Union, NY
SHEPARD William H. of Albany, NY	September 13, 1865
CHURCH Adelaide dau of I. V. Church	New York City
BUTTS Charles H. of Bath, NY	September 21, 1865
PLATT Charlotte A. of Bath, NY	Bath, NY
ROGERS Noah N. of Cornwall, Ct.	September 21, 1865
DUDLEY Ann E. of Bath, NY	Bath, NY
CLARK Asa of Howard, NY	September 26, 1865
HATHAWAY Mrs. Lucinda of Towlesville, NY	

RUSSELL Peter B. of Urbana, NY	September 30, 1865
OSTRANDER Mrs. Emily of Urbana, NY	Pulteney, NY
HARE Henry C.	October 1, 1865
WILSON Mrs. Mary	Centerville, NY
DURFEE Elon G. of Hornellsville, NY	October 3, 1865
TAYLOR Emily D. dau of W. C. Taylor of Elmira, NY	Elmira, NY
CHURCH Frederick L. of Rathbone, NY	August 23, 1865
BUTLER Julia L. of Rathbone, NY	Cameron, NY
DE PUY W. R. of Campbell, NY	October 10, 1865
CRANDALL Ella of Springville, NY	Springville, NY
CLARK Lewis of Fall Brook, Pa.	October 11, 1865
STRATTON Eliza of Fall Brook, Pa.	Fall Brook, Pa.
WILLDRAKE Solomon L. of Woodhull, NY	October 10, 1865
HALLETT Eliza of Cameron, NY	Cameron, NY
PINNEY Martin	October 19, 1865
SMITH Mrs. Bishop	Prattsburgh, NY
BRIGGS Charles of Urbana, NY	October 25, 1865
BRUSH Harriet of Kanona, NY	Bath, NY
PHELPS David of Corbit Hollow, NY	October 20, 1865
BENNETT Harriet of Wayne, NY	Wayne, NY
WILLSON John H.	October 25, 1865
BULL Carrie D. dau of Col. W. H. Bull	Bath, NY
SMEAD Edwin S. of Bath, NY	October 24, 1865
AYLER M. F. of Baltimore, Md.	Baltimore, Md.
BAPTIS George of Brooklyn, NY	July 25, 1865
ROBERTSON Nellie M. of Dansville, NY	Dansville, NY
HOUSE Ansel of Howard, NY	September 12, 1865
PHILLIPS Mrs. Miranda of Howard, NY	Howard, NY
HOLDEN Joseph of Fremont, NY	September 26, 1865
BARBER Fanny D. of Fremont, NY	Howard, NY
HOWARD Cooley D. of Avoca, NY	October 17, 1865
HOAGLAND Mrs. Samantha of Avoca, NY	Howard, NY
BUMP Onatus of Cameron, NY	October 28, 1865
QUICK Alvira of Cameron, NY	Rathbone, NY

HARRISON Daniel C. of Avoca, NY   November 5, 1865
CLARK Julia of Howard, NY   Howard, NY

PARKER Charles L. of Thurston, NY   November 9, 1865
STOCKING Elizabeth P. of Thurston, NY   Thurston, NY

DANIELS Orrin P. of Bath, NY   (Newspaper date) November 29, 1865
NILES Mary E. of Bath, NY at res. of Mrs. Silva BORDEN

THOMAS Stephen S. of the 86th Reg. NYS Vol.   October 27, 1865
SCHENCK Sarah M. of Bath, NY   Savona, NY

CLAWSON Lt. John M. of the 107th Reg. NYS Vol.   October 21, 1865
DRAKE Lucinda R. of Bath, NY   Bath, NY

CLARKE A. J. of the 161st Reg. NYS Vol.   November 18, 1865
NOBLES Emeline of Bath, NY   Bath, NY

NOBLES Isaac of Bath, NY   November 19, 1865
ALLERTON Annetta of Bath, NY   Bath, NY

BOARDMAN Louis of Hornellsville, NY   December 6, 1865
READ Lizzie of Bath, NY   Bath, NY

BURRELL Roger H. of Halls Corners, NY   November 29, 1865
KENNEDY Barbara Ann dau of John Kennedy   Italy Hill, NY

CORYELL John of Paulteney, NY   November 30, 1865
SEDDICK Rosette of Marenge, Ill.   Prattsburgh, NY

VAN ORSDALE Allen A. of Jasper, NY   December 13, 1865
DECK Sarah P. dau of Dr. Solomon Deck of Jasper, NY   Jasper, NY

HALL Jerry of the 107th Reg. NYS Vol.   December 9, 1865
HOLLEY Jennie of Savona, NY   Savona, NY

PUTNAM Enos of Cooper's Plains, NY   December 13, 1865
RUTHERFORD Hattie of Thurston, NY   Thurston, NY

HELM Z. S. of the 50th Reg.   December 25, 1865
ABEL Anna of Bath, NY   Bath, NY

BOSTWICK Hiram W. of New York City   December 27, 1865
JOHNSON Louise dau of T. A. Johnson   Corning, NY

SLY John of Corning, NY   December 28, 1865
BONHAM Mrs. A. of Corning, NY

HENDERSHOTT William A. of Bath, NY   January 1, 1866
COSS Leah B. of Bath, NY   Bath, NY

JOHNSTON Hector M. of Caton, NY
COSS Delia B. of Bath, NY

January 1, 1866
Bath, NY

BENNETT John R. of Bath, NY
GRAY Katie E. of Kanona, NY

December 27, 1865
Kanona, NY

DERRICK Ohillip
DARICK Margaret

December 13, 1865
Wheeler, NY

CARPENTER Harlow of Addison, NY
HAMMOND Della of Coopers Plains, NY

December 23, 1865
Coopers Plains, NY

BUCHANAN William M. of Caton, NY
WIDGER Minerva E. of Caton, NY

December 24, 1865
Painted Post, NY

CHAPPELL Oliver N. of Prattsburgh, NY
GELDER Mary A. of Prattsburgh, NY

January 2, 1866
Prattsburgh, NY

PIERCE John of Parishville, NY
GREEN Lucy dau of J. B. Green

January 18, 1866
Prattsburgh, NY

WAGGONER Nicholas of Cohocton, NY
DEWEY Caroline O. of Cohocton, NY

February 4, 1866
Cohocton, NY

TITUS Charles of Rathbone, NY
LANNING Mary C. of Woodhull, NY

January 20, 1866
Bath, NY

TURNER Isaac L. of Canandaigua, NY
BURROUGHS S. Amelia of Prattsburgh, NY

February 8, 1866

VAN KEUREN Joshua of Savona, NY
PARKER Mary E. of Savona, NY

February 17, 1866
Bath, NY

HALL Peter of Hammondsport, NY
LARROWE Clarrie of Hammondsport, NY

February 26, 1866
Bath, NY

QUAKENBUSH Willson W. of Bath, NY
BRIGGS Frankie O. dau of William S. of Penn Yan, NY

March 7, 1866
Penn Yan, NY

HELM J. S. of Thurston, NY
BREWSTER Libbie A. of Bath, NY

March 7, 1866
Bath, NY

RENCHARD Frank of Wheeler, NY
GREEN Jane dau of J. B. Green

March 1, 1866
Prattsburgh, NY

WIXOM Guy D.
HOTCHKIN Hattie R.

March 16, 1866
Prattsburgh, NY

SMITH A. V. of Savona, NY
MOORE Annette of Savona, NY

March 13, 1866
Savona, NY

SHEPARD John F. of New York City
DUTCHER Pamelia W. of Bath, NY

March 20, 1866

TALBOT George W. of Jasper, NY
CLARK Aseneth E. of Canisteo, NY

March 14, 1866
Bath, NY

DUSENBERRY Dwight of Thurston, NY
COLLIER Terzah of Bath, NY

March 17, 1866
Bath, NY

JONES Albert F.
LEWIS Kate dau of Groton Lewis

March 21, 1866
Prattsburgh, NY

HADLEY George F. of Bath, NY
BUTLER Julia of Bath, NY

March 22, 1866
Bath, NY

BENNETT Stephen Gates of Bluff Pt., NY
STYLES Hattie A. of Penn Yan, NY

March 21, 1866
Bath, NY

GRAHAM Miles G. of Bath, NY
RUTHERFORD Sarah J. of New York City

March 19, 1866
New York City

RUSSELL Lewis P. of Howard, NY
ROBINSON Mary E. of Avoca, NY

March 26, 1866
Avoca, NY

BRUNDAGE Gratton H. of Bath, NY
GRAY Clara niece of L. F. **MYRTLE** of Wheeler, NY

March 27, 1866
Wheeler, NY

WILSON James H. of Bath, NY
MARTIN Lizzie of Avoca, NY

March 27, 1866

LONGWELL Frank of Barrington, NY
BABCOCK Susan of Bradford, NY

March 14, 1866
Bradford, NY

BROWN A. U. formerly of the 161st Reg. NYV
STANTON Vinnie of Howard, NY

March 28, 1866
Howard, NY

TOWNER Charles S. of Campbell, NY
EDGAR Mary M. of Bath, NY

April 19, 1866
Sonora, NY

MARSH Washington of Elmira, NY
STEWART Carrie of Bath, NY

April 25, 1866
Bath, NY

HILL Monroe of Caton, NY
CRANDALL Henrietta M. of Cameron, NY

May 28, 1866
Bath, NY

CHIDSEY William H.
WAGSTAFF Josephine E. of Pulteney, NY

May 16, 1866
Pulteney, NY

WOOD Ira N. of Wayne, NY formerly of the 141st Reg.
FULLER Sarah O. of Bradford, NY

May 27, 1866
Weston, NY

SUTHERLAND John of Bath, NY   June 5, 1866
SHAUT Clara of Bath, NY   Bath, NY

STANTON Clark of Oxford, Mi.   June 14, 1866
JACKSON Fidelia dau of Stephen A. Jackson   Prattsburgh, NY

BRINK Judson of Mn.   June 19, 1866
ST JOHN Jennett of Pulteney, NY   Pulteney, NY

BROOKS James F. of Troupsburgh, NY   June 24, 1866
WILCOX Carolin B. of Troupsburgh, NY   Jasper, NY

POOLE James of Bath, NY   July 1, 1866
SCOTT Elizabeth of Bath, NY   Bath, NY

TAYLOR Irving of Bath, NY   July 3, 1866
HARRIS Abby H. of Bath, NY   Bath, NY

HOTCHKISS Mortimer   July 4, 1866
KISHBAUGH Nettie of S. Bristol, NY   Prattsburgh, NY

JONES Frank Z. of New York City   July 28, 1866
DE WOLFE Mara E. of Bath, NY   Bath, NY

DE WITT Jacob C. of Bath, NY   July 28, 1866
GAY Emily J. of Bath, NY   Bath, NY

ARMSTRONG John D. of Bath, NY   August 25, 1866
POLMATEER Sarah Ann of Avoca, NY

BENTON Norman of Bath, NY   August 22, 1866
FINCH Lydia A. of Bath, NY   Bath, NY

HALL Samuel of Almond, NY   August 26, 1866
PAGE Levica of Bath, NY   Bath, NY

LOGHRY Joseph B. of Bath, NY   August 17, 1866
CHAPMAN Mrs. Emma N. of Bath, NY   Bath, NY

CHESLER Charles of Naples, NY   August 18, 1866
HUBER frederica of Bath, NY

QUAKENBUSH George of Bath, NY   September 5, 1866
DAVISON Anna of Bath, NY   Bath, NY

DILDINE Alfred of Groveland, NY   September 5, 1866
BALEY Isabel of Groveland, NY   Bath, NY

FERRIS Isaac H.   July 3, 1866
GREEK Mary Jane   Bath, NY

COATS Chester H.
STRATTON Mate

August 30, 1866
Bath, NY

JORDAN Henry M.
PELHAM Rosela

September 8, 1866
Wheeler, NY

HERRON Robert of Bath, NY
CLARK Hattie A of Howard, NY

September 16, 1866
Howard, NY

DORSEY Daniel H. of Bath, NY
STORY Diantha C. of Bath, NY

September 13, 1866

ANGELL Joseph of Brooklyn, NY
HARDENBROOK Libbie of Bath, NY

September 26, 1866
Bath, NY

SMITH Dr. Ira P. of Bath, NY   (Newspaper date) October 24, 1866
SMITH Hattie E. dau of John J. Smith of Bath, NY

SHATTUCK Harrison A. of Bath, NY
TOWNSEND Charlotte of Bath, NY

October 14, 1866
Bath, NY

MONTGOMERY James of Dansville, NY
WILEY Elizabeth B. of Woodhull, NY

October 17, 1866
Troupsburgh, NY

CROMMER Oliver of Wayne, NY
COOK Mary of Wayne, NY

October 13, 1866
Wayne, NY

PARK R. C. of Canisteo, NY
COUNTRYMAN Kittie dau of Solomon of Jasper, NY

October 3, 1866
Jasper, NY

VAN ORSDALE Charles J. of Jasper, NY
COUNTRYMAN Nellie E. dau of Solomon of Jasper, NY

October 3, 1866
Jasper, NY

DANIELS William H. of Bath, NY
SITTERLY Eliza Ann of Bath, NY

October 25, 1866
Bath, NY

HEILER L. G. of Conneaut, Oh.
CLARK Franc A. of Prattsburgh, NY

October 31, 1866
Bath, NY

EDWARDS Jacob of Corning, NY
CARTER Adelaide of Bath, NY

October 24, 1866
Bath, NY

COATES Charles M. of Wheeler, NY
LA FARGE Frank of Bath, NY

November 1, 1866
Bath, NY

BRYANT Hicks
BROWN Eliza

November 1, 1866
Bath, NY

BRYAN D. B. of Sonora, NY
KNIGHT Mrs.Jane B. of Farmer Village, NY

November 8, 1866
Farmer Village, NY

ORMSBY Orman W.
WALLACE Clementine

November 1, 1866

KING Charles F. of Savona, NY
HUGHES Mrs. Sarah C. of Savona, NY

November 8, 1866
Savona, NY

WHITE Martin L. of Cameron, NY
HALLETT Savannah of Adrian, NY

November 7, 1866
Adrian, NY

BABCOCK Wilson W. of Elmira, NY
HOVEY Catherine of Liberty, NY at father's

November 14, 1866
Liberty, NY

MATTESON W. H. of Ronald, Mi.
VAN WORMER Zilpha of Liberty, NY

November 14, 1866
Liberty, NY

WINNIE C. W.
SHEPARD Fannie dau of George

November 8, 1866
Hammondsport, NY

CORR Jaline of Urbana, NY
SPRAGUE Susan E. of Urbana, NY

November 8, 1866
Urbana, NY

WALSH James H. of Tyrone, NY
WASHBURN Annie H. of Tyrone, NY

November 24, 1866
Bath, NY

SYLIMON Peter of Urbana, NY
MOWERS Phebe E. of Bath, NY

December 2, 1866
Bath, NY

MERRING George E. of Rathbone, NY
COLE Jane P. of Rathbone, NY

December 1, 1866
Bath, NY

ROLFE De Forest P. of Nebraska City, Neb. Terr.
GILMORE Susan of Bath, NY

December 6, 1866
Bath, NY

ELLSWORTH Stewart S. of Penn Yan, NY
MAGEE Hebe P. dau of John of Watkins, NY

December 12, 1866
Watkins, NY

BIGELOW Samuel O. of Buffalo, NY
PERRY Mary L. of Buffalo, NY

December 12, 1866
Bath, NY

FRENCH Philemon of Wheeler, NY
BRUSH Helen of Wheeler, NY

October 3, 1866

RICE William C. of Wheeler, NY
FRIES Nancy C. of Wheeler, NY

October 24, 1866

EELLS Horace of Bath, NY
SMITH Anna E. of Bath, NY

December 5, 1866

ALDRICH Leonard of Thurston, NY
RUMSEY Hattie C. of Thurston, NY

December 12, 1866
Risingville, NY

UNDERHILL Edward H. of Bath, NY		December 22, 1866
NORTHRUP A. of Canadensis, Pa.		Canadensis, Pa.
PARKER E. W. of St. Louis, Mo.		December 13, 1866
BROWN Emeline dau of Morris of Penn Yan, NY		Penn Yan, NY
RICHARDSON Edward M. of Bath, NY		December 5, 1866
KNAPP Augusta of Bradford, NY		Bradford, NY
LOCKWOOD Francis H. of Pulteney, NY		December 3, 1866
HERVEY Elizabeth of Pulteney, NY		Hammondsport, NY
MILLER Joseph of Howard, NY		November 21, 1866
FOOT Emma Elizabeth of Howard, NY		
HARRIS William T. of Bath, NY		December 12, 1866
SMITH Ann Eliza of Bath, NY		Bath, NY
MC NEIL Gillis of Bath, NY		December 18, 1866
PLATT Kate of Bath, NY		Bath, NY
VAN WIE James of Howard, NY	(Newspaper date)	December 26, 1866
DAWSON Louisa N. of Bath, NY		Bath, NY
SHAWGER William H. of Thurston, NY		December 23, 1866
MARTIN Maggie		Cosse's Corners, NY
MC ALLISTER Erastus of Wallace, NY		December 15, 1866
OUDERKIRK Sarah S. of Wallace, NY		
BROWNELL Amos of Fremont, NY		December 15, 1866
MILLE Hicks of Bath, NY		
HEVINER Allen D. of Medina, NY		January 1, 1867
BULLARD Ella A. of Bath, NY		Bath, NY
BARRETT William W. of Cameron, NY		December 31, 1866
NILES Louise J. of Bath, NY		Bath, NY
PAYNE Midow W. of Bath, NY		January 1, 1867
CHASE Annis R. of Cameron, NY		
HAIGHT Peter J. of Savona, NY		December 26, 1866
ACKERSON Mary Clara of Savona, NY		Savona, NY
NEWMAN Preston F. of Porter, NY		January 1, 1867
COVERT Hannah Mary of Bradford, NY		Savona, NY
PITTS James M. of Painted Post, NY		January 1, 1867
HOUGHTALING Mary Jane of Painted Post, NY		Savona, NY

SCOFIELD Milton M. of Urbana, NY January 2, 1867
HOAGLAND Margaret A. of Urbana, NY Savona, NY

SMITH Charles W. of Urbana, NY January 5, 1867
SNYDER Eliza M. of Bath, NY

WRIGHT Charles of Bath, NY December 25, 1866
BROOKS Henrietta of Bath, NY Bath, NY

GAGE Elmer of Painesville, Oh. January 1, 1867
SMITH Frances of Bath, NY Bath, NY

LEWIS Joseph of Prattsburgh, NY January 3, 1867
EMERSON Helen C. of Bath, NY Bath, NY

GRIFFITH George G. of Wayne, NY January 9, 1867
COSS Matilda of Bath, NY Bath, NY

GRAY Frederick Stewart of New York City January 2, 1867
HARLOW Julia dau of Rev. M. Harlow of Bath, NY Bath, NY

MILLER George M. of Pulteney, NY January 9, 1867
HOLDEN Harriet P. of Pulteney, NY Pulteney, NY

TRENAMEN George J. of Rochester, NY January 22, 1867
CHASE Melinda of Liberty, NY Liberty, NY

SPRAKER Alexander of Bath, NY January 18, 1867
GLEASON Hannah of Bath, NY Bath, NY

MC ELWEE James G. of Savona, NY January 23, 1867
KING Joie A. of Hedgesville, NY Hedgesville, NY

GRIMES Philander of Bradford, NY January 26, 1867
RICHARDSON Mary of Bradford, NY Savona, NY

BOWERS Benjamin of Thurston, NY January 29, 1867
EDSALL Sarah C. of Thurston, NY Campbell, NY

HOLMES John V. January 29, 1867
DAVIS Eunice P. of Thurston, NY Campbell, NY

WHEELER Clayton M. of Wayland, NY January 20, 1867
GUSTIN Julia A. of Cohocton, NY Liberty, NY

WILLSON Paul of Cohocton, NY January 30, 1867
PARKS Esther V. of Cohocton, NY Liberty, NY

SECOR Isaac W. of Wayland, NY January 30, 1867
WETMORE Frances E. of Cohocton, NY Liberty, NY

STARKS Allen M. of Gainsville, NY
MURRAY Emma L. of Bath, NY
January 30, 1867
Gainsville, NY

TAYLOR William of Wheeler, NY
DAVIS Mrs. Mary of Bath, NY
February 15, 1867
Bath, NY

BURCHARD Melvin of Prattsburgh, NY
KEELER Sarah A. of Avoca, NY
February 20, 1867
Liberty, NY

GREENE Alfred E.
BOYD Betsey
February 20, 1867
Prattsburgh, NY

REYNOLDS Hiram P. of Cuba, NY
FAUCETT Sarah of Bath, NY
March 3, 1867
Bath, NY

DICKEY Erastus of Canisteo, NY
CARRIER Lydia of Canisteo, NY
February 26, 1867
Bath, NY

BURTON P. of Port Byron, NY
HEDDEN Mary E. of Hammondsport, NY
March 4, 1867
Hammondsport, NY

MORSE Garrett C. of Wheeler, NY
BREWER Emma of Wheeler, NY
February 24, 1867

STULL Alber of Newton, NJ
COVERT Alice of Hammondsport, NY
March 10, 1867
Bath, NY

HUBER John A.
RIAN Mary E.
March 21, 1867
Bath, NY

PUTNAM Richard of Wheeler, NY
BROOMON Anna of Prattsburgh, NY
March 20, 1867
Bath, NY

BROOMON James R. of Wheeler, NY
MIDDLETON Jennie of Prattsburgh, NY
March 20, 1867
Bath, NY

MORRISON David H. of Bath, NY
SCARVELL Fannie of Bath, NY
March 29, 1867

MC CARRICK Andrew J. of Southport, NY
CHAPMAN Louisa at res of Samuel Chapman
March 20, 1867
Bath, NY

DEAN George R. of Unionville, Nev. (Newspaper date)
GODFREY Jennie M. of Pulteney, NY
April 10, 1867
Pulteney, NY

RIDDELL William of Canisteo, NY
JONES Helen C. of Avoca, NY at res of David Jones
March 26, 1867
Avoca, NY

BACON John H. of Wheeler, NY
OVERHISER Kate of Wheeler, NY
March 9, 1867
Avoca, NY

HORTON Levi E. of Cameron, NY   April 6, 1867
HICOK Maggie M. of Bath, NY   Bath, NY

GRAHAM Dugald C. of Bath, NY   April 6, 1867
O'CONNOR Mary J. of Bath, NY

WAGGONER A. C. of Wheeler, NY   April 24, 1867
WAGGONER C. C. of Bath, NY   Bath, NY

SPRAGUE Edward of Urbana, NY   April 17, 1867
FERGUSON Anna J. of Webb's Crossing, NY

BUTLER Silas W. of Wheeler, NY   April 27, 1867
TOWNSEND Mrs. Mary A. of Wheeler, NY

STEPHENS Frazier of Canisteo, NY   May 5, 1867
TAILOR Elizabeth A. of Hornellsville, NY   Bath, NY

GREEN Samuel S. of Bath, NY   May 11, 1867
SPRAGUE Hulsa J. of Thurston, NY   Thurston, NY

DRAHMER William of Dansville, NY   June 2, 1867
NICHOLS Libbie of Bath, NY   Bath, NY

OSBORNE George W. of Cameron, NY   June 2, 1867
BORDEN Olive M. of Thurston, NY   Thurston, NY

GREEN John   May 15, 1867
COOLBAUGH Cynthia A.   Savona, NY

RICE Wilder of Howard, NY   May 28, 1867
TOWNER Ella of Avoca, NY   Savona, NY

DORMAN John L. of Bath, NY   June 9, 1867
GANNON Mary A. of Bath, NY   Savona, NY

RENDT Eugene L.   June 12, 1867
FRENCH Josephine A.   Campbell, NY

EDDY N. P. Md. of Geneva, Ill.   June 26, 1867
GREGG Mrs. Ruth E. of Urbana, NY   Bath, NY

BREWER Randall of Bradford, NY   May 19, 1867
INSCHO Permelia A. of Bradford, NY

FAY George B. W. of Bath, NY   June 9, 1867
FLUENT Mrs. Maria J. of Bath, NY

BAUTER John M. of Wheeler, NY   June 13, 1867
THOMPSON Jennie M. of Wheeler, NY

VAN LOON William V. of Prattsburgh, NY	June 23, 1867	
NORTHRUP Adina of Prattsburgh, NY	Pulteney, NY	
ALLEN Duncan S. Md. of Quincy, Mi.	June 26, 1867	
CHASE Anna M. dau of N. B. Chase of Avoca, NY	Avoca, NY	
JOHNSON James of Bath, NY	July 7, 1867	
CALKINS Mary of Thurston, NY at res of Sally **CONCORD**	Thurston, NY	
RUNION J. Bird of Shiawasse, Mi.	August 15, 1867	
WHITE Henrietta dau of J. White Jr.	Bath, NY	
TRACY Benjamin J. of Townsend, NY	July 31, 1867	
FAIRCHILD Franc E. dau of Corydon Ed. of Ovid Bee	Ovid, NY	
SACKETT Rockanbean of Cameron, NY	July 29, 1867	
PECK Frances of Canisteo, NY	Cosse's Corners, NY	
THARP Charles of Thurston, NY	August 17, 1867	
KNICKERBOCKER Eliza A. of Thurston, NY	Cosse's Corners, NY	
BUNDA George of Cameron, NY	August 28, 1867	
ANABLE Mary J. of Cameron, NY	Cameron, NY	
CARRINGTON Charles Frederick of Philadelphia, Pa.	September 4, 1867	
SOMERVILLE Mary dau of Rev. O. R. of Howard, NY	Bath, NY	
GATES David W. Pastor M. E. Church Mitchellville, NY	September 4, 1867	
PURDY Marion H. dau of Charles Purdy of Bath, NY	Bath, NY	
SEAGER William L. of Thurston, NY	September 5, 1867	
CREVELING Eleanor of Thurston, NY	Savona, NY	
SEAGER Roselle of Sonora, NY	September 11, 1867	
KING Georgietta of Sonora, NY	Bath, NY	
LAKE James of Hannibal, NY	September 19, 1867	
WIXON Urania of Bath, NY	Bath, NY	
PRATT S. D. of Bradford, NY	September 15, 1867	
ANGELL A. A. of Penn Yan, NY at William **JORDAN** res	Tyrone, NY	
WILLIAMS John J. of S. Dansville, NY (Newspaper date)	October 2, 1867	
TYLER Mattie A. of Savona, NY		
MC CHESNEY James of Howard, NY	October 6, 1867	
MINTERE Harriet of Howard, NY	Bath, NY	
OTIS Austin H. of Kanona, NY	October 9, 1867	
HILL Elizabeth of Kanona, NY	Kanona, NY	

HOSFORD Seymour A. of Thurston, NY
KNAPP Mary L. of Bath, NY

October 12, 1867
Bath, NY

CUMMINGS Daniel L. of Bath, NY
GAGE Alice of Cameron, NY

October 16, 1867
Bath, NY

WHITEHEAD Alexander of Bath, NY
WILLIAMS Susan A. of N. Cameron, NY

October 9, 1867
N. Cameron, NY

WARNER Orren P. of Emporium, Pa.
ATWATER Mary R. of Jerseyshore, Pa.

October 18, 1867
Bath, NY

PRENTISS Adams of Pulteney, NY
CARPENTER Ellen of Pulteney, NY

October 15, 1867
Pulteney, NY

SAVAGE Rev. Eleazor of Rochester, NY formerly of Bath
TUTTLE Mrs. Ellen F. of Bath, NY

October 23,1867
Bath, NY

BRAUGHT Henry of Bath, NY
HOTCHKISS Sarah A. of Bath, NY

October 30, 1867

ALLEN Eugene C. of Bath, NY
HAVENS Rachel of Bath, NY

October 31, 1867
Bath, NY

CLARK John of Campbell, NY
BARIT Judith of Campbell, NY

October 29, 1867

VAN GELDER E. Clinton
JACOBUS Julia A. at res of Isaac Jacobus

October 30, 1867
Bath, NY

FAGENS Jeremiah of Bath, NY
GARDNER Sarah of Bath, NY

October 31, 1867
Bath, NY

BALLARD Cyrus of Tyrone, NY
KNICKERBOCKER Catherine A. of Orange, NY

November 14, 1867
Bath, NY

WALTERS Willis J.
GRISWOLD Lisetta of Avoca, NY

October 10, 1867
Avoca, NY

ROBBINS F. D. of Dansville, NY
KNAPP M. L. dau of H. T. of Ossian, NY

November 5, 1867
Ossian, NY

AUSTIN Dayton C. of Marshall, Mi.
BAILEY Maggie A. of Cameron, NY

November 24, 1867
Bath, NY

CASTOR Charles of Wheeler, NY
STEVENS Rhoda M. of Wheeler, NY

November 17, 1867
Avoca, NY

RIDENOUR John M. of Union Co. Ind.
HEES Catherine of Avoca, NY

November 27, 1867
Avoca, NY

HAMILTON Lewis of Campbell, NY   (Newspaper date) December 4, 1867
BARRETT Mahetabel of Campbell, NY   Campbell, NY

VUNCK William H. of Avoca, NY   December 5, 1867
SPRAKER Maggie of Bath, NY   Bath, NY

WOODWORTH Alfred B. of Ulysses, NY   December 18, 1867
NICHOLS Clara dau of Rev. S. Nichols of Bath, NY   Bath, NY

YOST Charles W. of Cameron, NY   (Newspaper date) January 1, 1868
GAGE Phebe E. of Cameron, NY   Bath, NY

CRANE William of Cameron, NY   November 24, 1867
SABIN Fanny of Cameron, NY   Cameron, NY

BREWER William of Wheeler, NY   December 11, 1867
ALLEN Mary Jane of Bath, NY

WISE George W. of Bath, NY   December 25, 1867
CLARK Annie K. of Bath, NY

HINES Anthony of Bath, NY   December 26, 1867
WILSON Parmelia J. of Bath, NY

TOWLE P. Stewart of Bath, NY   December 12, 1867
BROTHER Mary dau of Henry Brother of Bath, NY   Bath, NY

HALL Francis L. of Barrington, NY   December 31, 1867
HINES Catherine C. of Cameron, NY   Bath, NY

PIERCE Stephen B. of Covert, NY   December 31, 1867
CLARK Sarah E. of Jasper, NY   Bath, NY

SPRINGSTEAD Prof. O. of Saybrook, Ill.   December 25, 1867
CARTER M. E. of Bath, NY   Bath, NY

TOMLINSON Watson M. of N. Urbana, NY (News. date)   January 8, 1867
DYKES Mrs. Amanda O. dau of Rev. A. **ORCUTT**   Sonora, NY

MOTHERSELL D. T. of Middlesex, NY   December 25, 1867
CROSS A. M. of Pulteney, NY

HAWE James of Bath, NY   January 18, 1868
EARLE Sarah J. of Bath, NY

NILES Jerome H. of Bath, NY   January 15, 1868
WAGNER Catherine of Bath, NY   Bath, NY

NEWTON Dallas of Birdsall, NY   January 1, 1868
BAILEY Roxie of Urbana, NY   Wayne, NY

FORD George of Barrington, NY   January 15, 1868
HALL Mary F. of Barrington, NY   Wayne, NY

DOXTADER John   January 9, 1868
WHEELER Clara of Avoca, NY   Avoca, NY

MURRAY Lindley of New York City   January 15, 1868
MC CAY Sarah dau of W. B. Mc Cay of Bath, NY   Bath, NY

ELLIS Ebenezer of Bath, NY   January 22, 1868
WARD Sarah A. dau of Dr. L. A. Ward of Hornellsville, NY   Hornellsville, NY

REED J. C. of Bolivar, NY   January 28, 1868
ROLFE Perthenia J. of Avoca, NY   Lawrenceville, Pa.

CAMPBELL Robert of Bath, NY   February 5, 1868
CURTIS Frances A. of Bath, NY   Bath, NY

LOCKWOOD Samuel of Tyrone, NY   February 23, 1868
GRACE Catherine of Wayne, NY   Bath, NY

SHARP David   February 24, 1868
CHARLTON Rebecca   Bath, NY

BAILEY Charles L. of Hammondsport, NY   February 26, 1868
BACHUS Lydia of Savona, NY   Bath, NY

MC FIE Alexander B. of Urbana, NY   March 3, 1868
BRUNDAGE Eliza H. of Urbana, NY   Urbana, NY

OVENSHIRE Henry C. of Urbana, NY   March 4, 1868
SCOFIELD Sally A. of Urbana, NY   Urbana, NY

DART Henry of Pulteney, NY   March 7, 1868
MC CHESNEY Miss ____ of Howard, NY   Bath, NY

ABBOTT Theodore H. of Urbana, NY   March 8, 1868
BARRETT Ann B. of Urbana, NY   Bath, NY

FAUCETT Henry of Bath, NY   March 11, 1868
BRUNDAGE Kate of Bath, NY

CLEMMONS George of Dansville, NY   March 11, 1868
CHICHESTER Dora of Wheeler, NY   Wheeler, NY

ESBORN Lorenzo of Albion, NY   March 11, 1868
HORR Orna A. of Cohocton, NY   Cohocton, NY

ALLEN William of Avoca, NY   March 11, 1868
RIDER Lucinda B. of Avoca, NY   Avoca, NY

EDMOND John F. of Cohocton, NY — March 11, 1868
MATHEWSON Eunice of Avoca, NY — Avoca, NY

POTTER John H. of Troupsburgh, NY — March 11, 1868
CARD Juliette of Troupsburgh, NY — Woodhull, NY

BRINK Peter of Otego, NY — March 5, 1868
VANDERWARKER Mary Aurelia of Thurston, NY — Thurston, NY

SELY Milo W. of E. Saginaw, Mi. — March 16, 1868
SEAGER Phebe S. of Sonora, NY — Bath, NY

GANUNG Clark B. of Bradford, NY — March 18, 1868
FOLSUM Emma B. of N. Urbana, NY — Bath, NY

SCHUYLER George of Wayne, NY — March 18, 1868
FOLSOM Irene L. of N. Urbana, NY — Bath, NY

GUNN George D. of Bath, NY — April 16, 1868
MAJOR Mary Jane of Gaines, NY — Gaines, NY

BROWN James W. of Bradford, NY — April 3, 1868
GRANT Julia of Bath, NY — Bath, NY

WILHELM Seth E. of Thurston, NY — April 15, 1868
EDSALL Deborah C. of Thurston, NY — Savona, NY

COX William of Bath, NY — May 11, 1868
GRISWOLD Ruth W. of Bath, NY — Bath, NY

FRENCH Joseph W. of Thurston, NY — May 17, 1868
BEATON Mary E. of Thurston, NY — Savona, NY

BAUTER Dewitt C. — June 10, 1868
ECKLER Julia of Wheeler, NY — Wheeler, NY

MARCH Stillman of Naples, NY — June 11, 1868
PARTRIDGE Purley of Cohocton, NY — Cohocton, NY

VAN TUYLE B. F. of Petrolia, Canada W. — June 18, 1868
CHENEY Kate V. dau of Dr. W. S. of Prattsbrugh, NY — Prattsburgh, NY

VAN GORDER A. B. of Cameron, NY — May 31, 1868
EMERSON H. S. of Bath, NY — Bath, NY

FAY H. Orvillo son of Dr. Fay of Wayland, NY — July 1, 1868
REDMOND Vietta A. of Wayland, NY — Wayland, NY

ROSS John M. of Handy, Mi. — July 2, 1868
GLEASON Anna of Bath, NY — Bath, NY

BARRETT Henry of Campbell, NY — July 4, 1868
COSS Mrs. Matilda of Campbell, NY — Bath, NY

DOUD Seth L. of Wheeler, NY — July 1, 1868
MILLIMAN Janette of Dansville, NY — Dansville, NY

GOLDEN Owen J. — June 28, 1868
BRINK Jennie of Avoca, NY — Avoca, NY

DEYO Ellery C. of Naples, NY — July 8, 1868
WOOD Mayola of Naples, NY — Avoca, NY

SMITH Nathaniel of Gorham, NY — July 21, 1868
HOOD Rachel of Bath, NY — Bath, NY

WOODARD William A. of Owasso, Mi. — July 29, 1868
PIERCE Eliza S. of Cohocton, NY — Cohocton, NY

TUBBS Halsey S. of Tyrone, NY — August 2, 1868
RICE Melissa of Bath, NY — Bath, NY

EDSALL Selim of Campbell, NY — August 8, 1868
BUCKINGHAM Delphine of Campbell, NY — Savona, NY

SWEET John H. of Avoca, NY — August 2, 1868
SEVERANCE Susan E. of Avoca, NY — Avoca, NY

WHITE A. B. of Bath, NY — August 27, 1868
WHITE Mary Ann of Howard, NY — Bath, NY

HENDERSON John C. — August 26, 1868
MC FIE Jeanette — Urbana, NY

PADDOCK John N. — August 2, 1868
HENDERSON Hannah E. — Pleasant Valley, NY

YOUNGLOVE O. H. — September 17, 1868
MYRTLE Maggie of Hammondsport, NY — Hammondsport, NY

BAILEY William Wallace of Wayne, NY — September 22, 1868
STODDARD Emma Annette of Bath, NY — Bath, NY

BURT M. M. H. of Savona, NY — September 23, 1868
MERCHANT Ellen E. of Savona, NY at res of S. **MC ELWEE**

CAMPBELL Adam G. of Havana, NY — September 17, 1868
LAWRENCE Jane O. dau of Samuel of Catherine, NY — New York City

PIERCE William of Troupsburgh, NY — October 7, 1868
TAYLOR Cynthia of Deerfield, Pa. — Bath, NY

BOYD Daniel of Hornellsville, NY   October 8, 1868
WHITE Jennie C. of Howard, NY

CHURCH Edwin L. of Bath, NY   October 20, 1868
BULL Augusta Ellen dau of Col. William H. of Bath, NY   Bath, NY

SHARP John of Bath, NY   October 6, 1868
ROBINSON Mrs. Maria of Bath, NY   Bath, NY

HUBER Charles of Naples, NY   October 7, 1868
MEHLENBACKER Kate

LONGCOY William of S. Bradford, NY   October 4, 1868
BENNETT Mary of S. Bradford, NY   Savona, NY

TAYLOR Almeron of S. Bradford, NY   October 4, 1868
BEARD Adie of S. Bradford, NY   Savona, NY

BEDELL J. E. of Bath, NY   October 15, 1868
MC DOWELL E. F. of Bath, NY   Bath, NY

DUNHAM Jerome B. of Howard, NY   October 6, 1868
CARTER Mary J. of Canisteo, NY   Bath, NY

ELLIOTT Orlando F. of Wayland, NY   October 13, 1868
ARMSTRONG Victoria of Pulteney, NY   Bath, NY

SILLIMEN James W. of Urbana, NY   October 20, 1868
EMMONS Jean of Wheeler, NY   Bath, NY

LANE Charles O. of Bath, NY   October 20, 1868
WEBSTER Phidelia of Bath, NY   Bath, NY

PURDY W. H. of Bath, NY   October 21, 1868
DRAKE Amanda of Jasper, NY   Jasper, NY

HOLLANDS William of Mansfield, Pa.   October 28, 1868
BAILEY Clara V. of Mansfield, Pa.   Bath, NY

SMITH Jerome of Howard, NY   November 4, 1868
BELLINGER Lydia of Avoca, NY   Avoca, NY

FAY Lewis M. of Bath, NY   November 12, 1868
WELLS Mary A. of Bath, NY   Bath, NY

BRAMBLE Sylvester E. of Prattsburgh, NY   November 17, 1868
DANIELS Mrs. Sarah M. of Bath, NY

FIELD Benjamin F. of Binghamton, NY   November 14, 1868
TAYLOR Almeda of Campbell, NY   Campbell, NY

KYSER Warren P. of Bath, NY   Novemer 24, 1868
FRAYLEY Christina of Bath, NY

MOULTON James H. of Cohocton, NY   November 24, 1868
VAN WORMER Mabel A. of Cohocton, NY   Avoca, NY

ORMSBY Richard of Bath, NY   (Newspaper date) December 9, 1868
GULLIVER Eliza of Howard, NY   Howard, NY

VAUGHN R. C. of Cameron, NY   November 17, 1868
YOUNG Addie of Cameron, NY   Bath, NY

ARNOLD J. W. of Avoca, NY   (Newspaper date) December 9, 1868
FORD Emma M. of Howard, NY   Howard, NY

SHULTS J. E. of Cooper's Plains, NY   November 25, 1868
CRAWFORD Mary E. dau of James G. of Middletown, NY   Middletown, NY

MORSE Charles L. of Wheeler, NY   December 10, 1868
JOLLEY Lucretia of Wheeler, NY   Wheeler, NY

SMITH Simon P. of Howard, NY   December 9, 1868
DILLENBECK Charlotte of Avoca, NY   Avoca, NY

HATHAWAY Alfred   December 6, 1868
HODGE Hane   Cosses Corners, NY

SMITH Charles A. of Barrington, NY   December 22, 1868
LEWIS Emma E. of Barrington, NY

NORTHRUP Benjamin F. of Italy, NY   December 24, 1868
VAN LOON Sarah E. of Italy, NY   Bath, NY

PELHAM L. W. of Wheeler, NY   December 25, 1868
ROBBINS Emma S. of Wheeler, NY   Wheeler, NY

JEWETT Ames of Hornby, NY   December 8, 1868
PLATT Sarah L. of Campbell, NY   Campbell, NY

FOX Christopher   December 23, 1868
MATHEWSON Zilpha   Avoca, NY

ROSENCRANS A. D. of Avoca, NY   December 27, 1868
HEAD Annette of Avoca, NY   Avoca, NY

SNELL De Witt of Bath, NY   December 30, 1868
MARKELL Katherine of Avoca, NY   Avoca, NY

LYKE Josiah of Bath, NY   December 31, 1868
GRAY Caroline of Avoca, NY   Avoca, NY

WALKER James of Howard, NY   December 16, 1868
EVANS Kate of Howard, NY at bro Charles LANG

STEBBINS A. R. of Watsontown, Pa.   December 29, 1868
BAKER Emma of Painted Post, NY   Painted Post, NY

CINCERBOX Edgar of Virdin, Ill.   December 23, 1868
ORGAN Servilla of Virdin, Ill.   Virdin, Ill.

BENNETT D. C. H. of Oxford, Mi.   January 5, 1869
MATHER Charlotte L. dau of N. B. Mather of Bath, NY   Bath, NY

CRUM Henry A. of Bath, NY   December 31, 1868
SCOTT Hellen of Bath, NY   Bath, NY

TAFT Merrit W. of Jasper, NY   December 24, 1868
FAILING N. M. of Jasper, NY   Jasper, NY

OUTMAN Jonah of Troupsburgh, NY   January 2, 1869
STONE Melissa of Troupsburgh, NY

DIMMICK M. D. Md. of Burns, NY   January 14, 1869
SMITH Mrs. Elizabeth of Bath, NY   Bath, NY

VAN LOON David H. of Bath, NY   January 14, 1869
MC COLLOUGH Margaret of Bath, NY

BURLEY William of Cameron, NY   December 27, 1868
REYNOLDS Susanna of Cameron, NY   W. Cameron, NY

GUNSOLOS Joseph of Avoca, NY   January 13, 1869
BRASTED Viola M. of Howard, NY   Howard, NY

SNELL Jake of Avoca, NY   January 17, 1869
JOLLEY Della of Kanona, NY   Kanona, NY

MORROW John W. of Thurston, NY   January 27, 1869
STOCKING Marietta of Thurston, NY   Bath, NY

BENNETT Ira of Howard, NY   January 26, 1869
VAN WIE Elizabeth of Howard, NY   Howard, NY

WILLIS William S.   January 24, 1869
RICE Lydia dau of Seth Rice of Towlesville, NY   Towlesville, NY

BEVIER John A. of Fon Du Lac, Wis.   January 20, 1869
DOCKSTADER Mattie N. of Kanona, NY   Bath, NY

GRANBY George R.   February 10, 1869
ACKER Alice   Avoca, NY

HOLLY Judson of Wayne, NY	February 9, 1869
LOGHRY Mrs. Nancy of Bath, NY	Bath, NY
CHASE Lewis of Cameron, NY	February 13, 1869
FENTON Minerva A. of Lindley, NY	Bath, NY
KENNEY William of Honeoye, NY	February 11, 1869
BIRCH Jennie of Bath, NY	Bath, NY
JACOBUS Samuel of Urbana, NY	February 11, 1869
O'BRIEN Mary Jane of Bath, NY	Bath, NY
BRYAN Judson of Bath, NY	February 11, 1869
LONGWELL Anna of Bath, NY	Bath, NY
CARR Charles D. of Bradford, NY	February 25, 1869
TOMER Adelaide E. of Campbell, NY	Campbell, NY
WHEATON Henry of Bath, NY	February 17, 1869
EARL Loisa of Bath, NY	Bath, NY
ELLAS Addison F. of Bath, NY	February 25, 1869
LITTLE Jennie C. of Bath, NY	Bath, NY
SANDERSON Robert of Pulteney, NY	February 17, 1869
HADDEN Anna R. of Pulteney, NY	Bath, NY
GRISWOLD Frank of Avoca, NY	March 1, 1869
BEERS Mary E. dau of Rev. N. N. Beers of Avoca, NY	Avoca, NY
SMITH J. L. of Bath, NY	March 9, 1869
SCARVELL H. of Bath, NY	Corning, NY
MORRISON Hiram of Bath, NY	March 13, 1869
MAXWELL Fanny of Bath, NY	Bath, NY
RICHARDSON Charles M. of Bath, NY	March 24, 1869
FISH Sarah E. of Bath, NY	Bath, NY
LARROWE L. A. of Severne, NY	March 17, 1869
AYERS Hattie dau of Hiram Ayers of Norway, NY	Norway, NY
MAGILL Alexander M. of Bath, NY	April 15, 1869
WHITE Esther of Howard, NY	Howard, NY
SNELL William of Bath, NY	April 22, 1869
DOCKSTADER Hellena M. of Bath, NY	Bath, NY
WHITTAKER W. C. of Kalamazoo, Mi.	April 23, 1869
DAVID Mary A. of Savona, NY	Savona, NY

ROBIE Levi of Bath, NY	May 5, 1869
CALKINS Helen A. dau of Ira M. Calkins of Bath, NY	Bath, NY
SMITH Gileas of Steuben Co., NY	May 19, 1869
SMITH Carrie A. of Steuben Co., NY	
RUSCO Phillip of Monterey, NY	May 23, 1869
DAVISON Bell of Bath, NY	Bath, NY
SINSEBOX George E. of Urbana, NY	May 16, 1869
CHASE Ella E. of Urbana, NY	Bath, NY
SPRAGUE Elijah of Urbana, NY	May 25, 1869
HOFFMAN Mary of Bath, NY	Bath, NY
STILLSON Lyman of Elmira, NY	June 1, 1869
GARDNER Jennie M. of Elmira, NY	
BONHAM J. C. of Campbell, NY	June 2, 1869
JESSOP Katie of Campbell, NY	Campbell, NY
CONKLIN James of Bath, NY	June 5, 1869
SMITH Polly of Bath, NY	Cosses Corners, NY
THARP Philander P. of Bath, NY	June 9, 1869
GILBERT Urania A. of Bath, NY	Bath, NY
MOREITY Josiah of Hornellsville, NY	July 3, 1869
O'BRINE Anna E. of Bath, NY	Bath, NY
BIRDSALL Henry of Cohocton, NY	July 4, 1869
BRUNDAGE Eloisa F. of N. Urbana, NY	N. Urbana, NY
COSS John B. of Marcalene, Io.	July 15, 1869
PERRY Jenny of Dansville, NY	Bath, NY
WILLIAMS George of Bath, NY	July 21, 1869
POWELL Mary of Bath, NY	Bath, NY
FAIRCHILD Harvey A. of Bath, NY	August 25, 1869
KIEHLE Mary E. of Dansville, NY	Dansville, NY
LENT Wilbur P.	August 29, 1869
WHITTEMORE Elizabeth Agnes	Jasper, NY
YOUNG William H. of Bath, NY	August 18, 1869
BRUNDAGE Polly of Bath, NY	Bath, NY
HENICA George W. of Deerfield, Mi.	September 8, 1869
CRANDALL Mrs. Lucy L. of Cameron, NY	Cameron, NY

BOUTON Valentine of Avoca, NY　　　　　　　　September 14, 1869
CLARK Mary E. of Bath, NY

WOOD James F. of Cohocton, NY　　　　　　　September 12, 1869
BERGETT Mary E. of Rathbone, NY　　　　　　Avoca, NY

BALCOMB Henry S. of Cameron, NY　　　　　　September 16, 1869
WILBER Ella M. of Cameron, NY　　　　　　　Bath, NY

NILES Ezra of Bath, NY　　　　　　　　　　　September 25, 1869
JACK Carrie of Thurston, NY　　　　　　　　Bath, NY

SCHELL George W. of Howard, NY　　　　　　　October 13, 1869
BRASTED Marietta dau of John C. Brasted of Howard, NY　Howard, NY

BULKLEY S. of Bath, NY　　　　　　　　　　　October 6, 1869
MORS Anna of Bath, NY　　　　　　　　　　Savona, NY

DRAKE R. H. of Bradford, NY　　　　　　　　October 7, 1869
COVERT Agnes of Bradford, NY　　　　　　　Savona, NY

VELEY Peter of Monterey, NY　　　　　　　　October 17, 1869
BAKER Sarephina of Corning, NY　　　　　　Savona, NY

HARRIS John L. of Montoursville, Pa.　　　　　October 25, 1869
PAYNE Hannah E. of Savona, NY　　　　　　　Bath, NY

BROWN Benjamin of Italy, NY　　　　　　　　October 9, 1869
MAXFIELD Mrs. Almeda of Italy, NY

AULLS Lyman C. of N. Urbana, NY　　(Newspaper date) November 3, 1869
DREW Louise J. of Hammondsport, NY

MC MULLEN Daniel of Bath, NY　　　　　　　November 1, 1869
GREEN Jennie of Bath, NY　　　　　　　　　Bath, NY

TOWNSEND Joshua of Prattsburgh, NY　　　　　November 1, 1869
CHILSON Abby L. of Prattsburgh, NY

JONES William　　　　　　　　　　　　　　October 20, 1869
DRAKE Katie　　　　　　　　　　　　　　　Bath, NY

HICKS William of Bath, NY　　　　(Newspaper date) November 3, 1869
MULHOLLEN Emily Jane of Bath, NY

WATERMAN Joshua Whitney of Detroit, Mi.　　　November 10, 1869
DAVENPORT Fanny dau of late Col. Davenport　Riverside, NY

COWLEY Abram E. of Corning, NY　　　　　　October 27, 1869
ORCUTT Alice of Corning, NY

CONINE Lorenzo D. of Canisteo, NY   November 13, 1869
HATHAWAY Mary L. of Canisteo, NY

VAN GELDER Almon M. of Bath, NY   November 24, 1869
LOCKWOOD Harriet of Urbana, NY   Urbana, NY

MAGILL James M. of Howard, NY   October 28, 1869
VAN LOON Nancy Maria of Bath, NY   Howard, NY

HOFFMAN Elijah W.   November 28, 1869
HATHAWAY Mrs. Sarah J.   Bath, NY

SHULTS Arnold of Bath, NY   November 24, 1869
GREY Ella of Bath, NY at res of Grattan **BRUNDAGE**

CLARK Amasa of Bath, NY   December 1, 1869
FRIES Anna of Bath, NY   Bath, NY

CHAPMAN Elias K. of Bath, NY   December 2, 1869
SCOFIELD Lucy of Urbana, NY   Bath, NY

RILEY Richard A. Jr.   December 16, 1869
KING Lizzie adopted dau of Mrs. Smith   Geneseo, NY

HONEYMAN Austin of Bath, NY   December 15, 1869
MC ELWEE Lucy of Bath, NY   Bath, NY

EELLS Carlton of Bath, NY   December 22, 1869
NIVER Clarissa of Bath, NY   Bath, NY

WALKER Grier of Howard, NY   December 22, 1869
CLARK Judith A. of Bath, NY   Bath, NY

BALDWIN W. W.   December 23, 1869
BENNETT Sarah   Campbell, NY

TOWNER Aaron E.   September 29,1869
LAPE Sarah E.   Avoca, NY

SHAUT Hiram   October 18, 1869
BAUTER Magelia of Wheeler, NY   Avoca, NY

THOMAS James C. of Prattsburgh, NY   December 8, 1869
BROOKMAN Mary E. of Prattsburgh, NY   Avoca, NY

PIATT Charles A. of Howard, NY   December 11, 1869
FRANCE Alice of Howard, NY   Avoca, NY

MERRILL Albert B. of Campbell, NY   December 24, 1869
PADDOCK Maggie of Wheeler, NY

MILES M. of Kansas City, Mo. January 9, 1870
ROWLETTE Hannah M. Bath, NY

POWERS Asa D. of Troupsburgh, NY December 5, 1869
SWAN Rhoda P. of Troupsburgh, NY Troupsburgh, NY

CHAMPLAIN Robert of Westfield, Pa. December 30, 1869
GILE Eliza of Westfield, Pa. Troupsburgh, NY

WEBSTER F. C. of Urbana, NY January 15, 1870
LONGWELL Susan M. of Urbana, NY Bath, NY

FEAGLES Franklin M. of Benton Center, NY February 15, 1870
RACE Henrietta of Benton Center, NY Prattsburgh, NY

SILSBEE Charles Edward of Detroit, Mi. February 16, 1870
GILMORE Lydia A. dau of P. Gilmore of Bath, NY

MAXWELL Thomas S. of Bath, NY February 24, 1870
MORTON Lucy A. of Bath, NY Bath, NY

MC INTYRE Robert S. of Reading, NY February 22, 1870
BRIGGS Elizabeth of Wheeler, NY Bath, NY

MAY Edward S. Md. of Campbell, NY February 28, 1870
WOODRUFF Tilla dau of late J. B. Woodruff at Mother's Ann Arbor, Mi.

BARDEEN Charles of Bath, NY March 10, 1870
BEAM Henrietta of Bath, NY Bath, NY

MILLARD C. H. of Adrian, NY February 26, 1870
ELLIS Kate of Urbana, NY Hammondsport, NY

HUSTON Seymour H. of Bath, NY March 9, 1870
SNELL Nancy of Bath, NY Bath, NY

HINSDALE Eugene of Binghamton, NY March 15, 1870
BENJAMIN Hattie S. of Bath, NY Bath, NY

LITTLE Phillip M. of Bath, NY March 16, 1870
CALKINS Emma dau of Ira M. Calkins of Bath, NY Bath, NY

ARMSTRONG Charles Andrew of Pulteney, NY March 17, 1870
SULLIVAN Sarah of Pulteney, NY Pulteney, NY

SPRAGUE Joseph W. of NJ March 20, 1870
DAMOTH Mary of Bradford, NY

GENUNG Franklin D. of Bath, NY March 30, 1870
MOWERS Susan J. of Bath, NY

CLARK George of Howard, NY	April 14, 1870
WHITE Margaret A. of Howard, NY	Bath, NY
WOODRUFF Edward F. of Bath, NY	April 18, 1870
VELEY Celestia E. of Bath, NY	Savona, NY
JOHNSON William B. of Bath, NY	April 28, 1870
WILCOX Mary of Bath, NY	Bath, NY
CLARK Cyrus of Dansville, NY	May 3, 1870
JONES Hannah J. of Bath, NY	Bath, NY
WALTERS Charles D. of Bath, NY	May 25, 1870
DAVISON Ella E. dau of T. C. of Bath, NY	
LOWLY A. E. of Bath, NY	May 25, 1870
MILLS Mrs. Esther E. of Bath, NY	
CORNWALL Truman of Howard, NY	June 1, 1870
LOGHRY Lucretia of Cameron, NY	Cosses Corners, NY
WHITE Ezra M. of Cohocton, NY	June 1, 1870
VAN WORMER Mary E. of Cohocton, NY	Cohocton, NY
BIRCH Eugene of Bath, NY	July 4, 1870
GRIFFITH Amanda of Bath, NY	Bath, NY
SEARLS J. Wesley of Pulteney, NY	June 30, 1870
GULICK Hattie of Pulteney, NY	Pulteney, NY
WAKEMAN Seth B. of Lawyersville, NY	July 13, 1870
DANS Helen A. of Cobleskill, NY at res of Harry **COLE**	Savona, NY
RISING Willis H. of Merchantville, NY	July 31, 1870
MASTERS Alice J. of Merchantville, NY	Merchantville, NY
DECK Solomon of Jasper, NY	August 3, 1870
DAVIS Anna of Cameron, NY	Thurston, NY
DECK Uriah of Jasper, NY	August 3, 1870
PECK Mrs. Mary of Jasper, NY	Thurston, NY
MORTON Eugene of Bath, NY	August 11, 1870
GRIFFITH Alice of Rockville, Pa.	Rockville, Pa.
HUBBARD Byron of Campbell, NY	October 12, 1870
EMMONS Amanda of Maple Grove, NY	Savona, NY
COOTS David of Howard, NY	October 7, 1870
ROBERTS Harriet of Howard, NY	Bath, NY

CHASE Bonaparte of Bath, NY   October 14, 1870
FENTON Angeline O. of Lindley, NY

CROOKSTON William H. of Wayne, NY   October 9, 1870
BRUNDAGE Salina of Wayne, NY   Savona, NY

MOSS William F. of Campbell, NY   October 11, 1870
MORSE Sarah J. of S. Bradford, NY   Savona, NY

KEELER Cyrus of Bath, NY   October 23, 1870
VAN GELDER Polly Ann of Bath, NY   Savona, NY

JANES William A. of Bath, NY   October 19, 1870
VROOM Jennie L. of Bath, NY   Bath, NY

EELLS Willard of Wheeler, NY   October 16, 1870
PUTMAN Adelia D. of Wheeler, NY   Bath, NY

BRUNDAGE Addison   October 24, 1870
TAGGART Lizzie dau of John W.

CRAIG J. M. of Elmira, NY   October 26, 1870
BRUNDAGE Mary C. dau of Hiram Brundage of Bath, NY   Bath, NY

MILLER John G. of Bath, NY   (Newspaper date) November 2, 1870
WALKER Helen of Bath, NY

KEMADY A. C. of Bath, NY   (Newspaper date) November 2, 1870
WALKER Melissa of Bath, NY

MC KIBBEN William Henry of Howard, NY   October 27, 1870
SHARP Eliza Jane of Howard, NY   Howard, NY

ABER Daniel of Bath, NY   November 22, 1870
BOOTH Mrs. A. S. of Bath, NY   Bath, NY

WELTER Zachariah of Himrods, NY   November 10, 1870
MARGESON Deborah Ann of Wayne, NY   Wayne, NY

COYLE Edward of Bath, NY   November 20, 1870
SMITH Emma of Bath, NY   Bath, NY

FAY Frank A. of Bath, NY   November 3, 1870
GAY Eliza M. of Bath, NY at res of M. V. **BARTON**

CHURCHILL Riley of Middlebury, Pa.   December 1, 1870
BOWLBY Alice E. of Bath, NY   Bath, NY

DUTCHER George of Dundee, NY   December 9, 1870
FRANCISCO Emma of Barrington, NY   Hammondsport, NY

CASTERLINE David of Hammondsport, NY	December 14, 1870
GLANN Mrs. Mary L. of Hammondsport, NY	Bath, NY
HADDEN James L. of Urbana, NY	December 14, 1870
SILLIMAN Eliza A. of Urbana, NY	Bath, NY
GIBSON George F. of Pulteney, NY	November 24, 1870
CROSS Mary E. of Pulteney, NY	
COMPTON Andrew of Friendship, NY	November 28, 1870
GREEN Mrs. Sarah W. of Pulteney, NY	Pulteney, NY
PRENTICE William A. of Pulteney, NY	December 14, 1870
PARKER Jennie T. of Pulteney, NY	Pulteney, NY
MORRIS Squire M. of Pulteney, NY	December 10, 1870
BUCK Clara N. of Pulteney, NY	Pulteney, NY
BOILEAU Almeron D. of Bath, NY	December 21, 1870
BARRETT Mary E. of Bath, NY	Bath, NY
STEWART Thomas W. of Howard, NY	December 22, 1870
MOORE Ida of Bath, NY	Howard, NY
LOUNSBERRY Albert of Pulteney, NY	December 22, 1870
SCUTT Nettie of Tyrone, NY	S. Pulteney, NY
FORD George W. of Middlesex, NY	December 31, 1870
DRAKE M. of Prattsburgh, NY	
FLYNN Angevine E. of Bath, NY	January 3, 1871
ABER Ann of Howard, NY at res of James Aber	
BROWNRIGG George of Kanona, NY	January 5, 1871
HOUSTON Hattie of Kanona, NY	Kanona, NY
VAN BUSKIRK R. of Avoca, NY	January 1, 1871
MANN Mrs. Susan of Bath, NY	Bath, NY
SMITH Phillip A. of Fishkill Landing, NY	January 2, 1871
CLELAND L. V. of Liberty, NY	
LOGHRY Charles 2nd of Bath, NY	January 23, 1871
LONGWELL Zilla of Bath, NY	Cosses Corners, NY
GRISWOLD Fred E. of Naples, NY	January 25, 1871
ADAMS Jennie C. of Naples, NY	Bath, NY
EDGAR Alden S. of Benton, NY	January 25, 1871
MATHEWS De Ett C. of Bradford, NY	Bradford, NY

FINCH James M. of Rochester, NY   January 25, 1871
PETERSON Clara M. of Savona, NY   Savona, NY

HERBERT John of Thurston, NY   January 30, 1871
WITHEY Amanda of Cameron, NY   Bath, NY

HERSH Jacoba of Hornellsville, NY   March 12, 1871
LAIN Helen of Bath, NY

TRIPP F. G. of Wayland, NY   March 5, 1871
TRIPP Mrs. Rachel of Wayland, NY

MC KAY Orange of S. Dansville, NY   March 8, 1871
CLARK Hulda dau of James P. of Cohocton, NY   Cohocton, NY

LEWIS George W. of Wheeler, NY   March 14, 1871
MILLETT Mary F. of Wheeler, NY   Kanona, NY

WARREN Clarence H.   March 16, 1871
WEBSTER Allie of Bath, NY   Bath, NY

PHILLIPS L. H. of Thurston, NY   March 22, 1871
BOOTH Mrs. Olive M. of Thurston, NY   Thurston, NY

STEWART John of Howard, NY   March 30, 1871
STEWART Mary Anna of Howard, NY at res of Samuel Stewart

CLARK Henry of Prattsburgh, NY   March 29, 1871
CARHART Henrietta of Prattsburgh, NY   Prattsburgh, NY

HESS Henry R. of Pulteney, NY   January 29, 1871
HOTCHKIN Anna W. of Pulteney, NY   Pulteney, NY

BACHMAN John L. of Pulteney, NY   February 23, 1871
COVELL Samantha A. of Prattsburgh, NY   Prattsburgh, NY

TOMER Webster of Pulteney, NY   March 8, 1871
HYATT Mrs. Louisa of Pulteney, NY   Pulteney, NY

SCOTT Jacob H. of Onieda Co., NY   April 1, 1871
CULVER L. of Bath, NY   Bath, NY

CULVER Orrin of Bath, NY   April 1, 1871
WATSON A. of Bath, NY   Bath, NY

PAGE James of Bath, NY   April 15, 1871
DORSEY Mary J. of Bath, NY   Bath, NY

WILHELM Jackson of Bath, NY   April 16, 1871
CARR Lettie of Bath, NY   Bath, NY

THOMPSON W. H. of Bath, NY (Newspaper date) May 3, 1871
WILCOX Sarah of Bath, NY Bath, NY

ALLERTON George of Bath, NY May 14, 1871
TRUMBULL Sarah M. of Bath, NY

SMITH Dr. W. W. of Howard, NY April 23, 1871
RICE Lydia J. of Howard, NY Howard, NY

GRAVES E. L. of Batavia, NY May 13, 1871
CLEVELAND Nettie of Wayne, NY at res of John **ERNEST**

SOUTHWORTH W. H. H. of Dryden, NY May 24, 1871
WARD Ellen E. dau of Fred Ward of Bath, NY Bath, NY

NICHOLS Peter L. of Sharon, Pa. June 25, 1871
AUSTIN Cynthia Ann

TERRIBURY Judson of Hartsville, NY July 4, 1871
SMITH Catherine of Hartsville, NY Towlesville, NY

SNELL George of Bath, NY July 3, 1871
BENSON Kittie A. of Clinton, Iowa Clinton, Iowa

NORTHRUP Nirom of Bath, NY August 20, 1871
MORSE Mrs. Eliza of Wheeler, NY Bath, NY

WELCH George of Webster, NY August 15, 1871
WHEAT Christina M. of Webster, NY Spencer Springs, NY

WEBSTER Alva of Savona, NY August 6, 1871
BURROWS Hannah C. of Horseheads, NY Savona, NY

SHATTUCK C. E. of Cleveland, Ohio August 31, 1871
LARROWE Arabella of Cohocton, NY Bath, NY

WARRICK Isaac of Thurston, NY August 24, 1871
MARTIN Mrs. Phebe J. of Thurston, NY Thurston, NY

WIXSON Milton B. of Bath, NY August 23, 1871
CLAWSON Laura A. of Campbell, NY Campbell, NY

GRAY Albert of Tyrone, NY September 7, 1871
DUNN Mary of Campbell, NY Campbell, NY

HINDS Freeman of Bath, NY September 20, 1871
YOST Flora E. of Thurston, NY

PIERCE Reuben of Urbana, NY October 4, 1871
SMALLIDGE Dell of Urbana, NY Urbana, NY

ORDWAY M. C. of Adrian, NY   October 8, 1871
VAN GORDER Anna of Adrian, NY

ELLIS Clark of Urbana, NY   October 8, 1871
WELCH Tilla of Urbana, NY

WEBSTER Byron A.   October 4, 1871
JAYNES Mary C.   Urbana, NY

HURLBURT Charles J. of Chicago, Ill.   October 5, 1871
ROGERS Susan Mariott dau of Dr. G. A. of Chicago, Ill.   Chicago, Ill.

DAVIS Joshua D. of W. Union, NY   October 22, 1871
MC FALL Elizabeth of W. Union, NY at Amasa **TANNER**   Troupsburgh, NY

CHENEY Walter S. Md. of Auburn, NY   (Newspaper date) November 1, 1871
FRENCH Mary J. dau of Robert French of Benton, NY   Benton, NY

SCOTT Winfield son of J. J. **ERNEST**   October 16, 1871
SUNDERLIN Auretta of Wayne, NY   Wayne, NY

NELLIS Charles H. of Campbell, NY   November 4, 1871
EDDY Celia R. of Campbell, NY   Savona, NY

BEDFORD E. L. of Warren, Ill.   November 8, 1871
EVANS Ettie of Savona, NY   Savona, NY

ST PETERS Charles of Bath, NY   November 22, 1871
BILLINGTON Mary of Bath, NY   Bath, NY

JOLLEY James L. of Wheeler, NY   November 22, 1871
PALMER Oliett of Wheeler, NY   Wheeler, NY

JAYCOX George E. of Binghamton, NY   November 22, 1871
FOLSOM Emma of N. Urbana, NY   N. Urbana, NY

MARGESON Eber J. of Wayne, NY   December 4, 1871
JACKSON Mrs. C. J. of Bath, NY   Bath, NY

DERRICK Dennis   December 13, 1871
AULLS Mary of Wheeler, NY

IDE Charles Henry   December 18, 1871
KNAPP Aurelia dau of William Knapp   Orange, NY

ROBARDS Allen of Howard, NY   December 25, 1871
VAN VLECK Jane of S. Dansville, NY   Avoca, NY

CONKRITE Frank M. of Hornellsville, NY   December 13, 1871
KELLINGER Laura of Hornellsville, NY   Hornellsville, NY

MORTON Maj. Thomas H. of New York City
WHEELER Nannie dau of Grattan H. Wheeler

December 29, 1871
Hammondsport, NY

OXX Steuben C. of Avoca, NY
BAKER Sarah J. of Fremont, NY

December 30, 1871
Avoca, NY

CAMPBELL Robert J.
OSWELL Virginia Bacon

December 20, 1871
Ogdensburgh, NY

LOUNSBURY Jacob of Bradford, NY
GARDINER Lydia Ann of Wayne, NY

December 24, 1871
Wayne, NY

OLMSTEAD S. of Avoca, NY
HOPKINS C. of Avoca, NY

January 1, 1872
Bath, NY

MC BETH David of Howard, NY
MC KIBBEN Nancy W. of Howard, NY

January 10, 1872
Howard, NY

CRUTHERS William J.
WALTERS Amanda W. of Prattsburgh, NY

December 30, 1871
Avoca, NY

LEWIS Joseph of Prattsburgh, NY
BREST Josephine of Prattsburgh, NY

January 1, 1872

LANE Daniel F. of Prattsburgh, NY
MAGEE Sarah A. of Avoca, NY

December 27, 1871
Avoca, NY

BALIUEL George of Washington DC
VICKERY Mrs. Clara of Avoca, NY

January 25, 1872
Avoca, NY

HOLDEN Timothy S. of Prattsburgh, NY
STEWART Viola M. of Pulteney, NY

January 17, 1872
Pulteney, NY

POWELL Alexander of Bath, NY
GOFF Mrs. Nancy of Howard, NY

January 24, 1872
Howard, NY

RUMSEY William of Bath, NY
MOORE Ella of Brooklyn, Ny

February 1, 1872
Brooklyn, NY

BALDWIN E. W. of Phelps, NY
RICE Mary of Avoca, NY

January 24, 1872
Avoca, NY

ALDEN Ward of Howard, NY
VAN DUSEN Susan of Howard, NY

February 15, 1872
Howard, NY

SHULTS Rev. James of Avoca, NY
SHILL Livonia of Avoca, NY

February 15, 1872

GILBERT George of Bath, NY
GENUNG C. C. of Bath, NY

February 1, 1872

SMITH W. A. of Bath, NY   February 27, 1872
GRANT Susie of Bath, NY

RICE Austin S. of Avoca, NY   February 29, 1872
WALLACE Frances of Avoca, NY   Avoca, NY

CROSS Lamar of Hornellsville, NY   March 6, 1872
HORTON Julia E. of Howard, NY   Howard, NY

WEST William H. of Merchantville, NY   March 11, 1872
CHAPLE Ella of Merchantville, NY   Bath, NY

STICKNEY Charles C. of Wheeler, NY   March 6, 1872
JONES Mrs. Julia of Bath, NY   Bath, NY

CORYELL S. W. of Pulteney, NY   January 11, 1872
COGSWELL S. C. of Pulteney, NY   Pulteney, NY

STEVER Rupert of Pulteney, NY   March 5, 1872
GAY Sarah of Pulteney, NY   Pulteney, NY

BURT W. S. of Corning, NY   March 2, 1872
SANFORD Martha A. of Sonora, NY   Savona, NY

WEBSTER Charles W. of Bath, NY   March 13, 1872
WARREN Mary A. of Bath, NY   Bath, NY

SIMMONS Ira of Thurston, NY   January 21, 1872
LOVE Phlena of Thurston, NY   Thurston, NY

JONES George W. of Bath, NY   March 16, 1872
MULHOLLEN Emma Jane of Thurston, NY   Thurston, NY

MERRILL T. F. of Bath, NY   March 13, 1872
DANIELS Zubia of Bath, NY

CORWIN O. F. of Merchantville, NY   April 11, 1872
COOLBAUGH Loma A. of Merchantville, NY   Merchantville, NY

PURDEN Urias of Campbell, NY   April 14, 1872
TAYLOR H. Mary of Bradford, NY   Savona, NY

SHULTS J. D. of Bath, NY   April 17, 1872
CARTER Eva of Bath, NY   Bath, NY

ST JOHN Horace F. of New York City   May 14, 1872
WHEELER Elisa of Bath, NY   Bath, NY

WEEKS Hiram of Bath, NY   April 24, 1872
BORDEN Maria of Bath, NY   Bath, NY

ARGAS John of Hammondsport, NY — June 17, 1872
TRAUM Dorothy of Hammondsport, NY — Bath, NY

PECK Lucien W. of Arcade, NY — June 19, 1872
CURTIS Ellie M. at Father's — Bloomville, NY

BAILEY M. J. of N. Cameron, NY — June 26, 1872
WILLIAMS H. C. of N. Cameron, NY — N. Cameron, NY

TRUMBULL A. A. of Bath, NY — June 27, 1872
COMSTOCK Mrs. E. of Bath, NY — Bath, NY

FERRIS John H. of Howard, NY — July 4, 1872
HILL Alida S. of Howard, NY — Avoca, NY

HALL Isaac of Howard, NY — July 2, 1872
HIGGINS Juliette of Howard, NY — Howard, NY

GURNSEY Charles of Howard, NY — July 4, 1872
COLE Martha of Howard, NY — Howard, NY

CHARLESWORTH James of Wheeler, NY — July 7, 1872
DYER Sarah Jane of Avoca, NY — Howard, NY

HALL Robert of Howard, NY — July 15, 1872
KEEGANS Lizzie of Howard, NY — Howard, NY

CORNWELL William of Urbana, NY — July 15, 1872
FLYNN Fannie of Bath, NY — Bath, NY

WAGSTAFF Henry — July 17, 1872
GODFREY Mrs. Sarah T. — Pulteney, NY

MARGESON B. P. of Urbana, NY — August 17, 1872
MC GOWAN Emma J. of Urbana, NY — Bath, NY

WATKINS M. F. of Burns, NY — August 15, 1872
CARNEY Lett H. of Dansville, NY — Dansville, NY

HART Edmond M. of Dunkirk, NY — September 2, 1872
MERRILL R. Anna of Kansas City, Mo. — Campbell, NY

BARNES J. P. of Rock Stream, NY — August 29, 1872
BROWN Maggie J. — Hammondsport, NY

JENKS W. H. — September 4, 1872
GATES Eliza — Coopers Plains, NY

ANNABEL Albert of N. Cameron, NY — August 18, 1872
CHASE Luna of N. Cameron, NY — Bath, NY

GAY George H.	September 5, 1872
LOCK Frankie O.	Pulteney, NY
WILLIS Festus of Towlesville, NY	September 15, 1872
HOAGLAND Hattie of Towlesville, NY	Bath, NY
WAGONER George A.	September 13, 1872
BAKER Mary A.	Pulteney, NY
MC CLURE D. G. of Altay, NY	September 20, 1872
WALTON Libbie M. of Cameron, NY	Cameron, NY
BENNETT Richard T. of Bradford, NY	September 15, 1872
TOMER Julia H. of Campbell, NY	Campbell, NY
HARTRUM John S. of Greenwood, NY	September 11, 1872
ORCUTT Belinda of Bath, NY	Savona, NY
VAN HOUTEN Isaac	September 21, 1872
HATCH Maria dau of Silas Hatch	Canisteo, NY
CARRIER Nathaniel W. of Rochester, NY	September 30, 1872
BRUNDAGE Mary of Bath, NY	Bath, NY
HOWARD Charles E.	October 9, 1872
MATHEWS Louise F.	Philadelphia, Pa.
HART Frank P. of Elmira, NY	October 17, 1872
FINCH Mary E. of Elmira, NY	Elmira, NY
CASE Charles G. of Thurston, NY	October 7, 1872
ABEL Dora L. of Savona, NY	Savona NY
STODDARD H. of Webster, NY	October 30, 1872
EMERY Aggie of Webster, NY	Webster, NY
TOWNSEND C. of Bath, NY	October 30, 1872
DAVIS V. M. of Urbana, NY	Urbana, NY
DRYER Rev. C. H. of West. NY Conference	November 5, 1872
FRENCH C. Arabella of Bath, NY	Bath, NY
LEE Cyrus of Bloods, NY	November 2, 1872
BENNETT Electa of Bath, NY	Avoca, NY
SMITH William T.	October 30, 1872
ROSE Margelia dau of late Col. Martin F. Rose	New York City
(Grand dau of Gen. O. F. **MARSHALL** of Wheeler, NY)	
HUNTER V. J. of Bath, NY	November 12, 1872

MURPHY Katie of Sunnyside, Iowa — Sunnyside, Iowa

DEMOREST D. L. of Avoca, NY — November 14, 1872
ROOT Alice of Cohocton, NY — Cohocton, NY

STEWART Alfred P. of Campbell, NY — November 21, 1872
PLATT Mary E. of Campbell, NY — Savona, NY

MAHALAN Deloss of Thurston, NY — December 1, 1872
TAYLOR Mary of Thurston, NY — Merchantville, NY

ARMSTRONG J. P. of Bath, NY — December 9, 1872
RUTHERFORD Lizzie of Merchantville, NY — Merchantville, NY

JOHNSON George W. — December 11, 1872
KEYSOR Bernice J. — Howard, NY

BLAKESLEE Floyd S. of Coopers Plains, NY — November 20, 1872
DYGERT Anna dau of James S. Dygert of Kanona, NY — Kanona, NY

HAVEN Charles D. of Racine, Wis. — December 16, 1872
HIGGINS Sarah dau of Late J. D. Higgins Md. — Bath, NY

BRAYTON Sweet of Fremont, NY — December 15, 1872
MAXWELL Fanny of Bath, NY — Bath, NY

BIRKETT John of Thurston, NY — November 27, 1872
PETERSON Sophia of Thurston, NY — Thurston, NY

CARR W. J. of Barrington, NY — December 4, 1872
GREEK Harriet of Thurston, NY — Thurston, NY

SITTERLY Luther of Bath, NY — December 18, 1872
NORRIS Fida F. dau of Seth Norris of Bath, NY — Bath, NY

DE GRAFF William of Howard, NY — December 18, 1872
KINKADE Christaine of Bath, NY — Bath, NY

WHEELER Don Duane — December 19, 1872
ROSE Mary at res of late Sherman Rose

BENTON W. H. of Spencer, NY — December 24, 1872
PRAY Ellen of Danby, NY — Danby, NY

BROOMHALL George of Albany, NY — December 25, 1872
STINSON M. J. of Bath, NY — Bath, NY

WOOD Thomas of Mt. Washington, NY — December 18, 1872
LONGWELL Rose of Mt. Washington, NY — Mt. Washington, NY

CORYELL Josiah of Pulteney, NY
PIERCE Libbie of Racine, Wis.

December 26, 1872
Pulteney, NY

MC CONNELL William Dexter
GURNSEY Lucy M.

November 20, 1872
Howard, NY

COLE Alvah P.
ROBERTS Ellen

December 22, 1872
Howard, NY

WASHBURN H. Addison
DEAN Susie A.

December 25, 1872
Pulteney, NY

ROBERTS Ervin
VAN DUSEN Sarah

December 31, 1872
Howard, NY

HOUSE James A.
WESSELS Mary E.

December 31, 1872
Howard, NY

CROSS Curtis C. of Urbana, NY
BREWER Allie of Urbana, NY

December 29, 1872

VAN TUYLE Abram of Jerusalem, NY
MC ENTYRE Augusta of Bradford, NY

December 30, 1872
Bath, NY

GREEN William S. of Bath, NY
PADDOCK Mrs. Mary of Bath, NY

January 1, 1873
Cameron, NY

GREEN Horatio T. of Prophetstown, Ill.
MAY Sarah B. dau of Samuel May

January 1, 1873

DOLSON Charles A. of Andover, NY
HARMON Alice of Andover, NY

January 2, 1873
Andover, NY

LINNELL C. H. of Corning, NY
WHEELER Mary of Cameron, NY

December 25, 1872
Cameron, NY

CALKINS Ira F. of Bath, NY
WOODS Clara B. of Rushford, NY at bro Rev. H. C. Woods

January 6, 1873
Holley, NY

BRIGLIN E. R. of Hopewell, NY
FOX Kate of Avoca, NY

December 26, 1872
Avoca, NY

ROBBINS Josiah of Bath, NY
REAMER Catherine Maria of Bath, NY

January 25, 1873
Bath, NY

FAUCETT James of Bath, NY
BRUNDAGE Elizabeth of Urbana, NY

January 23, 1873
Urbana, NY

VAN WORMER Emory L. of Liberty, NY
MOORE Addie C. of Avoca, NY

January 22, 1873
Avoca, NY

HIGGINS Oramel H.
ALDEN Clarissa A.

January 14, 1873
Howard, NY

DANIELS Frank of the Detroit Free Press
PAGE Fanny dau of James Page of Cohocton, NY

January 29, 1873
Cohocton, NY

DIEMOND George
LEECH Mary Jane

January 2, 1873
Bath, NY

YOUNG Henry of Bath, NY
LEECH Bessie of Bath, NY

February 2, 1873
Bath, NY

STEWART Daniel J. of Bath, NY
NUTTING Carrie J. of Elmira, NY

February 6, 1873
Elmira, NY

SAGER William H. of Avoca, NY   (Newspaper date) February 26, 1873
SQUIRES Addie F. at res of A. J. **MC CALL**   Bath, NY

BARNES Augustus F. of Wellsboro, Pa.
BULL Sarah B. dau of Col. William H. Bull of Bath, NY

February 19, 1873
Bath, NY

LEECH Thomas of Bath, NY
CARSON Maria of Bath, NY

February 20, 1873
Bath, NY

SNELL John Albert of Bath, NY
DILLENBACK Celestia of Avoca, NY

February 20, 1873
Bath, NY

VAN SCOOTER P. of Hornellsville, NY
DONAHE Mrs. Margaret at Father's John J. **SMITH**

February 20, 1873

NIEL P. H. of Avoca, NY
FOX Julia A. of Avoca, NY

February 12, 1873
Avoca, NY

DAWSON Lancelot of Howard, NY
ANNABLE Lydia dau of Frederick Annable of Howard, NY

February 26, 1873
Howard, NY

SMITH Delanson of Bath, NY
CLARK Abbie of Bath, NY

February 27, 1873
Towlesville, NY

CRAKES W. S. of Campbell, NY
RUMSEY Carrie A. of Campbell, NY

February 22, 1873
Savona, NY

HOOD Lucius of Avoca, NY
COOPER Elizabeth D. of Avoca, NY

February 26, 1873
Avoca, NY

SHARDLOW Winfield S. of Avon, NY
LYON S. Louisa dau of D. W. Lyon of Mt. Morris, NY

March 13, 1873
Mt. Morris, NY

HORTON Luther T. of Howard, NY
PATTERSON Adelphia of Howard, NY

March 5, 1873
Howard, NY

ROE Joseph of Canisteo, NY   March 11, 1873
BOURNE Mary of Howard, NY   Howard, NY

DUNHAM John of Troupsburgh, NY   February 18, 1873
GIFFORD Angalia of Howard, NY   Howard, NY

DARLING John W. of Hornellsville, NY   February 16, 1873
CARY Nettie M. of Hornellsville, NY   Howard, NY

LOUCKS Henry C.   February 18, 1873
BALDWIN Caroline   Avoca, NY

VAN DUESEN Reuben of Bath, NY   March 20, 1873
MILLS Lucinda of Bath, NY

MILLARD Edward of Campbell, NY   February 20, 1873
BIXBY Irene L. of Campbell, NY   Campbell, NY

BEEMAN C. H. of Hornellsville, NY   March 27, 1873
HAND Josephine of Bath, NY   Bath, NY

DENNIS A. D. of Bath, NY   March 25, 1873
JONES Clara C. of Covington, Pa.   Mansfield, Pa.

CASTLE John W. of Bath, NY   April 8, 1873
BURT Harriet of Bath, NY   Bath, NY

HUNN James L. of Avoca, NY   April 10, 1873
CLARK Phoeba J. of Avoca, NY   Avoca, NY

BACKMAN C. M. of Elmira, NY   May 15, 1873
DANIELS Mary E. of Elmira, NY   Bath, NY

WORKMAN Elijah of Bradford, NY   May 17, 1873
HELM Libbie A. of Bath, NY   Bath, NY

GRANT George H. of Bath, NY   May 25, 1873
HADDEN Emma of Cold Springs, NY

BROWN Levi of Big Flats, NY   May 28, 1873
BROWN M. Jennie at res of M. C. **BENNETT**   Big Flats, NY

FOLLETT Erwin of Great Bay, Wis.   May 20, 1873
BROWN Rosamond dau of L. H. Brown of Bath, NY   Bath, NY

LEAVENWORTH S. S. of Orange, NY   May 21, 1873
SISSON Marion of Cohocton, NY

HOAGLAND Charles of Bradford, NY   May 28, 1873
LAMPSON Mrs. Mary J. of Bath, NY   Bath, NY

MC ENNY Henry of Campbell, NY   (Newspaper date) June 4, 1873
TIGH Mary Ann of Campbell, NY   Bath, NY

BECKWITH C. of Bath, NY   June 12, 1873
WEDGE Lottie of Scio, NY   Bath, NY

WOOD Simeon   June 11, 1873
SMALL Fanny at res of Hiram Small

FRENCH N. B. of Elmira, NY   June 2, 1873
SANFORD Anna of Mt. Washington, NY   Mt. Washington, NY

DE PUYSTER Augustus   June 12, 1873
HESS Minnie   Bath, NY

GAY D. E. of Bath, NY   June 18, 1873
BRUNDAGE Sophia

LEGRO S. D. of Bath, NY   June 19, 1873
MINER Emma of Bath, NY   Bath, NY

MASON Orlim J. of N. Cameron, NY   June 19, 1873
MC CHENNY Margaret L. of Bath, NY   Bath, NY

VROOM Charles W. of Leroy, Mi.   June 30, 1873
SILSBE Maggie H. of Leroy, Mi.   Leroy, Mi.

MOORE John of Dixon, Ill.   June 26, 1873
LEGRO Lydia E. of Bath, NY   Bath, NY

BRASTED Orlando of Howard, NY   July 3, 1873
HAMILTON Edith E. of Howard, NY   Howard, NY

STEWART J. of Bath, NY   July 9, 1873
COYL Mrs. Emma of Bath, NY   Howard, NY

BORDEN A. of Hornellsville, NY   July 9, 1873
STEWART S. of Howard, NY   Howard, NY

HEWLETT E. P. of Guernville, Cal. formerly of Savona, NY   August 7, 1873
ALLERTON Sophia of Savona, NY   San Jose, Cal.

CHICHESTER Henry of Wheeler, NY   August 14, 1873
DILDINE D. Jennie of Urbana, NY at res of E. FRY

MAXSON Prof. Cyrus of Bath, NY   August 31, 1873
SCOTT Mary of Bath, NY   Bath, NY

AINSWORTH George B. of Prattsburgh, NY   August 27, 1873
OSBORN Alice of Pulteney, NY   Pulteney, NY

PERINE Clarence of New York City   September 23, 1873
RIPLEY Mrs. Christina F. of Bath, NY   Bath, NY

BISCOE Rev. George S. of Tipton, Iowa   September 16, 1873
ENSIGN Emma P. of Tipton, Iowa

JACK Amos of Thurston, NY   September 2, 1873
MERRILL Mary A. of Campbell, NY   Campbell, NY

CAPLE L. D. of Branchport, NY   September 4, 1873
PARIS Mary E. of Branchport, NY   Prattsburgh, NY

FULKERSON George W. of Thurston, NY   September 28, 1873
EDWARDS Ella L. of Erwin, NY   Erwin, NY

COVELL Nelson of Bath, NY   September 23, 1873
HUFFMAN Jennie of Bath, NY   Bath, NY

COATS S. M. of Wheeler, NY   October 3, 1873
ALLEN Melissa S. of Wheeler, NY   Bath, NY

RICHARDSON F. M. of Bath, NY   October 3, 1873
BOUTON Mrs. E. E. of Prattsburgh, NY   Prattsburgh, NY

FOSTER Edward L. of Barrington, NY   October 1, 1873
STRAIT Lola of Campbell, NY   Savona, NY

CRANSTON James R. of US Army   October 9, 1873
KING Mrs. Sarah E. at res of Y. H. WHEELER   Hammondsport, NY

YOUMANS Oliver B. of Savona, NY   October 11, 1873
ALLEN Frances P. of Eagle Valley, NY   Thurston, NY

BIEBER Charles of Rochester, NY   October 16, 1873
GELBRICH Anna of Hammondsport, NY   Bath, NY

DE PUE James H. of Bath, NY   October 15, 1873
LYON Sate of Pulteney, NY   Pulteney, NY

WASHBURN Daniel F. of Pulteney, NY   October 8, 1873
MC NELLA Mary I. of Pulteney, NY   Pulteney, NY

BRUSH William H. of Pulteney, NY   October 22, 1873
CLARK Ellen C. of Prattsburgh, NY   Prattsburgh, NY

SNYDER William H. H. of Elmira, NY   October 23, 1873
WHITCOMB Hattie A. of Merchantville, NY   Merchantville, NY

DIETZEL George C. of Livonia, NY   October 1, 1873
FLORA Rhoda of Wayland, NY   Bath, NY

MAYNARD Frank H. of Elmira, NY
CRAIG Anna dau of Robert B. Craig of Cold Springs, NY

November 8, 1873
Cold Springs, NY

TILLOTT Thomas R. of Savona, NY
HUBBARD Mary of Campbell, NY

November 4, 1873
Coopers Plains, NY

DE WITT Orlando of Monterey, NY
RANDALL Nancy of Monterey, NY

November 15, 1873
Coopers Plains, NY

HICOK Samuel S. of Cameron, NY
AGAR Jane of Urbana, NY

November 11, 1873
Bath, NY

STARKS Daniel C. of Hermitage, NY
MURRAY Mary E. of Bath, NY

October 21, 1873
Hermitage, NY

GRIMES James of Urbana, NY
GIBSON Laura of Wayne, NY

October 31, 1873
Mt. Washington, NY

HALL Frank of Bath, NY
BULL Mary A. of Bath, NY

November 19, 1873
Bath, NY

GOFF Luke R. of Howard, NY   (Newspaper date) December 17, 1873
FERRIS Lora of Howard, NY

Howard, NY

KINGKADE C. S.
SHAVER Addie

December 2, 1873
Avoca, NY

WRIGHT Alpheus N. of Tuscarora, NY
MARGESON Maria of Wayne, NY

November 27, 1873
Wayne, NY

INSCHO James of Orange, NY
EDWARDS Lois S. of Orange, NY

November 22, 1873
S. Bradford, NY

MC DOWELL J. L. of Elmira, NY
EDSALL Clara of Elmira, NY

December 10, 1873
Bath, NY

WEBBER Frederick of Hornellsville, NY
RUNEY Annie E. of Howard, NY

December 15, 1873
Howard, NY

WOOD James of Bath, NY
LONGWELL Lorena of Urbana, NY

December 17, 1873
Savona, NY

VAN HOUSEN B. of Prattsburgh, NY
HOUSE Ettie of Howard, NY

December 31, 1873
Howard, NY

GILLETT William R. of Thurston, NY
NOLES Eunice of Thurston, NY

December 21, 1873
Bath, NY

TRUMBULL Emmons T. of Bath, NY
GILLETT Frances of Bath, NY

December 21, 1873
Bath, NY

TUELL James of Avoca, NY   December 31, 1873
HUNN M. J. of Avoca, NY   Avoca, NY

PIERSON Samuel H. of Urbana, NY   January 13, 1874
MILLS Eliza of Urbana, NY   Bath, NY

JAYNES Austin S. of Sonora, NY   January 21, 1874
MACK Mrs. Betsey M. of Bath, NY   Bath, NY

NICHOLS Nyre of Bath, NY   January 24, 1874
ROBBINS Emma S. of Wheeler, NY   Bath, NY

BENEDICT Daniel L. of Theeler, NY   January 14, 1874
BARRETT Mary E. of Urbana, NY   Bath, NY

GIVEANS Samuel S. of Vernon, NJ   January 15, 1874
HOAGLAND Sarah L. of Howell, Mi.   Bath, NY

FLUENT James R. of Bath, NY   February 3, 1874
SMITH Harriet of Bath, NY   Cameron, NY

VELIE Abraham J. of Orange, NY   February 7, 1874
HARRIS Ella of Howard, NY   Howard, NY

MILLER J. B. of Wayland, NY   February 11, 1874
MC CROSSEN Deborah T. of Richmond, NY   Richmond, NY

BROWN Joseph of Bath, NY   February 18, 1874
HAIGHT Phebe of Bath, NY   Bath, NY

BOYD David M. of Woodhull, NY   February 25, 1874
BRUNDAGE Sarah of Pleasant Valley, NY   Pleasant Valley, NY

BENNETT Theodore of Wayne, NY   February 26, 1874
REED Libbie of Wayne, NY   Hammondsport, NY

BAKER Joseph L. of Covington, Pa.   February 10, 1874
SIMONS Amanda J. of Savona, NY   Covington, Pa.

BALL Edward J.   February 25, 1874
CLARK Clara A.   Bath, NY

MANN George   March 18, 1874
DIAMOND Emily   Bath, NY

SINCERBOX James W. of Pulteney, NY   March 19, 1874
AUSTIN Marion of Pulteney, NY   Bath, NY

DILDINE Jeptha L. of Urbana, NY   March 19, 1874
DREW Eliza W. of Urbana, NY   Bath, NY

CLARK Charles A. of Bath, NY — March 18, 1874
HOLBROOK Susie B. of Hammondsport, NY — Hammondsport, NY

CRANS James of Bath, NY — March 24, 1874
WILLOUR Fanny Adeline dau of Alonzo Willour of Bath, NY

WILLIAMS H. B. Sheriff of Steuben Co. NY — March 12, 1874
BARBER Amanda of E. Avon, NY — E. Avon, NY

DE GRAFF Frank of Howard, NY — April 17, 1874
KINKADE Susan of Avoca, NY — Bath, NY

JOY Lewis B. of Buffalo, NY — April 14, 1874
WILLSON Mrs. Caroline (**DUDLEY**) — Bath, NY

STEARNS George Herbert of Cincinnati, Oh. — April 15, 1874
WELD Isabella Mary of Boston, Mass. — Bath, NY

BOULON Adoneram Judson of Peoria, Ill. — April 16, 1874
KNOX Miss Mary dau of Conrad **WELCH** — Dansville, NY

LEWIS Jesse of Bath, NY — March 26, 1874
BURCH Mrs. Nancy J. of Bath, NY — Mt. Washington, NY

BERRY Henry of Hector, NY — May 6, 1874
EVERTS Maggie of Hector, NY — Hector, NY

COOPER George of Howard, NY — April 8, 1874
GILCHRIST Emma of Howard, NY — Howard, NY

COLCORD M. B. of Thurston, NY — May 5, 1874
MORRISON S. D. of Thurston, NY — Thurston, NY

DUDLEY S. J. of Bath, NY — May 14, 1874
BRUNDAGE Emma of Thurston, NY at res of Charles Brundage

WRIGHT A. J. of Angelica, NY — (Newspaper date) May 20, 1874
ANDREWS Nancy of Bradford, NY — Bradford, NY

GRAY Aaron — (Newspaper date) June 10, 1874
COLBATH Emma — Bath, NY

SMALLIDGE Charles R. of Urbana, NY — May 27, 1874
BORDEN Mary of Bath, NY — Bath, NY

GILBERT Francis Bachus of Urbana, NY — June 10, 1874
MC CAY Sabra (**ELLSWORTH**) — Brooklyn, NY

ANGEL Eli T. of Wheeler, NY — June 27, 1874
BOOTH Eliza of Wheeler, NY — Bath, NY

DAVIS W. R. of Bath, NY   July 2, 1874
MARTIN Catherine of Avoca, NY   Avoca, NY

BROWN C. R.   July 3, 1874
MC CANN Mary   Bath, NY

HADLEY G. F. of Bath, NY   July 12, 1874
VELEY Emma A. of Bath, NY

MERRILL E. S.   June 27, 1874
CLARK Dell A. of Cameron, NY   Cameron, NY

JONES Thomas of Bath, NY   August 2, 1874
THOMAS Phebe of Bath, NY

PLACE Reuben of Shiawasso, Mi.   August 6, 1874
KNAPP Mrs. A. J. of Bath, NY   Savona, NY

MASON Enoch D. of Cameron, NY   September 10, 1874
AGOR Mary E. of Urbana, NY   Bath, NY

GREGORY B. L. Danbury, Ct.   August 12, 1874
CUMMINGS Jennie S. of Bath, NY   Bethel, Ct.

GLEASON Warren   September 8, 1874
DOCKSTADER Mrs. Eliza C.   Bath, NY

CANFIELD Edward of Bath, NY   September 17, 1874
HASTINGS Jennie M. dau of Maj. D. M. of Baltimore, Md.   Baltimore, Md.
    (groom was accidently drowned soon after marriage)

CLARK Perry of Kanona, NY   September 16, 1874
MILLER Susie of Bath, NY   Bath, NY

HUY L. Grant of Corning, NY   September 22, 1874
RIDENOUR Kate Hess of Avoca, NY   Avoca, NY

BRYANT Dr. Joseph D. of New York City   September 29, 1874
CRUM Annette A. dau of Samuel Crum of Bath, NY   Bath, NY

SEARS Harley age 76y of Thurston, NY   October 11, 1874
PALMER Mrs. Rachel age 73y of Potter Co. Pa.   Bath, NY

PHILLIPS William of Thurston, NY   November 4, 1874
CLARK Margarite A. of Thurston, NY

CHAPMAN Charles E. of Elmira, NY   November 12, 1874
STOCUM Osie Kate dau of Maj. John Stocum   Bath, NY

SHARP L. B. of Howard, NY   October 29, 1874

CLARK Eunice of Bath, NY   Bath, NY

STEWART Ezekiel L. of Howard, NY   (Newspaper date) November 18, 1874
HOAGLAND Mary J. of Howard, NY   Howard, NY

WARNER John S. of Medina, Oh. formerly of Bath, NY   November 21, 1874
WOODWARD Clara dau of Judge Woodward   Medina, Ohio

JACOBUS G. R. of Bath, NY   November 18, 1874
WEBSTER Marilla of Urbana, NY

EMERSON W. H.   November 18, 1874
WOOLEVER Jennie

COCHRAN James of Howard, NY   November 25, 1874
MAXWELL Hattie of Howard, NY   Bath, NY

SWITZER Wallace of Bath, NY   November 26, 1874
KNOWLES Hattie of Bath, NY   Bath, NY

SPAULDING Lewis of Hornellsville, NY   October 8, 1874
ZIELLY Orinda of Avoca, NY   Avoca, NY

FOX Oscar L. of Bath, NY   November 24, 1874
EGGLESTON Eugene of S. Pulteney, NY   S. Pulteney, NY

WHITEWOOD Luther of Canisteo, NY   December 16, 1874
BODGE Annette of La Port, Ind.   Bath, NY

BARNES J. N. of Canisteo, NY   December 24, 1874
MARTIN Diantha of Bath, NY   Bath, NY

MC CLOUGH R. of Bath, NY   December 24, 1874
LOOK Julie of Bath, NY   Bath, NY

GEARY Edward of Bath, NY   December 24, 1874
ASHLEY Jennie of Bath, NY   Bath, NY

MC DONALD James of Penn Yan, NY   December 23, 1874
GARDNER Ellen   Bath, NY

PEACOCK Henry of Wayne, NY   December 24, 1874
STINSON Ellen A. dau of George Stinson of Bath, NY   Bath, NY

FRALEY Fred of Howard, NY   December 8, 1874
DE GRAFF Eunice of Howard, NY   Howard, NY

EMERY J. J. of Bath, NY   December 30, 1874
HARVEY Julia E. of Bath, NY   Bath, NY

HERRICK Rilla W. of Bradford, NY   January 4, 1875
NICHOLS Frank T. of Dundee, NY   Bradford, NY

HAMLIN Albert H. of Fowlerville, NY   December 23, 1874
MAGEE Emily C. of Fowlerville, NY at parents   Avoca, NY

BAILEY John F. of Prattsburgh, NY   January 9, 1875
WELCH Ella of Urbana, NY   Bath, NY

ACKERMAN John D. of Cameron, NY   January 27, 1875
MORROW Deborah M. of Thurston, NY   Bath, NY

CHURCHILL Frank D. Editor Wellsboro Gazette   February 8, 1875
HALL Ida dau of Alexander Hall of Bath, NY   Bath, NY

CARNOCHAN Samuel of Bath, NY   February 3, 1875
LOOMIS Gertrude of Bath, NY   Bath, NY

HARDING J. Matt of Fremont, NY   February 17, 1875
WILLIS Nora of Howard, NY   Howard, NY

KIMBALL C. P. of Maine   February 18, 1875
SPARHAWK Mrs. Helen J. dau of H. F. **GETCHELL**   Chicago, Ill.

RICHARDSON Clinton W. of Bath, NY   February 16, 1875
DAVIS Della May dau of R. W. Davis of Long Is. City, NY   Long Is. City, NY

TAGGART Frank A. of Brooklyn, NY   February 17, 1875
SUTTON Tillie M. of Brooklyn, NY   Brooklyn, NY

KINNER William of Cameron, NY   February 24, 1875
WHEELER Abbie of Bath, NY at James **MORRISON** res   Cameron, NY

LITTLE Andrew formerly of Milwaukee, Wis.   January 28, 1875
GREENE Laura M. dau of John E. of New York City   New York City

MILLARD George of Canisteo, NY   March 17, 1875
ROSE Hattie of Canisteo, NY   Bath, NY

MILLER Hiram H. of Bath, NY   March 10, 1875
SEAGER Emma L. of Bath, NY   Bath, NY

RINE John of Wallace Station, NY   March 18, 1875
SUMMERVILLE Mattie A. of Wallace Station, NY   Bath, NY

MATTOON Dewitt of Avoca, NY   March 17, 1875
CLARK Thankful of Bath, NY   Bath, NY

WASSER Abraham of Kanona, NY   March 11, 1875
SLATTERY Mary of Kanona, NY

SCOFIELD G. M. of Bath, NY	March 30, 1875
KEELER Emma of Bath, NY	Bath, NY
SHUMAN Mathew of Avoca, NY	April 15, 1875
MC NEIL Mary of Avoca, NY	Avoca, NY
BREWSTER John A. of Bath, NY	April 14, 1875
NICHOLS M. Helen of Bath, NY	Bath, NY
SALT Wellington of Bath, NY	January 27, 1875
ALLISON Mercy E. of Bath, NY	Bath, NY
FEAGLES Jacob H. of Orange, NY	April 18, 1875
OAKLEY Carolee of Bradford, NY	Savona, NY
COTTON Russell of Bath, NY	March 16, 1875
PURDY Esther A. of Bath, NY	Bath, NY
AUSTIN James A. of Prattsburgh, NY	May 2, 1875
HULTS Martha of Pulteney, NY	Italy Hollow, NY
LARROWE A. of Cohocton, NY	April 28, 1875
MORGAN Kittie of Lima, NY	Lima, NY
SMITH Frank D. of Mitchellville, NY	May 1, 1875
TOWNSEND Libbie of Mitchellville, NY	Hammondsport, NY
BEYER William W. of Bath, NY	February 28, 1875
PURDY Emma L. of Bath, NY	Bath, NY
WILLIAMS Durand of Hornellsville, NY	April 28, 1875
HELMES Emma V. of Canisteo, NY	Canisteo, NY
SLINEY Thomas Emmett	May 19, 1875
CARNEY Nora	Bath, NY
TUBBS Thurston W. of Hartsville, NY	May 2, 1875
DENNIS Charlotte of Canisteo, NY	Canisteo, NY
ROBERTSON Charles B. of Howard, NY	June 2, 1875
GLOVER Lydia of Howard, NY	Howard, NY
PALMER Frank of Bath, NY	May 22, 1875
MOWERS Evalina of Bath, NY	Campbell, NY
HILL Charles W. of Pulteney, NY	May 20, 1875
STONE Flora A. of Pulteney, NY	
GLEASON Joseph F. of Towlesville, NY	July 4, 1875
BORDEN Lydia E. of Bath, NY	Bath, NY

AGOR Thomas of Urbana, NY	June 26, 1875
SMALLEY Lizzie of Urbana, NY	Bath, NY
WHITNEY Edward M.	June 29, 1875
LONG Florence dau of John E. Long of US Navy	Astoria, NY
MC CHESNEY Alexander of Howard, NY	July 17, 1875
FOLLANSBEE Ettie of Howard, NY	Bath, NY
ORCUTT Frank W. of Savona, NY	August 21, 1875
HAWKINS Dora E.	Bath, NY
MOSS Frank of Bath, NY	August 29, 1875
FLEWELLYN Mary F. of Bath, NY	Bath, NY
TOWNSEND Burdette of Bath, NY	August 21, 1875
PETRIE Mary E. of Bath, NY	Bath, NY
GIFFORD Adelbert L. of Vineland, NY	August 24, 1875
ACKERSON Helen of Bath, NY	Bath, NY
KENMUIR James of Kansas City, Mo.	February 3, 1876
ROWLETTE Celia of Steuben Co. NY	Kansas City, Mo.
SWITZER B. C. of Campbell, NY	February 17, 1876
BENNETT Ella dau of George T. of Campbell, NY	Campbell, NY
MILLER George H. of Wheeler, NY	January 19, 1876
OVERHISER Lydia A. of Wheeler, NY	Wheeler, NY
MILLER Derrick V. of Wheeler, NY	February 17, 1876
LEWIS Jennie of Wheeler, NY	Wheeler, NY
HORTON Theodore F. of Bath, NY	February 16, 1876
STINSON Maggie J. of Bath, NY	Savona, NY
ABER George W. of Urbana, NY	March 1, 1876
BAKER Margelia of Urbana, NY	Savona, NY
POTTER Alanson C. of Wheeler, NY	March 1, 1876
LORD Hattie E. of Wayne, NY	Savona, NY
BURNAP Perley of Hornby, NY	February 17, 1876
MATTOON Adeline of Avoca, NY	Hornby, NY
VAN HOUSEN John H. of Howard, NY	March 16, 1876
HANABLE Sarah E. of Howard, NY	Howard, NY
RUMSEY Lorenzo W. of Campbell, NY	March 22, 1876
BURGETT Ruth A. of Thurston, NY	Savona, NY

BARNES Dr. Charles A. of Rochester, NY	February 29, 1876
SMITH Susan M. of Bath, NY	Watkins, NY
HOPKINS F. D. of Bath, NY	February 22, 1876
HAMMOND Ruth E. of Erwin Center, NY	Erwin Center, NY
FLEWELLYN E. B. of Bath, NY	March 4, 1876
ANDERSON Caroline of Cameron, NY	Bath, NY
SHULTS A. J. of Wheeler, NY	March 30, 1876
GRAY Mary E. of Avoca, NY	Avoca, NY
BROTHER Valentine of Bath, NY	April 16, 1876
CUNNINGHAM Mary of Bath, NY	Bath, NY
TAYLOR Bennett of Howard, NY	April 5, 1876
STEWART Matilda E. of Howard, NY	Buena Vista, NY
MILLER Peter of Howard, NY	March 23, 1876
MC BETH Harriet E. of Howard, NY	Howard, NY
MUNSON Cyrus of Bradford, NY	April 26, 1876
MATHEWS Le Ella of Bradford, NY	Bradford, NY
CHASE Thomas C. of Avoca, NY	April 26, 1876
WARD Mrs. Sarah A. of Hornby, NY	Corning, NY
PETERSON Charles H. of Savona, NY	May 24, 1876
SANDERS Elma of Savona, NY	Savona, NY
RICHARDS Albert of Avoca, NY	June 24, 1876
MAYNARD Sarah of Avoca, NY	
DRAKE William S. of Bath, NY	July 29, 1876
KELLOGG Julia C. of Elmira, NY	Bath, NY
TRAVIS Absolom M. of Howard, NY	August 13, 1876
HATHAWAY Lorra E. of Howard, NY	Towlesville, NY
THOMPSON Orville M. of Wheeler, NY	August 16, 1876
STRONG Alvina of Wheeler, NY	Bath, NY
MC CARTNEY A. Clarence of Bath, NY	August 24, 1876
JONES L. Anna of Bath, NY	Bath, NY
VOSBURGH Alonzo of Bath, NY	August 30, 1876
STEWART Mary of Bath, NY	Bath, NY
JAYNES W. A. of Urbana, NY	September 11, 1876
SMITH Lucinda C. of Urbana, NY	Cold Springs, NY

HOUGH Martin of Lenox Co. Ontario, Canada   September 20, 1876
SHULTS Anna dau of Josiah of Avoca, NY   Avoca, NY

MUDGE Edgar R.   September 6, 1876
MORRISON Libbie   Pulteney, NY

STONE Stephen A.   September 10, 1876
FARR Mary B.   Pulteney, NY

PARKER Adam of San Francisco, Cal.   September 27, 1876
ALLERTON Frank C. of Savona, NY   Savona, NY

MOSS David of Savona, NY   September 25, 1876
STEWART Mary Jane of Howard, NY   Howard, NY

ACKERSON John of Bath, NY   September 24, 1876
PLATT Lydia S. dau of Ira of Bath, NY   Bath, NY

LOCKWOOD Jacob F. of Urbana, NY   October 1, 1876
ABER Anna M. of Urbana, NY   Bath, NY

KETCHUM E. T. of Wayne, NY   (Newspaper date) October 4, 1876
FENTON Mariah of Hornellsville, NY

HULL Henry of Bath, NY   (Newspaper date) October 11, 1876
HAYDEN Charlotte E. of Rochester, NY at Mother's   Rochester, NY

BAKER Isaac E. of Bath, NY   September 9, 1876
LONGWELL Maria E. dau of George of Bath, NY   Bath, NY

RETAN O. S.   October 4, 1876
LYON Emma   S. Pulteney, NY

FRY Wesley of Barrington, NY   October 26, 1876
FAUCETT Martha dau of Richard of Bath, NY

COTTON Albert of Fremont, NY   October 25, 1876
WHITE Hannah C. of Howard, NY   Howard, NY

CLEMMONS S. E. of Bath, NY   October 26, 1876
GRAY Elida A. of Avoca, NY   Avoca, NY

GAY John J. of Howard, NY   October 31, 1876
MC KIBBEN Susan of Howard, NY   Bath, NY

MC KIBBEN Andrew of Howard, NY   October 31, 1876
GAY Hattie of Howard, NY   Bath, NY

DYE Orton of Avoca, NY   October 18, 1876
COOPER Sarah of Avoca, NY   Bloods, NY

SCOTT George T. of Avoca, NY   November 12, 1876
MILLER Elizabeth E. of Bath, NY   Bath, NY

LAINE A. B. of Canisteo, NY   October 10, 1876
WHITE Maggie of Howard, NY   Hornellsville, NY

CROWE William Le Ray   November 29, 1876
KNAPP Ella M. formerly of Steuben Co. NY   Owasso, Mi.

GRAY Ambrose of Avoca, NY   December 26, 1876
CONWAY Mary of Avoca, NY   Bath, NY

WHITE Daniel Jr. of Bath, NY   December 27, 1876
SANFORD Nannie of Cold Springs, NY   Cold Springs, NY

ULLYETTE Lambert T. of W. Sparta, NY   December 21, 1876
KYSOR H. Augusta of Howard, NY   Howard, NY

HALSEY Leonard of Howard, NY   July __. 1876
STANTON Sophia of Brookfield, Pa.   Howard, NY

BURLESON John R. of Howard, NY   December __, 1876
COLE Martha A. of Howard, NY   Howard, NY

COLE George B. of Bath, NY   January 19, 1877
EVANS Amy of Bath, NY   Bath, NY

KEELER F. J. of Kanona, NY   December 27, 1876
GAMBEE Laura E. of Romulus, NY   Romulus, NY

SALT Daniel T. of Bath, NY   January 1, 1877
WHITE Jennie of S. Howard, NY   S. Howard, NY

OXX Warren W. of Bath, NY   January 18, 1877
MC FIE Louise J. of Bath, NY   Bath, NY

ROBARDS James of Avoca, NY   January 24, 1877
ROCKWELL Alice E. of Savona, NY   Savona, NY

TAFT Henry C. of Oakland, Cal.   February 13, 1877
MAXWELL Lizzie of Dansville, NY

MITCHELL George of Norwich, NY   January 3, 1877
BRADLEY Carrie

YOUNGS George of Elmira, NY   January 1, 1877
THOMSON Hannah A.

FORD J. N. of Bath, NY   February 23, 1877
COYKENDALL Mary J. of Bath, NY   Bath, NY

MANVILLE C. M. of Towanda, Pa.   February 18, 1877
BARRON Ella T. dau of C. H. of Penn Yan, NY   Penn Yan, NY

WARREN W. D. of Bath, NY   March 4, 1877
BENNETT Sate of Bath, NY   Bath, NY

DYER Thomas of Avoca, NY   March 7, 1877
FAUCETT Mary dau of Richard Faucett   Mt. Washington, NY

ABER E. E. of Bath, NY   March 24, 1877
BRUNDAGE Mary E. of Prattsburgh, NY   Prattsburgh, NY

ALLEN Oscar F. of Canaseraga, NY   March 22, 1877
PIERCE Mary A. of Hornellsville, NY   Hornellsville, NY

HARTMAN Charles E. of S. Dansville, NY   March 11, 1877
WAINWRIGHT Gertrude E. of Stephens Mills, NY   Stephens Mills, NY

BROOKS Levi of Bath, NY   April 15, 1877
MONELL Helen M. of Bath, NY   Bath, NY

EDWARDS Lewis of New York City   April 19, 1877
GANSEVOORT Helen dau of late Duncan **MAGEE**   Livingston, NY

KYSER James F. of Bath, NY   May 5, 1877
WAGNER Nora C. of Bath, NY   Bath, NY

CARR George H. of Mc Graw, Pa.   April 22, 1877
DICKINSON Mary M. of Bradford, NY   Bradford, NY

TAYLOR Henry of Bradford, NY   June 7, 1877
LONGWELL Hannah of Urbana, NY   Savona, NY

HUBER James S. of Bath, NY   July 14, 1877
RYDER Marie E. of Bath, NY   Corning, NY

TOPPING Perry of Bath, NY   July 15, 1877
ROBARDS Mary M. of Howard, NY   Howard, NY

BURGET James T. of Thurston, NY   August 5, 1877
DENSMORE Carrie of Thurston, NY   Thurston, NY

MC GLOTHLIN George of Urbana, NY   August 4, 1877
DUNN Maggie of Wheeler, NY   Bath, NY

SMITH George W. of Bradford, NY   August 11, 1877
WARRING Frankie E. of Bath, NY   Bradford, NY

ELLIS Charles A. of Bath, NY   September 25, 1877
ABER Jennie dau of G. Aber of Bath, NY   Bath, NY

LAKE Martin F. of Hornellsville, NY
DAILEY Annie of Fremont, NY

September 27, 1877
Bath, NY

COYE Alvah D. of Hornby, NY
KRESS Sarah E. of Orange, NY

October 2, 1877
Monterey, NY

SUTTON John of Prattsburgh, NY
CORNUE Sarah of Prattsburgh, NY

October 9, 1877

STEWART George of Howard, NY
MC ADAMS Alidia of Howard, NY

October 17, 1877
Bath, NY

FERGUSON Milson E. of Cameron, NY
FRENCH Sarah of Cameron, NY

November 4, 1877
Bath, NY

PETERS David of Thurston, NY
MYERS Fidelia of Bath, NY

November 13, 1877
Savona, NY

SANFORD Alonzo of Bradford, NY
CLARK Emma E. of Bath, NY

November 26, 1877
Savona, NY

SHEPHERD Horace B.
PATTERSON Jennie M.

November 27, 1877
Kanona, NY

FORD Elisha B. of Pulteney, NY
GUNTERMAN Mary of Bath, NY

November 28, 1877
Bath, NY

MILLER W. P. of Bath, NY
REED Elizabeth M. of Bath, NY

December 2, 1877
Bath, NY

THOMAS Lemuel H. of Bath, NY
PERRY Anna of Bath, NY

December 6, 1877
Bath, NY

COVELL Lafayette of Bath, NY
TOWSLEY Mary of Wheeler, NY

December 10, 1877

BENNETT George of Pulteney, NY
LUNGER Kate of Pulteney, NY

November 21, 1877
Pulteney, NY

VAN AMBURG William J.
FOREMAN Elizabeth H.

December 9, 1877
Pulteney, NY

WHEELER R. W. of Bath, NY
SCARVELL Louisa of Bath, NY

December 25, 1877
Bath, NY

WARD B. C. of Bath, NY
BLACK Mrs. Caroline W. of Bath, NY

December 30, 1877
Bath, NY

BROOKS Murray of Bath, NY
INGERSOLL Emma of Bath, NY

December 24, 1877
Bath, NY

DECKER E. O. of Elmira, NY   December 31, 1877
MARTINETT Anna G. of Bath, NY   Bath, NY

GLOVER Myron of Howard, NY   January 1, 1878
WALKER Sarah Jane of Howard, NY   Howard, NY

FAUCETT John S. of Bath, NY   January 23, 1878
TOWNSEND Rosalie of Barrington, NY   Barrington, NY

PARKER James A. of Merchantville, NY   January 24, 1878
JONES Dellie M. dau of Edward of Merchantville, NY   Merchantville, NY

WYGANT Lyman of Hedgesville, NY   January 19, 1878
COSS J. L. of Hedgesville, NY

BOWES John of Bath, NY   February 5, 1878
CAVANAUGH Maggie of Bath, NY

MC ELWAIN Robert   February 12, 1878
PALMER Hattie L.   Hammondsport, NY

CURTIS Edwin E. of Altoona, Pa.   February 20, 1878
BOVIER Helen D.   Bath, NY

COOK Charles C. of Wellsboro, Pa.   February 27, 1878
HALL Lettie dau of Alexander Hall   Bath, NY

BEEBE Willis of Urbana, NY   February 25, 1878
STORMS Fannie of Urbana, NY   Bath, NY

WARNER David J. of Corning, NY   January 29, 1878
L'AMOUREAUX Carrie M. of Bath, NY   Bath, NY

LONGWELL George of Bath, NY   February 28, 1878
WHEELER Maria A. of Bath, NY   Bath, NY

WESSELS Charles of Howard, NY   March 6, 1878
SMITH Sara of Howard, NY   Howard, NY

EMERSON E. A. of Bath, NY   February 28, 1878
MILLARD Libbie of Mt. Morris, NY   Mt. Morris, NY

O'BRIEN Robert   (Newspaper date) March 21, 1878
GAY Libbie at res of William Gay   Towlesville, NY

SALTSMAN Elijah   March 13, 1878
TOWNER Lydia A. of Avoca, NY   Avoca, NY

VAN ORDER Lyman H. of Howard, NY   March 14, 1878
MC GONEGAL Frank H. of Avoca, NY   Coopers Plains, NY

ELLAS Clark of Urbana, NY	March 17, 1878
BLIVEN Mary of Mitchellville, NY	Mitchellville, NY
HENDERSON Henry A. of Avoca, NY	March 14, 1878
HANKS Sarah E. of Kanona, NY	Kanona, NY
GLANN George of Avoca, NY	March 22, 1878
HAMMOND Ida E. of Avoca, NY	Avoca, NY
BAILEY Lafayette C.	March 23, 1878
BAILEY Carrie dau of Capt. C. P. Bailey	Hammondsport, NY
BOWLBY George K. of Bath, NY	March 27, 1878
HARDENBROOK Sarah E. of Bath, NY	Bath, NY
LUMBARD Franklin M. of Elmira, NY	March 28, 1878
MC KIBBEN Elizabeth of Howard, NY	Howard, NY
BENNETT John W. of Howard, NY	March 27, 1878
GLOVER Nancy of Howard, NY	
AUSTIN Le Grand S.	March 27, 1878
KELLY Adda	Bradford, NY
DODGE Albert W.	March 27, 1878
KELLY Flora	Bradford, NY
FAULKNER Thomas of Bath, NY	April 21, 1878
GENUNG Adda B. of Bath, NY	Bath, NY
HUNTINGTON Lewis K. of Painted Post, NY	March 20, 1878
RAYMOND Josephine R. dau of Amos of Raymond, Pa.	Raymond, Pa.
LONG David A. of Troupsburgh, NY	April 14, 1878
LAMPHIER Mrs. Mary E. of Troupsburgh, NY	Troupsburgh, NY
LONG Gilbert G. of Troupsburgh, NY	April 14, 1878
PIERCE Martha A. of Troupsburgh, NY	Troupsburgh, NY
LAMPHIER W. R. of Troupsburgh, NY	April 17, 1878
LONG Betsey A. of Troupsburgh, NY	Troupsburgh, NY
HARVEY Marvin C. of Bath, NY	April 10, 1878
RUDD Ida of Bath, NY	Bath, NY
GURNSEY Fred H. of Howard, NY	April 21, 1878
THOMPSON Kate M. of Thurston, NY	Thurston, NY
BROWN George W. of Hornellsville, NY	April 15, 1878
RARRICK Jennie of Painted Post, NY	

SMITH J. Willett of Bath, NY April 23, 1878
PACE Ella A. of Bath, NY Hornellsville, NY

VAN DUSEN William B. of Howard, NY April 17, 1878
BENNETT Mary of Howard, NY Howard, NY

WHEELER John D. of Cameron, NY April 11, 1878
SANTEE Dell E. of Cameron, NY Cameron, NY

BENNETT Charles E. April 11, 1878
DE LANEY Sarah E. Canisteo, NY

COCHRAN George of Howard, NY April 24, 1878
MC KIBBEN Christina of Howard, NY Howard, NY

EADE Frank of Wheeler, NY April 9, 1878
TYLER Emegene of Wheeler, NY Wheeler, NY

FRY William Henry of Bath, NY April 17, 1878
SNYDER Augusta M. of Bath, NY Bath, NY

RHODES Frank D. of Potter, NY April 17, 1878
HUNLEY Ella L. of Bath, NY Potter, NY

CAMPBELL Rev. S. M. of Rochester, NY May 1, 1878
JUDSON Mrs. Mary P. of Prattsburgh, NY Prattsburgh, NY

SMITH J. D. of Bath, NY May 8, 1878
NILES Adelaide M. of Bath, NY Bath, NY

TEETER Harland of Wallace, NY May 5, 1878
DAVIS Estella of Avoca, NY Wallace, NY

HAWLEY Miles W. of Perry, NY formerly Hornellsville, NY April 30, 1878
GLEASON Mrs. Laura V. dau of N. B. **VAN SLYK** Madison, Wis.

BARTZ Frank of Wayland, NY April 27, 1878
POOR Flora B. of Wayland, NY Wayland, NY

GRISWOLD D. H. April 25, 1878
MC CULLUM Martha C. of S. Dansville, NY S. Dansville, NY

GESSNER John of Perkinsville, NY April 30, 1878
HAUCK Barbara of Dansville, NY Dansville, NY

BROTHER Martin R. of Johnstown, NY April 24, 1878
HOUSE Elizabeth C. of Kanona, NY Kanona, NY

COOK Jacob of Rathbone, NY May 21, 1878
DRAKE Sarah Ella of Howard, NY Howard, NY

CATTERSON Rev. William of Penn Yan, NY   May 14, 1878
ROSENBURY Emily dau of John J. of Penn Yan, NY   Penn Yan, NY

HAYWARD William H. of Jackson, Mi.   May 5, 1878
HOPKINS Libbie L. of Penn Yan, NY   Penn Yan, NY

EVANS B. Earl of Avon, NY   May 19, 1878
BAKER Ella of Hammondsport, NY   Hammondsport, NY

GLEASON H. F. of Wayne, NY   June 6, 1878
EARLL A. D. of Wayne, NY   Wayne, NY

HUBBS Melvin B. of Campbell, NY   June 22, 1878
WHEELER Minnie dau of James B. of Cameron, NY   Cameron, NY

BLANSETT Charles T. of Wheeler, NY   July 2, 1878
ROOT Nettie of Cohocton, NY   Hornellsville, NY

SEAGER William L. of Thurston, NY   July 7, 1878
TRUMBULL Lizzie of Thurston, NY   Savona, NY

BUNKER George W. of Canisteo, NY   July 4, 1878
DYON Catherine E. of Canisteo, NY   Canisteo, NY

LINLEY George of Rochester, NY   July 1, 1878
GOULD Favie of Bath, NY   Niagara Falls, NY

WHITEMORE Marshall   July 4, 1878
ROWLEY Fannie   Canisteo, NY

TEED Harry   July 4, 1878
HEAD Emma B.   Canisteo, NY

KILLERMAN Eliphalet of Conesus, NY   July 21, 1878
GRANGER Alma of Wayland, NY

BARDEEN Charles H. of Thurston, NY   August 3, 1878
SMITH Priscilla Emeline of Thurston, NY   Thurston, NY

MANNING C. S. of Greenwood, NY   August 7, 1878
BLAKE Libbie of Greenwood, NY   Greenwood, NY

CROWELL Charles R. of Ulysses, Pa.   September 5, 1878
TOWNER Celestia of Avoca, NY   Avoca, NY

SMALL Frank of Bath, NY   September 5, 1878
WEMPLE Lizzie of Bath, NY   Bath, NY

CLARK Hebron S. of Merchantville, NY   September 17, 1878
SHEPARD Corah E. of Mt. Washington, NY   Mt. Washington, NY

DOUGLASS Myron   September 19, 1878
WOOD Alice H. of Mt. Washington, NY   Mt. Washington, NY

CHRISTLER Richard   September 25, 1878
MUSGRAVE Agnes M.   Bath, NY

CRAFT Francis L. of Howard, NY   September 26, 1878
DIMMICK Martha E. of Howard, NY   Howard, NY

RIDER Charles A. of Bath, NY   October 1, 1878
CARPENTER Mrs. C. L. of Bath, NY formerly Elmira, NY   Bath, NY

TALBOT Dennis   September 29, 1878
SABIN Mrs. Mary E. of Adrian, NY   Jasper, NY

BROWN Frank of Hornellsville, NY   October 9, 1878
OLMSTEAD Addie of Hornellsville, NY

WALLACE T. N. of Hornellsville, NY   October 17, 1878
JONES Ida of Hornellsville, NY

ARNOLD Charles W. of Cohocton, NY   October 29, 1878
SLAYTON Clara of Cohocton, NY

TOBEY Elba of Caton, NY   October 23, 1878
BARTHOLOMEW Lizzie of Southport, NY   Southport, NY

MAY James S. formerly of Bath, NY   October 3, 1878
HUTCHINSON Augusta of Prophetstown, Ill.   Prophetstown, Ill.

FERRIS Charles of Bath, NY   October 13, 1878
DEAN Rose of Bath, NY   Bath, NY

EATON George of Cameron, NY   October 20, 1878
SPRAGUE Phena of Urbana, NY   Wayne, NY

ROBINSON Robert of Bath, NY   November 20, 1878
PLATT Lucinda J. of Bath, NY

STEWART George E. of Howard, NY   November 14, 1878
EMERSON Lydia J. of Bath, NY   Bath, NY

BUFFUM Charles J. of Cowelsville, NY   October 13, 1878
WHITTEMORE Julia A. dau of M. F. of Jasper, NY   Jasper, NY

BUCKLEY John C. of Sonora, NY   November 27, 1878
MANNING Lydia M. of Sonora, NY

LOVELAND Henry   October 31, 1878
WISLEY Mary E.   E. Wayland, NY

SMITH Daniel S. of Bristol Hill, NY
FRENCH Hattie L. of Naples, NY
November 17, 1878
N. Cohocton, NY

COREY Orson M. of N. Cohocton, NY
HEWITT Minerva F. of N. Cohocton, NY
November 13, 1878
N. Cohocton, NY

HEMINGWAY William H. of Urbana, NY
STRATTON Kittie of Urbana, NY
November 24, 1878
Wheeler, NY

HORTON Lucius
WINTERMUTE Ruth Allie dau of Arthur
November 20, 1878
Pulteney, NY

SEELEY Albert
LEE Mrs. Loretta
November 20, 1878
Pulteney, NY

DABOLL Frank A.
ACKERMAN Alice of Prattsburgh, NY
November 28, 1878

HALL Emmett A. of Bath, NY
TOLES Emogene dau of John of Cameron Mills, NY
November 27, 1878
Cameron Mills, NY

EMERSON Alfred of Bath, NY
GRAY Mary of Bath, NY
November 30, 1878
Bath, NY

COVERT L. H. of Bath, NY
INSCHO Bell W. of Watkins, NY
December 7, 1878
Bath, NY

MOORE George of Campbell, NY
SHAVER Nannie of Campbell, NY
December 4, 1878
Campbell, NY

ALLEN V. D. of Avoca, NY
LAKE U. S. of Bath, NY
November 10, 1878
Thurston, NY

FAUCETT Anthony of Savona, NY
SKINKLE Delphine of Savona, NY
November 28, 1878
Campbell, NY

MANNING George of Savona, NY
DIMMICK Ella J. of Thurston, NY
December 1, 1878

ABER George G. of Bath, NY
FRINK Sarah A. of Bath, NY
December 11, 1878
Unionville, NY

KEITH Charles of Thurston, NY
WILLARD Grace of Cameron, NY
December 25, 1878

JENKINS Charles of N. Adams, Mass.
HOWARD Mary of Hornellsville, NY
December 17, 1878

COGSWELL Clark
BOYD Minnie of Prattsburgh, NY
December 24, 1878

HAMLIN Lawrence A. of Owasso, Mi. December 25, 1878
WYGANT Minnie J. of Cohocton, NY

SMITH Rufus E. December 23, 1878
BURKITT Alice Bath, NY

PLATT Jansan P. of Bath, NY December 25, 1878
ROBINSON Susan J. dau of Thomas of Bath, NY Bath, NY

VEEDER Byron G. of Cohocton, NY December 16, 1878
MC CARTNEY Mary C. of Bath, NY Bath, NY

SANFORD Frank A. of Sonora, NY December 26, 1878
HEWEY Maggie dau of James of Sonora, NY Sonora, NY

RANCHAN Charles M. of Wheeler, NY December 24, 1878
PARKHILL May of Howard, NY Howard, NY

CLARK Lavern S. of Canisteo, NY December 25, 1878
WARD Libbie E. of Rathbone, NY Rathbone, NY

HANAAN Daniel J. of Thurston, NY December 22, 1878
INSCHO Elizabeth M. of Bradford, NY Mt. Washington, NY

HUEY John S. of Orange, NY (Newspaper date) January 9, 1879
YAPLE Mary S. of Hornby, NY Hornby, NY

VAN DEUSEN Judson of Corning, NY November 28, 1878
WHITE Alice J. of Bath, NY

CARPENTER Ansel of Wayne, NY December 21, 1878
EAGLESTON Sarah of Tyrone, NY Weston, NY

POLMATEER Heman of Prattsburgh, NY December 28, 1878
SHULTS Fannie of Prattsburgh, NY Prattsburgh, NY

DOCKSTADER Benjamin of Avoca, NY January 1, 1879
BLACKENEY Helen M. of Wheeler, NY Avoca, NY

WILLOUR Charles M. of Bath, NY January 1, 1879
DOWNS Hannah A. of Canisteo, NY

AUDINWOOD George J. of Lindley, NY December 12, 1878
WHITE Emma M. of Caton, NY

DUVALL Charles of Hornellsville, NY January 6, 1879
WYLIE Kate of Hornellsville, NY

GIBSON Fred R. of Pulteney, NY January 1, 1879
PROSSER Emma J. of Jerusalem, NY

STINSON John F. of Bath, NY	January 15, 1879
MC DONNELL Sarah of Bath, NY	Campbell, NY
LONGWELL Charles G.	January 16, 1879
CARPENTER Emma N. dau of late B. S. of Elmira, NY	Bath, NY
ZIELLY Henry L. of Avoca, NY	January 21, 1879
SQUIRES Belle of Avoca, NY	Avoca, NY
BROWN Aalon of Hornellsville, NY	January 22, 1879
ABER Mrs. Lucy of Savona, NY	Savona, NY
DILLENBECK Leroy of Prattsburgh, NY	January 16, 1879
OVERHISER Belle at sister's	Borden Valley, NY
AINSWORTH Isaac of Prattsburgh, NY (Newspaper date)	January 30, 1879
SMITH Mrs. Emma of Corning, NY	Corning, NY
PEROW Wenwell	December 25, 1878
NILES Belle C.	E. Cohocton, NY
LONGWELL Eugene B. of Bradford, NY	January 29, 1879
MURDOCK Gustie dau of Rev. S. H. of Urbana, NY	Urbana, NY
BROWN Edgar G.	January 22, 1879
WAGENER Adele M.	Pulteney, NY
MATSON Nelson P. of Woodhull, NY	January 29, 1879
WILCOX Carrie of Woodhull, NY	Woodhull, NY
DEMENT A. E. of Bath, NY	February 4, 1879
FITZPATRICK Hattie of Bath, NY	
BROWN Edgar G. of Bradford, NY	January 28, 1879
TRAVIS Mary of Bradford, NY	S. Bradford, NY
ROFF David J. of Pulteney, NY	February 18, 1879
BALL Julia A. of Pulteney, NY	Pulteney, NY
HILL George W. of Caton, NY	February 6, 1879
BREES Stella C. of Caton, NY	
MYRTLE Clarence of Bath, NY	February 13, 1879
STANTON Adelia dau of Col. N. B. of Hornby, NY	Hornby, NY
WILCOX Albert of Bath, NY	February 25, 1879
ROOT Thena of Cohocton, NY	Avoca, NY
WILCOX Edward of Bath, NY	February 19, 1879
HEINAMAN Emma J. of Kanona, NY	Kanona, NY

BULLOCK John N. of Penn Yan, NY
WILLIS Julia A. of Bath, NY

February 20, 1879
Kanona, NY

SHULTS Timothy of Wheeler, NY
DAVIS Anna D. of Wheeler, NY

February 19, 1879
Bath, NY

BAULCH William H. of Bath, NY
LOUCKS Delia of Avoca, NY

February 26, 1879
Avoca, NY

PALMER Bradley of Howard, NY
MATTOON A. M. of Howard, NY

February 9, 1879
Towlesville, NY

SMITH Charles B. of Prattsburgh, NY
MANNING Sarah J. of Italy Hollow, NY

March 9, 1879
Wheeler, NY

CLINEBURG Ignatius of Lindley, NY
BUCK Mary E. of Tuscarora, NY

February 19, 1879
Tuscarora, NY

STONE Charles D. of Pulteney, NY
TURNER Kittie of Jerusalem, NY

March 11, 1879
Jerusalem, NY

GREEN Lyman D. of Bath, NY
WOODHOUSE Alice F. of Bath, NY

February 28,1879
Kanona, NY

FOLSOM Otis F.of Urbana, NY
BENSON Louesa of Tyrone, NY

March 5, 1879
Tyrone, NY

CHAMPLIN Ebenezer of Wayne, NY
GILBERT Rosa A. of Tyrone, NY

March 6, 1879
Tyrone, NY

DECKER John of Urbana, NY
BARRETT Julia A. of Urbana, NY

March 12, 1879
Bath, NY

TATE Will W. of Wayne, NY formerly Gaines, Pa.
WHITEHEAD Frances L. of Jersey Shore, Pa.

March 9, 1879
Bradford, NY

FRANCIS Nelson C. of Canisteo, NY
FOSTER Nettie E. of Jasper, NY

March 12, 1879
Addison, NY

BLAKESLEY John W. of Jerusalem, NY   (Newspaper date) April 3, 1879
FINGER Mary E. of Jerusalem, NY

Prattsburgh, NY

FOSTER Frank M. of Prattsburgh, NY
LORD Flora L. of Gorham, NY

February 25, 1879
Canandaigua, NY

BURLEY W. A. of Cameron, NY
BLIVEN Mary of Bath, NY

March 30, 1879
Bath, NY

NICHOLS W. H. of Bath, NY
BIRDSALL Hattie A. of Bath, NY

March 20, 1879

DENNIS David A. of S. Bradford, NY — March 16, 1879
FEAGLES Grace D. of S. Bradford, NY — S. Bradford, NY

MONNELL Alfred of Bath, NY — March 26, 1879
MORROW Anna of Corning, NY formerly of Avoca, NY — Corning, NY

TAYLOR B. F. of Prattsburgh, NY — March 9, 1879
COLLIER May E. of Bath, NY — Bath, NY

PHILLIPS J. M. of Avoca, NY — March 26, 1879
FLYNN Mary L. of Bath, NY — Bath, NY

SMITH Eli of the Soldiers and Sailors Home Bath, NY — April 1, 1879
WELLS Mrs. Harriet B. of Bath, NY

DEMING Marvin of Howard, NY — March 17, 1879
PECK Martha J. of Howard, NY — Howard, NY

VAN GELDER William E. of Pulteney, NY — March 30, 1879
BENNITT Pru Dell J. of Pulteney, NY — Pulteney, NY

JANES Edwin W. of Canisteo, NY — April 2, 1879
BARTLETT Fannie of Addison, NY (will move to Ohio)

DIBBLE A. J. of Wayne, NY — April 19, 1879
HILL Ada D. of Wayne, NY — Wayne, NY

GALE Webster E. of Union Twp. — April 2, 1879
DICKINSON Anna E. of Bath, NY — Union City, Pa.

BARBER Edward of Groveland, NY — April 13, 1879
RUSSELL Edna dau of Henry of Caton, NY

WILSON George M. of Howard, NY — April 20, 1879
WELLS Hattie of Howard, NY

HECKERS Jacob of Hartsville, NY — April 17, 1879
WHITING Ida E. of Hartsville, NY — Hartsville, NY

BUSH J. W. of Bloods, NY — April 26, 1879
LOWELL M. J. of Bloods, NY — Bloods, NY

SEAMAN A. N. of N. Urbana, NY — April 19, 1879
GRAY Lillie of N. Urbana, NY — Hammondsport, NY

DEWAINE C. D. of Thurston, NY — April 17, 1879
CARMAN Emma M. of Campbell, NY — Bath, NY

STRATTON A. B. of Urbana, NY — May 3, 1879
CRAIG Martha C. of Urbana, NY — Cold Springs, NY

HOLLENBECK C. J.
PECK Mollie E. of N. Cohocton, NY

April 27, 1879

ACKERSON Frank H. of Bath, NY
ELLIS Sadie A. of Bath, NY

May 3, 1879
Hornellsville, NY

HELM John V. of Thurston, NY
ELLIOTT Mrs. Alice of Thurston, NY

May 4, 1879
Eagle Valley, NY

GRISWOLD Joel W. of Bath, NY
ROBIE Fanny of Bath, NY

May 14, 1879
Bath, NY

PALMER Loren H. of Howard, NY
SILLSBEE Clara J. of Howard, NY

May 20, 1879
Haskinsville, NY

BORDEN Charles of Campbell, NY
COSS Delia of Campbell, NY

May 25, 1879
Campbell, NY

COLLIER William of Greenwood, NY
HANNAH Maria R. of Greenwood, NY

May 21, 1879
Hornellsville, NY

WHITING Mark of Derrick City, Pa.
JONES Ada of Hornellsville, NY

May 22, 1879

HULL Nathan E.
DONALDSON Mary E.

May 18, 1879
Hartsville, NY

DUNN (or **DIVEN**) Frank of Canisteo, NY
KING Flora of Canisteo, NY

May 29, 1879

OLDFIELD G. G. of Hornby, NY
QUINN Hattie M.

(Newspaper date) June 12, 1879
Catlin, NY

EGGLESTON W. Paul of Corning, NY
MILLER Anna of Caton, NY

June 1, 1879
Caton, NY

LEWIS Willis H. of Duke Center, Pa.
RATHBUN Lucretia of Corning, NY

June 4, 1879

LEAVENWORTH Rev. H. of Big Flats, NY
CUNNINGHAM Hattie of Corning, NY

May 29, 1879

KEITES Gilbert of Wayland, NY
SHERMAN Annie of Wayland, NY

May 29, 1879
Wayland, NY

RIDGEWAY J. Arthur of Monroeton, Pa.
HIGMAN Jennie dau of John of Corning, NY

May 28, 1879
Corning, NY

TORRENCE Charles E.
MARSH Ava E.

June 8, 1879
Bath, NY

MC ENTEE William
ADAMS Nancy of Charleston, Pa.
June 5, 1879
Corning, NY

ROAT Alonzo
HAVENS Alida
July 7, 1879
Prattsburgh, NY

FROST Rufus S. of Boston, Mass.
WILLARD Mrs. C. Emily dau of B. C WICKHAM of Tioga
June 18, 1879
Corning, NY

LOVELESS Edward H. of Bath, NY
SEAGER Rebecca of Grove, NY
June 18, 1879
Grove, NY

HUSTED Clark
PATTERSON Emma A.
July 3, 1879
Woodhull, NY

SNELL L. B. of Avoca, NY
WILBUR Mary of Thurston, NY
July 3, 1879
Bath, NY

WHITEHEAD Cyrus of Wayne, NY
CRANS Susan J. dau of William of Wayne, NY
June 24, 1879
Wayne, NY

CLARK Albert E. of Jasper, NY
HECKMAN Rosie S. of Jasper, NY
June 25, 1879
Jasper, NY

WILSON John R. of Howard, NY
HARRIS Mary Jane of Howard, NY
July 2, 1879
Greenwood, NY

PECK Cassius J. of Wallace, NY
BURK Gertrude C. of Wheeler, NY
July 4, 1879
Hammondsport, NY

CANFIELD Jonas of Wayne, NY
ROBBINS Eva of Wayne, NY
June 29, 1879
Wayne, NY

WARNER S. L. of Naples, NY
MANN Ida V. of Bath, NY
July 14, 1879
Bath, NY

LA COSTE Benjamin of Avoca, NY
SNOW Lodema V. of Avoca, NY
July 29, 1879

COTTON James C. of Fremont, NY
BURDICK Carrie E. of Hornellsville, NY
July 30, 1879

SPRAGUE William of Urbana, NY
HUNT Mrs. Emily of Urbana, NY
(Newspaper date) August 7, 1879

BURNS James W. of Hornellsville, NY
TOWNER Helen L. of Avoca, NY
July 30, 1879
Avoca, NY

VENIS Grant of Corning, NY
BOOTH Anna of Corning, NY
July 20, 1879

KIRKHAM John W. of Bath, NY
PLATT Louise H. of Bath, NY

August 13, 1879
Bath, NY

LACEY George E.
EGGLESTON Aggie

August 18, 1879
Corning, NY

BURNS James of Howard, NY
STEWART Susie of Howard, NY

August 27, 1879
Cohocton, NY

ACKERMAN George E. of Kendall, NY
VAN WORMER Eugena of Cohocton, NY

August 26, 1879
Cohocton, NY

LOCKWOOD Francis M. of Wheeler, NY
GILBERT Evylena of Wheeler, NY

August 28, 1879
Wheeler, NY

STROUD Frank J. of Woodhull, NY
NEWMAN Bertha A. of Tuscarora, NY

August 27, 1879
Woodhull, NY

COLBY William J. of Troy (NY or Pa,?)
DUSENBERRY Jennie F. of Avoca, NY

September 2, 1879

O'BRYAN Thomas
FRITZ Mary

September 1, 1879
Corning, NY

CHAPIN Benjamin F. of Bath, NY
SMITH Sarah of Mitchellville, NY

September 4, 1879
Bath, NY

POST Jacob of Corning, NY
MARSHALL Jennie of Caton, NY

September 7, 1879

WHITFORD Ausustus L. of Hornellsville, NY
HUNT Mrs. Frances A. of Fremont, NY

August 31, 1879
Fremont, NY

HOWELL William J. of Antrim, Pa.
MULFORD Mary dau of late John H. **STOTHOFF**

September 4, 1879
Burdett, NY

ALMY Willis of Hartsville, NY
CALL Eva of Hartsville, NY

August 30, 1879
Hartsville, NY

WOODARD Charles H. of Blood Station, NY
ARNOLD Lovilla H. of Naples, NY

September 25, 1879
Naples, NY

LOUNSBURY Mark G. of Prattsburgh, NY
NORTHRUP Mary A. of Prattsburgh, NY

September 13, 1879
Prattsburgh, NY

HANKS George F. of Kanona, NY
SHULTS Arvilla M. dau of T. A. of Prattsburgh, NY

September 24, 1879
Prattsburgh, NY

O'CONNOR James of Corry, Pa.
KEATING Maggie of Corning, NY

September 18, 1879

ALDRICH Henry of Osceola, Pa. September 23, 1879
SMITH Lillie of Tuscarora, NY

HOPKINS William of Milo, NY October 2, 1879
KENNEDY Ellen of Italy Hollow, NY Bath, NY

BECK Henry of Corning, NY October 2, 1879
GITHLER Matilda of Painted Post, NY Painted Post, NY

BROWNELL Jerome of Prattsburgh, NY October 2, 1879
WEEKS Abbie J. of Prattsburgh, NY

PUTNAM Sylvester L. of Wheeler, NY October 2, 1879
DILLENBECK Emma A. of Prattsburgh, NY

SEAMAN Edward W. of Thurston, NY October 8, 1879
BOYCE Estella of Savona, NY Savona, NY

SCARVELL Henry of Bath, NY October 19, 1879
STOUT Addie of Bath, NY Cameron, NY

JOHNSON George W. of Troupsburgh, NY October 18, 1879
SIMMONDS Elva M. of Troupsburgh, NY Troupsburgh, NY

EDDY Ethan P. of Brookfield, Pa. October 21, 1879
THOMAS Jane of Troupsburgh, NY Troupsburgh, NY

SCRIPTURE Acquila of Howard, NY October 25, 1879
HARRIS Nancy A. of Howard, NY Bath, NY

DECKER George M. of Bath, NY October 29, 1879
SUTLIFF Mary M. of Bath, NY Bath, NY

STITES Mortimer L. of New York City October 22, 1879
DISBROW Ann Delephine dau of C. R. of Bath, NY

VAN CAMPEN Orlando S. of Corning, NY November 5, 1879
SANFORD Delia dau of late Alfred of Corning, NY Corning, NY

HOOD Cyrus S. of Corning, NY November 6, 1879
GAMMAN Nina E. dau of Charles M. of Corning, NY Corning, NY
IRELAND F. B. of Cohocton, NY November 5, 1879
RIDER Harriet A. of Fremont, NY Avoca, NY

LOOMIS Charles November 25, 1879
CLARK Fannie of Bath, NY Bath, NY

KILPATRICK Edward F. of Naples, NY November 25, 1879
ALLIS Alida dau of Jerry Allis

SMITH Phillip of Catlin, NY   November 20, 1879
KNEALE Alice dau of Arthur of Big Flats, NY   Catlin, NY

WHEAT Henry of Hornby, NY   November 19, 1879
HUMPHREY Jessie of Hornby, NY

PARK Robert F. of Corning, NY   November 26, 1879
COWAN Emma B. of Corning, NY   Gibson, NY

PIERCE C. A. of Dundee, Ill.   November 20, 1879
DEAN Annie E. of E. Campbell, NY   E. Campbell, NY

GURNSEY Frank of Branchport, NY   November 19, 1879
HORTON Abigail S. of Pulteney, NY   Pulteney, NY

SANFORD George W. of Bath, NY   December 3, 1879
WOODRUFF Eva L. of Bath, NY   Mt. Washington, NY

CHAPMAN Francis of Prattsburgh, NY   (Newspaper date) December 4, 1879
BOGGS Lovica H. of Prattsburgh, NY

DUNNING L. O. of Prattsburgh, NY   November 25, 1879
TURNER Sarah A. of Prattsburgh, NY   Bradford, NY

CHAPMAN Dwight of Wheeler, NY   November 26, 1879
FRANCIES Rosa of Wheeler, NY   Avoca, NY

SCHRYVER Judson B. of Caton, NY   December 10, 1879
UPDYKE Mary of Odessa, NY   Corning, NY

LANE George W. of Beaver Dams, NY   December 3, 1879
UNDERWOOD Leila H. dau of G. L. of Hornby, NY   Hornby, NY

HATHAWAY H. H. of Oriskany Falls, NY   December 11, 1879
DAVISON Ida of Canisteo, NY   Canisteo, NY

REYNOLDS W. D. of Seneca, NY   December 16, 1879
JENKS Lettie M. of Cameron, NY   Cameron, NY

CADE Charles Derby of Caton, NY   December 6, 1879
CRAWFORD Emma L. of Caton, NY

CARMER Clarence of Clarence, NY   December 10, 1879
STROUD Marion of Woodhull, NY

KEELER Seth of Cohocton, NY   December 19, 1879
KITCH Mary of Cohocton, NY

STAFFORD S. W. of Westfield, Pa.   December 17, 1879
GOULD Maggie M. of Bath, NY   Bath, NY

MATTICE Edward V. of Cohocton, NY
MAXFIELD Nancy A. of Avoca, NY

December 17, 1879
Bath, NY

SMITH S. W. of Rome, NY
HOUSE E. A. of Avoca, NY

December 24, 1879
Bath, NY

PLATT William A. of Bath, NY
HANKINSON Julia dau of late Dr. G. A. at Mother's

December 24, 1879
Hoboken, NJ

FOWLER George S. of N Cohocton, NY
ADAMS Linda M. of Bloods Depot, NY

December 20, 1879
Bloods Depot, NY

STEWART Morey
PUNCHES Jane A.

December 20, 1879
Jasper, NY

WILKINS Fred H. of Canisteo, NY
GOFF Dora dau of M. Goff of Howard, NY

December 31, 1879
Howard, NY

ARMSTRONG G. M. of Wayne, NY
BAILEY Mary M. of Bath, NY

December 31, 1879
Wayne, NY

MORRISON Syrena F. of Bath, NY
HUGHES Lottie of Avoca, NY

December 31, 1879
Bath, NY

JUDD E. Eugene of Thurston, NY
SMITH Arvilla C. of Thurston, NY

January 1, 1880
Savona, NY

WALTON W. F. of Dundee, NY
PATTERSON Clara of S. Bradford, NY

January 11, 1880
S. Bradford, NY

BARNES L. F. of Cohocton, NY
OXX Emma of Avoca, NY

December 28, 1879
Haskinsville, NY

DUNHAM Ransom H. of Troupsburgh, NY
PAGE Elizabeth J. of Troupsburgh, NY

January 5, 1880
Troupsburgh, NY

KEELER Leroy
THARP M. Eva

January 7, 1880
Bath, NY

ANDREWS J. M. of Syracuse, NY
BEATON Mrs. Emma A.

January 14, 1880
Thurston, NY

STEWART H. W. of Howard, NY
BURNEY Mary of Chicopee, Mass.

January 1, 1880
Howard, NY

ROSE Walter S. of Wheeler, NY
WHEELER Emma dau of W. H. of Cameron, NY

January 14, 1880
Cameron, NY

SHAW Jefferson L. of Barrington, NY
ANGEL Amanda of Barrington, NY

January 15, 1880
Cameron, NY

MC KIBBEN Thomas of Howard, NY
HATHAWAY Miss ____ of Bath, NY

January 21, 1880
Bath, NY

BAULCH R. A. of Bath, NY
ALLISON Louie R. of Bath, NY

January 23, 1880

SHULTS Charles of Bath, NY
DAVISON Fanny of Bath, NY

January 29, 1880
Bath, NY

PRATT Rev. S. W. of Bath, NY
MC KAY Sarah M. dau of Col. Janus S. of Campbell, NY

February 25, 1880
Campbell, NY

DANIELS Edgar A. of Conesus, NY
SHARPSTEEN Sarah L. of Springwater, NY

February 14, 1880
Springwater, NY

GRAY William F. of Wayland, NY
THORP Florence E. of Wayland, NY

February 18, 1880
Wayland, NY

KING William H. of Orange, NY
VAN VLEET Louella of Bath, NY

February 19, 1880
Bath, NY

DE GROAT G. R. of Italy, NY
COPELAND Josie of Bath, NY

February 17, 1880
Bath, NY

GRAY W. S. of Avoca, NY
FRANCIS Ida of Bath, NY

February 24, 1880
Bath, NY

BULL R. C. of Bath, NY
FRANCIS Flora A. of Bath, NY

February 24, 1880
Bath, NY

LOGHRY J. W. of Bath, NY
STEWART Sarah A. of Howard, NY

February 25, 1880
Bath, NY

VAIL Charles of Hammondsport, NY
NORTHRUP Dessie of Hammondsport, NY

February 25, 1880
Bath, NY

OVERHISER Henry S. of Wheeler, NY
STANTON Lottie of Cohocton, NY

February 11, 1880
Bloods Depot, NY

CRANS John
KNOWLES Lizzie of Bath, NY

February 25, 1880

CROW Germain
SHEPARD Rosia of Bath, NY

March 3, 1880
Bath, NY

SMITH Silas
CHERDEVOINE Mrs. Cynthia M. of Battle Creek, MI.

March 10, 1880
Fremont, NY

MC PHEE Frank of Hornellsville, NY
COOLEY Mary C. of Hornellsville, NY

March 14, 1880
Hornellsville, NY

SERLES Amsi of Wheeler, NY
CURTIS Ida L. of Prattsburgh, NY

March 9, 1880
Prattsburgh, NY

BRIGLIN William of Prattsburgh, NY
SMITH Anna of Prattsburgh, NY

February 19, 1880
Avoca, NY

BENNETT James G. of Wayland, NY
PARTRIDGE Julia M. of Fremont, NY

March 4, 1880

SEAGER George of Sonora, NY
MC CALMONT Lucy E. of Bath, NY

March 10, 1880
Bradford, NY

HECKMAN George W. of Thurston, NY
BAILEY Flora E. of Orange, NY

March 14, 1880
Risingville, NY

MC DONNELL John
O'DELL Addie

February 29, 1880

HALL W. W. of Savona, NY
BRUNDAGE Josephine of Urbana, NY

March 18, 1880

ELLISON Andrew of Orange, NY
DENNIS Anney A. of S. Bradford, NY

March 18, 1880
S. Bradford, NY

WELD O. W.
SMITH E. May

March 24, 1880
Prattsburgh, NY

WOODARD Charles M. of Bath, NY
HILLA Amanda W. of Bath, NY

March 24, 1880
Bath, NY

BURT Morris H. of Bluff Point, NY
BLOOM Ella M. of Sonora, NY

March 24, 1880
Sonora, NY

FOWLER John of Corning, NY
DAVIS Mrs. Mary of Bath, NY

March 15, 1880
Corning, NY

COOK Uri De Loss of E. Campbell, NY
SCOTT Ellen Louisa of E. Campbell, NY

March 21, 1880
Painted Post, NY

TOBEY Wayland of Caton, NY
AUSTIN Rose M. of New Milford, Pa.

March 2, 1880
New Milford, Pa.

MC CHESNEY George of Bath, NY
BORDEN Minnie B. of Bath, NY

March 25, 1880
Bath, NY

WOOD Charles F. of Painted Post, NY
CHASE Ida E. dau of Rev. A. B. of Corning, NY

March 17, 1880
Corning, NY

GLEASON Edgar J. of Wayne, NY
BAKER Sarah E. of Wayne, NY

March 28, 1880
Wayne, NY

ROSE Charles O.   March 31, 1880
BABCOCK Addie E. at parents

BARNARD Fred of Caton, NY   March 25, 1880
CASS Libbie of Caton, NY   Corning, NY

FLEET A. B. of Tiflin, Oh.   February 25, 1880
WOOD Harriet at res of Joel Wood   Orange, NY

EUNIS George of Swartwood, NY   (Newspaper date) April 15, 1880
JOHNSON Mary A. of Howard, NY   Howard, NY

STARING Daniel of Stark, NY   April 15, 1880
RIDER Susie M. of Haskinsville, NY   Haskinsville, NY

CHURCH C. W. of Canisteo, NY   April 11, 1880
STEVENS Amanda of Canisteo, NY   Bath, NY

PRATT Herbert B. of Hornellsville, NY   March 21, 1880
BENTON Georgia of Hornellsville, NY   Hornellsville, NY

SIMPSON Dewitt C. of Jasper, NY   April 9, 1880
CROSBY Lois of Jasper, NY   Hornellsville, NY

MORGAN Stephen of Bath, NY   March 17, 1880
GOULD Jennie of Bath, NY   Savona, NY

GELDER Thomas of Prattsburgh, NY   April 15, 1880
GRAHAM Mrs. ____ of Italy Hollow, NY   Italy Hollow, NY

KING George O. of Canisteo, NY   April 21, 1880
BRASTED Augusta of Howard, NY   Canisteo, NY

ELDRED Frank of Campbell, NY   May 1, 1880
CHAPIN Carrie E. of Addison, NY   Savona, NY

WOLCOTT F. C. of Avoca, NY   April 29, 1880
CASS Elvira D. dau of late Maj. Charles of Campbell, NY Campbell, NY

CLARK Joel of Campbell, NY   April 25, 1880
ROGERS Sarah A. of Campbell, NY   E. Campbell, NY

SIMMONS R. Fulton of Canandaigua, NY   May 5, 1880
GRAY Mary N. of Painted Post, NY   Painted Post, NY

THOMAS Daniel C. of Canisteo, NY   May 5, 1880
CRAWFORD Libbie of Canisteo, NY   Canisteo, NY

STANNARD Charles of Hornellsville, NY   May 5, 1880
TERRY Della of Hornellsville, NY

STOCUM John of Bath, NY	May 12, 1880
MARKS Eva of Geneva, NY	Cleveland, Oh.
LILLY Henry of Canisteo, NY	May 31, 1880
PYE Sarah E. of Canisteo, NY	
KETCHUM L. W.	June 1, 1880
ROSS Martha A. of Hornellsville, NY	Hornellsville, NY
LARKIN Thomas of Cohocton, NY	June 8, 1880
WOODARD Clara of Leroy, NY	Leroy, NY
OBERT C. B. of Bath, NY	June 9, 1880
LYON Anna P. at aunt's Mrs. **TOWLE**	Clinton, Io.
DENSMORE P. F. of Woodhull, NY	June 12, 1880
LYON Amelia J. of Woodhull, NY	Woodhull, NY
STOGA John H. of Caton, NY	June 18, 1880
GRAHAM Susan H. of Caton, NY	Caton, NY
MILLER De Forest of Belmont (Newspaper date)	June 25, 1880
PIERCE Dora of Hornellsville, NY	Hornellsville, NY
SEARLES Rev. William E. of Harrison Valley, Pa.	June 22, 1880
KETCHUM Emma S. of Urbana, NY	Urbana, NY
BOND Charles of Watkins, NY	June 23, 1880
GILBERT Jennie E. of Bath, NY	Bath, NY
HENDRICK J. of Canisteo, NY	June 30, 1880
WIXSON Lydia of Wayne, NY	Wayne, NY
HAMMOND Oscar of Cohocton, NY	July 4, 1880
HAMMOND Cynthia L. of Cohocton, NY	Haskinsville, NY
COLLINS Henry of Bath, NY	June 23, 1880
HENREHAN Maggie of Risingville, NY	Bath, NY
ROBERTS Leslie C.	July 3, 1880
ROBARDS Franc B.	Haskinsville, NY
BLANE R. E. of Hammondsport, NY	July 4, 1880
MAY Eliza of Hammondsport, NY	Bath, NY
HEYSHAM George of Osceola, Pa.	July 18, 1880
ABBOTT Laura of Troupsburgh, NY	Troupsburgh, NY
OSGOOD Darwin S. of Bradford, NY	July 22, 1880
SWITZER Melissa	Bradford, NY

BENNETT Geno of Hammondsport, NY
DAMOTH Josephine of Hammondsport, NY

July 24, 1880
Bradford, NY

MC NEIL I. C. of Avoca, NY
HEDGES Estella dau of William of Bradford, NY

August 20, 1880
Bradford, NY

STEVENS Chester of Osceola, Pa.
FRENCH Frank of Savona, NY

August 4, 1880
Painted Post, NY

THOMAS George S. of Wheeler, NY
BARRETT Lydia L. of Wheeler, NY

August 18, 1880
Wheeler, NY

HYLER Alvin E. of Avoca, NY
FOSTER Eva A. of Howard, NY

August 21, 1880
Bath, NY

CARROLL John of Bath, NY
MC KIBBEN Jennie at res of Thomas Mc Kibben

August 26, 1880

ALDEN Eliot of Bath, NY
HOYT Charlotte dau of William C. of Bath, NY

September 2, 1880

ALLEN Seth of Barrington, NY
CHAPMAN Ida of Wayne, NY

August 31, 1880
Wayne, NY

SEAMANS Frank S. of Savona, NY
DAVIS Herma P. of Savona, NY

August 31, 1880
Savona, NY

HOUGH Charles of Campbell, NY
EASTERBROOK Florence M. of Campbell, NY

September 1, 1880
Savona, NY

RAPLEE H. M. of Dundee, NY
WHEELER Eva J. of Bath, NY

September 1, 1880
Bath, NY

DECKER Charles M. of Bath, NY
DE WITT Ettie of Bath, NY

September 5, 1880
Bath, NY

SMITH W. H. of Bath, NY
GENUNG Ida R. of Bath, NY

September 8, 1880
Bath, NY

PLATT B. D. of Bath, NY
SALT Mary H. of Bath, NY

September 8, 1880
Bath, NY

STOCKING Hervey of Bath, NY
SMITH Milla of Bath, NY

September 12, 1880
Bath, NY

SUTHERLAND George R. of Campbell, NY
MC KAY Hester A. dau of Col. James S. of Campbell, NY

September 8, 1880
Campbell, NY

THOMAS Melvin I. of Woodhull, NY
ABER Ellen E. of Urbana, NY

August 8, 1880
Urbana, NY

MARGESON Alva A. of Canisteo, NY — September 12, 1880
COVERT Ettie of N. Urbana, NY — Urbana, NY

CURRAN Albert of Wayne, NY — September 14, 1880
MC GLOTHLIN Nettie of Bath, NY — Bath, NY

SWEEZEY Thomas E. of Bath, NY — September 12, 1880
TRUMBULL Ettie of Bath, NY — Bath, NY

VAN GELDER E. L. of Bath, NY — September 4, 1880
GOUNDRY Mary A. dau of Joseph of Orange, NY — Orange, NY

CLEAVER E. J. of Corning, NY — September 15, 1880
RISING Mary R. of Thurston, NY — Thurston, NY

SPACE J. W. of Addison, NY — September 15, 1880
HAWLEY Alice of Merchantville, NY — Merchantville, NY

STICKLES J. W. of Jasper, NY — September 22, 1880
PATTERSON Alma of Kanona, NY — Woodhull, NY

WAGNER S. of Savona, NY — September 21, 1880
BAKER Allie P. of Savona, NY — Savona, NY

CHURCHILL Fred of Bath, NY — September 19, 1880
SCHUYLER Helen of Bath, NY — Hammondsport, NY

SEAMANS Charles R. — September 21, 1880
BENNETT Mary C. — Savona, NY

MC NEIL G. P. of Avoca, NY — September 29, 1880
SHAUT Ella of Avoca, NY — Hammondsport, NY

SULLIVAN John W. of Prattsburgh, NY — September 30, 1880
BROWNELL Alice M. of Prattsburgh, NY — Bath, NY

HASLETT Samuel of Woodhull, NY — September 29, 1880
BRENNAN Kate of Addison Hill, NY — Merchantville, NY

SHULTS W. D. formerly of Bath, NY — September 23, 1880
NEWMAN Mrs. A. R. of Tarrytown, NY

SCOTT J. W. of Bath, NY — September 29, 1880
ANDERSON Annette of Cameron, NY — Bath, NY

DEVENDORF Seth M. of Hamlin, NY — October 14, 1880
HOAGLAND Hattie M. of Howard, NY — Howard, NY

SCHOFIELD Ralph R. of Campbell, NY — November 11, 1880
MALLORY M. Delia — Savona, NY

CASTON O. G. of Wheeler, NY　　　　　　　　November 15, 1880
LEWIS S. A. of Avoca, NY　　　　　　　　　　Bath, NY

COLE A. H. of Bath, NY　　　　　　　　　　November 18, 1880
BENNETT Alma A. of Savona, NY　　　　　　Savona, NY

MERRILL Ward B. of Hornellsville, NY　　　　November 25, 1880
SEAMANS M. Alfa dau of Alvin of Thurston, NY

MILLER Judston A. of Savona, NY　　　　　　November 26, 1880
SCHUYLER Alidia J. of Bath, NY　　　　　　　Bath, NY

BOWERS Edward J. of Campbell, NY　　　　　November 21, 1880
GREEK Olive of Campbell, NY　　　　　　　　Savona, NY

JOHNSON Byron R. of Bath, NY　　(Newspaper date) December 3, 1880
COLSON Eunice A. of Thurston, NY　　　　　　Howard, NY

CHURCHILL George Henry of Elmira　(Newspaper date) December 3, 1880
GOULD Beulah dau of A. R.　　　　　　　　　Bath, NY

SMITH Walter J. of Howard, NY　　　　　　　November 24, 1880
EDGETT Maria of Howard, NY at res of George WILSON

GRAY D. W. of Hammondsport, NY　　　　　　December 23, 1880
COGSWELL Belle of Hammondsport, NY

EDWARDS Webster of Cohocton, NY　　　　　November 11, 1880
CLAPP Alice of Cohocton, NY

SNYDER William of Hunts Hollow, NY　　　　December 24, 1880
LIST Esther of Lyons Hollow, NY

STEPHENS Dr. C. B. of Avoca, NY　　　　　　December 22, 1880
BROWN Florence of Avoca, NY　　　　　　　Stephens Mills, NY

HAYES W. H. of Troupsburgh, NY　　　　　　December 13, 1880
SEE Elizabeth C. of Addison, NY　　　　　　E Troupsburgh, NY

MILES John of Cohocton, NY　　　　　　　　October 27, 1880
BLEYMEHIL Kate of Cohocton, NY

LOCKWOOD Serville H. of Wheeler, NY　　　December 27, 1880
CHANDLER Mary J. of Dansville, NY　　　　Dansville, NY

NICHOLS Amasa J.　　　　　　　　　　　December 30, 1880
OSBORNE Edna　　　　　　　　　　　　　Pulteney, NY

OSBORN George of Prattsburgh, NY　　　　December 25, 1880
POTTER Anna of Prattsburgh, NY　　　　　Wheeler, NY

HOOD Edward of Corning, NY
REED Jessie E. of Corning, NY

January 6, 1881

GUNDERMAN Watson of Cameron, NY
REYNOLDS Cora E. of Cameron, NY

January 1, 1881
Rathbone, NY

GIBSON William of Cohocton, NY
CHAPMAN Esther of Naples, NY

January 11, 1881
Naples, NY

WALLING Daniel of Bradford, NY
GILMORE Sarah E. of Bradford, NY

January 9, 1881
S. Bradford, NY

MATTOON W. L. of Wallace, NY
VAN HASEN Adelia of Wallace, NY

January 19, 1881

ROBIE Reuben E. of Bath, NY
BABCOCK Anna W. of Canton, Ill.

February 2, 1881
Canton, Ill.

WALLING Charles of Bradford, NY
BENNETT Lida of Bradford, NY

February 9, 1881
Middlesex, NY

NOXON George R. of Wheeler, NY
TOWNER Della J. of Avoca, NY

February 14, 1881
Avoca, NY

CONINE G. Lavall
MC ANDREW Emma L. dau of John of Bath, NY

February 16, 1881
Bath, NY

WINDNAGLE W. J. of Prattsburgh, NY
WILLETT Francis E. of Jerusalem, NY

February 10, 1881

DUDLEY Benjamin formerly of Bath, NY
ERWIN Lizzie dau of late Arthur H. of Painted Post, NY

February 16, 1881
Painted Post, NY

GRAVES Bradley of Prattsburgh, NY
BURKE Flora of Naples, NY

February 15, 1881

HOPKINS Arthur W. of Prattsburgh, NY
PARKER Ellen C. of Pulteney, NY

February 17, 1881

WALTHER Henry of Rushville, NY
GELDER Minnie L. of Prattsburgh, NY

February 17, 1881

BRUNDAGE De Witt
KNOWLES Mary

February 24, 1881

SPENCER Joseph of Barrington, NY
FREEMAN Harriet of Bath, NY

February 23, 1881
Bath, NY

EDSON Mortimer of N. Cohocton, NY
THOMPSON Lydia of N. Cohocton, NY

March 10, 1881
N. Cohocton, NY

LEE Orville H. of Prattsburgh, NY   March 22, 1881
WARREN Mrs. Amanda C. of Prattsburgh, NY   Wheeler, NY

WOOD Ira M. of Wayne, NY   March 15, 1881
LEONARD Anna E. of Bradford, NY   Bradford, NY

HUDSON Frank of Bath, NY   (Newspaper date) April 8, 1881
LOGHRY Helen of Bath, NY   Bath, NY

HAVENS George of S. Bradford, NY   March 30, 1881
CHRISLER Mary A. of Bath, NY   Bradford, NY

STEWART Charles D. of Borden, NY   March 20, 1881
BAXTER Minnie A. of Addison, NY

CARROLL Ward D. of Bath, NY   March 30, 1881
WALKER Rose M. of Bath, NY   Cohocton, NY

MILLER Orren of Howard, NY   March 30, 1881
MC BETH Martha E. of Howard, NY   Howard, NY

DILLENBACK Alexander of Avoca, NY   April 9, 1881
THARP Caroline of Howard, NY

HOYT Daniel of Jasper, NY   April 16, 1881
BENEWAY Carrie of Jasper, NY

PAGE Esek of Hornellsville, NY   May 8, 1881
HUNT Mrs. Mary of Hornellsville, NY   Stephens Mills, NY

CRANE Perry B. of Naples, NY   April 28, 1881
GREEK Anna M. of Painted Post, NY   Painted Post, NY

BIRD Charles A. of Bradford, Pa.   May 10, 1881
RICE Mollie dau of late Capt. Burrage Rice of Bath, NY   Bath, NY

WARD Charles W. of Savona, NY   May 19, 1881
ROGERS Mary A. of Savona, NY   Savona, NY

KNOWLES E. L. of Thurston, NY   May 16, 1881
JACOBIE Julia of Addison, NY

CALKINS I. W.   May 21, 1881
BRUNDAGE Jennie C.

SMITH Harry of Irving, Mass.   May 22, 1881
MILLER Jennie of Cohocton, NY   Cohocton, NY

WILLIAMSON D. S. of Cameron, NY   May 26, 1881
ROBBINS Minnie of W. Cameron, NY   Cameron, NY

BRUSH Horton L. of Pulteney, NY	May 25, 1881
HORTON Lillie T. of Pulteney, NY	Pulteney, NY
RAYFORD Edward of Corning, NY	May 30, 1881
RAY Fanny of Palmura, NY	Palmyra, NY
TRUE John	June 8, 1881
STAR Satie J.	Hornellsville, NY
BOTTOM George of Tuscarora, NY	May 25, 1881
CRANDALL Lotta of Nelson, Pa.	
SMITH Frank of Elkland, Pa.	May 25, 1881
EVERETT Ada of Woodhull, NY	Osceola, Pa.
BOLTON William B. of Elmira, NY	June 2, 1881
SHEARER Mary A. dau of W. L. of Corning, NY	
WELTS Milton S. of Addison, NY	June 8, 1881
FLETCHER Mrs. Harriet A. of Monterey, NY	Painted Post, NY
HURD William L. of Bath, NY	June 8, 1881
BROOKINS Ada C. of S. Dansville, NY	S. Dansville, NY
SHULTS Arnold of Bath, NY	June 16, 1881
BUCK Annie of Bath, NY	Bath, NY
STONE Ora R. of Dansville, NY	June 16, 1881
SPONABLE Hattie of Dansville, NY	Dansville, NY
BABCOCK Willoughby W. of Prattsburgh, NY	June 15, 1881
BRUNDAGE Celia A. dau of Ira R. of Penn Yan, NY	Penn Yan, NY
DIMMICK E. W. of Howard, NY	June 24, 1881
MANHART Rachel of Howard, NY	Bath, NY
MARTIN Theodore of Ovid, NY	June 21, 1881
BREWER Georgia A. of Caton, NY	
BAILEY Addison E. of Wayne, NY	June 26, 1881
FOLSOM Mary F. of Wayne, NY	
WALDO Frank of Canisteo, NY	June 23, 1881
TAYLOR Nellie of Elmira, NY	Elmira, NY
BAILEY Lewis of Caton, NY	June 19, 1881
CRAWFORD Mary E. of Caton, NY	
CHAPE James M. of St. Louis, Mo.	June 15, 1881
CHAPE Nellie G. dau of W. H. of Corning, NY	St. Louis, Mo.

RATHBUN Chester H. of Mt. Morris, NY
BAKER Eliza M. of Haskinsville, NY

July 3, 1881
Haskinsville, NY

MOORE A. J. of Savona, NY
GATES C. E. of Savona, NY

July 6, 1881
Savona, NY

LEE Henry R. of Andover, NY
WHITE Minnie A. of Howard, NY

July 4, 1881
Howard, NY

BEST Charles W. of Hornellsville, NY
BATES Jennie V. of Hornellsville, NY

June 28, 1881

BAUTER Charles A.
SHARPSTEEN Carrie J. of Woodhull, NY

July 3, 1881
Woodhull, NY

POTTER A. J. of Worthington, Oh.
VAN HOUSEN Jennie dau of A. H. of Prattsburgh, NY

July 2, 1881
Prattsburgh, NY

SAMPLE D. H.
COOPER Jennie of Hornby, NY

July 4, 1881
Dix, NY

THRALL Byron of Corning, NY
BOOT Bertha of Middleboro, Pa.

July 2, 1881

SPARKS Joseph M. of Corning, NY
BOOTH Emma D. of Corning, NY

July 16, 1881
Knoxville, NY

BENEDICT William of Savona, NY
VAN GELDER Emma of Savona, NY

July 27, 1881
Savona, NY

SMITH Richard A.
PECK Alfreda

August 6, 1881
Cohocton, NY

EATON George S.
PATCHALL Mina

August 3, 1881
Corning, NY

FLACK John of Corning, NY
MARTIN Mrs. Jennie of Corning, NY

August 16, 1881

JONES M. J. of Wheeler, NY
RAYMOND Harriet C. of Wheeler, NY

August 27, 1881
Mitchellville, NY

OSBORNE Charles of Canisteo, NY
THORP Mary of Canisteo, NY

August 24, 1881

DAVIS William M. of Waterbury, Ct.
SCOFIELD Nellie of Bath, NY

September 6, 1881
Campbell, NY

VELEY Peter of Bath, NY
SMITH Mrs. Sarah J. of Bath, NY

September 25, 1881

TREIBER M. Collins of Harrisburg, Va.   September 27, 1881
READ Eugena   Bath, NY

NASH Frank   September 14, 1881
ROBINSON Margery   Bath, NY

CLARK James of Bath, NY   August 18, 1881
VAN LOON Mrs. James of Bath, NY   Bath, NY

SANFORD O. S. of Prattsburgh, NY   September 25, 1881
STRONG Ida of Prattsburgh, NY   Pulteney, NY

WHEELER Robert W. of Cameron, NY   September 28, 1881
RISING Minnie D. of Thurston, NY   Thurston, NY

CRANE Floyd E. of Corning, NY   October 4, 1881
JONES Amy of Corning, NY   Corning, NY

FISHER Perlee M. of Prattsburgh, NY   October 5, 1881
VUNCK Fanny M. of Prattsburgh, NY

BEACH Charles H. of Hornby, NY   October 5, 1881
CLARK Melissa W. of Big Flats, NY   Corning, NY

RAZEY James   October 5, 1881
CLARK Delia dau of D. D. of N. Cohocton, NY   N. Cohocton, NY

BELL Robert of Pulteney, NY   September 27, 1881
PIERCE Alida of Jamestown, NY

CLAWSON C. H. of Red House, NY   October 12, 1881
SMITH R. Jennie of Prattsburgh, NY   Prattsburgh, NY

FAULKNER Fraser of Mitchellville, NY   October 16, 1881
HEDGER Retta M. of Prattsburgh, NY   Rochester, NY

HUNGERFORD John N. of Corning, NY   October 18, 1881
FORRESTER Mrs. Susan M. of Elmira, NY   Corning, NY

CRAIG Charles E. of Orange, NY   October 10, 1881
DECKER Mary E. of Bradford, NY   Wayne, NY

MAXSON Milton R. of Hornellsville, NY   October 17, 1881
VAN ALSTINE Mary O. of Hornellsville, NY

BUTLER George of Dundee, NY   October 24, 1881
JONES Phoebe of Bath, NY   Bath, NY

ROBERTS Thomas of Hornellsville, NY   November 8, 1881
LEWIS Elizabeth of Elmira, NY   Elmira, NY

CHILVERS Albert of Corning, NY   November 3, 1881
CURTIS Nettie of Corning, NY

HADDEN Jacob B. of Pulteney, NY   November 5, 1881
STEWART Cornelia L. of Pulteney, NY   Prattsburgh, NY

SCHOONOVER Thad   November 1, 1881
CHILSON Clara of Knoxville, NY   Woodhull, NY

EDWARDS Nathan B. of W. Union, NY   November 6, 1881
BAKER Polly of W. Union, NY   Independence, NY

JARVIS George W. of Corning, NY   October 31, 1881
TURRILL Clara of Corning, NY   Corning, NY

BROCKWAY Walter H. of Prattsburgh, NY October 31, 1881
SMITH Sarah M. of Prattsburgh, NY   Prattsburgh, NY

JERRY Emron J. of Thurston, NY   November 2, 1881
YOST Millie of Thurston, NY   Thurston, NY

WINEGAR William W. of Bath, NY   November 23, 1881
BRUNDAGE Mrs. Ella of Bath, NY

PRESTON Homer M. of Hornellsville, NY   November 23, 1881
SEARLES Mary T. of Addison, NY   Hornellsville, NY

BURNS Michael J. of Dansville, NY   November 23, 1881
HENDERSHOT Jennie dau of D. H. of Hornellsville, NY Hornellsville, NY

GRANT Byron S. of Painted Post, NY   November 16, 1881
WATERS Effie J. of Campbell, NY

BONNER Melvin of Painted Post, NY   November 16, 1881
WATTERS Adelia E. of Campbell, NY

BEEBE Albert P.   November 23, 1881
AINSWORTH Emma formerly of Prattsburgh, NY Salt Lake City, Ut.

WOODRUFF John C. of Naples, NY   November 5, 1881
DRAKE Rosa of N. Cohocton, NY

HENDERSON Rice of Corning, NY   November 22, 1881
GRANGER Anna E. of Big Flats, NY   Wellsburgh, NY

ZIMMERMAN Arthur of Jasper, NY   November 16, 1881
JACKSON Diana of Jasper, NY

HUBBARD D. S. of Syracuse, NY   November 22, 1881
HUBBARD Emily of Cameron, NY   Cameron, NY

CLELAND of Cohocton, NY
HOYT Louise of Cohocton, NY

November 23, 1881
Cohocton, NY

ARLAND Charles R. of Pleasant Valley, NY
STRATTON Delphina of Pleasant Valley, NY

December 2, 1881
Cold Springs, NY

LAW William H. of Pittston, Pa.
KENYON Jennie L. of Savona, NY

December 10, 1881
Savona, NY

CHISSOM I. B. of Prattsburgh, NY
BRUNDAGE Clara L. of Prattsburgh, NY

December 1, 1881

PECK Ripley of N. Cohocton, NY
BALDWIN Mrs. Ann of Howard, NY

December 1, 1881

MARTIN W. H. of Rathbone, NY
KELLOGG Ella of Addison, NY

November 27, 1881
Woodhull, NY

ACKERSON Henry A. of Prattsburgh, NY
GRAVES Mrs. Christina of Prattsburgh, NY

December 6, 1881

SHOEMAKER Oliver of Wayne, NY
CROOKSTON Emma F. of Wayne, NY

December 17, 1881
Wayne, NY

BAILEY Montraville of Wheeler, NY
INGERSOLL Mary of Bath, NY

December 15, 1881
Bath, NY

MANDEVILLE Austin Md. of Rochester, NY
UNDERHILL Emma Louise dau of A. L. of Bath, NY

December 15, 1881
Bath, NY

MARGESON Alonzo
BLUNT Joanna of Cameron, NY

November 26, 1881
Bath, NY

BENNETT D. R. of Howard, NY
HIGGINS Louise of Howard, NY

December 7, 1881

RAYMOND Delos Q. of Havana, NY
OADDEN May of Tuscarora, NY

December 6, 1881

COOPER Levi of Painted Post, NY
HARE Margaret of Centreville, NY

December 14, 1881

WILLIAMS Herbert E. of Owego, NY
VOGEL Willimina of Corning, NY

December 13, 1881
Knoxville, NY

CONDERMAN Lester of Fremont, NY
WILBER Emma F. of Avoca, NY

December 22, 1881

CALKINS Elba S. of Avoca, NY
MATTOON Adell C. of Avoca, NY

December 14, 1881

BURTON Arthur D. of Milo, NY   December 28, 1881
ASPELL Ella of Milo, NY

WOOD Charles S. of Tyrone, NY   December 28, 1881
LANE Emma F. of Beaver Dams, NY

HALSEY Charles of Hornellsville, NY   December 24, 1881
CLARK Phebe J. of Groveland, NY

HODENCAMP Perry of Caton, NY   December 25, 1881
MILLER Nellie of Caton, NY

HUNT Mathew of Hammondsport, NY   December 22, 1881
HALLIDAY Mary of Hammondsport, NY

ROSA Fred of Canisteo, NY   December 27, 1881
STANTON Ida E. of Canisteo, NY

HADDEN F. S. of Otsego, Mi.   December 24, 1881
SMITH Eva of Prattsburgh, NY

LAMPHIRE Benjamin M. of Prattsburgh, NY December 24, 1881
COLEGROVE Mary S. of Prattsburgh, NY

LEWIS Joseph W. of Wheeler, NY   December 26, 1881
JOHNSON Esther A. of Wheeler, NY

BRIGGS Eugene of N. Cohocton, NY   December 21, 1881
RIKER Kate of N. Cohocton, NY   N. Cohocton, NY

RATHBUN Lavay of Howard, NY   January 1, 1882
CULVER Libbie of Fremont, NY   Howard, NY

MEAD Edward of Haskinsville, NY   January 1, 1882
COLE Imogene of Howard, NY

DAVIS Charles of Howard, NY   January 12, 1882
TAYLOR Helen of Howard, NY   Howard, NY

BENNETT Charles F. of Campbell, NY   January 1, 1882
MATHEWS Delia M. of Bradford, NY   Savona, NY

ARGUE William   January 18, 1882
DONOVAN Ellen of Corning, NY

GRAVES Will of Hornellsville, NY   January 20, 1882
DOYLE Helen of Howard, NY

BROWN G. E. of Hornellsville, NY   January 23, 1882
OLIVEY Georgia of Elmira, NY   Elmira, NY

PACE John B. of Hornellsville, NY   January 27, 1882
HATHAWAY Rosa L. of Hornellsville, NY

MYERS George H. of Bradford, NY   January 25, 1882
HORTON Alva A. of Savona, NY   Savona, NY

SLATTERY Will T.   January 25, 1882
ARDELL Franc C. of Bloods, NY

UNDERWOOD A. B. of Canisteo, NY   February 6, 1882
DE LAND Clara of Canisteo, NY

FOWLER Frank C. of N. Cohocton, NY   February 2, 1882
RICE Jessie of Bloods, NY

MC MANUS Charles E. of Avoca, NY   January 29, 1882
BROWN Sarah E. of Cohocton, NY   Cohocton, NY

SQUIRES Charles W. of Hedgesville, NY   January 30, 1882
PERRY Lodee of Rathbone, NY   Rathbone, NY

ALLERTON George E. of Savona, NY   January 18, 1882
COLE Flora E. dau of Harry of Savona, NY   Savona, NY

YOKUM Jacob of Hornellsville, NY   February 4, 1882
BARBER Malvina of Hornellsville, NY

JAYNES Frank E. of Barrington, NY   February 8, 1882
BIGELOW Viola J. of Bradford, NY   Bradford, NY

OSBORNE Edwin B. of Hornellsville, NY   February 14, 1882
HIXON Jennie of Trumansburgh, NY

BROWN Chauncey A. of Bath, NY   February 22, 1882
DANIELS Mary E. of Bath, NY   Bath, NY

HANSE Willis of Bradford, NY   February 19, 1882
HALL Emma dau of Richard of Wayne, NY   Wayne, NY

DUSENBERRY Alfred of S. Bradford, NY   February 22, 1882
JOHNSON Addie of Bath, NY   Savona, NY

GOODESON Alfred of England   February 23, 1882
GREGG Kate Shults dau of Edward W. of Bath, NY   Bath, NY

NIXSON James S.   March 8, 1882
WAGER Katie Ann   Bath, NY

TOWNER Walter L. of Prattsburgh, NY   March 1, 1882
NOXON Edith P. of Wheeler, NY

MC PHERSON William of Seneca, NY   March 8, 1882
THOMAS Ella of Savona, NY   Savona, NY

EMERSON John of Fulton, Oh.   March 11, 1882
WHITCOMB Ettie of Savona, NY   Savona, NY

BOSINBACK William of Sonora, NY   (Newspaper date) March 17, 1882
KRESS Lizzie of Sonora, NY   Sonora, NY

DUDLEY Sidney of Cohocton, NY   March 11, 1882
CLARK Jennie of Cohocton, NY

CLARK Charles of Riker Hollow, NY   March 14, 1882
COLE Olive of N. Cohocton, NY

VAN RIPER Frank of N. Cohocton, NY   March 15, 1882
PORTER Ella of Naples, NY

ERWAY Benjamin of Bath, NY   March 16, 1882
WESTCOTT Lisette of Lindley, NY   Lindley, NY

PINNEY Phide of Prattsburgh, NY   March 16, 1882
BEAL Kit E. of Prattsburgh, NY   Prattsburgh, NY

SMITH David of Savona, NY   March 25, 1882
STOWELL Emma of Savona, NY   Savona, NY

SHAVER Aaron M. of Avoca, NY   March 29, 1882
BUCK Frankie A. of Avoca, NY   Avoca, NY

TRAVIS David of S. Bradford, NY   April 4, 1882
EDSALL Ella of Thurston, NY   Savona, NY

ALDRICH Samuel of Cameron, NY   March 19, 1882
JERRY Dora H. of Thurston, NY   Cameron, NY

LEWIS Fred L. of Wheeler, NY   April 5, 1882
COOK Kate R. dau of Adam of Wheeler, NY   Wheeler, NY

MOWERS William   March 22 1882
PALMER E. formerly of Bath, NY   Carson City, Mi.

JONES David D. of Avoca, NY   April 4, 1882
SQUIRES Mary E. of Avoca, NY   Bath, NY

MARGESON William J. of Wayne, NY   April 9, 1882
MARIM Minnie of Sonora, NY   Sonora, NY

FRENCH David H. of Cameron, NY   January 29, 1882
CHASE Mary Lida of Bath, NY   Bath, NY

PEAK Frank H. of Waverly, NY
GARRISON Belle of Corning, NY

April 18, 1882

SMITH Alonzo of Addison, NY
SYMONDS Mrs. Celestia

March 13, 1882
Addison, NY

HAMILTON William of Campbell, NY (Newspaper date) April 28, 1882
HOUGH Ophelia of Campbell, NY

Campbell, NY

BURGEY Maurice P
BERRY Lucy M. dau of Spicer of Corning, NY

April 19, 1882
Corning, NY

GALLAGHER Charles of S. Pulteney, NY
CURRAN Katie of Prattsburgh, NY

April 19, 1882
Prattsburgh, NY

GILLETT George of Naples, NY
BELL Hattie dau of Philo of Prattsburgh, NY

April 16, 1882
Prattsburgh, NY

WHEELER Henry of Kanona, NY
SILLENBECK Mary E. of Kanona, NY

April 16, 1882
Prattsburgh, NY

BUTLER Hoyt P. of Bath, NY
WILLIS Hattie S. of Bath, NY

April 16, 1882
Bath, NY

JUDD Eugene of Thurston, NY
SPRAGUE Jennie of Bath, NY

April 6, 1882
Bath, NY

BROWN Arthur of Bristol, Eng.
DINGLEY Josephine dau of Mrs. W. R. of Thurston, NY

April 30, 1882
Thurston, NY

MACAULEY Nelson of Greenwood, NY
MILLER Mary R. of Bath, NY

April 27, 1882
Bath, NY

JACOBY John D. of Bradford, NY
DYER Rissie L. of Orange, NY

May 14, 1882
Savona, NY

SLATER William of Bradford, NY
JACOBY Rosa M. of Bradford, NY

May 14, 1882
Savona, NY

TRAVIS Ensley B. of Wayne, NY
MORELAND Mary dau of William of Wayne, NY

May 3, 1882
Wayne, NY

RAYMOND Alexander of Bath, NY
KNIFFEN Clara of Bath, NY

May 7, 1882
Hammondsport, NY

BOLT Charles E. of Tuscarora, NY
MANLEY M. Alice of Tuscarora, NY

June 7, 1882
Tuscarora, NY

CROUCH Joel A. of Bloods Depot, NY
VOSBURGH Ana A. of Rochester, NY

June 10, 1882
Bloods Depot, NY

WILKINSON Park of Cohocton, NY　　　　　June 10, 1882
TRAVERSE Nora of Prattsburgh, NY　　　　Prattsburgh, NY

MC CREERY Joseph of Thurston, NY　　　　June 11, 1882
PERRY Ordelia D. of Limestone, NY　　　　Thurston, NY

GILLETT Edward C. of Prattsburgh, NY　　June 14, 1882
DOOLITTLE Mary V. of Easton, Pa.

FULLER Nupolion of Campbell, NY　　　　July 2, 1882
PATTERSON Kate of Campbell, NY　　　　　Campbell, NY

BAILEY Delbert of Wheeler, NY　　(Newspaper date) July 7, 1882
TYLER Nora E. of Wheeler, NY　　　　　　Hammondsport, NY

SPRAGUE John L. of Pleasant Valley, NY　June 29, 1882
RETAN Sylvina of Pulteney, NY　　　　　　Penn Yan, NY

BUCK Philo H. of Merchantville, NY　　　July 19, 1882
LINK Emma F. of Merchantville, NY　　　　Savona, NY

MONELL E. F. of Bath, NY　　　　　　　　July 19, 1882
COWLES Cora A. of Bath, NY　　　　　　　Bath, NY

KIMBALL C. L. of N. Cohocton, NY　　　　August 2, 1882
EVERETT Lillie of N. Cohocton, NY　　　　N. Cohocton, NY

MORAN Edwin of Rochester, NY　　　　　　August 16, 1882
HOFFMAN Mary of Bath, NY　　　　　　　　Bath, NY

WATSON Joseph of Bath, NY　　　　　　　August 21, 1882
BUTLER Hattie of Sylvania, Pa.　　　　　　Sylvania, Pa.

HATHAWAY Robert R. of Cameron, NY　　　September 6, 1882
PIERCE Martha A. of Jordanville, NY　　　Bath, NY

LOUCKS Nathaniel S. of Avoca, NY　　　　September 7, 1882
ROBINSON Carrie C. of Avoca, NY　　　　　Avoca, NY

JORDAN William D. of Troupsburgh, NY　　September 6, 1882
NORTHRUP Louise G. of Troupsburgh, NY　Troupsburgh, NY

CRAIG Thomas　　　　　　　　　　　　　September 20, 1882
SUTHERLAND Mrs. Maria　　　　　　　　　Bath, NY

BRACE James of Bradford, NY　　　　　　October 7, 1882
INSCHO Dora of Bradford, NY　　　　　　　Bradford, NY

TORRENCE Oliver A. of Thurston, NY　　　October 8, 1882
HAND Lena M. of Bath, NY　　　　　　　　Bath, NY

SCOFIELD Andrew R. of Sonora, NY	October 1, 1882
SEAGER Ella C. of Sonora, NY	Sonora, NY
LEGRO John of Bath, NY	October 12, 1882
DAVIS Lucy of Avoca, NY	Bath, NY
WIXSON Alba K. of Bath, NY	October 18, 1882
VAN VLEET Helen dau of J. of Bath, NY	Bath, NY
TOLLIVER Lewis of Bath, NY	October 24, 1882
STEPHENS Mary of Bath, NY	Bath, NY
SMALLIDGE Fred S.	November 15, 1882
WAGNER Lizzie dau of M. T.	Bath, NY
LINDSAY John S.	November 8, 1882
ROTH Miss ____	Bath, NY
CONINE Frank of Bath, NY	November 8, 1882
SINCLAIR M. Adell of Bath, NY	Bath, NY
JACKSON James of Coventry, Pa.	November 9, 1882
NELSON Nettie of Bath, NY	Bath, NY
KREIDLER Samuel of Hornellsville, NY	November 9, 1882
WOOD Sarah E. of Hornellsville, NY	Hornellsville, NY
MC CANN Richard of Thurston, NY	November 5, 1882
COLE Mary E. of Thurston, NY	Thurston, NY
SHULTS Chauncey D. of Bath, NY	November 27, 1882
WOODARD Ida M. of Bath, NY	Bath, NY
SHOEMAKER Phillip	December 5, 1882
FAUCETT Mollie	Bath, NY
STEVER George W. of Pulteney, NY	December 14, 1882
LEPPER Mrs. Louisa of Unionville, NY	Bath, NY
KINGSLEY Newton L. of S. Dansville, NY	December 13, 1882
EVELAND Lizzie D. of S. Dansville, NY	S. Dansville, NY
MILLER Nelson J. of Prattsburgh, NY	November 26, 1882
PORTER Hattie E. of Prattsburgh, NY	Kanona, NY
FRINK F. H. of Naples, NY	December 3, 1882
HAIGHT Mrs. Katie of Prattsburgh, NY	Prattsburgh, NY
COOK Cephas S. of Thurston, NY	November 29, 1882
CRANS Alice A. of Thurston, NY	Merchantville, NY

SUMMERSON David of Campbell, NY   December 24, 1882
PLATT Martha A. of Bath, NY   Merchantville, NY

EVERETT George W. of Hornellsville, NY   December 24, 1882
TROWBRIDGE Mary E. of Fremont, NY   Hornellsville, NY

SIMMS William B. of Hornellsville, NY   December 25, 1882
BENTLEY Christina T. of Hornellsville, NY   Hornellsville, NY

GRAVES Charles P. of Dansville, NY   December 20, 1882
OWEN Mrs. Mary M. of Dansville, NY   Beechville, NY

SEAMANS Melvin L. of Savona, NY   December 30, 1882
BISHOP Sarah E. of Savona, NY   Savona, NY

BRUNDAGE S. H. of Pleasant Valley, NY   January 10, 1883
LEWIS Anna of Cold Springs, NY   Cold Springs, NY

YOUNG George C. of Wayland, NY   January 13, 1883
ROOT Helen of Wayland, NY   Wayland, NY

COBURN Martin B. of Wyoming Co. NY   January 17, 1883
RICHARDSON Lottie E. dau of George of Bath, NY   Bath, NY

TAYLOR Henry B. of Howard, NY   January 10, 1883
MC CARTNEY Ellen J. of Bath, NY   Bath, NY

DIMMICK Martin of Bath, NY   January 17, 1883
SMITH Mrs. Anna of Bath, NY   Bath, NY

NORTHRUP Eugene of Pulteney, NY   January 7, 1883
WALTERS Annie of Pulteney, NY   Pulteney, NY

SWITZER G. W. of Bradford, NY   January 14, 1883
AXTELL Jeanette of Bradford, NY

MILLER Oliver H. of Bath, NY   January 4, 1883
HEINAMAN Katie M. of Bath, NY   Bath, NY

CASS Solomon A   January 17, 1883
DANNALS Josephine of Bath, NY   Bath, NY

HODGE William of Monroe, Pa.   (Newspaper date) February 2, 1883
BARBER Martha E. of Corning, NY

CRAM Benjamin M. of Boston, Mass.   February 7, 1883
HUNT Olive O. dau of Jerome of Bath, NY at sister's Auburn, NY

BURDETT Allen of Hornellsville, NY   (Newspaper date) February 23, 1883
COLLINS May of N. Almond, NY

JONES George W. of Gang Mills, NY	(Newspaper date)	February 23, 1883
KNAPP Flora M. of W. Erwin, NY		
RANDALL Calvin D. of Smithport, Pa.	(Newspaper date)	February 23, 1883
WETMORE Louella of Fremont, NY		
MC CHESNEY Charles of Bath, NY		February 14, 1883
KELLOGG Mary of Howard, NY		Howard, NY
ROGERS Hiram of Savona, NY		March 17, 1883
THOMPSON Phebe of Savona, NY		Savona, NY
CROOKSTON William of Wayne, NY		January 14, 1883
COVEY Mrs. Louisa C. of Winona, Mn.		Bath, NY
HOUSE Frank of Howard, NY		February 15, 1883
SMITH Vinnie A. of Howard, NY		Howard, NY
WOODARD Bonum of Dix, NY		March 9, 1883
HAWKINS Mary of Urbana, NY		Savona, NY
CODY Frank A. of E. Campbell, NY		March 7, 1883
HAMILTON Sarah of Corning, NY		E. Campbell, NY
HORTON Lyman S. of Scuttsville, NY		March 11, 1883
SCUTT Sarah M. of Scuttsville, NY		Kanona, NY
SAXTON Fay of Howard, NY		March 23, 1883
CLARK Ada M. of Cameron, NY		Towlesville, NY
WIXSON William of Bath, NY		March 11, 1883
HAYES Sarah E. of Bath, NY		Savona, NY
WALLACE James of Bath, NY		March 28, 1883
WOODRUFF Helen A. of Bath, NY		Savona, NY
STEWARD John A. of Savona, NY		April 7, 1883
AUSTIN Charlotte of Savona, NY		Savona, NY
LE MUNYON George of Bath, NY		April 5, 1883
LINDSAY Fannie of Bath, NY		Bath, NY
JARVIS William A. of Elmira, NY		April 10, 1883
WILLMORE Mrs. Amanda of Bath, NY		Bath, NY
WHITMAN Fred of Hornellsville, NY		March 28, 1883
HARRINGTON Sarah of Hornellsville, NY		
KING Wilson of Deerfield, Pa.		April 17, 1883
COOLEY Mrs. Dora of Erwin, NY		Painted Post, NY

IDE Erwin of Smithboro, NY	April 16, 1883
COURTWRIGHT Phena of Urbana, NY	Urbana, NY
SUTTON John of Bath, NY	April 17, 1883
CASLER Nora of Thurston, NY	
CASE Albert of Jasper, NY	April 1, 1883
FREELAND Cora of Greenwood, NY	
VAN RIPER Abram of Cohocton, NY	April 19, 1883
EVELAND Mrs. H. of Rogersville, NY	
ENNIS Lamont O. of Erin, NY	April 25, 1883
JOHNSON Ella of Howard, NY	Howard, NY
WASHBURN James of Bradford, NY	April 26, 1883
KING Nettie of Bradford, NY	
THOMAS Martin G. of Bath, NY	April 24, 1883
WILLIAMS Rose of Bath, NY	Howard, NY
LEE Joseph of Pulteney, NY	May 3, 1883
NEVYUS Maggie of Pulteney, NY	Pulteney, NY
MASON R. H. of Woodhull, NY	May 18, 1883
WARD Lucy E. of Savona, NY	Savona, NY
ROBINSON Asher E. of Lindley, NY	May 5, 1883
TERRELL Mrs. Mary of Painted Post, NY	
MC CANN Fred of Thurston, NY	May 20, 1883
FERO Celia of Addison, NY	Addison, NY
MILLER Adrian F. of Wheeler, NY	May 12, 1883
POTTER Helen of Prattsburgh, NY	
BAUTER Charles H. of Towlesville, NY	May 29, 1883
FRALEY Belle of Bath, NY	Bath, NY
COBB Charles H. of Westfield, Pa.	May 20, 1883
HOUGHTALING Susan M. of Erwin, NY	
SANTEE Dr. W. L.	May 31, 1883
HOWELL Isabelle	Hammondsport, NY
FRANCISCO C. M. of Rushville, NY	June 12, 1883
LEWIS Clara B. of Prattsburgh, NY	
MOREDYKE Rev. Peter of Grand Rapids, Mi.	June 4, 1883
PERRY Matie of Troupsburgh, NY	

RUNNER Ward of Campbell, NY **VAN HOUSEN** Lena of Prattsburgh, NY	June 13, 1883
COLE J. H. of Bath, NY **MC KEEN** Lillie of Canisteo, NY	June 17, 1883 Canisteo, NY
RUNNER Olin Fisk of Wayne, NY **HARDENBROOK** Martha Eva dau of A. S. of Bath, NY	June 26, 1883 Bath, NY
WAYNE Alexander of Geneseo, NY **ROBINSON** Cynthia of Bath, NY	June 19, 1883 Geneseo, NY
GEARY James Jr. of Sonora, NY **CHASE** Olive of Bath, NY	July 29, 1883 Bath, NY
WELCH Frank B. of Erwin, NY **YARRINGTON** Florence A. of Hornby, NY	August 5, 1883 Savona, NY
RUTH Erwin of Delaware Water Gap, Pa. **WARD** Mary of Savona, NY	August 13, 1883
FAY Frank A. of Bath, NY **JOHNSON** Ella of Bath, NY	August 18, 1883 Bath, NY
SPEARS Charles A. of Pulteney, NY **SALMON** Maggie of Pulteney, NY	August 15, 1883 Penn Yan, NY
PEACOCK Ephraim L. of Penn Yan, NY **WAY** Eva A. of Jerusalem, NY	September 12, 1883 Hammondsport, NY
MAYBE Joseph of Howard, NY **ABER** Mary of Howard, NY	October 3, 1883
MEEKER Frank Worrell **JOY** Jennie Radcliffe	October 2, 1883 Bath, NY
MC CORMICK Walter B. of Pulteney, NY **HALL** Ardelissa of Pulteney, NY	September 26, 1883 Pulteney, NY
FLETCHER James M. of Avon, NY **EMERSON** Harriet of Bath, NY	October 10, 1883
WALLING E. L. of S. Bradford, NY **CARR** Melissa of S. Bradford, NY	September 22/3, 1883 S. Bradford, NY
CHRISCADEN Hugh **COOK** Elizabeth	October 12, 1883 Pulteney, NY
SHEPARD Lee V. of Bath, NY **SIMMONS** Clara A. of Bath, NY	October 17, 1883 Bath, NY

EDSALL Philo M. of Thurston, NY
CONKLING Elizabeth L. of Roseville, Pa.

November 11, 1883
Savona, NY

HEINAMAN Edward
MAGEE Molly

November 7, 1883
Bath, NY

CLARK Lewis H. of Avoca, NY
BARTON Helene May of Bath, NY

November 15, 1883
Bath, NY

SNYDER Frank J. of New Milford, Pa.
BUTLER Ida May of Bath, NY

November 15, 1883
Bath, NY

HITCHCOCK H. H. of Buffalo, NY
VAN NESS Ella M. of Corning, NY

October 30, 1883
Bath, NY

MILLER Willis L. of Orange, NY
WALLACE Libbie J. of Orange, NY

November 21, 1883
Bradford, NY

LEWIS William F. of Cameron, NY   (Newspaper date) November 30, 1883
OSBORNE Mary F. of Cameron, NY

Cameron, NY

HILTON J. H. Frank of Hornby, NY
LEAVENWORTH Ida M. of Hornby, NY

November 3, 1883

PLATT Cephas F. of Painted Post, NY
ERWIN Mary dau of Gen. Francis E. Erwin

November 28, 1883

DILLENBECK Stewart H. of Prattsburgh, NY
SANFORD Clara D. of Prattsburgh, NY

December 12, 1883
Prattsburgh, NY

WITHEY Delos of Cameron, NY
WHITE Almira of Cameron, NY

November 4, 1883
Cameron, NY

STUART Joshua of Howard, NY
STEWART Annie of Howard, NY

November 15, 1883
Howard, NY

MC ELWEE Charles N. of Hornby, NY
MOORE Sarah L. of Hornby, NY

December 7, 1883

HUNTER Giles F. of Harwardon, Io.
WILKES Anna Shannon of Bath, NY

December 19, 1883
Bath, NY

MERRILL S. B. of Bath, NY
WYGANT Susan of Risingville, NY

December 26, 1883
Risingville, NY

HOUSE William A.
DUSENBERRY Mary H.

December 25, 1883

BAILEY Charles of Wheeler, NY
CARMAN Lizzie of Wheeler, NY

December 23, 1883

RAYMOND Silas of Wheeler, NY   December 25, 1883
KELLY Carrie of Wheeler, NY

MOWER Robert G. of Bolivar, NY   December 25, 1883
RILEY Edith of Pulteney, NY

MORSE Ebenezer E. of Lindley, NY   December 23, 1883
NOYES Emma of Howard, NY

DUSENBERRY Jarvis of Avoca, NY   December 25, 1883
OJERS Clara B. of Avoca, NY

WHEATON Albert Z. of Cohocton, NY   December 25, 1883
TUCKER Mattie J. of Avoca, NY

HUGHES Charles of Avoca, NY   December 31, 1883
LYKE Anna C. of Howard, NY

CHUBBOCK Vernon R. of Fremont, NY   (Newspaper date) January 4, 1883
PENNELL Emma E. of Honeoye, NY   nr Fairport, NY

MC KENZIE Ralph D. of Cameron, NY   January 1, 1884
WHITE Addie of Cameron, NY

WHITEHEAD Charles   December 19, 1883
PATTERSON Carrie   Hammondsport, NY

HAFFNER Augustus of Philadelphia, Pa.   December 29, 1883
SCHMOKER Mrs. U. of Hammondsport, NY

BRACE L. B. of Hornellsville, NY   January 7, 1884
KEEFE Maggie of Hornellsville, NY

JOHNSON George B. of Prattsburgh, NY   December 29, 1883
MOORE Anna C. of Cohocton, NY

KNAPP Homer of Corning, NY   January 2, 1884
GRAHAM Mary E. of Caton, NY

TAYLOR Monroe of Greenwood, NY   December 30, 1883
BLAIR Carrie of Greenwood, NY

BILLSON Francis V. of Avoca, NY   January 17, 1884
OLMSTEAD Amanda A. of Bath, NY   Bath, NY

GILMORE Arthur W. of Bradford, NY   January 15, 1884
KETCHUM Eliza H. of Urbana, NY   Urbana, NY

HAVENS Frank D. of Bradford, NY   January 15, 1884
WALLING Delia S. of Bradford, NY   Bradford, NY

ROCKEFELLOW William of Avon, NY
COLE Eva of Campbell, NY formerly of Cohocton, NY
January 7, 1884

SEAGER A. N. of Savona, NY
FAUCETT Katie of Savona, NY
January 23, 1884
Savona, NY

WYCKOFF John R. of Savona, NY
BEACH Emma of Savona, NY
January 27, 1884
Savona, NY

FAUCETT Richard of Savona, NY
SNYDER Myra A. of Bath, NY
January 24, 1884
Bath, NY

KUDER C. A. of Dansville, NY
ROGERS Kate W. of Risingville, NY
January 22, 1884
Rogersville, NY

LAYTON John R. of Urbana, NY
WIXON Jennie of Urbana, NY
January 16, 1884

HORTON Charles W. of Hammondsport, NY
RAY Sarah A. of Hammondsport, NY
January 18, 1884

SCHOFIELD James of Hammondsport, NY
SNOW Cornelia M. of Hammondsport, NY
January 16, 1884

SMITH Orren B. of Prattsburgh, NY
BODINE Sara P. dau of Amasa of Prattsburgh, NY
January 23, 1884

EDWARDS William H. of Hammondsport, NY
WRIGHT Mary of Hammondsport, NY
January 16, 1884
Bath, NY

JENNINGS Thomas
GILES Fanny dau of B. J.
January 27, 1884
Hornellsville, NY

BATHRICK Charles E.
SMITH Carrie
January 28, 1884
Hornellsville, NY

WHITTENHALL Uri
LEACH Clara H.
February 3, 1884
Woodhull, NY

MC GOODWIN John of Howard, NY
RICE Sarah of Howard, NY
January 29, 1884

REAMER William H. of Prattsburgh, NY
WRAIGHT Alice M. of Wheeler, NY
February 3, 1884

WILKINS George H. of Canandaigua, NY
BREWER Margaret E. of Caton, NY
February 2, 1884
Elmira, NY

CONDERMAN A. J. of Fremont, NY
WALLACE Nettie J. of Fremont, NY
February 5, 1884
Fremont, NY

ANDREWS Frank
O'NEIL Allie

February 2, 1884
Hornellsville, NY

DONNELLY George of Avoca, NY
MAGEE Lizzie of Avoca, NY

February 11, 1884

MANNING Richard of Richburg, NY
MC CARTHY Mary of Hornellsville, NY

February 25, 1884
Hornellsville, NY

BUTTS Willard of Wheeler, NY
LITTLE Edith of Bath, NY

January 3, 1884
Wheeler, NY

HARDENBROOK William Emery of Bath, NY
GAYALL Delia of Bath, NY

March 5, 1884
Bath, NY

WHEELER T. H. of Wheeler, NY
PARMER Eva of Urbana, NY

February 18, 1884
Wheeler, NY

PIXLEY Lavern
CURTIS Mattie

February 27, 1884
Avoca, NY

EVERETT Charles W. of Avoca, NY
CALKINS Nellie G. of Avoca, NY

February 26, 1884

DE GOLYER William of Gloversville, NY
SCOTT Emma E. of Wayland, NY

February 19, 1884

SHARER Jonah of E. Wayland, NY
MC NISH Cora dau of Mathew of Springwater, NY

February 24, 1884

WOODBURY Fred C. of Bath, NY
MONELL Hattie B. of Kanona, NY

March 12, 1884
Kanona, NY

CLARK Frank of Brookfield, Pa.
MURDOCK Libbie of Troupsburgh, NY

February 17, 1884

FENTON Ira of Woodhull, NY
MOREHOUSE Mrs. Sophrona nee **QUIGLEY** of Woodhull, NY

January 26, 1884

WILDER Glen C. of Painted Post, NY
GOODSELL Norma of Painted Post, NY

March 13, 1884

SMITH Elmer E. of Fremont, NY
BURDETT Lena M. of Fremont, NY

March 12, 1884

ACOMB William H. of S. Dansville, NY
MC CURDY Margaret of Ossian, NY

March 12, 1884

WARREN Charles B. of Dundee, NY
EVERTS Mate of Orange, NY

March 12, 1884
Orange, NY

MOSIER Lewis of Tuscarora, NY   March 14, 1884
BREWER Electa of Addison, NY

ELLISON Mitchell of Cameron, NY   March 26, 1884
STEWART Mara of Bath, NY   Bath, NY

GAY Hugh of Towlesville, NY   (Newspaper date) April 4, 1884
LANE Jennie of Bath, NY   Bath, NY

BEMON Harvey of Towlesville, NY   April 2, 1884
COOLEY Mary A. of Bath, NY   Bath, NY

SHADER William H. of Wheeler, NY   April 2, 1884
SMITH Sarah E. of Savona, NY   Savona, NY

FLOREY William of Wayland, NY   March 12, 1884
SMITH Mrs. Nora L. of Wayland, NY

CARR Ardean of Hector, Pa.   March 12, 1884
HERRINGTON Emma G. of Woodhull, NY   Osceola, Pa.

STURDEVANT J. Beals of Avoca, NY   April 6, 1884
YEISLEY Minnie of Avoca, NY

FERGUSON Charles of W. Cameron, NY   April 9, 1884
PALMATER Carrie of W. Cameron, NY

BEACH Charles H. of Cohocton, NY   April 16, 1884
PECK Zerlie of Wolcott, NY

JOHNSON George   April 14, 1884
BOOTH Dora dau of Myron of Wayland, NY

RUMSEY John H. of Campbell, NY   April 10, 1884
WRIGHT Surrena of Campbell, NY   E. Campbell, NY

BURLEY David of Cameron, NY   April 13, 1884
HARVEY Nettie of Thurston, NY   Merchantville, NY

CONKLIN William E. of Bath, NY   April 8, 1884
SHIESLEY Susie of Bath, NY   Bath, NY

SHEPARD Henry of Kanona, NY   (Newspaper date) April 18, 1884
LAYTON Jane of Kanona, NY   Kanona, NY

WHITMAN Rev. E. H. of Duboiston, Pa.   April 16, 1884
EDGETT Lillian dau of A. B. of Hornellsville, NY

BROTHER Henry H. of Kanona, NY   April 8, 1884
DAWSON Carrie of Kanona, NY   Kanona, NY

KINCAID Ezra of Kanona, NY — April 30, 1884
SHAVER Mrs. Franc M. of Kanona, NY — Kanona, NY

PLATT Benton of Bath, NY — April 30, 1884
CHAPIN Lily E. of Campbell, NY — Savona, NY

SMITH Stewart of Avoca, NY — May 4, 1884
HERRON Maggie of Bath, NY — Bath, NY

BEECHER William of Buffalo, NY — April 23, 1884
LYKE Josie of Howard, NY

BULLOCK Charles E. of Bath, NY — May 7, 1884
GOFF Belle R. of Chilton, Wis. — Chilton, Wis.

KING W. N. of Knoxville, NY — May 4, 1884
SANFORD Mrs. Mary A. of Knoxville, NY

BASSETT Benjamin of Painted Post, NY — May 7, 1884
LAMBERT Helen of Painted Post, NY — Painted Post, NY

ANGELL W. H. of St. Paul, Mn. — May 8, 1884
BRADLEY Mary B. dau of George B. of Corning, NY — Corning, NY

ALDERMAN Alvin C. of Berlin, Mi. — April 13, 1884
WRIGHT Mrs. Eliza A. of Hornellsville, NY

COLEMAN Stephen G. of Elmira, NY — May 7, 1884
SMITH Effie L. formerly of Prattsburgh, NY — Livonia, NY

WEAVER Robert of Corning, NY — May 9, 1884
STEWART Ida E. of Hornellsville, NY

EMERSON Charles P. of Bath, NY — May 25, 1884
COOTS Eliza of Howard, NY — Hornellsville, NY

YOUNG William G. of Greenwood, NY — May 15, 1884
WHITE Mrs. Mary A. of Howard, NY — Howard, NY

HIGGINS L. B. of Bath, NY — June 4, 1884
REYNOLDS Mary A. of Bath, NY — Bath, NY

GROBE John C. of Dansville, NY — May 27, 1884
BILLS Cora W. of Wayland, NY — Wayland, NY

HOWE Will L. of Prattsburgh, NY — June 23, 1884
NOXON J. Eudora of Wheeler, NY — Wheeler, NY

WALLBRIDGE George of Hornellsville, NY — June 26, 1884
CROSS Carrie of Hornellsville, NY — Hornellsville, NY

PRUDEN Uriah of S. Bradford, NY
TAYLOR Libbie of S. Bradford, NY
July 6, 1884
S. Bradford, NY

CLARK Isaac M. of Troupsburgh, NY
ORR Mrs. Louisa of Addison, NY
July 2, 1884

BURDETT John of Elmira, NY
REDFORD Emma J. of Hornellsville, NY
July 4, 1884
Hornellsville, NY

HUBBARD E. A. of Prattsburgh, NY
WALLACE Valeria of Pulteney, NY
July 10, 1884
Pulteney, NY

ELLIS Edwin of Addison, NY
SMITH Fanny of Addison, NY
July 13, 1884
Troupsburgh, NY

PIERCE Alvin S. of Addison, NY
JENKS Olive M. of Bath, NY
July 30, 1884
Bath, NY

HOUSE Reuben
WILLSON Allie
July 20, 1884

SMITH George B. of Hornby, NY
SEELEY Ada of Monterey, NY
July 13, 1884

FOSTER William of Wheeler, NY
REED Rachel of Wheeler, NY
August 2, 1884
Wheeler, NY

BOTTOM C. A.
AUSTIN Ida
July 2, 1884
Troupsburgh, NY

CASTLE Floyd F. of Woodhull, NY
GREEN Cora B. of Woodhull, NY
July 26, 1884

PIERCE Thadeus S. of Hedgesville, NY
CASE Anna E. of Hedgesville, NY
July 3, 1884

VAN NORMAN Prof. of Jasper, NY
LOSEY Cora of Lawrenceville, Pa.
July 30, 1884

SAMPLE Luke G. of Gillett, Pa.
THOMPSON Julia of Bath, NY
August 10, 1884
Wellsburg, NY

EMERSON Herbert S. of Kanona, NY
READ Marjorie A. of Kanona, NY
August 10, 1884
Bath, NY

JOHNSON Prof. Walter
WOODWORTH Sena of N. Cohocton, NY
July 31, 1884
Bareboo, Wis.

PETERSON Ferdinand C.
EVERLING Anna K.
August 6, 1884
Hornellsville, NY

CHRISTIAN John of Cohocton, NY
KRUG Mary of Cohocton, NY

August 12, 1884

RUMSEY Casper of Rathbone, NY
ROSELL Delia of Mi.

August 5, 1884
Thurston, NY

BASSETT Charles of Urbana, NY
ROGERS Jennie

August 20, 1884
Hammondsport, NY

ABBY Albert T. of Watkins, NY
WILLIS Sarah W. of Howard, NY

September 3, 1884
Howard, NY

ZELINER George M. of Grand Rapids, Mi.
AUSTIN Eva M. dau of Henry of Savona, NY

August 27, 1884
Savona, NY

LOUNSBERRY L. of Potter, NY
HOPKINS Charlotte E. of Bath, NY

September 10, 1884
Bath, NY

HALL Walter O. of Avon, NY
RISING Hattie R. of Campbell, NY

September 24, 1884
Campbell, NY

KRESS Henry
MC GREW Kate

September 23, 1884
Corning, NY

MOORE George B. of Dundee, NY
CRANS Amanda of Bath, NY

October 2, 1884
Bath, NY

EARL Frank E. of Savona, NY
JACK Mary of Savona, NY

October 4, 1884
Savona, NY

FINCH William of S. Troupsburgh, NY
COHAN Sophia of S. Troupsburgh, NY

October 1, 1884
Addison, NY

WILCOX Ralph of Troupsburgh, NY
HUSTED Carrie of Woodhull, NY

October 17, 1884

HOUSE George W. of Howard, NY
EARLY Clara of Avoca, NY

September 24, 1884

WESTFIELD Henry H.
HYDE Agnes E.

October 1, 1884
Hornellsville, NY

DOTY Ward G.
ROOF Stella C

October 2, 1884
Hornellsville, NY

UNDERHILL Edwin Stewart of Bath, NY
ALLEN Minerva Elizabeth dau of William W. of Bath, NY

October 9, 1884
Bath, NY

STEWART Edward J. of Bath, NY
BAILEY Ella E. of Hammondsport, NY

October 9, 1884
Hammondsport, NY

ALLEN Thomas Jr. of Hornellsville, NY   October 5, 1884
SCHRADER Emma of Dunkirk, NY   Bradford, NY

METTS Oliver of Hornellsville, NY   October 8, 1884
KESSLER Lena of Dunkirk, NY   Dunkirk, NY

GLEASON Ezra of Urbana, NY   October 14, 1884
LOVERIDGE Ida of Urbana, NY

PURDY Isaac of Pulteney, NY   October 1, 1884
ROFF Carrie of Penn Yan, NY   Corning, NY

BARTLETT Courtland F. of Almond, NY   October 7, 1884
CURRY May C.   Hornellsville, NY

GREEN Arthur of Hornby, NY   October 15, 1884
ROOT Fanny of Hornby, NY

HUBER H. A. of Jasper, NY   October 18, 1884
HOLT Amanda of Jasper, NY

BURNS David of Howard, NY   October 21, 1884
CORNELL Helen of Howard, NY

SMITH Sylvester of Erwin, NY   October 12, 1884
MORSE Mary F. of Addison, NY

FENTON Lewis W. of Woodhull, NY   October 16, 1884
BISSELL Ida M. of Woodhull, NY   Elkland, Pa.

STAFFORD Smith of Woodhull, NY   October 16, 1884
FENTON Kate R. of Woodhull, NY   Elkland, Pa.

CAMERON Jacob of Buffalo, NY   October 22, 1884
PARKS Mrs. Harriet M. of Hornellsville, NY

WALDEN Wilson R. of Caton, NY   October 27, 1884
BATES Nettie S. of Caton, NY

ALBEE Herman   October 28, 1884
FREEMAN Mary   Corning, NY

DARRIN J. W.   October 14, 1884
HILTON Mary   San Francisco, Cal.

COMASH John   October 27, 1884
CAMPBELL Jospehine   Corning, NY

MOCKER Victor   October 24, 1884
RUFF Anna C.   Corning, NY

CROFT William of Urbana, NY   October 31, 1884
CONNELLY Mary Jane of Urbana, NY

WEBSTER Julius of Arkport, NY   October 22, 1884
WALKER Margaret O. of Arkport, NY

MC DANIELS John W. of Howard, NY   November 5, 1884
TUTTLE Ella B. of Howard, NY

FRITZ George T. of Wheeler, NY   October 28, 1884
JONES Mate of Arkport, NY

KENYON Herbert of Hornellsville, NY   November 2, 1884
PHELPS Carrie B. of Hartsville, NY

HUTCHES Andrew C. of Mt. Washington, NY   October 30, 1884
LONGWELL Addie E. of Mt. Washington, NY

SHAW Hiram F. of Palmyra, NY   October 30, 1884
JONES Georgie of Wheeler, NY   Hammondsport, NY

SMITH Delmer of Tyrone, NY   November 11, 1884
HAMMER Lena of Tyrone, NY   Almond, NY

WOOD Lewis W. of Orange, NY   (Newspaper date)   November 21, 1884
SMITH Carrie M. of Tyrone, NY   Almond, NY

ORCUTT Charles W.   November 13, 1884
MALLORY Minnie H. dau of Rev. Mallory   Savona, NY

VAN GELDER Monroe of Urbana, NY   November 18, 1884
CASTLE Lizzie of Urbana, NY   Urbana, NY

DAVENPORT George   November 26, 1884
GREEK Emma   Peinted Post, NY

ALDRICH George of Risingville, NY   November 26, 1884
SHULTS Lizzie dau of George of Risingville, NY

WILLIAMSON George of Avoca, NY   December 3, 1884
BREWER Julia of Wheeler, NY   Bath, NY

DECKER Charles D. of Branchport, NY   November 19, 1884
PARKER Rena C. dau of Charles L. of Pulteney, NY   Pulteney, NY

STEPHENS J. Duane of Fremont, NY   November 27, 1884
WHITE Rose C. of Howard, NY   Howard, NY

WHITE John of Howard, NY   November 27, 1884
WALSH Ettie of Cameron, NY   Howard, NY

HALLINAN James of Tuscarora, NY   December 1, 1884
FRAWLEY Mary of Thurston, NY   Addison, NY

PARK Henry of Rathbone, NY   December 4, 1884
YOUNG Mary B. dau of William of Rathbone, NY   Rathbone, NY

SIMPSON E. of Jasper, NY   December 3, 1884
WYCKOFF Allie C. of Jasper, NY   Jasper, NY

PLAISTED David of W. Union, NY   December 3, 1884
WYCKOFF Lucy E. of Jasper, NY   Jasper, NY

TAYLOR Lafayette of Howard, NY   December 1, 1884
PRENTISS Mrs. Eleanora of Pulteney, NY   Pulteney, NY

HARTMAN Peter of Seeley Creek NY   November 27, 1884
CARR Katie of Seeley Creek, NY   Caton, NY

SANFORD W. W. of Thurston, NY   December 14, 1884
LYON Eva E. of Thurston, NY   Savona, NY

RILEY James G. of Pulteney, NY   November 29, 1884
BEACH Lizzie of Pulteney, NY   S. Pulteney, NY

INGRAHAM Hiram of Wayland, NY   December 16, 1884
OLNEY Mattie of Cohocton, NY   Cohocton, NY

MANNING J. F. of Havana, NY   December 9, 1884
HEYNA C. of Avoca, NY   Havana, NY

GILBERT Dr. W. H. of Lawrenceville, Pa.   December 6, 1884
VAN NORMAN Lizzie A. of Jasper, NY   Tioga, Pa.

SMITH Frank of Arkport, NY   December 15, 1884
THOMPSON Anna M. of Burns, NY   Hornellsville, NY

BROOKMAN Thomas M. of Elmira, NY   December 14, 1884
TERWILLIGER Clara E. of Lindley, NY   Lindley, NY

ROBERTS Luell J. of Sabins, Pa.   December 20, 1884
MOSHER Cordelia M. of Howard, NY

WHITE E. M. of Dundee, NY   December 18, 1884
WHEELER Ida M. of Bath, NY   Bath, NY

ROLESON Lester of Hornby, NY   December 14, 1884
GARDNER Susie A. of Hornby, NY   Hornby, NY

WOOD William of Urbana, NY   December 21, 1884
ANDREWS Laura of Wheeler, NY   Mitchellville, NY

Steuben Farmers Advocate (Bath, NY)
Wednesday
January 5, 1831 - November 14, 1866

BRUNDAGE Jesse son of Capt. Abram of Bath, NY December 30, 1830
WHEELER Sarah dau of Gratton H. of Wheeler, NY Wheeler, NY

SMITH Solomon December 30, 1830
EMERY Eliza Urbana, NY

QUIN Edward of Tioga Co. NY January 5, 1831
KERNAN Margaret Mary dau of Gen. William Tyrone, NY

SPAULDING Philo B. (Newspaper date) February 2, 1831
METCALFE Catherine (Thursday last) Bath, NY

SHAVER John (Newspaper date) February 2, 1831
DROWN Lucinda

EMERSON John January 27, 1831
BLACKMAN Ruby

BEALS Ezra January 27, 1831
KATNER Catherine Wheeler, NY

SMITH Griffin of Bath, NY February 13, 1831
FLUENT Elizabeth of Canisteo, NY Canisteo, NY

FURMAN Josiah H. of Bath, NY February 8, 1831
WELLS Fanny of Bloomsbury, Pa. Bloomsbury, Pa.

SALYER Daniel of Tyrone, NY February 21, 1831
SALYER Luthena of Tyrone, NY Tyrone, NY

THOMPSON Smith February 22, 1831
JORDAN Angelina

OVETT Milton of Jersey, NY February 22, 1831
DAYMONTH Polly of Jersey, NY

WHITE Capt. Ira A. of Tyrone, NY February 15, 1831
JOHNSON Fidelia of Cedarville, NY Cedarville, NY

CARNAHAN Henry February 25, 1831
FLUENT Susan Cameron, NY

WATKINS Edmond G. March 3, 1831
STRONG Catherine Bath, NY

MAGEE John Mem. of Congress
SNOWDEN Mrs. Arabella of Washington DC

February 22, 1831
Washington DC

COTTON Henry G. Atty. of Painted Post, NY
MC BURNEY Maria of Painted Post, NY

March 8, 1831

MILLARD Edward of Campbell, NY
LAYCOST Eliza of Campbell, NY

February 18, 1831
Campbell, NY

ROSENCRANS Elijah
DILDINE Nancy

March 16, 1831
Pulteney, NY

GARDNER William of Penn Yan, NY
BIDWELL Emelia C.

February 20, 1831
Prattsburgh, NY

LA D'MINER Homer   (Newspaper date) March 30, 1831
HALL Amanda   (Sunday eve)   Prattsburgh, NY

PHILLIPS John   (Newspaper date) March 30, 1831
MADOLE Betsey   (Sunday last)   Howard, NY

ALEXANDER Moses age 95y
TOMPKINS Mrs. Frances age 105y

April 11, 1831
Bath, NY

NICHOLS William son of Judge Nichols of Bath, NY
BENNETT Adeline dau of Jacob of Howard, NY

April 20, 1831
Howard, NY

BOYD John of Wheeler, NY
WILCOX Prudence of Wheeler, NY

April 20, 1831
Bath, NY

SEYBOLT William H.
WOODARD Sally

April 23, 1831
Jersey, NY

BUMP Joseph
PHILLIPS Betsey

May 4, 1831
Bath, NY

HARTWELL James L.
EATON Mary Jane

May 14, 1831
Urbana, NY

SHURTLEFF J. B. Editor of Tioga Co. Gazette
TAYLOR Elizabeth C. dau of George W.

May 11, 1831
Wheeler, NY

FULTON Maj. Caleb P. of Bath, NY
SIMPSON Eliza of Cameron, NY

June 3, 1831
Cameron, NY

CAMERON George
PAULING Betsey

June 26, 1831
Bath, NY

SAMPSON William C. of Utica, NY
BARKER Mary of Utica, NY

July 7, 1831
Utica, NY

MANDEVILLE Homer formerly of Chenango Co. NY	July 17, 1831	
MANLEY Abigail formerly of Chenango Co. NY	Addison, NY	
LAUGHRY Charles of Canisteo, NY	August 14, 1831	
BROWN Juliet E. of Cameron, NY	Cameron, NY	
BROWN Emmett E. of Cameron, NY	August 14, 1831	
LAUGHRY Mary of Canisteo, NY	Canisteo, NY	
CAMPBELL Sylvanus of Howard, NY	August 16, 1831	
HUNT Electa of Howard, NY	Howard, NY	
CROSS John of Pulteney, NY	August 25, 1831	
PERKINS Louis dau of Capt. John of Pulteney, NY	Pulteney, NY	
MUNDAY David of Wheeler, NY	August 28, 1831	
WOOD Ann	Prattsburgh, NY	

SMITH James — September 8, 1831
IRWIN Sarah — Bath, NY

LANE Edmond — September 21, 1831
HARRIS Melissa — Wheeler, NY

WARNER William — September 24, 1831
CHASE Naomi

DOTY Jacob — September 18, 1831
MOORE Sarah Maria — Canisteo, NY

WELLS David of Howard, NY — October 6, 1831
HANNA Polly of Bath, NY — Bath, NY

WHITE Alexander — October 26, 1831
CORNELL Esther — Bath, NY

REEVE Isaac of Bath, NY — November 3, 1831
ARNOLD Ann of Penn Yan, NY — Penn Yan, NY

MC BURNEY John of Painted Post, NY   (Newspaper date) November 16, 1831
KNOX Almaria of Painted Post, NY — Painted Post, NY

STEWART Oliver of Bath, NY — November 21, 1831
PARKER Abigail of Bath, NY — Bath, NY

TOURTELOTTE S. K. of Hammondsport, NY — November 22, 1831
MC CLURE Eleanor of Bath, NY — Bath, NY

FOGLE George — November 23, 1831
METCALFE Ann W. — Bath, NY

CALKINS Ira of Pulteney, NY
WHITING Harriet of Bath, NY

December 20, 1831
Bath, NY

MC ELWEE James of Bath, NY   (Newspaper date)
SEAMANS Savanna of Bath, NY

December 28, 1831
Hornby, NY

CRUGER Washington
BROWN Jane Ann of Poughkeepsie, NY

July 23, 1831
Poughkeepsie, NY

CRUGER Jefferson
SHERWOOD Mary

December 17, 1831
Poughkeepsie, NY

SCHUYLER George
PRINDLE Susan of Wayne, NY

December 21, 1831
Bath, NY

BURRETT Dr. Harvey
BABCOCK Anner

December 13, 1831
Campbell, NY

THOMAS William W.
GILMORE Maria

December 13, 1831
Coventry, NY

WOODRUFF Edwin late of Canandaigua, NY
GILMORE Lydia A. of Coventry, NY

January 1, 1832
Coventry, NY

HASKIN Cyrus of Addison, NY
NASH Betsey of Addison, NY

January 12, 1832
Addison, NY

ORMSBY William of Wheeler, NY
GARDNER Minerva of Urbana, NY

January 21, 1832
Wheeler, NY

THOMAS Obed S.
ANDREWS Lowly dau of Ichabod Andrews

February 15, 1832
Reading, NY

CARNER Hiram P.
COLE Lydia A.

February 29, 1832
Bath, NY

HOUGHTALING Aaron
LIBBY Mary

March 8, 1832
Bath, NY

WANNENBURG Francis Jr.
PAGE Sophronia

March 11, 1832
Cohocton, NY

TOWNSEND Ira L. of Prattsburgh, NY
DE LONG Catherine of Hammondsport, NY

March 27, 1832
Hammondsport, NY

BAKER Joseph of Wheeler, NY
BUSKIRK Susannah of Cohocton, NY

April 3, 1832
Cohocton, NY

ANDREWS Maj. John T. of Reading, NY
ANDREWS Eliza of Reading, NY

April 2, 1832
Reading, NY

MC CLURE John of Erwin, NY
LYON Mary of Erwin, NY

March 20, 1832
Erwin, NY

SMITH Moses
BROAT Lanah Ann

April 4, 1832
Bath, NY

MATHEWS Samuel R.
MC BURNEY Caroline

April 9, 1832
Painted Post, NY

BACON James W.   (Newspaper date) April 18, 1832
PIGG Nancy

Rennsalaer, NY

ROCHESTER William B. of Buffalo, NY
POWERS Mrs. Eliza widow of Gershom of Auburn, NY

April 9, 1832
Auburn, NY

HOTCHKISS Marshall of Wayne, NY
FRENCH Maria of Bath, NY

May 6, 1832
Bath, NY

HAMMOND Lazarus of Hammondsport, NY
PRENTICE Mary of Bath, NY

May 8, 1832
Bath, NY

SKINNER Daniel G. of Bath, NY
GLASS Laura dau of Erastus of Bath, NY

May 20, 1832
Bath, NY

METCALFE Franklin
HESS Mary Ann

September 4, 1832
Bath, NY

HAWLEY Adna S.
STOCKING Mary Ann

September 6, 1832
Bath, NY

BURLEY William
CARNAHAN Susan

September 17, 1832
Cameron, NY

MARLATT Christopher
TUBBS Cynthia

October 7, 1832
Woodhull, NY

HOYT Robert H.   (Newspaper date) October 24, 1832
EASTERBROOK Mary

Painted Post, NY

BISHOP Dr. William   (Newspaper date) October 24, 1832
MC CULLOCK Lucretia

Painted Post, NY

BROUGHTON Urial
YORK Mrs. Naomi

October 28, 1832
Bath, NY

HOWE Haran of Ann Arbor, Mi.
VAN GORDER Polly of Wheeler, NY

October 21, 1832
Wheeler, NY

AULLS Ephraim son of Thomas Aulls
MIRTAL Katherine

October 25, 1832
Wheeler, NY

SMITH Ephraim   October 31, 1832
MILLER Lydia   Wheeler, NY

MADOLE Jesse   November 7, 1832
CONDERMAN Anna   Howard, NY

CONDERMAN Jacob   November 8, 1832
CONDERMAN Lydia   Howard, NY

WATKINS Milo late of Buffalo, NY   November 10, 1832
STEELE Burnet Ann of Painted Post, NY   Painted Post, NY

GOFF Job of Howard, NY   November 15, 1832
HANKS Rosilla of Howard, NY   Howard, NY

BEAMAN Henry C. of Jersey, NY   November 18, 1832
ROWLEY Martha dau of John S. of Bath, NY   Bath, NY

COSS Joseph   November 29, 1832
BUTLER Delia   Bath, NY

RUTHERFORD William M.   December 2, 1832
CREVELLING Margaret   Bath, NY

missing issues

LEE Avery S. of Avoca, NY   December 28, 1834
LOOP Sally of Avoca, NY   Urbana, NY

RHODES Amasa of Painted Post, NY   December 28, 1834
WILCOX Almira of Painted Post, NY   Painted Post, NY

BURNHAM George of Avoca, NY   February 1, 1835
SILSBE Caroline dau of James of Avoca, NY   Avoca, NY

SANDERSON William A. of Prattsburgh, NY   January 19, 1835
ALLEN Mageen of Prattsburgh, NY   Prattsburgh, NY

BAYLES William of Urbana, NY   February 18, 1835
HAMILTON Jane of Urbana, NY   Urbana, NY

SHUMWAY Rev. G. R. H. of Palmyra, NY   February 17, 1835
FORD Emily C. dau of James of Lawrenceville, Pa.   Lawrenceville, Pa.

HOVER David of Tyrone, NY   February 22, 1835
EMERY Sarah of Bristol Center, NY   Tyrone, NY

CHASE Asa   February 23, 1835
BOGARDUS Sarah   Bath, NY

CLISBE James — January 25, 1835
LINKLETTER Sarah — Howard, NY

WILBER Benjamin S. of Howard, NY — March 3, 1835
TOWLE Sophia of Howard, NY — Howard, NY

DUPARKO William of Howard, NY — March 8, 1835
OSBORN Juliet of Howard, NY — Howard, NY

STONE Jason H. — March 13, 1835
SMITH Harriet — Bath, NY

NASH Rier of Bath, NY — April 20, 1835
SCOTT Mrs. Anna of Benton, NY — Benton, NY

BROWN George M. — April 22, 1835
GRISWOLD Caroline — Bath, NY

BARNEY Nathan — April 28, 1835
MC WHORTER Ann — Avoca, NY

HOWELL William of Bath, NY — April 29, 1835
ADAMS Frances Adelphia of W. Avon, NY — W. Avon, NY

HIGGINS James G. — May 6, 1835
BURNS Maria E. — Bath, NY

HENRY H. O. of Bath, NY — June 18, 1835
GIBSON Phebe Maria of Rome, NY — Rome, NY

LOOP James L. of Avoca, NY — August 6, 1835
STEPHENS Parmelia of Almond, NY — Almond, NY

TERRY Daniel of Urbana, NY — August 22, 1835
LAUGHLIN Mrs. Catherine of Urbana, NY — Urbana, NY

BECKWITH Elijah late of Bath, NY — July 30, 1835
WYATT Ann of Bangor, Maine

BARNEY Nelson of Otsego, NY — September 6, 1835
BECKWITH Phylancy T. of Bath, NY — Bath, NY

BILLINGTON Mathias — September 27, 1835
WENTWORTH Mary — Kennedyville, NY

RUE Schuyler — September 27, 1835
ROTH Hannah — Bath, NY

FORD John of Bath, NY — September 26, 1835
TEMPLAR Anna of Bath, NY — Bath, NY

PRATT Shumway	September 13, 1835
WARREN Anna	Bath, NY
HENRY Josiah of Bath, NY	October 1, 1835
LOGAN Mrs. Polly of Bath, NY	Bath, NY
HALL John	September 25, 1835
HALL Elmira	Painted Post, NY
KING Edgar son of Samuel late of Ithaca, NY	May 28, 1835
HARMON Jemima of Andover, NY	Andover, NY
HARMON Cyrus H. of Andover, NY	October 2, 1835
KING Louisa dau of Samuel late of Ithaca, NY	Andover, NY
FRANCIS Spencer of Prattsburgh, NY	October 4, 1835
LINCOLN Monice of Bristol, NY	Bristol, NY
PRENTISS J. G. of Angelica, NY	October 11, 1835
ROLO Frances of Cortlandville, NY	Cortlandville, NY
HEMENWAY Aaron of Bath, NY	October 27, 1835
MILLS Minerva of Bath, NY	Bath, NY
BALL Benjamin	November 12, 1835
BURGE Eunice	Wayne, NY
GRAY Daniel	November 19, 1835
MYRTLE Lydia	Wheeler, NY
RANDALL William of Hammondsport, NY	November 22, 1835
READ Hannah	Urbana, NY
FRANCIS James K.	December 10, 1835
CLAPP Catherine	Bath, NY
WILLIAMS Abram of Hector, NY	December 21, 1835
HAVENS Elizabeth of Pulteney, NY	Bath, NY
BRIDGES Edmond E. of Prattsburgh, NY	December 17, 1835
GUNSOLUS Sarah dau of Emanuel of Wheeler, NY	Wheeler, NY
NILES Addison Md. of Prattsburgh, NY	December 17, 1835
MILLS Martha dau of Elisha of Naples, NY	Naples, NY
THAYER Simeon of Cameron, NY	December 31, 1835
PATTERSON Amarilla of Bath, NY	
HARRISON Phillip A. of Urbana, NY	January 7, 1836
THOMPSON Dolly of Bath, NY	Bath, NY

WOODRUFF Stepto of Almond, NY
REED Ann of Richmond, NY

December 13, 1835
Richmond, NY

WILBER John
GLEASON Lena Ann

January 14, 1836
Bath, NY

MORSE Mr. ____
FULLER Marilla

January 14, 1836

SMITH Elias H.
PARKER Polly

January 21, 1836
Bath, NY

FERRIS Hubbard of Howard, NY
HAMILTON Mary dau of John of Howard, NY

January 1, 1836

WAGENER W. W. of Pulteney, NY
FRENCH Elizabeth dau of J. of Wayne, NY

February 2, 1836

GARRISON George of Cameron, NY
WATKINS Lucy Ann of Bath, NY

February 7, 1836
Bath, NY

ABER Henry
TUTTLE Mary Jane

February 6, 1836
Bath, NY

CRITTENDEN Alva E. of Burns, NY
WENTWORTH Harriet of Bath, NY

February 14, 1836
Bath, NY

MATHER M. B.
DAVIS Catherine

February 18, 1836
Bath, NY

DREW Noah
LYON Amy

December 30, 1835
Pulteney, NY

DEWEY Hiram
OSBORN Mabel dau of Ard

February 23, 1836
Cohocton, NY

MORRISON Jesse of Great Valley, NY
MERRITT Amanda of Asylum, Pa.

February 29, 1836
Bath, NY

HENDERSHOTT Charles
ROBINSON Caroline

March 3, 1836
Hornellsville, NY

REYNOLDS Calvin J.
CAREY Betsey

March 3, 1836

NICHOLSON John of Hornellsville, NY
BENNETT Narcissa of Hornellsville, NY

March 3, 1836

GARDNER Nelson W.
LOGAN Elizabeth

March 9, 1836
Bath, NY

BOWER Richard	March 9, 1836
WHITCOMB Clarry Ann	Bath, NY
WHEELER David N. of Campbell, NY	March 17, 1836
STANIFORD Sarah G. of Campbell, NY	Bath, NY
DUNHAM Jonathan	March 31, 1836
NEWTON Elmina	Howard, NY
FENTON William M. of Pontiac, Mi.	April 11, 1836
BIRDSALL Adelaide S. dau of James of Addison, NY	Addison, NY
GUERNSEY Edmund of Woodhull, NY	April 13, 1836
BAXTER Hannah of Woodhull, NY	Woodhull, NY
MC QUIGG Jesse of Cohocton, NY	May 10, 1836
HILL Sarah of Cohocton, NY	Cohocton, NY
SELDEN Oscar B. of Bath, NY	June 8, 1836
WALKER Sarah of Howard, NY	Howard, NY
HALLETT Nathan of Cameron, NY	June 15, 1836
CLARK Maria of Cameron, NY	Bath, NY
CHATFIELD Andrew J.	June 27, 1836
BEEMAN Eunice E. dau of Almon of Addison, NY	Big Flats, NY
DEMONET Dominque of Seneca Falls, NY	July 30, 1836
SAPONT Eliza of Seneca Falls, NY	Bath, NY
UNDERHILL R. L.	August 25, 1836
STOUT Frances Minerva	Bath, NY
ROGERS Emerson of Wayne, NY	August 28, 1836
COYKENDALE Clorinda of Wayne, NY	
CONN Samuel of Bath, NY	September 4, 1836
FOWLER Orissa Ville of Cohocton, NY	Cohocton, NY
HAVERLING George S. of Bath, NY	September 22, 1836
BESLY Ruby dau of Samuel Besley	Campbell, NY
BEARD James of Painted Post, NY	September 22, 1836
PEEBLES Mary of Painted Post, NY	Painted Post, NY
JOHNSON Hiram	September 2, 1836
BUNDY Almira	Cameron, NY
GUYON Elijah of Canisteo, NY	September 22, 1836
JAMISON Mrs. Persis	Mt. Morris, NY

MEAD Samuel | October 30. 1836
SWARTHOUT Hulda | Tyrone, NY

OVERHISER Casper | November 4, 1836
WIXSON Caroline | Orange, NY

PURDY Joseph age 64 yrs of Steuben Co. (Newspaper date) | November 30, 1836
SILSBE Hansy age 64 yrs of Wayne, NY | Wayne, NY

TOLBERT Jesse of Bath, NY | November 5, 1836
TAYLOR Phebe of Bradford, NY | Mud Creek, NY

RICHARDSON Henry S. of Bath, NY | November 10, 1836
ROBERTS Eunice | Chemung, NY

YOUNGS James | November 23, 1836
PARKER Permelia | Howard, NY

ARMSTRONG Aaron of Pulteney, NY | December 17, 1836
MAKER Eunice of Wheeler, NY | Prattsburgh, NY

EDWARDS James M. of Bath, NY | December 27, 1836
TULLY Anna Maria of Bath, NY

HULBERT Silas of Cohocton, NY (Newspaper date) | January 11, 1837
SHEPARD Polly dau William of Cohocton, NY | Cohocton, NY

MANHART John | January 29, 1837
GOFF Hily | Howard, NY

HAGARDY Isaiah | February 6, 1837
HAWKINS Zilpha | Urbana, NY

COOK Joseph D. of Urbana, NY | February 19, 1837
THOMPSON Mary Ann of Urbana, NY

OWEN Elijah B. of Big Flats, NY | February 28, 1837
STEELE Mary | Painted Post, NY

WELLS Charles E. | March 11, 1837
COMPTON Hannah Maria of Bradford, NY | Tyrone, NY

PATTERSON John of Howard, NY | April 23, 1837
CROSIER Elizabeth of New York City | Howard, NY

MOORE John 2nd | April 20, 1837
KEYSER Catherine | Avoca, NY

MILLER Charles K. | April 25, 1837
MC BURNEY Mary dau of John | Painted Post, NY

LOOMACE Theron of Prattsburgh, NY
HANKS Eleanor

April 20, 1837
Kennedyville, NY

CAMPBELL John M. of Bath, NY
HALLOCK Eliza dau of Joshua of Bath, NY

May 10, 1837
Bath, NY

BARTLETT Phillip
HALE Eliza H. dau of Stephen of Hartwick, NY

June 1, 1837
Hornellsville, NY

AYERS Elias
JONES Miss _____ dau of John

June 8, 1837
Arkport, NY

BENGIE Stephen of Howard, NY
BEACH Phebe of Cohocton, NY

June 9, 1837
Bath, NY

RUTHERFORD James
SMITH Elizabeth

June 14, 1837

GRAY Henry
LOUCKS Catherine

June 18, 1837
Howard, NY

CLARKE Thomas of Bath, NY
WARDNER Harriet N. of Andover, NY

July 2, 1837
Andover, NY

DAWSON Bonham of Bath, NY
BARTINE Sally of Bath, NY

July 13, 1837
Bath, NY

ROSE James of Bath, NY
CASTERLINE Catherine of Painted Post, NY

July 20, 1837
Painted Post, NY

JONES John S. Md. of Bath, NY
WHEELER Charlotte dau of George of Bath, NY

August 2, 1837
Bath, NY

SYLVESTER Enoch
COOK Sally dau of Andrew Cook

July 25, 1837
Dansville, NY

HOTCHKIN John N. of Prattsburgh, NY
BULL Phebe S. of Marshall, NY

July 22, 1837
Marshall, NY

OVERTON Israel H.
HIX Phebe

August 2, 1837
Cohocton, NY

KENNARD John
WHITING Mary dau of Col. John Whiting

September 13, 1837
Bath, NY

ROBIE Harvey W. of Canastota, NY
STEVENS Parlynea M. of Bath, NY

September 28, 1837
Bath, NY

GOFF Maj. Henry of Howard, NY
SMITH Minerva dau of late Reuben Smith

October 12, 1837
Bath, NY

ELLSWORTH Joshua of Italy, NY	October 15, 1837
FRANCIS Martha of Prattsburgh, NY	Prattsburgh, NY
ROCKWELL Nathan O. of Orange, NY	October 9, 1837
JANES Sarah A. of Orange, NY	Orange, NY
GUINNIP Joseph J. of Campbell, NY	October 9, 1837
PATCHEN Sarah of Hornby, NY	Hornby, NY
ROBERTS Charles of Reading, NY	October 15, 1837
LEAVENWORTH Matilda of Reading, NY	Reading, NY
COTTON Henry G. of Painted Post, NY	November 8, 1837
BACON Mary of Painted Post, NY	Painted Post, NY
MURPHY Jeremiah of Ill.	December 21, 1837
VAN VELIE Clarissa of Cameron, NY	Cameron, NY
BUTLER Alva of Bath, NY	January 27, 1838
BOYER Letitia of Bath, NY	Bath, NY
ALLERTON Townsend of Bath, NY	February 1, 1838
CHAPIN Ann of Bath, NY	Bath, NY
RELETT Rev. W. of Wayne, NY	February 8, 1838
MITCHELL Mary Ann dau of John B. of Wayne, NY	Wayne, NY
SPICER Thomas S. of Bath, NY	March 3, 1838
CRANS Elizabeth of Bath, NY	Bath, NY
ROSE Sherman	March 23, 1838
STRIKER Mahala G.	Wheeler, NY
HASTINGS Timothy Revolutionary Pensioner of Wayne, NY	April 7, 1838
ABEL Mrs. Hannah of Bath, NY	
BEEMAN Almon of Addison, NY	April 16, 1838
BOSTWICK Almira of Hornellsville, NY	Angelica, NY
ELLAS Francis S. teacher at Clinton Istitute	May 9, 1838
HOYT Sarah E. formerly of Buffalo, NY	Stamford, Ct.
HALSEY Peter of Bath, NY	May 31, 1838
JOHNSON Lucia of Bath, NY	Bath, NY
PENDLETON Charles H.	June 10, 1838
SEARS Charity	Greenwood, NY
KNIGHT Daniel of Bath, NY	July 4, 1838
WARREN Emily of Bath, NY	Bath, NY

BORST Joseph   July 5, 1838
WARD Nancy   Erwin, NY

HUGHES Thomas Pancoast of Mud Creek, NY   July 12, 1838
FRENCH Mary of Bath, NY   Bath, NY

COWEN Nelson of Mansfield, Pa.   July 17, 1838
WHITNEY Emeline dau of Abraham L. of Painted Post, NY   Painted Post, NY

CHISSOM George of Wheeler, NY   July 28, 1838
WILLIAMSON Ruth dau of David form. of Montgomery Co.   Wheeler, NY

REED Dr. Randall of Allegany Co. NY   August 7, 1838
ALLEN Eliza Ann of Fleming, NY   Fleming, NY

FORT Henry of Orange, NY   August 4, 1838
DOANE Hannah of Orange, NY   Orange, NY

MILLER Harry of Barne, Mi.   August 27, 1838
STANLEY Jane F. G.   Avoca, NY

RICE John of New York City   September 4, 1838
SMITH Sarah of Hammondsport, NY   Hammondsport, NY

MILLER Mark of Towanda, Pa.   August 30, 1838
STEWART Sarah dau of Richard B. Stewart   Bath, NY

OTIS Ralph of Almond, NY   August 25, 1838
SMITH Mary (after courtship of 20 minutes)   Hornellsville, NY

SEARLES William   September 22, 1838
HADDEN Sybia   Pulteney, NY

HUBBARD Austin   October 11, 1838
CHAPIN Laura   Prattsburgh, NY

WILLARD Peter R. of Greenwood, NY   October 11, 1838
HUNT Jane of Greenwood, NY   Greenwood, NY

BACHUS John of Newark, NY   October 9, 1838
PATTERSON Theodosia of Painted Post, NY

ROSE Martin H. of Hammondsport, NY   November 22, 1838
MARSHALL Eliza Ann dau of Gen. O. F. Marshall   Wheeler, NY

STRYKER Benjamin F.   October 31, 1838
LEWIS Jane   Wheeler, NY

MAKER Archilus   November 3, 1838
WILLIAMSON Mary Ann

DRAKE Luther — November 10, 1838
JOHNSON Charlotte

MYRTLE Benjamin — November 14, 1838
SMITH Arabella

DUTCHER William A. of Geneva, NY — January 21, 1840
WOODS Mary dau of late William Woods — Bath, NY

BROWN William Henry Harrison of Cameron, NY — January 19, 1840
TOWNSEND Jane dau of late Uriah Townsend of Dresden, NY

MILLS Daniel — February 9, 1840
BORDEN Polly

RICE Seth H. of Howard, NY — February 12, 1840
WHEELER Gratia dau of Jeremiah Wheeler of Bath, NY — Bath, NY

MC CAY James Stewart late of Co. Antrim, Ireland — March 12, 1840
HAMLIN Hester a ward of W. W. Mc Cay — Bath, NY

BOON David of Ithaca, NY — February 17, 1840
RACE Jane of Painted Post, NY

BOWEN Moses — February 4, 1840
BRIGGS Adelia — Painted Post, NY

TAYLOR Stephen of Naples, NY — March 12, 1840
MAGOWAN Mary E. of Jerusalem, NY

WARREN Steward K. — March 25, 1840
WILLOUR Maria L. — Bath, NY

BODINE Lewis — April 13, 1840
READ Maria — Mud Creek, NY

COLEGROVE George of Addison, NY — April 22, 1840
ROBINSON Emma A. of Addison, NY — Addison, NY

MICKS William G. Md. of Portsmouth, Va. — May 7, 1840
RATHBONE Cornelia M. dau of Gen. R. of Rathbone, NY — Rathbone, NY

CAMPBELL Luther — May 30, 1840
BURTON Mrs. Elizabeth — Greenwood, NY

GREGORY David son of Stephen of Campbell, NY — June 7, 1840
MILLER Julia of Bath, NY — Campbell, NY

MC BURNEY Thomas of Painted Post, NY — June 4, 1840
MILLS Jane A. dau of late Elisha T. Mills — Fairfield, Ct.

IVES Augusta M. of Homer, NY   June 3, 1840
RIGGS Caroline dau of Dr. Lewis Riggs of Homer, NY   Homer, NY

ALLEN Israel B. of Howard, NY   June 24, 1840
VAN HOUSEN Eliza Ann of Howard, NY

BENTLEY William of Cohocton, NY   July 12, 1840
CROSBY Betsey of Cohocton, NY   Cohocton, NY

BOARDMAN Isaac   July 7, 1840
DIXON Mary   Dixson's Ferry, Ill.

STEWART Eleazer of Bath, NY   August 8, 1840
BARTON Lorinda of Bath, NY   Bath, NY

STEWART Robert   August 9, 1840
ABER Fanetta of Bath, NY   Bath, NY

BECKWORTH Richard B. of Erwin, NY   August 2, 1840
LEE Martha Ann of Erwin, NY

MOWERS Mathias of Bath, NY   August 24, 1840
COON Mary of Bath, NY

WAY Asa late of Saratoga Co. NY   September 5, 1840
BECKWITH Mrs. Fanny   Bath, NY

BAKER Ebenezer of Hammondsport, NY   September 6, 1840
TYLER Harriet of Pulteney, NY   Pulteney, NY

WOOD Berry C.   (Newspaper date) September 16, 1840
FEGALS Mary Ann   Painted Post, NY

PALMER G. W. of Howard, NY   September 17, 1840
BURDON Eunice of Howard, NY

WIXOM William of Prattsburgh, NY   September 12, 1840
GULICK Elizabeth of Pulteney, NY   Pulteney, NY

FLUENT Lucien of Cameron, NY   October 7, 1840
DANIELS Zuba of Bath, NY   Bath, NY

MAGEE Calvin of Bath, NY   October 7, 1840
SMITH Harriet of Bath, NY

ONGLEY William H. of Jefferson, NY   October 17, 1840
HICKMOTT Mary H. of Lockport, NY   Sennett, NY

BALDWIN William J. of Bath, NY   October 22, 1840
DOW Catherine of Bath, NY   Bath, NY

REXFORD Charles of Troupsburgh, NY   November 5, 1840
JEFFERS Lavina of Troupsburgh, NY   Troupsburgh, NY

WALLACE Cydney   November 5, 1840
JONES Mary Ann   Hornellsville, NY

BUTLER Joseph   December 24, 1840
ROYER Catherine   Bath, NY

DECKER Alexander of Urbana, NY   December 30, 1840
ALLISON Almira L. of Urbana, NY   Bath, NY

CHILDS Luther formerly of Bradford, NY   January 10, 1841
COATES Angeline of Bradford, NY   Bradford, NY

FRAZEE Barnet of Geneva, NY   January 7, 1841
WHEATON Alice Maria formerly of Seneca Falls, NY   Geneva, NY

COLEGROVE William J. of Norwich, Pa.   January 20, 1841
WRIGHT Eunice of Bath, NY   Bath, NY

SUNDERLIN D. of Tyrone, NY   January 17, 1841
WOLVERTON Lydia of Bradford, NY   Bradford, NY

BAILEY Wright of Tyrone, NY   January 19, 1841
BODOIN Margaret of Tyrone, NY   Tyrone, NY

BULLARD Otis A. of Hartford, Ct.   January 21, 1841
OLMSTEAD Angeline A. of Howard, NY   Howard, NY

NILES Edward of Dansville, NY   January 27, 1841
MC CLURE Martha J. dau of Finla Mc Clure   Bath, NY

LONGWELL Lewis of Urbana, NY   January 28, 1841
RETAN Rachel of Pulteney, NY   Pulteney, NY

HILL Charles of Hammondsport, NY   January 27, 1841
ROBINSON Eliza of Addison, NY   Addison, NY

BONHAM William   February 16, 1841
COOK Eliza   Campbell, NY

WOOD William of Addison, NY   February 21, 1841
HOLDEN Nancy of Bath, NY   Bath, NY

HOTCHKIN William H. of Pulteney, NY   February 27, 1841
PERKINS Ann Eliza of Pulteney, NY   Pulteney, NY

HURD Zopher of Painted Post, NY   February 8, 1841
MARLATT Almira of Troupsburgh, NY   Troupsburgh, NY

HISCOCK William H. of Branchport, NY	March 14, 1841
SELDEN Helen A. of Cameron, NY	Cameron, NY
COOK Paul C.	March 18, 1841
ROSENCRANS Margaret	Cohocton, NY
ROBERTS Ira of Reading, NY	March 18, 1841
EDGAR Hulda Maria of Reading, NY	
EDGETT George of Howard, NY	March 27, 1841
JONES Sarah J. of Howard, NY	Howard, NY
WHITTEMORE Moses F. Publisher of the Constitutionalist	April 8, 1841
WEBSTER Sarah	Bath, NY
ERWAY Ira of Barton, NY	March 5, 1841
MONELL Louisa of Bath, NY	
FENNO Samuel of Tyrone, NY	April 12, 1841
BURNELL Ann Eliza of Canandaigua, NY	Canandaigua, NY
SHAUT Joseph	April 22, 1841
HENDRYX Jane Ann	Bath, NY
HOPKINS Edward H. of Bath, NY	May 4, 1841
FOSTER Therese of Hammondsport, NY	Hammondsport, NY
MILLER Hiram	March 25, 1841
SMITH Harriet dau of David of Bonny Hill, NY	Bath, NY
LATTY James of Potter Co. Pa.	April 27, 1841
SEARS Perlina dau of Harley Sears of Cameron, NY	Cameron, NY
FORREST Calvin B. of Aurelius, NY	May 15, 1841
ONGLEY Mary E. of Sennett, NY	Sennett, NY
ANDREWS F. C. of Reading, NY	May 26, 1841
SMITH Euphema of Bath, NY	Bath, NY
BORDEN Azariah	June 6, 1841
ROSE Sally	Howard, NY
BISHOP John of Troupsburgh, NY	June 3, 1841
HASKINS Eliza Ann of Troupsburgh, NY	Troupsburgh, NY
DENNIS John of Jasper, NY	May 13, 1841
TAYLOR Amanda of Jasper, NY	Jasper, NY
PROSSER David B. Atty. of Penn Yan, NY	June 10, 1841
WEST Loisa H. of Milo, NY	Milo, NY

SHAYER Reuben of Cameron, NY
FIFE Julia of Jasper, NY

July 1, 1841
Jasper, NY

BORDEN Ambrose of Howard, NY
STEWART Loisa of Pulteney, NY

July 6, 1841
Wheeler, NY

JONES Thomas W. of Bath, NY
SHIDEMAN Derinda L. of Perry, NY

July 26, 1841
Perry, NY

ALDRICH Rodolphus
NOTTINGHAM Mrs. Catherine

August 2, 1841
Bath, NY

KING Charles of Greenwood, NY
JEFFERS Eunice of Jasper, NY

August 5, 1841
Jasper, NY

HILL Isaac H. of Dryden, NY
MOORE Elizabeth S. of Kennedyville, NY

August 21, 1841
Kennedyville, NY

GOODSELL Isaac P. of Hornby, NY
WOODARD Christiana of Hornby, NY

August 25, 1841

WHITE George of Albany, NY
TAYLOR Helen Ann dau of George W. of Wheeler, NY

September 9, 1841
Bath, NY

PERRY William of Cameron, NY
SELDEN Harriet E. of Cameron, NY

September 12, 1841
Cameron, NY

BURLEY Elijah of Bath, NY
QUANT Cornelia of Cameron, NY

September 7, 1841
Cameron, NY

ELLIS John A. of Urbana, NY
AGUR Mehitabel of Urbana, NY

September 19, 1841

BLOOD Samuel F. formerly of Bath, NY
COLE Lydia S. of Howard, NY

September 22, 1841
Howard, NY

WARREN Marcus C.
LOGAN Nancy

September 23, 1841
Bath, NY

COOTS Henry C. of Bath, NY
MILLER Mary of Bath, NY

September 26, 1841

BADGER Harvey of Elmira, NY
POTTER Louisa dau of Hiram Potter

September 29, 1841
Bath, NY

LANNING Albert P. of Hammondsport, NY
PULLING E. N. of Hammondsport, NY

September 29, 1841

BROCKWAY Walter of Wheeler, NY
BEAL Dolly of Wheeler, NY

October 20, 1841
Wheeler, NY

ARROWSMITH Sidney of Monroe Co. NY   September 20, 1841
CADY Lucinda of Cohocton, NY   Cohocton, NY

RICE Joel H. of Jackson, Mi.   November 9, 1841
BUTLER Caroline L. dau of Joseph Butler of Avoca, NY   Avoca, NY

NORTON Dr. George of Shelba, NY   November 17, 1841
ELLAS Sarah dau of Dr. Simpson E. Ellas   Bath, NY

ARMSTRONG Ackerson of Pulteney, NY   November 18, 1841
WHEELER Eliza dau of Grattan H. Wheeler   Wheeler, NY

REXFORD Alanson of Troupsburgh, NY   November 14, 1841
GRIGGS Martha Ann of Greenwood, NY   Greenwood, NY

FOSTER Jonathan B. of Greenwood, NY   November 18, 1841
CAMPBELL Harriet of Greenwood, NY

SHAYER Alfred   November 21, 1841
HAUBER Eleanor of Greenwood, NY   Canisteo, NY

BRYANT Joshua   November 17, 1841
ALLERTON Mary Jane   Bath, NY

BRINE Cornelius   November 28, 1841
HALLOCK Nancy   Erwin, NY

MARKHAM Norris of Cohocton, NY   December 8, 1841
PATTERSON Mary Jane of S. Dansville, NY   S. Dansville, NY

PARKER Alexander L. of Pulteney, NY   December 8, 1841
TOWNSEND Sarah dau of Rev. Joel Townsend   Jerusalem, NY

BAKER Edy   December 30, 1841
BUMP Lilly   Cameron, NY

MC DOWELL Thomas of Howard, NY   January 4, 1842
SICKFORD Felinda of Cohocton, NY   Cohocton, NY

COOK William A. of Bath, NY   December 28, 1841
COOK Ellen C. of Pike, NY   Pike, NY

CLARK Charles R. of Wheeler, NY   February 26, 1842
BAILEY Sarah dau of Nicholas of Urbana, NY   Urbana, NY

PELHAM John of Wheeler, NY   February 24, 1842
WARNER Susan of Urbana, NY   Urbana, NY

JOHNSON William B.   March 1, 1842
WILDER Clarissa A.   Bath, NY

JOHNSON Lewis of S. Dansville, NY   February 24, 1842
LOUCK Patience of S. Dansville, NY   S. Dansville, NY

WHEELER Mr. ____ of Richfield, NY   abt.February 24, 1842
MACK Rhoda of S. Dansville, NY

BROCKWAY Abner of Wheeler, NY   April 3, 1842
WHITE Mary Ann of Wheeler, NY   Wheeler, NY

HURD Gilbert of Lyndon, Ill.   March 13, 1842
BENSON Sarah dau of late Holbrook Benson of Starkey, NY   Starkey, NY

STEARNS Col. Marcus P. formerly of Bath, NY   March 28, 1842
CLARKE Margaret Elizabeth of Chicago, Ill.   Chicago, Ill.

WILBER Hoxie H.   April 12, 1842
LEGRO Patience   Bath, NY

BORDEN John   April 14, 1842
ANDRUS Caroline   N. Cohocton, NY

COOK Edmond   April 14, 1842
CHAPMAN Zyporah   Canisteo, NY

WARD James F.   April 15, 1842
WHEELER Lydia Ann   Cohocton, NY

LYMAN Elias of Burlington, Vt.   April 14, 1842
HALL Cornelia J. dau of Timothy of Troy, NY   Troy, NY

PERKINS Lemuel of Campbell, NY   April 17, 1842
LOOP Orpha Maria of Lenox, NY   Cameron, NY

THOMAS John of Bath, NY   May 6, 1842
HILL Caroline of Bath, NY   Bath, NY

SCIDMORE George C. of Dansville, NY   May 20, 1842
WING Sarah Ann of Cohocton, NY   Cohocton, NY

MEACH Henry   May 12, 1842
CHAPIN Luthera   Hume, NY

BENTON Norman of Bath, NY   June 15, 1842
DANIELS Mary D. of Bath, NY   Bath, NY

BELL Amos of Cortland Co. NY   June 15, 1842
RUGER Eliza Ann of Urbana, NY   Urbana, NY

SAYLES Stephen age 54 yrs   July 3, 1842
RATHBUN Eunice age 21 yrs   Howard, NY

BRUNDAGE Alfred of Urbana, NY   July 3, 1842
LEE Sarah Jane dau of David R. Lee   Bath, NY

HUBBARD Charles of Penn Yan, NY   July 4, 1842
LAMB Lucy of Bradford, NY   Bath, NY

HOUGHTALING Ira   July 10, 1842
SWEENEY Jane   Bath, NY

MILLER William of Mt. Washington, NY   July 24, 1842
STOUT Lydia of Mt. Washington, NY   Avoca, NY

HILL Mr. ___ of Wayne Co. NY   July 27, 1842
DILLENBECK Mrs. ___ of Kennedyville, NY   Avoca, NY

BASSETT Isaac of Avoca, NY   July 27, 1842
LYLE Sally of Mongomery Co. NY   Avoca, NY

BUTLER Mr. ___ of Bath, NY   July 31, 1842
EMERSON Miss ___ of Bath, NY   Avoca, NY

WHEATON Cyrus   July 29, 1842
CHASE Julia   Prattsburgh, NY

BLANCHARD Elijah   September 14, 1842
TYLER Rhoda   Bath, NY

HUNTER James of Bath, NY   September 21, 1842
VELIE Catherine of Elmira, NY   Elmira, NY

HOBART W. C. of Bath, NY formerly E. Bloomfield, NY   September 29, 1842
WILLIS Mary Ann of Howard, NY   Howard, NY

BRADLEY Zera of Bath, NY   October 1, 1842
OSBORN Emily S. of Andover, NY formerly of Bath, NY   Andover, NY

REEVE Lt. J. D. V.   September 27, 1842
SHEPARD Elizabeth dau of late Joshua Shepard   Dansville, NY

WALLACE William A.   September 17, 1842
MARSHALL Sarah D. dau of Gen. O. G. Marshall   Wheeler, NY

JANSEN Miles H. of Bath, NY   October 30, 1842
BETRON Belinda of Bath, NY   Bath, NY

WAGONER Jacob of Pulteney, NY   November 3, 1842
BUTTS Orrelia of Newark, NY   Pulteney, NY

MC CAY James of Woodhull, NY   November 6, 1842
MILLER Sarah A. of Pulteney, NY

SHANNON James of Bath, NY   November 22, 1842
ROSEBOOM Lucy of Cherry Valley, NY   Cherry Valley, NY

WHITING Levi C.   November 23, 1842
WOODS Pamelia N. dau of late William Woods   Bath, NY

JOHNSON Dr. L. B. of Bath, NY   November 30, 1842
HUBBARD Catherine of Bath, NY

STOCKING John A. of Cameron, NY   November 30, 1842
BUTLER Betsy of Cameron, NY   Cameron, NY

MONIER James L. of Naples, NY   December 6, 1842
ANDREWS Margaret of Naples, NY

WHEELER O. P.   December 11, 1842
ERWIN Mary   Bath, NY

                        missing issues

TRIPP Henry G. of Hammondsport, NY   December 29, 1844
FOSTER Alcina of Cohocton, NY   Kenndyville, NY

ROOSY Daniel of Cameron, NY   December 28, 1844
MOORE Lydia Jane of Cameron, NY   Cameron, NY

MAYORS Josiah of Cohocton, NY   January 1, 1845
LEGARE Susan of Cohocton, NY   Cohocton, NY

PAGE Charles H. of Almond, NY   December 25, 1844
MARGESON Matilda of Urbana, NY   Urbana, NY

CLEAVELAND Andrew W. of Naples, NY   January 1, 1845
GOODRICH Almyra of S. Bristol, NY   Cohocton, NY

SHULTS Andrew J.   January 1, 1845
HAVENS Lucretia S.   Bath, NY

BARNEY Thomas H. of Wheeler, NY   January 8, 1845
RICE Lucy dau of Oliver Rice of Avoca, NY   Avoca, NY

BOUTON Henry H. of Avoca, NY   December 31, 1844
WILLIS Laura S. of Howard, NY   Avoca, NY

RHODES William C. a Jr. Editor of Elmira Gazette   January 7, 1845
MAXWELL Fanny P. dau of Thomas Maxwell of Elmira, NY Elmira, NY

GILBERT Hiram D.   January 26, 1845
BORDEN Emma   Bath, NY

BROOKS David B. of Bath, NY
PELTON Nancy of Bath, NY
January 19, 1845
Kennedyville, NY

BASSETT John C.
GERMOND Mary T. of Hunts Hollow, NY
February 9, 1845
Kennedyville, NY

DILDINE Levi of Pulteney, NY
BOYD Mary of Pulteney, NY
January 23, 1845

METZ William late of Corning, NY
DUNTON Adeline of Avoca, NY
February 13, 1845
Mud Creek, NY

STEPHENS Charles C. of Greenwood, NY
CHAPMAN Martha A. of Greenwood, NY
February 9, 1845
Greenwood, NY

MORROW Henry
TOLLES Harriet A.
March 15, 1845
Urbana, NY

PATCHIN T. J. of Bradford, NY
SUTTON Sophrona of Bradford, NY
March 19, 1845
Bradford, NY

AINSWORTH D. W. C. of Prattsburgh, NY
COLE Aurelia J. of Prattsburgh, NY
May 3, 1845
Prattsburgh, NY

HAWES Charles of Starkey, NY
DISBROW Ann Maria of Barrington, NY
May 7, 1845
Tyrone, NY

VAN GELDER Barney of Urbana, NY
PARKER Hannah of Urbana, NY
June 8, 1845
Urbana, NY

BAILEY Lewis of Wayne, NY
HOLLENBACK Delia of Wayne, NY
June 7, 1845
Wayne, NY

PRATT Elijah
TARNEY Eliza
June 16, 1845
Bath, NY

FOX Major Luster of Cuba, NY
WIXON Hannah of Wayne, NY
June 11, 1845
Wayne, NY

BROWN Lucius H.
HUBBARD Mrs. Harriet dau of Phillip **COOK**
July 31, 1845
Cohocton, NY

EDWARDS Ira P. of Bath, NY
DAWSON Margret of Bath, NY
May 11, 1845
Pulteney, NY

VAN SCOTER Elias of Dansville, NY
FOOT Jane of Grove, NY
September 7, 1845
Dansville, NY

INGALLS Solon of Dansville, NY
STONE Mary A. of Dansville, NY
September 11, 1845
Dansville, NY

CAMPBELL S. Miner of Campbell, NY
BURTON S. Louisa dau of G. E. Burton of Prattsburgh, NY
September 18, 1845
Prattsburgh, NY

CLARK Ashbury of Wheeler, NY
BUDD Eliza Ann dau of Joseph Budd
September 3, 1845
Monticello, NY

ROSE S. H. of Avoca, NY
BARTO Adeline of Avoca, NY
September 17, 1845
Avoca, NY

COOK J. of Wheeler, NY
SNEATMAN M. of Wheeler, NY
September 29, 1845
Wheeler, NY

FERRIS F. of Howard, NY
SHAVER A. of Avoca, NY
September 29, 1845
Avoca, NY

MECARC J. B. of Candor, NY
PATTERSON Sophiah T. of Erwin, NY
October 1, 1845
Erwin, NY

MC CHESNEY Hugh of Howard, NY
DAVISON Mary Ann of Bath, NY
October 7, 1845
Bath, NY

BRIGGS Henry of Avoca, NY
WHITING Hannah dau of James Whiting
September 28, 1845
Cohocton, NY

MALLORY Erastus T.
KELLEY Mary J.
October 9, 1845
Jasper, NY

JOHNSON Nelson of Broome Co. NY
CRAIG Lauraett of Jasper, NY
September 17, 1845
Jasper, NY

LAMB J. of Auburn, NY
SANDERSON Margaret of Prattsburgh, NY
October 24, 1845
Prattsburgh, NY

WILTSEY William H. of Barrington, NY
HOUCH Caroline of Wayne, NY
November 6, 1845
Wayne, NY

BROWN Asahel of Shelby, NY
PECK Orilla M. of Avoca, NY
November 11, 1845
Avoca, NY

BACON Isaac M. of Big Flats, NY
GARDNER Emily A. of Corning, NY
December 11, 1845
Corning, NY

BARNARD Asher of Corning, NY
GARDNER Abigail of Newville, NY
December 11, 1845
Corning, NY

BRUNDAGE James of Urbana, NY
DAVIS Jerusha of Urbana, NY
January 6, 1846
Wayne, NY

RUTHERFORD George of Bath, NY
FRENCH Lida of Bath, NY
January 4, 1846

SMITH Justice M. of Painted Post, NY
DAVIS Rebecca Y. of Hornellsville, NY

January 20, 1846
Hornellsville, NY

FORD Morris of Penn Yan, NY
SPENCER Laura of Penn Yan, NY

January 14, 1846
Bath, NY

QUIN George E. of Jefferson, NY
KERNAN W. E. of Tyrone, NY

January 20, 1846
Tyrone, NY

THOMAS Levi E. of Bath, NY
WILLOUR Margaret E. of Bath, NY

January 24, 1846
Bath, NY

SMITH Thomas J. of Liberty, NY
INGALLS Harriet Eliza of Liberty, NY

February 4, 1846
Liberty, NY

VAN GELDER Jonathan of Bath, NY
SILSBE Semantha of Wayne, NY

February 15, 1846
Wayne, NY

WIXOM William Md. of Italy, NY
DOUBLEDAY Semantha dau of E. Doubleday of Italy, NY

February 15, 1846
Italy Hill, NY

BENNETT Alkali of Howard, NY
GOFF Harriet M. of Howard, NY

February 25, 1846
Howard, NY

NEELY James D. of Howard, NY
HAMILTON Miranda of Howard, NY

February 26, 1846
Howard, NY

MILLER David A. of Bath, NY
COSS Matilda of Bath, NY

February 24, 1846
Bath, NY

HANNA John
DUNKLEBURGH Catherine

April 9, 1846
S. Dansville, NY

COOPER Christopher of Avoca, NY
HAMMOND Esther of Cohocton, NY

May 3, 1846
Avoca, NY

KROMER Levi Y.
PERKINS Lydia Lucretia

May 24, 1846
S. Dansville, NY

PRUSIA Jesse B.
TRUMAN Olive H.

May 20, 1846
S. Dansville, NY

WEDGE Benjamin of Howard, NY
STARR Polly of Howard, NY

June 8, 1846
Howard, NY

SHAVER John L. of Lodi, NY
ROSE Polly dau of J. Rose of Greenwood, NY

April 25, 1846
Canisteo, NY

SHAVER Jeremiah of Canisteo, NY
SAWTELL Ursala formerly of Greene, NY

May 30, 1846
Canisteo, NY

VAN WINKLE Simeon of Bath, NY	June 24, 1846
LOOK Mary Jane dau of Dr. S. Look of Prattsburgh, NY	Bath, NY
WHITFIELD James	June 21, 1846
BUCK Jane	Penn Yan, NY
GROVES Erastus C. of Angelica, NY	July 6, 1846
HARDING Theresa R. of Hornellsville, NY	Hornellsville, NY
BARTON Chester	July 4, 1846
VAN GELDER Eliza	Bath, NY
SHULTS George of Prattsburgh, NY	July 16, 1846
HOES Susan Cornelia of Prattsburgh, NY	
CLEVELAND John of S. Dansville, NY	July 12, 1846
BERRY Nancy of S. Dansville, NY	Dotys Corners, NY
HADLEY George of Canisteo, NY	August 15, 1846
HALLETT Clarissa of Cameron, NY	Cameron, NY
WHITCOMB M. C. of Howard, NY	August 26, 1846
HOADLEY Lucina of Avoca, NY	Avoca, NY
LAFORGE Martin of Bath, NY	September 2, 1846
BAIN Susan M. of Bath, NY	Bath, NY
WILIAMSON William C.	October 3, 1846
PHOENIX Malissa	Rathbone, NY
SHERMAN Bradley of Angelica, NY	October 6, 1846
BROWN Adelia of Bath, NY	Bath, NY
REDDINGTON Thomas of Cameron, NY	October 4, 1846
PIERSON Marion of Cameron, NY	Canisteo, NY
WOOLBERT Elijah	October 8, 1846
VAN ORMAN Hannah of Genessee, Pa.	Canisteo, NY
LEWIS John of Bath, NY	October 17, 1846
HAND Mary Elizabeth of Bath, NY	Avoca, NY
FASSETT John of Tyrone, NY	October 22, 1846
ELLISON Ann of Tyrone, NY	Reading, NY
BOWEN Col. L. E. of Troupsburgh, NY	October 29, 1846
PERRY E. A. of Troupsburgh, NY	Greenwood, NY
DE GRAW George W.	October 31, 1846
BIGSBY Mary Jane	Barrington, NY

BALDWIN J. Davis of Elmira, NY   November 10, 1846
MAXWELL Elizabeth T. dau of S. H. of Corning, NY   Corning, NY

FERGUSON Solomon of Pulteney, NY   November 3, 1846
ST JOHN Susan M. of Pulteney, NY   Pulteney, NY

SNYDER Anthony of Italy, NY   (Newspaper date) November 18, 1846
SMITH Eliza of Italy, NY   Italy, NY

COOK Nehemiah   (Newspaper date) December 2, 1846
BILLSON Helen Ann of Kennedyville, NY   Kennedyville, NY

BENJAMIN John of Bath, NY   November 26, 1846
CAMPBELL Lydia of Bath, NY   Bath, NY

INGERSOLL Nicholas of Bath, NY   December 2, 1846
SCARVELL Rosana of Bath, NY   Bath, NY

BELLAS George of Bath, NY   December 13, 1846
ABER Jane of Bath, NY   Bath, NY

PALMER Joseph E. of Erwin, NY   December 7, 1846
VANCE Elizabeth M. of Dansville, NY   Dansville, NY

FRANCIS John M. Editor of Troy Budget   December 8, 1846
TUCKER Harriet E. of Palmyra, NY   Palmyra, NY

REYNOLDS Julius of Bath, NY   December 24, 1846
CONKLIN Elizabeth of Bath, NY   Bath, NY

LOUCKS John of Avoca, NY   December 30, 1846
ZIELLY Nancy C. of Avoca, NY

COLE Franklin   January 1, 1847
CLARK Hannah Mariah   Howard, NY

PICKLE Peter   December 6, 1846
CLARK Clarissa   Howard, NY

RAYMOND John C. of Italy, NY   January 6, 1847
CORY Sarah A. of Italy, NY   Italy, NY

RICHARDSON Thomas J. of Bath, NY   January 14, 1847
ABER Amanda of Bath, NY   Bath, NY

PATTERSON S. A. of Dansville, NY   January 18, 1847
CANFIELD Rhoda Ann of Hornellsville, NY   Hornellsville, NY

CORNING Alexander of Corning, NY   (Newspaper date) February 3, 1847
BLOOD Indianna dau of Capt. Asa Blood of Bath, NY   Napoleon, Mi.

WENTWORTH George of Burns, NY	January 13, 1847
CRITTENDEN Eunice of Burns, NY	Burns, NY
WING Elnathan H. of Cohocton, NY	January 1, 1847
OLIVER Sally of Dansville, NY	Dansville, NY
DERVEL Daniel of Bristol, NY	February 11, 1847
STRICKLAND Mrs. Lucia Ann of Bath, NY formerly of Ct.	Kennedyville, NY
KAUSCH Christian of S. Dansville, NY	February 4, 1847
BRAUNSCHWEIG Maria E. of S. Dansville, NY	S. Dansville, NY
HOUCK Asel of Bath, NY	February 25, 1847
DISBROW Angeline of Tyrone, NY	Tyrone, NY
SMITH Capt. John L. of Bath, NY	March 4, 1847
LEGRO Lois M. of Bath, NY	Bath, NY
DYER Patrick of Bath, NY	March 2, 1847
TOWNER Mary of Bath, NY	Avoca, NY
HARTY John	March 2, 1847
CRAWFORD Harriet	Addison, NY
BRINK James L. of Mud Creek, NY	March 3, 1847
PRATT Hanrieta of Mud Creek, NY	Mud Creek, NY
CARR Asaph of Corning, NY	March 9, 1847
HANDY Cordelia A. of Corning, NY	Elmira, NY
KINGSBURY Heman W. of Dansville, NY	March 11, 1847
HAMMOND Elizabeth of Elkland, Pa.	Elkland, Pa.
YORTAN James of Howard, NY	March 15, 1847
SMITH Laura M. of Howard, NY	Howard, NY
BURK Horace of Italy, NY	March 27, 1847
NOBLE Sarah Ann of Prattsburgh, NY	Prattsburgh, NY
PARKER Allen J. of Dansville, NY	March 25, 1847
ASHLEY Harriet M. of Springwater, NY	Springwater, NY
BELLIS George C. of Bath, NY	May 10,1847
ABER Jane of Bath, NY	
JOLLEY James of Wheeler, NY	May 20, 1847
BAKER Hannah of Wheeler, NY	Wheeler, NY
CLARK Hiram G. of Prattsburgh, NY	May 15, 1847
BARDEEN Mary C. of Prattsburgh, NY	Prattsburgh, NY

KNAPP John of Italy, NY   May 15, 1847
EDSON Martha of Italy, NY   Italy, NY

JACOBUS John D. of Westchester Co. NY   May 23, 1847
ALDERMAN Janet of Urbana, NY   Bath, NY

SOUTHWELL John B. of Monterey, NY   June 13, 1847
GOODON Jane E. of Corning, NY   Corning, NY

WHITE Samuel B. of Starkey, NY   June 24, 1847
TOMES Amanda of Pulteney, NY   Pulteney, NY

MILLS John H. of Liberty, NY   July 4, 1847
BLOOD Amelia I. of Liberty, NY   Bath, NY

COATS Leonard G. of Bath, NY   July 5, 1847
GRANT Nancy W. of Bath, NY   Bath, NY

CASE John Jr. of Bath, NY   February 19, 1847
RECTOR Adeline of Rome, NY   N. Dansville, NY

BUNDY Peter of Otsego, NY   June 24, 1847
FRENCH Charlotte J. of Bath, NY   Bath, NY

SNYDER Hiram of Bath, NY   July 1, 1847
SMITH Elsa A. of Bath, NY   Bath, NY

COVELL Willis of S. Dansville, NY   July 1, 1847
CUSTOR Mary of S. Dansville, NY   S. Dansville, NY

PAYNE Niles of Orange, NY   September 1, 1847
LEWIS Patty of Orange, NY   Orange, NY

RUSSELL Daniel of Castleton   September 23, 1847
HUNTER Maria of Wayne, NY   Wayne, NY

CURTIS George W. of Wayne, NY   September 29, 1847
SWARTHOUT Isabel of Wayne, NY   Wayne, NY

SANDFORD Russell of Wayne, NY   September 30, 1847
CHAPMAN Laura of Pulteney, NY   Pulteney, NY

HALLOCK George of Bath, NY   October 13, 1847
HUBBELL Mary dau of W. S. Hubbell of Bath, NY   Bath, NY

missing issues

TOLLIVER D. T. of Bath, NY   November 29, 1848
NICHOLS Elizabeth of Bath, NY   Kennedyville, NY

SMITH Rev. Howell of Penn Yan, NY	December 12, 1848
DE GOLIA Frances of Prattsburgh, NY	Prattsburgh, NY
BEEMAN William M.	December 16, 1848
FISHER Elizabeth	Italy, NY
HOPKINS John C.	January 23, 1849
BUTLER Laura B.	Avoca, NY
CALKINS John C. of Avoca, NY	January 30, 1849
MACK Abigail of Bath, NY	Bath, NY
STEWART Andrew of Howard, NY	February 3, 1849
REACHER Susan of Bath, NY	Bath, NY
HARVEY Holms of Tompkins Co. NY	February 14, 1849
WILLOUR Mrs. Sarah of Bath, NY	Bath, NY
SWEET Edward A. of Urbana, NY	March 3, 1849
GREGORY Meribah of Urbana, NY	Avoca, NY
VANDERWARKIN Jacob of Wheeler, NY	March 3, 1849
ELLIOTT Temma of Wheeler, NY	Wheeler, NY
FLEMING John D. Md. of Bath, NY	March 7, 1849
BROWN Hannah C. of Bath, NY	Bath, NY
NICHOLSON Ambrose of Howard, NY	March 27, 1849
ELLIS Sophia of Lodi, NY	Lodi, NY
MASON George W. Editor of Elmira Gazette	March 25, 1849
COLLINGWOOD Elizabeth	Elmira, NY
STINSON George of Mud Creek, NY	April 11, 1849
JOHNSON Catherine of Dansville, NY	Bath, NY
JEROME Leonard Walter of Rochester, NY	April 5, 1849
HALL Clarissa dau of Ambrose Hall of Palmyra, NY	Palmyra, NY
FIFE Hiram of Bath, NY	April 19, 1849
SMITH Matilda of Elmira, NY	Elmira, NY
BIRD George J. of Canisteo, NY	April 23, 1849
DAGGERT Nancy of Cameron, NY	Cameron, NY
WOODS James of Elmira, NY	June 19, 1849
VAN DUSER Susan dau of William Van Duser of Veteran, NY	
PARMER Elias of Hammondsport, NY	July 3, 1849
AULLS Hannah of Bath, NY	Bath, NY

BIXBY Simon of Hornby, NY   July 9, 1849
LUKE Phebe T. of Bath, NY   Bath, NY

PATRICK Benjamin T. of Norwalk, Oh.   June 28, 1849
MAXWELL Eliza P. dau of Thomas Maxwell of Elmira, NY   Milan, Oh.

WELCH Adolphus of Starkey, NY   July 29, 1849
GRAHAM Helen Marr of Starkey, NY   Bath, NY

WILHELM John of Bath, NY   August 13, 1849
NOBLES Emeline of Bath, NY   Bath, NY

WEBSTER Ithamar of Bath, NY   August 23, 1849
NIXON Harriet of Bath, NY   Bath, NY

CLARK Thomas Sr. age 99y of Starkey, NY   August 30, 1849
ASPELL Phebe age 72y widow of Richard of Starkey, NY   Starkey, NY

SHINEBARGER William of Hornellsville, NY   September 16, 1849
COBURN Phebe of Hornellsville, NY   Hornellsville, NY

SHINEBARGER George of Hornellsville, NY   October 1, 1849
HILL Harriet of Hornellsville, NY   Hornellsville, NY

BUSH John of Reading, NY   October 16, 1849
BENNETT Huldah A. of Urbana, NY   Urbana, NY

RATHBUN Hiram of Howard, NY   October 11, 1849
SHEARER Louisa dau of Robert Shearer of Howard, NY

CHURCH Edwin F. of Bath, NY   December 26, 1849
ANDRUS Catherine of Ithaca, NY   Ithaca, NY

PARSONS Darwin A. of Bath, NY   January 15, 1850
WALLING Lucy Jane of Campbell, NY   Bath, NY

WHEELER John G. formerly of Bath, NY   January 8, 1850
WAIT Emily E. of Janesville, Wis.   Janesville, Wis.

CAIN Joseph L. of Wayne, NY   January 27, 1850
TYLER Nancy of Mud Creek, NY   Wayne, NY

BALLARD Alpheus R. of Wheeler, NY   February 17, 1850
COOPER Emeline of Wheeler, NY   Bath, NY

MC GONEGAL Ira of Bath, NY   March 2, 1850
OWEN Mary of Bath, NY   Bath, NY

ELLAS George H. of Decatur, Ind.   February 20. 1850
BRONSON Phebe of Urbana, NY   Urbana, NY

SELOVER John R.	February 27, 1850
LEWIS Mary Frances	Prattsburgh, NY
WARREN Joseph Butler of Bath, NY	March 11, 1850
BROOKS Elizabeth of Bath, NY	Bath, NY
ABER Aaron of Bath, NY	March 26, 1850
CORNWELL Elizabeth Ann of Bath, NY	Bath, NY
PARKS Amos	April 9, 1850
LA FARGE Mary Jane	Prattsburgh, NY
NORRIS Henry	April 29, 1850
WHEELER Lucy	Bath, NY
ROSE Daniel H. of Howard, NY	April 28, 1850
GOFF Martha Ann of Howard, NY	Howard, NY
BENNETT Hiram of Hornellsville, NY	May 1, 1850
DOTY Eliza of Hornellsville, NY	Hornellsville, NY
EMERSON Amos of Bath, NY	April 18, 1850
EGGLESTON Helen Cornelia of Bath, NY	Bath, NY
CASE George of Howard, NY	May 25, 1850
GRAVES Harriet of Howard, NY	Howard, NY
LEWIS Abraham Q.	June 5, 1850
DOWNS Catherine B.	Prattsburgh, NY
PARK Henry of Addison, NY	June 6, 1850
MC NULTY Mary E. of Big Flats, NY	Elmira, NY
ROSS William of Reading, NY	May 16, 1850
REED Sarah C. of Hornellsville, NY	Hornellsville, NY
LANDERS Frederick B. of Hornellsville, NY	June 4, 1850
MULHOLLEN Sarah W. of Canisteo, NY	Canisteo, NY
OSTERHOUT John C. of Corning, NY	June 12, 1850
KELLY Mary of Corning, NY	Albany, NY
HARRIS Joseph H.	June 18, 1850
COOLEY Mary Wallbridge dau of Maj. L. J. Cooley	Elmira, NY
ZIELLY Thomas H. of Peterborough, Canada W.	July 15, 1850
TOOKER Ann of Elmira, NY	Avoca, NY
RUGER John	July 21, 1850
ALDEN Jane	Bath, NY

AMIDON Shepherd formerly of Greenwood, NY   July 31, 1850
RAZEY Betsy Maria of Almond, NY   Hartsville, NY

DYGERT Samuel of Canisteo, NY   July 27, 1850
DYGERT Mary Ann of Cameron, NY   Cameron, NY

RICE Joel H. of Bath, NY   August 18, 1850
TURNER Mrs. C. H. of Waterloo, NY   Waterloo, NY

DANIELS Kendrick of Bath, NY   September 5, 1850
WARREN Sarah H. dau of Phineas Warren of Bath, NY   Avoca, NY

SMITH William of Troupsburgh, NY   October 10, 1850
PERSONS Lucinda H. of Woodhull, NY

PERSONS William of Woodhull, NY   June 30, 1850
MC PHERRONS Amy of Cameron, NY   Jasper, NY

GRAHAM Samuel of Woodhull, NY   August 20, 1850
WILHELM Hannah of Woodhull, NY

DURKEE John of Bath, NY   October 12, 1850
ERWIN Adeline of Bath, NY   Hammondsport, NY

AULLS Ephraim of Bath, NY   October 13, 1850
BRYANT Mary of Bath, NY   Bath, NY

VAN DUSEN William Henry   October 17, 1850
BELLINGER Nancy   Wheeler, NY

HULL Luther of Howard, NY   October 23, 1850
SMITH Louisa E. of Howard, NY   Howard, NY

VAN GELDER Henry of Bath, NY   October 31, 1850
VELEY Polly of Bath, NY

EATON Benjamin of Bath, NY   November 21, 1850
YOST Mrs. Mercy of Cameron, NY   Gibson, NY

VAN ALLEN William H. of Scio, NY   November 19, 1850
WHITE Nancy M. dau of Luther White of Dansville, NY   Dansville, NY

HALLETT Nehemiah of Wellsville, NY   November 17, 1850
SMITH Harriet dau of T. J. Smith   Bath, NY

DYGERT Walter of Bath, NY   November 24, 1850
WILLIS Rhoda of Bath, NY   Bath, NY

JACKSON J. C. of Otis, Mass.   November 27, 1850
MILLER H. M. of Rochester, NY   Bath, NY

BROWN Myron W. of Thurston, NY — December 11, 1850
STEWART Calcina E. of Campbell, NY — Campbell, NY

GARLINGHOUSE John of Mi. — (Newspaper date) December 25, 1850
BENEDICT Mary Jane of Urbana, NY

BRECK Joseph of Elmira, NY formerly of Bath, NY — January 15, 1851
CAHILL Mrs. ___ of Elmira, NY — Elmira, NY

PERRY Gilbert M. of Caniadea, NY — January 27, 1851
ELLIS Martha of Bath, NY — Bath, NY

SKINKLE Isaac of Thurston, NY — January 22, 1851
COLLIER Catherine V. of Bath, NY

ALLEN Vestus D. of Bath, NY — December 8, 1850
POLMATEER Mrs. Rachel of Avoca, NY

COLLIER Richard of Bath, NY — February 12, 1851
CROSBY Mary of Bath, NY

HOVEY Jacob C. of Bath, NY — March 18, 1851
OLMSTEAD Mary E. dau of Aaron Olmstead of Wayne, NY — Wayne, NY

SEXTON John L. Jr. — May 28, 1851
PATTERSON Grace A. dau of Benjamin of Lindley, NY — Lindley, NY

WOODRUFF Alfred S. of Urbana, NY — June 12, 1851
PRINDLE Serepta of Wayne, NY — Wayne, NY

BAKER Edward B. of Wilkesbarre, Pa. — June 27, 1851
ELLIS Charlotte of Bath, NY — Bath, NY

ROWE Anson — September 14, 1851
PRESTON Julia Ann — Bath, NY

WATSON Lawrence — September 14, 1851
WELCH Ann — Bath, NY

STINSER Michael — September 14, 1851
O'BRIEN Catherine — Bath, NY

FOSTER John B. of Prattsburgh, NY — October 1, 1851
FISHER Hannah Elizabeth of Barrington, NY — Hammondsport, NY

HOWELL Freeman of S. Dansville, NY — October 2, 1851
WEIDMAN Tharessa of Cummingsville, NY — Patchinsville, NY

WHITE Isaac S. of S. Dansville, NY — October 2, 1851
COVERT A. E. of S. Dansville, NY — Patchinsville, NY

KENMORE Rev. Charles of Andover, NY   September 28, 1851
COMFORT Sarah Elizabeth dau of Eli of Howard, NY   Howard, NY

DEERLOVE William of Prattsburgh, NY   October 14, 1851
CASTER Polly of Prattsburgh, NY   Avoca, NY

MILLER William H. of Howard, NY   October 26, 1851
GRAHAM Jerusha of Howard, NY   Howard, NY

ALLEN Samuel H. of Cohocton, NY   October 26, 1851
HOWARD Jane of Howard, NY   Howard, NY

SINCLEAR John A. of Bath, NY   October 30, 1851
EMERSON Celinda of Thurston, NY   Thurston, NY

MILLER William H. of Howard, NY   November 17, 1851
MILLER Elizabeth H. of Garrettsville, NY   Garrettsville, NY

MORRIS Israel   October 12, 1851
WILLIS Mrs. Eunice of Bath, NY   Howard, NY

THOMAS William   November 23, 1851
PIERCE Maria of Bath, NY   Bath, NY

MC ADAM John   November 12, 1851
STEWART Jane   Howard, NY

SHARP John of Howard, NY   November 12, 1851
FORRESTER Harriet E. of Howard, NY   Howard, NY

LOOD John of Elgin, Ill.   November 16, 1851
BACON Lucretia of Howard, NY

MERRILL Otis N. of Howard, NY   November 20, 1851
BENNETT Lydia R. of Howard, NY   Howard, NY

ALDRIDGE Fenner S. of Thurston, NY   December 3, 1851
MOREY Martha of Thurston, NY   Thurston, NY

MILLER Abram of Spencer, NY   January 6, 1852
MAXWELL Vie dau of Thomas Maxwell of Southport, NY

DREW George M. of Pulteney, NY   January 21, 1852
VAN NESS Abbie of Pulteney, NY   Pulteney, NY

VAN NESS Peter of Pulteney, NY   January 21, 1852
PELTON Caroline of Pulteney, NY   Pulteney, NY

CLARK Hiram of Urbana, NY   January 21, 1852
HYATT Laura of Pulteney, NY   Pulteney, NY

FAIRFIELD John of Urbana, NY	January 10, 1852
MC CARTER Betsy of Bath, NY	Bath, NY
SCOFIELD John L. of Pulteney, NY	January 27, 1852
PRENTISS Fredrika dau of John A. of Pulteney, NY	Pulteney, NY
HARRIS John of Howard, NY	January 21, 1852
STEWART Jane of Howard, NY	Howard, NY
CHISSOM David M. of Cameron, NY	March 1, 1852
BROWN Jane of Cameron, NY	Bath, NY
MORGAN Julius G. of Erwin Center, NY	March 11, 1852
GRIDLEY Sarah L. of Erwin Center, NY	Erwin Center, NY
DORR Robert L. Atty. of Dansville, NY	February 28, 1852
TOMPKINS Mary dau of Rice Tompkins of Wayne, NY	Wayne, NY
PURDY Truman P. of Bath, NY	April 22, 1852
HOPKINS Emily M. of Bath, NY	E. Ashford, NY
ROSENCRANS J. J. of Cohocton, NY	May 5, 1852
WEMPLE E. J. of Cohocton, NY	
GRANT B. F. of Bath, NY	April 15, 1852
BENEDICT Mary E. of Bath, NY	Bath, NY
BROWN Richard of Prattsburgh, NY	May 1, 1852
WILSON Maria of Prattsburgh, NY	Hammondsport, NY
LAWTON William of Cameron, NY	May 25, 1852
HIGGINS Rosetta of Cameron, NY	Bath, NY
CARRINGTON Russell of Dansville, NY	June 17, 1852
GILBERT Ellen of Dansville, NY	Hartsville, NY
MUNSON Edgar of Bradford, NY	June 15, 1852
CURTIS Lucy Maria dau of Amos Curtis of Meridan, Ct.	Meridan, Ct.
HARRIS Robert F. of Bath, NY	July 7, 1852
BRACE Seneca V. of Bath, NY	Bath, NY
RAYMER Henry H.	July 5, 1852
SHARPE Henrietta A. dau of John Sharpe	New York City
OVERHISER John Casper of Wheeler, NY	September 9, 1852
WRAIGHT Caroline of Wheeler, NY	Bath, NY
HARMON Henry H. of Howell, Mi.	September 8, 1852
BANCROFT Esther dau of R. Bancroft Md.	Elmira, NY

HARVEY William B. of Addison, NY — September 14, 1852
BARKER Mary E. of Thurston, NY — Thurston, NY

LEONARD Richard of Avoca, NY — September 19, 1852
GREEN Mrs. Mary E. of Avoca, NY — Avoca, NY

SALMON Joel of Avoca, NY — October 3, 1852
WHITNEY Mary formerly of Burns, NY — Avoca, NY

PURDY M. C. of Bath, NY — October 14, 1852
BAUTER Betsey of Bath, NY — Bath, NY

SPRING James of Towlesville, NY — October 21, 1852
JOHNSTON Lavina of Towlesville, NY

COOLEY Jesse — October 28, 1852
STEPHENS Mary of Elmira, NY — Elmira, NY

HOLLIDAY Homer Atty. of Hornellsville, NY — October 31, 1852
HAWLEY Sarah Jane dau of William M. of Hornellsville, NY Hornellsville, NY

OLMSTEAD Erastus of Avoca, NY — October 27, 1852
BELLINGER Margaret of Wheeler, NY — Kennedyville, NY

LAKE Thomas of Urbana, NY — October 25, 1852
BAILEY Huldah of Urbana, NY — Urbana, NY

DRAKE Reuben of Cameron, NY — November 7, 1852
MOORE Elizabeth dau of Aris Moore of Independence, NY

WELCH William of Mitchellville, NY — December 22, 1852
WARNER Nancy of Mitchellville, NY — Mitchellville, NY

IRELAND Merritt of Owego, NY — January 4, 1853
WEBSTER Caroline of Bath, NY — Owego, NY

EARLS S. of Wheeler, NY — January 21, 1853
SIMERSON Susan of Pulteney, NY — Naples, NY

WISNER Jeffrey A. of Elmira, NY — February 2, 1853
GOULD Jeannette dau of A. R. Gould of Bath, NY — Bath, NY

HOAGLAND James William of Bath, NY — January 27, 1853
PAYNE Samantha of Avoca, NY — Avoca, NY

THOMAS Orville E. — February 16, 1853
COSS Loiza G. — Bath, NY

RICHARDSON George B. of Bath, NY — February 27, 1853
WILLOUR Eliza R. of Bath, NY

RHODES John Clark of Dansville, NY　　　March 17, 1853
HENRIE Maria Bunyan of Dansville, NY

DONEGAN John　　　April 10, 1853
DONAHE Mary　　　Bath, NY

EMERSON John P. from the sea　　　March 31, 1853
BENNETT Mrs. Mary J. of Weston, NY　　　Weston, NY

VAN ETTEN Daniel of Elmira, NY formerly of NJ　　　May 8, 1853
VADER Mary Ann dau of Cornelius Vader of Avoca, NY　　　Avoca, NY

DOUBLEDAY J. of Yates Co. NY　　　April 21, 1853
NEFF M. E. of Bath, NY　　　Prattsburgh, NY

MORENT Aaron　　　June 1, 1853
PORTER Esther of Ossian, NY　　　Ossian, NY

BAKER Jedediah M. of Canisteo, NY　　　May 24, 1853
OLIN Ann V. of Hornellsville, NY　　　Hornellsville, NY

THOMPSON Edward C. of Bath, NY　　　June 15, 1853
TERRY Sonora J. dau of Dr. M. Terry　　　Savona, NY

BISHOP Seely of Bradford, NY　　　July 3, 1853
MITCHELL Emily of Bradford, NY　　　Elmira, NY

POTTER E. K.　　　July 13, 1853
SEARS Orilla　　　Kanona, NY

BACON Hiram of Bradford, NY　　　July 28, 1853
STAMP Mrs. Mariat of Bath, NY　　　Bath, NY

TAYLOR James of Greenwood, NY　　　July 25, 1853
PUTNAM Antoinette of Greenwood, NY　　　Hornellsville, NY

LEWIS Frank of Angelica, NY　　　August 2, 1853
MULHOLLEN Mary E. of Canisteo, NY　　　Canisteo, NY

WHITFORD Nathan of S. Dansville, NY　　　August 8, 1853
ROBINSON Lulalia of S. Dansville, NY

SHULTS Theodore A. of Wheeler, NY　　　September 1, 1853
DERRICK Abby Jane of Wheeler, NY　　　Bath, NY

THOMPSON Milton of Wheeler, NY　　　September 8, 1853
HANKINSON Catherine A. of Wheeler, NY　　　Wheeler, NY

EAGLESTON Frederick of New York City　　　September 3, 1853
LOREE Mary of Wayne, NY　　　Wayne, NY

CARPENTER Burkly of Tyrone, NY
FREEMAN Cornelia of Bath, NY

September 14, 1853

FOSTER Myron of Elmira, NY
GRADY Margaret of Elmira, NY

September 20, 1853
Elmira, NY

PARKHILL A. T. of Howard, NY
BROWN Elizabeth of Chester, Oh.

September 20, 1853

DOUBLEDAY Evert M. of Batavia, NY
GLOAD Sarah A. of Pulteney, NY

October 6, 1853
Pulteney, NY

TOMPKINS John H. of Hornellsville, NY
HOWARD Emeline D. dau of Capt. Nathaniel Howard

October 19, 1853
Perry Center, NY

FINCH Andrew J. of Bath, NY
LAYTON Judith A. of Hammondsport, NY

December 1, 1853
Avoca, NY

HATHAWAY Leander of Howard, NY
COMSTOCK Mrs. Lucinda of Bath, NY

October 23, 1853
Bath, NY

EMERSON Robert R. of Bath, NY
SMITH Sophrona of Bath, NY

November 16, 1853
Bath, NY

BEACH Samuel Jr. of Hammondsport, NY
BELL Mary of Hammondsport, NY

January 2, 1854
Monterey, NY

LOOMIS Henry
HAYLOR Susan

January 25, 1854
Bath, NY

DERRICK Warren of Wheeler, NY
CLARK Mary of Wheeler, NY

January 12, 1854
Avoca, NY

MC CASLIN Peter of Cohocton, NY
VAN ATTEN Livona of Cohocton, NY

January 27, 1854

NORRIS Seth R. of Bath, NY
MANLEY Sarah E. of Howard, NY

January 27, 1854
Howard, NY

HAYES George of Buffalo, NY
WEEKS Mary R. of Prattsburgh, NY

January 20, 1854
Prattsburgh, NY

HASKINS William P. of Howard, NY
PHILLIPS Nancy Ann dau of A. S. of Hornellsville, NY

January 23, 1854
Hornellsville, NY

WILBUR Reuben
DUDLEY Caroline

March 22, 1854
Bath, NY

POND Joseph of Big Flats, NY
KING Sarah Jane of Hornby, NY

April 8, 1855
Hornby, NY

HAZEN Alexander T. of Cameron, NY	May 14, 1855
WHITE Melissa of Canisteo, NY	Canisteo, NY
QUICK Hiram of Campbell, NY	May 26, 1855
BURGET Lydia of Campbell, NY	Cameron, NY
RICE Horace of Avoca, NY	May 31, 1855
SHULTS Sarah M. of Avoca, NY	Avoca, NY
BRUNDAGE John of Urbana, NY	June 13, 1855
SHEPARD Lucy of Wheeler, NY	Wheeler, NY
CLARK William of Pulteney, NY	September 12, 1855
NORRIS Hester of Pulteney, NY	Bath, NY
SMITH Ten Eyck G. of Ill.	September 12, 1855
HALLETT Louisa of Canisteo, NY	Bath, NY
BARTON E. P. of Bath, NY	October 10, 1855
PETTIBONE Frances dau of Col. E. J. of Elba, NY	Elba, NY
DE WOLFE T. S. of Bath, NY	November 24, 1855
MC BEATH Caroline A. of Bath, NY	Avon, NY
FOSTER Hial J.	Thanksgiving Day
RICHARDS Mary E.	Prattsburgh, NY
EMERSON Oliver H. of Bath, NY	December 12, 1855
JONES Isabel of Bath, NY	Bath, NY
RUNNELS John of Dunkirk, NY	January 19, 1856
TARNEY Mary A. dau of Bartholomew Tarney of Bath, NY	Bath, NY
JONES William B. of Bath, NY	January 30, 1856
DUNLAP Mrs. Ann of Pulteney, NY	Pulteney, NY
WINFIELD Morris of Howard, NY	February 9, 1856
MISNER Mrs. H. L. of Bath, NY	Bath, NY

missing issues

MAGEE George J. of Watkins, NY	June 28, 1865
STOTHOFF Emma S. of Hector, NY	
GRISWOLD John E. of Avoca, NY	June 29, 1865
FERRIS Susan M. of Avoca, NY	Avoca, NY
MC PHERSON Edward of Ft. Atkinson, Wis.	July 13, 1865
HEES Maria of Avoca, NY	Avoca, NY

GIBBS James E. of Catlin, NY   August 8, 1865
MIDDAUGH Ann of Catlin, NY   Coopers Plains, NY

MIDDAUGH John of Catlin, NY   August 8, 1865
SMITH Sarah of Catlin, NY   Coopers Plains, NY

CORWIN O. F. of Havana, NY   August 9, 1865
ALDERMAN L. M. of Thurston, NY   Thurston, NY

CORNISH James M. of Prattsburgh, NY (Co. G. 10th Cav.)   December 7, 1865
DARLING Sopronia of Odessa, NY   Odessa, NY

MC LIN Frank of New York City   December 21, 1865
MC LEAN Rosa dau of Gen. Mc Lean   Prattsburgh, NY

RUTHERFORD L. G. of Savona, NY   December 30, 1865
BEATY Charlotte of Tyrone, NY   Tyrone, NY

LEWIS D. D.   January 24, 1866
BLISS Ellen E.

BOYER Amos of Bath, NY   April 12, 1866
READ Mrs. Elizabeth of Bath, NY   Bath, NY

WHEELER Oliver H. of Urbana, NY   April 18, 1866
READ Mary L. of Bath, NY   Bath, NY

WILSON Edward P. of Delaware   July 2, 1866
MUNSON Lucy dau of Rufus Munson of Bradford, NY   Bradford, NY

VAN AMBURG Edgar S. of Bath, NY   July 3, 1866
GREEK Hannah of Urbana, NY   Bath, NY

KNOWLES Oliver of Crosswick, NJ   July 12, 1866
OSTRANDER Statia dau of R. Ostrander of Honeye Falls, NY Bath, NY

CORBETT John of Cohocton, NY   September 15, 1866
FAIRBROTHER Sarah A. of Cohocton, NY   Wayland, NY

OSTRANDER Samuel of Campbell, NY   September 29, 1866
CHRISLER Sarah E. of Campbell, NY   Campbell, NY

Canisteo Times

October 7, 1880 - December 25, 1884

PALMER William of Hornellsville, NY   September 30, 1880
HUNTSBURGER Minnie of Erie, Pa.   Erie, Pa.

FULKERS John R. of Addison, NY   September 19, 1880

STONE Emma C. of Canisteo, NY

Hartsville, NY

SIMPSON Asa Eugene of Jasper, NY
FREELAND Ella Maria of Jasper, NY

October 2, 1880
Canisteo, NY

CUMMINS Charles R. of Troupsburgh, NY
ACKER Orpha of Hartsville, NY

October 3, 1880
Canisteo, NY

SLY Ameria H. of Hornellsville, NY
CLARK Jennie E. of Hornellsville, NY

September 28, 1880
Hornellsville, NY

SHEEHAN James of Addison, NY
MC TAMNEY Maggie A. of Addison, NY

September 19, 1880
Addison, NY

MAYO T. A. of Lindley, NY
JORDAN Theresa of Tuscarora, NY

September 22, 1880
Tuscarora, NY

ZIELLY A. L. of Avoca, NY
CHASE Libbie of Avoca, NY

September 23, 1880

INSCHO Jesse of Tioga, Pa.
BROWN Clara of Caton, NY

October 14, 1880
Caton, NY

RAWSON William S. of Jacksonville, Fl.
STEPHENS Sarah of Canisteo, NY

October 8, 1880
Canisteo, NY

WARNER W. W. of Canisteo, NY
MURPHY Ellen of Canisteo, NY

October 7, 1880
Canisteo, NY

LANDERS William S. of Afton, NY
BIRDSALL Mary E. du of H. H. Birdsall of Addison, NY

October 6, 1880

LANGWORTHY W. I. of Alfred Center, NY
BRANCHARD Emma O. of Belmont, NY

September 29, 1880
Belmont, NY

VEEDER Luther of Wallace, NY
WARD Maggie of Wallace, NY

September 29, 1880
Avoca, NY

HOUSE Wesley of Jasper, NY
WAGNER Lizzie of Jasper, NY

October 7, 1880
Jasper, NY

JONES Henry B. of Addison, NY
JONES Sarah Elizabeth of Addison, NY

October 13, 1880
Addison, NY

MC KAY Harry C. of Addison, NY
ELDRICH Nellie C. of Brooklyn, NY

October 6, 1880
Brooklyn, NY

FOX Charles N. of Howard, NY
PERSONIUS Lottie D. of Beaver Dams, NY

October 13, 1880
Watkins, NY

HUBBARD Chauncey G. Md. of Hornellsville, NY   October 14, 1880
PRENTISS Flora of Canisteo, NY   Canisteo, NY

ROLOSON Melvin P. of Hornby, NY   October 13, 1880
TYLER Sarah C. dau of Sarah E. Tyler   Corning, NY

HAUFF Jacob   September 30, 1880
TAGGART Emma dau of N. Taggart of Corning, NY   Corning, NY

HOWELL Amos W. of Hornby, NY   October 12, 1880
MORGAN Addie M. of Hornby, NY   Corning, NY

SIMMONS Frank of Hornellsville, NY   October 20, 1880
HOUCK Anna of Hornellsville, NY   Hornellsville, NY

WHITE Silas H. of Lindley, NY   October 10, 1880
JOHNSON Jennie M. of Lindley, NY   Lindley, NY

FURMAN Frank H. of Hornellsville, NY   October 19, 1880
STILLMAN Elva E. of Hornellsville, NY   Hornellsville, NY

LOID Daniel of Corning, NY   October 14, 1880
WEBBER Mary D. of Big Flats, NY   Elmira, NY

WIHN Edward of Corning, NY   October 13, 1880
BUDD Rebecca of Corning, NY   Corning, NY

HERBERT William of Bath, NY   October 17, 1880
TOWNSEND Maggie of Bath, NY   Corning, NY

MC CARRICK George M. of Big Flats, NY   October 20, 1880
VAN GORDER Kitty of Big Flats, NY   Corning, NY

RUMSEY Isaac of Campbell, NY   September 26, 1880
PARSELLS Anna E. of Addison, NY   Addison, NY

BOOTHE Isaac C. of Canaseraga, NY   October 28, 1880
GRAHAM Mrs. Helen L. of Canaseraga, NY   Canaseraga, NY

FENDERSON Scott of Corning, NY   (Newspaper date) November 4, 1880
VAN WERT Sadie of Corning, NY   (Wednesday eve.) Corning, NY

SMITH Charles E. of Canisteo, NY   November 4, 1880
WHITING Laura of Jasper, NY   Bath, NY

BUTTON Charles of Jasper, NY   October 27, 1880
ROWLEY Estella of Jasper, NY   Cameron, NY

COTTON Mr. ____ of Lindenwood Cottage   November 4, 1880
HERBERT Ida of Cohocton, NY   Fremont, NY

MOSHER Orson A. of Hornellsville, NY October 26, 1880
GIBSON Mrs. Kate R. of Buffalo, NY Buffalo, NY

MC MAHON M. of Elmira, NY October 22, 1880
CAMERON Lizzie of Hornellsville, NY Hornellsville, NY

DAWSON John of Woodhull, NY November 2, 1880
PARKER Mary F. of Woodhull, NY Woodhull, NY

WRIGHT Edward L. of Painted Post, NY November 3, 1880
KIRKLAND Mary E. of Painted Post, NY Painted Post, NY

WILEY Lyman of Emporium, Pa. November 9, 1880
ROWLEY Willa L. of S. Addison, NY S. Addison, NY

KLICE William C. of Italy Hill, NY November 8, 1880
CLARK Mrs. U. E. of N. Cohocton, NY Bath, NY

MYERS John N. November 10, 1880
SHAFFER Mary E. Hornellsville, NY

WILCOX Mortimer of Ossian, NY November 9, 1880
SMITH Nellie of Arkport, NY Arkport, NY

HAUBER Simeon of Troupsburgh, NY October 26, 1880
LOOMIS Adelia of Troupsburgh, NY W. Union, NY

DIGNEN Michael of Tuscarora, NY November 10, 1880
PERKINS Estella S. of Tuscarora, NY S. Addison, NY

DIGNEN Charles F. of Tuscarora, NY November 10, 1880
NICHOLS Rachel of Tuscarora, NY S. Addison, NY

LOPER Albert E. of Rathbone, NY November 17, 1880
MARTIN Nellie of Rathbone, NY Rathbone, NY

BRIGGS Henry of Fremont, NY March 17, 1880
SHIPMAN Leola E. of S. Dansville, NY

BURTIS D. L. of Hornellsville, NY November 18, 1880
BEAVER E. E. of Binghamton, NY Binghamton, NY

VAN GELDER Theodore of Bath, NY November 17, 1880
GOUNDRY Dora dau of Francis Goundry of Tyrone, NY Tyrone, NY

COLDER James of Lindley, NY November __, 1880
STEWART Maria of Lawrenceville, Pa. Lawrenceville, Pa.

MINER Albert W. of Canisteo, NY November 24, 1880
CLEMENTS Ella J. of Brockton, NY Brockton, NY

BURGETT William H. of Rathbone, NY   November 14, 1880
CONLEY Mary of Rathbone, NY   Woodhull, NY

HARRY James L. of Grand Rapids, Mi.   November 22, 1880
FREEMAN Estella A. of Tuscarora, NY   Tuscarora, NY

GARY Benjamin   November 15, 1880
SCHIRMER Anna M. of Rogersville, NY

LEVERS G. Frank of S. Dansville, NY   November 16, 1880
RIVETT Anna

WILLARD Joseph R. of Alfred, NY   November 17, 1880
KELLER Nellie of Alfred, NY   Alfred, NY

HARRIS Isaiah of Canisteo, NY   November 19, 1880
CRANDALL Sarah L. of Howard, NY   Howard, NY

BEACH Asa I. of Canaseraga, NY   November 12, 1880
HATHAWAY Mrs. Jennie of Buffalo, NY   Canaseraga, NY

HOGAN Thomas of Hornellsville, NY   November 12, 1880
LEDDIN Delia of Salamanca, NY   Salamanca, NY

STILLMAN O. of W. Union, NY   November 17, 1880
FRAIER Mary of Independence, NY   Independence, NY

LANGWORTHY Orra of Alfred, NY   November 13, 1880
HENDEE Ella of Hartsville, NY   Hartsville, NY

GENUNG Frank L.   November 8, 1880
VEITH Jennie L. dau of Frank Veith of Corning, NY   Corning, NY

BATTERSON Seymour of Wallace, NY   November 12, 1880
PINCHIN Eliza A. of Almond, NY   Avoca, NY

HOOD James C. formerly of Corning, NY   November 24, 1880
CARPENTER Carrie   Indianapolis, Ind.

SIMPSON John M. of Cameron, NY   November 20, 1880
GALLATIAN Carrie L. of Cameron, NY   Woodhull, NY

YOUNG Leslie of New York City formerly of Addison, NY   November 21, 1880
MASTERSON Nellie of Brooklyn, NY   New York City

CAMPBELL Joseph B. of Lindley, NY   November 8, 1880
TAFT Mrs. Amelia E. of Addison, NY   Addison, NY

CASTLE Erwin of Rathbone, NY   November 15, 1880
BEST Lizzie of Colesville, NY

ROBINSON Cassius L. of Hornellsville, NY
MC NAUGHTON Lillian of Hornellsville, NY
December 6, 1880
Hornellsville, NY

BROWN Charles of Canandaigua, NY
MILLIMAN Cora of Wayland, NY
November 27, 1880
Dansville, NY

COON Henry C. Prof. Alfred University
HILL Mrs. Mary E. of Alfred Center, NY
December 6, 1880
Alfred Center, NY

LANGLEY D. W. of Canisteo, NY
ROBINSON Hattie dau of J. S. of Bothwell, Ontario Can.
December 15, 1880
Hamilton, Ontario

FLETCHER Fred E. of Corning, NY
PATCHALL Ann M. dau of O. C. Patchill of Corning, NY
December 8, 1880
Corning, NY

HAWLEY Juster B. of Hornellsville, NY
ADAMS Jennie L. dau of David of Hornellsville, NY
December 25, 1880
Hornellsville, NY

AVERY H. A. of Hornellsville, NY
PIERCE Clara L. of Hornellsville, NY
December 22, 1880
Hornellsville, NY

HOPPOUGH H. D. of Canadice, NY
LAWTON Margarate A. of Dansville, NY
December 19, 1880
Bath, NY

MOWRY W. M. of Bath, NY
VAN GELDER Ella of Bath, NY
December 15, 1880
Bath, NY

BREWER Charles of Rochester, NY
FERGUSON Cecelia M. of Canisteo, NY
December 25, 1880
Canisteo, NY

CARPENTER Ralph of Troupsburgh, NY
MOYER Alice of Troupsburgh, NY
December 25, 1880

HUSTED Charles of Woodhull, NY
BROWN Abbie L. of Woodhull, NY
December 25, 1880

ZIMMERMAN John C. of Bradford, NY
READ Alma of Woodhull, NY
November 28, 1880

GRIEF Frank of Hornellsvill, NY
ANSON Rose of Wellsville, NY
December 29, 1880
Wellsville, NY

WARNER Austin E. of Addison, NY
EVERTS Christina of S. Addison, NY
December 27, 1880
Addison, NY

ELWELL Edwin of Troupsburgh, NY
YEOMANS Sarah E. of Troupsburgh, NY
December 25, 1880
Westfield, Pa.

WELCH Albert J. of Westfield, Pa.
TUBBS Emma R. of Westfield, Pa.
December 25, 1880
Troupsburgh, NY

WEST Emmett of Wells, Pa. December 22, 1880
REASER Eva A. of Corning, NY Corning, NY

MC BURNEY John B. of Corning, NY August 4, 1880
BRYAN Rose B. of Canandaigua, NY Painted Post, NY

SORNBERGER Aaron of Rochester, NY December 26, 1880
EASTERBROOK Mrs. Miranda of W. Almond, NY W. Almond, NY

HAMMOND J. A. December 29, 1880
PEASE Grace A. of Hornellsville, NY Hornellsville, NY

LANGS William W. of Hartsville, NY (Newspaper date) January 6, 1881
COOK Celestia of N. Fenton, NY Andover, NY

MILES John of Cohocton, NY October 27, 1880
BLEYMEHIL Kate of Cohocton, NY Bath, NY

EDMOND Webster of Cohocton, NY November 11, 1880
CLAPP Alice of Cohocton, NY Bath, NY

GRAY D. W. of Hammondsport, NY December 23, 1880
COGSWELL Bell of Hammondsport, NY Bath, NY

BROWN Mervin E. of Avoca, NY December 29, 1880
WILSON M. Ella of Avoca, NY

PARTRIDGE Roy of N. Cohocton, NY December 29, 1880
KIMBALL Minnie of Cohocton, NY

ADAMS Charles D. of Hornellsville, NY December 21, 1880
CLARK Ida M. of Buffalo, NY Buffalo, NY

AVERY Herbert A. of Hornellsville, NY December 22, 1880
PIERCE Clara L. of Hornellsville, NY Hornellsville, NY

BRADFORD E. R. of Cedar Rapids, Io. December 29, 1880
JONES A. E. of Avoca, NY Canisteo, NY

STEDMAN Frank of Dansville, NY (Newspaper date) January 6, 1881
LANGLEY Sarah of Canisteo, NY Canisteo, NY

ROSA Adelbert J. of Canisteo, NY December 29, 1880
GRANGER Sarah A. of Canisteo, NY Canisteo, NY

TURNER Mark J. of Canisteo, NY December 30, 1880
DELANY Maggie A. dau William Delany of Canisteo, NY Canisteo, NY

GOFF Floyd W. December 26, 1880
MORGAN Eva of Canisteo, NY late of Howard, NY Howard, NY

WALLACE E. E. Md. of Jasper, NY	January 5, 1881
METCALF Myra A. of Jasper, NY	Jasper, NY
TOBEY Rovellious of Caton, NY	December 19, 1880
DAVIDSON Emma of Caton, NY	Caton, NY
ROBINSON Charles B. of Reading Center, NY	January 3, 1881
ACKLEY Frances M. of Mansfield, Pa.	Corning, NY
MC CRAY R. W. of Alfred, NY	December 25, 1880
CHATFIELD Lillian	Painted Post, NY
RICE Edgar R. of Woodhull, NY	January 1, 1881
PICKETT Lucy A. of Troupsburgh, NY	Troupsburgh, NY
HOPPER Jerome A. of Troupsburgh, NY	January 1, 1881
SLOANE Martha E. of Mass.	Troupsburgh, NY
DENNIS R. P.	January 2, 1881
BARKLEY Tina of Bradford, NY	Bradford, NY
HUNTER D. C. of Jasper, NY	January 16, 1881
BARNES Anna of Jasper, NY	Woodhull, NY
PITTS Harry F. of Corning, NY	December 23, 1880
BEACH Jennie M. of Mansfield, Pa.	Mansfield, Pa.
HAYNES James G. of Catskill, NY	December 5, 1880
PATTERSON Frankie of S. Bradford, NY	S. Bradford, NY
WALTS Adelbert of Avoca, NY	January 19, 1818
CASTER Emma of Avoca, NY	Avoca, NY
HILL Sherman B.	January 20, 1881
SCHUTT Carrie dau of Dubois Schutt of Caton, NY	Caton, NY
BEARD Myron A. of Bath, NY	January 20, 1881
EMERSON Delphine L. of Campbell, NY	Bradford, NY
ANGELL N. J. of Chapinsville, NY	February 1, 1881
SCHOONMAKER Clara of N. Cohocton, NY	N. Cohocton, NY
VAN ETTEN Ambrose of Jersey City, NJ	January 12, 1881
HOFFMAN Nettie of Corning, NY	Corning, NY
BROWN Cornelius of Friendship, NY	January 20, 1881
HORTON Addie of Pulteney, NY	Pulteney, NY
SIMMS Elijah of Hornellsville, NY	February 3, 1881
ROBINSON Jennie of Hornellsville, NY	Hornellsville, NY

DREISBACH Joseph E. of Sparta, NY
HARTMAN Ida Adella of Dansville, NY
February 1, 1881
Dansville, NY

SAGER Charley of Avoca, NY
WAGNER Ina of Avoca, NY
February 4, 1881
Avoca, NY

WILCOX Isaac R. of Canisteo, NY
BARNES C. C. of Canisteo, NY
February 19, 1881
Greenwood, NY

WILCOX W. N. of Ithaca, NY
GRAUF Ida L. of Canisteo, NY
February 19, 1881
Greenwood, NY

BREWER Mark A. of Fargo, Dakota late of Hornellsville
RICE Tabbs of Howard, NY
February 10, 1881
Howard, NY

WATERS John of Johnsville, NY
WILLIAMSON Alida C. of Avoca, NY
February 9, 1881
Avoca, NY

FLOHR Charles of Canisteo, NY
O'MULLEN Sarah of Canisteo, NY
February 22, 1881
Greenwood, NY

SMITH E. D. of Canisteo, NY
HART Mary of Canisteo, NY
February 24, 1881
Canisteo, NY

MARTIN Charles H. of Bristol Springs, NY
WHEELER Mrs. Amelia A. of Naples, NY
February 10, 1881
Naples, NY

SABIN Ransom of Cameron, NY
WHITE Helen M. of Cameron, NY
February 27, 1881
Cameron, NY

VAUGHN Herman A.
DRAKE Fanny L. dau of Allen Drake of Jasper, NY
February 23, 1881
Jasper, NY

ROLLIN William of Canisteo, NY
CAMPBELL Lottie of Greenwood, NY
March 6, 1881
Greenwood, NY

FORMAN Lemuel R. of Bedford, Mi.
PUFFER Viola D. of Canisteo, NY
March 2, 1881
Canisteo, NY

COUNCELMAN Andrew J. of Olean, NY
ROOT Matilda of Hornellsville, NY
March 8, 1881
Hornellsville, NY

LUTHER Daniel M. of Fremont, NY
MAYNARD Minnie S. of Hornellsville, NY
March 2, 1881
Hornellsville, NY

DEMAREST James of Cohocton, NY
SMITH Ida O. of Naples, NY
February 26, 1881
Hammondsport, NY

WELDON Harvey of Lindley, NY
CROMMAN Deborah W. of Muncy, Pa.
March 6, 1881
Lindley, NY

COOPER E. S. of Avoca, NY	March 10, 1881
GLOVER Olive N. of Cohocton, NY	Avoca, NY
STANTON J. Amasa of Hornby, NY	March 15, 1881
KINGSLEY Ada A. dau of Amos of Hamilton, NY	Hamilton, NY
SINSEBOX Charles of Urbana, NY	March 16, 1881
SHERER Rachel of Howard, NY	Howard, NY
DECKER Frank L. of Alton, Pa. formerly Bath (News. date)	March 31, 1881
DAVIS Julia of Bath, NY	Van Etten, NY
VAN ORSDALE Fitch of Jasper, NY	March 10, 1881
CRAIG Grace dau of Maj. W. E. Craig of Lockport, NY	Lockport, NY
MONELL Alva of Bath, NY	March 16, 1881
WHITE Carrie of Howard, NY	Howard, NY
LOPER James A. of Saginaw, Mi.	March 22, 1881
STROUD Mary P. of Woodhull, NY	Woodhull, NY
STEWART John of Arkport, NY	March 27, 1881
PIERCE Ida M. of Hornellsville, NY	Hornellsville, NY
THOMAS William J. of Swains, NY	March 30, 1881
SHERMAN Lissie E. of Dalton, NY	Canisteo, NY
WASHBURN Solomon of Springwater, NY	March 20, 1881
HAVENS Martha of N. Cohocton, NY	Naples, NY
TAYLOR William F. of Canisteo, NY	March 23, 1881
YOUNG Tina of Cameron, NY	Cameron, NY
REED Smith W. of Corning, NY	April 5, 1881
VAN GORDER Jennie of Nelson, Pa.	Lindley, NY
HOSIER Menzo of Corning, NY	April 6, 1881
ADSIT Ann Eliza dau of O. F. Adsit	Corning, NY
CARROL Ward D. of Bath, NY	March 30, 1881
WALKER Rose M. of Bath, NY	Cohocton, NY
RUTAN Wilbur R. of Elmira, NY	April 17. 1881
HUNT Mrs. Jennie A. of Caton, NY	Elmira, NY
HOUSEN J. A. of Lindley, NY	March 30, 1881
WEAVER Mary A. of Tuscarora, NY	Osceola, Pa.
MORRISON William of Prattsburgh, NY	March 16, 1881
SIMMONS Hattie J. of Savona, NY	

HIGGINS Daniel Sr. April 20, 1881
SALLEY Catherine dau of late Barney Salley of Corning, NY Corning, NY

HAISCHER Anthony of Corning, NY April 15, 1881
FREEMAN Mary R. dau of W. H. Freeman of Corning, NY Corning, NY

HUNTINGTON Merritt of Jasper, NY April 28, 1881
CHAMBERLAIN Josie dau of Dr. C. P. of Canisteo, NY Canisteo, NY

KERNAN John of Rexville, NY April 26, 1881
DAILY Bridget of Andover, NY Andover, NY

STEVENS Charles of Lawrenceville, Pa. March 19, 1881
UTTER Anna of Woodhull, NY Osceola, Pa.

WOODWORTH Charles of Hartsville, NY April 3, 1881
HARTSMAN Carrie J. of Hartsville, NY Hartsville, NY

RICE Daniel T. of Canisteo, NY May 18, 1881
WARD Maggie E. of Rathbone, NY Rathbone, NY

GREEN Martin of Canisteo, NY June 5, 1881
WRIGHT Ina of Canisteo, NY Canisteo, NY

SMITH Frank L. of Canisteo, NY June 15, 1881
HOLMES Lillie of Canisteo, NY Canisteo, NY

JESSEN Martin of Wellsville, NY June 17, 1881
PATRIDGE Amanda of Hornellsville, NY Canisteo, NY

WALDO Frank R. of Canisteo, NY June 23, 1881
TAYLOR Nellie W. of Elmira, NY formerly Canisteo, NY Elmira, NY

CADY Ellery of Brookfield, Pa. June 14, 1881
BENNETT Sylvia Ann of Troupsburgh, NY Troupsburgh, NY

BEST Charles W. of Hornellsville, NY June 28, 1881
BATES Jennie V. of Hornellsville, NY Buffalo, NY

BAXTER Charles A. of Woodhull, NY July 3, 1881
SHARPSTEEN Carrie J. of Woodhull, NY Woodhull, NY

POTTER Albert J. of Niles, Mi. July 2, 1881
VAN HOUSEN Jennie dau of Abram Van Housen Prattsburgh, NY

BROWN Nelson J. of Lindley, NY July 4, 1881
MARYOTT Louisa A. of Morristown, NJ Canaseraga, NY

KNISLEY Horatio Seymour of Corning, NY July 2, 1881
PALMER Kittie of Knoxville, NY Corning, NY

VAN DYKE Charles E. of Lindley, NY — July 4, 1881
BRANEN Ella E. of Lindley, NY — Corning, NY

GRAHAM Benjamin of the Swale, NY — July 23, 1881
MILLS Frances of Rathbone, NY — Troupsburgh, NY

STEPHENS Hiram A. of Wallace, NY — July 17, 1881
O'HARA Mrs. M. E. of Wallace, NY — Stephens Mills, NY

COX William O. of Cleveland, Oh. — July 20, 1881
HORTON Anna E. dau of Charles T. Horton — Campbell, NY

STEVENS Alanson of Hornellsville, NY — July 22, 1881
PICKARD Mrs. P. of Hornellsville, NY — Corning, NY

BOWEN D. H. of Dansville, NY — August 10, 1881
FAULKNER Victoria S. of Wayland, NY — Wayland, NY

OSBORN Charles of Canisteo, NY — August 24, 1881
THORP Mary of Canisteo, NY — Canisteo, NY

KELLOGG Niles of Canisteo, NY — August 15, 1881
HICKEY Phebe R. of Howard, NY — Howard, NY

SCOTT William H. of Elmira, NY — August 23, 1881
DEYO Viola E. of Caton, NY — Painted Post, NY

LANG Eugene of Oneonta, NY — August 18, 1881
KEITH Mary C. of Hornellsville, NY — Hornellsville, NY

SEELY Mathew of Troupsburgh, NY — August 13, 1881
NYE Estella of W. Union, NY — Troupsburgh, NY

MILLIKIN Peter H. of Montgomery, NY — August 17, 1881
THOMSON Adelaide L. dau of Charles H. of Corning, NY — Corning, NY

ANDREWS Frank of Jasper, NY — August 28, 1881
PICKARD May of Smethport, Pa. — Smethport, Pa.

EDWARDS Artemus of Troupsburgh, NY — August 30, 1881
NORTHRUP May of Troupsburgh, NY — Troupsburgh, NY

COOK William of Troupsburgh, NY — September 1, 1881
CARPENTER Jennie of Woodhull, NY — Woodhull, NY

BOSS Benjamin of Woodhull, NY — August 27, 1881
MC FALL Susie of Troupsburgh, NY — Troupsburgh, NY

SLOCUM Ward of Greenwood, NY — September 20, 1881
WINGET Bertie of Greenwood, NY — Greenwood, NY

PARKER John R. of Monterey, NY   September 28, 1881
GEORGE Carrie M. of Troupsburgh, NY   Woodhull, NY

HOFFMAN Theodore of Canisteo, NY   (Newspaper date) October 20, 1881
MARSHALL Rena of Canisteo, NY   Hornellsville, NY

BRODIE Joseph of Angelica, NY   October 8, 1881
GRIEVES Maggie of N. Cohocton, NY   Haskinsville, NY

KELLEY Joseph of Hornellsville, NY   September 26, 1881
ELLIOTT Carrie of Canisteo, NY   Canisteo, NY

MURDOCK E. P. of Troupsburgh, NY   September 27, 1881
POWERS Mary of Troupsburgh, NY   Troupsburgh, NY

SMITH Rev. C. B. of E. Troupsburgh, NY   October 18, 1881
DIBBLE Estella of E. Campbell, NY   E. Campbell, NY

WORKS Will of Troupsburgh, NY   October 18, 1881
LOZIER Ella of Troupsburgh, NY   Troupsburgh, NY

DE LONG Russell J. of Woodhull, NY   October 19, 1881
SHAW J. M. of Woodhull, NY   Woodhull, NY

BRUNDAGE Frank of Greenwood, NY   October 4, 1881
VAN ORSDALE Helen of Jasper, NY   Jasper, NY

TURNER Robert E. of Waverly, NY   (Newspaper date) November 3, 1881
ROE Lizzie of Canisteo, NY   Canisteo, NY

SHERWOOD Wesley of Cameron, NY   October 19, 1881
HARGRAVE Hattie of Cameron, NY   Cameron, NY

JUNE Frank of Jasper, NY   October 19, 1881
PERRY Myra of Rathbone, NY   Rathbone, NY

KEEMER Joseph   (Newspaper date) November 3, 1881
KRESS Mary of Hornellsville, NY   (Wednesday Eve) Hornellsville, NY

NOLTE George E. of Alamosa, Col.   October 20, 1881
LOPER Mrs. Susannah of Golden, Col. formerly Canisteo   Golden, Col.

YOUNG Charles H. of Bath, NY   November 2, 1881
WILLIAMS Eva E. of Naples, NY   Naples, NY

EDWARDS Nathan B. of W. Union, NY   November 6, 1881
BAKER Polly of W. Union, NY   Independence, NY

HENDRICK Eugene of Troupsburgh, NY   October 26, 1881
BUCK Olive of Harrison, Pa.   Westfield, Pa.

SMITH Louis W. of Troupsburgh, NY
DALY Addie L. of W. Union, NY

November 15, 1881
Troupsburgh, NY

PECKHAM W. H. of Canisteo, NY
TURNER Kate E. grand dau of George Turner of Canisteo

November 17, 1881
Canisteo, NY

BABCOCK S. C. of Fremont, NY
ACOMB Mary A. of S. Dansville, NY

November 24, 1881

TIMMERMAN Arthur of Jasper, NY
JACKSON Diana of Jasper, NY

November 16, 1881
Jasper, NY

ABBOTT Daniel F.
THOMAS Minnie M.

November 10, 1881
Hornellsville, NY

BURNS Michael of Dansville, NY
HENDERSHOTT Jennie of Hornellsville, NY

November 23, 1881
Hornellsville, NY

PRESTON Homer M. of Hornellsville, NY
SEARLS Mary T. of Addison, NY

November 23, 1881
Hornellsville, NY

KENNEDY Isaac of Morton, Ill.
KENNEDY Mrs. Lou of Howard, NY

December 2, 1881
Hornellsville, NY

CUMMINGS John of Woodhull, NY
HIBBARD Olive of Woodhull, NY

November 23, 1881
Addison, NY

MURRAY Daniel D. of Corning, NY
JONES Lillie A. of Corning, NY

November 24, 1881
Corning, NY

REYNOLDS Wesley of Canisteo, NY
BAKER Anna of Greenwood, NY

December 11, 1881
Savona, NY

PECK Ripley C. of N. Cohocton, NY
BALDWIN Mrs. Anna of Howard, NY

December 1, 1881
Howard, NY

COSTON M. Emmet of Greenwood, NY
WILLIAMSON Addie of Greenwood, NY

December 1, 1881

WEBB George A. of Milwaukee, Wis.
CASTLE Mary A. of Woodhull, NY

December 12, 1881
Woodhull, NY

BRADLEY Frank W. of Oxford, NY
VICKERS Clara E. of Hornellsville, NY

November 30, 1881
Hornellsville, NY

TYLE Lafayette of Corning, NY
WILSON Hattie D. of Avoca, NY

December 6, 1881
Naples, NY

FRANCE Frank L. of Canisteo, NY
EVANS Clara E. of Canisteo, NY

December 21, 1881
Darien, NY

FAIRBROTHER Eugene of Cohocton, NY   December 14, 1881
SLAYTON Laura of Cohocton, NY   Avoca, NY

CALKINS Elba of Avoca, NY   (Newspaper date) January 5, 1882
MATTOON Adell of Avoca, NY   Avoca, NY

STONE John of Kansas   December 25, 1881
HUDSON Mrs. Julia of Woodhull, NY   Woodhull, NY

NEWMAN Erwin of Jasper, NY   December 25, 1881
CRAIG Maria of Jasper, NY   Woodhull, NY

TEMPLER William H. of Tyrone, NY   December 25, 1881
ABER Hattie of Wheeler, NY

CADY Willis O. of Hornellsville, NY   December 27, 1881
TURNER Josephine of Hornellsville, NY   Hornellsville, NY

GRAY George E. of Hornellsville, NY   December 19, 1881
LEWIS Adeline E. of Hornellsville, NY   Hornellsville, NY

CONKLIN John E. of Hornellsville, NY   December 17, 1881
ALLIS Alida E. of Hornellsville, NY   Hornellsville, NY

DUBOIS Rev. Mr. ____ of Kanona, NY   December 21, 1881
CULVER Emma of Howard, NY   Howard, NY

CONKLIN B. F. of Hornellsville, NY   December 21, 1881
TRENCHARD Maggie A. of Hornellsville, NY   Hornellsville, NY

AGNEW William H. of Salamanca, NY   December 21, 1881
RYNO Florence of Hornellsville, NY   Hornellsville, NY

SCHAUMBERG Joseph L. of Hornellsville, NY   December 22, 1881
KIMBALL Ettie E. of Hornellsville, NY   Hornellsville, NY

BROWN Bona J. of Woodhull, NY   December 21, 1881
DAWLEY Mate M. of Woodhull, NY   Woodhull, NY

GOFF Fred of Canisteo, NY   January 5, 1882
BURRELL Ella of Canisteo, NY   Canisteo, NY

GLEASON Lemuel of Wayne, NY   December 29, 1881
BELLIS Alida of Bath, NY   Bath, NY

TUCKER Orville A. of Ward, NY   (Newspaper date) January 12, 1882
IVES Martha of W. Almond, NY

SORGE Henry of Dansville, NY   January 4, 1882
DEAN Libbie M. of Hornellsville, NY

HUNT John of Corning, NY
O'SHAUGHNESSY Mary of Corning, NY

January 4, 1882
Corning, NY

MC KIE David J. of Penn Yan, NY
LESHURE Lottie of Dresden, NY

January 2, 1882
Corning, NY

FELLER James W. of Hornellsville, NY
RISINGER Catherine B. of Corning, NY

December 31, 1881
Corning, NY

BLAKESLEE Prof. James of Hammondsport, NY
BASSETT Mary dau of Clark Bassett of Campbell, NY

December 29, 1881
Painted Post, NY

EMERSON Thomas of Bath, NY
MC NEIL E. B. of Naples, NY

December 14, 1881
Naples, NY

COCHRANE A. W. of Hamonton, N. S.
HALLIDAY Ida D. of Bath, NY

December 28, 1881
Bath, NY

TOWNER A. J. of Avoca, NY
FERRIS Clarissa of Howard, NY

January 11, 1882
Howard, NY

WATSON Horace of Bath, NY
CROW Caroline of Bath, NY

January 12, 1882
Bath, NY

SMITH Martin of Bath, NY
WALKER Arvilla of Bath, NY

January 10, 1882
Bath, NY

MC GRADY S. D. of Canisteo, NY
CONVERSE Linda of Canisteo, NY

January 25, 1882
Canisteo, NY

UNDERWOOD A. B. of Canisteo, NY
DE LAND Clara M. of Canisteo, NY

February 6, 1882
Canisteo, NY

ALLEN James F. of Howard, NY
BARTLETT Lou V. of Howard, NY

February 21, 1882
Howard, NY

POPE James of Hartsville, NY
ASHBAUGH Addie E. of Hornellsville, NY

February 1, 1882
Alfred Center, NY

WICKHAM Joseph P. Jr. of Tioga, Pa.
CROPSEY Virginia D. of Lawrenceville, Pa.

February 15, 1882
Lawrenceville, Pa.

ROBERTSON Rev. D. J. of Canisteo, NY
TAYLOR Mary dau of William B. Taylor of Canisteo, NY

March 1, 1882
Canisteo, NY

SHERWOOD Homer of Jasper, NY
WYCKOFF Generva of Jasper, NY

February 15, 1882
Jasper, NY

HOUSE Will of Jasper, NY
GRINNOLDS Genevieve of E. Troupsburgh, NY

February 18, 1882
Jasper, NY

SUTTON Dr. Frank R. of Canisteo, NY   February 21, 1882
SMITH Emily of Bath, NY   Bath, NY

HORTON Martin S. of Hornellsville, NY   February 8, 1882
STEVENSON Carrie E. of Howard, NY   Howard, NY

DYER James of Avoca, NY   February 9, 1882
LINDSAY Barbara of Bath, NY   Canisteo, NY

BAKER Jerry of W. Union, NY   February 12, 1882
OSMAN Rebecca J. of W. Union, NY   Independence, NY

WARD Waldo of Canisteo, NY   March 8, 1882
ELLISON Adeline of Canisteo, NY   Canisteo, NY

DYGERT W. H. of Kanona, NY   March 1, 1882
LOUCKS Belle of Avoca, NY   Avoca, NY

WORKS Arthur formerly of Troupsburgh, NY (News. date)   March 16, 1882
GREY Marion of Richburg, NY   Richburg, NY

HAXTON Wilson T. of Troupsburgh, NY   March 6, 1882
GRINNOLDS Cora of Troupsburgh, NY   Troupsburgh, NY

STEPHENS H. M. of Canisteo, NY   March 15, 1882
GEER Mrs. H. J. of Fleming, NY   Fleming, NY

COOK Dwight of Canisteo, NY   March 22, 1882
WALDO Aggie   Canisteo, NY

GROFF George A. of Canisteo, NY   April 2, 1882
HEPINSTALL Nettie J. of Canisteo, NY

JAMISON M. S. of Canisteo, NY   March 28, 1882
PIERSON Mary M. of Canisteo, NY   Jasper, NY

MAY Fred W. of Hornellsville, NY   April 5, 1882
WOOD Inez M. of Painted Post, NY   Painted Post, NY

BRASTED Horace K. Md. of Lima, NY   April 12, 1882
CARTER Rose E. of Canisteo, NY   Canisteo, NY

TOMER Harvey S. of Hornellsville, NY   April 12, 1882
HUNTINGTON Helen Mary dau of E. T. of Rochester, NY   Rochester, NY

MC CARTY William of Hornellsville, NY   April 19, 1882
HAZLETON Edith F. of Elmira, NY   Canisteo, NY

CRIPPEN Truman W. of Howard, NY   April 23, 1882
SWEEZEY Lizzie A. of Canisteo, NY   Canisteo, NY

BAILEY William T. of Canisteo, NY   April 26, 1882
BALDWIN Belle of Canisteo, NY   Canisteo, NY

PEAK William of Canisteo, NY   May 13, 1882
SLOCUM Ruby of Canisteo, NY   Andover, NY

STEPHENS C. S. of Canisteo, NY   May 14, 1882
KING E. of Howard, NY

CROSS S. S. of Canisteo, NY   May 10, 1882
WILSON Carrie adopted dau of Prentice and Polly   Canisteo, NY

WALDO L. A. of Canisteo, NY   May 24, 1882
LEWIS Jennie of Prattsburgh, NY   Prattsburgh, NY

LAIN Edwin L. of Canisteo, NY   May 27, 1882
SMITH Emma of Canisteo, NY   Prattsburgh, NY

MC GUIRE John B. of Canisteo, NY   May 25, 1882
TERRY Jessie of Hornellsville, NY   Canisteo, NY

CLEMENT Albert S. of New York City   June 1, 1882
ROSS Maud of Watkins, NY   Watkins, NY

ALLEY Frank B. of Hornellsville, NY   June 4, 1882
JOHNSON Isabel of Hornellsville, NY   Hornellsville, NY

SLAUGHT L. F. of Canisteo, NY   (Newspaper date) June 15, 1882
WHITLEY Mrs. B. J. of Canisteo, NY   Canisteo, NY

CAMPBELL W. F. of Canisteo, NY   July 6, 1882
CRAMER Cora M. of Buffalo, NY   Buffalo, NY

CLEMENT Bloomfield of Canisteo, NY   July 12, 1882
CONRAD Georgie E. of Fenton, Mi.   Fenton, Mi.

ARMSTRONG Charles H. of Avon, NY   July 12, 1882
BERNHAM Carrie of Hornellsville, NY

KING Van Amburgh of Hornellsville, NY   July 4, 1882
WEBB Cora D. of Hornellsville, NY

FURMAN William of Hornellsville, NY   July 4, 1882
KING Sarah E. of Fremont, NY   Hornellsville, NY

JEFFERS A. B. of Hornellsville, NY   July 12, 1882
WOODS Ida I. of Litchfield, Mi.   Hornellsville, NY

JORDAN Marcus M. of Knoxville, Pa.   July 4, 1882
SCHOONOVER Lena E. of Knoxville, Pa.   Woodhull, NY

DYER George S. of Addison, NY
WELLS Delia of Woodhull, NY

July 5, 1882
Jasper, NY

CULVER Joseph W. of Burns, NY
TROWBRIDGE Augusta of Hornellsville, NY

July 13, 1882
Burns, NY

BONNEY Eugene of Brookfield, Pa.
FISH Eliza of Brookfield, Pa.

July 9, 1882
Troupsburgh, NY

CONINE Charles S. of Keeneyville, Pa.
TYLER Rua E. of Prattsburgh, NY

July 15, 1882

ROBERTS Cameron of Hornellsville, NY
CROPSER Lottie A. of Hornellsville, NY

July 29, 1882
Almond, NY

LEVERIDGE G. W. of Salamanca, NY
HAGADORN Jennie M. of Hornellsville, NY

July 30, 1882
Canisteo, NY

BLAIR S. H. of Woodhull, NY
BROWN Elizabeth E. of Knoxville, Pa.

July 16, 1882
Knoxville, Pa.

WAGNER Jay P. of Risingville, NY
SPENCER Carrie May of Risingville, NY

July 27, 1882
Campbell, NY

WILSON James of Canisteo, NY
SNOW Jennie dau of Rev. F. A. Snow of Canisteo, NY

August 20, 1882
Rowleyville, NY

SMITH James of Cameron, NY
HEMINGWAY Sarah of Addison, NY

July 1, 1882
Cameron, NY

FORD F. E. of Canisteo, NY
PALMER Libbie of Union City, Pa.

August 25, 1882
Union City, Pa.

BOWDISH J. W. of Canisteo, NY formerly Marion Io.
ALLISON Lottie S. of Canisteo, NY

September 6, 1882
Canisteo, NY

HALLETT Frederick M. of Canisteo, NY
DEAN Ida M. of Canisteo, NY

September 2, 1882
Canisteo, NY

STEVENS James P.
PALMER Mrs. Ophelia A. dau of W. W. **GOFF**

September 7, 1882
Canisteo, NY

HAVENS James L. of Bath, NY
MERRILL Sarah of Bath, NY

September 3, 1882
Campbell, NY

BENNETT Judson of Bath, NY
TRACY Mary of Bath, NY

August 24, 1882
Bath, NY

CRANE Warren of Cameron, NY
EMERSON Eva of Cameron, NY

August 24, 1882
Bath, NY

GILES Prof. Arthur H. of Cazenovia, NY	September 2, 1882
BISSELL Mary Gertrude dau of Rev. T. J. Bissell	Corning, NY
BAUTER George W. of Wheeler, NY	September 11, 1882
PERRY Hermie C. of Avoca, NY	Avoca, NY
DENNIS Samuel F. of Jasper, NY	September 12, 1882
BOWEN Mrs. Mary A. of Addison, NY	Addison, NY
ELLS J. W. of Hartsville, NY	September 18, 1882
BURDICK Irene O. of Hornellsville, NY	Hornellsville, NY
CHAMBERLAIN Harvey of Little Genessee, NY	September 26, 1882
BROTZMAN Ella of Troupsburgh, NY	Jasper, NY
BUCK Henry W. of Jasper, NY	October 11, 1882
BRUTSMAN Ada E. of Troupsburgh, NY	Jasper, NY
CHARLES Lewis T. of Hornellsville, NY	October 10, 1882
SHELLY Isabel A. of Albany, NY	Albany, NY
SHAUT Frederick of Canisteo, NY	October 18, 1882
AYRES Carrie B. of Hornellsville, NY	Hornellsville, NY
CHAPIN D. S. of Saginaw, Mi.	October 17, 1882
CONDERMAN Rose of Hornellsville, NY	Hornellsville, NY
WYNGART Jacob of Hornellsville, NY	October 29, 1882
HOFFMAN Lena of Hornellsville, NY	Hornellsville, NY
DE GRAFF Edward of Towlesville, NY	October 24, 1882
FOOTE May of Towlesville, NY	Towlesville, NY
ALLEN Wesson of Hornellsville, NY	October 29, 1882
HARTMAN Sarah of Dansville, NY	Hornellsville, NY
HILL Charles P. of Lindley, NY	October 26, 1882
GAMMEN Anna M. dau of Charles M. of Corning, NY	Corning, NY
COVELL William A. of Hornellsville, NY	November 12, 1882
KRING Alice A. of Hornellsville, NY	Hornellsville, NY
HACKETT W. L. of Canisteo, NY	October 11, 1882
DULTON Carrie H. of W. Union Io. at Charles Hackett res	Canisteo, NY
SAUSMAN Floyd W. of Hornellsville, NY (Newspaper date)	November 16, 1882
PLIMPTON Fannie dau of A. J. of Hornellsville, NY	
PHINNEY Henry R.	November 1, 1882
CLANCY Katie	Hornellsville, NY

TUCKER Seth R. of Hornellsville, NY
GAISER Jennie L. of Hornellsville, NY

November 8, 1882
Hornellsville, NY

SEELEY Jasper E. of Hornellsville, NY
RICKEY Mrs. Letha M. of Greenwood, NY

November 22, 1882

SNELL Thomas of Hornellsville, NY
WASHBURN Eliza J. of Buffalo, NY

November 21, 1882
Buffalo, NY

VAN SCOTER A. of Canaseraga, NY
BROWN Ida of Canaseraga, NY

November 14, 1882
Canisteo, NY

GREEN Ray of Canisteo, NY
NORTON Florence of Hornellsville, NY

December 5, 1882
Canisteo, NY

DERRICK James of Troupsburgh, NY
STONE Minnie of Troupsburgh, NY

November 21, 1882
E. Troupsburgh, NY

COYKENDALE Edwin F. of Hornellsville, NY
ROSS Ida G. of Hornellsville, NY

December 6, 1882
Hornellsville, NY

FURMAN D. Wylie of Gaines, Pa.
ACKER Eliza A. of Hartsville, NY

December 6, 1882
Canisteo, NY

BOSSARD William D. of Townsend, NY
ALLEN Sarah A. of Canisteo, NY at res of J. F. Allen

December 10, 1882
Canisteo, NY

JOYCE Charles Fay of Buffalo, NY
WALKER Hattie E. dau of C. C. B. Walker

December 13, 1882

BRASTED M. C.
ORDWAY Delle dau of William H. Ordway of Canisteo, NY

December 13, 1882
Canisteo, NY

HEALY B. W. of Troupsburgh, NY
BULLEN Jennie of Woodhull, NY

December 3, 1882
Troupsburgh, NY

GAY Frank O. of Bath, NY
DURNIAN Adelle of Bath, NY

December 5, 1882
Bath, NY

JOHNSON Elnathan of Hornellsville, NY
HELMER Hattie B. of Hornellsville, NY

December 13, 1882
Hornellsville, NY

REED Elmer of Mt. Desert Island Me.
GOSS Nellie A. of Hornellsville, NY

December 12, 1882
Hornellsville, NY

COONS William A. of Hornellsville, NY
KNAPP Ella of Hornellsville, NY

December 22, 1882
Hornellsville, NY

SAUSMAN Albert G.
HAKES Hattie of Hornellsville, NY

December 27, 1882
Hornellsville, NY

VAN GORDON Edward K. **AYERS** Martha of Hornellsville, NY	December 27, 1882 Hornellsville, NY
WALLACE George D. of Canisteo, NY **BURD** Amy of Canisteo, NY	January 2, 1883 Hammondsport, NY
WETMORE Willard M. of Canisteo, NY **EASON** Flora dau of Smith Eason of Canisteo, NY	January 11, 1883 Canisteo, NY
DILLENBECK Henry I. of Wheeler, NY **WELCH** Alice E. of Avoca, NY	January 7, 1883
HASKELL Alfred of Port Crescent, Mi. (Newspaper date) **WHEELER** Emma of Hornellsville, NY	January 25, 1883 Hornellsville, NY
GOTTSCHALL Fred L. of Fremont, NY **VOLTZ** Laura C. of Dansville, NY	January 25, 1883 Arkport, NY
BENNETT James C. of Wayland, NY **NEWSOM** Jane of Hornellsville, NY	January 25, 1883 Hornellsville, NY
PRICE Alonzo R. of Harrisburg, Pa. **JOHNSON** Danna of Addison, NY	January 22, 1883
HIBBARD Cherick of New Albany, Pa. **FERGUSON** Mary M. formerly of Cameron, NY	January 10, 1883 New Albany, Pa.
LANGS Jacob of Hornellsville, NY **HARTMAN** Mrs. Mary E. of Hornellsville, NY	January 21, 1883 Fremont, NY
PRESTON J. R. of Canisteo, NY **MANHART** Mary of Canisteo, NY	February 4, 1883 Canisteo, NY
MYERS Lewis of Howard, NY **OYER** Frankie M. of Howard, NY	January 27, 1883 Howard, NY
KAUSCH Edward of Wayland, NY **WALKER** Rosa B. of Hornellsville, NY	February 1, 1883 Hornellsville, NY
METZ William of Troupsburgh, NY **SAUNDERS** Mrs. Finetta P. of Richburg, NY	January 19, 1883 Richburg, NY
BROOKS A. R. of Canisteo, NY **HODGES** Kittie of Starkey, NY	February 1, 1883 Watkins, NY
HUNTER Edgar of Hornellsville, NY **REYNOLDS** Carrie E. of Watkins, NY	February 7, 1883 Hector, NY
WRIGHT Charles of Canisteo, NY **CLARK** Dolly of Canisteo, NY	February 22, 1883

FANTON F.
GARDNER Eunice P. of Tuscarora, NY
February 8, 1883
Cameron Mills, NY

NEWMAN David H. of Canisteo, NY
BENNETT Hulda M. of Canisteo, NY
February 28, 1883
Canisteo, NY

LAWRENCE Mart D. of Woodhull, NY
WILEY Lucy C. of Woodhull, NY
February 25, 1883
Woodhull, NY

GREEN Frank of Canisteo, NY
HAMILTON Jennie of Canisteo, NY
March 8, 1883
Canisteo, NY

MARLATT Charles of Troupsburgh, NY
WILCOX Jennie of Troupsburgh, NY
March 6, 1883
Troupsburgh, NY

JOHNSON Frank of Woodhull, NY
NORTHRUP Ella of Rathbone, NY
March 14, 1883
Rathbone, NY

JOHNSON H. W. of Canisteo, NY
CLEMENT Abbie of Canisteo, NY
March 27, 1883
Canisteo, NY

SMITH Harley of Jasper, NY
SPENCER Fannie of Jasper, NY
April 15, 1883
Tuscarora, NY

COLE Jesse of Canisteo, NY
COLE Kate of Canisteo, NY
April 18, 1883
Addison, NY

TRAVER John F. of Painted Post, NY
SAYER Lucy A. of Painted Post, NY
April 17, 1883
Painted Post, NY

TOBIAS Frank D. of Troupsburgh, NY
HOLLISTER Mrs. Mary of Troupsburgh, NY
April 12, 1883
Troupsburgh, NY

CARLTON James L. of Campbell, NY
CHAMBERS Mrs. Emily L. of Painted Post, NY
April 3, 1883
Campbell, NY

CLARK Wilbur of Canisteo, NY (Newspaper date) May 10, 1883
CRONE Jennie of Canisteo, NY
Canisteo, NY

PARKER J. Elliott of Woodhull, NY
HARDER A. Lida of Woodhull, NY
May 9, 1883
Woodhull, NY

PAXTON Harry of Addison, NY
NORTHRUP Lizzie of Cameron Mills, NY
May 16, 1883

AYERS M. J. of New York City
UPSON Adda dau of William Upson of Canisteo, NY
May 23, 1883
Canisteo, NY

DOUGLAS Henry C. of Hartford, Ct.
GARDNER Viola B. of Hornellsville, NY
May 24, 1883
Hornellsville, NY

COWLES J. H. of Bath, NY
MC KEEN Lillie of Canisteo, NY

June 17, 1883
Bath, NY

POTTER Edward J. of Savona, NY
ACKERSON Amanda of Savona, NY

June 9, 1883
Savona, NY

HAMMER Andrew of Canisteo, NY
FRENCH Carrie of Canisteo, NY

July 3, 1883
Canisteo, NY

BUTTON Albert L. of Jasper, NY
FREELAND Frank of Jasper, NY

June 27, 1883
Hedgesville, NY

FAIRBANKS Elmer of Hornellsville, NY
STOCUM Hattie of Canisteo, NY

July 4, 1883
Canisteo, NY

SWEET Dr. Eli Jr. of Canisteo, NY
BAKER Lottie of Canisteo, NY

July 12, 1883
Canisteo, NY

ALLEN Joseph H. of Susquehanna, Pa.
BROWN Jessie A.

July 15, 1883
Canisteo, NY

SMITH Carl W.
BAKER Amelia dau of John Baker

(Newspaper date) July 26, 1883

DE LANEY Frank T. of Canisteo, NY
SMITH Rosella G. of Canisteo, NY

July 29, 1883
Canisteo, NY

BRONSON Isaac T. of Hornellsville, NY
WHITE Belle of S. Dansville, NY

July 13, 1883
Arkport, NY

PRESTON John N. of Adrian, NY
BOX Jennie L. of Adrian, NY

August 5, 1883
Adrian, NY

DENNIS Boardman of Jasper, NY
ORDWAY Vira dau of J. L. Ordway of Jasper, NY

August 15, 1883
Jasper, NY

CARTER Charles A. of Howard, NY
GUYON Anna M. of Canisteo, NY

August 22, 1883
Canisteo, NY

JAMISON T. E. of Canisteo, NY
GUYON Carrie E. of Canisteo, NY

August 22, 1883
Canisteo, NY

BALDWIN Thomas D. of Nelson, Pa.
CAMPBELL Susie dau of Robert Campbell of Nelson, Pa.

September 5, 1883
Nelson, Pa.

GRIGGS Cass of Troupsburgh, NY
HOPPER Hattie N. of Troupsburgh, NY

September 11, 1883
Troupsburgh, NY

CALKINS Richard of Woodhull, NY
PERRY Belle E. of Woodhull, NY

September 12, 1883

DENNIS Will F. of Jasper, NY   September 13, 1883
MARLATT Ida J. dau of Hamilton Marlatt of Woodhull, NY

VORHIS John T. son of Rev. Stephen Vorhis of Spencer, NY   September 26, 1883
BAKER Carrie dau of Nathan Baker of Canisteo, NY   Canisteo, NY

PERRY William of Canisteo, NY   September 12, 1883
STEWART Anna L. of Howard, NY   Campbell, NY

CARDWILL Charles of Bath, NY   (Newspaper date) October 4, 1883
MC CANN Abbie of Risingville, NY   Campbell, NY

MEEKER Frank W. of Binghamton, NY   October 2, 1883
JOY Jennie R. of Bath, NY   Bath, NY

WAIGHT Frank of Jasper, NY   October 7, 1883
RUTHERFORD Christina of Troupsburgh, NY   Troupsburgh, NY

REYNOLDS Ralph of Troupsburgh, NY   October 7, 1883
SCHOONOVER Ella L. of Troupsburgh, NY   Troupsburgh, NY

CRANE Charles of Canisteo, NY   October 18, 1883
ADAMS Mrs. B. A. of Andover, NY formerly Canisteo   Andover, NY

JACKSON O. D. of Bingham, Pa.   September 26, 1883
MARLATT May E. of Woodhull, NY   Coudersport, Pa.

PLAISTED Walter of W. Union, NY   October 10, 1883
BALEY Mate E. of Young Hickory, NY   Young Hickory, NY

SMITH Charles of Woodhull, NY   October 16, 1883
SULLIVAN Josie of Rathbone, NY   Addison, NY

BRASTED Joseph H. of Canisteo, NY   October 17, 1883
CARTER Allie M. dau of George W. Carter of Canisteo   Canisteo, NY

MATTESON George M. of Greenwood, NY   October 26, 1883
CARPENTER Minnie of Tioga Center, NY   Tioga Center, NY

POTTER Darwin F.   October 17, 1883
STEVENS Fannie B.   Hornellsville, NY

DASCOM William A. of Binghamton, NY   October 17, 1883
STEWART Mary J. of Bath, NY   Penn Yan, NY

MURRAY Samuel of Bath, NY   October 22, 1883
GREENFIELD Lydia of Bath, NY   Wellsboro, Pa.

COLLIER Charles P. of Avoca, NY   October 17, 1883
WHEATON Fannie of Avoca, NY

HUNT Horace of Avoca, NY
TOWNER Minnie of Avoca, NY

October 18, 1883

PAGE Edmond of W. Union, NY
MUNGER Mrs. Mary of Wellsville, NY

October 27, 1883
Andover, NY

AUSTIN N. of Greenwood, NY
PARSHALL Maria of Hornellsville, NY

October 21, 1883
Greenwood, NY

KNIGHT Merritt of Greenwood, NY
SPRINGER Estell of Greenwood, NY

October 23, 1883
Greenwood, NY

HEALY D. of Bevins, NY
DAY Ida B. of S. Dansville, NY

November 1, 1883
S. Dansville, NY

GARDNER Ellsworth of Troupsburgh, NY
PODGETT Ella of Troupsburgh, NY

November 4, 1883
Troupsburgh, NY

STROUD Edwin M. of Woodhull, NY
OLIN Vella of Woodhull, NY

November 1, 1883
Woodhull, NY

COOPER David of Bolivar, NY
COLVIN Nancy of Sheakleyville, Pa.

November 4, 1883
Woodhull, NY

BATCHELDER E. J. of Jasper, NY
BENEDICT Flora of Canisteo, NY

November 3, 1883
Canisteo, NY

ORCUTT Alvah B. of Canisteo, NY
AMES Emma A. of Savona, NY

November 7, 1883
Canisteo, NY

PLAINTON James E. of Addison, NY
HINE Lottie C. of Addison, NY

November 7, 1883
Addison, NY

SHELLECK Zeno E. of Cameron, NY
WARDEN Ida of Cameron, NY

October 20, 1883
Cameron, NY

STEWART Robert of Howard, NY
FIELDS Mary late of Illinois

November 27, 1883

SIMONS Charles of Perkinsville, NY
ENGLE Elizabeth

November 20, 1883
Wayland, NY

BAKER Fay of Fremont, NY
TENNEY Lizzie of Almond, NY

December 11, 1883

COLVIN Willis of Woodhull, NY
BATES Maggie of Deposit, NY

November 6, 1883
Deposit, NY

O'BRIEN James of Corning, NY
HOGAN Annie of Corning, NY

November 27, 1883
Corning, NY

SIMONSON Edward of Corning, NY   December 2, 1883
STUART Mary F. of Cameron, NY   Corning, NY

ATCHISON Thomas of Corning, NY   November 27, 1883
FITZPATRICK Lizzie of Corning, NY   Corning, NY

PIERSON Horace G. of Corning, NY   November 28, 1883
ALEXANDRE Julia of Corning, NY   Corning, NY

MARTIN William of Bath, NY   November 28, 1883
PLOW Emma of Bath, NY   Bath, NY

JACOBUS Frank of Bath, NY   November 29, 1883
SMITH Mary L. of Bath, NY at res of O. M. Smith

PETERS Merchant of Canisteo, NY   December 23, 1883
MC KEEN Effie of Canisteo, NY   Canisteo, NY

ELDRETT Lorimer of Mt. Morris, NY   December 25, 1883
SWARTZ Elizabeth of Mt. Morris at uncle's A. J. ALDRICH Canisteo, NY

ACKER William C. of Hartsville, NY   December 27, 1883
CLARK Hattie of Hartsville, NY   Canisteo, NY

WILLIAMS Orrin of Canisteo, NY   December 25, 1883
ROSA Eva of Canisteo, NY   Adrian, NY

BURD Lysander J. of Hornellsville, NY   January 3, 1884
STEWART Abbie L. of Howard, NY   Howard, NY

WICKHAM Joseph D. of Canisteo, NY   (Newspaper date) January 10, 1883
EDGETT Sarah J. of Canisteo, NY   Hornellsville, NY

PECK Charles of W. Cameron, NY   February 6, 1884
THOMAS Mrs. Sarah of Adrian, NY   Adrian, NY

MEAD Amos of Canisteo, NY   (Newspaper date) February 28, 1884
POTTER Nancy J. of Canisteo, NY   Canisteo, NY

WARD George of New York City   February 19, 1884
BOVIER Rachel of Canisteo, NY   Hornellsville, NY

LINES Jacob B. of Woodhull, NY   February 25, 1884
ODDSON Carrie B. of Woodhull, NY   Woodhull, NY

NEWMAN Burr S. of Tuscarora, NY   March 30, 1884
MILLER Delia of Woodhull, NY   Woodhull, NY

JACKSON Thomas J. of Jasper, NY   March 23, 1884
HAYES Melissa of Jasper, NY   Jasper, NY

DENNIS Will of Jasper, NY	March 27, 1884
SHAWL Allie of Jasper, NY	Jasper, NY
WARNER A. D. of Canisteo, NY	April 2, 1884
WOODMANCY Florence of Canisteo, NY	Canisteo, NY
HEDGES Wilson M. of Canisteo, NY	April 13, 1884
HARPER Mary of Meadville, Pa.	Canisteo, NY
MILLARD Philo of Woodhull, NY	April 2, 1884
JONES Mrs. Sarah E. of Addison, NY	Addison, NY
STEPHENS Emmett of Canisteo, NY	April 21, 1884
STEPHENS Ettie of Hornellsville, NY	
LANTZ James R. of Woodhull, NY	April 10, 1884
REDDINGTON Rebecca R. of Woodhull, NY	Woodhull, NY
WOOD Willard R. of Woodhull, NY (Newspaper date)	April 24, 1884
NEWELL Mary E. of Woodhull, NY	Hedgesville, NY
BURLEY David of Cameron, NY	April 13, 1884
HARVEY Nettie of Thurston, NY	Merchantville, NY
LOPER Emmett of Canisteo, NY	April 27, 1884
NICHOLSON Ida of Hornellsville, NY	
HAVENS James of Painted Post, NY (Newspaper date)	May 1, 1884
WHEELER May of Dalton, NY	Canisteo, NY
ORCUTT Lorenzo of Savona, NY	April 24, 1884
HENDERSHOTT Martha N. of Canisteo, NY	Canisteo, NY
SHERMAN William H. of Canisteo, NY	April 24, 1884
BENNETT Lura R. of Canisteo, NY	Canisteo, NY
DUNHAM Ralph E.	May 21, 1884
ORDWAY Roxie	Canisteo, NY
POWELL Mr. ___ of Cuba, NY	May 23, 1884
JEFFERS Arabella of Canisteo, NY	Canisteo, NY
BALLARD Earl of Westfield, Pa.	May 21, 1884
SMITH Nellie of Mixtown, Pa.	
WALKER Charles L. of Angelica, NY	May 22, 1884
CARPENTER Flora A. of Angelica, NY	Angelica, NY
JACOBS Frank H. of Hornellsville, NY	May 30, 1884
WALBRIDGE Ida of Hornellsville, NY	

CASE Abner of Woodhull, NY	May 29, 1884
MOREHOUSE Amanda of Sodus, NY	Addison, NY
ALLEN Edgar of Rock Stream, NY	June 11, 1884
DAVISON Eva of Canisteo, NY	Canisteo, NY
MAC DOUGAL Avery of Hornellsville, NY	June 18, 1884
NYE Jennie E. of Elmira, NY	Elmira, NY
LAKE Myron R. of Canisteo, NY	June 19, 1884
CARTER Addie A. dau of John of Canisteo, NY	Canisteo, NY
GRISWOLD Will D. of Hornellsville, NY	June 11, 1884
SHULTZ Edith of Belmont, NY	Belmont, NY
FOULTS William H. of Avoca, NY	June 19, 1884
SHARP Cora of Avoca, NY	
DAY De A. of Canisteo, NY	June 26, 1884
CARRINGTON Flora of Fremont, NY	Fremont, NY
EDDY George B. of Hornellsville, NY	July 5, 1884
CARNEY Lena of Hornellsville, NY	Hornellsville, NY
PETTIBONE Hawley S.	July 5, 1884
TROWBRIDGE Anna	Hornellsville, NY
WEBB James L. of Hornellsville, NY	June 22, 1884
MONROE Edith M. of S. Addison, NY	Friendship, NY
TRAVIS David H. of Woodhull, NY	July 1, 1884
MILLER Anna E. dau of A. & J. Miller of Canisteo, NY	Canisteo, NY
DURYEA William A. of Perry Center, NY	July 22, 1884
HEMMINGWAY Mrs. Martha E. of Hornellsville, NY	Hornellsville, NY
LYNN Rev. P. T. of the Genessee Conference	July 10, 1884
MOULTON Ida J. of Batavia, NY	Batavia, NY
MC MINDES Henry	July 4, 1884
PRUTZMAN Susan	Troupsburgh, NY
DE MUNN John of Fremont, NY	July 5, 1884
BREWER Ella M. of Woodhull, NY	Woodhull, NY
STURDEVANT Edwin E. of Corning, NY	July 4, 1884
ORCUTT Mary E. of Painted Post, NY	Painted Post, NY
SWEEZEY Edwin T. of Canisteo, NY	July 23, 1884
LANGDON Emma of Oswayo, NY	Greenwood, NY

JENKINS Jared W. of Hartsville, NY
HARTRUM Ella F. of Hornellsville, NY

July 27, 1884
Hornellsville, NY

CRANE E. L. of Cameron, NY
COCHRANE Carrie E. of Hornellsville, NY

July 20, 1884
W. Cameron, NY

SHERWOOD Orson of Canisteo, NY
MC MINN Maggie of Howard, NY

August 17, 1884
Hartsville, NY

SMITH W. W. of Rexville, NY
JANES Nellie dau of Julius Janes of Mendon, NY

August 20, 1884
Mendon, NY

EDWARDS Charles G.
WALDO Emma A. of Prattsburgh, NY

August 20, 1884
Prattsburgh, NY

CLARK Walter B. of Addison, NY
CLINTON Ida B. dau of S. D. Clinton of Addison, NY

August 20, 1884
Addison, NY

ROWE John of Canisteo, NY
BEATTY Maggie of Canisteo, NY

September 4, 1884
Canisteo, NY

COATS John H. of Howard, NY
COBB Addie L. of Howard, NY

September 10, 1884
Howard, NY

BRUNDAGE B. S. of Greenwood, NY
WILLIAMSON Jennie of Hornellsville, NY

September 30, 1884
Hornellsville, NY

BENNETT Ambert of Troupsburgh, NY
COON Jennie of Troupsburgh, NY

September 21, 1884
Troupsburgh, NY

BRASTED Clement M. of Troupsburgh, NY
SCHOONOVER Nettie of Troupsburgh, NY

October 1, 1884
Hornellsville, NY

WATSON George G. of Hornellsville, NY
TAYLOR Jennie of Hornellsville, NY

September 30, 1884
Hornellsville, NY

WAGNER Leroy M. of Knoxville, Pa.
BROWN Maggie E. of Hornellsville, NY

September 30, 1884
Hornellsville, NY

FLEET Edgar of Elmira, NY
JOHNSON Anna of Hornellsville, NY

September 30, 1884
Elmira, NY

WILCOX Ralph of Troupsburgh, NY
HUSTED Carrie of Woodhull, NY

September 17, 1884
Woodhull, NY

JONES Thomas G. of Blossburg, Pa.
GRASSOM Mary D. of Corning, NY

September 30, 1884
Elmira, NY

LOSEY W. E. of Middlebury, Pa.
ROUNDSVILLE Mattie of Erwin Center, NY

September 24, 1884
Charleston, Pa.

MEAD W. D. of Sylvester, Pa.   September 26, 1884
MOSHER Libbie of Caton, NY   Caton, NY

MEEKS Seymour of Howard, NY   October 7, 1884
CORNELL Fannie dau of Peter Cornell of Howard, NY   Howard, NY

MOORE George B. of Dundee, NY   October 2, 1884
CRANS Amanda of Bath, NY   Bath, NY

CORWIN Samuel M. of Jasper, NY   October 5, 1884
GUILE Minnie R. of Woodhull, NY   Woodhull, NY

HOBER H. A. of Jasper, NY   October 18, 1884
HOLT Amanda of Jasper, NY   Greenwood, NY

BURNS David of Howard, NY   October 21, 1884
CORNELL Helen of Howard, NY   Howard, NY

GLAZIER Charles E. of Hornellsville, NY   October 23, 1884
ALLEY Flora dau of S. M. Alley of Hornellsville, NY Hornellsville, NY

MEEKS James Adolphus of Howard, NY   October 22, 1884
BAXTER Grace J. of Howard, NY   Howard, NY

PACKARD Stephen D. of Hornellsville, NY   October 22, 1884
BAXTER Alice F. of Howard, NY   Howard, NY

JONES William E. of Corning, NY   October 16, 1884
MANNING Ida B. dau of L. B. Manning of Corning, NY   Corning, NY

KENYON Herbert of Hornellsville, NY   November 2, 1884
PHELPS Carrie B. of Hartsville, NY   Canisteo, NY

LANG Horatio Seymour of Hornellsville, NY   October 29, 1884
BABCOCK Lizzie C. of Hornellsville, NY   Hornellsville, NY

FULLER Spencer T. of Cleveland, Oh.   November 17, 1884
DE MASON Mary P. of New York City   Canisteo, NY

JACKSON Charles G. of Canisteo, NY   November 12, 1884
LAWTON Hattie E. of Newell, Iowa   Newell, Iowa

TOUSLEY J. R. of Jasper, NY   November 27, 1884
STONE Addie Layton dau of Prentice Stone of Jasper, NY   Jasper, NY

BRASTED Dr. Charles M. of Hornellsville, NY   December 10, 1884
BEEBE Alida L. of Canisteo, NY   Canisteo, NY

HALLETT W. J. of Howard, NY   December 7, 1884
HALLETT Flora of Adrian, NY   Canisteo, NY

GILBERT W. H. Md. of Lawrenceville, Pa.   December 6, 1884
VAN NORMAN Lissa J. of Jasper, NY   Tioga, Pa.

SIMPSON E. of Jasper, NY   December 3, 1884
WYCKOFF Allie C. of Jasper, NY   Jasper, NY

PLAISTED David of W. Union, NY   December 3, 1884
WYCKOFF Lucy E. of Jasper, NY   Jasper, NY

EDWARDS Burt of Woodhull, NY   December 14, 1884
SAULSMAN Alfarette of Norfolk, Va.   Woodhull, NY

CLARK Leroy of Hartsville, NY   December 8, 1884
MORGAN Ida of Canisteo, NY   Canisteo, NY

SMITH J. J. of Jasper, NY   December 16, 1884
DABOLL Mrs. Lucinda dau of D. H. EDWARDS

Corning and Blossburg Advocate

August 21, 1840 - September 6, 1843

WHEAT Lyman C. of Hornby, NY   August 28, 1840
WARNICK Mary of Hornby, NY   Hornby, NY

BALCOM Uriah of Erwin, NY   September 8, 1840
BESLEY Jane A. dau or Samuel Besley of Campbell, NY   Campbell, NY

COOK John of Lawrenceville, Pa.   September 10, 1840
SOMERS Elizbeth M. of Lawrenceville, Pa.   Lawrenceville, Pa.

BECKWITH A. B. of Bath, NY   September 29, 1840
THOMPSON Martha C. of Painted Post, NY   Painted Post, NY

TOBEY Samuel of Caton, NY   September 30, 1840
SPENCER Charlotte of Caton, NY   Caton, NY

CRANE Charles of Erwin, NY   October 11, 1840
NOBLES Mrs. Sarah of Erwin, NY   Erwin, NY

BACON Alvin of Avon, Ohio   October 14, 1840
NORTHWAY Almeria of Hornby, NY   Hornby, NY

WYNKOOP N. F. of Corning, NY   October 15, 1840
HEERMANS Sarah A. of Providence, Pa.   Chemung, NY

WATKINS Daniel I. of Mississippi   October 15, 1840
WYNKOOP Cornelia A. of Chemung, NY   Chemung, NY

SARLE Richard
MANN Lucina

October 19, 1840
Tioga, Pa.

GRIDLEY Eli of Caton, NY
ROUE Eliza of Caton, NY

November 15, 1840
Caton, NY

JACOBS David of Caton, NY
HUBBARD Susan of Caton, NY

November 20, 1840
S. Corning, NY

NOYES Joseph of Southport, NY
COREY Prudence of Southport, NY

November 29, 1840
Southport, NY

CLARK Samuel M.
BURNS Mary Ann

December 3, 1840
Centreville, NY

TRAVER Dr. Robert M.
YOUNG Eliza

October 29, 1840
Centreville, NY

MALLORY John
LAMB Mary

November 5, 1840
Knoxville, NY

ALWORTH William of Corning, NY
GUERNSEY Eliza of Mill Creek, NY

January 7, 1841

TRACY N. U. of Corning, NY
DEPEW J. A. of Litchfield, Ct.

December 29, 1840
Barrington, NY

BARNARD Rufus of Milford, NY
WATERS Harriet of Milford, NY

January 6, 1841
Milford, NY

POTTER Willis of Erwin, NY
SEE Mary of Erwin, NY

January 21, 1841
Erwin, NY

FALES Atwood of S. Corning, NY
PIERCE Adeline of S. Corning, NY

December 28, 1840
S. Corning, NY

STANTON Russell of Caton, NY
NORTHWAY Lucy C. of Hornby, NY

March 25, 1841
Hornby, NY

WYMAN H. H. of Corning, NY
SRONS Ruth S. of Walkill, NY

May 24, 1841
Corning, NY

FULLER L. T. of Corning, NY
CARD A. Jane of Woodstock, NY

May 30, 1841
Woodstock, NY

LINDSAY Merritt of Caton, NY
APGAR Emeline of Caton, NY

June 2, 1841
Caton, NY

SWEET John W. of Corning, NY
RACE Maria of Corning, NY

June 13, 1841
Erwin, NY

CRUM Rev. Gardner of Dix, NY
PARKER Mrs. Nancy of Addison, NY

June 9, 1841
Addison, NY

CORNELL Luke of Hornby, NY
CUSHING Martha of New Bedford, Mass.

July 7, 1841
Painted Post, NY

BRITTAIN William of Auburn, NY
CLARKE Charity of Centreville, NY

September 19, 1841
Centreville, NY

PIERCE Hiram of Corning, NY   (Newspaper date) September 22, 1841
PERRY Susan of Corning, NY

Corning, NY

WOODRUFF Gurdin of Lawrenceville, Pa.
CADY Betsey of Lawrenceville, Pa.

September 30, 1841
Painted Post, NY

KINGSBURY A. F. of Rochester, NY
CALKINS Hannah Mary of Corning, NY

October 11, 1841
Corning, NY

ARNOLD William J. of Corning, NY
KRESS Harriet of Covington, Pa.

October 26, 1841
Covington, Pa.

CHATFIELD T. I. of Owego, NY
BUNDY Mary P. of Elmira, NY

November 9, 1841
Owego, NY

BILLINGHURST Lucien of Corning, NY
FELLOWS Hannah dau of Col. J. Fellows of Corning, NY

February 3, 1842
Corning, NY

MORSE Daniel W. of Preble, NY
HULL Harriet M. of Corning, NY

February 7, 1842
Corning, NY

DEGOLIER Anthony of Painted Post, NY
SEELY Mary Jane of Painted Post, NY

February 10, 1842
Painted Post, NY

DUNN Andrew of Caton, NY
SPENCER Emeline of Caton, NY

February 13, 1842
Caton, NY

FERENBAUGH Charles of Hornby, NY
SWEET Lucy of Caton, NY

February 16, 1842
Corning, NY

HAWLEY James M. of Corning, NY
PRESTON Eunice of Corning, NY

March 2, 1842
Corning, NY

GILMORE Benjamin of Nornby, NY
ROBBINS Mariah of Hornby, NY

February 23, 1842
Hornby, NY

EARLS William of Newfield, NY
VAN ETTEN Anna of Danby, NY

March 9, 1842
Knoxville, NY

VAN ETTEN Robert H.
BAKER Lavina

March 10, 1842
Knoxville, NY

WILSON Robert of Geneva, NY　　　　　　　March 13, 1842
CORIELL Sarah Jane of Hornby, NY　　　　　Hornby, NY

METZ William of Corning, NY　　　　　　　April 3, 1842
RHYME Mary Ann of Corning, NY　　　　　　Big Flats, NY

HOOD William of Corning, NY　　　　　　　April 23, 1842
SMITH Catherine of Corning, NY

ENOS Eben E. of Painted Post, NY　　　　　May 4, 1842
CRONKHITE Amanda of Painted Post, NY　　Painted Post, NY

SMITH Andre of Geneva, NY　　　　　　　　May 18, 1842
CLARK Elizabeth of Geneva, NY　　　　　　Corning, NY

PEEBLES Dr. C. of Corning, NY　　　　　　June 15, 1842
WINANS Mrs. Catherine M. dau of Judge **STEELE**　　Corning, NY

LOVELAND George P. of Corning, NY　　　　July 14, 1842
DEAN Marietta of Laurens, NY　　　　　　Laurens, NY

BROWN Clark of Corning, NY　　　　　　　August 10, 1842
DODGE Mary Elizabeth of Corning, NY　　　Corning, NY

CHATFIELD Charles J.　　　　　　　　　　August 15, 1842
FOSTER Sarah D. dau of Robert W. Foster　　Lebanon, Pa.
　　(adopted dau of Sylvester **SMITH** of Painted Post, NY)

COBURN Joseph T. of Caton, NY　　　　　　September 4, 1842
ROBERTS Mary of Barton, NY　　　　　　　Caton, NY

BONHAM D. H. of Campbell, NY　　　　　　September 7, 1842
REYNOLDS Sarah G. of Big Flats, NY　　　Big Flats, NY

LAND Chauncey P. of Corning, NY　　　　　October 12, 1842
BRADLEY Harriet E. of Greene, NY　　　　Greene, NY

BARNES Washington of Bath, NY　　　　　　October 25, 1842
BIRDSALL Louisa of Greene, NY　　　　　　Greene, NY

HALL Samuel of Elmira, NY　　　　　　　　December 22, 1842
DICKINSON Eliza D. dau of A. B. Dickinson of Hornby, NY　Hornby, NY

POWERS Charles H. of Corning, NY　　　　January 1, 1843
PRESTON Caroline A. of Corning, NY　　　Veteran, NY

WESTCOTT Charles of Caton, NY　　　　　　January 5, 1843
PRATT Adeline of Addison, NY　　　　　　Addison, NY

REMER Abram L. of Hornby, NY　　　　　　January 5, 1843

BATES Mary A. of Hornby, NY — Corning, NY

HAMILTON Lewis of Campbell, NY — February 1, 1843
BALCOM Mary E. dau of Lyman Balcom of Campbell, NY — Campbell, NY

GRAHAM George — January 26, 1843
ANDREWS Ann Eliza — Jasper, NY

TAYLOR Henry — February 15, 1843
LONGWELL Phebe — Bath, NY

DOW John of Bath, NY — March 8, 1843
MARSHALL Miss ____ of Bath, NY

CLARKE William brother of Charles of Corning, NY — March 9, 1843
MOORE Susan sister of Francis Moore Jr. — Houston, Texas

SLOAN George of Elmira, NY — March 28, 1843
ROWLEY Harriet of E. Painted Post, NY — E. Painted Post, NY

PERRY Upton R. of Tioga, Pa. — April 28, 1843
BUMP Leah of Tioga, Pa. — Corning, NY

HOLLENBECK Joseph of Corning, NY — June 15, 1843
NEWTON Sarah of Corning, NY — Corning, NY

BIRD Loring Grant of Elmira, NY — June 25, 1843
BROWNELL Eunice of Corning, NY — Corning, NY

Corning Journal

July 21, 1847 - December 27, 1872

KELLOGG Cyrus of Corning, NY — July 14, 1847
COOPER Rhoda Ann of Corning, NY — Corning, NY

SANFORD K. — July 19, 1847
ALSEN E. M. — Corning, NY

WHEELOCK M. M. of Corning, NY — April 5, 1848
ROCKWELL Olive of Corning, NY — Corning, NY

QUINSY Squire M. of Jacksonville, Pa. — April 10, 1848
FENTON Jane E. of Rathbone, NY — Knoxville, NY

STURDEVANT Horatio N. — April 12, 1848
WOLCOTT Mary S. — Corning, NY

DELAMATER Stephen D. of Corning, NY — April 15, 1848

FILKINS Minerva of Corning, NY

Corning, NY

WILSON Joseph K. of Bradford, NY
HUTCHINSON Maria of Bradford, NY

May 17, 1848
Corning, NY

CUMMINGS Henry of Harrison, Pa.
DODGE Angeline of Harrison, Pa.

May 31, 1848
Harrison, Pa.

MATHEWSON Russell
JOHNSON Emma Cornelia

June 28, 1848
Corning, NY

HUSTED Wilson of Troupsburgh, NY
PEASE Abigail dau of Oliver Pease of Troupsburgh, NY

July 16, 1848
Troupsburgh, NY

CHAPMAN James H. of Jefferson, NY
DENTON Frances dau of S. B. of Corning, NY

August 3, 1848
Corning, NY

KNAPP Elder William of Corning, NY
ROCKWELL Eunice of Monterey, NY

August 6, 1848
Monterey, NY

MOORE David of Corning, NY
MORRIS Mrs. Sarah of Corning, NY

August 29, 1848
Corning, NY

CUSHING Leland of Campbell, NY
MOWRY Catherine of New York City

September 3, 1848
Corning, NY

MERRIWEATHER Mr. Doctor of Geneva, NY
BLAKE Mary A. of Buffalo, NY

August 25, 1848
Corning, NY

CAMPBELL George of Knoxville, NY
WEDGE Emily of Knoxville, NY

September 22, 1848
Corning, NY

WASHINGTON George
HARDY Julia

September 23, 1848
Corning, NY

DENTON Seymour F. of Corning, NY
MORSE Lucretia of Corning, NY

October 19, 1848
Corning, NY

LANPHEAR Amasa J. of Corning, NY
PERSONS Louise of Corning, NY

October 19, 1848
Corning, NY

STURDEVANT D. B. of Brookfield, Ct.
DAVIS Mary of Corning, NY

October 31, 1848
Corning, NY

HASTINGS Charles of Corning, NY
HARRISON Lucinda of Corning, NY

December 9, 1848
Corning, NY

HUNT Rollin B. of Harrison, Pa.
GILL Mary Melinda of Harrison, Pa.

December 23, 1848
Elkland, Pa.

JOHNSON Washington
CLARK Elinor

January 2, 1849
Corning, NY

GILROY William of Bath, NY
LEWIS Sarah of Corning, NY

December 6, 1848
Corning, NY

CORNELL John L. of Painted Post, NY
LOVELL Sarah of Buena Vista Plains

January 1, 1849
Buena Vista Plains

TUPPER Virgil
PARCEL Juliette

January 25, 1849
Corning, NY

DRYER A. C. of Addison, NY
BILES Mrs. Mary of Bath, NY

February 15, 1849
Painted Post, NY

BOWEN John of Otsego, NY
PATCHEN Mrs. Phebe

February 24, 1849
Hornby, NY

MILLER William of Orange, NY
BRONSON Marando of Dix, NY

February 22, 1849
Dix, NY

VAN ETTEN John
LAWRENCE Mary Louisa

March 11, 1849

CHILDS William
MC CREA Eliza of Corning, NY

April 6, 1849
Corning, NY

CLARK Jesse S. of Corning, NY
PERSON Eunice of Corning, NY

April 12, 1849
Corning, NY

MESSENGER William H. of Corning, NY
NEWTON Charlotte of Corning, NY

April 19, 1849
Painted Post, NY

ROWLEY Alvah of E. Painted Post, NY
HEART Caroline of Big Flats, NY

April 17, 1849
Corning, NY

THOMPSON George W. of Addison, NY
VAN VLECK Elizabeth of Addison, NY

April 29, 1849
Hornby, NY

RUMSEY Levi M.
WILLIAMS Sophia

May 30, 1849
Corning, NY

LYON Asher H. of Woodhull, NY
PIERCE Alice of Hornby, NY

May 23, 1849
Hornby, NY

WILBUR Thomas of Friendship, NY
BELDEN Ann of Hornellsville, NY

September 10, 1849
Hornellsville, NY

GREGORY Christopher of Hornellsville, NY
REDFIELD Betsey Jane of Hornellsville, NY

September 11, 1849
Hornellsville, NY

TURK David of Addison, NY   January 23, 1850
WEST Henrietta of Corning, NY   Corning, NY

OVIATT Lorenzo of Corning, NY   January 12, 1850
HUNT Mary M. of Corning, NY

COOPER William H. of Corning, NY   February 17, 1850
CARR Mary Ann of Corning, NY   Corning, NY

RYANT Dennis of Corning, NY   February 15, 1850
CASTERLINE Eunice D. of Corning, NY   Corning, NY

ROCKWELL Lemuel Prof. of Music of Rushford, NY   March 4, 1850
VAN SCOTER Mary   Hornellsville, NY

MABIE William B. of Sullivan, Pa.   March 3, 1850
DIMMICK Candace of Corning, NY   Corning, NY

VERNOOY Samuel of Elmira, NY   March 11, 1850
MC BRIDE Amelia C. of Elmira, NY   Corning, NY

BURTON Sylvester of Sullivan Co.   March 24, 1850
CLARK Eunice E. of Corning, NY

BROWN Civilian of Elmira, NY   March 26, 1850
NORTON Harriet R. of Elmira, NY   Corning, NY

FULLER D. K. of Rathbone, NY   April 4, 1850
ARNOLD Lucia E. of Corning, NY   Corning, NY

SPENCER Timothy of Corning, NY   April 20, 1850
BRIGGS Mary of Corning, NY   Painted Post, NY

WHITMORE O. S. of Rathbone, NY   April 18, 1850
WILSON Martha J. of Binghamton, NY   W. Addison, NY

PERKINS Gilman W. of Painted Post, NY   June 23, 1850
HUNTLEY Mariah M. of Corning, NY

MC CARN Henry of Corning, NY   June 30, 1850
WEDGE Ruby of Corning, NY   Corning, NY

LADIEU William of Hornby, NY   July 4, 1850
MANWARING Phebe J. of Hornby, NY   Hornby, NY

BURLEY Sheldon of Corning, NY   August 10, 1850
SMITH Mary Jane of Corning, NY   Corning, NY

ERWIN Samuel S. son of F. E. of Painted Post, NY   August 7, 1850
SHAW Amelia of Painted Post, NY   Painted Post, NY

TEEL Jacob of Horseheads, NY
DARRIAN Melissa of Gibson, NY

August 31, 1850
Gibson, NY

WRIGHT S. of Seneca Falls, NY
POWERS Caroline A. of Corning, NY

September 5, 1850
Corning, NY

PARKS Augustus S. of Corning, NY
SHIELDS Sarah A. of Corning, NY

September 4, 1850
Big Flats, NY

DASKANE William H. of Caton, NY
CUMMINGS Aseneth of Caton, NY

September 15, 1850

WHEAT James of Lindon, Ill.
SMITH Brittania of Campbell, NY

September 17, 1850

HUTCHINS Elias of Cortland Co. NY
TYLER Charlotte of Painted Post, NY

September 20, 1850
Painted Post, NY

HAMLIN Ira C. of Caton, NY
CRAWFORD Sheloneth of Caton, NY

October 7, 1850
Corning, NY

ROSENCRANS Harvey of Catlin, NY
LIVINGSTON Roana of Catlin, NY

October 10, 1850
Corning, NY

MIDDAUGH H. D. of Lawrenceville, Pa.
SOMERS Julia A. of Corning, NY

October 10, 1850
Corning, NY

THORNSON Robert
SWARTHOUT Mrs. Juliette

October 14, 1850
Addison, NY

COOK James N. of Hornellsville, NY
SQUIRE Susan of Cooperstown, NY

October 14, 1850
Addison, NY

WHEELOCK George A. of Corning, NY
LYON Amelia of Corning, NY

October 29, 1850

WILLIAMS John Henry of Corning, NY
COLMAN Elizabeth of Batavia, NY

October 29, 1850
Batavia, NY

BERRY Charles H. of Corning, NY
HUBBELL Frances of Corning, NY

November 14, 1850

CURTIS E. Lewis B. of Danby, NY
MILLS Anna K. of Corning, NY

November 13, 1850

MITCHELL Thadeus of Lawrence, Pa.
WARNER Margaret M. of Waverly, NY

October 29, 1850
Waverly, NY

PARKER James W. of Corning, NY
RICE Charlotte of Corning, NY

November 24, 1850

DODGE William F. of Corning, NY   December 12, 1850
CROSLY Louise E. of Corning, NY   Corning, NY

HOWELL William N. of Elmira, NY   January 8, 1851
BONHAM Emily of Knoxville, NY

DANA Brazilla of Corning, NY   February 12, 1851
WEEKS Ann Eliza of Corning, NY

POWERS David S. of Coopers Plains, NY   April 2, 1851
BUSSEY Abigail M. of Beaver Dams, NY   Beaver Dams, NY

PENSTON M. of Liberty, NY   April 23, 1851
QUIGLEY Ann of Hornellsville, NY   Hornellsville, NY

TERBELL Douglas Md. of Corning, NY   May 1, 1851
ROBINSON Celena N. of Corning, NY

BROWN Frederick D. of Woodhull, NY   May 4, 1851
WILLIAMS Hannah M. of Woodhull, NY

LEWIS Dennis of Corning, NY   May 20, 1851
JACKSON H. A. of Corning, NY   Corning, NY

MC KINNEY Comet of Great Bend, Pa.   August 5, 1851
GRAY Mary E. dau of Isaac Gray of Corning, NY   Corning, NY

SLY Mathew M. R.   July 29, 1851
MAXWELL Harietta A. dau of Thomas Maxwell

CUMPSTON C. P. of Corning, NY   August 21, 1851
JENNINGS Sarah A. of Corning, NY   Corning, NY

WHEELER Lewis C. of Elmira, NY   August 2, 1851
GARR Rosetta of Elmira, NY   Corning, NY

CHAPLIN William L.   August 12, 1851
GILBERT Theodorcia at the Water Cure   Glen Haven, NY

PEW Theodore of Corning, NY   September 4, 1851
WELLS Adaline L. of Corning, NY   Corning, NY

MATTIMORE Patrick of Corning, NY   September 3, 1851
FITZPATRICK Ann of Corning, NY   Elmira, NY

ROWLEY Salmon B. of Corning, NY   October 7, 1851
LOMBARD Anna J. dau of Charles Lombard of Corning, NY

ATWATER D. of Corning, NY   October 13, 1851
CURTIS Jane M. of Corning, NY   Corning, NY

POTTER Cranston T. of Corning, NY
MALLORY Louisa of Knoxville, NY

October 13, 1851

MILLS Daniel of Bath, NY
EGGLESTON Esther Eliza of Bath, NY

November 15, 1851

BUTTS William E. of Helena, Ark.
LINDSLEY Catherine A. of Lindley, NY

December 3, 1851
Lindley, NY

ARMSTRONG Edward of Campbell, NY
WALLEN Mary L. of Campbell, NY

December 7, 1851
Campbell, NY

RIGBY William T. of Corning, NY
ROWLEY Marietta dau of Alvah of E. Painted Post, NY

December 11, 1851

BAILEY Abner A. of Corning, NY
SANFORD Adelia of Corning, NY

December 30, 1851

THOMPSON George of Corning, NY
OAKS Martha dau of Lucius WARNER

December 31, 1851

THURBER F. C. of Corning, NY
SPRAGUE Melissa B. of Westfield, Pa.

December 31, 1851

BUNDY George W. of Cameron, NY
LANE Hannah of Cameron, NY

January 29, 1852
Bath, NY

HURD Rev. Isaac N. Pres. Church of Big Flats, NY
BASSETT Mary of Hector, NY

February 4, 1852
Peach Orchard, NY

WAY William T. of Corning, NY
MC LEAN Jane of Painted Post, NY

February 19, 1852
Painted Post, NY

HERRINGTON N. M. Md. of Corning, NY
GENUNG Julia A.

March 10, 1852
Almond, NY

LUMBARD H. J. of Corning, NY
EDMISTER Catherine dau of Lewis of Big Flats, NY

March 4, 1852
Big Flats, NY

FORD James P. of Penn Yan, NY
BARNETT Catherine A. of Greene, NY

February 18, 1852
Greene, NY

DODGE Erastus of Corning, NY
LUCE C. of Albany, NY

March 26, 1852
Albany, NY

MC CANN John of Painted Post, NY
GARDNER Ann M. of Painted Post, NY

March 18, 1852
Knoxville, NY

DARMEEKET Martin of Corning, NY
STEINBRENNER Christiana of Corning, NY

March 27, 1852
Corning, NY

WHEELER Edwin R. of Corning, NY
STEERE Joana A. of Smithfield, RI
March 29, 1852
Woonsocket, RI

LOCKWOOD Nathaniel of Binghamton, NY
FRY Louisa of Corning, NY
April 6, 1852
Corning, NY

JONES John R.
WISNER Cornelia P.
April 12, 1852
nr Elmira, NY

BONNEL D. of New York City   (Newspaper date)
PEW Adeline of Corning, NY
April 30, 1852

HUDSON George W. of Jackson, Pa.
KEMP Eunice of Jackson, Pa.
April 29, 1852
Southport, NY

DREW James S. of Urbana, NY
CLARK Mary of Urbana, NY
May 13, 1852
Hammondsport, NY

WILLER George of Corning, NY
BRIGGS Matilda of Corning, NY
June 3, 1852
Corning, NY

NEWELL James K. of Corning, NY
HUNT Julia A. dau of Russell Hunt of Corning, NY
June 28, 1852
Corning, NY

BOWERS William of Campbell, NY
CORNELL Elizabeth of Campbell, NY
July 4, 1852
Campbell, NY

CORNELL John B. of Campbell, NY
CARTER Samantha of Campbell, NY
July 4, 1852
Campbell, NY

DAILY Philo B. of Post Creek, NY
STRAIT Mary J. of Post Creek, NY
July 5, 1852
Coopers Plains, NY

THOMAS L. S. of Corning, NY
YOUNG Charlotte R. of Corning, NY
September 8, 1852
Corning, NY

DODGE Charles F. of Owego, NY
SMITH Matilda P. of Corning, NY
September 16, 1852
Corning, NY

ROBINSON J. N. of Corning, NY
BARTON W. A. of Corning, NY
September 5, 1852
Corning, NY

THOMPSON La Rue P. of Corning, NY
HAYT Martha C. dau Dr. J. C. Hayt of Corning, NY
October 6, 1852
Corning, NY

KELLY Ora of Jackson, Pa.
JOHNSON Sarah A. dau of William A. of Corning, NY
October 18, 1852
Corning, NY

MILLER Alanson of Corning, NY
CULVER Louisa of Corning, NY
October 18, 1852
Corning, NY

KELLY Thomas of Blossburg, Pa. October 19, 1852
HAYS Mary of Blossburg, Pa.

SMITH Gilbert of Painted Post, NY October 14, 1852
MILLIGAN Margaret of Elmira, NY Elmira, NY

SPICER D. A. Md. of Greenwood, NY October 7, 1852
MC CLAY A. J. of Greenwood, NY Greenwood, NY

HAVENS Charles W. of Corning, NY October 19, 1852
EMMONS Margaret L. of Corning, NY Corning, NY

DAVIS N. D. of Corning, NY October 28, 1852
WESTCOTT Adelaide M of Caton, NY Wheeler, NY

HAYT William W. of Corning, NY December 23, 1852
HART Mary H. dau William Hart of Corning, NY Corning, NY

ROE Andrew J.of Elmira, NY December 19, 1852
JOHNSTON Lucinda of Caton, NY Caton, NY

POWERS Dyer of Lawrence, Pa. December 30, 1852
WHITNEY Maria D. of Caton, NY Caton, NY

WOOD Lewis (Newspaper date) January 7, 1853
MARTIN Lavina

JENNINGS W. S. January 1, 1853
HALL Mary dau of B. B. Hall Monterey, NY

TUCKER Smith of Avoca, NY January 10, 1853
FOLWELL Hannah Corning, NY

PECK David S. of Avoca, NY January 10, 1853
EDWARDS Emeline Corning, NY

WATKINS Charles December 25, 1852
TAYLOR Louisa Erwin, NY

CHAMBERS William December 27, 1852
CONNELLY Margaret Addison, NY

SMITH William A. December 31, 1852
OTIS Mariette

BILES Filander January 1, 1853
WHITE Elizabeth

WHITE Samuel January 16, 1853
LUCKY Mary Ann

DRUMMOND William B. of Corning, NY	January 23, 1853
WEEKS Mary of Corning, NY	Corning, NY
CAMPBELL John of Erwin, NY	February 2, 1853
JONES Mary Jane of Erwin, NY	
WISNER Jeffrey A. of Elmira, NY	February 2, 1853
GOULD Jeannette dau of A. R. Gould of Bath, NY	Bath, NY
KIMBALL Nathaniel D. of Corning, NY	March 20, 1853
EUNISON Janette of Corning, NY	Corning, NY
BRIGGS Alfred of Corning, NY	March 18, 1853
ELLISON Lucinda of Corning, NY	Corning, NY
BEECHER William H. of Angelica, NY	March 2, 1853
WHITE Helen of Hamburg, NY	Hamburg, NY
MALLORY Milton J. of Knoxville, NY	March 30, 1853
BUCKLEY Laura of Knoxville, NY	Knoxville, NY
ROBBINS I. R. of Horseheads, NY	April 12, 1853
BROWN Catherine of Painted Post, NY	
SPENDLOVE James R. of Geneva, NY	April 16, 1853
OSTRAM Sarah A. of Geneva, NY	Geneva, NY
BARKER Henry J. of Adams, Mass.	May 23, 1853
ADAMS E. of Ransomville, NY	Corning, NY
PRESTON George W. of Corning, NY	June 30, 1853
WEST Amamda R. of Corning, NY	Corning, NY
SANDERSON Charles M. of Corning, NY	June 19, 1853
BURDGE Ann C. of Corning, NY	Corning, NY
GOULD Jacob of Knoxville, NY (Newspaper date)	July 1, 1853
THOMAS Sarah of Knoxville, NY	Big Flats, NY
PERRY William W. formerly of Dresden, NY	June 2, 1853
WHEELER Susan dau of Jno. F. of Ft. Smith, Ark.	Ft. Smith, Ark.
HARVEY Uri of Campbell, NY	July 3, 1853
CORNELL Lucy C. of Campbell, NY	Campbell, NY
TOWNER W.	August 7, 1853
LYON Harriet	Corning, NY
UNDERWOOD Josiah of Hornby, NY	August 4, 1853
GAYLORD Adeline dau of Willis H. of Hornby, NY	Hornby, NY

HAYT William A. of Corning, NY PUGSLEY Eveline	August 24, 1853 Patterson, NY
MOORE Joseph F. of Corning, NY CLARK Adele D. of Corning, NY	August 31, 1853 Corning, NY
BROWN Chauncey of Horicon, Wis. SMITH Ann M. of Kenosha, Wis.	August 9, 1853 Kenosha, Wis.
CALDWELL Edwin of Newark, Wis. HAYT Martha of Patterson, NY	August 25, 1853 Patterson, NY
HALL Alfred A. VAN GELDER Abby Jane dau of Mathew Van Gelder	September 7, 1853 Painted Post, NY
RUSSELL Henry of Caton, NY GORTON Betsey A. of Caton, NY	July 17, 1853 Caton, NY
STARNER John of Elkland, Pa. RICHARDS Mary Ann of Caton, NY	September 1, 1853 Caton, NY
LEAVENWORTH A. E. of Corning, NY GRIGGS Mary A. of Corning, NY	September 14, 1853 Corning, NY
ROWLEY Levi Jr. of Corning, NY FARNHAM Emma	September 14, 1853 Elbridge, NY
CRANE E. Leroy of Woodhull, NY WILLIAMS Frances L. of Woodhull, NY	September 14, 1853 Jasper, NY
EDMISTER William H. of Dryden, NY HATCH Martha E. of Addison, NY	September 10, 1853 Addison, NY
GEORGE Edward E. of Painted Post, NY FREELAND Jane L. of Seneca Falls, NY	September 14, 1853 Seneca Falls, NY
BROWN D. C. of Addison, NY GRISWOLD Susan of Addison, NY	September 26, 1853 Addison, NY
GREEN James of Corning, NY KINNERY Eliza of Addison, NY	September 25, 1853 Addison, NY
HURD Orlando of Watkins, NY TOWNSEND Julia dau of L. G. Townsend of Geneva, NY	September 12, 1853 Geneva, NY
HOOD John D. of Corning, NY CRIST Rebecca R. of Corning, NY	October 9, 1853
EDMISTER Lewis of Big Flats, NY TEETER Mary of Big Flats, NY	October 8, 1853 Corning, NY

SMITH Nathan T.   October 10, 1853
BARROWS Emeline A. dau of Capt. Chester of Buffalo, NY   Corning, NY

VAN DEREN Phillip B. of Elmira, NY   October 10, 1853
GREGG Ellen A. of Elmira, NY   Elmira, NY

PELTON Nelson of Caton, NY   October 2, 1853
GREGORY Amamda C. dau of Orlando of Caton, NY   Caton, NY

ABRAMS George H. of Charleston, Pa.   October 17, 1853
WILKINS Martha dau of William Wilkins of Caton, NY   Caton, NY

BENTLEY Romulus R. of Milport, NY   October 20, 1853
MC GAIREY Elizabeth Teresa of Milport, NY

KIMBALL Nathan H. of Corning, NY   October 27, 1853
LACY Harriet A. of Corning, NY   Corning, NY

MC LEAN George of Lawrence, Pa.   November 1, 1853
LICTENTHALER Effie A. of Lawrence, Pa.   Corning, NY

HAWKINS W. L. of Corning, NY   October 26, 1853
CLOUGH Mary J. of Dover, NH   New York City

MC CEWEN Alexander of Corning, NY   November 3, 1853
MC CARTY Catherine of Knoxville, NY   Corning, NY

KERRICK Cornelius of Hornby, NY   November 3, 1853
ODMAN Hannah of Centreville, NY   Centreville, NY

THROOP Benjamin M. M. of Palmyra, NY   November 30, 1853
WALKER Harriet E. of Corning, NY   Corning, NY

KELLEY Charles of Jackson, Pa.   November 26, 1853
MERRILL Esther of Thurston, NY   Corning, NY

MESSENGER George   October 6, 1853
DAVIES Caroline H. formerly of Athens, Pa.   Troy, Pa.

WEST Charles Francis of Corning, NY   November 18, 1853
GERMAN R. A. of Burdett, NY   Burdett, NY

WOODARD Ephraim of Cohocton, NY   December 8, 1853
ANDREWS Catherine of Cohocton, NY   Corning, NY

BURDICK W. S. of Corning, NY   December 20, 1853
DAVIS Isabella of Corning, NY   Corning, NY

HUG Henry of Corning, NY   January 2, 1854
MAYER Verona of Corning, NY

REED Rial of Campbell, NY	January 3, 1854
MC INTOSH Betsy of Campbell, NY	Corning, NY
KINNEY Charles A. of Hornellsville, NY	December 29, 1853
WILLIAMS Marion of Knowlesville, NY	Knowlesville, NY
HILTON Henry of Hornby, NY	January 1, 1854
REMER Eliza of Hornby, NY	Hornby, NY
POMEROY M. M. of Corning, NY	January 26, 1854
WHEELOCK A. A. of Corning, NY	Corning, NY
ARNOLD Gilbert C. of Green Bay, Wis. formerly of Corning	January 16, 1854
FOSTER Grace C. of Owego, NY	Dapere, Wis.
WILSON George R.	February 5, 1854
WEEKS Sarah	Corning, NY
WALKER Charles B. of Corning, NY	March 2, 1854
TOWNSEND Maria B. of Palmyra, NY	Palmyra, NY
HINGON Stephen of Veteran, NY	February 28, 1854
STURDEVANT Almira of Dix, NY	Dix, NY
BAGLEY H. of Catlin, NY	March 12, 1854
HAM Emeline of Catlin, NY	Catlin, NY
HICKS John of Catlin, NY	March 12, 1854
ROSE Mary of Catlin, NY	Catlin, NY
CRIPPEN Alex	March 12, 1854
WHITNEY Maria of Watkins, NY	
ADAMS Thomas W. of Corning, NY	March 27, 1854
LYON Adelia dau of Asa Lyon formerly of Corning, NY	Keelersville, Mi.
CHERRY James of Lindley, NY	March 15, 1854
BISSELL Helen dau of P. Z. W. Bissell of Sharon, Ct.	Sharon, Ct.
FOSS Aaron	March 20, 1854
LOVE Elizabeth	Corning, NY
MARSHALL James A. of E. Randolph, NY	March 20, 1854
DARLING Mary of Napoli, NY	Corning, NY
HOWARD Stanley R. of Ithaca, NY	March 23, 1854
CAMPBELL Martha of Corning, NY	Corning, NY
THORN Lawrence of Corning, NY	March 28, 1854
CLARK Martha of Horseheads, NY	

HODGE Andrew Jackson of Corning, NY   March 31, 1854
PLATT Mary of Hornby, NY   Hornby, NY

PARKS Joel   March 30, 1854
HARFORD Melissa   Corning, NY

BURTIS James W. of Winnebago, Ill.   April 19, 1854
MORGAN Mrs. Margaret of Mansfield, Pa.   Corning, NY

JOHNSON Henry   April 11, 1854
MC INTOSH Mary E.   Knoxville, NY

PHELPS Elijah of Peoria, Ill.   (Newspaper date) April 28, 1854
HARMON Mary E. of Leroy, NY   Corning, NY

ERNISSE Henry of Corning, NY   April 23, 1854
RIGHTMIRE Mary of Corning, NY   Corning, NY

BARR Thomas of Painted Post, NY   April 26, 1854
KINNEY C. of Painted Post, NY   Painted Post, NY

CLOUGH Ira L. of Pittsfield, Mass.   May 15, 1854
RICE Mary L. of Gibson, NY   Gibson, NY

ROBINSON William W. of Corning, NY   May 24, 1854
VANDERVOORT Jennie of Kinderhook, NY   Kinderhook, NY

DEMING Hiram D. of Lindley, NY   May 24, 1854
COLTON Juliaette of Wellsboro, Pa.   Corning, NY

HARRINGTON A. M. of Jamestown, NY   May 23, 1854
WHITAKER Catherine V. of Jamestown, NY   Nunda, NY

FRAVER Nathaniel   June 4, 1854
BUTTS Elizabeth   Corning, NY

DUMARS R. R. R. of Elmira, NY   June 6, 1854
DAVIDSON M. Henrietta of Elmira, NY   Chemung, NY

RECORD John B. of Knoxville, NY   June 6, 1854
LATTIN Betsey E. of Knoxville, NY

HENSEL John of Knoxville, NY   May 28, 1854
MONROE Helen of Knoxville, NY

WALKER Nelson A. of Corning, NY   June 12, 1854
JACOBS Almira of Corning, NY

WORDEN L. J. of Veteran, NY   June 7, 1854
WORMLEY J. E. of Corning, NY   Corning, NY

HARRIS Orville of Washington Co. NY	June 20, 1854
BOYER Arabella E. dau of Judge Boyer of Painted Post, NY	Painted Post, NY
BELL J. M. of Athens, Pa.	June 22, 1854
SOMERS Helen E. dau of James Somers of Corning, NY	Corning, NY
NORTON J. W. of Phillipsville, NY	July 3, 1854
HOFFMAN C. A. of Phillipsville, NY	Corning, NY
TALLENT D. G. of Corning, NY	July 4, 1854
FRAZER A. D. of York, NY	York, NY
DELAMATER John D. of corning, NY	July 3, 1854
SEAES Sabrina J. of Corning, NY	
SOULE William L. of Farmington, Pa.	July 4, 1854
GILMAN Susana of Painted Post, NY	
ROBINSON Oscar F. of Corning, NY	July 2, 1854
RIGHTMIRE Harriet A. of Corning, NY	
YOUNG Edward T. of Hornellsville, NY	July 12, 1854
MC CONNELL Cornelia of Howard, NY	Howard, NY
HOWELL A. J. of Corning, NY	July 22, 1854
DUNHAM Cally of Farmington, Pa.	Farmington, Pa.
BRADLEY John F. of Elmira, NY	July 19, 1854
WILMARTH Louisa F. of Corning, NY	Binghamton, NY
GLEASON John S. of Wayne, NY	July 29, 1854
BURDGE Deborah of Wayne, NY	
DATES George of Leroy, NY	July 17, 1854
GORTON Frances dau of W. H. of Corning, NY	
ROSA Rev. E. D. late of Troy, Pa.	August 11, 1854
CORY Letitia of Corning, NY	Elmira, NY
MIDDLEBROOK J. H. (Newspaper date)	August 25, 1854
LINDSEY M. L.	Lindley, NY
BARGESS Elwood of Caledonia, NY	August 31, 1854
SINCLAIR Mary of Caledonia, NY	Corning, NY
WOOD Isaac of Corning, NY	September 6, 1854
WELTON Flavilla A. of Weltonville, NY	Weltonville, NY
RHODES Silas R. of Caton, NY	September 6, 1854
OSBORN Amelia A. of Caton, NY	Caton, NY

LOOK Ransom of Bath, NY
HAVENS Elizabeth of Bath, NY

September 10, 1854
Corning, NY

PHELPS Charles R. of Addison, NY
CRUM Ann Augusta of Beaver Dams, NY

September 13, 1854
Beaver Dams, NY

THORN George W. of Ft. Ann, NY
BAILEY Helen P. dau of B. P. of Corning, NY

September 20, 1854
Corning, NY

BURDICK Alanson
FREME Mrs. Elizabeth

September 19, 1854
Corning, NY

KRIEGER Jacob of Corning, NY
KREENER Christina D. of Corning, NY

September 20, 1854

LANE David
WADSWORTH Helen M. of Elmira, NY

September 23, 1854
Corning, NY

PAUL George of Erwin, NY
PHENIS Mary of Erwin, NY

September 25, 1854
Corning, NY

OWEN Sherman W. of Danby, NY
HOLLY Mary Jane of Knoxville, NY

September 22, 1854
Knoxville, NY

MALLORY John of Corning, NY
HOLCOMB Mrs. Lemira of Leroy, Pa.

October 11, 1854
Leroy, Pa.

NUTE Edward of Barrington, Ill.
JEWETT Sylvia A. dau of Thomas Jewett of Hornby, NY

October 5, 1854
Hornby, NY

BIGELOW W. L. of Corning, NY
MALLORY Harriet M. dau of Lauren of Corning, NY

October 18, 1854
Corning, NY

CLARK Roswell of Canisteo, NY
CLARK Mrs. Electa B. of Jerusalem, NY

October 10, 1854
Corning, NY

ROBINSON Carlos D. of Corning, NY
DUNNING Mary of Corning, NY

October 20, 1854
Corning, NY

BURR William of Covington, Pa.
SEYMOUR A. of Corning, NY

November 5, 1854
Corning, NY

PHELPS Andrew J. of Corning, NY
KETCHUM Sarah M. of Harford, NY

November 22, 1854
Harford, NY

YOUNG Clark D. of Horseheads, NY
SOULE Abby of Big Flats, NY

November 18, 1854
Corning, NY

NORTH Theodore of Elmira, NY
BRADLEY Ann of Elmira, NY

December 13, 1854
Elmira, NY

BERRY Spicer S.
REED Olive E. of Corning, NY

December 6, 1854
Caton, NY

NOWLEN George H. of Avon, NY
FOWLER Helen dau of J. W. Fowler

December 26, 1854
Bath, NY

HELMES Ziba of Blakley, Pa.
HOLMES Phebe of Addison, NY

December 25, 1854
Knoxville, NY/Pa.

DAVISON Osmer L. of Catherine, NY
DAVIS Mary Jane of Corning, NY

December 27, 1854
Corning, NY

SMITH Simeon S. of Caton, NY
JENNINGS Harriet N. of Southport, NY

January 1, 1855
Elmira, NY

BLISS Charles of Corning, NY
MILLIGAN Ann of Corning, NY

December 31, 1854
Corning, NY

HICKEY Luke of Oswego, NY
BARRY Honora of Corning, NY

January 2, 1855
Corning, NY

WOLCOTT Charles 3rd of Corning, NY
GILLETT Huldah Jane dau of Aaron H. of Corning, NY

January 1, 1855
Corning, NY

GRAY Orrin D. of Maine, NY
WOLCOTT Margaret of Cameron, NY

January 30, 1855
Cameron, NY

VAN ATTEN Thompson of Newton, NJ
STRUBLE Mary D. of Union, NY

February 3, 1855
Binghamton, NY

RIGHTMIRE Lewis of Corning, NY
EMISSE Elizabeth of Corning, NY

February 11, 1855

PRATT Nelson of Tioga, Pa.
ABBOTT Ann of Tioga, Pa.

March 1, 1855
Corning, NY

TOWNER Oliver R. of Avoca, NY
SQUIRE Sarah J. of Avoca, NY

February 25, 1855
Avoca, NY

FARNUM Rollin
DOUD Emily L.

March 1, 1855
Corning, NY

WOLCOTT John
BERRY Phebe

March 13, 1855
Corning, NY

SMITH Henry D. Jr. of Caton, NY
WESTCOTT Elizabeth C. of Caton, NY

March 13, 1855
Corning, NY

MYRES James D. of Waverly, NY
KRESS Elizabeth of Corning, NY

March 14, 1855
Corning, NY

WALKER John of Howard, NY	March 7, 1855
MARSH Elizabeth L. of Bath, NY	Bath, NY
OWEN Alvin	March 14, 1855
REMINGTON Emily	Painted Post, NY
RICE Daniel O. of Elmira, NY	March 26, 1855
MILES Leonora C. of Elmira, NY	Elmira, NY
DENISON Charles G. of Tioga, Pa.	April 10, 1855
LAND Martha E. dau of Robert Land of Corning, NY	Corning, NY
HAYES James of Corning, NY	April 8, 1855
HAYES Della B. of Corning, NY	
GARDINER Harrison of Wheeler, NY	April 6, 1855
ROBINS Delia of Wheeler, NY	Corning, NY
STEWART Anthony	April 28, 1855
SHERWOOD Ann H.	Corning, NY
HOWELL Sidney B. of Painted Post, NY	May 22, 1855
SWARTWOOD Isabel of Starkey, NY	Starkey, NY
DAY John of Painted Post, NY	May 28, 1855
LINDLEY Abby W. of Dudley, Mass.	Dudley, Mass.
BUCK H. T. of Cortlandville, NY	June 18, 1855
HUNTER Catherine of Corning, NY	Elmira, NY
WOOD Harvey of Caton, NY	July 3, 1855
HARDENBURGH Veletta of Caton, NY	Caton, NY
VAN HORN Welcome of Corning, NY	August 12, 1855
BULLOCK Elizabeth of Corning, NY	Corning, NY
DAWSON Franklin of Caton, NY	August 9, 1855
TREAT Abby R. of Bridgeport, Ct.	
BRIGGS Walter of Middlebury, Pa.	August 20, 1855
GOODWIN Roana of Middlebury, Pa.	Corning, NY
WATTS William of Elmira, NY	July 24, 1855
DWYER Mary of Elmira, NY	Corning, NY
MIDDAUGH Joel of Catlin, NY	August 27, 1855
ALLEN Susan of Ithaca, NY	Corning, NY
HAVILAND James of Cleveland, Oh.	August 20, 1855
HALL Carrie of Cleveland, Oh.	Elmira, NY

EMMONS T. H. of Corning, NY
SQUIRES Janette M. dau of Henry of Kirkwood, NY
September 4, 1855
Kirkwood, NY

BARNARD Charles D. of Corning, NY
GORTON Mary S. of Corning, NY
September 9, 1855
Painted Post, NY

HUNT Smith R. of Corning, NY
MUFFLY Louisa of Coopers Plains, NY
September 9, 1855
Painted Post, NY

HOWARD Albert S. of Painted Post, NY
HORNING Sarah C. of Addison, NY
September 1, 1855
Painted Post, NY

LONG Henry I. of Corning, NY
BLAIR Martha J. dau of John Blair of Seneca Falls, NY
September 17, 1855
Seneca Falls, NY

MARTIN A. J.
PALMER C. I. of Corning, NY
September 23, 1855
Corning, NY

CRESTLEY Francis of Corning, NY
DAILEY Helen of Corning, NY
September 20, 1855
Horseheads, NY

TOMSON Charles Horatio of Corning, NY
JOHNSON Adelaide dau of Thomas A. of Corning, NY
September 26, 1855
Corning, NY

DAVENPORT Scott of Newark, NY
WHEAT Anna E. of Painted Post, NY
September 25, 1855
Painted Post, NY

BURLEY Charles of Corning, NY
WELDEN Maria of Corning, NY
September 28, 1855
Corning, NY

DAVIS Erastus of Caton, NY
HARRISON Mary of Caton, NY
October 3, 1855
Caton, NY

TUTHILL T. Jefferson of Southport, NY
STEELE Charlotte D. of Corning, NY
October 4, 1855
Elmira, NY

KUGH Patrick of Bath, NY late of Ireland
STINSON Jane of Bath, NY
October 8, 1855
Corning, NY

GOLDSMITH Vincent of Erin, NY
JOHNSON Electa of Corning, NY
October 3, 1855
Corning, NY

PHILLIPS L. of Addison, NY
YOUNG Margaret of Addison, NY
October 5, 1855
Lawrenceville, Pa.

PARKER S. J. of Corning, NY
CALHOUN Eliza of Lawrenceville, Pa.
October 2, 1855
Lawrenceville, Pa.

BUNDY Simeon of Horseheads, NY
HARRINGTON Mary M. of Corning, NY
October 9, 1855
Elmira, NY

GOODSELL William B. of Corning, NY	October 8, 1855
CHIDESTER Jane of Corning, NY	Corning, NY
MILAGE Arthur J. of Corning, NY	October 8, 1855
OSBORNE Helen of Horseheads, NY	Corning, NY
MILLARD J. E. of Campbell, NY	October 17, 1855
HAMMOND Hannah D. of Campbell	Campbell, NY
MANDEVILLE Marlon H. of Columbia, SC	November 1, 1855
ARFORD Maria of Corning, NY	Corning, NY
RIGBY William T. of Corning, NY	November 1, 1855
PEARSE Susan of Corning, NY	Avon, NY
BUTTS Joseph of Elmira, NY	November 12, 1855
RILEY Harriet of Caton, NY	Corning, NY
HUBBARD M. S. of Candor, NY	November 13, 1855
DODGE Caroline M. of Corning, NY	Corning, NY
TROUT G. W. of Elmira, NY	November 14, 1855
BECHTOL Rachel of Caton, NY	Caton, NY
CALKINS J. G. of Victor, NY	November 28, 1855
DOWSER Lueena of Painted Post, NY	Painted Post, NY
YOUMANS William C. of Coopers Plains, NY	December 5, 1855
MILLER Betsey C. of Campbell, NY	Campbell, NY
WHITE William S. of Corning, NY	December 17, 1855
STEWART Sylvia M. of Caton, NY	Caton, NY
LITTLEFIELD James W.	December 17, 1855
COUNTERMAN Phebe A. of Corning, NY	Caton, NY
CARPENTER Franklin P. of Campbell, NY	December 23, 1855
GOODRICH Ann Jenette of Campbell, NY	Coopers Plains, NY
GARDNER William H. of Hornby, NY	December 31, 1855
HOLMES Margaret of Homer, NY	Homer, NY
DARLING Hexekiah of Corning, NY	December 26, 1855
MC INTOSH Frances of Corning, NY	Corning, NY
EMERSON Oliver H. of Bath, NY	December 12, 1855
JONES Isabel of Bath, NY	Bath, NY
STRADELLA William	January 1, 1856
WOMBOUGH Pamela dau of Henry of Addison, NY	Addison, NY

COLEMAN Henry O. of Bellona, NY	January 9, 1856
MILES Mrs. Laura of Elmira, NY	Elmira, NY
FREEMAN Richard of Bath, NY	January 9, 1856
GILLETT Elvira L. of Corning, NY	Shiawassee Co. Mi.
KELLY C. B. of Gaines, Pa.	January 7, 1856
BURLEY Isabella J. of Charleston, Pa.	Tioga, Pa.
BURLEY E. R. of Charleston, Pa.	January 7, 1856
CHURCHILL Martha J. of Chatham, Pa.	Tioga, Pa.
HAVENS John B. of Corning, NY	February 1, 1856
BREWER Helen A. of Milport, NY	Horseheads, NY
EDWARDS James of Cameron, NY	February 20, 1856
PATTERSON Caroline of Maumee City, Ph.	Hornellsville, NY
BROWN Michael of San Francisco, Cal.	March 3, 1856
MORRISON Rebecca J. of Granville, Pa.	
MOORE Carlonus of Corning, NY	March 6, 1856
BARBER Lydia Ann of Corning, NY	Corning, NY
PAGE Anthony of Corning, NY	March 4, 1856
VINEGARD Adeline of Corning, NY	Corning, NY
PARKER Rev. James of Hornby, NY	March 6, 1856
HALLIDAY Mrs. Hannah M. of Thurston, NY	Coopers Plains, NY
LYON Jesse of Catherine, NY	March 6, 1856
GAYLORD Elizabeth J. of Penn Yan, NY	Penn Yan, NY
WHITNEY Philou of Horseheads, NY	April 16, 1856
ZEAK Ann Eliza of Horseheads, NY	
SAILES Erastus of Veteran, NY	April 13, 1856
VAN GORDER Catherine of Horseheads, NY	
HILL Charles W. of Caton, NY	April 2, 1856
RILEY Adelia C. of Corning, NY	Corning, NY
HARRISON William C. of Caton, NY	April 27, 1856
GRIDLEY Caroline A. of Caton, NY	Corning, NY
HAYT Sanford of Dryden, NY	May 1, 1856
DANIELS Sarah A. of Hartford, Pa.	Corning, NY
BUNT Simon P. of Colesville, NY	May 9, 1856
KIMBLE Sarah E. of Corning, NY	Hornby, NY

MC KINDLEY John G. of Kenosha, Wis.   April 22, 1856
HALE Harriet P. dau of Samuel Hale of Corning, NY

ROBINSON William of Hornellsville, NY   May 8, 1856
MAYNARD Indiana of Dansville, NY   Hornellsville, NY

MC KAY George M. of Hornellsville, NY   May 11, 1856
BELDEN Cordelia M. dau of Dr. E. of Hornellsville, NY   Hornellsville, NY

ROBINSON Rev. James A. of Hornellsville, NY   May 14, 1856
HALE Sarah T. dau of John K. Hale of Hornellsville, NY   Portland, Me.

OLCOTT Alexander of Corning, NY   May 21, 1856
MALLORY Catherine A. of Corning, NY   Corning, NY

PARKHURST Joel of Elkland, Pa.   May 14, 1856
STEELE Mrs. Martha dau of B. **HARROWER**   Lawrenceville, Pa.

COOPER O. O. of Ceres, NY   May 28, 1856
BUCK H. Jane of Woodhull, NY   Elkland, Pa.

CLARK George B.   June 4, 1856
MAXWELL Harriet E. dau of Thomas Maxwell   Elmira, NY

LOWE U. S. of Elmira, NY   June 11, 1856
BOYNTON Mary Jane dau of Dr. N. of Elmira, NY   Owego, NY

WALTERS Charles   June 10, 1856
BOWER Anna Regina   Corning, NY

SMITH Henry P. of Corning, NY   June 29, 1856
MULLIGAN Eliza of Corning, NY   Corning, NY

BORST John of Painted Post, NY   July 10, 1856
VAN GELDER Nancy of Bath, NY   Kanona, NY

BOOTH A. E. of Mitchellville, NY   July 10, 1856
WYGANT Susan of Painted Post, NY   Kanona, NY

ALDRICH Loring of Addison, NY   July 10, 1856
HOUGHTALING Hulday of Woodhull, NY   Corning, NY

SOUTHARD William H. of Hornby, NY   July 13, 1856
PERRY Ruana of Corning, NY   Corning, NY

BARTON Col. J. L. of Buffalo, NY   July 23, 1856
MANN Mrs. Harriet of Lawrenceville, Pa.   Lawrenceville, Pa.

MIDDAUGH Garret of Big Flats, NY   August 4, 1856
SIMONS Iantha L. of Big Flats, NY   Corning, NY

HUBBELL E. T. of Philadelphia, Pa.   August 14, 1856
BENNETT F. E. of Elmira, NY   Elmira, NY

GIBSON Luke of Prattsburgh, NY   September 4, 1856
PALMER Adeline dau of I. G. Palmer of Corning, NY   Corning, NY

JONES Yost   July 1, 1856
PAUL Lana   Erwin, NY

BARTHOLOMEW James M. of Big Flats, NY   August 31, 1856
BAKER Frances A. of Painted Post, NY   Painted Post, NY

MORRISON W. F. of Rochester, NY   September 9, 1856
WRIGHT Lottie A. dau of Rev. A. Wright of Corning, NY   Corning, NY

FAIRMAN S. B. Editor of Elmira Advertiser   September 4, 1856
NEARING Lois M. dau of Phillip Nearing of Smyrna, NY   Smyrna, NY

CRIDDLE William of Corning, NY   September 16, 1856
COLE Hannah of Corning, NY   Corning, NY

COX John of Veteran, NY   September 18, 1856
BENNETT Margaret of Catherine, NY   Catherine, NY

MALLORY Rev. J. C. of Savona, NY   September 30, 1856
BAKER Mary M. dau of David Baker of Corning, NY   Corning, NY

WELCH Joseph B. of Angelica, NY   September 24, 1856
WELLS Julia dau of Henry Wells of Penn Yan, NY   Penn Yan, NY

MILLS Edwin of Marshall, Mi.   October 2, 1856
BENEDICT Mary A. of Elmira, NY   Elmira, NY

OLCOTT Theodore of Corning, NY   October 2, 1856
MAYNARD Annie H. of Corning, NY   Corning, NY

EVANS John E. of Painted Post, NY   October 8, 1856
PATTERSON Jane Eliza of Lindley, NY at res of Benjamin Patterson

COLE Augustus of Oconto, Wis.   October 9, 1856
DAVIS Frank M. of Poughkeepsie, NY   Poughkeepsie, NY

MESSEREAU Samuel J. of Portville, NY   October 21, 1856
MC ARTHUR Mrs. C. A. of Riga, NY   Riga, NY

WEED Joseph M. of Middlebury, Pa. formerly Havana, NY   October 21, 1856
MITCHELL Mary E. of Tioga, Pa.   Tioga, Pa.

BUSH George W. of Erin, NY   October 20, 1856
HARRINGTON Paulina M. of Horseheads, NY   Horseheads, NY

DIDCOCK Henry D. of Corning, NY   October 29, 1856
WOOSTER Mary M. of Great Valley, NY   Great Valley, NY

KELSEY Edwin S. of Corning, NY   November 5, 1856
HARRISON Nancy M. of Caton, NY   Painted Post, NY

SPAULDING Edwin of Corning, NY   October 29, 1856
MILLER Lucy M. dau of Dr. Miller of Dix, NY   Dix, NY

SIMMONS M. B. of Corning, NY   November 25, 1856
WHITEHEAD Jennie O. of Penfield, NY

HAYT Stephen T. of Corning, NY   November 19, 1856
TOWNSEND Margaret C. dau of Edward S. of Palmyra, NY   Palmyra, NY

GARRETT James K. of Keeseville, NY   November 24, 1856
CHAFFEE Nancy of Corning, NY   Corning, NY

GILLETT George of Caton, NY   November 23, 1856
HOLMES Susan M. of Caton, NY   Caton, NY

WITT Henry of Corning, NY   November 30, 1856
GREEN Jane of Corning, NY   Corning, NY

EMPIE John H. of Middleport, NY   (Newspaper date) December 4, 1856
GRICE Clemantha of Tazewell Co. Ill.   Tremont, Ill.

SAXTON D. W. of St. Catherine, Canada W.   November 19, 1856
WHEELER Celia of Elmira, NY   Elmira, NY

STANCLIFF L. J. of Elmira, NY   November 20, 1856
ELDRICH Julia T. dau of Dr. Eldrich of Southport, NY   Elmira, NY

MAYNARD John of Corning, NY   December 4, 1856
JOHNSON Anna B. dau of T. A. Johnson of Corning, NY   Corning, NY

WOODWORTH Allen   November 20, 1856
SMITH Mandaette dau of H. D. Smith   Caton, NY

COOPER Ezra of Waterford, Pa.   December 15, 1856
RUMSEY Jennie of Kanona, NY   Kanona, NY

MILLER James H. of Jackson, Pa.   December 10, 1856
DUNHAM Martha of Southport, NY   Southport, NY

GILBERT Rufus H. Md.   December 24, 1856
MAYNARD Bertha dau of late John of Auburn, NY   Corning, NY

TURNER David Jr. of Veteran, NY   December 17, 1856
LYON Mary C. of Catherine, NY   Catherine, NY

FORCE David of Jennings Co. Ind.
DAY Mrs. Sarah of Jennings Co. Ind.

December 15, 1856
Tyrone, NY

BUNN Daniel M. of Dix, NY
COOPER Charlotte S. of Corning, NY

December 22, 1856
Corning, NY

CANFIELD E. R. of Portville, NY
RICHARDS Lucretia S. of Caton, NY

December 18, 1856
Caton, NY

REDFIELD J. A. of the Williamsport & Elmira RR
ROSE Anna C. of Auburn, NY

December 24, 1856
Auburn, NY

KENEDA Robert of Corning, NY
WOODRUFF Sarah Jane of Corning, NY

December 26, 1856
Corning, NY

KINNER John B. of Elmira, NY
TROUP Lucy Ann of Painted Post, NY

January 1, 1857
Elmira, NY

SMITH Charles of Gibson, NY
BAKER Roby of Gibson, NY

December 31, 1856
Gibson, NY

KERN Lewis of Lawrenceville, Pa.
HOW Secelia of Lawrenceville, Pa.

January 1, 1857
Painted Post, NY

HILL Henry S. of Peoria, Ill.
KEYS Addie A. dau of Dr. D. C. Keys of Peoria, Ill.

January 3, 1857
Elmwood, Ill.

MOSIER Charles
MARTIN Anna Catherine late of Wellsboro, Pa.

January 9, 1857
Corning, NY

SCHERMER Julius of Corning, NY
MALLORY Mary J. dau of L. Mallory of Corning, NY

January 15, 1857
Corning, NY

LEEPER John W. of Big Flats, NY
CAMPBELL Cordelia of Big Flats, NY

January 18, 1857
Big Flats, NY

ELLIS Elisha of Caton, NY
WELDON Lavina of Corning, NY

January 3, 1857
Caton, NY

MC INTYRE Henry E. of Corning, NY
HATCH Vie T. adopted dau of Capt. W. B. Hatch

February 4, 1857
Bath, NY

BENJAMIN George J. of Ithaca, NY
WELCH Sarah L. of Elmira, NY

February 25, 1857
Elmira, NY

RIPLEY George N. of Corning, NY
GARDNER Harriet E. of Corning, NY

February 25, 1857
Corning, NY

VINCENT Joseph N. of Elmira, NY
SPENCER Polly W. of Corning, NY

March 10, 1857
Corning, NY

MURPHY Charles A.   March 11, 1857
LAWRENCE Jane N. dau of Whitehead Lawrence   Gibson, NY

DAVIS Norris of Caton, NY   March 12, 1857
HILL Mrs. Lucy A. of Mc Donough, NY   Corning, NY

HURD Phineas of York Co. Wis.   March 30, 1857
HAM Almena of Caton, NY   Caton, NY

GILLETT Joseph of Corning, NY   April 8, 1857
THOMAS Eliza of Addison, NY   Addison, NY

CARD Henry J. of Sullivan, Pa.   April 17, 1857
BELKNAP Eliza J. of Sullivan, Pa.   Corning, NY

WOODARD William Md. of Big Flats, NY   May 4, 1857
ELWELL Margaret C. of Big Flats, NY   Elmira, NY

THOMPSON La Rue P. of Corning, NY   May 20, 1857
BEACH Harriet A. of Whitneys Point, NY   Whitneys Point, NY

TUTHILL Henry G. of Corning, NY   May 20, 1857
TOWSLEY Kate A. of Corning, NY   Corning, NY

CASTLE P. H. of Gibson, NY (Wash. Co. papers please copy)May 17, 1857
VAN ETTEN Louisa of Gibson, NY   Coopers Plains, NY

WELLINGTON Quincey W. of Corning, NY   May 13, 1857
WICKHAM Matilda B. of Tioga, Pa.   Tioga, Pa.

HOTCHKIN Samuel   May 19, 1857
GRAY Mary Ann dau of Hiram Gray of Elmira, NY

VAN SCOTER L. B. of Corning, NY   May 26, 1857
GORTON Sarah F. dau of Rufus Gorton of Corning, NY

FINCH J. B. of Hornellsville, NY   May 27, 1857
MATTERSON Ann S. dau of John Matterson of Painted Post, NY

HETFIELD Jacob of Lawrenceville, Pa.   June 5, 1857
CARPENTER Azuba of Horseheads, NY   Horseheads, NY

WHEELER William of Corning, NY   June 13, 1857
GRANT Mary L. of Corning, NY   Corning, NY

ROBINSON Ezekiel L. of Corning, NY   June 11, 1857
BUNNELL Catherine of Elmira, NY

DICKINSON A. B. of Hornby, NY   June 18, 1857
GENUNG Mrs. Abigail of Hornby, NY   Hornby, NY

MINER Charles of Wayland, NY	July 4, 1857
ROOT Ruth A. of Dansville, NY	Corning, NY
VAN GORDER John of Painted Post, NY	July 4, 1857
PECK Sylvina of Corning, NY	
WORTZ Leonard of Painted Post, NY	July 5, 1857
CHERRY Mary of Painted Post, NY	Addison, NY
MC CORD George of Corning, NY	July 8, 1857
MERRICLE Louisa of Corning, NY	Big Flats, NY
SHULTS John B. of Campbell, NY	July 16, 1857
MITCHELL Mrs. C. A. of Caton, NY	Corning, NY
BISHOP Hoyt C. of Corning, NY	July 19, 1857
TRUAX Amelia of Corning, NY	Corning, NY
BURNETT A. H. of Corning, NY	July 29, 1857
SMITH M. J. of Palmyra, NY	Palmyra, NY
WILSON Henry M. of Hinesburg, Vt.	September 3, 1857
GRIGGS Sarah A. of Corning, NY	Corning, NY
TATOR John of Hudson, NY	September 3, 1857
HOW Adeline of Caton, NY	Caton, NY
PLIMPTON Albert M. of Corning, NY	September 19, 1857
METCALF Delia M. of Corning, NY	Corning, NY
PHELPS Lorenzo D. of Corning, NY	September 18, 1857
BELCHER Mrs. Anna of Corning, NY	Corning, NY
GARABRANT Richard of Elmira, NY	September 19, 1857
HOFFMAN Saloma of Geneva, NY	Corning, NY
FOREST William E. of Minneapolis, Mn.	September 24, 1857
HUY Margaret of Big Flats, NY	Big Flats, NY
YOUNG Sylvester of Painted Post, NY	September 27, 1857
ZIMMERMAN Mary E. of Painted Post, NY	
HOLLENBECK Joseph of Corning, NY	October 1, 1857
FOWLER Martha of Corning, NY	
SOUTHARD Philander G. of Catlin, NY	October 3, 1857
SMITH Adelia of Big Flats, NY	
PARKS Alonzo of Corning, NY	October 17, 1857
MORGAN Mrs. Lana of Corning, NY	Corning, NY

SECOR Adam of Savannah, NY   October 22, 1857
KNAPP Harriet A. of Corning, NY   Corning, NY

BROWN Delos of Poals Brook, NY   (Newspaper date) November 5, 1857
DICKENS Angeline of Gibson, NY   Corning, NY

BURROWS Josiah T. of Campbell, NY   November 25, 1857
NUTE Amanda dau of M C. Nute of Campbell, NY Campbell, NY

BEVIER W. of Caton, NY   November 10, 1857
DEAN Mrs. Betsy of Caton, NY   Caton, NY

WOLCOTT Charles N. of Caton, NY   November 25, 1857
VAN ORSDALE Isabel formerly of Ithaca, NY   Caton, NY

JEFFRIES K. A. formerly of Corning, NY   (Newspaper date)November 26, 1857
KIMBALL Alice of Corning, NY   Detroit, Mi.

MURRAY John of Hornby, NY   November 21, 1857
KING Jane Ann of Hornby, NY   Hornby, NY

POWER Dyer   November 18, 1857
SEELEY Marion L. of Lindley, NY   Lindley, NY

HARRINGTON Cornelius of Addison, NY   November 30, 1857
CONSTABLE Mary E. of Tompkins, NY   Corning, NY

ARMSTRONG W. Albert of Hornby, NY   December 3, 1857
CARTER H. Maria of Elmira, NY   Elmira, NY

DAYTON Erastus of Catlin, NY   December 10, 1857
WOOLSEY Filetta A. of Catlin, NY   Big Flats, NY

SMITH J. M. of Corning, NY   December 30, 1857
SORNBERGER Mrs. C. A. of Corning, NY   Corning, NY

DE MUNN Mathias T. of Trumansburg, NY   January 5, 1858
DEARMAN Jennie of Corning, NY   Corning, NY

THOMPSON Andrew of Gibson, NY   January 1, 1858
VAN ETTEN Susan of Gibson, NY   Big Flats, NY

BROWN Prof. A. K. formerly of Otsego Co. NY   December 31, 1857
WHEELOCK Marion dau of M. M. late of Corning, NY   Lock haven, Pa.

MOREHOUSE Gideon of Campbell, NY   January 1, 1858
READ Jane of Campbell, NY   Coopers Plains, NY

THOMAS George W. of Ottawa, Ill.   January 7, 1858
TAYLOR Martha of Caton, NY   Corning, NY

HOWE James T. of Corning, NY   (Newspaper date) January 21, 1858
WHITMAN Sarah of Sullivan, Pa.   Lisle, NY

WILLIAMS H. N. of Woodhull, NY   January 22, 1858
AUSTIN Lucy A. of Wellsboro, Pa.   Wellsboro, Pa.

EATON Henry of Hornby, NY   February 18, 1858
DUNHAM Cornelia A. of Breesport, NY   Breesport, NY

WESTCOTT Edwin   February 27, 1858
CLEMENS Martha   Addison, NY

JONES B. R. of Big Flats, NY   March 12, 1858
SMITH Margaret of Cameron, NY

TOOKER Prof. D. T. of Belfast, NY   March 18, 1858
NUTTEN Mary J. dau of Rev. D. Nutten   Hornellsville, NY

LEWIS Julius M. of Caton, NY   March 17, 1858
COOPER Mary F. dau of Anson formerly of Corning, NY   Caton, NY

JOHNSON Augustus of Caton, NY   March 23, 1858
QUAKENBUSH Jane of Caton, NY   Caton, NY

CROTZER Andrew J. of Mifflinburg, Pa.   March 24, 1858
SOMERS Antoinette dau of Charles C. Somers   Lawrenceville, Pa.

BROWN Lyman of Caton, NY   March 27, 1858
LUCE Ada Eliza of Corning, NY   Painted Post, NY

STURDEVANT Estes A. of Hornellsville, NY   March 29, 1858
BROWN Elmina R. of Erwin, NY   Hornellsville, NY

HOGG Samuel of E. Maine, NY   April 7, 1858
HARE Mary Jane of Centerville, NY   Centerville, NY

GALLUP Rufus B. of Corning, NY   April 16, 1858
BLAIN Phebe Ann of Corning, NY   Corning, NY

BULMER John of Corning, NY   April 21, 1858
TERWILLIGER Elvira A. dau of A. of Preble, NY   Preble, NY

WILKINS Charles of Caton, NY   April 14, 1858
RILEY Maria E. of Caton, NY   Caton, NY

WESTON Wallace W.   May 3, 1858
MERSEREAU Harriet E. dau of J. G. of Portville, NY   Portville, NY

RICHARDS George   May 11, 1858
SMITH Lucinda R. dau of Titus Smith of Caton, NY   Caton, NY

PRIEST Carlton	May 16, 1858
HOWE Eveline A. dau of William P. Howe of Caton, NY	Caton, NY
JOHNSON Chalres N. of Buffalo, NY	June 1, 1858
MURPHY Fanny L. of Corning, NY	Corning, NY
TANNER John of Centerville, NY	June 13, 1858
TEYLEUR Ann of Centerville, NY	Centerville, NY
SMITH James M. C. of Plainfield, NJ	June 28, 1858
PAYNE Persis of Corning, NY	Corning, NY
ATWOOD Abraham of Catlin, NY	July 4, 1858
LIVINGSTON Betsy of Catlin, NY	Catlin, NY
REASOR William of Big Flats, NY	July 6, 1858
BAILEY Phebe Ann of Big Flats, NY	Big Flats, NY
REDFIELD Martin of Milwaukee, Wis.	July 24, 1858
HOFFMAN Minnie of Milwaukee, Wis.	Milwaukee, Wis.
MATHEWS George of Corning, NY	August 29, 1858
WHEELER Harriet of Corning, NY	Corning, NY
WILBUR Harrie O. of Corning, NY	September 1, 1858
LAWRENCE Hattie A. of Pepperell, Mass.	Pepperell, Mass.
CLAY Nathaniel J. of Conquest, NY	September 11, 1858
CRAWFORD Susan J. of Waverly, NY	Corning, NY
HOUGH Edwin H. of Hornellsville, NY	September 11, 1858
LOOK Emma B. of Prattsburgh, NY	Prattsburgh, NY
HOLMES Isaac of Shippen, Pa.	October 20, 1858
BROUGHTON Amelia of Shippen, Pa.	Wellsboro, Pa.
COLE C. S. of Corning, NY	November 2, 1858
WHEAT Addie of Painted Post, NY	Painted Post, NY
HAINZER Joakim	November 1, 1858
WEBSTER Ann	Corning, NY
BOUGHTON Henry M. of Campbell, NY	November 4, 1858
BROWN Alice M. of Campbell, NY	Campbell, NY
NEWMAN Asa E. of Addison, NY	November 9, 1858
WING Mrs. Lydia F. of Campbell, NY	Coopers Plains, NY
ANGELL Frank M. of Hornellsville, NY	November 10, 1858
MORILL C. A. of Hornellsville, NY	Hornellsville, NY

STORY Joseph T. of Hornellsville, NY
MC GOWAN Margaret of Hornellsville, NY

November 10, 1858
Hornellsville, NY

KING Samuel of Wellsboro, Pa.
ROOT Maria L. of Wellsboro, Pa.

November 18, 1858
Corning, NY

SHARP Rev. William of Hornby, NY
MASTERS Cynthia A. dau of N. Masters of Hornby, NY

November 18, 1858
Hornby, NY

PRITCHARD T. S. of Corning, NY
MC CARTY Mary W. dau of William of Corning, NY

December 1, 1858
Corning, NY

WEEKS Charles of Corning, NY
GORTON Lydia of Corning, NY

January 19, 1859
Corning, NY

BENTLEY Daniel T. of Beaver Dams, NY
MILLS Catherine of Beaver Dams, NY

January 30, 1859
Beaver Dams, NY

RHODES John of Dix, NY
CALKINS Mahala J. of Dix, NY

February 10, 1859
Corning, NY

JORALEMON John H. of Columbia, Pa.
BROWN Ambrosia of Painted Post, NY

February 13, 1859
Wellsboro, Pa.

SEELEY Charles of Southport, NY
MC INTOSH Mahala of Big Flats, NY

February 22, 1859

WORMLEY Simeon L. of Corning, NY
HUBBARD Lucy A. of Caton, NY

February 27, 1859
Caton, NY

KIBLER Anthony of Corning, NY
MINEN Mary of Rochester, NY

March 8, 1859
Corning, NY

COBB M. H.
BIGBY Betsy O.

March 3, 1859
Wellsboro, Pa.

GALLUP William H. of Corning, NY
CLING Mariah of Corning, NY

March 22, 1859
Corning, NY

CONOVER Daniel R. of Hornby, NY
SHULTS Nancy M. of Hornby, NY

March 30, 1859
Hornby, NY

GREEN William Md.
MILLS Kate H. dau of Rev. Sidney Mills

April 13, 1859
Lawrenceville, Pa.

MILLARD W. O. of Campbell, NY
CROUCH Mary S. of Carroll Co. Ill.

March 31, 1859
Carroll Co. Ill.

NORTON Edward D. of the Ithaca Journal Office
CARR Aramintha C. of Ithaca, NY

May 24, 1859
Ithaca, NY

NORTON George W.
KELSEY Sarah M.
May 19, 1859
Olean, NY

DAVISON J. B. of Caton, NY
PECK Miranda of Reading, NY
May 16, 1859
Reading, NY

GILBERT Horace E. of Caton, NY
DEYO Eunice of Caton, NY
May 26, 1859
Caton, NY

HENDERSON James A. of New York City
MASON Mrs. Harriet T. of Portland, Me.
May 18, 1859
Addison, NY

WHEAT John L. of Louisville, Ky. late of Corning, NY
FELLOWS Mary E. dau of Rev. Nathan of Rochester, NY
May 17, 1859
Rochester, NY

CADY Franklin of Dix, NY
ADSIT Sophia of Hornby, NY
May 31, 1859
Corning, NY

BOYNTON Edwin M. Md. formerly of Elmira, NY
MORRISON Winnie of Vallejo, Cal.
April 25, 1859
San Francisco, Cal.

STEERE E. P.
MERSEREAU Anna
June 1, 1859
Tioga, Pa.

WALKER William of Corning, NY
BOSTWICK Helen C. of Corning, NY
June 16, 1859
Corning, NY

HUNGERFORD John N. of Corning, NY
GANSEVOORT Mary W. dau of late Dr. Teneyck Gansevoort of Bath, NY
June 22, 1859

SEELEY Dr. N. R. of Corning, NY
STUART Mary C. of Painted Post, NY
June 22, 1859
Painted Post, NY

SWEENEY James of Urbana, NY
LOUCKS Amelia of Erwin, NY
June 17, 1859
Corning, NY

LAMBERT W. M. of Burdett, NY
MC ELHENNY Isabelle J. dau of Rev. T. of Burdett, NY
July 4, 1859
Burdett, NY

AUSTIN Richard of Corning, NY
FORBES Isabella of Corning, NY
July 27, 1859
Corning, NY

WILEY David of Woodhull, NY
HUGGINS Maria of Willing, NY
August 9, 1859
Corning, NY

GREEK Henry H. of Corning, NY
MARTIN Eleanor E. dau of Jacob Martin of Corning, NY
August 18, 1859
Corning, NY

COOLEY Levi J. of Elmira, NY
CARPENTER Mrs. E. A. dau of Jonathan **BLAKE**
August 23, 1859
Owego, NY

(formerly of Springfield, Mass.)

DARRIN Knapp of Lansing, Mi.	August 31, 1859
COOK Jane A. of Hornellsville, NY	Addison, NY
YOUNG Hugh the Editor Tioga Co. Agitator	September 22, 1859
BUTTERWORTH L. A. of Coudersport, Pa.	Coudersport, Pa.
WAY J. H. of Corning, NY	October 16, 1859
PEW Augusta of Corning, NY	Berien, Mi.
TUPPER John of Corning, NY	October 17, 1859
COWAN Adelia M. of Corning, NY	Caton Ctr. NY
BRAGG Frederick S. of Corning, NY	October 30, 1859
WARNER Mary of Corning, NY	Corning, NY
HARROWER Col. G. T. of Lindley, NY	November 5, 1859
PARKHURST Helen dau of Dr. Parkhurst of Lawrenceville	Lawrenceville, Pa.
BALCOM Benjamin of Campbell, NY	November 16, 1859
CUNKLEE Eliza Malvina of Campbell, NY	Coopers Plains, NY
HOBER Frederick C.	November 20, 1859
WOMBOUGH Eliza dau of Henry Wombough	Addison, NY
PACKER James M. of the Corning Journal Office	November 28, 1859
CHAPMAN Helen D. dau of Ichabod of Humphrey, NY	Corning, NY
TERWILLIGER A. H. of Corning, NY	December 6, 1859
PHELPS Martha E. dau of H. G. Phelps of Corning, NY	Corning, NY
RHOADES Lyman of Auburn, NY	December 13, 1859
ROBINSON Barbara C. dau of R. E. of Corning, NY	Corning, NY
STEPHENS William B. of Fremont, NY	December 8, 1859
VAN SCOTER Samantha A. of Hornellsville, NY	Corning, NY
CUSHMAN C. M. (Newspaper date)	December 22, 1859
CLARK Emeline S. dau of Charles formerly of Corning, NY	Minneapolis, Mn.
HIBBARD Solon A. of Williamsport, Pa.	December 26, 1859
VREDENBURGH Elizabeth of Rathbone, NY	Corning, NY
CHAPMAN Hiram of Watkins, NY	January 4, 1860
WOLCOTT Mrs. Ann M. of Gibson, NY	Corning, NY
DRAKE Philo S. of Painted Post, NY	January 2, 1860
GILLETT Diadama of Corning, NY	

RUMSEY Charles W. of Thurston, NY   December 25, 1859
JACK Rachel J. of Thurston, NY   Savona, NY

STOTENBUR John A. of Havana, NY   December 31, 1859
PATCHIN Frank M. of Granville, Pa.   Savona, NY

AUSTIN James of Sonora, NY   January 2, 1860
WOODRUFF Phebe of Mt. Washington, NY   Savona, NY

COOPER William W. of Washington DC   January 5, 1860
REYNOLDS Ellen J. dau of Nathan Reynolds of Elmira, NY   Elmira, NY

SYMONDS James of Thurston, NY   December 14, 1859
COSS Sarah Jane of Bath, NY   Bath, NY

SPENCER Frank of Thurston, NY   January 7, 1860
STOCUM Susan L. of Cameron, NY   Thurston, NY

HOLLIS Eugene T. of Addison, NY   January 25, 1860
SHERMAN Loretta of Addison, NY

HARRADON Horatio B. of Hornby, NY   February 2, 1860
CASE Frances D. of Corning, NY   Corning, NY

DEWERLETS John of Elmira, NY   February 12, 1860
PRINCE Erndst of Coopers Plains, NY   Coopers Plains, NY

HOLSON Francis of Seneca, NY   February 13, 1860
RUSSELL Fannie of Coopers Plains, NY   Coopers Plains, NY

MAYNARD Charles of Geneva, NY   February 19, 1860
SHAPPIE Elmira of Wellsburg, NY   Corning, NY

PATTERSON Alfred D. of Painted Post, NY   March 5, 1860
MC GRATH Ada of Painted Post, NY   Painted Post, NY

STORMS Asa of Big Flats, NY   March 18, 1860
PHILLIPS Ann R. of Big Flats, NY   Painted Post, NY

FRANCISCO Hiram   March 20, 1860
PIESTER Fanny   Corning, NY

KNAPP Hiram of Hopewell, NY   March 27, 1860
BERRY Lizzie E. of Caton, NY

HOWELL Daniel E.   March 20, 1860
MINIER Fatima   Big Flats, NY

LAWRENCE Montivill of Tioga, Pa.   March 26, 1860
COLESTOCK Helen of Tioga, Pa.   Corning, NY

CRANDALL Robert F. of Corning, NY	April 4, 1860
DODGE Marion of Corning, NY	Corning, NY
WILSON William J. of Knoxville, NY	April 7, 1860
WELDEN Mary Jane of Knoxville, NY	Knoxville, NY
PRATT Daniel R.	April 11, 1860
MURDOCK Isabella G. dau of Rev. Murdock of Elmira, NY	Elmira, NY
WOLCOTT Timothy S. of Caton, NY	April 3, 1860
TORREY Adelia L. dau of Amaziah Torrey of Caton, NY	Caton, NY
MINAR Shubael P. of Caton,NY	April 1, 1860
RATHBONE Julia of Caton, NY	Caton, NY
WOLCOTT W. M. of Caton, NY	April 17, 1860
LEWIS Julia E. of Caton, NY	
TIFFANY J. M. of Norwich, NY	April 11, 1860
HERRICK Hannah M. dau of G. W. Herrick of Corning, NY	Corning, NY
DE WITT Orlando of Corning, NY	April 26, 1860
KING Adeline of Corning, NY	Knoxville, NY
HART William of Phildelphia, Pa. formerly Corning, NY	April 25, 1860
PORTER Mrs. Mary of Farmington, Ct.	Farmington, Ct.
MILLER G. B. of Caton, NY	May 23, 1860
TOBEY Mary of Caton, NY	Caton, NY
GORTON Peleg of Corning, NY	May 24, 1860
BURNAP Eliza of Hornby, NY	Hornby, NY
COBB James of Gang Mills, NY	June 11, 1860
WHIPPLE Mary M. of Beartown, NY	Painted Post, NY
THOMPSON Henry of Thurston, NY	June 10, 1860
MACKEEL Mary A. of Thurston, NY	Savona, NY
KNAPP Duran of Addison, NY	June 18, 1860
YOUNG Elizabeth of Addison, NY	Corning, NY
BROOMHALL Henry of Corning, NY	June 18, 1860
YOUNG Hannah of Addison, NY	Corning, NY
BRAZEE Abram of Corning, NY	June 8, 1860
MC CANN Fanny of Corning, NY	Corning, NY
BRASTED Levi W. of Howard, NY	July 2, 1860
KIMBALL Lydia A. of Catlin, NY	Corning, NY

DEAN Oliver S. Princepal of Towanda Academy   July 12, 1860
KELLOGG Mrs. Anna C. dau of James **COOPER**   Corning, NY

MORRISON William of Gibson, NY   July 11, 1860
HUNT Martha L. of Gibson, NY   Elmira, NY

FRENCH Edwin of Corning, NY   July 8, 1860
DAVIS Cynthia Ann dau of Norris Davis of Caton, NY   Caton, NY

PIERSON Lucius C.   August 8, 1860
BRIGGS Charlotte of Cameron, NY   Corning, NY

STEWART Myron of Lawrenceville, Pa.   August 18, 1860
MYERS Betsy of Lawrenceville, Pa.   Caton, NY

GORTON Rufus Jr. of Corning, NY   September 10, 1860
RICHARDS Theresa E. of Caton, NY   Caton, NY

BACON Lewis of Caton, NY   September 13, 1860
ASHTON Emma of Caton, NY   Caton, NY

LIPPS Henry   September 16, 1860
BAKER Louisa   Knoxville, NY

YOUNG J. F. of Painted Post, NY   September 24, 1860
FREEMAN Delia of Corning, NY

DEYO Alonzo   October 3, 1860
COOPER Charlotte M. of Caton, NY   Caton, NY

BAKER Zury of Lawrenceville, Pa.   (Newspaper date) October 11, 1860
PETSLEY Catherine of Lawrenceville, Pa.   Corning, NY

PARKHURST P. D. of Mainesburg, Pa.   September 20, 1860
YOUNG S. Ophelia of Painted Post, NY   Painted Post, NY

SMITH William J. of Corning, NY   October 23, 1860
TIFFANY Elizabeth of Jamestown, NY   Tiffanyville, NY

HOWE Jervis P. of Caton, NY   October 25, 1860
COLE Elizabeth J. of Caton, NY   Caton, NY

STANLEY Newton G. of Stanley Corners, NY   October 31, 1860
RENIFF Mrs. Lucinda of Corning, NY   Corning, NY

ROSE David of Corning, NY   October 31, 1860
BUNKER Adeline of Corning, NY

WELCH Charles of Cayuga Co. NY   November 3, 1860
STEVENS Hannah B. of Corning, NY   Corning, NY

BEACH J. T. of Dansville, NY
HAINES Annie of Dansville, NY

November 7, 1860

DECKER George of Corning, NY
STEVENS Charlotte of Corning, NY

November 3, 1860
Corning, NY

KNIGHT George of Bath, NY
BIDWELL Mary of Bath, NY

November 14, 1860
Painted Post, NY

SAGE John B.of Southport, NY
STREETER Esther E. of Southport, NY

November 15, 1860
Caton, NY

HOSIER Henry of Rochester, NY
BABCOCK Amanda H. of Centerville, NY

December 3, 1860
Corning, NY

CLARK David H. of Mansfield, Pa.
KELTZ Catherine of Lawrenceville, Pa.

December 4, 1860
Corning, NY

TUTTLE John of Dix, NY
GRANT Mary of Corning, NY

December 8, 1860
Corning, NY

CORNELL Samuel J. of Campbell, NY
DEAN Catherine M. of Campbell, NY

October 20, 1860
Savona, NY

CROMER James of Thurston, NY
EDSALL Maria of Thurston, NY

November 27, 1860
Savona, NY

LEWIS Isaac S. of Mt. Washington, NY
LINDSLEY Mary of Mt. Washington, NY

December 6, 1860
Savona, NY

EMMONS T. H. of Corning, NY
HARROWER N. A. dau of John of Farmington, Pa.

December 12, 1860
Lindley, NY

WORMLEY John G.
BURROWS Mary E. of Big Flats, NY

December 20, 1860
Corning, NY

COLBY Henry H. of Corning, NY
BARTON Emma J. of Corning, NY

December 25, 1860
Corning, NY

CLARK George M. of Corning, NY
MALLORY Minerva of Knoxville, NY

December 24, 1860

HUNT Thadeus E. of Corning, NY
BRAGG Elizabeth E. of Corning, NY

December 9, 1860
Rochester, NY

MC BURNEY John Jr. of Corning, NY
SEAMAN Mary A. of Knoxville, NY

December 25, 1860
Knoxville, NY

ELLISON Nelson J.
FOWLER Caroline R.

December 31, 1860

CUNNINGHAM Mc Leod W. of Corning, NY   December 31, 1860
FOWLER Catherine A. of Corning, NY   Corning, NY

WOODRUFF Ezra of Erwin, NY   January 4, 1861
FOOT Angeline of Addison, NY

CURLEY Fred of Corning, NY   January 6, 1861
SNYDER Julia Ann of Corning, NY

WEAVER Peter of Southport, NY   November 7, 1860
BROOKS Sarah E. of Southport, NY   Southport, NY

BOWERS George   December 15, 1860
WEAVER Emily of Southport, NY   Southport, NY

TOBEY J. W. of Caton, NY   January 6, 1861
RANSOM Jennett of Groveland, NY

MC KINNEY Jesse of Elmira, NY   January 23, 1861
SWEET Mary E. dau of Rev. Sweet late of Chemung, NY   Addison, NY

PAYNE Alvin T. of Corning, NY   January 31, 1861
BROWN Martha dau of Esek A. Brown of Caton, NY   Caton, NY

BROWN Augustus of Erwin, NY   February 2, 1861
WOODRUFF Susan of Erwin, NY   Corning, NY

ROBINSON O. J. of Corning, NY   February 13, 1861
FULTON Carrie C. of Stanleys Corners, NY   Stanleys Corners, NY

TOWNSEND L. G. of Geneva, NY   (Newspaper date) February 21, 1861
BRADLEY Mrs. Julia A. of Corning, NY   Corning, NY

SHEPHERD Charles of Lindley, NY   February 14, 1861
COOK Phebe A. of Lindley, NY   Painted Post, NY

WELDEN David of Corning, NY   February 27, 1861
BRIGGS Sybil of Corning, NY   Caton, NY

WATROUS Charles B. of Tioga Co. Pa.   February 21, 1861
HURD Harriet of Caton, NY   Caton, NY

WALDON Hiram of Caton, NY   February 24, 1861
WESTCOTT Gertrude P. of Caton, NY

TOBEY Edwin   March 6, 1861
CLARK Louisa

NEWTON George of Corning, NY   March 6, 1861
TALLMADGE Irena of Woodhull, NY   Woodhull, NY

CRAWFORD James M. of Rathbone, NY	March 17, 1861	
STURDEVANT Alice M. of Hornellsville, NY	Hornellsville, NY	
AUSTIN Isaiah of Campbell, NY	March 24, 1861	
BREWER Mrs. Elizabeth of Campbell, NY	Campbell, NY	
BILLINGTON M. L. of Savona, NY	February 21, 1861	
CLARK Eliza M. of Campbell, NY	Savona, NY	
ADAMS John D. of Bath, NY	March 12, 1861	
NILES Viorna E. of Bath, NY	Bath, NY	
BROWN Jerome of Corning, NY	March 20, 1861	
LEE Charlotte of Campbell, NY	Savona, NY	
RHODES P. Watson of Troy formerly of Bath, NY	March 26, 1861	
SUTTON Allie of Troy, NY/Pa.		
COLE Harvey of Post Creek, NY	March 20, 1861	
HUMPHREY Elizabeth J. of Hornby, NY	Hornby, NY	
WENTZ H. M. of Binghamton, NY	April 9, 1861	
REESE Louise M. of Gibson, NY	Corning, NY	
BUNDY E. D. of Corning, NY	April 24, 1861	
DOLIVER Orcelia J. of Corning, NY	Caton, NY	
HARRINGTON Nelson B. of Knoxville, NY	April 22, 1861	
MERRICK Maria F. of Knoxville, NY	Corning, NY	
EDWARDS H. S. of Knoxville, NY	April 25, 1861	
QUAKENBUSH Arietta V. of Knoxville, NY	Knoxville, NY	
FAY W. W. of Painted Post, NY	June 12, 1861	
HURLBURT Maggie L. dau of H. M. of Corning, NY	Elmira, NY	
PRESTON George W.	July 31, 1861	
BURTON Electa Ann dau of G. E. of Corning, NY	Corning, NY	
SAWYER Sylvester R. of Campbell, NY	July 20, 1861	
GRIDLEY Mary E. of Caton, NY	Caton, NY	
GRAY Guy of Big Flats, NY	August 11, 1861	
CATLIN Sarah M. of Big Flats, NY	Corning, NY	
SOULE Charles H. of Corning, NY	August 18, 1861	
PATCHEN Hattie A. of Elmira, NY	Elmira, NY	
PATTERSON George W. Jr. of Corning, NY	September 17, 1861	
TODD Frances D. of Corning, NY	Corning, NY	

MYERS James P. of Bradford, NY
COOK Alice of Wayne, NY

September 12, 1861
Savona, NY

RICHARDSON John of Bradford, NY
GOBLE Eliza Jane of Bradford, NY

September 15, 1861
Savona, NY

HUKE George D. of Geneva, NY
HAVENS Mary J. of Corning, NY

September 25, 1861
Corning, NY

WILSON John of Corning, NY
MURRAY Annie E. dau of Capt. Thomas Murrey of Corning

October 10, 1861
Corning, NY

STEWART Edwin S. of Corning, NY
BROAKMAN Lavina M. dau of Rev. S. M.

October 15, 1861
Caton, NY

BONHAM Amos of Caton, NY
TOBEY Mrs. Nancy M. of Caton, NY

October 16, 1861
Caton, NY

DENNINGTON Moody of Clyde, NY
CALKINS Louisa of Corning, NY

October 24, 1861
Corning, NY

VAN ALSTINE Stewart R. of Farmerville, NY
ROBINSON Henrietta C. of Corning, NY

October 29, 1861
Corning, NY

MC DONALD G. E. of S. Livonia, NY
HILL Sarah L. dau of Rev. H. F. of Corning, NY

November 6, 1861
Corning, NY

ERWIN Eugene H.
COOK Elizabeth at res of James Cook

November 13, 1861
Erwin, NY

COOK Ralph of Erwin, NY
SMITH Mary L. of Erwin, NY

November 13, 1861

WING Thomas of Caton, NY
SHEPARD Mrs. Maria L. of Milford, NY

November 17, 1861
Caton, NY

BAILEY Clarence P. son of Col. B. P. Bailey
ROBINSON Kate E. dau of R. E. late of Corning, NY

November 20, 1861
Brookfield, Mo.

FAY H. G. Md. of Painted Post, NY
FENDERSON Mrs. Amanda M. of Painted Post, NY

October 17, 1861
Savona, NY

VELIE Franklin of Campbell, NY
HOLLENBECK Emily of Campbell, NY

October 19, 1861
Savona, NY

LONGWELL Hosea Jr. of Bradford, NY
COLE Mary C. of Bradford, NY

November 13, 1861
Bradford, NY

BANCROFT Harrington of Thurston, NY
EDSALL Sarah Catherine of Thurston, NY

November 25, 1861
Savona, NY

ROWLEY Charles K. of Caton, NY — December 4, 1861
FRANKLIN Esther of Campbell, NY — Corning, NY

SMITH Andy L. of Hornellsville, NY — December 12, 1861
TRAVER Mrs. Eliza T. widow of Dr. Robert M. of Painted Post, NY

ROBINSON W. H. of Corning, NY — December 21, 1861
PLATT Lucy E. of Havana, NY — Corning, NY

LILLY Edward of Susquehanna, Pa. — December 24, 1861
KETCHUM Lucy M. of Corning, NY — Corning, NY

KENYON Menzo A. of Corning, NY — December 31, 1861
TRAVER Ella of Corning, NY

BAKER Lt. Arthur S. of the 86th Reg. — December 25, 1861
PATTENGILL Leona H. dau of Rev. H. late of Hornellsville, NY

HOLLENBECK Joseph of Corning, NY — January 5, 1862
HUNT Sarah dau of Thomas of Caton, NY — Caton, NY

CALKINS Charles T. of Owego, NY — January 9, 1862
SAWYER Roena P. of Owego, NY — Corning, NY

ATKINSON Frank H. — January 15, 1862
DUNN Helen Mar dau of Judge Dunn — Elmira, NY

BURTON Marshall G. of Corning, NY — February 5, 1862
KELLY Marion dau of Joel of Corning, NY — Corning, NY

GANNON Ansel of Bradford, NY — February 25, 1862
WIXSON Hannah of Friendship, NY — Corning, NY

JACOBS Alonzo of Corning, NY — March 29, 1862
RICE Cynthia of Corning, NY

STONE D. F. of Wellsboro, Pa. — April 16, 1862
BARLOW Carrie L. of Charleston, Pa. — Charleston, Pa.

HEWLITT William J. of Corning, NY — April 26, 1862
GRINNELL Olive Frances of Corning, NY — Corning, NY

HEATH Harrison of Corning, NY — April 24, 1862
GRINNELL Angeline of Corning, NY

RHODES Thomas H. of Caton, NY — May 1, 1862
DE WATERS Sarah of Caton, NY — Caton, NY

BURLEIGH Ithiel A. of Gibson, NY — May 11, 1862
SPENCER Sarah E. of Gibson, NY

MILLS Ellsworth D. of New York City	May 21, 1862
WELLINGTON A. Eliza sister of Q. W. of Corning, NY	Corning, NY
SHECKLES R. L. S.	May 22, 1862
READER Christianna	Corning, NY
FRYMIRE Samuel of Corning, NY	June 3, 1862
MUMFORD R. L. dau of Dr. O. of Corning, NY	Corning, NY
GILBERT Horace E. of Caton, NY	June 5, 1862
GRIDLEY Jennie C. dau of Lewis of Caton, NY	Caton, NY
GREEN James of Chemung, NY	June 6, 1862
EAMS Mary of Chemung, NY	Corning, NY
WHEELER Elias of Corning, NY	June 8, 1862
GREGORY Betsey of Savona, NY	
BEACH Daniel	June 4, 1862
MAGEE Angelina C. dau of Hugh of Watkins, NY	Watkins, NY
SMITH Jeffrey Jr. of Woodhull, NY	June 3, 1862
KNAPP Mrs. Josephine B. dau of William **WESTCOTT** of Addison, NY	
DONEHUE James J. of Wellsburg, NY	June 14, 1862
MARLEY Emma Jane of Wellsburg, NY	
TOBEY Ransford of Caton, NY	July 1, 1862
THOMPSON Jennie of Vestal, NY	Vestal, NY
VAN GORDER Albert of Erwin, NY	July 4, 1862
ZELIH Lucy of Erwin, NY	Corning, NY
DECKER William of Corning, NY	July 8, 1862
STEVENS S. Sophronia of Corning, NY	
DEYO James L. of Caton, NY	July 6, 1862
DAVENPORT Luana dau of Henry of Caton, NY	Caton, NY
RICHARDS Rev. William H. of Mi.	August 6, 1862
WILKES Mrs. Eleanor of Corning, NY	
SIMONS Benona of Caton, NY	July 20, 1862
CHURCHILL Sabina of Big Flats, NY	Gibson, NY
WHITING George C. of Hornby, NY	August 21, 1862
BIXBY Catherine L. of Hornby, NY	Hornby, NY
SHEARER W. L. of Knoxville, NY	September 15, 1862
PALMER E. A. of Knoxville, NY	Knoxville, NY

STEWART William C.   September 20, 1862
CLARK Hattie of Olean, NY dau of late Harvey of Corning, NY

CUTLER James   September 28, 1862
HARRINGTON E. A. of Jamestown, NY   Corning, NY

GATES Henry P. of Rochester, NY   September 14, 1862
CAMPBELL Elizabeth of Rochester, NY   Knoxville, NY

CAMPBELL S. C. of Waverly, NY   October 8, 1862
FARWELL M. A. dau of Benjamin of Painted Post, NY   Painted Post, NY

KENNEDY George H.   October 15, 1862
HERRINGTON Alice E. dau of Dr. N. M. of Corning, NY   Corning, NY

HERRINGTON George of Southport, NY   September 21, 1862
FERRAN Harriet E. of Caton, NY   Caton, NY

THOMPSON John   October 22, 1862
ENGLISH Mary E. dau of William English   Caton, NY

ELMORE Sanford of Corning, NY   October 28, 1862
CLUTE Mary M. of Corning, NY   Elmira, NY

BURT Morris H. of Orange, NY   December 4, 1862
WEBB Angenoria of Orange, NY   Monterey, NY

HUNT Thomas of Caton, NY   December 25, 1862
HUNT Julia of Caton, NY

GREGORY Erwin of Caton, NY   December 24, 1862
HILDRETH Laura

WHEAT John   December 28, 1862
DOLIVER Mary   Caton, NY

GREEN David S. of New York City   January 6, 1863
BROWN Sarah dau of Jonathan of Corning, NY   Corning, NY

RUSSELL Samuel Jr. of Corning, NY   January 8, 1863
CLARK Emma D. dau of late Jesse of Corning, NY   Corning, NY

BROWN Charles D. of Corning, NY   January 8, 1863
HOLCOMB Marion L. of Corning, NY

BAKER William T. of Co. A. 28th NYV of Seneca Falls, NY January 11, 1863
PALMER Rosa O. dau of I. G. of Corning, NY   Corning, NY

CARR John P. of Corning, NY   January 20, 1863
JEFFREY Mary Elizabeth dau of E. A. form. Corning, NY   New Haven

SIMONS Martin of Caton, NY — December 30, 1862
OSTRANDER Lydia of Corning, NY — Corning, NY

DAVID Charles of Corning, NY — December 30, 1862
OSTRANDER Jane of Corning, NY — Corning, NY

VORHEES D. D. of NJ — September 24, 1862
KEYES Mary J. dau of Dr. D. C. of Corning, NY — Oakland, Cal.

BIDLEY William A. of Dix, NY — January 15, 1863
MATHEWS Sarah Jane of Coopers Plains, NY — Dix, NY

KIMBALL John H. of New York City — January 21, 1863
GAYLORD Helen S. dau of Alonzo of Orange, NY — Orange, NY

HARE William of Centerville, NY — January 20, 1863
ROOT Lydia of Knoxville, NY — Knoxville, NY

HILL Richard L. Adjt. 24th NYV — March 19, 1863
HAVENS Julia A. dau of William P. of Corning, NY — Corning, NY

PALMER Henry B. son of I. G. of Corning, NY — April 15, 1863
WESTCOTT Emma J. sis of Mrs. J. SEVERANCE — St. Joseph, Mo.

EDMISTER Barton of Erwin, NY — April 23, 1863
ROWLEY Eliza of Corning, NY — Corning, NY

BEACH William of Whitneys Point, NY — May 7, 1863
ROOKS Mary D. of Corning, NY at Father's — Harrison, Pa.

BRYEN John of Jackson, Pa. — March 25, 1863
RUSSELL A. Zubee E. of Jackson, Pa. — Caton, NY

TOBEY Christopher 2nd — May 12, 1863
SEYTER Mary P. of Corning, NY

WHITCOMB Samuel P. of Portageville, NY (News. date) — May 21, 1863
HAMMOND Julia E. dau of Simeon of Corning, NY — Corning, NY

KIMBER Henry of Canandaigua, NY — May 18, 1863
MORRISON Mary A. of Corning, NY — Corning, NY

BECK Robert of Corning, NY — May 20, 1863
TOWNLEY Ellen J. of Corning, NY — Corning, NY

WELLMAN James R. of Caton, NY — May 20, 1863
SPENCER Charlotte of Caton, NY — Big Flats, NY

WELLS Robert R. of US Army formerly of Corning, NY — May 13, 1863
EBAUGH Amanda J. dau of Jerome of Hampsted, Md. — Hampsted, Md.

DURAND Louis A. formerly 23rd Reg. NYV — May 28, 1863
WESTCOTT Helen L. dau of Arthur Sr. of Caton, NY — Big Flats, NY

KETCHUM Arthur H. of Corning, NY — May 27, 1863
SMITH Mary B. dau of James E. of Corning, NY — Corning, NY

DAVIS D. A. of Mansfield, Pa. — June 14, 1863
HELNER Louisa of Corning, NY — Corning, NY

SHAY William of Corning, NY — June 14, 1863
DICKERSON Sarah J. of Corning, NY — Corning, NY

SEARS Lewis of Thurston, NY — June 17, 1863
HILTON Mrs. Eliza of Hornby, NY — Corning, NY

MC KAY Samuel of Hornellsville, NY — June 8, 1863
WESTCOTT Emmi S. of Addison, NY — Hornellsville, NY

HUNT H. H. of Corning, NY — June 24, 1863
HARRISON Hannah F. of Williamsport, Pa.

THOMAS O. P. of Corning, NY — May 31, 1863
WHEELOCK C. P. of Corning, NY — Big Flats, NY

COWAN A. W. of Gibson, NY — June 28, 1863
OAKLEY S. A. of Gibson, NY

REED B. B. — July 9, 1863
HILL Diantha dau of W. P. of Caton, NY — Caton, NY

JONES Joshua of Elmira, NY — July 14, 1863
DENTON Harriet C. dau of S. B. of Elmira, NY — Elmira, NY

PEARSON William of Erwin, NY — July 23, 1863
PAPENEE(?) Rhoda Ann of Erwin, NY

WHEAT H. L. formerly Corning, NY 11th Cav. Mo. Vol. — July 18, 1863
GREENMAN L. M. of Cazenovia, NY — Pana, Ill.

BONHAM R. A. of Corning, NY — July 21, 1863
TILLINGHAST Maggie A. of Corning, NY — Corning, NY

FOX H. C. Supt Buffalo & Erie RR — August 6, 1863
MONIER Gertrude L. dau of James of Naples, NY — Naples, NY

WILKINS Guy of Caton, NY — August 20, 1863
TOBEY Hannah of Caton, NY — Caton, NY

MUNGER Rev. R. D. W. of E. Genessee Conf. — September 2, 1863
HINMAN Estella dau of Dr. Hinman of Havana, NY — Havana, NY

WAITE Neville E. of Corning, NY   September 24, 1863
BADGER Angie F. of Brooklyn, NY   Brooklyn, NY

GALLATIAN Charles B. of Corning, NY   September 24, 1863
HILTON Drusilla dau of V. E. of Corning, NY   Corning, NY

GREEN William H. late of US Army   September 22, 1863
GARR Marion M. of Elmira, NY

JOHNSON George B. of Lockhaven, Pa.   September 20, 1863
LOVELESS Mary M. of Corning, NY   Corning, NY

ALLEN Calvin of Corning, NY   September 20, 1863
BARBER Sarah Ann of Corning, NY   Corning, NY

WESTCOTT Daniel P. of Jamestown, NY   September 10, 1863
WILSON Sarah R. of Jamestown, NY   Jamestown, NY

WILCOX M. H. of Corning, NY   October 6, 1863
KIMBLE Fanny H. dau of I. W. of Corning, NY   Corning, NY

HEWITT J. S. of Moravia, NY   October 8, 1863
JOHNSON Malinda A. of Caton, NY   Corning, NY

DEMING Charles W. of 16th Pa. Cav.   October 6, 1863
GRIDLEY Emma dau of Lewis of Caton, NY

JONES Alfred of Corning, NY   October 21, 1863
ANTHONY Martha H. dau of Edward of Brooklyn, NY   Brooklyn, NY

FURNAM William of Elmira, NY   October 21, 1863
HORTON Arabella of Coopers Plains, NY   Coopers Plains, NY

COOPER Jacob C. of Corunus, Mi.   October 29, 1863
CARR Susan D. of Knoxville, NY   Knoxville, NY

OLDFIELD William J. of Post Creek, NY   November 12, 1863
WOOLEVER Emily of Post Creek, NY   Post Creek, NY

SMITH S. H. Jr. of Caton, NY   July 4, 1863
DAVENPORT Helen L. dau of Henry of Caton, NY   Corning, NY

BRUNDAGE David of Gibson, NY   November 21, 1863
HAVENS Amanda A. of Gibson, NY   Coopers Plains, NY

WOOD George of Caton, NY   November 15, 1863
BUCHANAN Sarah of Caton, NY   Caton, NY

BERRY T. J. of Tioga, Pa.   November 20, 1863
MERSEREAU Frankie of Tioga, Pa.   Tioga, Pa.

LONGWELL A. of Corning, NY	December 20, 1863
OWENS Josephine of Tyrone, NY	Tyrone, NY
BULMER Charles A.	December 31, 1863
LEWIS S. Maria dau of late Rev. R. G. of Corning, NY	Corning, NY
YOUNG Clement H. of NYC formerly of Painted Post, NY	December 22, 1863
SOULE Frank dau of D. E. of Corning, NY	New Brunswick, NY
SAGER James of Corning, NY	January 20, 1864
BARTO Mattie J. of N. Chemung, NY	N. Chemung, NY
PHINNEY John of Co. K. 86th Reg. NYV	January 15, 1864
CURTIS Abbie of Addison, NY	Addison, NY
WOLCOTT George of Corning, NY	January 27, 1864
FERENBAUGH Amanda S. of Corning, NY	Corning, NY
BOUCER John of Blossburg, Pa.	January 1, 1864
EVANS Mary of Blossburg, Pa.	
BRIGGS Charles W. of Elmira, NY	February 2, 1864
NEWKIRK Josephine of Corning, NY	Corning, NY
HOGOBOOM David of New Lebanon, Ill.	February 10, 1864
BROWN Harriet J. dau of Ira of Corning, NY	Corning, NY
CAMPBELL S. A.	February 1, 1864
GAMBLE Emeline dau of Col. William formerly of Bath, NY	Painted Post, NY
BROWN Henry E. of Painted Post, NY	February 22, 1864
FROST Mary E. dau of Jacob of Monterey, NY	Monterey, NY
VINCENT Capt. Nathan H. of Co. D. 86th Reg. NYV	February 15, 1864
ELLSWORTH Angeline D. sis of late Capt. D. S.	Hornellsville, NY
RUSSELL H. D. of Caton, NY	February 20, 1864
BORTLE Charity M. of Caton, NY	Caton, NY
MANCE Charles of Painted Post, NY	February 22, 1864
HUDSON Adah of Elmira, NY	Caton, NY
BUTLER William M.	February 28, 1864
PUTNAM Eliza dau of Cornelius of Southport, NY	Southport, NY
MERCHANT W. H. of Corning, NY (Newspaper date)	March 3, 1864
ADAMS Lottie of Lawrenceville, Pa.	Lawrenceville, Pa.
HILL George J. of Caton, NY	March 10, 1864
SCUTT Maria of Caton, NY	Caton, NY

WHITE Thompson S. of Corning, NY   March 13, 1864
WARNER Philena of Corning, NY   Corning, NY

GORTON John of Corning, NY late of Co. D. 23rd Reg.   March 17, 1864
WORMLEY Emma B. dau of William of Big Flats, NY   Big Flats, NY

WHEELER Thadeus R. of E. Bloomfield, NY   April 6, 1864
STANTON Emma Augusta dau of Col. N. B. of Hornby, NY   Hornby, NY

RAMSDELL H. J. of Washington DC formerly Tioga, Pa.   April 13, 1864
GARRETTSON Emily M. of Tioga, Pa.   Tioga, Pa.

HART William R. of Philadelphia, Pa. formerly Corning   April 20, 1864
WILCOX Hattie dau of William of Buffalo, NY   Buffalo, NY

DE WATERS Dwight of Caton, NY   April 7,1864
COOPER Martha E. of Caton, NY   Caton, NY

HARDENBURGH Lyman M. of Caton, NY (50th Reg.)   May 15, 1864
PEW Mrs. Mary M. of Caton, NY   Caton, NY

LAND Charles of Virginia City, Nev. formerly Corning   May 31, 1864
POWERS Carrie L. dau of late Charles of Corning, NY   Corning, NY

LAASS Emil of Blossburg, Pa.   June 7, 1864
JAMES Jennie D. dau of John of Corning, NY   Corning, NY

WARD J. B. of Elmira, NY   June 6, 1864
ERWIN Lizzie dau of William of Painted Post, NY   Painted Post, NY

TRANSUE Jeremiah of Big Flats, NY   June 29, 1864
SEYMOUR Marietta of Big Flats, NY   Corning, NY

JONES Samuel of Painted Post, NY   July 3, 1864
FREEMAN Louise of Corning, NY   Corning, NY

FREEMAN William H. of Syracuse, NY   July 3, 1864
DREW Sarah of Syracuse, NY   Corning, NY

COMSTOCK John D. of Catlin, NY   July 5, 1864
WOODRUFF Susan C. of Corning, NY   Corning, NY

BARSE Levi J. of Elkland, Pa.   July 17, 1864
BENNETT Jane of Elkland, Pa.   Caton, NY

ARTHUR Robert of Watkins, NY   July 19, 1864
JOHNSON Hattie of Watkins, NY   Gibson, NY

FULLERTON William of Jackson, Pa.   July 17, 1864
BRAGG Lucie A. of Albion, Mi.   Jonesville, Mi.

LEACH Romain W. of New York City	August 8, 1864
FREEMAN Mary L. of Corning, NY	Corning, NY
FURMAN Miles of Corning, NY	July 31, 1864
ELLISON Mrs. Annette of Corning, NY	Big Flats, NY
SMITH George H. of Milo, NY	September 11, 1864
BREESE Hattie L. of Caton, NY	Caton, NY
KNAPP Rev. Nathan B. of Sandy Creek, NY	September 27, 1864
HAZEN Celina T. dau of D. C. of Ithaca, NY	Ithaca, NY
PALMER F. W. of Auburn, NY	October 6, 1864
SHEPHERD Emma W. of Corning, NY	Corning, NY
BELL Rev. J. D.	September 7, 1864
ARNOLD Anna E. dau of Rev. J. T. of E Genessee Conf.	Lima, NY
FERRIS J. E. of Corning, NY (Newspaper date)	October 13, 1864
ROBLYER Hannah of Corning, NY	Corning, NY
LESNURE C. W. of Hornby, NY	October 23, 1864
HARRINGTON Lydia A. of Corning, NY	Corning, NY
STORMS Uri of Corning, NY (Newspaper date)	November 3, 1864
RHODES Isabel of Big Flats, NY	Big Flats, NY
ATWATER Dwight of Elmira, NY (Newspaper date)	November 17, 1864
LEWIS Mary H. at res of Harrison **GRIDLEY**	Canandaigua, NY
ALLEN Oscar of Corning, NY	October 30, 1864
ROSENCRANS Alice of Corning, NY	Corning, NY
STILLSON Hiram of Owego, NY	November 26, 1864
SHELLMAN Sarah E. of Owego, NY	Erwin, NY
RICH John J. of Cairo, Ill.	November 19, 1864
WILLIAMS Ella L. formerly of Corning, NY	Bowling Green, Oh.
JAYNES Eugene of Corning, NY	November 30, 1864
BROWN Rosina J. of Corning, NY	Corning, NY
ROWLEY J. W.	November 30, 1864
EDMISTER Emma	Erwin, NY
PARKER Andrew of Buffalo, NY	November 30, 1864
GRAVES Helen dau of L. W. of Corning, NY	Corning, NY
PAGE George W.	December 7, 1864
BROWN Martha J. of Corning, NY	Corning, NY

FAY Lt. Charles M. of Prattsburgh, NY
GILBERT Helen of Painted Post, NY

December 13, 1864
Painted Post, NY

CRANS William D. of Waverly, NY
BOOTH Sarah M. of Waverly, NY

December 21, 1864
Corning, NY

WOOD Thomas E. of Rochester, NY
VOUGHT Ameda S. of Waverly, NY

December 21, 1864
Corning, NY

LAWSON Edward S. of New York City
GRAVES Lucy E. dau of Dr. J. B. of Corning, NY

December 22, 1864
Corning, NY

MILLER Michael of Orange, NY
DAVIS Hannah of Campbell, NY

(Newspaper date) January 5, 1865

MITCHELL George W. of Jackson, Pa.
ROCKWELL Anna of Lawrenceville, Pa.

December 28, 1864

LEWIS George A. of Cameron, NY
SCOTT Jennie of Blossburg, Pa.

December 21, 1864
Blossburg, Pa.

ARNOLD Capt. John K. late of 7th Reg.
BECKOUT May T. dau of John Beckout

December 22, 1864
Akaman, Wassea Co.

SHERMAN Orra of Watkins, NY
PAYNE Mary A. of Elmira, NY

December 31, 1864
Knoxville, NY

DE WATERS Algie L. of Southport, NY
COOPER Dellie P. dau of Anson of Caton, NY

January 1, 1865
Caton, NY

HOWE Delos of Brookfield, Pa.
SAMPLE Elizabeth of Middleburg, Pa.

December 31, 1864
Lawrenceville, Pa.

BROWN Frank D. of Corning, NY
SKINNER Melissa A. of Corning, NY

March 6, 1865
Corning, NY

SLIE Prof. J. S. of Corning Academy
HUBBARD Martha M. of Corning, NY

April 6, 1865
Corning, NY

WOLCOTT Jacob H. of Caton, NY
WELTS Mary E. of Corning, NY

April 1, 1865

CUSHING H. S. of Blossburg, Pa.
BULLOCK Sarah of Corning, NY

April 12, 1865
Beaver Dams, NY

DAVISON Clifton A. of Caton, NY
TOBEY Theresa A. of Caton, NY

May 20, 1865
Corning, NY

HAZEN John C. of Ithaca, NY
HALL Emelie dau of Benjamin of Auburn, NY

May 31, 1865
Auburn, NY

MINER James A. of Corning, NY   May 31, 1865
SMITH Dell of Wellsville, NY

BREWER Thomas of Campbell, NY   June 30, 1865
CUNNINGHAM Frances of Erwin, NY   Painted Post, NY

GIFFORD Nelson of Watkins, NY   July 10, 1865
MC GIVEN Mary of Corning, NY   Corning, NY

LOVELL Carlton H. of Corning, NY   July 2, 1865
CARLTON Sarah A. of Bath, NY   Corning, NY

SWEETLAND William Henry of Corning, NY   July 12, 1865
GROTON Emily Adelaide dau of Hiram of Corning, NY   Corning, NY

WILDER G. A. of Corning, NY   July 24, 1865
DE GROAT Alice of Erwin, NY

MC COLLOUGH George of Corning, NY   July 25, 1865
CRAWFORD Kate of Caton, NY   Gibson, NY

KINNAN Henry of Caton, NY   July 3, 1865
PALMER Sarah L. of Caton, NY   Caton, NY

VEAZIE Thomas of Penn Yan, NY   August 17, 1865
HUKE Mrs. G. D. dau of Jabez HAVENS of Corning, NY   Corning, NY

RICHARDS Damon H. of Caton, NY   August 6, 1865
VEAZIE Nancy A. of Augusta, Me.   Corning, NY

BECKET Henry of Corning, NY   August 23, 1865
SPENCER Amanda dau of David of Corning, NY   Corning, NY

SULLIVAN Thomas   September 2, 1865
CHAMPLAIN Adelia of Tioga, Pa.

DEXTER George of Owego, NY   September 6, 1865
BICKNELL Cornelia   Corning, NY

SMITH George W. of Corning, NY   September 6, 1865
ALLEY Rhoda Falley dau of James Alley   Hornellsville, NY

BUTLER Jerome of Corning, NY   September 6, 1865
MACK Mary of Corning, NY   Corning, NY

BURT John B. of Corning, NY   September 13, 1865
WORMLEY Jennie E. of Corning, NY   Corning, NY

VESTBINDER Horace of Lindley, NY   September 17, 1865
HARRISON Ethie of Caton, NY   Corning, NY

CHAMBERS Archibald of Fallbrook, Pa. September 19, 1865
JACK Elizabeth of Fallbrook, Pa. Corning, NY

WHITAKER James M. of 141st Reg. NYV September 3, 1865
WEBSTER Julia R. of Vestal, NY Savona, NY

LEAVENWORTH Daniel D. of Thurston, NY September 17, 1865
THORP Sarah of Thurston, NY Savona, NY

CLUTE Lt. George N. of Corning, NY (late of 86th Reg.) September 21, 1865
WRIGHT Ruth A. of Canton, Pa. Canton, Pa.

LOVELL Elijah G. of Watkins, NY September 30, 1865
PAGE Adelia W. of Watkins, NY Corning, NY

DECKER William of Wellsburg, NY September 30, 1865
CLARK Nettie of Elmira, NY Corning, NY

CUNNINGHAM John V. of Noperville, Ill. September 1, 1865
LEWIS Hattie N. dau late Rev. R. G. of Corning, NY Adrian, Mi.

FOX Col. William F. late of 107th Reg. September 28, 1865
SHATTUCK Mary A. dau of L. H. Shattuck Corning, NY

HOLLANDS John S. of W. Troy, Pa. October 3, 1865
SMITH Millie B. dau of Thomas R. Smith W. Troy, Pa.

HILTON Josiah P. of Hornby, NY October 19, 1865
CUSHING Elvera C. of Campbell, NY Campbell, NY

BUMP Oscar W. of Corning, NY October 17, 1865
BAILEY Ethelaide of Addison, NY Addison, NY

DICKINSON Walter S. of Corning, NY November 1, 1865
ROSE Emma dau of John of Corning, NY Corning, NY

PAGE Henry of Williamsport, Pa. October 11, 1865
BUCHLER Matilda of Williamsport, Pa.

HOWE Harrison of Caton, NY October 22, 1865
GREGORY Melissa of Caton, NY

BONHAM Henry of the 141st Reg. of Corning, NY October 31, 1865
SMITH Sarah of Corning, NY Corning, NY

WEBB Henry of Maine, NY September 26, 1865
SHEVALIER Olive M. of Maine, NY Corning, NY

BROWN Nathan November 4, 1865
SEARLS Maggie Corning, NY

CORZETT William A.	November 6, 1865
GARRISON Maggie	Corning, NY
ROCKWELL Levi A.	November 6, 1865
HACKETT Jane	Corning, NY
FREEMAN Charles H. of Corning, NY late of 141st Reg.	November 21, 1865
KING Monnie C. of New York City	New York City
BACHMAN Capt. late of 161st Reg. of Horseheads, NY	December 20, 1865
MORGAN Kate dau of A. C. Morgan	Lindley, NY
RIGHTMIRE Isaac S. of Chicago, Ill.	December 13, 1865
BARNES Louisa B. of Corning, NY	Corning, NY
FOSTER George W. of Niles Valley, Pa. late of Corning	December 13, 1865
LAKE Nida of Poughkeepsie, NY	Poughkeepsie, NY
WESTCOTT Bailey of Corning, NY	December 17, 1865
CRAMER Mayella of Corning, NY	Monterey, NY
PRATT Tobias L. of Caton, NY	November 27, 1865
TOBEY Lucy M. of Caton, NY	Caton, NY
STILLSON Nehemiah W. of Caton, NY	December 17, 1865
TOBEY Louisa E. of Caton, NY	Caton, NY
DUNKLER James of Campbell, NY	December 19, 1865
BENTON Maggie of Erwin, NY	
KINNEY Henry L. of Lindley, NY	December 24, 1865
MATHER Catherine of Campbell, NY	
SCOTT John of Campbell, NY	December 25, 1865
CHRISTLER Catherine of Campbell, NY	

missing issues

SMITH David P.	April 16, 1868
JEWETT Almira dau of Thomas Jewett	Hornby, NY
FORCE Edwin J.	April 18, 1868
BIDELER Lottie J.	Caton, NY
GRAVES George R. of Corning, NY	April 22, 1868
JOHNSON Carrie Park dau of Birdsall N. Johnson	Binghamton, NY
SNYDER George W. of Lindley, NY	April 26, 1868
MULFORD Nettie of Lindley, NY	Lawrenceville, Pa.

GREEN Alvaro of Corning, NY
WHITWOOD V. Adelaide of Canisteo, NY

May 19, 1868
Canisteo, NY

PERRY George A. of Corning, NY
WINTON Lizzie of Corning, NY

June 2, 1868
Corning, NY

BROWN David P. of Worcester, Mass.
SMITH Mary C. dau of Elias H. of Corning, NY

June 3, 1868
Corning, NY

MILLS W. H. of Orange, NY
OLNEY Celia dau of Rev. P. Olney

June 3, 1868
Weston, NY

HOUGH Leroy S. of Hornellsville, NY
REWALT Annie C. of Hornellsville, NY

May 28, 1868
Hornellsville, NY

BEMIS Horace
WASHBURN Sarah J.

June 1, 1868
Hornellsville, NY

EASTERBROOK Orrin of Corning, NY
JONES M. Libbie of Corning, NY

June 30, 1868
Corning, NY

ROWLEY Washington of Corning, NY
NOLAN Mary adopted dau of Rev. B. F. **BALCOM**

June 11, 1868
Corning, NY

FARWELL John K. of Chicago, Ill.
ROSE Hattie of Painted Post, NY

June 22, 1868
Painted Post, NY

VAN DEMARK William of Caroline, NY
LINDSAY Addie C. dau of D Merrit of Caton, NY

June 30, 1868
Caton, NY

SABINS Charles of Catlin, NY
TENBROOKS Maggie of Big Flats, NY

July 8, 1868

BADGER H. M.
GILLETT Mrs. L. M.

August 19, 1868
Elmira, NY

JACOBS Braziel W.   (Newspaper date)
THOMA Eveline S. dau of Jacob of Corning, NY

September 3, 1868
Corning, NY

CHERRY James B. of Painted Post, NY
SAVORY Sarah of Painted Post, NY

September 21, 1868
Elmira, NY

LAKE Martin of Hornellsville, NY
SMITH Melissa dau of Abram L. of Hornellsville, NY

August 30, 1868
Haskinsville, NY

VAN GORDER Homer of Corning, NY
CANFIELD Abigail J. of Corning, NY

September 17, 1868

GILLETT Aaron of Tioga, Pa.
SANDERS Kate of Tioga, Pa.

September 24, 1868
Corning, NY

DOUGLAS Charles G. of Corning, NY	October 7, 1868
BROWN Mary R. dau of D. F. of Corning, NY	Corning, NY
KIRKENDALL Thompson of Campbell, NY	October 8, 1868
RUMSEY Ellen of Campbell, NY	Coopers Plains, NY
MATHEWS Henry of Lindley, NY	October 10, 1868
CHRISLER Margaret of Campbell, NY	Coopers Plains, NY
VAN ORSDALE George of Caton, NY	September 20, 1868
HOWE Lottie of Caton, NY	Caton, NY
BALCOM Mark of Corning, NY	October 21, 1868
CAMPBELL Anna L. of Corning, NY	Corning, NY
ROWLAND D. B. of Eau De Clair, Wis.	October 21, 1868
MILLER E. Eleanora of Corning, NY	Corning, NY
TUCKER Ira of Avoca, NY	Novembr 8, 1868
VAN SCOTER Sarah dau of Rufus **GORTON** of Corning	Corning, NY
WHEELER Nelson of Corning, NY	November 10, 1868
BAXTER Mary dau of Duncan of Corning, NY	Corning, NY
FARNSWORTH Marcellus of Caton, NY	November 20, 1868
GILE Mary A. of Caton, NY	
HORTON Alfred F.	November 18, 1868
BERGER Almina	Campbell, NY
REED Thomas of Corning, NY	November 26, 1868
TOWNLEY Frances L. of Corning, NY	Corning, NY
PARKS James W.	November 3, 1868
HEERMANS Mary E. dau of John of Corning, NY	Kingwood, W. Va.
ROTSELL William of Corning, NY	December 5, 1868
WINNER Delia of Corning, NY	Corning, NY
HILL Merrill D. of Hornellsville, NY	December 23, 1868
BATES Hettie of Hornellsville, NY	Hornellsville, NY
GRIFFIN Anthony of Elmira, NY	December 20, 1868
MAGRANN Maggie of Elmira, NY	Elmira, NY
STOUT Byron J. of Pontiac, Mi.	December 30, 1868
FARNHAM Hanna C. of Addison, NY	Addison, NY
CONOVER Merritt C.	December 30, 1868
CLARK Mary C.	Corning, NY

CURTIS Thomas W.
SCHRYVER Sarah E.

January 3, 1869
Corning, NY

HOLLITT I. W. of Corning, NY
SMITH Arvilla of Corning, NY

January 22, 1869
Corning, NY

HARE John T. of Corning, NY
ALLEN Ella A. of Corning, NY

February 17, 1869
Corning, NY

SMITH Charles H. of Corning, NY
ELLIOTT Harriet A. of Corning, NY

February 18, 1869
Corning, NY

ELLIOTT W. H. W.
BAILEY Matilda

February 18, 1869
Corning, NY

THOMPSON Henry of Caton, NY
BILLINGTON Mrs. Nancy of Lansing, NY

February 21, 1869
Caton, NY

STEWART Charles of St. Joseph, Mo.
PERKINS Helen L. dau of Col. Janes of Lima, NY

February 25, 1869
Lima, NY

RUTHERFORD W. H. of Addison, NY
ALDERMAN E. M. dau of Rev. O. P. of Lewisburgh, Pa.

March 11, 1869
Lewisburgh, Pa.

JUDD Jasper B. of Owego, NY
HUMPHREY Sarah B. of Ithaca, NY

March 25, 1869
Ithaca, NY

ARMINE Aaron M. of Hornellsville, NY   (Newspaper date)
DUNHAM Laura of Howard, NY

April 22, 1869
Haskinsville, NY

WOODWARD William E. of Watkins, NY
ROBINSON Eliza dau of late L. H. of Corning, NY

April 28, 1869
Corning, NY

RIPLEY Joseph F. of Lambs Creek Pa.
KOHLER Mary A. of E. Charleston, Pa.

April 22, 1869
Corning, NY

IREDELL Charles Jr. formerly of Bristol, Pa.
ERWIN Annie M. dau of late Arthur H. of Painted Post

April 8, 1869
Painted Post, NY

KRIEGER E. A. of Cameron, NY
SMITH Mary A. dau of Justin M. of Cameron, NY

May 19, 1869
Cameron, NY

FRENCH Horace
REDFIELD Ernestine dau of Jared A. of Elmira, NY

May 20, 1869
Elmira, NY

GOODSELL H. L. of Hornby, NY
RHODES Mrs. Anna of Knoxville, NY

May 14, 1869
Knoxville, NY

MOWRY Sullivan of Knoxville, NY
BARNES Martha of Coopers Plains, NY

May 25, 1869
Knoxville, NY

MERRILL Frank P. of Salisbury, Mass.   May 30, 1869
GILBERT Jennie L. dau of Dr. Joseph D. of Corning, NY   Corning, NY

FLOWER Lucius L. of Lambs Creek, Pa.   May 26, 1869
COLES Stella of Lambs Creek, Pa.   Corning, NY

SMITH Edward E. of Corning, NY   May 27, 1869
SMITH Emma W. of Burdett, NY   Burdett, NY

BORLAND G. Judson   June 9, 1869
SEDGEWICK Ellen dau of William of Painted Post, NY   Painted Post, NY

STARKEY Levi A. of Mansfield, Pa.   June 15, 1869
WHITE Mrs. Amelia L. of Mansfield, Pa.   Corning, NY

VAN SCOTER A. C. of Hornellsville, NY   June 18,1869
SMITH Carrie E. of Hornellsville, NY   Corning, NY

SILL Cyrus D. of Corning, NY   June 10, 1869
BOURNE Mary A. of Lyons, NY   Lyons, NY

DAYBOLL Alfred of Corning, NY   June 23, 1869
WISEMAN Elizabeth of New York City   Corning, NY

DEUEL James F. of Lawrenceville, Pa.   August 17, 1869
MEADE Sarah A. of Caton, NY   Caton, NY

DIVEN Eugene   August 23, 1869
PARTRIDGE Julia A. dau of Henry M. Partridge   Elmira, NY

BREESE Lee S.   August 23, 1869
BATES Madge A. dau of Rev. J. H. Bates   Lincoln, Ill.

BLAKELY Daniel of Neenah, Wis.   September 3, 1869
PRATT Sarah M. of Knoxville, NY   Knoxville, NY

REYNOLDS Theodore L.   September 15, 1869
STEWART Fannie A. dau of Mrs. Elizabeth Stewart   St. Joseph, Mo.

HIGMAN William E. of Corning, NY   September 15, 1869
HOKE Adell of Leavenworth, Ks.   Leavenworth, Ks.

CUNNINGHAM Haines D. of Ithaca, NY   September 14, 1869
WARNER Fannie Louise dau of Dr. L. Warner   W. Winfield, NY

BOND Thomas of Campbell, NY   September 25, 1869
QUIMBY Frances of Campbell, NY   Corning, NY

BARRY P. J. of Corning, NY   September 24, 1869
REILLY Rebecca of Girard, Pa.   Buffalo, NY

ORSER A. W. of Addison, NY
SPRAGUE H. P. of Corning, NY

September 29, 1869
Corning, NY

SWIFT Rev. Isaac of New York City
JAYNES Emma A. dau of E. A. of Hornby, NY

October 12, 1869
Hornby, NY

YOUNG Jefferson of Rathbone, NY
SMITH Susan of Corning, NY

October 9, 1869
Rathbone, NY

RIDER William of Corning, NY
HOFF Christiana J. of Rochester, NY

October 13, 1869
Corning, NY

POND Horace N. of Corning, NY
SPENCER Hattie A. dau of George T. of Corning, NY

October 20, 1869
Corning, NY

HOOPER Joseph B. of Corning, NY
CUNNINGHAM Martha A. of Corning, NY

November 3, 1869
Corning, NY

GOODSELL William of Corning, NY
GARDENER Emma of Hornby, NY

November 7, 1869
Hornby, NY

SHURWIN Melville A. of Dunkirk, NY
BAKER Mary E. of Painted Post, NY

November 10, 1869
Painted Post, NY

STALL James A. of Corning, NY
HAVENS Helen E. dau of William P. of Corning, NY

November 17, 1869
Corning, NY

MILLER Horace W.
MINIER Hannah E. dau of Chrisjohn of Caton, NY

November 24, 1869
Caton, NY

THRALL Simeon J. of Little Flats, NY
SMITH Frances A. of Caton, NY

December 15, 1869
Corning, NY

NIGHTHART John J. of Mecklinburgh, NY
BOYCE Mary E. of Mecklinburgh, NY

December 25, 1869
Mecklinburgh, NY

WALSTER C. C. of Corning, NY
CONOVER L. S. of Corning, NY

December 29, 1869
Corning, NY

WALLACE John of Elmira, NY   (Newspaper date)
CARPENTER Lucy of Chemung, NY

December 30, 1869
Corning, NY

FRALIC D. L. of Lambs Creek, Pa.
SHERWOOD Anna M. of Mansfield, Pa.

January 12, 1870
Corning, NY

HORMET Jewit of Pittsburg, Pa.
MALLORY Sarah A. dau of John of Knoxville, NY

January 18, 1870
Corning, NY

ADAMS William W. of Corning, NY
DE WOLF Frances dau of Hiram of Corning, NY

January 6, 1870
Corning, NY

BRONSON William C. of Painted Post, NY   December 7, 1869
CASTERLINE Jennie of Painted Post, NY   Addison, NY

CULVER Chauncey of Mecklinburgh, NY   January 13, 1870
LAMBERT Harriet of Mecklinburgh, NY   Mecklinburgh, NY

RUNDALL A. D. of Corning, NY   January 20, 1870
LUTHER A. A. of Corning, NY   Corning, NY

GREGORY Wellington E. of Caton, NY   January 19, 1870
ROSE Emily E. of Jacksonville, NY   Jacksonville, NY

PATTERSON George of Troy, Pa.   January 26, 1870
HUFF Mary of Troy, Pa.   Corning, NY

BEEMAN Eli of Caton, NY   October 31, 1869
ACKERMAN Prudence J. dau of Richard and Caroline   Caton, NY

BORTLE William H. of Caton, NY   December 19, 1869
CRETHERS Nettie of Caton, NY   Caton, NY

KIMBLE James D. of Catlin, NY   February 1, 1870
LANE M. E. of Hornby, NY   Hornby, NY

BOGDEN W. of Wayland, NY   December 28, 1869
PIERCE Sarah of Wayland, NY   Haskinsville, NY

LOVELL Phillip of Wayland, NY   December 28, 1869
RAZEY Lucinda of Fremont, NY   Haskinsville, NY

RAZEY Charles of Fremont, NY   December 28, 1869
LOVELL Ella of Wayland, NY   Haskinsville, NY

DYE Adelbert of Fremont, NY   January 1, 1870
HAMMOND Diantha of Fremont, NY   Haskinsville, NY

ROWLAND Henry of Conesus, NY   February 3, 1870
MAYNARD Jennie of Elmira, NY   Corning, NY

GORTON Silas W. of Corning, NY   February 10, 1870
BUNDY Eva A. of Corning, NY   Corning, NY

WHITNEY Thomas E. of New York City   February 7, 1870
PAGE Kate E. of Williamsport, Pa.   Corning, NY

CALKINS David T.   February 17, 1870
SMITH Emma dau of George of Little Flats, NY   Little Flats, NY

HANLEY Samuel L. of Peach Orchard, NY   March 3, 1870
STILWELL Julia A. of Reynoldsville, NY   Hector, NY

JEWETT Nelson M. of Hornby, NY
FARRINGTON Hattie A. of Hornby, NY

March 13, 1870
Hornby, NY

SMITH Francis W. of Mecklinburgh, NY
SMITH Betsey of Mecklinburgh, NY

March 9, 1870
Mecklinburgh, NY

PIERCE Byron Md. of Coopers Plains, NY
STETSON Sophia E. of Franklin, NY

March 9, 1870
Franklin, NY

ROBBINS Leman of Caton, NY
JOHNSTON Laura of E. Guilford, NY

March 13, 1870

TABER P. T. of Horseheads, NY
WELLER Helen M. dau of T. V. of Knoxville, NY

March 17, 1870

GORTON George
MC CONNELL Mary dau of Henry of E. Corning, NY

March 10, 1870
E. Corning, NY

BALCOM Henry A. of Corning, NY
PERHAM Lucy dau of L. W. of Owego, NY

March 22, 1870
Owego, NY

AULLS Thomas H. of Wheeler, NY
WILLIAMS Mary A. of Wheeler, NY

March 26, 1870
Corning, NY

HEIN Arnold B. of Corning, NY
FALK Clara dau of Henry of Corning, NY

April 14, 1870
Elmira, NY

YOUNG Benjamin of Corning, NY
LANAHAN Julia of Corning, NY

April 14, 1870
Corning, NY

BRYNE E. of Corning, NY
DICKERSON Maggie of Corning, NY

April 20, 1870
Corning, NY

MILLS Henry of Elmira, NY
BROWN Phoebe of Hector, NY

April 26, 1870
Hector, NY

BROWN William E. of Hector, NY
FREEMAN Catherine of Waterburg, NY

April 30, 1870
Mecklinburgh, NY

STEVENS Gilbert of Hornby, NY
RIBBLE Augusta of Tyrone, NY

May 23, 1870
Corning, NY

MALTBY Jerome B. of Corning, NY
BEERS Mary dau of Andrew of Corning, NY

May 26, 1870
Corning, NY

QUICK Charles of Corning, NY
TILLINGHURST Elizabeth M. of Knoxville, NY

May 31, 1870
Knoxville, NY

CREECH Thomas P. of Corning, NY
SMITH Catherine A. of Corning, NY

June 25, 1870

JOHNSON Dewitt C. of Corning, NY — July 10, 1870
BUNNELL Mary of Corning, NY — Corning, NY

HALEY Jonathan of Corning, NY — (Newspaper date) July 14, 1870
CHURCH Hattie of Corning, NY — Painted Post, NY

HAM Chancey of Southport, NY — July 22, 1870
MILLER Electa of Southport, NY — Painted Post, NY

HATHAWAY H. C. — July 12, 1870
BARKLEY Mary — Coopers Plains, NY

JENKS C. of Coopers Plains, NY — July 20, 1870
SHULTS Maggie of Coopers Plains, NY — Coopers Plains, NY

VAN VLEET John of Hammondsport, NY — August 2, 1870
ERSLEY Ettie of Greenwood, NY — Corning, NY

GORTON Orley R. of Corning, NY — August 4, 1870
BUNDY Orcelia J. of Corning, NY — Lawrenceville, Pa.

MC ARTHUE Rev. Robert S. of New York City — August 4, 1870
FOX Mary E. dau of late Rev. Norman Fox — Painted Post, NY

MC CONNELL Elijah of Corning, NY — August 4, 1870]
LOVELESS Melvina dau of Daniel of Corning, NY — Corning, NY

NEWARK Charles of Owego, NY — August 12, 1870
ALEXANDER Mary Jane of Painted Post, NY — Painted Post, NY

VAN GELDER Charles J. of Wellsboro, Pa. — August 3, 1870
FORSYTHE Clara of Wellsboro, Pa. — Wellsboro, Pa.

HASTINGS George P. of New York City — August 18, 1870
DENTON Emma of Hammondsport, NY — Hammondsport, NY

BAKER Isa of Fremont, NY — August 14, 1870
BARBER Betsey M. of Fremont, NY — Haskinsville, NY

HOOD A. Melvin of Corning, NY — August 31, 1870
O'DONNELL Kate of Corning, NY — Corning, NY

VAN GORDON Harrison of Erwin, NY — (Newspaper date) September 8, 1870
CANFIELD Mary Ella of Corning, NY

WHITE John C. of Caton, NY — February 20, 1870
DAVIS Lucy E. of Caton, NY — Painted Post, NY

UPSON Nelson of Corning, NY — October 12, 1870
SAYLER Julie E. dau of Andrew of Moreland, NY — Moreland, NY

TOWNSEND Joseph G. of Ill.　　　　　　October 13, 1870
GIFFORD M. Louise dau of William H. Gifford　　Hudson, NY

KIMBALL Wallace S. of Knoxville, NY　　October 23, 1870
PECK Lucinda of Gibson, NY　　　　　Gibson, NY

VAN VLEET P. P. Md. of Shortsville, NY　　October 19, 1870
FULTON Anna M. dau of J. S. of Stanley Corners, NY　Stanley Corners, NY

VEAZIE C. H. of Caton, NY　　　　　October 26, 1870
BIDELER Alice E. of Coopers Plains, NY　　Coopers Plains, NY

PADDOCK James of Bath, NY　　　　　November 2, 1870
CRANDALL Josephine of Hammondsport, NY　Corning, NY

CLARK Edward D. of Corning, NY　　　November 15, 1870
ROGERS Haidee L. dau of Dr. Wm. E. formerly of Corning　Central City, Col.

SCHUTT Martin E. of Caton, NY　　　November 20, 1870
HURD Mary of Caton, NY　　　　　　Corning, NY

BUTLER Ralph of Painted Post, NY　　November 16, 1870
SAYLES Mary A. of Painted Post, NY　　Painted Post, NY

HEINYMAN Benjamin of Avoca, NY　　November 17, 1870
GRAY Nettie of Avoca, NY　　　　　Avoca, NY

MARTIN William of Avoca, NY　　　　November 22, 1870
WALLACE Mattie of Avoca, NY　　　　Avoca, NY

WILLIAMS J. C. of Avoca, NY　　　　November 24, 1870
NEIL Nancy of Avoca, NY　　　　　　Avoca, NY

COLE Nathan of Cal.　　　　　　　December 20, 1870
MILLER N. M. of Knoxville, NY　　　Knoxville, NY

ROLINSON Oren of Hornby, NY　　　December 21, 1870
GOODSELL Ella E. dau of Isaac of Hornby, NY　Hornby, NY

LEAR Joseph of Corning, NY　　　　December 22, 1870
BARNES Kate of Corning, NY　　　　Corning, NY

RINEVAULT William of Corning, NY　　December 21, 1870
FULLER Emma of Corning, NY　　　　Corning, NY

ALDRICH William W. of New York City　December 22, 1870
DUNNING Ella C. dau of M. L. of Corning, NY　Corning, NY

RICE Joseph A. of Gibson, NY　　　　December 25, 1870
HELLER Sarah D. of Gibson, NY　　　Gibson, NY

MIDDAUGH Truman C. of Lawrenceville, Pa. January 1, 1871
TILFORD Addie S. of Eaton Rapids, Mi. Corning, NY

SAMPSON William J. of Franklin, Pa. January 3, 1871
HUSBAND Margaret of Corning, NY Corning, NY

DYE John W. of Cohocton, NY January 4, 1871
FAIRBROTHER Elizabeth F. of Cohocton, NY Avoca, NY

BRIGGS Jerome of Cohocton, NY January 4, 1871
OVERHISER Anna M. of Avoca, NY Avoca, NY

MIDDICK George A. of Avoca, NY January 5, 1871
SHAVER Alice of Kanona, NY Kanona, NY

HYNA Samuel of Wheeler, NY January 4, 1871
WAGNER Alice of Wheeler, NY Wheeler, NY

GREEN William Sheldon of Corning, NY January 18, 1871
GRAVES Maggie A. of Corning, NY Corning, NY

DAVENPORT A. B. of Onieda, NY January 30, 1871
HOLMES Mary S. of Corning, NY Corning, NY

EARL Frank P. of Big Flats, NY February 12, 1871
FARR Mary of Big Flats, NY Corning, NY

BURDICK Sylvester of Corning, NY February 15, 1871
DICKERMAN Nancy of Corning, NY Corning, NY

TABOR Harris of Corning, NY February 26, 1871
KEMP Mrs. Clara of Corning, NY Corning, NY

JONES George W. March 1, 1871
CROAKER Eliza E. Corning, NY

HARRIS George of Corning, NY March 2, 1871
SNOOK Martha F. of Corning, NY Corning, NY

MABEE Jacob of Big Flats, NY March 9, 1871
BROWN Albina of Big Flat, NY Corning, NY

EDSALL H. P. of Thurston, NY April 1, 1871
KELLY Rosette of Campbell, NY Corning, NY

DE GROOT Edward of Erwin, NY April 9, 1871
VAN ZYLE Julia A. of Erwin, NY Knoxville, NY

FRARY Frank W. of Three Rivers, Mi. April 12, 1871
COOK Mary A. formerly of Campbell, NY at parents Three River, Mi.

WHITE James L. of Caton, NY   April 24, 1871
VAN ORSDALE Marium dau of John of Caton, NY

CLARK Lucius of Campbell, NY   April 27, 1871
WAKEMAN Sarah J. by Rev. Joel Wakeman   Campbell, NY

TAYLOR E. G.   May 11, 1871
HAYES M. E.   Knoxville, NY

ALEXANDER George of Pontiac, Mi.   January 25, 1871
WORMLEY Belle C. dau of Jacob Wormley   E. Corning, NY

CAMPBELL John of Boston, Mass.   May 30, 1871
HALEY Mary Jane of Corning, NY   Corning, NY

CATER John M. of Corning, NY   May 25, 1871
WINANS Stella O. of Leroy, NY   Elmira, NY

GOLDEN Appleton L. of Corning, NY   June 4, 1871
WILLIAMS Marietta of Corning, NY   Corning, NY

LITTS Merton D. of Corning, NY   June 4, 1871
MILLARD Alice of Corning, NY   Corning, NY

AINSWORTH Dr. H. R. of Addison, NY   May 25, 1871
YOUNGLOVE Emma dau of T. M. of Hammondsport, NY   Hammondsport, NY

RAWSON A. H. of Preston, Ill.   June 1, 1871
WRIGHT Celestia of Nelson, Pa.   Nelson, Pa.

SOUTHERLAND Dr. Leander of Campbell, NY   June 7, 1871
TEEPLES Ruth dau of George of Campbell, NY   Campbell, NY

NOOMAN James of Elmira, NY   June 7, 1871
FITZPATRICK Kate dau of John of Havana, NY   Watkins, NY

COMPTON Lewis   June 8, 1871
FOLBERT Eliza   Bradford, NY

FANTON Hull   June 8, 1871
SKELLENGER Mary Thom   Havana, NY

SLATER Augustin of Horseheads, NY   June 14, 1871
STURDEVANT Helen of Dix, NY   Dix, NY

WELLER G. F. of Waverly, NY   June 13, 1871
POLLEYS Frances of Waverly, NY   Waverly, NY

BERGSTROM C. J. of Corning, NY   July 2, 1871
MULFORD Mrs. H. of Corning, NY   Corning, NY

JEWELL H. M.
BENNER Mary of Urbana, NY

June 29, 1871
Corning, NY

JIMERSON Herbert T. of Hornby, NY
HENDRICK Bertha E. of Hornby, NY

June 28, 1871
Hornby, NY

HADLEY Judson A. of Big Flats, NY
KIMBALL Mattie of Mitchell, Pa.

July 1, 1871
Corning, NY

KRESS Clymer of Wellsboro, Pa.
BACHE Mary Adeline dau of William of Wellsboro, Pa.

June 29, 1871
Wellsboro, NY

MORSE William R. of Saginaw, Mi.
CHURCH Hattie L. dau of S. M. of Coopers Plains, NY

July 31, 1871
Lansing, Mi.

BILLINGHURST Charles of Knoxville, NY
PIERCE Ida D. of Knoxville, NY

August 16, 1871
Knoxville, NY

EDGER William P. of Corning, NY
GILLETT Frankie of Corning, NY

August 22, 1871
Corning, NY

THURBER W. H. of Greene, NY
TURK Florence of Addison, NY

August 30, 1871
Addison, NY

NORTON T. A. of Hartwick, NY
FRENCH Augusta C. dau of Mrs. A. G. of Caton, NY

September 6, 1871
Caton, NY

JENCKS William of Erwin, NY
WANCISE Lettie of Erwin, NY

September 17, 1871
Coopers Plains, NY

DUNCKLEE E. Lansing of Coopers Plains, NY
LEWIS Grace I. of Brooklyn, NY

September 25, 1871
Coopers Plains, NY

NEWCOMB Frank H.
ROBERTS Helen M. of Rock Stream, NY

October 12, 1871

POST Henry of Covington, Pa.
HOLDREN Emma C. of Corning, NY

October 19, 1871

HINDS Warren L. formerly of Corning, NY
HIGGINS Jennie of New York City

October 10, 1871
York, Pa.

FINCH Hiram of Campbell, NY
BAILEY Anna E. of Urbana, NY

November 8, 1871
Elmira, NY

COWAN Henry of Corning, NY
GORTON Sarah E. dau of S. D. of Corning, NY

November 2, 1871

EDSON Herbert S. of Corning, NY
HAZELTON Delia of Corning, NY

November 15, 1871
Johnstown, NY

HOWELL William D. of Painted Post, NY　　　November 11, 1871
ADAMS Olive of Painted Post, NY　　　Big Flats, NY

FITCH H. L. of New Hampton, Io.　　　November 7, 1871
STREETER Mrs. Mary M. R. dau of George L. **RYON**　　　Lawrenceville, Pa.

HARRIS Theodore R. of Cohocton, NY　　　November 10, 1871
LYON H. Ella dau of D. W. of Hamilton Sta., NY　　　Hamilton Sta., NY

PERRY Edwin F. of Woodhull, NY　　　November 24, 1871
OWENS Elmira of Rathbone, NY　　　Addison, NY

SPONATRE Adelbert of Dansville, NY　　　November 2, 1871
COLLINS Kittie of Dansville, NY　　　Dansville, NY

RICE Charles of Fremont, NY　　　November 15, 1871
GALLUP Lottie of Fremont, NY　　　Fremont, NY

KINER John of Mi.　　　December 7, 1871
GILLETT H. Josephine of Big Flats, NY　　　Big Flats, NY

SACKETT Emerson of Corning, NY　　　November 30, 1871
CALKINS Delia of Corning, NY

BROWN Lorenzo of Jasper, NY　　　December 6, 1871
PRUTZMAN Laura E. of Jasper, NY　　　Jasper, NY

STOWELL Marcus of Lindley, NY　　　December 20, 1871
HART Helen A. of Catharine, NY　　　Elmira, NY

HUDSON Michael of Farmerville, Canada　　　December 12, 1871
MARCH Emma of Corning, NY　　　Corning, NY

SEYMOUR Elbert B. of Corning, NY　　　December 20, 1871
TODD Emma L. dau of Maj. L. of Corning, NY　　　Corning, NY

SKINKLE Abram F. of Savona, NY　　　January 1, 1872
MERRILL Mary E. of Corning, NY

PECKHAM Charles M. of Binghamton, NY　　　December 28, 1871
GREGORY Nellie M. dau of Emerson of Canton, NY　　　Caton, NY

KIFF David of Hornby, NY　　　December 27, 1871
GOODSELL Delia C. of Hornby, NY　　　Hornby, NY

REMMEL Valentine of Corning, NY　　　December 31, 1871
QUANDT Augusta of Corning, NY　　　Painted Post, NY

CARR Charles A. of Albion, NY　　　January 4, 1872
PALMER Ella R. dau of Wilson of Coopers Plains, NY　　　Corning, NY

GRAY Edward F. of Cambridgeport, Mass.
DORSEY Lizzie dau of Mrs. M. D. **SMITH** of Corning, NY

November 29, 1871
Boston, Mass.

NIVER Weller of Caton, NY
HUNT Nellie M. dau of Arad J. of Caton, NY

January 10, 1872

GERON M. of E. Charleston, Pa.
NIVER Marion L. dau of E. D. of Caton, NY

January 16, 1872
Caton, NY

PIERCE Russell E. of Knoxville, NY
CONOVER Jennie K. of Knoxville, NY

February 5, 1872
Knoxville, NY

WESTCOTT Byron
TERWILLIGER Mary dau of Serene of Lindley, NY

December 17, 1871
Lindley, NY

HILL S. J. Md. of Caton, NY
SOULE Anna A. Md. of Ft. Dodge, Io.

February 2, 1872
Geneva, NY

MORRISON William of Corning, NY
MC GOVERN Kate of Corning, NY

February 7, 1872
Corning, NY

SIRINE Oscar of Watkins, NY
SOULE Olive A. of Watkins, NY

February 14, 1872
Corning, NY

REED W. Wallace of Corning, NY
FULLER Mary L. dau of Mrs. L. T. of Corning, NY

February 1, 1872
Corning, NY

HEESE Abraham of Corning, NY
MINIER Mary Ophelia dau of John of Big Flats, NY

February 14, 1872

MARLAND George of Corning, NY
MARSHALL Elmira of Corning, NY

February 22, 1872
Corning, NY

SEELEY Jesse of Coopers Plains, NY
WOOLEVER Mrs. Charlotte M. of Hornellsville, NY

February 29, 1872
Hornellsville, NY

PECK Thomas R. of Corning, NY
BRIGGS Hattie L. of Gibson, NY

March 26, 1872
Gibson, NY

POND Edward C. of Corning, NY
MECARG Helen E. dau of J. B. of Corning, NY

April 6, 1872
Corning, NY

STEARNS A. C. of Corning, NY
HOWARD Mrs. A. J. of Rochester, NY

April 16, 1872
Rochester, NY

HALLIDAY James H. of Thurston, NY
WILBER Sarah M. of Bath, NY

April 10, 1872
Savona, NY

BURNAP John Seneca of Hornby, NY
BIXBY Lydia Ann dau of Rev. A. of Frewsburg, NY

April 15, 1872
Hornby, NY

HUNGERFORD Elias B. of Corning, NY (Newspaper date) May 9, 1872
HILL Emily dau of William P. of Corning, NY   Corning, NY

MARTIN Edward S. of Dundee, NY   May 8, 1872
SAYLES Inez M. dau of Alexander of Painted Post, NY   Painted Post, NY

SMITH Amasa   May 8, 1872
CHRISTIAN Libbie dau of Thomas of Corning, NY   Corning, NY

COCHRAN J. H. of Corning, NY   May 24, 1872
WICKS Annie dau of Hiram of Corning, NY   Corning, NY

TAYLOR Rev. Banjamin F.   June 2, 1872
STEVENS Margaret A. of Lawrenceville, Pa.   Elmira, NY

WILLSON J. R. of Rushville, NY   June 12, 1872
HALL Mrs. A. of Cohocton, NY   Corning, NY

SQUIRES Edward N. of Corning, NY   June 20, 1872
DUNNING Euretta S. dau of William R. Dunning   Geneva, NY

GREENLEAF G. W. of Mansfield, Pa.   July 3, 1872
PORTER Angeline of Mansfield, Pa.   Corning, NY

SUTHERLAND George B.   (Newspaper date) July 11, 1872
JUDSON Louise C. dau of late Rev. David F. of Addison   Prattsburgh, NY

MELONEY James of Campbell, NY   July 4, 1872
SHAW Anna of Campbell, NY   Corning, NY

WILLIAMS H. H. of Thurston, NY   July 3, 1872
CORNELL Emma M. of Thurston, NY   Knoxville, NY

BEEMAN Oliver of Ft. Ann, NY   July 16, 1872
ADAMS Mary C. dau of S. W. of Corning, NY   Corning, NY

AHLE Valentine of Corning, NY   July 18, 1872
QUANDT Anna of Corning, NY   Corning, NY

DRAKE David S. of Corning, NY   August 14, 1872
TILLOTSON Mary E. of Corning, NY   Corning, NY

GRIDLEY Albert L. of Caton, NY (Newspaper date) August 15, 1872
WOOD Prue D. of Carlisle, Oh.   Carlisle, Oh.

THOMPSON Alanson of Montour, NY   September 1, 1872
SPENCER Louise dau of Smith Spencer of Corning, NY   Big Flats, NY

GREEN E. B. of Tioga, Pa.   September 11, 1872
NICHOLS M. D. of Tioga, Pa.   Corning, NY

KING William of Corning, NY **BAKER** Emma of Corning, NY	September 14, 1872 Corning, NY
CLEVELAND Ordine M. of Elmira, NY **BACON** Mary dau of Joseph T. of Corning, NY	September 19, 1872 Corning, NY
BAXTER Duncan H. of Corning, NY **SORNBERGER** Mina F. step dau of Justin M. **SMITH**	September 19, 1872 Corning, NY
GREENFIELD Charles E. of Corning, NY **GILBER** Julia E. of Corning, NY	September 16, 1872 Corning, NY
SLY P. R. of Hornby, NY **CUTLER** S. J. dau of James E. of Big Flats, NY	September 25, 1872 Big Flats, NY
BALLARD M. O. of Horseheads, NY **VEDDER** A. H. of Covington, Pa.	September 26, 1872 Corning, NY
MILLARD Miles H. of the Corning Journal Office **CORCORAN** Julia C. of Corning, NY	October 16, 1872 Corning, NY
HARRISON Henry of Hornby, NY **TAYLORSON** Hannah dau of Thomas of Corning, NY	October 16, 1872 Corning, NY
MC MULLEN George of Corning, NY (Newspaper date) **HELSER** Lizzie of Corning, NY	October 24, 1872 Elmira, NY
CROOLEY Arthur of Corning, NY **VAN WELT** Mary E. of State Line, Pa.	October 28, 1872 Corning, NY
MORSE Roswell of Addison, NY **BELLINGER** Nancy C. of Addison, NY	October 30, 1872 Painted Post, NY
BURGET Henry of Coopers Plains, NY **WEAVER** Annie of Bradford, NY	November 6, 1872 Coopers Plains, NY
ANGEL Prentice of Hornellsville, NY **BABCOCK** Lois of Cameron, NY	October 19, 1872 Cameron, NY
BAILEY L. L. of Wellsboro, Pa. **HILL** Lizzie C. of Lindley, NY	November 7, 1872 Lindley, NY
GREGORY B. L. of Caton, NY **HUNT** Mary E. of Caton, NY	November 7, 1872 Caton, NY
KING William S. of Corning, NY **CHURCHER** Mary J. of Corning, NY	December 17, 1872 Corning, NY
COOPER Fred S. of Coopers Plains, NY **MERRILL** Frankie J. of Painesville, Oh.	November 27, 1872 Painesville, Oh.

JONES Henry B. of Dexter, Mi.
ALEXANDER Kittie M. of Corning, NY

December 24, 1872
Corning, NY

Hammondsport Herald

May 7, 1874 - December 31, 1884

WOLCOTT James E. of Rochester, NY
CHASE Ida J. of Rochester, NY

September 30, 1874
Rochester, NY

CATCHPOLE James of Bath, NY
SIMONS Phoebe L. of Hammondsport, NY

October 3, 1874
Hammondsport, NY

LE BRITON Charles of Urbana, NY
MOSSER Maria Barbara of Urbana, NY late of France

November 18, 1874
Hamondsport, NY

RICHARDS F. J. of Bath, NY
BOWES Delia of Bath, NY

June 8, 1874
Elmira, NY

POWERS Thomas of Bath, NY
SHANLEY Mary of Bath, NY

November 29, 1874
Bath, NY

CROOKSTON Manley S. of Wayne, NY
JACOBUS Mary E. of Wayne, NY

December 30, 1874
Wayne, NY

NICHOLS Frank T. of Dundee, NY
HARRICK Ritta W. of Bradford, NY

January 11, 1875
Bradford, NY

GLEASON Alfred of Wayne, NY
COYL Almeda A. of Bath, NY

January 18, 1875
Hammondsport, NY

LONGWELL Ira T. of Hammondsport, NY
HOLLY Sarah M. of Rochelle, Ill.

December 17, 1874
Flag, Ill.

HORTON John of Wayne, NY
BAILEY Amanda E. of Urbana, NY

February 25, 1875
Bath, NY

VAN GELDER Frank of Hammondsport, NY
LAUGHLIN Theresa of Hammondsport, NY

March 27, 1875
Prattsburgh, NY

KEELER George of Hammondsport, NY
QUICK Eva of Hammondsport, NY

March 31, 1875
Hammondsport, NY

BENHAM L. C. of Penn Yan, NY
MOSHER Frank S. of Penn Yan, NY

April 17, 1875
Penn Yan, NY

SULLIVAN Prof. J. D. of Hammondsport, NY
ARCHER Hattie of Hemlock Lake, NY

April 11, 1875
Hemlock Lake, NY

WALTON G. B. of Dundee, NY
DOUGLAS E. Emma of Mt. Washington, NY

April 25, 1875
Mt. Washington, NY

BENHAM Henry of Hammondsport, NY
SMITH Mrs. Sarah C. of W. Bloomfield, NY

April 21, 1875
W. Bloomfield, NY

SMITH Frank B. of Mitchellville, NY
TOWNSEND Libbie of Mitchellville, NY

May 1, 1875
Hammondsport, NY

TOZER Andrew G. of Troupsburgh, NY
SANFORD Esther A. of Hammondsport, NY

May 5, 1875
Hammondsport, NY

HAWLEY Dr. E. H. of New York City
BAKER Kate of Hammondsport, NY

April 28, 1875
Pleasant Valley, NY

DAINS George W. of Urbana, NY
SHERMAN Helen T. of Urbana, NY

May 27, 1875
Urbana, NY

RETAN Albert
CHUBB Melissa formerly of Hammondsport, NY

April 14, 1875
Grand Rapids, Mi.

CLARK A. Darwin of Prattsburgh, NY
CARPENTER Emma J. dau of Franklin M of Pulteney, NY

June 29, 1875
Pulteney, NY

HALL Milon H. of Hammondsport, NY
WOOD Lydia A. of Hammondsport, NY

September 1, 1875
Hammondsport, NY

DICKEY Mathew of Cameron, NY
REESE Anna M. of Cameron, NY

October 6, 1875
Hammondsport, NY

CUMMINGS Scott of Farmersville, NY
HOLBROOK Carrie B. of Wayne, NY

October 13, 1875
Wayne, NY

REYNOLDS Samuel Sidney of Hammondsport, NY
DUNNING Mary Frank of Hammondsport, NY

October 21, 1875
Hammondsport, NY

CHRISLER Alverne of Bradford, NY
WOOD Lavinia M. of Orange, NY

October 21, 1875
Orange, NY

SMITH William C. of New York City
MOORE Mary E. dau of Col. S.

December 16, 1875
Lake Keuka, NY

LAYTON Tyler of Urbana, NY
DIMMICK G. E. of Thurston, NY

December 15, 1875
Bath, NY

HONEYMAN Reading
WOOD Mary H. of Urbana, NY

December 8, 1875
Urbana, NY

DE PEW William of Pulteney, NY
SHUART Margelia of Pulteney, NY

December 29, 1875
Pulteney, NY

COVERT Charles Edward of Potter, NY — February 6, 1876
JOHNSON Emma Rosalie of Pulteney, NY — Hammondsport, NY

BURROUGHS Edward Beardsley of Bridgeport, Ct. — April 19, 1876
GARDNER Harriet Foote dau of Rev. H. V. — Hammondsport, NY

JUMP Rensalaer of Hammondsport, NY — June 1, 1876
YOUNGLOVE Libbie Hoyt of Hammondsport, NY — Hammondsport, NY

CROSS Albert S. — June 21, 1876
BRUSH Sarah — Pulteney, NY

PIERCE Frank of Urbana, NY — July 5, 1876
VAN GELDER Mary E. of Urbana, NY — Mt. Washington, NY

MAYERS Joe of New York Ciry — July 12, 1876
BAKER Ettie formerly of Hammondsport, NY — Corning, NY

COMPTON Charles of Bradford, NY — August 31, 1876
WILLOVER Ella of Wayne, NY

HORTON Emmett of Barrington, NY — November 2, 1876
SWARTS Lizzie of Barrington, NY — Hammondsport, NY

MOORE Trevor — November 16, 1876
BRINK Anna

WHITE Walter Otis of Chicago, Ill. — December 12, 1876
RUNNER Csarina dau of Dr. Runner of Hammondsport, NY — Hammondsport, NY

HAWLEY Charles M. — January 29, 1877
FRAZEE Mary — Hammondsport, NY

WHITE A. A. of Wellsville, NY formerly of Hammondsport — March 8, 1877
OSBORNE Carie E. of Pulteney, NY — Corning, NY

VAN GELDER J. C. — May 17, 1877
EVANS Idelya — Hammondsport, NY

MOORE Hobart J. — June 6, 1877
HALL Le Retta dau of James Hall — Hammondsport, NY

MAXON Edward J. of Augusta, Ky. — July 3, 1877
CUSHING Maude dau of Rev. J. T. of Hammondsport, NY — Augusta, Ky.

LOVERIDGE Rev. D. E. of Norwich, NY — July 31, 1877
ALCOCK Ellen of Hammondsport, NY — Hammondsport, NY

COLEGROVE George Benjamin of Prattsburgh, NY — September 28, 1877
FOX Elnora of Prattsburgh, NY

LAPHAM John of Penn Yan, NY
LOCKWOOD Anna R. of Hammondsport, NY
October 7, 1877
Bath, NY

WAGSTAFF J. T. of Pulteney, NY (Newspaper date)
DUBOIS Lilly dau of Rev. J. G. of Pulteney, NY
October 24, 1877
Pulteney, NY

KEELER J. William of Bath, NY
READ Lizzie P. dau of late Dr. Read of Bath, NY
October 17, 1877
Bath, NY

DYER Eugene Benjamin of Hammondsport, NY
MANHART Margaret Maddia of Howard, NY
November 25, 1877
Hammondsport, NY

FAIRCHILD S. B.
HAMMOND Mary
February 12, 1878
Hammondsport, NY

FULLER Henry S. of Syracuse, NY
BEYEA Fanny dau of A. T. of Wayne, NY
February 18, 1878
Wayne, NY

LONGWELL James R. of Urbana, NY
GILBERT S. A. of Tyrone, NY
February 28, 1878

SANFORD John of Hammondsport, NY
SANFORD Mary of Hammondsport, NY
March 27, 1878

SPRAGUE George of S. Addison, NY
MC DOWELL Helen of Tuscarora, NY
May 3, 1878

BRUNDAGE Frank of Urbana, NY
STEWART Mate of Urbana, NY
October 16, 1878
Bath, NY

MILLS John C. of Pleasant Valley, NY
SHOEMAKER Jennie of Dundee, NY
March 21, 1879
Dundee, NY

DAVENPORT John of Bath, NY
LYON Sarah of Bath, NY
June 11, 1879
Bath, NY

HUBBARD E. A. of Prattsburgh, NY
SMITH Cornelia A. of Prattsburgh, NY
July 30, 1879

HILL Dr. Joseph B. of Picton, Ontario, Can.
PECK Lizzie L. of Pulteney, NY
August 3, 1879
Pulteney, NY

HARPER Thomas of Hammondsport, NY
NORTHRUP Kittie of Hammondsport, NY
August 30, 1879
Hammondsport, NY

WAGNER Charles of Pulteney, NY
VAN GELDER Jennie dau of Joseph of Pulteney, NY
October 21, 1879
Pulteney, NY

MANDEL Edward formerly of Spier, Germany
WALTERS Mrs. widow of Charles Walters
October 30, 1879
Bath, NY

ST JOHN G. S. of Clarendon, NY
WAGSTAFF Nettie of Pulteney, NY

December 7, 1879
Pulteney, NY

BABCOCK Dewitt of Branchport, NY
ARMSTRONG Nettie of Pulteney, NY

December 19, 1879
Prattsburgh, NY

PLUMB Orville L. of Canandaigua, NY
WOOD Ida M. of Hammondsport, NY

November 27, 1879
Hammondsport, NY

WARD W. Fred of Hammondsport, NY
QUICK Jennie V. of Hammondsport, NY

February 4, 1880
Hammondsport, NY

BEDELL Hervey of Pulteney, NY
HILL Ella E. dau of C. C. S. Hill of Pulteney, NY

February 18, 1880
Pulteney, NY

HORTON H. Carson of Bath, NY
LYON Libbie of S. Pulteney, NY

March 10, 1880
S. Pulteney, NY

GIBSON George of Pulteney, NY
COGSWELL Mrs. Avesta of Prattsburgh, NY

March 24, 1880
Pulteney, NY

LYONS Samuel of S. Pulteney, NY
SCOTT Lindsay of Hemlock Lake, NY

April 7, 1880
Hemlock Lake, NY

BAILEY Cyrus of Hammondsport, NY
BROWN Josie of Hammondsport, NY

June 15, 1880
Hammondsport, NY

BALL Harry C. of Pulteney, NY
HORTON Ella R. of Pulteney, NY

June 19, 1880
Pulteney, NY

LOOK Frank H. of Bath, NY
UHL Matilda M. of Bonney Hill, NY

July 22, 1880
Hammondsport, NY

GENUNG Jacob L. of Bradford, NY
CROOKSTON Eliza D. of Wayne, NY

August 10, 1880
Hammondsport, NY

BARNES J. P.
ALLIS Gertrude

October 16, 1880
Hammondsport, NY

WHEELER Charles G. of Hammondsport, NY
LOZIER M. Adella of Dansville, NY

October 27, 1880
Dansville, NY

JACOBS William A. of Urbana, NY
WOOD Martha J. of Urbana, NY

November 3, 1880
Urbana, NY

GARLINGHOUSE L. A. Md. formerly of Cleveland, Oh.
COREY Hattie of Barrington, NY

November 8, 1880
Barrington, NY

SKINKLE Charles S.
HORR Mary A. of Pulteney, NY

December 1, 1880
Pulteney, NY

SEBRING John C. of Pulteney, NY	December 7, 1880
BELL Susie A. of Pulteney, NY	Pulteney, NY
BROWN Cornelius of Friendship, NY	January 20, 1881
HORTON Addie of Pulteney, NY	Pulteney, NY
EARLY Addison of Prattsburgh, NY	March 13, 1881
CHILSON Mollie A. of Prattsburgh, NY	Hammondsport, NY
WIXSON J. of Barrington, NY	April 6, 1881
MERRING Jennie of Rathbone, NY	Rathbone, NY
CONNELLY James of Hammondsport, NY	April 27. 1881
MARE Mrs. Mary C. of Liberty, NY	Pleasant Valley, NY
VOGT John of Hammondsport, NY	May 31, 1881
HILPADD Anna of Hammondsport, NY	Hammondsport, NY
DUNNING Wesley M. of Lindley, NY	July 3, 1881
BROOKHEART Belle J. of Hammondsport, NY	Hammondsport, NY
HANSON George of Hammondsport, NY	July 31, 1881
CHISSOM Sarah of Hammondsport, NY	Pulteney, NY
CARR Ed W. formerly of Hammondsport, NY	August 27, 1881
WEAVER Mollie of Elmira, NY at sis Mrs. Carman **CARR**	Pleasant Valley, NY
HONEYMAN Theodore of Mt. Washington, NY	December 1, 1881
WOOD Ida dau of Joseph of Hammondsport, NY	Hammondsport, NY
DUNNING William E. formerly of Hammondsport, NY	December 1, 1881
THOMAS Naomi K. of Colorado Spr., Col.	Colorado Spr. Col.
MARGESON Martin of Urbana, NY	December 18, 1881
NIVER Bell of Urbana, NY	Urbana, NY
BILLINGS Oscar C. of Wheeler, NY	December 16, 1881
FOX Emma C. of Wheeler, NY	Hammondsport, NY
BEAM Charles S. of Dundee, NY	December 31, 1881
INGERSOLL Minnie dau of Joseph form. of Hammondsport	Painted Post, NY
HAIGHT Dora	January 2, 1882
ROSENCRANS Emma of Burdett, NY	Burdett, NY
ABER Frank of Urbana, NY	January 25, 1882
BENNITT Elsie of Urbana, NY	Hammondsport, NY
VAN GELDER Frank of Bath, NY (Newspaper date)	February 1, 1882
EARLY Ruvy J. of Prattsburgh, NY	Prattsburgh, NY

FLAHERTY James of Prattsburgh, NY   February 7, 1882
HEFFERMAN Mary of Hammondsport, NY   Hammondsport, NY

FOX C. L. of Italy, NY   March 1, 1882
RETAN Alice E. dau of N. Retan of S. Pulteney, NY   S. Pulteney, NY

GRAY Clint   April 4, 1882
COGSWELL Mella

FREY Gotlieb E.   April 3, 1882
SCHMOKER Josephine

FRENCH Lewis D. of Hammondsport, NY   April 18, 1882
JAYNES Carrie dau of William of Hammondsport, NY   Hammondsport, NY

SMITH Moses of N. Urbana, NY   April 30, 1882
WELSH Edna M. of Urbana, NY   Hammondsport, NY

GILMER C. W. of Bradford, NY   May 27, 1882
BENNITT L. E. of Bradford, NY   Hammondsport, NY

ROFF William of Pulteney, NY   July 12, 1882
VAN GELDER Carrie of Urbana, NY   Urbana, NY

BROWN Lewellyn H.   October 12, 1882
BOSWORTH Louise Mary dau of Rev. B. of Hammondsport   Hammondsport, NY

FORT Truman of Thurston, NY   November 23, 1882
HILL Sarah of S. Pulteney, NY   S. Pulteney, NY

NORTON Maj. T. H. of Wheeling W. Va.   December 12, 1882
WHEELER Nellie dau of Gratton H. of Pleasant Valley   Pleasant Valley, NY

LOCKE Fred W. of Urbana, NY   November 29, 1882
SANFORD Ella M. of Sonora, NY   Sonora, NY

WOOD Frank of Hammondsport, NY   December 11, 1882
HALLIDAY Fanny of Hammondsport, NY   Buffalo, NY

EGGLESTON Fred of Hammondsport, NY   December 20, 1882
FRENCH Matie dau of Mrs. E. French of Hammondsport   Hammondsport, NY

PITCHER Hyatt of Avon, NY   December 23, 1882
HALLIDAY Sophia of Bath, NY   Hammondsport, NY

BUSH Melvin H. of Hammondsport, NY   December 21, 1882
FISKE Elizabeth M. of Hammondsport, NY   Hammondsport, NY

COREY Chester of N. Cohocton, NY   (Newspaper date) January 10, 1883
BALLARD Frances of Hammondsport, NY

LEWIS Charles V. of Hammondsport, NY — February 6, 1883 — Savona, NY
SMITH Nellie of Savona, NY

FOLSOM Frank B. — February 11, 1883 — N. Urbana, NY
HEMENWAY Mary E. of Hammondsport, NY

BEDELL Sanford R. of Pulteney, NY — February 21, 1883
DREW Annie J. dau of James of Hammondsport, NY

CORYELL Charles — March 15, 1883 — Urbana, NY
JOHNSON Carrie M. of Urbana, NY

ELLAS Harry S. of Hammondsport, NY — March 26, 1883 — Hammondsport, NY
FINCH Laura of Bath, NY

BENNITT Fred formerly of Hammondsport, NY — April 19, 1883 — Joliett, Ill.
REED Anna Earl of Joliett, Ill.

RAYMOND Homer M. of Penn Yan, NY — May 16, 1883 — S. Pulteney, NY
HANSON Bertha of S. Pulteney, NY

SANTEE Dr. W. E. — June 12, 1883 — Hammondsport, NY
HOWELL Isabelle

PARKER George H. of Hammondsport, NY — June 20, 1883 — Hammondsport, NY
BEEKMAN Lydia of Hammondsport, NY

TOWNSEND William B. of Penn Yan, NY — August 1, 1883 — Hammondsport, NY
LONGWELL Florence A. dau of David of Hammondsport

MANDEL Edward of Wheeling W. Va. — August 15, 1883 — Hammondsport, NY
WHEELER Mary dau of Grattan H. of Hammondsport, NY

RAY William E. of Hammondsport, NY — August 21, 1883 — Hammondsport, NY
DREW Melissa I. of S. Pulteney, NY

SMITH John of Hammondsport, NY — August 19, 1883 — Avoca, NY
MARGESON Mrs. Bradley of N. Urbana, NY

EARNEST Quincey of Wayne, NY — September 25, 1883 — Tyrone, NY
LOOK Ophelia of Wayne, NY

CARMAN Joseph of Pleasant Valley, NY — October 20, 1883 — Barrington, NY
HUNT Kate E. of Pleasant Valley, NY

STREHL Adam of Patterson, NJ — October 25, 1883 — Hammondsport, NY
ARGUS Appolonia dau of Martin of Hammondsport, NY

HOWELL George S. of Hammondsport, NY — November 22, 1883 — Prattsburgh, NY
BLACKINGTON Mrs. Susan at sis Mrs. James **WALDO**

FLEMING Thomas of Pulteney, NY   December 4, 1883
FAUCETT Kate of Pulteney, NY   Penn Yan, NY

VAN GELDER Henry   January 26, 1884
LONGWELL Mary E.   Mt. Washington, NY

HAUS Benjamin F. of Wayne, NY   March 2, 1884
HALL Ella M. of Wayne, NY   Wayne, NY

EARLY Elmor A. of Urbana, NY   March 28, 1884
DE PEW Nora M. of Urbana, NY   Hammondsport, NY

VAN GELDER Willard of Hammondsport, NY   April 16, 1884
MC LEAN Mary E. of Avoca, NY   Hammondsport, NY

WIXOM Albert of Urbana, NY   April 23, 1884
SHERMAN Adeline of Urbana, NY   Fairville, NY

CURTIS Christopher of Avoca, NY   (Newspaper date) May 14, 1884
WALTERS Jennie of Hammondsport, NY formerly of Bath Elmira, NY

BLODGETT J. Delos   May 13, 1884
CHIDSEY Mrs. Josie E. dau of George **WAGSTAFF** Pulteney, NY

HALLENBECK William A. of Urbana, NY   August 14, 1884
GOODENOUGH Ella E. of Hammondsport, NY   Hammondsport, NY

BOWES Michael of Brooklyn, NY   August 14, 1884
LAUGHLIN Mary of Hammondsport, NY   Hammondsport, NY

BROWN William S. of Hammondsport, NY   August 19, 1884
BAILEY Nettie of Hammondsport, NY   Hammondsport, NY

PIERCE Alfred P. of Kanona, NY   September 16, 1884
BUTTS Cornelia of Kanona, NY

PIPER Theodore H. of Niagara Falls, NY   November 18, 1884
STRYKER Emma E. of Hammondsport, NY   Hammondsport, NY

MC DOWELL Edward C. of Hammondsport (News. date) December 17, 1884
LOUNSBERRY Carrie E. of Hammondsport, NY   Hammondsport, NY

ROBINSON Willis H. of Hammondsport, NY   December 11, 1884
CHAPMAN Flora dau of George M. Chapman   Hammondsport, NY

SHANLEY James son of Patrick of Mt. Washington, NY December 15, 1884
TAYLOR Josephine of Spencer, NY   Hammondsport, NY

ROBBINS Edward of S. Pulteney, NY   December 24, 1884
LANDERS Nettie dau of H. D. of Pulteney, NY   Pulteney, NY

Hornell Daily Times

January 2, 1879 - June 30, 1881

BURDETT G. R. of Fremont, NY **VAN KEURAN** Mary of Fremont, NY	January 1, 1879 Fremont, NY
YOKUM Frank of Canaseraga, NY **LUCE** Lizzie of Canaseraga, NY	December 31, 1878 Canaseraga, NY
GRIGGS W. S. **HOPPER** Edith M.	December 24, 1878 Troupsburgh, NY
HOUSER Fayette V. of Woodhull, NY **HARRIS** Armenia of Woodhull, NY	December 25, 1878 Woodhull, NY
ROOT Erastus of N. Almond, NY **STODDARD** Mrs. Susan A. of N. Almond, NY	December 28, 1878 Byersville, NY
GALLAGHER James of Andover, NY **CANWELL** Belle of Andover, NY	January 7, 1879 Andover, NY
COMSTOCK Thomas M. of Andover, NY **BAKER** Mrs. Almira of Andover, NY	January 9, 1879 Andover, NY
PERRY Frank G. of Ithaca, NY **BREWSTER** Sarah E. of Greenwood, NY	January 9, 1879
WILLEY Loly of S. Dansville, NY **WEBB** Elizabeth of S. Dansville, NY	December 15, 1878 S, Dansville, NY
HALE Lewis of Hartsville, NY **CONRAD** Mary of Jasper, NY	January 20, 1879 Greenwood, NY
TUTTLE Gurnsey P. of Alfred, NY **THOMAS** Ida May of Alfred, NY	January 15, 1879 Alfred, NY
BROWN Aaron of Hornellsville, NY **ABER** Mrs. ____ of Savona, NY	January 20, 1879 Savona, NY
ZIELLY Henry L. of Avoca, NY **SQUIRES** Belle of Avoca, NY	January 21, 1879
HENRY Cassius M. of Birdsall, NY **MC FALL** Bohema S. of Ovid, NY	January 29, 1879 Elmira, NY
MAYS James of Hornellsville, NY **DEMMERY** Lydia A. of Hornellsville, NY	January 30, 1879 Hornellsville, NY

EDSON Wyman L. of Union, NY January 15, 1879
BARTLETT Emma R. Whitesville, NY

CLARK Edward of Wellsville, NY January 28, 1879
EARLY Nettie of Wellsville, NY Wellsville, NY

GOLLOBER Isaac of Hornby, NY (Newspaper date) February 7, 1879
TUCHLER Fena of Hornby, NY Hornby, NY

RAYMOND John L. of N. Bingham, Pa. January 28, 1879
CLARK Mate of Spring Mills, NY Whitesville, NY

CARTER J. of Almond, NY February 8, 1879
CORBETT Emma J. of Hartsville, NY Hornellsville, NY

HILL George W. of Caton, NY February 6, 1879
BREESE Stella C. of Caton, NY Corning, NY

HARTER Lafayette G. of S. Dansville, NY January 23, 1879
HECOX Lucy M. of Howard, NY Howard, NY

ALLUM Renaldo of Andover, NY February 2, 1879
GLOVER Mary A. of Andover, NY Wellsville, NY

BARROWS J. M. of Cameron, NY January 29, 1879
COATES Lillie V. of Cameron, NY

THATCHER Charles Rollin of Hornellsville, NY February 13, 1879
GRAVES Alice W. of Jacksonville, Ill. Lynnville, Ill.

WILLEY J. W. of S. Dansville, NY February 19, 1879
LOUCKS Jennie of Fremont, NY Fremont, NY

HAWLEY Adelbert of Cameron, NY February 18, 1879
BABCOCK Rose M. of Cameron, NY Cameron, NY

O'BRINE James of Bath, NY February 24, 1879
RYAN Bridget of Hornellsville, NY Hornellsville, NY

DEUEL Charles F. of Canisteo, NY Febauary 19, 1879
SNYDER Mary A. of Canisteo, NY Hornellsville, NY

WALLACE John T. of S. Dansville, NY February 23, 1879
MC GEE Maggie of Fremont, NY Fremont, NY

CLINEBURY Ignatius of Lindley, NY February 19, 1879
BUCK Mary E. of Tuscarora, NY Tuscarora, NY

PALMER Hiram E. of Hornellsville, NY March 1, 1879
HAGADORN Sophrona of Hornellsville, NY Hornellsville, NY

BEYEA Lewis S. of Hartsville, NY	March 1, 1879
WHITFORD Hattie E. of Hartsville, NY	Alfred Ctr., NY
KELLOGG J. H. Md.	February 22, 1879
EATON Ella E. of Alfred Ctr., NY	Battle Creek, Mi.
BECKER John M. of Hornellsville, NY	March 11, 1879
COOMBS Lottie of Hornellsville, NY	Hornellsville, NY
MORITZ Joseph of Hornellsville, NY	March 12, 1879
GREGG Ida of Wellsville, NY	Hornellsville, NY
ALLVORD Sidney V. of S. Dansville, NY	February 27, 1879
SHERMER Hannah of S. Dansville, NY	Canaseraga, NY
STAPLES Solon of Lewiston, Me.	March 4, 1879
PARKER Mrs. Cynthia A. of Lewiston, Me.	Hornellsville, NY
STEWART Adonijah	March 12, 1879
CRANDALL Eusebia	Greenwood, NY
NORTHRUP Watson F.	March 12, 1879
CLYDE Nancy	Cameron, NY
TRAVIS Nelson C. of Canisteo, NY	March 12, 1879
FOSTER Hattie E. of Jasper, NY	Addison, NY
PIERCE Francis M. of Painted Post, NY	March 11, 1879
ALBEE Eva M. of Addison, NY	Addison, NY
BURT S. W. of Corning, NY	March 22, 1879
TATOR Mrs. Adeline A. of Corning, NY	Corning, NY
BAILEY Henry M. of Fremont, NY	March 24, 1879
RATHBUN Maria L. of Mt. Morris, NY	Fremont, NY
THOMAS James H. of Hornellsville, NY	March 28, 1879
MORRISON Nellie H. of Warren Pa.	Bradford, Pa.
MILLER C. F. of Hornellsville, NY	March 31, 1879
DORSEY Penie F. of Bath, NY	Bath, NY
PHILLIPS J. M. of Avoca, NY	March 26, 1879
FLYNN Mary L. of Bath, NY	Bath, NY
SMITH Eli of Soldiers and Sailors Home, Bath, NY	April 1, 1879
WELLS Mrs. Harriet L. of Bath, NY	Bath, NY
JANES Edwin W. of Canisteo, NY	April 2, 1879
BARTLETT Fanny of Addison, NY	Addison, NY

BURNESS George W. of Fremont, NY   April 7, 1879
COTTON Alice L. of Adrian, NY   Hornellsville, NY

PALMER Eugene A. of Belmont, NY   April 13, 1879
STONE Lena B. of Belmont, NY   Hornellsville, NY

BENNETT Germon M. of Troupsburgh, NY   March 19, 1879
CHASE Fannie of Troupsburgh, NY   Troupsburgh, NY

BISHOP Jacob of Troupsburgh, NY   March 26, 1879
GRANDY Augusta of Troupsburgh, NY   Troupsburgh, NY

BAKER Charles H. of Alfred, NY   April 6, 1879
MABURY Mrs. Mary A. of Alfred, NY   Andover, NY

HIGGINS Justin V. R.   April 16, 1879
ELLIS Mary M. at res of Albert Ellis

ELLIS Hiram of Arkport, NY   April 16, 1879
EVANS Elnora L. of Arkport, NY at res of Albert Ellis   Arkport, NY

SHERMAN Henry P. of Canisteo, NY   April 23, 1879
VORHEES Miranda M. of Canisteo, NY   Hornellsville, NY

WILSON George M. of Howard, NY   April 20, 1879
WELLS Hattie of Howard, NY

CUNNINGHAM John of Hornellsville, NY   April 23, 1879
WELSH Nellie of Hornellsville, NY   Hornellsville, NY

HECKERS Jacob of Hartsville, NY   April 17, 1879
WHITING Ida E. of Hartsville, NY   Hartsville, NY

CRANE Sidney H. of Hornellsville, NY   April 30, 1879
JOHNSON Sarah of Hornellsville, NY   Hornellsville, NY

SCEARS James D. of Hornellsville, NY   April 20, 1879
TAYLOR Mary E. of Canisteo, NY

DE WITT A. E. of Hornellsville, NY   April 30, 1879
NORTHRUP Ella of Hornellsville, NY   Hornellsville, NY

WIGGINS Dr. Clarence S. of Hornellsville, NY   May 1, 1879
CRIDLER Emma L. dau of Dr. L. of Hornellsville, NY   Hornellsville, NY

BARNEY Alvin W. of W. Union, NY   April 27, 1879
RICHARDSON Clara Bell of Independence, NY   Independence, NY

MORGAN H. E. of Andover, NY   April 20, 1879
BERRY R. M. of Andover, NY   Wellsville, NY

FAULKNER John P. of S. Dansville, NY	May 6, 1879
RICHARDSON Mrs. Emma of Hornellsville, NY	Hornellsville, NY
DAVIS Eugene of New York City	April 29, 1879
RUTHERFORD Maggie of Bath, NY	Cobleskill, NY
WALLACE F. E. of Hornellsville, NY	May 5, 1879
REED Winnie E. of Almond, NY	Almond, NY
PETTINGER W. E. of Hornellsville, NY	May 8, 1879
TOWNSEND Carrie of Wellsville, NY	Wellsville, NY
KIRKUM Henry of Cameron, NY	April 27, 1879
KIRKUM Mrs. Mary of Cameron, NY	N. Cameron, NY
VICKERS Jacob of Hartsville, NY	March 17, 1879
WHITING Ida E. of Hartsville, NY	Hartsville, NY
GRINNOLDS Levi S. of Troupsburgh, NY	May 25, 1879
ACKLEY Charity S. of Troupsburgh, NY	Hornellsville, NY
GREEN Russell P. of Alfred, NY	May 24, 1879
CARR Drucilla W. of Aflred, NY	Alfred, NY
MITCHELL Dr. Samuel Jr. of Hornellsville, NY	May 28, 1879
O'CONNOR Isabella of Hornellsville, NY	Hornellsville, NY
MADISON James A. of Hornellsville, NY	May 26, 1879
WOODARD Mary A. of Hornellsville, NY	Canisteo, NY
DIVEN Frank of Canisteo, NY	May 29, 1879
KING Flora of Canisteo, NY	Canisteo, NY
BORDEN Charles of Campbell, NY	May 25, 1879
CASE Delia of Campbell, NY	Campbell, NY
O'HEARN Jerry of Hornellsville, NY	June 10, 1879
REGAN Mary of Hornellsville, NY	Hornellsville, NY
BAKER Frank F. of Hartsville, NY	June 9, 1879
FOWLER Florence E. of Alfred, NY	Hartsville, NY
THOMAS Charles of Addison, NY	June 18, 1879
MURRAY Mary of Addison, NY	Bath, NY
HOWLAND Frank of Arnot, Pa.	June 18,1879
REYNOLDS Fannie P. of Almond, NY	Almond, NY
HENDERSON W. J. of Scio, NY	June 8, 1879
BAKER Adah of Andover, NY	Wellsville, NY

PEASE Charles C. of Dunkirk, NY   June 24, 1879
HUFF Amelia C. of Hornellsville, NY   Hornellsville, NY

STEVENS Edward J. of Hornellsville, NY   June 25, 1879
ELLIS Clara B. of Hornellsville, NY   Hornellsville, NY

VAN DUSEN Melvin of Howard, NY   June 18, 1879
ELLIS Clara B. of Howard, NY   Howard, NY

MILLER Walter I. of Canaseraga, NY   June 18, 1879
MUNDY Kate A. of Canaseraga, NY   Canaseraga, NY

CAMPBELL Clarence of Bath, NY   June 25, 1879
HODGMAN Mary of Bath, NY   Bath, NY

INGHAM Kirkland W. of Hornellsville, NY   July 2, 1879
SMITH Annette dau of S. C. of Jamestown, NY   Jamestown, NY

BARRETT John of W. Almond, NY   July 4, 1879
BECKWITH Sarah Ann of W. Almond, NY   Alfred, NY

DUNNING Manuel R. of Burns, NY   July 9, 1879
MC INTOSH Delia J. of Almond, NY   Almond, NY

SWAIN Edward   July 6, 1879
WOOD Dora   Andover, NY

TOOMEY Michael of Hornellsville, NY   June 30, 1879
FINNEGAN Sarah of Addison, NY   Addison, NY

FRANCE James of Hornellsville, NY   July 14, 1879
HERRICK Addie of Hornellsville, NY   Hornellsville, NY

SNYDER Frank E. of Hornellsville, NY   July 4, 1879
AYERS Mrs. Louise of Avoca, NY   Prattsburgh, NY

DUNHAM T. Franklin of Prattsburgh, NY   July 4, 1879
HORTON Ida of Prattsburgh, NY   Prattsburgh, NY

GILMORE R. H. of Cedar Rapids, Io.   July 15, 1879
CRANDALL Mary C. of Almond, NY   Almond, NY

ELSTER Justus V. of Cincinnati, Oh.   July 18, 1879
SELPEL Mrs. Agnes E. of Cincinnati, Oh.   Hornellsville, NY

SULLIVAN Abraham W. of Alfred Ctr., NY   July 23, 1879
CATLIN Della May of Elm Valley, NY   Andover, NY

BAKER Daniel   July 13, 1879
HAWKINS May E.   Andover, NY

THOMAS J. Franklin of Alfred, NY
KING Ella C. of Hornellsville, NY

July 24, 1879
Hornellsville, NY

BUTLER Byron of Hornellsville, NY
MOSHER Eliza J. of Hornellsville, NY

June 22, 1879
Hedgesville, NY

WHITCOMB Francis Hale of Alfred, NY
PALMITER Minnie Almira of Alfred, NY

July 26, 1879
Alfred Ctr., NY

COTTON James C. of Fremont, NY
BURDICK Carrie E. of Hornellsville, NY

July 30, 1879
Hornellsville, NY

BURNS James W. of Hornellsville, NY
TOWNER Helen L.

July 30, 1879
Avoca, NY

MADISON Charles
EDWARDS Mrs. Frances of Hornellsville, NY

July 29, 1879
Wellsville, NY

ROCKWELL J. B. of Pembroke, NY
BENTON Mary E. of Hornellsville, NY

June 11, 1879
Hornellsville, NY

DONNELLY Michael of Hornellsville, NY
MURPHY Mary of Hornellsville, NY

August 18, 1879
Hornellsville, NY

LANDRETH Olin H. son of Rev. J. of Canisteo, NY
TAYLOR Kittie dau of William B. of Canisteo, NY

August 20, 1879
Canisteo, NY

GOULD William H. of Woodhull, NY
BRONG Ella of Woodhull, NY

August 17, 1879
Bradford, NY

ALMY Willis of Hartsville, NY
CALL Eva J. of Hartsville, NY

August 30, 1879
Hartsville, NY

BOOTH Isaac M. of Bath, NY
BACKUS Kate of Campbell, NY

August 21, 1879
Corning, NY

DUNHAM William C. of New Market, NJ
BURDICK Juliette of Alfred Ctr., NY

August 30, 1879
Alfred Ctr., NY

SCOTT Charles W. of Canisteo, NY
WELCH Emma F. of Lowell, Mass.

August 24, 1879
Angelica, NY

WILCOX Charles M. of Canaseraga, NY
BOYLAN Mary M. of Canaseraga, NY

August 23, 1879
Alfred Ctr., NY

POST Jacob of Corning, NY
MARSHALL Jennie of Caton, NY

September 7, 1879
Caton, NY

ANDRUS R. P. of Hornellsville, NY
DUNN Maggie of Binghamton, NY

September 9, 1879
Hornellsville, NY

CRANDALL Eugene T.	September 6, 1879
SATTERLEE Estella	Alfred Ctr., NY
BEATTIE Alonzo D. of Hornellsville, NY	September 22, 1879
QUIGLEY Ida M. of Hornellsville, NY	Hornellsville, NY
MC GRAW J. Wesley of Hartsville, NY	September 16, 1879
SNOW Alice of Whitesville, NY	Independence, NY
DAVIS George L. of Canisteo, NY	September 10, 1879
ISBELL Callie dau of Judge of Marion City, Io.	Marion City, Io.
STUART J. G. of Steuben Co. NY	September 23, 1879
WAMBOLD Annis R. of Sparta, NY	Sparta, NY
COOMBS Frank V. of Hornellsville, NY	September 29, 1879
WEST Nettie of Almond, NY	Almond, NY
THOMAS John F. of Wheeler, NY	September 6, 1879
SMITH Ella of Prattsburgh, NY	Wheeler, NY
LONGCORE Eugene S. of Wheeler, NY	September 19, 1879
YOUNGS Mrs. Emma of Wheeler, NY	Wheeler, NY
TENNEY Martin A. of Alfred, NY	September 28, 1879
HALSEY Bertha of Alfred, NY	Almond, NY
STEPHENS George of Canisteo, NY	September 30, 1879
BOVIER Mrs. Sarah A. of Canisteo, NY	Canisteo, NY
MC MULLEN Hugh of Greenwood, NY	September 19, 1879
MC HATTEN Mary of Greenwood, NY	Andover, NY
HADSALL Mark L. of W. Almond, NY	September 17, 1879
YOUNG Emma R. of Birdsall, NY	Birdsall, NY
THRALL Fayette of Corning, NY	September 21, 1879
MC INTYRE Libbie of Corning, NY	Corning, NY
REDFIELD George of Hornellsville, NY	September 25, 1879
STEWART Alice M. of Bath, NY	Bath, NY
MC NIERNEY Mathew	October 12, 1879
SMITH Maggie	Hornellsville, NY
BECK Henry of Corning, NY	October 2, 1879
GITHLER Matilda of Painted Post, NY	Painted Post, NY
DEYOE Clifford of Hornellsville, NY	September 22, 1879
PRESTON Augusta E. of Corning, NY	Big Flats, NY

HANN Claudius of Canisteo, NY
BAKER Nellie A. of Canisteo, NY
October 11, 1879
Knoxville, Pa.

VAN DEMARK Alpheus of Hornellsville, NY
NORTHROP Mary of Hornellsville, NY
October 7, 1879
Hornellsville, NY

COOK Andrus W. of Dansville, NY
HOWARD Nellie of S. Dansville, NY
October 8, 1879
S. Dansville, NY

JONES Orson of Canisteo, NY
HALNINEN Ella of Cameron, NY
October 15, 1879
Jasper, NY

SEAMANS Edward W. of Thurston, NY
BOYCE Estella of Savona, NY
October 8, 1879
Savona, NY

BEYEA James of Hartsville, NY
CARRINGTON Mary of Hartsville, NY
October 12, 1879
Hartsville, NY

BUCK William A. of Corning, NY
RADLEY Isabel A. of Corning, NY
October 16, 1879
Corning, NY

TEINNER William J. of Adrian, NY
HALLETT Libbie E. of Adrian, NY
October 15, 1879
Adrian, NY

FORNEROOK J. of Hermitage, NY
WRITER Kate C. of Hornellsville, NY
October 23. 1879
Hornellsville, NY

AYERS Omer H. of Hornellsville, NY
OSTRAM Minnie S. of Hornellsville, NY
October 28, 1879
Hornellsville, NY

ELLSWORTH Fred W. of Belfast, NY
RATHBUN Amanda of Almond, NY
October 28, 1879
W. Almond, NY

VAN HORN Charles W. of Canisteo, NY
ENOS Maude of Almond, NY
October 24, 1879
Almond, NY

WALTHERS Otto of Hornellsville, NY
KAUSCH Etta of Wayland, NY
October 28, 1879
Wayland, NY

HILL James M. of Canisteo, NY
PAYNE Jennie of Canisteo, NY
October 27, 1879
Canisteo, NY

WHITFORD Adelbert R. of Hartsville, NY
TULLES Ella M. of Hartsville, NY
November 2, 1879
Hartsville, NY

WYANT Charles H. of Arkport, NY
COLGROVE Ida M. of Arkport, NY
November 2, 1879
Hornellsville, NY

MC EWEN John
ALGER Emma of Wellsville, NY
October 30, 1879
Wellsville, NY

BURLEY Charles S. of Cameron, NY   October 31, 1879
QUICK Clara of Campbell, NY   Campbell, NY

COOLEY Chester W. of Hornellsville, NY   November 9, 1879
SMITH Ella J. of Hornellsville, NY   Hornellsville, NY

WILLIAMS John W. of Hornellsville, NY   November 11, 1879
KELTS Emma J. of Hornellsville, NY   Hornellsville, NY

DEWEY George L. of Hornellsville, NY   November 12, 1879
SHERIDAN Harriet A. of Hornellsville, NY   Hornellsville, NY

KILLEEN Cornelius of Hornellsville, NY   November 11, 1879
PARDON Ann of Hornellsville, NY   Hornellsville, NY

BENNETT P. P. of Howard, NY   November 16, 1879
RANDALL Julia M. dau of Samuel of Haskinsville, NY   Haskinsville, NY

LOVELL Flavius J. of Hornellsville, NY   November 19, 1879
HIGGINS Nellie M. of Cameron, NY   Cameron, NY

BERRY Erastus W. of Jasper, NY   November 21, 1879
WHITTEMORE Lillie D. of Jasper, NY   Hornellsville, NY

GREGORY Harvey R. of Hornellsville, NY   November 19, 1879
KRESS Nellie of Hornellsville, NY   Hornellsville, NY

NEWELL Joseph of Hornellsville, NY   November 19, 1879
HIGGINS Ella of W. Cameron, NY

COLBERT John   November 19, 1879
DONOVAN Mary   Hornellsville, NY

TRACY Joseph of Hornellsville, NY   November 24, 1879
HAYES Annie of Hornellsville, NY   Hornellsville, NY

VICKERS Ashworth of Hartsville, NY   November 23, 1879
HENRY Jennie of Hartsville, NY   Hartsville, NY

NEAR Ervin W. of Hornellsville, NY   November 26, 1879
STAPLES Mary E. of Watertown, NY   Watertown, NY

COON George L. of Hornellsville, NY   November 30, 1879
KENNEDY Eva of Wellsville, NY   Wellsville, NY

SHERMAN Harley P. of Alfred, NY   November 26, 1879
HEMPHILL Ruth of Hartsville, NY   Alfred Ctr., NY

BURDICK Peter of Alfred Ctr., NY   November 29, 1879
CARTWRIGHT Hannah C. of Hartsville, NY   Alfred Ctr., NY

PARK Robert F. of Corning, NY
COWAN Emma B. of Corning, NY

November 2, 1879
Gibson, NY

SANFORD George W. of Bath, NY
WOODRUFF Eva L. of Bath, NY

December 3, 1879
Mt. Washington, NY

CHAPMAN Francis of Prattsburgh, NY   (Newspaper date) December 9, 1879
WOODFORD Eva L. of Prattsburgh, NY

SCHOONOVER Amos of Troupsburgh, NY
VORHEES Mary M. of Wellsville, NY

November 23, 1879
Wellsville, NY

SACKETT Caleb E. of W. Almond, NY
GREEN Cora Dell of Alfred, NY

December 3, 1879
Alfred, NY

TORRENCE Jerome of Cameron, NY
BRINK Elizabeth of Thurston, NY

December 3, 1879
N. Cameron, NY

WINKLEMAN J. D. of Duke Ctr., Pa.
FOSTER Dora of Troupsburgh, NY

December 7, 1879
Troupsburgh, NY

missing issues

COLLINS Uberto J. of Alfred, NY
COOPER Minnie Bell of Hornellsville, NY

December 28, 1880
Batavia, NY

KARR Charles
MC HENRY Eugenie

December 30, 1880
W. Almond, NY

TEW Henry B. of Troupsburgh, NY
RIGBY Carrie of Troupsburgh, NY

December 8, 1880
Woodhull, NY

PAGE Charles H. of Hornellsville, NY
BRUNDAGE Mrs. _____ of Bath, NY

December 29, 1880
Bath, NY

HUGINER Perry S.
TOTTEN Nancy S.

December 15, 1880
N. Almond, NY

VAN NESS Orrin W. of Hornellsville, NY
HOFFMAN Martha D. of Hornellsville, NY

January 8, 1881
Hornellsville, NY

GIBBS William O. of Hornellsville, NY
TIFFANY Emma of Hornellsville, NY

January 13, 1881

SWAN Thomas O. of Jasper, NY
CONLEY Sarah of Jasper, NY

January 9, 1881
Jasper, NY

HALLETT Samuel of Canisteo, NY
LOGHRY Emma of Cameron, NY

January 8, 1881
Cameron, NY

ALLEGAR Truman E. of N. Jasper, NY
WOOD Ann Maria of N. Jasper, NY
January 20, 1881
N. Jasper, NY

KENYON Dell of Alfred, NY
BOWERS Estella A. of Troupsburgh, NY
January 16, 1881
Alfred, NY

WHITCOMB E. Henry of Alfred, NY
GREEN Gertrude of Alfred, NY
January 19, 1881
Alfred, NY

ALDEN E. N. of Hornellsville, NY
RICE Ella of Dundee, NY
January 23, 1881
Dundee, NY

GRISWOLD Homer of S. Dansville, NY
GUINNIP Paulina L. of S. Dansville, NY
January 29, 1881
Hornellsville, NY

PERRY Willis S. of Woodhull, NY
CARPENTER Alice C. of Woodhull, NY
January 20, 1881
Woodhull, NY

MARKELEY William G. of Almond, NY
KARR Maggie of Almond, NY
January 30, 1881
Almond, NY

MC HENRY Henry of W. Almond, NY
MARVIN Alida of Almond, NY
February 10, 1881
Almond, NY

WHITE J. B. of Owego, NY
HART Eva S. of Almond, NY
February 10, 1881
Almond, NY

SEELEY Horatio N. of W. Union, NY
WESTCOTT Clarissa of W. Union, NY
February 20, 1881
Whitesville, NY

RAZEY Andrew of Fremont, NY
LEWIS Jennie of Fremont, NY
February 26, 1881
Hornellsville, NY

DUNN John of Binghamton, NY
BRODERICK Mary of Hornellsville, NY
February 28, 1881
Hornellsville, NY

COSTEN Charles of Hornellsville, NY
TOTTEN Alice of Hornellsville, NY
March 7, 1881
Hornellsville, NY

HALLETT Leroy of Jasper, NY
BULLOCK Jennie H. of Jasper, NY
March 20, 1881
Jasper, NY

SWAIN James F. of Tuscarora, NY
BREWER Mollie C. of Farmington, Pa.
March 20, 1881

SMITH Devillo P. of Hornellsville, NY
SULLIVAN Anna of Hornellsville, NY
March 27, 1881
Hornellsville, NY

ROCKWELL Hobart H. of Hornellsville, NY
MITCHELL Lavina W. dau of Dr. Samuel of Hornellsville
March 29, 1881
Hornellsville, NY

WING John H. of Hornellsville, NY	March 30, 1881
PIERCE Lillian of Hornellsville, NY	Hornellsville, NY
HARRIS Alonzo D. of Fairfield, NY	March 26, 1881
THOMAS Lottie M. of Alfred, NY	Alfred, NY
SHAFFER W. E. of Hornellsville, NY	March 31, 1881
CROSS Mrs. Harriet of Hornellsville, NY	Hornellsville, NY
DRAKE Jospeh R. of W. Almond, NY	March 31, 1881
STEWART Anna of Birdsall, NY	Belmont, NY
PRENTISS Edson H. of Jasper, NY	March 23, 1881
ORDWAY Phoebe Minerva of Cameron, NY	Cameron, NY
HALE Daniel T. of Olean, NY	April 14, 1881
SAWYER Emma C. dau of John K. of Hornellsville, NY	Hornellsville, NY
BABCOCK Charles C.	April 20, 1881
GILDERSLEEVE Louise	Hornellsville, NY
PAINE Irving of Hornellsville, NY	April 25, 1881
REDFIELD Josephine of Hornellsville, NY	Hornellsville, NY
VAN SCOTER John of Hornellsville, NY	April 19, 1881
REAGAN Anna of Burns, NY	Canaseraga, NY
TIBBETS George of Hornellsville, NY	May 5, 1881
GARDNER Susan A. dau of John B. of Owego, NY	Owego, NY
COOK Leveritt M. of Guilford, Vt.	May 17, 1881
MAGEE Sarah J. of Hornellsville, NY	Hornellsville, NY
COOLEY Lester D. of Castile, NY	May 19, 1881
SHATTUCK Hattie dau of Dr. S. E. of Hornellsville, NY	Hornellsville, NY
MC CARTHY Michael of Hornellsville, NY	June 1, 1881
HANRAHAN Maggie of Wellsville, NY	Wellsville, NY
HEFTER Morris of Hornellsville, NY	June 1, 1881
SCHWARTZ Anna dau of Fabian of Elmira, NY	Elmira, NY

Steuben Signal (Hornellsville, NY)

April 4, 1883 - January 23, 1884

JOHNSON H. W. of Canisteo, NY	March 27, 1883
CLEMENT Abbie of Canisteo, NY	Canisteo, NY

FLETCHER Alfred T. of W. Almond, NY   March 25, 1883
BAKER Hattie of W. Almond, NY   W. Almond, NY

BIRMINGHAM William of Alma, Mi.   April 4, 1883
ALLEN Dora of Hornellsville, NY   Hornellsville, NY

HAWLEY J. H. of Hornellsville, NY   April 4, 1883
REGAN Anna of Hornellsville, NY   Hornellsville, NY

POTTER Charles F. of Almond, NY   April 3, 1883
VAN GELDER Anna of Bath, NY   Belmont, NY

WHITMAN Fred C. of Hornellsville, NY   March 28, 1883
HARRINGTON Sarah A. of Hornellsville, NY

LIEB Alexander of Hornellsville, NY   April 4, 1883
OWEN Lenora E. of Hornellsville, NY

LEONARD Wesley B. of Hornellsville, NY   April 11, 1883
BRAMBLE Minnie dau of Charles of Havana, NY   Havana, NY

HESELTINE Frederick I. of Alfred Ctr., NY   April 10, 1883
GEORGE Lulu S. of Alfred Ctr., NY   Alfred Ctr., NY

BRINK John A. of Alfred, NY   April 10, 1883
O'BRIAN Mary A. of Almond, NY   Almond, NY

FITZGIBBONS John of Hornellsville, NY   April 8, 1883
HILL Libbie of Hornellsville, NY   Hornellsville, NY

LIPPINCOTT George of Hiltonville, NY   April 8, 1883
BROWN Rose E. of Friendship, NY   Friendship, NY

YOHON Henry of Wayland, NY   April 10, 1883
KIRK Mary of Wayland, NY   Wayland, NY

BLOWERS Gilbert of Grove, NY   April 11, 1883
MESS Emma of Garwoods, NY   Hornellsville, NY

SMITH Harley of Jasper, NY   March 15, 1883
SPENCER Fanny of Jasper, NY   Tuscarora, NY

SMITH Herbert C. of Hornellsville, NY   April 18, 1883
LEONARD Belle H. of Howard, NY   W. Almond, NY

CROSS Howard E. of Hornellsville, NY   April 21, 1883
HOLMES Mattie dau of T. E. of Hornellsville, NY   Hornellsville, NY

WOODRUFF F. S. of Hornellsville, NY   May 1, 1883
BENNETT Jennie of Hornellsville, NY   Hornellsville, NY

OAKS Junius A. of Hornellsville, NY **STEVENS** Anna of Hornellsville, NY	April 25, 1883 Hornellsville, NY	
BABCOCK Wilson of Elmira, NY **SHAFFER** Nettie of Hornellsville, NY	March 10, 1883	
HARRINGTON Charles of Hornellsville, NY **GRAHAM** Florence P. of Hornellsville, NY	April 25, 1883 Hornellsville, NY	
THOMAS Martin **WILLIAMS** Rose	April 25, 1883 Cossville, NY	
PENNIMAN James of Milford, Mass. **YOUNG** Ermina of Hornellsville, NY	April 30, 1883 Hornellsville, NY	
HUGANIR Charles of Fremont, NY **SAXTON** Ettie of Howard, NY	May 2, 1883 Howard, NY	
NORTON Oscar of W. Almond, NY **NORTON** Laurie E. of W. Almond, NY	April 25, 1883 Friendship, NY	
GOSS Allen D. of Hornellsville, NY **CROSSETT** Belle of Hornellsville, NY	May 8, 1883 Hornellsville, NY	
WHITE William of Lindley, NY **WOODSTOCK** Ida of Addison, NY	May 5, 1883 Addison, NY	
BOWERS John of Troupsburgh, NY **MANDEVILLE** Cora of Addison, NY	May 6, 1883 Addison, NY	
ALLEN N. Frank of Alfred Ctr., NY **SISSON** Nellie G. of Almond, NY	May 2, 1883 Almond, NY	
NORTHRUP Mark E. of Hornellsville, NY **KRESS** Ella of Hornellsville, NY	May 31, 1883 Hornellsville, NY	
BOYNTON George L. of Hornellsville, NY **VAN ORSDALE** May of Friendship, NY	May 31, 1883 Friendship, NY	
CLARK Samuel P. of Attleboro, Mass. **STEPHENS** Gelia of Greenwood, NY	June 6, 1883 Greenwood, NY	
KETSER Frank **BURGEN** Kittie	June 6, 1883 Wayland, NY	
PRENTISS George A. of Hornellsville, NY **WATERS** Louella S. of Hornellsville, NY	June 13, 1883 Hornellsville, NY	
ROTSELL William M. of Harrison Valley, Pa. **SHORT** Flora of Hornellsville, NY	June 18, 1883 Hornellsville, NY	

ST JOHN Eustace of Elmira, NY
CARPENTER Linda of Hornellsville, NY

June 15, 1883
Hornellsville, NY

PARTRIDGE Charles E. of Lent Hill, NY (Newspaper date)
TERRY Victoria E. of Ingleside, NY

June 27, 1883
Wallace, NY

LYMAN A. S. of Eleven Mile, Pa.
DICKINSON Mrs. Mary A. of Bath, NY

June 9, 1883
Lyndonville, NY

BEATTIE Thomas Jr. of Hornellsville, NY
DOBSON Emma L. of Scranton, Pa.

June 17, 1883
Canisteo, NY

ROSS Charles A. of Bath, NY
SMITH Lillie of Cameron, NY

June 17, 1883
Canisteo, NY

CASTERLINE James T. of Painted Post, NY
TIMMERMAN L. of Painted Post, NY

June 27, 1883
Painted Post, NY

JERVIS Charles M. formerly of Hornellsville, NY
GRAY Lola of Wayland, NY

June 25, 1883

HAMMOND James M. of Hornellsville, NY
FRANKLIN Abbie of Howard, NY

June 28, 1883
Howard, NY

CLARK Jesse of Wayland, NY
MACUMBER Eva of Bloods, NY

July 4, 1883
Wayland, NY

DAVIDSON Adam of Hornellsville, NY
BEDDIE Alice A. of Rochester, NY

July 18, 1883
Rochester, NY

ROUP Barney C. of Coopers Plains, NY
BARAGER Mary E. of Hornellsville, NY

July 18, 1883
Dalton, NY

SIMONSON Fred of Coopers Plains, NY
AYERS Mrs. Mary E. of Painted Post, NY

July 11, 1883
Painted Post, NY

COOPER Hamilton of Dunkirk, NY
KINNE Kittie dau of George P. of Hornellsville, NY

August 1, 1883
Hornellsville, NY

TROWBRIDGE D. H. of Hornellsville, NY
HUNT Ella M. of Hornellsville, NY

July 24, 1883
Hornellsville, NY

BROWN A. D. of Andover, NY
KARR Helen M. of Almond, NY

August 8, 1883
Almond, NY

SEAGER S. G. of Wellsville, NY
PERRY Anna dau of R. P. of Corning, NY

August 22, 1883
Corning, NY

REIGELUTH J. J. of Waverly, NY
ELLISON Ida of Corning, NY

August 22, 1883
Corning, NY

COLEGROVE James F. of Burns, NY	August 22, 1883
HASKELL Belle M. of Hornellsville, NY	Hornellsville, NY
HICKEY Henry of Hornellsville, NY	August 8, 1883
KELLER Kate D. of Hornellsville, NY	Hornellsville, NY
SUTTON Charles P. of Hornellsville, NY	September 4, 1883
COMSTOCK Lillie J. of Andover, NY	Andover, NY
GRIFFIN Thomas of Olean, NY	September 4, 1883
CURTIN Maggie of Hornellsville, NY	Hornellsville, NY
GELTSER Jacob of Hornellsville, NY	September 4, 1883
HANTLEIN Katie of Hornellsville, NY	Hornellsville, NY
CARTWRIGHT Collins of Weltonville, NY	September 4, 1883
MC CAPES Minnie E. of Hornellsville, NY	Hornellsville, NY
WELSH John of Hornellsville, NY	September 10, 1883
HICKEY Maggie of Canaseraga, NY	Canaseraga, NY
CARPENTER Dr. E. S. of N. Cohocton, NY	September 14, 1883
PIERCE Mrs. Lauretta of N. Cohocton, NY	N. Cohocton, NY
MITCHELL Howard of Arnet, Pa.	September 12, 1883
REYNOLDS Mattie A. of Hornellsville, NY	Hornellsville, NY
KAPLE Marlan A. of Almond, NY	September 9, 1883
SCOTT Louisa of Almond, NY	W. Almond, NY
MULLIKIN William S. of Rushford, NY	September 18, 1883
BIXBY Blanche I. of Rushford, NY	Hornellsville, NY
CRATER Fred E. of Hornellsville, NY	September 15, 1883
FLESCHHUNT Louisa of Towanda, Pa.	Corning, NY
FITCH T. B. R. of Canaseraga, NY	September 12, 1883
SMELTZER Celestia of Hornellsville, NY	Hornellsville, NY
KREIDLER Walter R. of S. Dansville, NY	September 20, 1883
CLARK Letta of S. Dansville, NY	S. Dansville, NY
DOW Fred S. of Hornellsville, NY	September 19, 1883
WINNIE Leona M. dau of Dr. E. of Haskinsville, NY	Haskinsville, NY
GILDERSLEEVE George A. of Hornellsville, NY	September 25, 1883
BAXTER Millie of Hornellsville, NY	Hornellsville, NY
KELSEY Edward W. of Avoca, NY	September 12, 1883
SHULTS Lettie C. of Avoca, NY	Avoca, NY

PECK Charles E. of Eagle Lake, Mn.
LOUCKS Katie of Avoca, NY
September 18, 1883
Avoca, NY

HANSON A. F. of Hornellsville, NY
MC CREERY Dora of Ann Arbor, Mi.
September 25, 1883
Ann Arbor, Mi.

CORNELL Seneca A. of Troupsburgh, NY
POWERS Nettie of Troupsburgh, NY
September 15, 1883
Troupsburgh, NY

WILLIAMSON John C. of Cameron, NY
SUTTON Estella of Cameron, NY
September 26, 1883
Cameron, NY

GRISWOLD Frank H. of S. Dansville, NY
CARNEY Josie R. dau of M. H. of S. Dansville, NY
September 26, 1883
S. Dansville, NY

JACKSON O. D. of Bingham, Pa.
MARLETTE Mary E. of Woodhull, NY
September 26, 1883
Coudersport, Pa.

TUCKER Bayard of Wallace, NY
BROWN Fanny H. of Corning, NY
September 26, 1883
Corning, NY

WELCH Albert of Avoca, NY
COBIN Eva M. of Avoca, NY
September 26, 1883
Avon, NY

ATWOOD Delisle of Avoca, NY
MC CORD May of Avoca, NY
September 26, 1883
Avoca, NY

STROBEL Peter
ZIMMERMAN Mary
September 17, 1883
Cohocton, NY

ALVORD Homer of Troupsburgh, NY
MC FARLAND Julia A. of Troupsburgh, NY
September 29, 1883
Jasper, NY

SWARTZ William H. of Allen, NY
COLE Belle R. of Allen, NY
October 2, 1883
Allen, NY

WALL Thomas of Hornellsville, NY
QUIGG Ellen of Hornellsville, NY
October 2, 1883
Hornellsville, NY

BAHAM Frank M. of Hornellsville, NY
FOSTER Cora of Hornellsville, NY
October 3, 1883
Hornellsville, NY

HUMPHREYS J. H. of New York City
FLETCHER Olive formerly of Hornellsville, NY
October 3, 1883
New York City

SMITH Sidney of Bradford, Pa.
HAGGERTY Mary of Hornellsville, NY
October 3, 1883
Bradford, Pa.

JOHNSON Daniel R. of Woodhull, NY
STONE Lillie L. of Woodhull, NY
October 3, 1883
Woodhull, NY

HELLER George A. of Elmira, NY   (Newspaper date)   October 17, 1883
BARNES Orra Etta of Addison, NY   Addison, NY

HAMILTON Willis L. of Campbell, NY   October 10, 1883
PLATT Elizabeth   Painted Post, NY

HAIGHT Charles of Ovid, Mi.   October 8, 1883
SCHLY Sophie of Wayland, NY   Wayland, NY

JONES Frank A. of Hornellsville, NY   (Newspaper date)   October 17, 1883
BLOWERS Irene May of Paw Paw, Mi.   Paw Paw, Mi.

BLOSS Myron H. of Independence, NY   October 3, 1883
HARTRUM Frankie E. of Greenwood, NY   Greenwood, NY

LARROWE John of Hartsville, NY   October 2, 1883
KELLISON Emma of Hornellsville, NY   Canisteo, NY

POTTER Darwin F.   October 17, 1883
STEVENS Fannie B.   Hornellsville, NY

BROWN Chancey P. of Jasper, NY   October 24, 1883
JUNE Ida M. of Jasper, NY   Jasper, NY

GATES John A. of Fremont, NY   October 20, 1883
PARKS Emma A. of W. Almond, NY   Andover, NY

GERBER Frank of Hornellsville, NY   October 31, 1883
HAGGERTY Maggie of Hornellsville, NY   Hornellsville, NY

STEWART James of Hornellsville, NY   October 31, 1883
BARTLE Minnie of Hornellsville, NY   Hornellsville, NY

VAN ORMAN Duran T. of Jasper, NY   November 4, 1883
GLOYD Jane E. of Cameron, NY   Hornellsville, NY

CLARK D. Healy of Burns, NY   November 1, 1883
DAY Ida B. of S. Dansville, NY   S. Dansville, NY

LEONARD Dr. L. D. of Prattsburgh, NY   November 7, 1883
JUDSON Mary A. of Minneapolis, Mn.   Minneapolis, Mn.

DEXTER John M. of Mc Kean Co. Pa.   October 30, 1883
KURTZ Mary C. of S. Dansville, NY   S. Dansville, NY

PIERCE Frank G.   November 14, 1883
BRAYTON Mary A. of S. Dansville, NY   S. Dansville, NY

CARPENTER George A.   Novembr 8, 1883
DEAN Alethe   Pulteney, NY

MILLER Andrew of Hornellsville, NY	November 4, 1883
OLIN Clara of Hornellsville, NY	Hornellsville, NY
LA LONDE Maurice A. of Oil City, Pa.	November 11, 1883
PAGE Emma L. of Chardon, Oh.	Hornellsville, NY
INGALLS Ray of Fremont, NY	November 15, 1883
KURTZ Maggie of Cohocton, NY	Hornellsville, NY
LASON Julius C. of Canisteo, NY	November 11, 1883
PAGE Mary of Troupsburgh, NY	Troupsburgh, NY
SNYDER Frank J. of New Milford, Pa.	November 15, 1883
BUTLER Ida M. of Bath, NY	Bath, NY
PHILLIPS David Jr. of Addison, NY	November 14, 1883
MARTIN Carrie of Addison, NY	Addison, NY
WISE Edward of Neils Creek, NY	November 14, 1883
RICE Maggie of Neils Creek, NY	Neils Creek, NY
DOUGHERTY Daniel of Hornellsville, NY	November 27, 1883
FITZGERALD Jo of Hornellsville, NY	Hornellsville, NY
FISK Wallace G. of Troupsburgh, NY	November 21, 1883
PAUL Ida J. of Troupsburgh, NY	Troupsburgh, NY
HOFFMAN Samuel of Hornellsville, NY	November 21, 1883
GARDNER Edith E. of Hornellsville, NY	Hornellsville, NY
CHAPMAN Byron C. of Cohocton, NY	November 11, 1883
WAGER Mary of Cohocton, NY	Wallace, NY
LEWIS William F. of Cameron, NY	November 22, 1883
OSBORNE Mary F. of Cameron, NY	Cameron, NY
KIRKMIRE Joseph of Cohocton, NY	November 15, 1883
OYER Minnie of Cohocton, NY	Cohocton, NY
WEBER Valentine of S. Dansville, NY	November 28, 1883
TRIPP Viola M. of S. Dansville, NY	
MAXWELL Charles C.	November 27, 1883
LAWRENCE Mrs. M. A.	Hornellsville, NY
DENSMORE Frank E. of S. Dansville, NY	November 22, 1883
JACOBS Kate of S. Dansville, NY	S. Dansville, NY
CLARK Will J. of Hornellsville, NY	December 5, 1883
TOMPKINS Charlotte F. of La Salle, NY	La Salle, NY

MOSHER Clayton D. of Hornellsville, NY	December 5, 1883
HAWLEY Bertha A. of Hornellsville, NY	Jamestown, NY
CRANDALL George H. of Almond, NY	December 9, 1883
PERRY Huldah E. of Almond, NY	Almond, NY
SIMONSON Edward of Corning, NY	December 2, 1883
STUART Mary F. of Cameron, NY	Corning, NY
HIGGINS Byron D.of Arkport, NY	December 16, 1883
PALMER Minnie of Burns, NY	Hornellsville, NY
ANDREWS William H. of Belmont, NY	November 29, 1883
BARBER Ida Freelove of W. Almond, NY	W. Almond, NY
BAKER Fay of Fremont, NY	December 11, 1883
TENNEY Lizzie of Almond, NY	Canisteo, NY
DILLENBECK Stuart H. of Prattsburgh, NY	December 12, 1883
SANFORD Clara D. of Prattsburgh, NY	Prattsburgh, NY
MILLER Eugene L. of Howard, NY	December 18, 1883
ROOT Ella V. of S. Dansville, NY	Dansville, NY
WRIGHT John M. of Erwin Ctr., NY	December 17, 1883
VAN GORDON Mary S. of Addison, NY	Addison, NY
PHELPS W. A. of Allentown, NY	December 19, 1883
DAVIS Mary J. of Corning, NY	Corning, NY
HUDSON Harry of Hornellsville, NY	December 25, 1883
WINDSOR Delia of Hornellsville, NY	Hornellsville, NY
LAMPHIER A. W. of Ward, NY	December 20, 1883
POTTER Mary A. of W. Almond, NY	W. Almond, NY
HAMILTON Mort of Howard, NY	December 25, 1883
COTTON Josie dau of Samuel of Fremont, NY	Fremont, NY
STEVENS William L. of Woonsocket, Dak.	December 25, 1883
O'CONNOR Ella of Almond, NY	Almond, NY
EDGETT Emery of Troupsburgh, NY	December 22, 1883
DAVIS Emma of Troupsburgh, NY	Troupsburgh, NY
BROWNELL Willis H. of Jasper, NY	December 25, 1883
WOODWARD Mira J. of Jasper, NY	Woodhull, NY
GRINNOLDS Malon of Troupsburgh, NY	December 23, 1883
HOUSE Lena of W. Union, NY	Troupsburgh, NY

SHAFFER Frank of Hornellsville, NY	January 2, 1884
DOHERTY Mary E. of Hornellsville, NY	Hornellsville, NY
EDWARDS M. N. of Red Cliff, Col.	December 27, 1883
VAN BUSKIRK E. J. of Hornellsville, NY	Hartsville, NY
WALTERS Wilhelm of Hornellsville, NY	January 3, 1884
REITNAUER Mary of Hornellsville, NY	Hornellsville, NY
BURD Lysander J. of Hornellsville, NY	January 3, 1884
STEWART Abby L. of Howard, NY	Howard, NY
BRACE L. B. of Hornellsville, NY	January 7, 1884
KEEFE Maggie of Hornellsville, NY	Hornellsville, NY
BRAZEE Barnum of Campville, NY	January 9, 1884
HOWLAND Estella	Rathbone, NY

Painted Post Times

October 5, 1870 - September 27, 1871

ERWIN Arthur H. of Painted Post, NY	October 19, 1870
BROWN Gertie dau of Dr. Reuben P. Brown of Addison, NY	Addison, NY
BUTLER Ralph of Elmira, NY	November 16, 1870
SAYLES Mary A. of Painted Post, NY	Painted Post, NY
FARR Creon B. of Tioga, Pa.	December 13, 1870
WELLINGTON Ella of Tioga, Pa.	Tioga, Pa.
BURROUGHS Rev. David of Prattsburgh, NY	December 25, 1870
ADAMS Henrietta M. dau of Prof. S. W. of Corning, NY	Prattsburgh, NY
HOYT W. A. of Corning, NY	February 15, 1871
FERENBAUGH Mary dau of Joseph of Corning, NY	Corning, NY
SUPPLEE A. P. of Painted Post, NY	March 23, 1871
SEDGEWICK Mattie of Painted Post, NY	Painted Post, NY
ALDRICH Oscar E. of Painted Post, NY	March 22, 1871
DENSMORE Amanda M. of Painted Post, NY	Painted Post, NY
REMINGTON Daniel E. of Painted Post, NY	April 6, 1871
HARRISON Lucy of Hornby, NY	Coopers Plains, NY
SHORT Charles	April 19, 1871
BORST Celina	Painted Post, NY

SHAW John of Campbell, NY   April 29, 1871
SMITH Mamie of Campbell, NY   Painted Post, NY

JENNINGS William B. of Addison, NY   April 26, 1871
BAKER Mary A. of Painted Post, NY   Painted Post, NY

LINDNER Lewis of Corning, NY   May 16, 1871
GITHLER Annie of Painted Post, NY

BERRY Edward H. of Corning, NY   May 24, 1871
KIMBLE Ida of Painted Post, NY   Painted Post, NY

FANTON Hull   June 8, 1871
SKELLENGER Mary Thom   Havana, NY

JIMERSON Herbert of Hornby, NY   June 28, 1871
HENDRICK Bertha E. of Hornby, NY   Hornby, NY

BRYSON William of Mechanicsburg, Pa.   June 22, 1871
COOPER Charlotte E. dau of late Dr. of Coopers Plains   Coopers Plains, NY

COOPER A. E. of Coopers Plains, NY   September 18, 1871
BURCH Eliza of Towanda, Pa.   Towanda, Pa.

HIGMAN Harris C. of Painted Post, NY   September 27, 1871
VAN ALSTIN Martha E. of Corning, NY   Corning, NY

Prattsburgh News

December 12, 1872 - December 25, 1884

WALLING Edward E. of Orange, NY   December 1, 1872
SWITZER Eliza J. of Bradford, NY   Savona, NY

MORRISON James A. of Tyrone, NY   December 1, 1872
BARCLAY Addie of Orange, NY   Savona, NY

KENNEDY William A. of Italy, NY   November 7, 1872
DOUBLEDAY Emma of Starkey, NY   Italy Hill, NY

MERRITT Augustus B.   November 26, 1872
VORHEES Matilda of Prattsburgh, NY   Prattsburgh, NY

SHERDRICK Clinton   December 19, 1872
JOHNSON Sarah   Prattsburgh, NY

KNAPP Oscar of Prattsburgh, NY   December 17, 1872
SMITH Sarah J. of Prattsburgh, NY   Prattsburgh, NY

HEDGER D. A. of Prattsburgh, NY   December 11, 1872
DEIGHTON Lucinda of Prattsburgh, NY   Prattsburgh, NY

TAYLOR Charles E. of Italy, NY   January 1, 1873
EARLY Minnie A. of Prattsburgh, NY   Prattsburgh, NY

MIDDLETON James A. of Prattsburgh, NY   January 15, 1873
GRAVES Hannah of Prattsburgh, NY

ANDERSON Thomas of Urbana, NY   January 9, 1873
CARMER Kate of Urbana, NY   Prattsburgh, NY

REIDY Patrick formerly of Prattsburgh, NY   January 28, 1873
FLANIGAN Anna E. of Cleveland, Oh.   Cleveland, Oh.

LEWIS S. G. of Urbana, NY   January 30, 1873
DREW Mary of Urbana, NY   Urbana, NY

PIPE James of Prattsburgh, NY   February 5, 1873
CARHART Harriet of Prattsburgh, NY   Prattsburgh, NY

GELDER T. H. of Prattsburgh, NY   February 25, 1873
WELD Minerva of Prattsburgh, NY   Prattsburgh, NY

DEINHART John of Prattsburgh, NY   March 12, 1873
MC HENRY Mira of Prattsburgh, NY

HAYES Charles F. of Rockford, Ill.   June 24, 1873
SHAVER Mary M. of Kanona, NY   Kanona, NY

SKINNER Arthur T. of Watkins, NY   June 25, 1873
MC LEAN Mrs. Rosa dau of George MC LEAN of Prattsburgh, NY

WATERS Robert of Pulteney, NY   (Newspaper date) June 26, 1873
RILEY Dell dau of Owen of Pulteney, NY   Pulteney, NY

COOK James S. of Prattsburgh, NY   June 25, 1873
LOUNSBERRY Emma of Pulteney, NY   Pulteney, NY

MANNING Tallman of Branchport, NY   July 4, 1873
TURNER Elida of Branchport, NY   Prattsburgh, NY

NOBLE William E. S. of Prattsburgh, NY   June 24, 1873
HERE Elizabeth of Perry, NY   Perry, NY

LEE William S. of Prattsburgh, NY   June 25, 1873
MC FEE Margarette of Urbana, NY   Bath, NY

STANTON Charles A. of Prattsburgh, NY   July 12, 1873
MERRITT Mrs. Bell of Wayne, NY   Prattsburgh, NY

CLARK John W. of Middlesex, NY
EDDY Mary A. of Prattsburgh, NY

August 2, 1873
Prattsburgh, NY

CAPLE L. D. of Branchport, NY
PARRIS Mary E. of Branchport, NY

September 4, 1873
Prattsburgh, NY

MORSE Seymour E. of Sparta, NY
MERRITT Mary E. of Prattsburgh, NY

September 9, 1873
Prattsburgh, NY

MARTEN Owen of Jerusalem, NY
RHODES Ella L. of Jerusalem, NY

October 1, 1873
Prattsburgh, NY

JACKSON Wesley of Prattsburgh, NY
LOCY Ellen of Prattsburgh, NY

October 19, 1873
Prattsburgh, NY

PULVER George of Italy, NY   (Newspaper date)
HILL Bell of Rikers Hollow, NY

November 6, 1873
Rikers Hollow, NY

FOX Charles M. of Pulteney, NY
MILLER Caroline of Pulteney, NY

November 15, 1873
S. Pulteney, NY

HOTCHKISS Charles R. of Wellsville, NY
EARLY Alice L. of Prattsburgh, NY

November 16, 1873
Prattsburgh, NY

WILSON Charles S. of Pulteney, NY
DILDINE Dora E. of Pulteney, NY

December 17, 1873
Prattsburgh, NY

MC CONNELL Ira A. of Italy, NY
SCOTT Virginia of Prattsburgh, NY

December 24, 1873
Prattsburgh, NY

PERRY Eli
MILLS Eliza

December 25, 1873
Prattsburgh, NY

BENNETT James T. of Italy, NY
LANE Lettie of Prattsburgh, NY

December 25, 1873
Prattsburgh, NY

HAVENS Walter of Prattsburgh, NY
PELHAM Mary E. of Wheeler, NY

January 2, 1874
Prattsburgh, NY

HUBBARD Jackson K. of New York City
SMITH Maria of Prattsburgh, NY

January 3, 1874
Prattsburgh, NY

FOSTER George of Prattsburgh, NY
HORTON Selina of Prattsburgh, NY

January 8, 1874
Prattsburgh, NY

LAWRENCE W. A. of Parsons, Ks.   (Newspaper date)
HORR Ella formerly of Prattsburgh, NY

January 15, 1874
Parsons, Ks.

LUNGRAN P. J. of Prattsburgh, NY
SMITH Kate of Prattsburgh, NY

January 21, 1874
Prattsburgh, NY

NEALY Reuben of Belfast, NY   March 10, 1874
LOUNSBERRY Celia of Pulteney, NY   Pulteney, NY

WILLIAMS S. W.   March 26, 1874
OSBORNE Minerva P.   Prattsburgh, NY

JOLLEY Frank of Wheeler, NY   April 22, 1874
DERRICK Emma of Wheeler, NY   Wheeler, NY

VAN SCOY Frank E. of Italy, NY   May 10, 1874
WALLACE Ida of Italy, NY

DAY A. A. of E. Saginaw, Mi.   June 3, 1874
VAN TUYL Ella dau of Thomas of Prattsburgh, NY   Prattsburgh, NY

ROLESON L. of Pulteney, NY   July 2, 1874
COLEGROVE Margarette of Prattsburgh, NY   Prattsburgh, NY

JOHNSON Wesley of Italy, NY   July 24, 1874
LAMPHIER Eunice of Prattsburgh, NY   Pulteney, NY

INGRAHAM Oliver of Pulteney, NY   August 18, 1874
HUGHES Almira R. of Pulteney, NY   Pulteney, NY

HARRIS Nathan of Pulteney, NY   August 18, 1874
HUGHES Malinda Jane of Pulteney, NY   Pulteney, NY

WHEELER James C. of Streeter, Ill.   September 9, 1874
SHULTS Mattie dau of George of Prattsburgh, NY   Prattsburgh, NY

REED Lewis of Pulteney, NY   September 6, 1874
BRUSH Ruth of Prattsburgh, NY at res of Charles Brush

STODDARD P. L. of Prattsburgh, NY   October 7, 1874
BRUNDAGE Anna dau of C. W. of Prattsburgh, NY   Prattsburgh, NY

CHAMPLIN Melvin   September 30, 1874
REYNOLDS Livonia dau of W. H. of Italy, NY   Italy Hill, NY

RIPPEY William H. of Prattsburgh, NY   October 6, 1874
WILCOX Sarah M. of Prattsburgh, NY   Prattsburgh, NY

CHAPMAN Charles S. of Prattsburgh, NY   October 7, 1874
DRAKE Esther F. of Naples, NY   Prattsburgh, NY

BROWN James Edward of Prattsburgh, NY   October 14, 1874
STORMS Margaret of Wheeler, NY   Wheeler, NY

BISHOP David L. of Hillsdale, Mi.   September 30, 1874
FOSS Josephine of Hillsdale, Mi.   Hillsdale, Mi.

LOUNSBERRY James R. of Prattsburgh, NY October 25, 1874
CHILSON Hattie A. of Prattsburgh, NY Pulteney, NY

WINDNAGLE Jonas E. of Prattsburgh, NY November 4, 1874
ANDRUS Adelaide C. of Jerusalem, NY Rochester, NY

BOGGS Ira D. of Prattsburgh, NY November 22, 1874
SANDERS Elizabeth of Prattsburgh, NY Prattsburgh, NY

MC CANN Hanry H. of Pulteney, NY November 29, 1874
THOMAS Anna E. of Pulteney, NY

SARGEANT D. W. of Rochester, NY November 25, 1874
WILLIAMS Mary Jane of Avoca, NY Avoca, NY

HARRIS Philo J. of Pulteney, NY December 6, 1874
CHAPPELL Elizabeth E. of Rathbone, NY

SHAVER Henry of Prattsburgh, NY December 17, 1874
CORNUE Villa of Prattsburgh, NY

GOODRICH A. H. of Pulteney, NY December 20, 1874
WELLES Martha J. dau of B. F. of Pulteney, NY Pulteney, NY

LEWIS Flint H. of Prattsburgh, NY December 29, 1874
GILLETT Franc L. dau of H. M. of Italy, NY Italy, NY

LEWIS Samuel R. of Prattsburgh, NY December 31, 1874
ROSA Violetta O. of Prattsburgh, NY Prattsburgh, NY

CISLER Frank B. January 3, 1875
AINSWORTH Katie L. Salt Lake City, Ut.

GRAVES Willard I. January 17, 1875
MARTIN Helen of Mt. Pleasant, Mi.

NORRIS Jackson of Dewitt Clinton Co. Mi. January 13, 1875
FISHER Mary A. of Prattsburgh, NY Wolcott, NY

HORR Elisha P. of Parson, Ks. formerly Prattsburgh, NY December 27, 1874
HOLCOMB Clara M. of Parson, Ks. Parson, Ks.

BROWN Frank of Prattsburgh, NY January 21, 1875
BAILEY Helen E. of Prattsburgh, NY Prattsburgh, NY

FRY James W. of Syracuse, NY January 20, 1875
COWING Mary dau of Albert R. of Jerusalem, NY Jerusalem, NY

BONNEY B. F. of Pulteney, NY February 3, 1875
FARGO Sarah Irene of Pulteney, NY Pulteney, NY

GIFFIN John B. of Pulteney, NY   February 25, 1875
BENNETT Bell of Pulteney, NY   Pulteney, NY

GREENE Charles A. of Prattsburgh, NY   March 16, 1875
SQUIRES Ada M. of Prattsburgh, NY   Prattsburgh, NY

HORTON Ira S. of Pulteney, NY   March 25, 1875
BURLEW Clarissa S. of Prattsburgh, NY   Prattsburgh, NY

BRAMBLE Ezra of Prattsburgh, NY   March 30, 1875
WATERS Mrs. Sarah of Prattsburgh, NY   Prattsburgh, NY

LAMPHIER Russell P. of Italy, NY   April 25, 1875
THOMPSON Mary E. of Italy, NY   Italy Hollow, NY

SMITH J. H.   April 27, 1875
EDSON Jennie dau of Edmond of Medina, NY   Medina, NY

COGSWELL James B. of Prattsburgh, NY   May 29, 1875
BAILEY S. Arvesta of Prattsburgh, NY   Hammondsport, NY

SALISBURY L. A. of Prattsburgh, NY   July 3, 1875
THAYER Susan of Prattsburgh, NY   Prattsburgh, NY

MARSHALL Phillip S. of Prattsburgh, NY   July 20, 1875
BELL Mary L. of Prattsburgh, NY   Prattsburgh, NY

MC CLURE F. G. Md. of Watson, Pa.   August 18, 1875
MILLS Jennie of Lawrenceville, Pa.   Lawrenceville, Pa.

RODGERS Lawson of Jerusalem, NY   September 1, 1875
BROWN Sarah A. of Prattsburgh, NY   Prattsburgh, NY

REYNOLDS Vincent L. of Avoca, NY   September 26, 1875
RILEY Susan E. of Avoca, NY   Pulteney, NY

DREW Byron J. of Pulteney, NY   October 7, 1875
PARKER Rosa A. of Prattsburgh, NY

WINDNAGLE Frank M. of Prattsburgh, NY   October 3, 1875
PULVER Frances of Italy, NY   Italy, NY

WYGANT James G. of Denison, Io.   September 28, 1875
FAULKNER Lillie of Prattsburgh, NY   Prattsburgh, NY

BARRETT Josephus of Potter, NY   October 27, 1875
RICE Molira of Pulteney, NY

GAY John W. of Pulteney, NY   November 9, 1875
STONE Mattie R. of Pulteney, NY   Pulteney, NY

ANGELL Harvey E. of Italy, NY	November 10, 1875
FOSTER Mary of Prattsburgh, NY	Prattsburgh, NY
WATKINS John J. of Prattsburgh, NY	October 20, 1875
CHITTERING Flora L. of Hornellsville, NY	Dunkirk, NY
HOPKINS Frank H. of Chilicothe, Oh.	November 3, 1875
POWELL Nellie of Penn Yan, NY	Penn Yan, NY
BARTLETT James of Wheeler, NY	November 22, 1875
CLAYSON Mrs. Helen of Prattsburgh, NY	Prattsburgh, NY

BLISS Charles Seward of Wheeler, NY   (Newspaper date) December 2, 1875
JOHNSON Ida E. of Wheeler, NY

SHEDRIC Morris of Wheeler, NY   (Newspaper date) December 2, 1875
BLISS Mary E. of Wheeler, NY

MORRISON James W. of Pulteney, NY	December 31, 1875
BROWN Jennie of Pulteney, NY	Pulteney, NY
ALLEN Phillip W. of Prattsburgh, NY	December 29, 1875
MORGAN Lillian C. of Potter, NY	Potter, NY
WILSON John of Prattsburgh, NY	January 5, 1876
DE WITT Sarah of Italy, NY	Italy, NY
PADDOCK Lewis M. of Wheeler, NY	January 6, 1876
BORDEN Mrs. Ann of Wheeler, NY	Wheeler, NY
BAILEY Simmons J. of Wheeler, NY	January 19, 1876
DUNN Celia F. of Wheeler, NY	Prattsburgh, NY
HOTCHKIN Levi C. of Prattsburgh, NY	January 5, 1876
FEE Julia of Belfont, Pa.	Belfont, Pa.
STEWART Lyman of Pulteney, NY	January 25, 1876
CLARK Frances J. of Branchport, NY	Branchport, NY
FOWLER Arnold of Avoca, NY	January 27, 1876
OLNEY Prudence of Avoca, NY	Avoca, NY
EDSON Charles W.	February 22, 1876
EVANS Anna	Southern Ill.
NORTHRUP William W. of Italy, NY	March 9, 1876
HILL Emma C. of Pulteney, NY	Prattsburgh, NY
HARRIS E. B. of Pulteney, NY	March 15, 1876
BELL S. J. of Pulteney, NY	Prattsburgh, NY

TURNER Richard M. of Jerusalem, NY
AGARD Mary M. of Wayland, NY
March 30, 1876
Prattsburgh, NY

SCOTT William B. of Wheeler, NY
HOWE Mary S. of Prattsburgh, NY
April 6, 1876
Prattsburgh, NY

REYNOLDS J. M. of Cohocton, NY
ARDELL Etta formerly of Prattsburgh, NY
March 29, 1876
Williamsport, Pa.

WHITE Lewis P. of Greenwood, NY
EARLEY Mrs. Patience of Prattsburgh, NY
May 18, 1876
Prattsburgh, NY

FRIES John of Prattsburgh, NY
BEAUHALL Helen of Torrey, NY
May 28, 1876
Bellona, NY

DERRICK George E. of Wheeler, NY
BEAM Anna of Starkey, NY
May 24, 1876
Starkey, NY

MARTS George of Bloods Depot, NY
FOX Fanny of Avoca, NY at res of Jesse Fox
June 21, 1876
Avoca, NY

STICKNEY Julius of Wheeler, NY
BROWN Minerva E. of Whiting, Vt.
June 29, 1876
Prattsburgh, NY

CLARY John C. of Prattsburgh, NY
SMITH Ursala S. of Prattsburgh, NY
June 29, 1876
Prattsburgh, NY

SIMMONS Sylvester of Milo, NY
BONNEY Mrs. Louisa of Prattsburgh, NY
June 28, 1876
Prattsburgh, NY

LOSEY Frank of Wheeler, NY
TYLER P. A. of Wheeler, NY
August 3, 1876
Mitchellville, NY

WATKINS Elijah T. of Prattsburgh, NY
CLARK Mrs. Laura of Pulteney, NY
September 20, 1876
Pulteney, NY

CROSSMAN William J. of Prattsburgh, NY
FOSTER Ella R. of Prattsburgh, NY
October 14, 1876
Prattsburgh, NY

LAMPHIER Charles of Pulteney, NY
COLE Ida of Middlesex, NY
September 26, 1876
Prattsburgh, NY

KELLY Charles
BURLEW Ida of Bay Port, Mi. at res of U. D. Burlew
October 31, 1876
Bay Port, Mi.

BURLEW Henri
DE FOREST Jennie of Bay Port, Mi.
October 31, 1876
Bay Port, Mi.

GRISWOLD George W. of Jerusalem, NY
LARE Alice A. of Italy, NY
November 1, 1876
Prattsburgh, NY

HOWELL George W. of Long Island, NY   December 27, 1876
TRENCHARD Ida A. of Wheeler, NY   Wheeler, NY

LEWIS Charles of Naples, NY   January 10, 1877
CLARK Mary of Prattsburgh, NY   Prattsburgh, NY

TALL William of Prattsburgh, NY   January 3, 1877
CHANDLER Juliette of Waterloo, NY   Waterloo, NY

SNOKE Prof. A. J. of Princeton, Ind.   December 26, 1876
WALDO Alvira A. dau of Charles and Elizabeth   Prattsburgh, NY

MOORE John K. of Wheeler, NY   January 10, 1877
OVERHISER Fanny J. of Wheeler, NY   Wheeler, NY

CLARK Germane A. of Prattsburgh, NY   February 14, 1877
JOHNSON Emma F. of Prattsburgh, NY   Prattsburgh, NY

HOGAN John C. of Hornellsville, NY   April 4, 1877
DOUD Ella E. of Prattsburgh, NY   Prattsburgh, NY

LYON Willard A. of Penn Yan, NY   May 27, 1877
LEWIS Addie of Prattsburgh, NY   Prattsburgh, NY

JOHNSON Charles of Prattsburgh, NY   May 30, 1877
DORSEY Minerva of Bath, NY   Prattsburgh, NY

STODDARD Stephen of Prattsburgh, NY   August 25, 1877
PARKS Sarah C. of Prattsburgh, NY   Prattsburgh, NY

SCOTT William W. of Corning, NY   September 20, 1877
WATKINS Lotta of Prattsburgh, NY   Prattsburgh, NY

COLEGROVE Samuel of Wheeler, NY   September 30, 1877
SNYDER Anna Maria of Wheeler, NY   Prattsburgh, NY

STONE George of Syracuse, NY   October 18, 1877
NORTHRUP Eugenia of Rathbone, NY   Rathbone, NY

BABCOCK Walter of Helena, Ark.   November 1, 1877
HAMLIN Fanny of Prattsburgh, NY   Prattsburgh, NY

CHAPMAN Frank O. of Avoca, NY   December 18, 1877
VORHEES Rosa B. of Prattsburgh, NY   Prattsburgh, NY

DRUM Edwin   December 31, 1877
FULLER Alida M. of Prattsburgh, NY   Prattsburgh, NY

PADDOCK James S. of Italy, NY   December 25, 1877
KENNEDY Agnes M. of Prattsburgh, NY   Prattsburgh, NY

HAYES Gilbert of Prattsburgh, NY
JOHNSON Addie of Prattsburgh, NY

December 30, 1877
Prattsburgh, NY

WHEELER John of Prattsburgh, NY
WILDMAN Mary dau of Rev. F. A. of Pulteney, NY

December 27, 1877
Pulteney, NY

SMITH Artemus of Prattsburgh, NY
ANDERKIRK Sarah of Cohocton, NY

January 2, 1878
Cohocton, NY

FOSTER Mervin of Prattsburgh, NY   (Newspaper date)
SANFORD Ella of Prattsburgh, NY

January 17, 1878
Prattsburgh, NY

SIKE Alonzo of Howard, NY   (Newspaper date)
COTTON Ora of S. Dansville, NY

January 17, 1878
Prattsburgh, NY

STONE Henry M. of Pulteney, NY
SINSEBOX Minnie of Pulteney, NY

February 12, 1878
Pulteney, NY

ROUNDS Samuel of Rockford, Mi.
BROCKWAY Mary A. of Prattsburgh, NY

February 19, 1878
Prattsburgh, NY

AUSTIN Charles L. of Jerusalem, NY
TAYLOR Lenna J. of Jerusalem, NY

March 10, 1878
Prattsburgh, NY

WILLIAMS Stephen T. of Prattsburgh, NY
JONES Edith M. of Prattsburgh, NY

April 17, 1878
Prattsburgh, NY

STANTON Edward B. of Cohocton, NY
HUBBARD Dell dau of late E. T. of Prattsburgh, NY

May 6, 1878
Lyons Hollow, NY

HARD Rev. Edwin of Branchport, NY
VAN TUYLE Nettie dau of William C. of Branchport, NY

April 23, 1878
Branchport, NY

THOMAS Merton of Woodhull, NY
WAGENER Illian A. dau of Col. Jacob of Pulteney, NY

May 2, 1878
Pulteney, NY

HAINES Henry T. of New York City
MC LEAN Kittie E. of Prattsburgh, NY

June 4, 1878
Prattsburgh, NY

MC LEAN W. Frank of Prattsburgh, NY
VAN TUYL Eva I. dau of T. of Prattsburgh, NY

June 19, 1878
Prattsburgh, NY

WATKINS William A. of Prattsburgh, NY
LEWIS Jennie dau of Richard of Prattsburgh, NY

July 11, 1878
Prattsburgh, NY

BLODGETT R. Morgan of Cheshire, NY
FERGUSON Lovisa dau of Solomon of Pulteney, NY

September 11, 1878
Pulteney, NY

DUBOIS William of Pulteney, NY
HORTON Violet of Pulteney, NY

October 2, 1878

WOOD C. H. of Painted Post, NY — October 22, 1878
WHEELER Fanny dau of Addison of Wheeler, NY — Wheeler, NY

MERRITT William H. of Cohocton, NY — November 6, 1878
RYNDERS Belle of Prattsburgh, NY — Prattsburgh, NY

RINGROSE John Jr. of Prattsburgh, NY — November 6, 1878
SWENSON Elizabeth G. of Wheeler, NY — Wheeler, NY

SHERWOOD Henry F. of Bath, NY — January 1, 1879
RICE Mary C. of Pulteney, NY — Pulteney, NY

NIMS George of Riker Hollow, NY — January 9, 1879
CHAPMAN Sarah of Riker Hollow, NY — Prattsburgh, NY

MAHAN Frank of Prattsburgh, NY — January 30, 1879
NEFF Addie of Prattsburgh, NY — Prattsburgh, NY

THAYER Daniel B. of Prattsburgh, NY — February 1, 1879
WALRATH Levina of Prattsburgh, NY — Prattsburgh, NY

AUSTIN Benjamin B. of Prattsburgh, NY — February 1, 1879
SMITH Mrs. Betsey E. of Prattsburgh, NY — Prattsburgh, NY

DEARLOVE Henry of Sacramento, Ca. formerly Prattsburgh — February 27, 1879
DAVIS M. E. of Isleton, Ca. — Isleton, Ca.

STEVENS Daniel of Wheeler, NY — April 3, 1879
BARDEEN Mrs. Hannah of Prattsburgh, NY — Prattsburgh, NY

BRUCE Rev. L. D. of Potter, NY — April 3, 1879
PATCH Julia dau of Rev. A. of Prattsburgh, NY — Prattsburgh, NY

EDDY Ira H. of Prattsburgh, NY — April 9, 1879
BARKER Zelda E. of Italy Hollow, NY — Prattsburgh, NY

DUNHAM T. Franklin of Prattsburgh, NY — July 4, 1879
HORTON Ida of Prattsburgh, NY — Prattsburgh, NY

WYGANT Elias of Prattsburgh, NY — September 25, 1879
HILL Mrs. R. of Prattsburgh, NY — Prattsburgh, NY

CONINE G. T. of Dundee, NY — September 25, 1879
SHULTS Estella of Prattsburgh, NY — Prattsburgh, NY

GUNDERMAN Elmer of Bath, NY — October 21, 1879
LINDSAY Ella of Bath, NY — Prattsburgh, NY

VORHEES Zenus T. of Prattsburgh, NY — October 29, 1879
RING Mary L. of Trumansburg, NY — Trumansburg, NY

PARKER Austin B. of Elmira, NY formerly Prattsburgh September 20, 1879
LEWIS Winnie dau of Evan J. of Elmira, NY Elmira, NY

EDGETT Richard of Howard, NY November 6, 1879
WALDO Mary C. of Prattsburgh, NY Prattsburgh, NY

SANFORD Lyman P. of Prattsburgh, NY December 17, 1879
GRAVES Viola dau of C. D. of Prattsburgh, NY Prattsburgh, NY

NOBLE E. Maynard of Prattsburgh, NY December 25, 1879
BRIGLIN Elizabeth of Prattsburgh, NY Prattsburgh, NY

PRESLER Ira of Prattsburgh, NY December 25, 1879
POLMATEER Nora of Prattsburgh, NY

ALEXANDER James G. of Jerusalem, NY January 1, 1880
PADDOCK Sarah L. of Jerusalem, NY

EMERSON William of Jerusalem, NY January 1, 1880
MOON Hester of Milo, NY Italy Hollow, NY

HILL W. A. of Riker Hollow, NY (Newspaper date) January 8, 1880
WELD Mrs. Matilda of Penn Yan, NY Riker Hollow, NY

HOPKINS Sidney of Pulteney, NY December 31, 1879
LOUNSBERRY Hattie of Pulteney, NY Prattsburgh, NY

HOPKINS Willis Linsley son of Ralph W. Hopkins January 14, 1880
PRINCE Elizabeth dau of Charles Prince Havana, NY

PATCH William L. of Prattsburgh, NY January 21, 1880
INGHRAM Mary A. of Naples, NY Naples, NY

BELTS William of Hornellsville, NY February 2, 1880
MAUDSLEY Annie S. of Hornellsville, NY Prattsburgh, NY

SHOEMAKER George of Kanona, NY February 16, 1880
SHULTS Cora E. of Kanona, NY Hammondsport, NY

HALEY Charles A. of Prattsburgh, NY February 5, 1880
YOUNG Eva B. Bath, NY

TOURTELOTTE Floyd J. of Italy Hollow, NY March 21, 1880
RILEY Rosa of Wallace, NY Prattsburgh, NY

TUTHILL Spencer Francis of Prattsburgh, NY June 4, 1880
MC CORMICK Ella of Jerusalem, NY Naples, NY

SKINNER Henry G. Jr. of Prattsburgh, NY June 17, 1880
MURPHY Mary J. dau of Robert of Prattsburgh, NY Prattsburgh, NY

JOHNSON Thomas H. of Wheeler, NY
SMITH Ida May of Wheeler, NY

July 22, 1880
Wheeler, NY

GILLETT Frederick J. of Italy, NY
VOORHEES Ida E. dau of Lewis of Prattsburgh, NY

August 25, 1880
Prattsburgh, NY

ALBRIGHT Judson C. of Rushville, NY
SULLIVAN Tressa of Prattsburgh, NY

August 25, 1880
Prattsburgh, NY

RICE George D. of Prattsburgh, NY
BROCKWAY Aurelia of Prattsburgh, NY

September 30, 1880
Prattsburgh, NY

WINDNAGLE Ora S. of Prattsburgh, NY
HENERY Ada A. of Cohocton, NY

September 29, 1880
Canisteo, NY

ROGERS Irvin H. of Prattsburgh, NY
MACAFEE Ida E. of Athens, Pa.

October 16, 1880
Athens, Pa.

PRATT John W.
BAKER Jennie dau of Dr. C. C. of Batavia, NY

October 13, 1880
Batavia, NY

BARTLETT M. E. formerly of Clifton Springs, NY
COOKE Isabella G. dau of Aaron of Crookston, Mn.

November 3, 1880
Crookston, Mn.

CLARK Freeman of Mitchellville, NY
BIRD Libbie of Mitchellville, NY

November 13, 1880
Pulteney, NY

MOORE Clark of Wheeler, NY
HAWKINS Anna of Prattsburgh, NY

November 20, 1880
Prattsburgh, NY

TRUAX Frank E. of Prattsburgh, NY
ELLSWORTH Libbie of Prattsburgh, NY

December 26, 1880
Pulteney, NY

SISSON Benoni A. of Pulteney, NY
ANDRUS Ceola E. of Jerusalem, NY

January 1, 1881
Pulteney, NY

LAMPHIER Edmond L. of Canisteo, NY
LAMPHIER Sarah of Prattsburgh, NY

January 16, 1881
Prattsburgh, NY

FISHER John W. of Binghamton, NY
GREEN Ett dau of J. B. of Prattsburgh, NY

January 26, 1881
Prattsburgh, NY

MUDGE Edgar H. of Sullivan, Pa.
GELDER Henrietta dau of James of Prattsburgh, NY

January 25, 1881
Seneca Castle, NY

SMITH John H. of Naples, NY
PALMER Helen of Wheeler, NY

January 16, 1881
Wheeler, NY

HAYNER Eugene of Italy, NY
PHILLIPS Imelda of Prattsburgh, NY

March 6, 1881
Prattsburgh, NY

RYAN Michael of Cohocton, NY — March 6, 1881
DEARLOVE Anna of Naples, NY — Naples, NY

HUNTER Thomas A. of Jerusalem, NY — March 10, 1881
CARVEY Nellie Irene of Jerusalem, NY — Prattsburgh, NY

COOK William E. of Prattsburgh, NY — March 16, 1881
SQUIRES Jennie L. of Prattsburgh, NY — Prattsburgh, NY

ARNOLD Martin E. of Jerusalem, NY — March 27, 1881
FOSTER Myra of Prattsburgh, NY — Prattsburgh, NY

SKINNER William W. of Prattsburgh, NY — August 22, 1880
SCHOFIELD Hattie M. of Prattsburgh, NY — Naples, NY

MORRISON William E. of Prattsburgh, NY — March 16, 1881
SIMONS Hattie J. of Savona, NY — Addison, NY

EDSON Daniel of Rochester, NY — May 10, 1881
ELLSWORTH Eunice of N. Cohocton, NY — N. Cohocton, NY

BRUSH James of Pulteney, NY — May 4, 1881
BAILEY Eva L. of Pulteney, NY — Pulteney, NY

FULLER D. W. of Prattsburgh, NY — June 8, 1881
SCUTT Alida of Jerusalem, NY — Jerusalem, NY

CROSS Francis S. of Pulteney, NY — September 7, 1881
HORR Mattie L. of Prattsburgh, NY — Prattsburgh, NY

WILLIAMSON B. F. Md. of Friendship, NY — September 8, 1881
PINNEY Kate Ford of Prattsburgh, NY — Prattsburgh, NY

MORRISON William E. of Pulteney, NY — October 18, 1881
YONGE Arabella of Pulteney, NY — Potter, NY

ALLINGTON William C. of Penn Yan, NY — October 24, 1881
ROBINSON Sarah S. of Prattsburgh, NY — Prattsburgh, NY

WILDMAN John A. of Prattsburgh, NY — October 2, 1881
VELEY Mina E. of Bath, NY — Bath, NY

WHITE Otto of Jerusalem, NY — December 29, 1881
WILSON Ida of Prattsburgh, NY — Prattsburgh, NY

COLE Henry H. of Pulteney, NY — December 21, 1881
TYLER Cora M. dau of Darius of Pulteney, NY — Pulteney, NY

LEE Charles of Prattsburgh, NY — January 4, 1882
WILLIAMS Nett (or Delia M.) of Prattsburgh, NY — Prattsburgh, NY

AUSTIN W. K. of Prattsburgh, NY
STANHOPE Amy R. of Wayne, NY

January 26, 1882
Wayne, NY

SARLES Charles W. of Pulteney, NY
CORYELL Annetta dau of David of Woodhull, NY

February 22, 1882
Woodhull, NY

LEWIS J. E. of Naples, NY
WINNE Mary of Gorham, NY

March 2, 1882
Gorham, NY

WHEELER Crumbia of Wheeler, NY
MERRITT Lida M. dau of William of Prattsburgh, NY

March 14, 1882
Prattsburgh, NY

HAYES Thompson of Lycoming Co. Pa.
GLOSSER Mrs. Sarah Jane of Lycoming Co. Pa.

March 28, 1882
Prattsburgh, NY

ROFF David J. of Pulteney, NY
STRYKER Alice A. dau of William of Prattsburgh, NY

March 29, 1882
Prattsburgh, NY

BABCOCK D. D. of S. Dansville, NY
HOTCHKISS Villie dayu of L. P. of Potter, NY

March 24, 1882
Potter, NY

LEWIS Mark of Wheeler, NY
ROSE Eva of Wheeler, NY

March 26, 1882
Avoca, NY

DERRICK E. K. of Wheeler, NY
BENEDICT Carrie of Prattsburgh, NY

June 6, 1882
Prattsburgh, NY

SIMONS Henry of Ingleside, NY
AVERY Dell of Ingleside, NY

June 25, 1882
Prattsburgh, NY

JONES Labbius D. of S. Pulteney, NY
HOPKINS Mary E. of Prattsburgh, NY

July 4, 1882
Prattsburgh, NY

MAXFIELD Denison H. son of Hiram
LEWIS Minnie dau of J. V.

June 28, 1882
Naples, NY

CORWIN Charles A. of Keeneyville, Pa.
TYLER Rua of Prattsburgh, NY

July 15, 1882
Prattsburgh, NY

BRUSH Monroe J. of Kanona, NY
JONES Etta A. dau of Mrs. Wakefield Jones of Wheeler

August 26, 1882
Wheeler, NY

CURTIS Silliman B. of Prattsburgh, NY
EVANS Martha J. of Prattsburgh, NY

August 27, 1882
Prattsburgh, NY

VAUGHN Ernest E. of Dundee, NY
TYLER Celia dau of J. G. of Pulteney, NY

September 13, 1882
Pulteney, NY

MURRAY George of Bath, NY
HURD Adda of Bath, NY

November 1, 1882
Bath, NY

RYNDERS S. of Cohocton, NY
PICKETT M. E. of Cohocton, NY

November 4, 1882
Wheeler Ctr., NY

SQUIRES Nat of Italy, NY
ADAMS Maggie A. dau of Perry of Jerusalem, NY

November 8, 1882
Jerusalem, NY

JACKSON Frank E. of Cohocton, NY
STANTON Lottie A. of Wheeler, NY

November 15, 1882
Wheeler, NY

NORTHRUP James of Bristol, NY
JOHNSON Emma of Italy, NY

November 9, 1882
Prattsburgh, NY

RYNDERS Everett M. of Prattsburgh, NY
BROWN Dora B. dau of John A. of Prattsburgh, NY

November 29, 1882
Prattsburgh, NY

CREGO William G. of Italy, NY
BRAMBLE Emma A. dau of George of Prattsburgh, NY

November 26, 1882
Prattsburgh, NY

OLDS Rufus of Wheeler, NY
JONES Mrs. Maria of Wheeler, NY

December 11, 1882
Tyrone, NY

LOCKWOOD Lewis of Wheeler, NY
WAY Mrs. Jane T. of Pulteney, NY

December 24, 1882
Prattsburgh, NY

ELLSWORTH Stewart A. of Prattsburgh, NY
DINEHART Rebecca A. of Prattsburgh, NY

January 10, 1883
Prattsburgh, NY

BURNS Charles H. of Avoca, NY
ALLIS Addie L. dau of H. E. of Prattsburgh, NY

January 24, 1883
Prattsburgh, NY

BENNETT Elsworth U. of Himrods, NY
VAN DEVENTER Florence A. of Dresden, NY

February 10, 1883
Prattsburgh, NY

MC CONNELL John T. of Pulteney, NY
STONE Sarah J. of Pulteney, NY

February 8, 1883
Pulteney, NY

YONGE William D.
WINTERMUTE Jennie dau of Arthur Wintermute

March 13, 1883
Pulteney, NY

EDMONDS Arthur C. of Seward Co. Ks.
WILLIAMSON Alma R. of Cameron, NY

January 30, 1883
Dalton, NY

COOK Floyd H. of Prattsburgh, NY
LOOK Carrie A. of Prattsburgh, NY

March 10, 1883
Bloods Depot, NY

GELDER J. Wesley of Pratsburgh, NY
TYLER Mary of Prattsburgh, NY

March 18, 1883
Prattsburgh, NY

WILLSON Franklin of Italy, NY
KITTLE Mary of Prattsburgh, NY

March 25, 1883
Prattsburgh, NY

STEVER George W. of Pulteney, NY	December 14, 1882
LEPPER Eliza A. of Bath, NY	Bath, NY
BARRETT Michael of Bath, NY	April 19, 1883
FLYNN Mary dau of Mrs. Michael Flynn of Prattsburgh, NY	Prattsburgh, NY
DRUM Eugene	April 18, 1883
ANDREWS Mary J.	Pulteney, NY
LEE Joseph E. of Pulteney, NY	May 3, 1883
NEVYUS Maggie of Pulteney, NY	Pulteney, NY
SAWYER Edward F. of Bradford, Pa.	May 19, 1883
STODDARD Minnie dau of Dr. P. K. of Prattsburgh, NY	Prattsburgh, NY
CALKINS William H. of Painted Post, NY	June 27, 1883
WILSON Florence E. dau of Edwin of Prattsburgh, NY	Prattsburgh, NY
SULLIVAN Fred of Prattsburgh, NY	July 14, 1883
ALLEN Cora of Prattsburgh, NY	Prattsburgh, NY
ANDERSON Frank S. of Rushville, NY	August 8, 1883
FRANCIS Alice A. of Prattsburgh, NY	Prattsburgh, NY
FENTON Daniel of Hornellsville, NY	October 10, 1883
CURRAN Nellie of Prattsburgh, NY	
HORTON William of Pulteney, NY	November 13, 1883
BRUSH Mrs. Ellen dau of J. R. **CLARK** of Prattsburgh, NY	Prattsburgh, NY
PECK George W. of Prattsburgh, NY	November 14, 1883
GRISWOLD Flora of Darien, NY	Darien, NY
TRAVIS Lewis of Hornellsville, NY	November 18, 1883
MATTICE Lizzie of Prattsburgh, NY	Wheeler, NY
HERRICK Charles E. of Italy Hollow, NY	November 22, 1883
CLARK Carrie A. of Prattsburgh, NY	Prattsburgh, NY
HARRIS Alonzo of Wheeler, NY	November 29, 1883
BARRETT Emma of Bath, NY	Wheeler, NY
MUNRO William of Tioga Co. Pa.	Thanksgiving Day
BROWN Miss ____ of Prattsburgh, NY	Prattsburgh, NY
BATES Delbert of Urbana, NY	November __, 1883
REAMER Mary of Urbana, NY	Wheeler, NY
ARMSTRONG W. A. of Pulteney, NY	November 28, 1883
BROWN Julia of Pulteney, NY	Pulteney, NY

HALL G. T. of Pulteney, NY	November 28, 1883
BROWN Carrie of Pulteney, NY	Pulteney, NY
WATERS Frank A. of Oak Orchard, NY	December 25, 1883
FISH Carrie L. of Prattsburgh, NY	Prattsburgh, NY
BENEDICT W. H. of Jerusalem, NY	December 25, 1883
MC CONNELL Flora A. dau of Smith of Pulteney, NY	Pulteney, NY
SMITH Orren B. of Prattsburgh, NY	January 23, 1884
BODINE Sarah F. dau of Amasa of Prattsburgh, NY	Prattsburgh, NY
SCHOFIELD Herbert T. of Prattsburgh, NY	February 6, 1884
LEWIS Libbie dau of A. Q. of Prattsburgh, NY	Prattsburgh, NY
WILLIAMS Charles H. of Prattsburgh, NY	June 12, 1884
HORTON Hattie dau of Stephen of Pulteney, NY	Pulteney, NY
HORTON Freeman W. of Pulteney, NY	October 1, 1884
WHEATON Samantha dau of David of Italy, NY	
COLE Green of S. Pulteney, NY	October 26, 1884
RETAN Laura E. dau of Jeptha of S. Pulteney, NY	S. Pulteney, NY
DECKER Charles D. of Branchport, NY	November 19, 1884
PARKER Rena C. dau of Charles L. of Pulteney, NY	Pulteney, NY
HILL Adelbert of Prattsburgh, NY	December 11, 1884
DRAKE Adah of Naples, NY	Prattsburgh, NY
RANDALL John L. of Penn Yan, NY	December 18, 1884
BRIDGES Ella M. of Fenton, Mi.	Penn Yan, NY
HOAGLAND John C. of Howard, NY	December 24, 1884
BROCKWAY Jennie of Prattsburgh, NY	Prattsburgh, NY

371, 372, 417, 441
FOX 5, 30, 87, 90, 92, 137, 139,
    172, 190, 191, 199, 282,
    301, 379, 386, 395, 406,
    409, 410, 437, 442
FRAIER 304
FRALEY 199, 246
FRALIC 392
FRANCE 177, 313, 418
FRANCIES 222
FRANCIS 216, 224, 266, 271,
    286, 451
FRANCISCO 180, 246, 368
FRANKLIN 375, 428
FRARY 397
FRASER 9, 78
FRASIER 85
FRAVER 348
FRAWLEY 60, 258
FRAYLEY 172
FRAZEE 275, 406
FRAZER 135, 349
FREELAND 40, 246, 301, 323,
    345
FREEMAN 49, 76, 106, 113, 125,
    127, 129, 135, 147, 231,
    256, 298, 304, 310, 355,
    370, 382, 383, 387, 394
FREME 350
FRENCH 67, 96, 97, 104, 133,
    145, 160, 164, 169, 184,
    188, 193, 207, 213, 228,
    240, 263, 267, 272, 283,
    288, 323, 370, 390, 399,
    410
FREY 90, 410
FRIEDMAN 119
FRIES 160, 177, 442
FRINK 134, 213, 243
FRINKNER 41
FRISBEE 79
FRITZ 220, 257
FROMAN 3
FROST 219, 381
FRY 141, 193, 204, 210, 342, 439
FRYMIRE 376
FULKERS 300
FULKERSON 29, 118, 194
FULKINSON 37, 90
FULLER 8, 111, 121, 145, 157,
    242, 267, 330, 332, 338,
    396, 401, 407, 443, 448
FULLERTON 382
FULSOM 71
FULTON 260, 372, 396
FULTS 55
FUNK 108
FURMAN 41, 259, 302, 317, 320,
    383
FURNAM 380
GABRIEL 88
GAGE 34, 162, 166, 167
GAISER 320
GALE 217
GALLAGHER 241, 413
GALLATIAN 304, 380
GALLUP 363, 365, 400
GAMBEE 205
GAMBLE 68, 109, 132, 381
GAMMAN 221
GAMMEN 319

GANNON 164, 375
GANSEVOORT 101, 111, 137,
    142, 145, 206, 366
GANTZ 85
GANUNG 169
GARABRANT 361
GARDENER 392
GARDINER 15, 86, 185, 352
GARDNER 48, 49, 52, 54, 133,
    140, 166, 175, 199, 258,
    260, 262, 267, 283, 322,
    325, 341, 354, 359, 406,
    425, 432
GARLINGHOUSE 118, 293, 408
GARNET 109
GARR 340, 380
GARRABRANT 28
GARRETT 358
GARRETTSON 382
GARRISON 19, 131, 150, 151,
    241, 267, 387
GARY 304
GATES 113, 165, 187, 234, 377,
    431
GAWENS 105
GAY 20, 34, 98, 158, 180, 186,
    188, 193, 204, 208, 252,
    320, 440
GAYALL 251
GAYLORD 62, 116, 344, 355, 378
GEARY 199, 247
GEE 14, 18, 57, 63, 64
GEER 316
GELBRICH 194
GELDER 145, 156, 226, 231, 436,
    447, 450
GELTSER 429
GENNING 83
GENUNG 178, 185, 209, 228, 304,
    341, 360, 408
GEORGE 120, 312, 345, 426
GERBER 431
GERMAN 346
GERMOND 282
GERON 401
GESSNER 210
GETCHELL 200
GIBBS 7, 105, 300, 423
GIBSON 2, 7, 11, 44, 130, 181,
    195, 214, 231, 265, 303,
    357, 408
GIFFIN 440
GIFFORD 17, 65, 70, 78, 192,
    202, 385, 396
GILBER 403
GILBERT 21, 29, 75, 117, 128,
    175, 185, 197, 216, 220,
    227, 258, 281, 295, 331,
    340, 358, 366, 376, 384,
    391, 407
GILCHRIST 197
GILDERSLEEVE 425, 429
GILE 71, 178, 389
GILES 112, 250, 319
GILL 123, 336
GILLAN 63
GILLETT 2, 6, 19, 60, 74, 81, 87,
    128, 149, 195, 241, 242,
    351, 355, 358, 360, 367,
    388, 399, 400, 439, 447
GILLSON 151

GILMAN 349
GILMER 410
GILMORE 91, 137, 160, 178,
    231, 249, 262, 333, 418
GILROY 337
GITHLER 221, 420, 435
GIVEANS 196
GLANN 97, 181, 209
GLASS 81, 263
GLAZIER 330
GLEASON 39, 66, 145, 162, 169,
    198, 201, 210, 211, 225,
    256, 267, 314, 349, 404
GLENDENNING 39
GLENN 89, 90
GLOAD 298
GLOSSER 449
GLOVER 60, 104, 201, 208, 209,
    309, 414
GLOYD 102, 431
GOBLE 374
GODDARD 33
GODDEN 15
GODFREY 163, 187
GOFF 12, 85, 87, 105, 143, 185,
    195, 223, 253, 264, 269,
    270, 284, 291, 314, 318
GOFORTH 57
GOLDEN 12, 170, 398
GOLDSMITH 353
GOLIVER 148
GOLLOBER 414
GONSOLUS 115
GOODBY 20
GOODENOUGH 412
GOODESON 239
GOODON 288
GOODRICH 38, 74, 102, 133,
    281, 354, 439
GOODSELL 62, 71, 72, 87, 107,
    119, 141, 251, 277, 354,
    390, 392, 396, 400
GOODWIN 39, 72, 352
GORDON 6, 63
GORTON 72, 94, 345, 349, 353,
    360, 365, 369, 370, 382,
    389, 393-395, 399
GOSPER 13
GOSS 96, 320, 427
GOTTSCHALL 321
GOULD 16, 68, 78, 97, 102, 149,
    153, 211, 222, 226, 230,
    296, 344, 419
GOUNDRY 229, 303
GRACE 12, 168
GRADY 298
GRAHAM 2, 36, 40, 111, 127,
    132, 157, 164, 226, 227,
    249, 290, 292, 294, 302,
    311, 335, 427
GRAMES 70
GRANBY 173
GRANDIN 82
GRANDY 416
GRANGER 211, 236, 306
GRANT 4, 17, 23, 109, 142, 169,
    186, 192, 236, 288, 295,
    360, 371
GRASSOM 329
GRAUF 308
GRAVES 2, 21, 89, 99, 118,

SLAUGHT 317
SLAYTON 212, 314
SLEEPER 41
SLIE 384
SLINEY 201
SLINGLAND 14
SLITER 60
SLOAN 335
SLOANE 307
SLOCUM 311, 317
SLOSSON 111
SLY 155, 301, 340, 403
SMALL 76, 100, 193, 211
SMALLEY 97, 202
SMALLIDGE 125, 152, 183, 197, 243
SMALLY 143
SMEAD 23, 129, 146, 154
SMELTZER 429
SMITH 2, 4-6, 10, 12, 13, 15-17, 19, 20, 22, 25, 26, 30-34, 38, 40, 42, 44-46, 48, 54, 56-59, 61, 64, 65, 67, 69, 72, 74, 76, 79, 80, 81, 82, 83, 85, 86, 87, 88, 89, 90, 94, 97, 98, 102, 103, 108, 109, 112, 113, 115, 116, 119, 120, 122, 126, 129, 134, 135, 136, 137, 138, 139, 141, 142, 143, 144, 149, 150, 154, 156, 159, 160, 161, 162, 170, 172, 173, 174, 175, 180, 181, 183, 186, 188, 191, 196, 201, 203, 206, 208, 210, 211, 213, 214, 215, 216, 217, 220, 221, 222, 223, 224, 225, 228, 230, 232, 233, 234, 235, 236, 238, 240, 241, 244, 245, 250, 251, 252, 253, 254, 256, 257, 258, 259, 261, 263, 264, 265, 267, 270, 272, 273, 274, 276, 284, 286, 287, 288, 289, 292, 298, 299, 300, 302, 303, 308, 310, 312, 313, 315, 316, 317, 318, 322, 323, 324, 326, 327, 329, 331, 334, 338, 339, 342, 343, 345, 346, 351, 356, 358, 359, 361, 362, 363, 364, 370, 374, 375, 376, 379, 380, 383, 385, 386, 387, 388, 390, 391, 392, 393, 394, 401, 402, 403, 405, 407, 410, 411, 415, 418, 420, 422, 424, 426, 428, 430, 435, 437, 440, 442, 444, 445, 447, 452
SMYTH 20
SNAY 34
SNEATMAN 283
SNELL 26, 53, 59, 128, 153, 172-174, 178, 183, 191, 219, 320
SNIDER 76
SNOKE 443
SNOOK 105, 397
SNOW 107, 115, 219, 250, 318, 420

SNOWDEN 260
SNYDER 24, 106, 134, 162, 194, 210, 230, 248, 250, 286, 288, 372, 387, 414, 418, 432, 443
SOLES 9, 57
SOMERS 331, 339, 349, 363
SOMERVILLE 165
SORGE 314
SORNBERGER 306, 362, 403
SOULE 19, 115, 349, 350, 373, 381, 401
SOUTHARD 76, 107, 356, 361
SOUTHERLAND 68, 398
SOUTHWELL 288
SOUTHWICK 110
SOUTHWORTH 31, 183
SPACE 229
SPAFFORD 20
SPARHAWK 200
SPARKS 234
SPAULDING 8, 23, 32, 40, 75, 87, 199, 259, 358
SPEARS 247
SPENCER 12, 29, 30, 34, 88, 95, 131, 139, 152, 231, 284, 318, 322, 331, 333, 338, 359, 368, 375, 378, 385, 392, 402, 426
SPENDLOVE 344
SPICER 5, 271, 343
SPONABLE 233
SPONATRE 400
SPOOR 38
SPRAGUE 47, 60, 106, 126, 140, 146, 150, 160, 164, 175, 178, 212, 219, 241, 242, 341, 392, 407
SPRAKER 120, 123, 162, 167
SPRAUL 112
SPRING 1, 296
SPRINGER 130, 325
SPRINGSTEAD 167
SQUIRE 61, 84, 98, 102, 339, 351
SQUIRES 191, 215, 239, 240, 353, 402, 413, 440, 448, 450
SRONS 332
ST JOHN 135, 145, 158, 186, 286, 408, 428
ST PETERS 184
STACK 91
STACY 48
STAFFORD 222, 256
STAINER 10
STALL 392
STAMP 297
STANCLIFF 358
STANHOPE 449
STANIFORD 268
STANLEY 272, 370
STANNARD 226
STANTON 25, 50, 143, 146, 147, 157, 158, 205, 215, 224, 238, 309, 332, 382, 436, 444, 450
STAPLES 415, 422
STAR 233
STARING 226
STARKEY 391
STARKS 27, 100, 163, 195
STARNER 42, 345

STARR 96, 97, 100, 284
STEARNS 197, 279, 401
STEBBINS 30, 109, 173
STEDMAN 306
STEELE 92, 264, 269, 334, 353, 356
STEERE 342, 366
STEINBRENNER 341
STELLER 112
STEPHENS 5, 31, 44, 48, 62, 63, 88, 93, 119, 129, 164, 230, 243, 257, 265, 282, 296, 301, 311, 316, 317, 327, 367, 420, 427
STEPHENSON 47
STERNER 58
STETSON 65, 86, 394
STEVENS 19, 20, 25, 37, 38, 60, 71, 86, 93, 110, 112, 117, 121, 151, 166, 226, 228, 270, 310, 311, 318, 324, 370, 371, 376, 394, 402, 418, 427, 431, 433, 445
STEVENSON 111, 114, 316
STEVER 141, 186, 243, 451
STEWARD 245
STEWART 8, 39, 48, 62, 63, 68, 70, 74, 83, 85, 102, 104, 107, 110, 112, 115, 116, 130, 134, 143, 145, 157, 181, 182, 185, 189, 191, 193, 199, 203, 204, 207, 212, 220, 223, 224, 232, 236, 248, 252, 253, 255, 261, 272, 274, 277, 289, 293, 294, 295, 303, 309, 324, 325, 326, 352, 354, 370, 374, 377, 390, 391, 407, 415, 420, 425, 431, 434, 441
STICKLER 59
STICKLES 31, 57, 229
STICKNEY 123, 186, 442
STID 35
STILES 11, 53, 104
STILLMAN 302, 304
STILLSON 175, 383, 387
STILTS 105
STILWELL 393
STINSER 293
STINSON 27, 69, 189, 199, 202, 215, 289, 353
STITES 221
STOCKBRIDGE 77
STOCKING 15, 94, 146, 155, 173, 228, 263, 281
STOCUM 14, 59, 198, 227, 323, 368
STODDARD 5, 25, 52, 99, 100, 108, 119, 170, 188, 413, 438, 443, 451
STOGA 227
STOKES 133
STONE 3, 5, 52, 73, 131, 173, 201, 204, 216, 233, 265, 282, 301, 314, 320, 330, 375, 416, 430, 440, 443, 444, 450
STONEMETTS 51
STORMS 208, 368, 383, 438
STORY 152, 159, 365

Other Heritage Books by Mary S. Jackson and Edward F. Jackson:

1850 Census for the Town of Howard, Steuben County, New York, and Genealogical Data on the Families Who Lived There

Death Notices from Steuben County, New York Newspapers, 1797-1884

Death Notices from Washington County, New York Newspapers, 1799-1880

Marriage and Death Notices from Schuyler County, New York Newspapers

Marriage and Death Notices from Seneca County, New York Newspapers, 1817-1885

Marriage Notices from Steuben County, New York Newspapers, 1797-1884

Marriage Notices from Washington County, New York Newspapers, 1799-1880

Other Heritage Books by Mary S. Jackson:

Marriages and Deaths from Tompkins County, New York Newspapers